W9-AEE-674

UNIVERSAL ASSEMBLY LANGUAGE

No. 2730
$27.95

UNIVERSAL ASSEMBLY LANGUAGE

ROBERT M. FITZ AND LARRY CROCKETT

 TAB BOOKS Inc.

Blue Ridge Summit, PA 17214

FIRST EDITION
SECOND PRINTING

Copyright © 1986 by TAB BOOKS Inc.
Printed in the United States of America

Library of Congress Cataloging in Publication Data

Fitz, Robert M.
Universal assembly language.

Includes index.
1. Assembler language (Computer program language)
I. Crockett, Larry. II. Title.
QA76.73.A8F57 1986   005.13′3   86-5944
ISBN 0-8306-1730-2
ISBN 0-8306-2730-8 (pbk.)

Contents

15-3,001

Preface

The student, hobbyist, or computer professional who is convinced that assembly language is worth studying and using must face the question, "Which assembly language?" As the number of different kinds of computers on the market grows, the number of assembly languages one might learn is also increasing. As a result, one question that the student or assembly language programmer must face is which assembly language to choose. Choosing an assembly language is probably no easier than choosing which microcomputer to buy—there are so many and there are so many considerations to ponder before choosing.

It is in light of this dilemma that the authors of this book feel that this book is unique. This text is not about a particular assembly language; it isn't specifically an introduction, for instance, to Z80 or 8086 or 68000 AL. Instead, this text introduces the reader to assembly language in a general way so that the concepts and insights gained here can be applied to a host of assembly languages with a reasonable amount of effort. That's one reason why we call this text *Universal Assembly Language*.

The second reason is that the text introduces the concept of a universal assembly language that is machine independent. It shows how one universal assembly language has been implemented, and it proposes an assembly language standard. We believe, in short, that assembly language has advanced to the point that it rivals high level languages such as Pascal and BASIC in terms of ease of use and portability. This conviction and the excitement it generates is what motivates the writing of this book.

We would like to express our thanks to Larry Copes and Dennis Longar of Augsburg College, Minneapolis, and to Timothy Wilder of the University of Minnesota for numerous helpful suggestions. And we would like to express our thanks to the many other people who encouraged and helped make this book possible.

Introduction

Assembly language seems to many people to be a throwback to computing's yesteryear. It's suitable for the wizard hacker, perhaps, or the high-powered professional programming team, certainly, but few others. Micro user spokesman Jerry Pournelle, for example, extols the virtues of learning to program in a high level language but cautions that "learning to program in assembly language takes special skills, lots of practice, and much time. I've never learned how to do it and never will." * With perceptions such as these, it is no wonder that novice computer users and even some professional programmers try to avoid assembly language as long as possible.

The authors of this text believe that these perceptions are mistaken. We believe that assembly language study and use is appropriate and valuable for at least two reasons. First, assembly language remains the most powerful and efficient way to accomplish many programming tasks. Assembly language programs are fast and, in many respects, easier to write and maintain than high level language programs. Second, assembly language study remains without question the best way to learn how computers work. High level languages such as BASIC or Pascal mask the operation of the machine, they cover its features and characteristics. Assembly language, since it usually maps directly on to the hardware of the machine, reflects the workings of the machine, how it is organized and how it executes its programs.

More specifically, assembly language remains the most efficient way, both in the short run and the long run, to accomplish programming tasks. Several reasons stand

---

Popular Computing (August 1984).

out. First, like high level languages, assembly language has some unique advantages. It has speed, maintainability, and power. Unlike high level languages, however, it allows the programmer direct access to all the resources of the computer. As a result, even high level language programmers often have to use assembly language subroutines and procedures to get parts of their jobs done.

Second, assembly language is not nearly as difficult to learn and use as is widely claimed. It's often as simple and intuitive as saying, "Move that apple from basket 1 and put it in basket 2," or "See if basket 1 has the most apples; if it does, put it in the car." In many respects, the number of rules and cautions that one must keep in mind is fewer than is the case with high level languages. In contrast with high level language programmers, the competent assembly language (or "AL") programmer knows at all times exactly what a particular instruction will cause the machine to do.

Third, AL enables the programmer to control hardware devices such as printers and modems. High level languages are not suited for these functions since they use internal routines that send and receive data in specific formats.

Fourth, if a few good programming habits are maintained, at least some AL programs can be written nearly as quickly and prove to be as maintainable and nearly as portable as high level language programs. This is perhaps the most contentious claim we'll make, and it will take the rest of the book to substantiate it. Count it as an "IOU" that we'll pay up by the time you finish reading.

An additional consideration for using assembly language has to do with advances in the field. Recently introduced assemblers, such as MOPI from VOCS in Minneapolis, make it possible to define assembly language instructions in a machine independent fashion—which makes assembly language potentially quite portable from one machine to another. Lack of portability has been traditionally one of the chief shortcomings of AL. With the advent of machine independent, or universal, AL, books such as this become the most advantageous way to study assembly language.

USING THIS BOOK

We intend to make the text informative for both the AL novice and veteran. The text should be accessible for those who have had some experience with computers, particularly in programming. For those who have had no experience with assembly language, we urge that you read the book chronologically, making sure that you understand each section before you go on to the next one. On the other hand, if you have had experience with assembly language, it makes sense to skip those portions of the text that cover material you already understand.

It may be that you have particular interests in one microprocessor; there are tables in the back of the text that list the characteristics of many microprocessors. For instance, if you are interested in Z80 assembly language, consult the table in the appendix that spells out some of the features of the Z80. This text would be a natural introduction to more specialized texts.

The book can be used as a general introduction to AL computing, as a reference text, or both. The wealth of information in the tables in the Appendices should make this text a valuable reference work. If it is used as an instructional text, its use will be enhanced by using it in conjunction with MOPI, the universal assembler marketed by VOCS of Minneapolis, MN. It is available from VOCS at Box 3705, Minneapolis, MN, 55403. In particular, using the examples in the text with the assembler should speed comprehension.

THE ORGANIZATION OF THE BOOK

Chapter 1 discusses a number of the advantages of learning and using AL. Specifically, it surveys some of the history of programming and it highlights some of the recent advances in assembly language.

Chapter 2 discusses computer fundamentals. It discusses topics such as hardware and software, systems and application programs, the major hardware components, memory organization, registers, and the basic instruction cycle.

Chapter 3 discusses data representation, or how it is that we can represent the world and the problems we wish to solve with computers. Specifically, it introduces the different numbering systems and how to convert between them. It discusses how computers represent negative numbers and characters found on computer keyboards.

Chapter 4 introduces the reader to basic computer operations, the operations that enable computers to accomplish the tasks we assign them. Assembly language instructions and commands are introduced.

Chapter 5 details how programs should be written and presents some of the do's and don'ts of writing good programs and satisfactory documentation.

Chapter 6 surveys computer registers and how different registers are used. It explains general purpose registers, index registers, the uses of index registers on various micros, and special purpose registers.

Chapter 7 discusses addressing modes. In particular, it covers the basic content of AL instructions, addressing mode syntax, effective addresses, and the various addressing modes.

Chapter 8 explains in some detail the concept of a universal, machine-independent assembly language.

The Appendices include a proposed assembly language standard, micro instruction set tables, and a micro characteristics table.

Chapter 1

Advantages of
Assembly Language

Purpose of the Chapter: This chapter will introduce the concept of assembly language and the role it has played in computer programming. We'll also look at some of the history of assembly language and high level languages, such as FORTRAN and BASIC, to see how they compare. Then the chapter will assess some of the advantages and disadvantages of programming in assembly language. Last, we will introduce some of the new concepts that are being introduced in assembly language that will make it easier to learn and easier to use on different microcomputers.

THE DEVELOPMENT OF ASSEMBLY LANGUAGE

Just as a taxi-cab driver must be instructed if the passengers wish to reach their destination, computers must be instructed in order to accomplish their assigned tasks. If we wish a computer to sum a column of numbers, for example, it must be told, among other things, where to find the numbers, what arithmetic operation to perform on them, and where to store the result.

Instructions and Languages

An instruction must be expressed in a language that is intelligible to the computer being used. A Japanese man who speaks no English will smile graciously but unresponsively if we ask him in English to do something. Similarly, a computer will be content to sit idly and "twiddle its thumbs" if we cannot instruct it in a language it, so to speak, "understands." Instructions are not effective, therefore, unless the recipient of the instruction understands the language of the instructor.

Virtually all computers today are digital rather than analog machines. This means that machine functioning is based on discrete electronic impulses such as the presence or absence of a small voltage in an electronic circuit. The binary number system, with its two symbols 1 and 0, is ideally suited to representing the two states of a digital computer circuit—namely, on and off. What Japanese is to the Japanese man, the binary number system is to the computer; the computer, as it were, speaks binary.

The binary number 10 can represent a number, in this case, 2, or it can represent an instruction, for example, an instruction to add one value to another. In fact, the heart of the modern digital computer is its ability to represent both data and instructions as the presence of a pulse or its absence—what we understand as 1s and 0s. The idea of *representation* is pivotal here. As we are able to construct computer-compatible representations of data, instructions, and problems we wish to solve, we are able to get the computer to perform useful tasks. It is the computer's singular ability to manipulate rapidly the representations of problems we wish to solve that makes it so useful.

As a result, if we wish computer assistance, we are forced to represent the world and the problems we wish to solve in terms that are intelligible to the machine. As we are able to represent problems, data, and ways to solve problems in terms of a mass of 1s and 0s, the computer is able to return another set of 1s and 0s that, when properly interpreted, may be a solution to the problem we gave it.

A computer will have no difficulty making sense of 30 single-spaced pages of 1s and 0s, provided that they represent a well-formed computer solution to a problem. But no matter how well-formed the solution is, human eyes soon glaze over after just a few lines of 1s and 0s. Some of Shakespeare's richest prose can be represented as a set of 1s and 0s, but it loses everything in the translation as far as humans are concerned.

The Invention of Assembly Language

Early computers were instructed in terms of vast numbers of eye-glazing, mind-numbing 1s and 0s. Writing programs in binary proved to be not only terribly tedious and difficult to interpret and modify, but also error prone. As a result, it was a major breakthrough when programs that could translate English-like alphabetic symbols, such as ADD and MOV, into binary instructions were invented. Significantly, it meant that the computer assisted in its own programming.

As the lowest level symbolic language, assembly language was also the first translator of natural language symbols to machine binary numbers. With assembly language, for example, the programmer can write a source code program that uses ADD rather than 01. The assembly language program or assembler then translates the ADD in the *source code* to a 01 in the *object code*. Note the translation ratio. One assembly language instruction is translated into one binary instruction. This one-to-one translation ratio is characteristic of AL.

Consequently, although the invention of assembly language made computer programs more intelligible to people, by itself it did not reduce the number of instructions required to perform particular tasks. It still took one symbolic instruction to get the machine to perform one operation such as storing a value in a register or adding two values to produce a third.

Subroutines

As a result, though early assembly language made programming easier and more intelligible, it did not make programs shorter. Programs were still loaded with repetitive sets of instructions. An additional breakthrough, namely the idea of a *subroutine*, was required to address the repetitiveness of programming. Suppose we wish to write a program to determine payroll checks. If we have five employees, we could write a program which, among other things, did the following:

    A. Get first employee's name.
    B. Get first employee's hourly rate.
    C. Get first employee's number of hours worked.
    D. Multiply B times C.
    E. Store result in "FIRSTWAGE."
        ⋮

    A. Get fifth employee's name.
    B. Get fifth employee's hourly rate.
    C. Get fifth employee's number of hours worked.
    D. Multiply B times C.
    E. Store result in "FIFTHWAGE."

Now, this programming practice may be acceptable if a company has just a few employees, but if it employs hundreds or thousands, something has to change. The way to change it is to employ a subroutine that accepts and returns values to a program segment that calls on it when needed. Consider the advantages of the following alternative:

    If WAGE needs to be calculated
    Call Subroutine DETERMINEWAGE
        ⋮

    Subroutine DETERMINEWAGE:
      A. Get NAME.
      B. Get HOURLYRATE.
      C. Get HOURSWORKED.
      D. Multiply HOURLYRATE times HOURSWORKED.
      E. Store result in WAGE
    Return

Each time the subroutine is executed, it gets a new name from the list of names of employees to be paid. It returns a possibly different value in WAGE each time it is called. The subroutine named DETERMINEWAGE can be called as many times as it is needed. Hence, repetitive tasks can be accomplished by using one set of instructions repeatedly. Not only does this practice save typing and limit the possibility of error, it saves limited memory space as well.

Subroutines are "on call" programming services written by the programmer or possibly supplied with the programming software. Once written, they can be called repeatedly to accomplish routine tasks. A subroutine or a procedure is a programming solution to a particular component of a problem.

As a rule of thumb, it is best to think in terms of a subroutine performing one specific task. A subroutine should be thought of as executing a single task or a group of closely related tasks. It is generally advisable, for instance, to separate arithmetic procedures from output procedures. When a subroutine is called, the calling program (which may be either a main program or another subroutine), is put "on hold." Upon completion of the subroutine, the main program resumes execution at the point it had reached when the subroutine was called. It is possible, even common, for subroutines to call other subroutines.

External Subroutines and Linkers

Some subroutines are so useful that it is desirable to use them for more than one program. One solution is simply to enter the subroutine code in each new program. Another solution is an *external* subroutine—a subroutine that is not incorporated into the source code for the program but that may be called and used when needed. Since the external subroutine has to be combined with the main program and since the subroutine's location in memory cannot be predetermined, two new concepts are needed.

The first concept is that of a *linker*, which is sometimes called a *linking loader* or a *linkage editor*. A linkage editor combines the main program with the required subroutines so that they comprise an executable program. The various cross references between the main program and subroutines, for instance, have to be synchronized.

The second concept is that of *relocatable* programs or subroutines. This involves a new type of assembler, a relocatable assembler, which produces a relocatable *module* (a procedure) that the linker program can then store anywhere in memory. This is a matter of adding a number to all the program's addresses so that the relocatable program can run in a different area of main memory. The relocatable program, when assembled, is assumed to start at the location in memory whose address is zero. When executed, however, its starting location depends on where it is loaded into memory.

Macros

The development of subroutines solved the problem of repeating procedures. But what happens when a subroutine needs to be modified every time it is used or for every different program that uses it? It is unlikely that every program will require identical subroutines even for common tasks. The answer is a *macro*. A macro is a set of AL instructions with variable elements that are assigned a name. For example, a set of instructions that outputs characters to a printer might be named PRINT. Instead of typing the set of instructions each time we wish to output characters, we can simply invoke the macro named PRINT and specify the required variables that are to replace the variable elements.

So far, a macro sounds much like a subroutine. The difference is that an assembler with macro capabilities, a *macro assembler*, inserts the series of AL instructions into the program whenever it sees the name PRINT. At first, macros were inserted into a source code file by a separate program, called a *preprocessor*; later, it was combined with the assembler to form a macro assembler. A macro offers some of the same conveniences as the procedure-like instructions of higher level languages. For instance,

Pascal's WRITE instruction, which corresponds roughly to BASIC's PRINT, is explicitly called a *standard procedure* and not an instruction, since using it invokes an output procedure that is comprised of a series of instructions. Another difference between a macro and a subroutine is that the code for a subroutine occurs in the program code only once. The code for a macro, by contrast, is entered into the object code file each time the assembler encounters the macro's name.

Conditional Assembly

The external, relocatable subroutine and the macro were both attempts to reduce the amount of source code required to write a program in AL. Each solved a particular problem, but solved it only for simple procedures rather than for entire programs. As programs became more complex, and computer systems with minor differences became more common, another problem developed—namely, the case in which procedures differ only slightly from one program to another. As an analogy, consider the mason who constructs a wall. A brick wall with a window is a brick wall but it is not the same as a windowless brick wall since building the windowed wall requires additional steps. Hence, there are both similarities and differences between the two walls.

In a program, there may be two procedures that are similar yet not identical; one is followed in one case, the other in the other case. Instead of writing two separate procedures for each condition, it is simpler to include both in one program and delete at assembly time the procedure that is not used. This is called *conditional assembly*. With conditional assembly, whether a section of code is included or excluded depends on conditions that are external to the program.

The development of assembly language is illustrated in Fig. 1-1. To summarize the history of assembler development, *absolute assembly* means that code is generated for execution at fixed memory locations. *Relocatable assembly* means that the code generated may be relocated for execution anywhere in memory. A *macro* expands a single AL instruction into a set of AL instructions, while *conditional assembly* means that selected segments of code can be included or excluded as conditions require.

Another capability that developed historically was the generation of machine code for one machine on another; the code for a Zilog microcomputer, for example, could be generated on a DEC minicomputer. Assemblers that have this capability are called *cross assemblers* since they can develop code for different types of computers. Cross assemblers can be absolute assemblers, or they can include relocatable, macro, and conditional capabilities.

THE DEVELOPMENT OF HIGH LEVEL LANGUAGES

At this point in the history of assembly language, development came largely to a halt. The history of symbolic language development focused on a new endeavor, the so-called *higher level* languages (HLLs) such as Fortran and COBOL. The development of HLLs was made possible in part by the increasing speed and larger memories of newer machines.

High level languages usually consume large amounts of memory and produce relatively slow executable programs, a point we will have occasion to refer to several times.

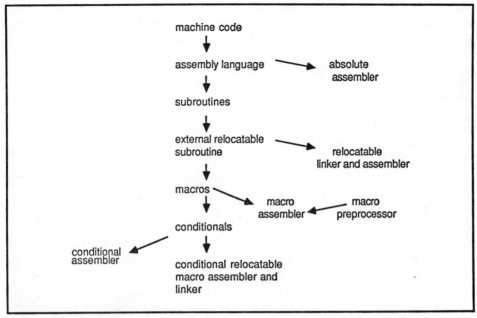

Fig. 1-1. The historical development of assembly language: Because no standard developed, a variety of assemblers implemented different combinations of these capabilities. The earliest assemblers were primitive. As time passed, assemblers came to support relocatable modules, conditional assembly, and macro assembly. A full fledged assembler today is a conditional relocatable macro assembler with a separate linker.

In their favor, nevertheless, HLLs enable the programmer to instruct the computer to do tasks rather than single operations. Consider the following example. Suppose a high school student is sitting in an algebra class. The teacher might say, "Go to the board and solve the equation 'x = 2a + 32' where a equals 9." The teacher doesn't need to specify, "First, get out of your seat, put one foot in front of the other until you reach the board, then pick up the chalk, . . ." The student will know how to do these subroutines, we might call them, in order to accomplish the assigned task. Likewise, with Pascal, for example, if we enter the command, Write (5 * 4), we don't need to specify all the steps of a multiplication routine, register usage, and output routines since the Pascal compiler does this for us.

The principal difference between a HLL compiler, such as a Pascal compiler, and a conventional, simple assembler, therefore, is that generally each Pascal statement is converted into several, possibly many, computer operations, while each assembly language instruction is converted into one computer operation. Note that the HLL instructions bear little direct relationship to actual machine operations; there is, for instance, no WRITE operation in the machine itself. The computer, by means of a procedure or subroutine, can be instructed to print something, but it can only do so by means of a series of machine operations, like the student who must put one foot in front of the other until he reaches the board.

It is sometimes argued that the advantage of a HLL compiler over an assembler is that the compiler contains a set of fully tested procedures that work without debugging, provided that they are used properly. The same, however, is at least potentially true of AL; once a subroutine has been written and debugged, it can be used repeatedly without further testing. The principal difference, therefore, between a compiler and an assembler in terms of this issue is that the procedures are integral to the compiler while they are external to the assembler.

Some Early High Level Language History

Historically, the first compiler was developed for and by engineers and scientists. Syntactically, its instructions looked, as one would expect, much like algebraic formulas. The first compiler, Fortran (*FORmula TRANslator*), was introduced in April, 1957, at IBM. It is interesting to note that, when Fortran was introduced, it was claimed that Fortran would largely eliminate coding and debugging! Of course, that claim proved to be quite false.

The next important compiler was developed in a business environment for use in record keeping and management. A committee was commissioned by the Department of Defense to develop a language that would be machine independent; the Pentagon wanted a language that would not be tied to a particular computer in the way that early assembly languages were. The resulting language, COBOL (*COmmon Business Oriented Language*) was released in 1960 and is one of the most widely used languages. (Note the role that machine-independence played in the development of COBOL—it's a topic we'll return to later.)

Generally speaking, each compiler was developed by and for a particular group or application. Scientific needs are addressed by Fortran while COBOL is better suited to business applications. Although the development of compiler languages made programming easier for specific applications, generally the compilers were not suitable for all applications. As the use of computers became more general, a wider variety of problem solving tasks were undertaken. Additional HLLs were developed to address these additional needs. Every variety of computer use, it seemed, required a different language or enhancement for its application. This resulted in a raft of high level languages; Fig. 1-2 indicates the relationship of some of these languages.

Fortran (1957): science and mathematical

COBOL (1960): business and administration

BASIC (1960): instructional/general purpose (mainly interpreted)
    CBASIC, HBASIC, Microsoft BASIC

Pascal (1970): instructional and general purpose
    Ada, Modula-2

C (1972): "portable pseudo-assembly language"

Lisp (1950s): list processing and artificial intelligence
    Prolog

Fig. 1-2. Some major high level languages: Fortran and COBOL developed first, helped along by interest in machine independent language processing. BASIC and Pascal followed in response to educational needs. C and Lisp are specialized languages that enjoy wide popularity.

Interpreters and Compilers

One feature of a compiled language is that all the source code file that will be compiled into an object code file must be completely written prior to compilation. This means, among other things, that errors such as syntax mistakes are not detected until *compile time*. One syntax error, for example, can result in many compile time errors. It is not uncommon that correcting one syntax error in the source file will result in 10 or 12 fewer errors at compilation.

This feature of compilers is particularly unwieldy for high level language instruction. One task to which a computer can be put is to check each line of the instructions for syntax errors interactively. An interpreter does just that. An interpreter differs from a compiler in that each instruction is converted into machine code as it is being executed. With a compiler, the entire program is converted into machine code first. Although an interpreter has good debugging capabilities, it drastically decreases the program's execution speed.

Interactive interpreters such as BASIC were developed in order to provide more immediate feedback in terms of correct instruction syntax. As a result, some believed it to be useful for instructional purposes—though others concluded that BASIC, since it did not discourage poor programming habits, was a poor instructional language compared to Pascal, which was also developed for use as a teaching language and incorporates a number of concepts developed as a result of three decades of programming experience.

As this brief survey suggests, both in fact and impression, most of the development of the last two decades or so has been in the high level languages. HLLs are task-oriented rather than operation oriented. Particularly as adults, we usually think in terms of tasks and not operations. This fact partly explains the widespread appeal of HLLs. Even a cursory look at the popular computer magazines shows widespread interest in BASIC, Pascal, Forth, and C, but only an occasional, surprisingly timid, reference to assembly language. All of the "action" seems focused on high level languages. Assembly language, by contrast, seems moribund, stagnant, perhaps headed for practical extinction.

THE ADVANTAGES OF ASSEMBLY LANGUAGE

In just the last few years, however, advances in assembly language and newfound appreciation for its power have resulted in a small but distinct revival for AL. This revival was triggered by the rapid introduction of microcomputers in household appliances, motorized vehicles, and specialized tools. AL proved to be well suited for such tasks and interest in it rebounded. Moreover, people came to recognize its value as a tool of instruction for how computers work. High level languages, precisely because they are designed to be machine independent and to do tasks rather than operations, tend to mask the workings of the computer. Assembly language maps directly on to machine operations and, as a result, allows the user to see directly into the workings of the computer.

In this section, we will survey some of the advantages of assembly language.

Simplicity

Contrary to widespread perception, assembly language is actually quite simple in many respects. Its simplicity stems directly from its explicit, direct relationship to the computer.

With HLLs, on the other hand, statements can mean one thing under some circumstances and another under other circumstances. "Go to the board" can mean one thing if the circumstance is an algebra classroom and quite another if it is a swimming pool. Likewise, WRITE(CONTINUE) in Pascal will result in one output format if CONTINUE is real and another if it is an integer. We'll have to remember what output format is associated with what variable type. The price that is paid for the luxury of writing task-oriented instructions, in other words, is a lot of rules. Assembly language, as an operation-oriented language, has far fewer rules for the programmer to remember. "Store value A in location B" will always mean just that—no more and no less.

In assembly language, each instruction generally causes one and only one operation to take place in the machine. Each instruction results in the performance of one easily understood operation. The ease of understanding stems from the explicitness of operation-based instructions. All the ambiguity and complexity of task-oriented instructions (really procedures) has been decomposed into the completely explicit and therefore simple. Once the work has been done up front, in other words, programming is relatively simple.

As the example of a student going to the blackboard to solve an algebraic equation attempted to illustrate, task solving and task solving languages presuppose a great deal. Philosophers call it "background knowledge" and farmers call it "common sense," but it comes down to this: human beings, in attempting various tasks or in instructing others to do tasks, have on hand a great deal of background knowledge and experience. We don't start from scratch each time we attempt a problem; rather, we have on hand a rich reservoir of experience and rules of thumb. We take such background knowledge for granted in attempting to solve problems or tell others how to solve problems.

This chapter has already cited the problem that computers speak a different language than humans. Computers "prefer" artificial languages such as binary arithmetic, while humans prefer natural languages such as English. Aside from arguable claims from the developers of artificial intelligence programs that their programs possess a reservoir of background knowledge, a computer programmer usually cannot assume that the computer has a reservoir of background knowledge to draw on. Computers start much closer to scratch, as it were, each time a problem is attempted, than we do. The result is that problem solving on a computer is often largely a matter of making fully explicit what is only implicit in human problem solving. This making explicit of the implicit is the heart of *problem decomposition* and hence of programming. Only when the problem has been decomposed and the implicit background knowledge made explicit should coding begin. It is one reason for perhaps the otherwise baffling adage, "The sooner you start coding, the longer it will take you to complete the program."

With assembly language programming, the process of making the implicit in problem solving explicit must be done completely. That is, the solution to a problem must be expressed fully in terms of computer operations rather than the computer tasks which high level languages allow. The price that is paid is more development time up front—even more time must be spent in AL than in HLL in designing the solution before coding can begin. More time should be spent in designing and conceptualizing the task than in coding and debugging it.

A problem that has been completely decomposed into its component operations is suitable for computer resolution only when all the requisite implicit background knowledge has been made explicit. It is at that point and only that point that actual machine coding is appropriate; coding, in other words, should be the last part of programming.

One advantage of assembly language is that, once the problem has been decomposed and all implicit knowledge made explicit, the machine can be instructed exactly what to do. A solution to a decomposed problem fully translated into explicit actions or operations doesn't need to concern itself about rules, for example, the rule not to assign a real number to an integer variable. Assembly language is as simple as saying, "Store value A in memory location B. Make a copy of the contents of B and add the copy to the contents of location C." There is not the long list of rules and conditions to remember that is characteristic of HLLs.

The work of decomposition and making the implicit explicit, once done, results in programming which is actually quite simple. Assembly language is operation based as opposed to procedure based—since operations are fully explicit, AL doesn't need the raft of rules that high level languages require.

Program Development and Execution Speed

One of the principal advantages of programming in a high level language is the speed with which a program can be written and debugged. Since high level languages utilize instructions that are more like procedures than machine level operations, programs in high level languages tend to be much shorter than AL programs. Other things being equal, shorter programs are more quickly written and more easily debugged.

Assembly language programs must use genuine instructions; typically, each instruction in an AL program assembles into one machine operation. This results in programs that are considerably longer than their high level language counterparts. Other things being equal, longer programs not surprisingly take longer to write and are more difficult to debug.

But there have been a number of advances in assembly language that make the productivity issue less clear. For instance, with the development of subroutines and macros, assembly language programming achieved some of the advantages of high level language programming; external subroutines in particular speed the writing of programs.

Even with these advances, however, assembly language programming still can be counted on to take longer than high level language programming. That is, it usually will take longer to write an AL program than a HLL program. This, however, is not the entire programming story. Programs rarely work correctly after the first coding. It is doubtful that any significant program has worked correctly after the first draft. Identifying AL errors in AL programs can be much faster than identifying HLL errors. One reason is that most computers are provided with an assembly language debugging program. Debuggers for high level languages are rare—a fact which suggests the relative difficulty of debugging in HLLs as compared to AL.

Another reason is the simplicity of each AL instruction. Instructions that correspond directly to machine operations are relatively simple—move a copy of one number to another place, compare two values, switch program control to another location. These are intrinsically simple operations with few unknown (or perhaps undocumented) side effects. Modular languages such as Pascal warn about side effects generated by procedures. In fact, HLL statements are procedures whose side effects are often not easily identified. An AL procedure can be readily examined—not so with HLLs. Moreover, with HLLs, the programmer is obliged to include extra display instructions to generate any diagnostic messages that might be required in the case of errors. This complicates the instruction (procedure) with further possible side effects.

As a result, while HLL programs typically prove faster to write initially because they use procedure-like instructions, they are much more difficult to debug—precisely because they use these kind of instructions. There is a price to be paid, in other terms, for the convenience of procedure-like instructions. As programs increase in complexity, that price grows exponentially.

As will be explained in this text, AL programming time can be reduced significantly by using *procedural instructions*, instructions that are converted into a series of machine code instructions rather than just one. This kind of AL programming, it should be noted, is possible only with the newer assemblers such as MOPI.

Assembly language programs typically execute much faster than the same program written in a compiler language—sometimes as much as ten times faster. The inefficiencies of compiler language programs might be thought acceptable since hardware, particularly RAM, has become cheap enough, and programming time expensive enough that we can afford to spend the former in order to save the latter. Compiler type languages are designed to shorten the amount of time it takes to write a program even though it means that the program will run more slowly.

It is generally agreed and widely assumed that programs can be written more quickly in high level languages. Since each HLL instruction is often equivalent to twenty or more assembly language instructions, it is true that a single HLL instruction can cause a computer to do a lot more than a single AL instruction.

But coding is only one part of the development of a good software package. Newer concepts of software development emphasize that coding is only one of several aspects of programming. In terms of coding, it is true that high level language programs can be written in less time. The design, documentation and testing of a program, however, are just as important, if not more important, than the actual coding. As a result, programming should be thought of as a *total development effort* and not just as coding. When the total development effort—and not simply coding—is taken into account, a different picture emerges. See Fig. 1-3 for a comparison.

It is often claimed that the coding for a HLL program will take half the time for the same task as for an AL program. Let's suppose that this is correct. Even if it is, however, it doesn't follow that programming in a high level language takes half the time it takes for assembly language. The design, documentation, and testing time requirements are roughly the same.

When it is taken into account that coding is only one part of programming, it turns out that the total development time advantage of HLL over AL is sometimes on the order of 10 percent or so, not the often claimed 50 or 100 percent. Moreover, the same small advantage can be realized in the maintenance or rewriting of existing programs. The advantage of HLL over AL in terms of software development expense, therefore, is real but often fairly modest.

In current discussions, in fact, too much attention is being paid to faster computer hardware in the quest for faster execution times. Good algorithms written in an effi-

	High Level	Assembly	Percent Difference
Design	40	40	--
Documentation	20	20	--
Coding	10	20	50
Testing	20	20	--
Total	90	100	10

Fig. 1-3. Total development effort: Coding is only one aspect of software development. When all aspects of programming are taken into account, including design, documentation, coding, and testing, the advantage of HLL over AL is much smaller than is often supposed, perhaps as little as 10 percent overall. Of course, the difference will depend on many factors, including the kind of program being written, the kinds of AL and HLL being used, and the skill of the programmer(s) involved.

cient language such as AL, we would argue, is a more promising ticket to faster execution. In fact, a program written in assembly language will generally run 4 to 10 times faster than a HLL program, doing the same task, on the same computer. High level languages are "fast," therefore, in a short-sighted way. HLLs are well-suited for programs that will be used infrequently or for programs where speed is not important. As Fig. 1-4 illustrates, AL execution speed means that there is a point at which using AL takes less time than using a HLL. That point is a function of the number and complexity of program executions.

Let's suppose, as may be true in certain circumstances, that a high level language program can be written in one half the time it takes to write a comparable assembly language program. If it takes 30 hours to write it in Pascal, for example, and it takes 60 hours to write it in AL, a savings of 30 hours has been achieved. But the AL version will execute faster. Suppose that it runs 5 times faster, say 2 minutes versus 10 minutes.

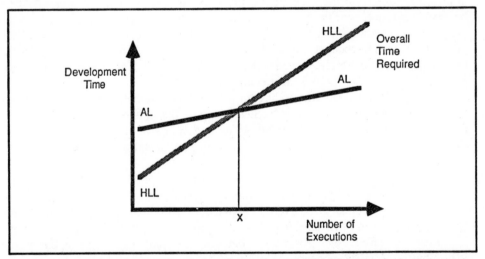

Fig. 1-4. AL programs will eventually take less time overall: AL's execution speed advantage means that there will be a point x, in terms of the number of times the program is used, at which an AL program will take less time overall in terms of development time and execution time. Where the x is reached will be a function of the number of executions and the kind of program being written and used.

We need to remember that programs are used as well as developed. As a result, we should be concerned with the overall time consumption of developing and using the program. As Fig. 1-5 illustrates, a program would take less overall time written in AL after just 225 executions, which could be as little as a few weeks of use. If the program is to be used often, assembly language programs will consume considerably less time overall, making the added development time of AL a sound investment.

Ease of Learning and Use

A common assembly language myth is that it is intrinsically difficult—to learn, to use, to debug. Often, it is believed that programming in AL requires special knowledge and training—a language for the experts and not hobbyists or occasional users. We believe that this myth is just that—an untrue belief. Admittedly, the programmer must specify in greater detail what the computer must do; there is, it might be said, an extra step of refinement to get down to machine level operations rather than compiler level procedural instructions. This extra step does require additional work and, in some cases, some experience. But once this programming "down payment" has been paid, AL programming in many ways is simpler to learn and to use. There are fewer rules associated with the use of AL instructions, and debugging can be simpler in many circumstances. As a result, it is not the case that HLLs are in every way easier to learn and use than AL. In many ways, just the reverse is true.

Machine Control

High level languages are deliberately microprocessor independent; they frost over the view into the computer system. The price paid for this independence is less control over the resources of each computer. In too many cases, programs have to be tailored to the limitations of a HLL rather than the full capabilities of the computer. This is especially true with the formatting of reports and the organization of input data.

With assembly language, by contrast, the computer is more transparent to the programmer. AL is more like a window in to the programming capabilities of the computer. As a result, the limitations are those of the programmer rather than the language.

Many functions that the computer is capable of performing can be controlled only via assembly language or HLLs, such as C and Modula-2, that support AL-like instruc-

	HLL	AL	Difference
Development:	30	60	30 (hours)
Execution Time:	10	2	8 (minutes)
Executions Needed to Recover the Difference:		225	

Fig. 1-5. Overall time consumption: Even if an AL program takes much longer to develop, with its faster execution it will take a relatively small amount of program use to recover the greater initial development time. In this hypothetical case, in which a program took twice as long to develop in AL but executes five times as fast, it would take as little as 225 executions to recover the difference in terms of time (30 hours longer × 60 minutes, divided by 8 = 225). As a result, in many situations, AL will enjoy an advantage in overall time consumption.

tions. When using most HLLs, the programmer is limited to performing only those functions that the language supports. Assembly language has no such restrictions. A prime example is the generation of reports and displays. High level languages typically restrict programs to a limited number of data formats or fields. The result is often a compromise between what the programmer wants and the language will permit. With AL, on the other hand, the programmer can produce any type of format and is therefore able to generate the desired result.

The fact that assembly language offers total control, versatility, and maximum speed makes using assembly language necessary in many instances. It is often the only language that can be used. Additionally with high level languages, special procedures, those with time critical functions, have to be done in AL.

Choices generally involve trade-offs. The choice of a truck over a four-door sedan, for instance, probably means greater load capability but less riding comfort. The choice of a computer language also involves trade-offs. Higher level languages offer some advantages over assembly language—if they didn't, it is unlikely they would have been developed and widely used. On the other hand, as we intend to argue throughout, high level languages have significant disadvantages as well.

In fact, the disadvantages of assembly have been exaggerated. Both some of those who use it and those who don't have pointed to its disadvantages. As it turns out, many of AL's disadvantages stem from inadequate implementation and utilization rather than anything inherent in the language itself. Ironically, some AL disadvantages are the product of the inadequate implementation and use by those who point to its disadvantages most consistently!

Portability

It is widely believed that high level language programs are easily transported from one kind of machine to another, say from an IBM PC to an Apple *II*e. It is also widely supposed that assembly language programs are not easily transported. But let's distinguish fact from fancy in terms of relative portability.

In fact, there is some truth to the claim that high level languages possess a measure of portability. This fact should not be surprising since, historically, one motivation for the development of HLLs was portability across machines with different CPUs. One motivation for the Defense Department's adaptation of Ada, for instance, was portability on the wide variety of systems it uses.

The problem with portability as an expressed goal is that it stands in some conflict with the evolution, the progress, of a language. Programs written in older versions of a language typically will run on upgraded compilers but programs written in the later versions usually will not run on the older compilers—that is, there is *upward* but not *downward* compatibility. The result is that, today, we know of no language which can claim full portability. Choose the language you wish, the odds are good that programs written in it for one machine will have to undergo some modification in order to run on other machines.

Assembly language has traditionally been identified as the nonportable language. Since 1) AL instructions are assembled on a one to one basis into machine instructions and 2) every kind of computer uses a different set of instructions, it has been thought that assembly language is and must be nonportable. In fact, most of the instructions of any given instruction set are quite machine dependent. This is a consequence of the fact the instructions are based on the unique internal architecture of the kind of machine.

The idea of the "architecture" of a machine really means the following. First, it refers to the characteristics of the electronic circuitry, especially the kind and number of registers. Second, it refers to the addressing modes available to the programmer—how it is that instructions access data and other instructions in memory. Last, these two, in part, generate the instruction set which is supported by the system. Clearly, architecture varies dramatically from one kind of machine to another. What complicates matters even more is the practice of many manufacturers of using different instructions to represent the same computer operation. Historically, there has been little effort to achieve a standard that would mitigate this practice.

This unfortunate practice stemmed from a couple of factors. First, new assemblers often were based on earlier assemblers with the result that incompatibility was perpetuated rather than reduced. Second, the desire to produce new and presumably better assemblers often resulted in the production of difference rather than improvement. None of the assemblers were based on an accepted standard.

Recently, however, a few independent suppliers have attempted to implement something approximating uniformity in their assemblers. As the principal case in point, this book attempts to introduce a standard set of instructions that can be used with all the 8, 16 and 32 bit micros as implemented by the MOPI assembler, which was developed by VOCS of Minneapolis.

NEW, ADVANCED ASSEMBLERS

Assembly language has survived in spite of considerable stagnation for two reasons: 1) it is the "native language" of every computer; 2) for some applications it is the only language that can be used. After nearly a decade of stagnation in assembly language development, new advances indicate that assembly language is being brought up to date. Current computer science ideas are finally being implemented in AL—a fact that should revitalize the language. The result should be greater use and acceptance.

Achieving acceptance of new innovations is slippery business in the computer field. It takes time to publicize new developments, and get their merits verified and then accepted by those who have been trained in older technology. The newer advancements should not only guarantee its survival, they should guarantee greater use and acceptance. We will briefly consider some of them now, specifically standardization, machine-independent instructions, and, of course, universal assembly language.

A Standardized Assembly Language

In the past, much of the confusion that characterized AL use stemmed from the lack of a standard. Many incompatible instruction codes and formats represented either identical or similar machine operations. Complicating standardization was the use of arcane, difficult-to-decipher symbols to represent instructions and addressing modes. Historically, people supposed that assembly language could not be standardized because of the nature of the language itself—since AL instructions map directly onto machine hardware and since hardware differs dramatically, people concluded that standardization was inconceivable.

To a degree, this conclusion is correct. On the other hand, similar machine operations, operations that are essentially the same even though they are done on different kinds of computers, can be represented by similar mnemonics and formats. Standard formats can be used to represent similar machine conditions. This book, in fact, introduces a standardized assembly language instruction set that can be used with all microprocessors currently available. This standard has been implemented on the MOPI assembler.

Machine-Independent Instructions

Some instructions are found on all computers. These instructions can easily be represented by standard format instructions that can be used with all assemblers and all computers. Additionally, while it's the case that some operations differ from machine to machine, there are sequences of instructions that can be used to accomplish the same commonly used functions. While the series of instructions that are required to perform these functions may vary from machine to machine, the functions are still the same.

Some of the newer computers will contain special instructions to perform some of these basic functions. Examples include multiplication, moving and comparing a string, and filling a string with a constant. Some of the newer assemblers allow a single assembly language instruction to be converted into a series of machine instructions.

A large part of any program consists of a few basic procedures. Although the code that is required to perform these procedures may vary from computer to computer, the procedure is the same. As a result, a standard set of mnemonics can be used to represent those procedures that are common to all microprocessors.

Universal Assembly Language

Current assemblers for the various microcomputers use different instruction mnemonics and formats for exactly the same operation. In fact, a single assembler will often use several mnemonics for the same basic operation. This not only complicates porting a program from one computer to another, but it also makes learning assembly language needlessly difficult. By using a standard or universal set of mnemonics and instruction formats, AL is not only easier to learn and use, it is simpler to transfer programs from one computer to another.

Chapter 8 explains universal assembly language mnemonics in detail.

Chapter 2

Computer Fundamentals

Purpose of the Chapter: This chapter reviews the fundamentals of computers for those who could use a short refresher. In this chapter, we will explain what a microcomputer is in general terms, going into as much detail as an assembly language programmer needs for most work. The chapter will cover the different sizes of computers, the different levels of a computer, data and software, the basic components that comprise a computer system, microcomputer memory and input/output, and the basic instruction cycle of a computer.

MICROS, MINIS, AND MAINFRAMES

The term *microprocessor* continues to take on new meaning as computer technology advances. Historically, it originated with the introduction of the integrated circuit. This technology enables entire sections of a computer, which in the early days of computing occupied many cubic feet, to be put on one silicon chip, which is smaller than a fingernail. As a result of this miniaturization, the processor section of the computer came to be called a *microprocessor*.

Though exact dividing lines are increasingly blurred, often people still distinguish between microcomputers, minicomputers, and mainframes. For a period of time, it was thought that micros were computers that cost less than $10,000, while minis cost from $10,000 to $50,000 and mainframes cost more than $50,000. A better way to distinguish them is by word size—micros use 4-, 8-, and 16-bit words; minis use 16 and 32 bit words; mainframes typically use 32- and 64-bit words. Additionally, micros are usually single user systems, while minis often support 2 to 40 users (each with a separate terminal), and mainframes sometimes support as many as several hundred users at the same time. About the only constant in these comparisons is that micros are smaller and less powerful than minis, which are smaller and less powerful than mainframes. It should be remembered, however, that some of today's micros are more powerful than minis from just 10 years ago. As a result, the meaning of these terms is fluid and depends on the year in which they are used.

Microprocessors are designed in many different ways and possess somewhat different relative capacities—however, their components are quite often similar. The design of a micro, the way in which various components are arranged, as well as the way the hardware and software interact, is referred to as its *architecture*. A micro's architecture is a major factor in determining which operations it can perform.

THE FOUR LEVELS OF A COMPUTER SYSTEM

There are lots of way to peel an apple and lots of ways to analyze things like computers. One useful way to analyze computers is in terms of four *functional levels*, of what function or basic task gets done at what level of the computer system (see Fig. 2-1 on the next page).

First, the most conspicuous computer level to a user is often an application program such as a word processor or a spreadsheet. Application programs *interface* with— they connect directly with—the user by means of a terminal or with an external device, such as a printer, to perform a specific task. One kind of application program is a language processor. An *assembler*, for example, is a language processor that converts instructions that people can readily understand into instructions that computers can readily understand.

Second, these programs, in turn, require *systems software* or, as it is sometimes called, an *operating system*. The systems software provides all the services needed by the application program; it is the link between the application program and the computer's hardware. For some simple applications such as controlling the operation of a printer, the operating system is also the application program. In any event, the operating system consists of a number of procedures and utilities that are used by both the programmer and application software.

Third, the machine instructions specify the actions executed by the computer. As will be explained, machine instructions are represented using *machine code*, which is the native language of a computer. Machine code directly causes a computer to execute operations—no translation is needed.

All of these first three levels are usually implemented using software. However, the dividing line between software and hardware is not fixed, and many computer operations can be implemented using either hardware or software. An analogy may help. Software has the same amount of mass, of physical stuff, as an idea—namely, none. Like an idea, it can cause something with mass to behave in a certain way even though it has no mass itself. What ideas are to brains and bodies, roughly speaking, software is to computers—information informing action.

Last, at the most basic level, is the computer's hardware— its circuitry and components that determine its capabilities. Just as cars are designed in a variety of ways— some are front wheel drive automatics while others are rear wheel drive manuals— computers are designed in a variety of ways. Some are relatively simple, with no extra

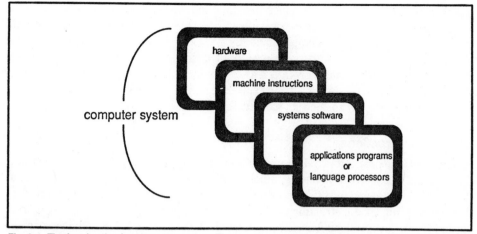

Fig. 2-1. The four levels of a computer system: The most apparent part of a computer to a user is usually an application program or a language processor. But underneath this part is systems software, machine instructions, and hardware, all of which reflects a system design.

processors and few registers (see below) and some enjoy the aid of math coprocessors and special timing or control circuitry.

The *hardware* of a computer system is all the parts of it that can be touched or carried across the room—including the terminal, disk drives, and the like. The *software*, by contrast, cannot be touched (though the media is on which it is stored, such as floppy disks, can) and consists of the programs, commands, and instructions that drive the computer.

As shown in Fig. 2-1, an application program or language processor runs "on top of" the operating system, which controls the hardware by means of machine instructions. The visibility of lower levels to the user is determined by the transparency of the higher levels. Application programs and high level languages, for instance, deliberately obscure the details of the operating system, the machine language, and the hardware. As we will see, these details are both more transparent and accessible with assembly language.

DATA AND SOFTWARE

There are two basic types of information stored in a computer's memory. The first type of information is a series of *instructions,* which tells the computer which operations to perform. A computer without a program, to draw an analogy, is even less useful than a piano without a pianist. Instructions exist in the computer as numbers or codes, with each code specifying one operation. A series of such instructions is called a *program.* Since each single instruction is capable of only one simple operation, it usually takes many thousands of instructions to perform useful tasks. The second type of information stored in memory is the *data,* which is to be processed in some fashion. Once the data has been processed, usually it is *written* or stored in memory. Conversely, a *memory read* operation retrieves data that has been previously stored in the memory. It should be noted that, to the computer, there is no difference between the way instructions and data appear, since both are just a series of electronic 1s and 0s; the com-

19

puter must be instructed as to which are data and which are instructions.

Both instructions and data can be stored permanently and internally in the computer or they can be stored semipermanently and externally on a device such as a disk drive. Alternately, data can be gotten as input during program execution on an "as-required" basis, and it can be produced as output on an "as-finished" basis. This practice is referred to as *real time* processing since the data is processed or generated (usually to a printer or screen) as soon as it is available.

Machine Instructions

Assembly language (or "AL") instructions should be distinguished from *machine instructions*. AL instructions use symbolic terms and numeric representation such as MOV (move data) and 50H (50 hexadecimal which equals 80 decimal—see chapter 3). By contrast, machine instructions are represented with binary numbers, that is, with 1s and 0s. For example, an AL instruction would look like "Add B, 8" while a machine instruction would look like "01001001."

Machine instructions correspond directly to the specific operations that the hardware can perform. They are the only instructions that are external to the computer that the computer can use directly. In older computers, these instructions activated the individual hardware components directly. In contemporary computers, these instructions activate a series of commands that are internal to the computer called *microinstructions*. Some computers allow the programmer to use these microinstructions. In most computers, however, they are treated as part of the hardware and are not used directly by the programmer.

Systems Software and the Operating System

System software, which acts as an interface between the hardware and other programs, is used to perform many of the commonly required hardware procedures that must be used to accomplish most tasks. Many of these procedures are complicated and require specialized training to write. As a result, AL programmers use these procedures but usually do not write them or rework them. They are, however, built into the systems software so that they are available to the programmer. The systems software also consists of the set of programs that link and coordinate various parts of the computer. On some computers, the system software that is permanently included in the hardware is often called *firmware* since it is a hybrid between hardware and software.

One function of the systems software is to provide an interface that makes it easier for a wide variety of programs to operate on different computer systems. The *operating system* (or OS) provides a standardized set of instructions at one end and a computer specific set of instructions at the other. (See Fig. 2-2). The OS is able to translate standard instructions into specific machine instructions. This makes the standard set of instructions more *hardware independent*. Programs can then be written for an operating system, such as CP/M or MS-DOS, rather than for a specific computer, such as an Apple II or an IBM PC.

Application Programs

In contrast to the systems programs that control the computer, application pro-

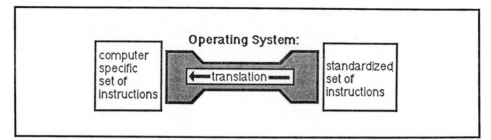

Fig. 2-2. The operating system: As well as providing the interface between an application program and a hardware system, and providing many procedures and utilities that can be used by both programmers and users, an operating system provides a general environment that masks some of the specifics of any particular micro so that programs can be written for the OS rather than the particular micro. It does it by translating the standardized set of instructions in which the application programs are written into the specific set of instructions required by the microprocessor.

grams are designed to solve specific problems or perform a task. Spreadsheets, databases, word processors and desktop utilities are all examples of application programs. Application programs are usually thought of as "running on top of" the systems software, since the application programs require the presence of the systems software in the computer in order to execute.

Language Processors: Assemblers, Compilers and Interpreters

The native tongue of computers is machine language, the series of 1s and 0s that specify computer operations. Since people find machine language impractical, and computers find English impossible, compromises are constructed in the form of various programming languages. Early computers were instructed in machine language, but this proved tedious and error-prone. It was discovered that programs can be used to translate symbolic languages that people can understand into the machine language computers can use.

The first symbolic language was assembly language. The symbolic instructions of an AL program must be assembled or converted into machine language. Usually, assembly language instructions are converted into machine instructions on a one-for-one basis—one assembly language instruction is translated into one machine instruction. Consequently, unless it is a universal AL or is translated by a special program called a *cross assembler* so it will run on other microprocessors, it is tied to one particular microprocessor.

High level languages such as BASIC and Pascal are more removed from machine language and bear a greater relationship to natural languages such as English than AL. A *compiler* converts high level language (HLL) instructions into machine language; typically one high level language statement such as BASIC's PRINT statement will translate into as many as 30 or more machine instructions. A compiler permanently converts a HLL program to machine code. An *interpreter*, on the other hand, is an alternate way of implementing a HLL. When a program is interpreted, each HLL statement is translated into machine code as the program runs. This means that each time the program is run, it must be translated again, statement by statement, as the program executes. This makes interpreted programs easier to debug but much slower in terms of execution speed.

THE THREE MAJOR HARDWARE COMPONENTS

Microcomputers are composed of three basic components, a *central processing unit, memory,* and *input/output.* The processing done by a computer occurs in the central processing unit, or CPU. In order for the the computer to know what to do and to remember what it has done, a memory system is needed. And in order for a computer to receive instructions and data, or for it to communicate its results, an input/output, or I/O system is needed. See Fig.2-3 for an illustration of the three major computer components.

The CPU

In a microprocessor, the CPU is on a single integrated circuit chip with the memory and I/O added as external components. In a complete microcomputer, all or part of the memory and I/O are on the same chip. In either case, our description of the basic components still applies.

As the heart of the computer, the central processing unit, or CPU, controls all computer operations, including the control of the memory and I/O sections. As illustrated in Fig. 2-4, it consists of three basic units, the control section, the arithmetic logic unit, and a number of registers. In the CPU, the *control section,* which we designate as the "computer chief executive," interprets program instructions and sends timing signals to the rest of the computer. This unit is responsible for directing every action between the various computer components. The *arithmetic logic unit,* or ALU, the "assistant to the chief executive," performs arithmetic operations, such as addition, and logical

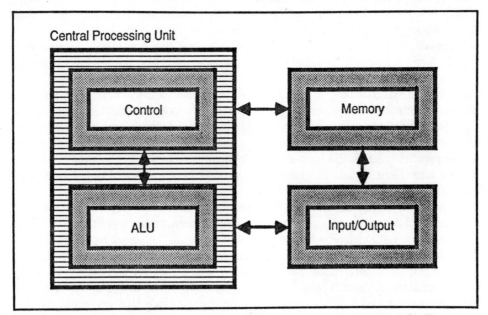

Fig. 2-3. The three major computer components: CPU, memory, and input/output (I/O). The control and ALU components of the CPU communicate and they, in turn, communicate with memory and I/O. In the CPU, the control unit determines what is done when, and the ALU does much of the actual computing. Memory is needed to store and retrieve programs and data. I/O is needed to get and send data—to people and other devices such as disk drives and other computers.

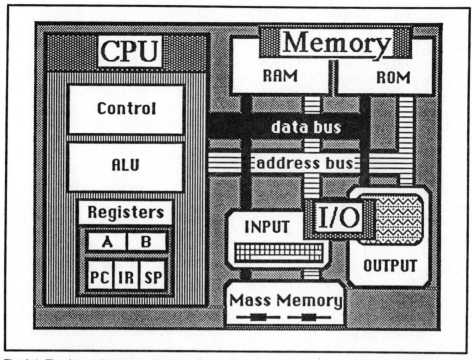

Fig. 2-4. The three microcomputer components: CPU, memory, and I/O sections and their principal components. Each of the three major components is comprised of more specific components. All of these components are connected by both a data bus and an address bus. Memory consists of both RAM and ROM (see text), while typical I/O devices include input keyboard, output screen, and a mass storage device such as a disk drive. Usually, the address bus is larger than the data bus in terms of the number of wires each has. Micros have one or more general purpose registers, which we have labeled A and B, and several purpose registers, the PC, IR and SP.

operations such as AND and OR, which are used to manipulate individual bits (*bit* is a contraction of *bi*nary digi*t*, or the 1s and 0s computers use) stored in the computer.

The principal circuit element in a CPU is a register. A register is a memory location used to store and manipulate fixed-length binary words. Data can be written to or read from a register, and like RAM, the contents of a register are only temporarily stored. Registers are unlike most RAM memory cells in that they are often used directly to manipulate data, they are more directly involved in instruction execution, they are much faster to use than a memory location, and each register is given a symbolic name and not a numeric address. The only part of the CPU that really concerns the programmer is the registers, since operation of the other two sections is automatic.

Since they are part of the CPU, registers are used to store frequently used data or data that is used to control the computer's operation, primarily because they are faster and they are directly accessible by the control unit and the ALU. While reading data or instructions from RAM is much faster than from an external device, such as a disk drive, reading it from a register is faster still. Reading the data from RAM takes on the order of 300 to 600 *nanoseconds* (a nanosecond is one billionth of a second). Reading it from a register often takes less than 100 nanoseconds. Because the CPU doesn't have to determine a memory location address as would be done if RAM were used, a register read is often three to six times faster than a RAM read. These are such small intervals that it might be thought useless to be concerned about them, but when you consider that computers perform thousands or millions of reads and writes in order to execute a typical program, these relative speed differences become important.

Registers are often arranged in an array as illustrated in Fig. 2-5 so that individual registers can be combined to form larger registers that can hold larger chunks of data. For example, if registers B through G are 8 bit registers, registers B and C could be combined to form a 16 bit register called BC. Not all registers are either the same size or multiples of some basic size. Some special purpose registers such as the Stack Pointer and Program Counter are assigned a fixed size—which depends on the function they serve. Registers have their data transferred over an internal data bus, which is part of the CPU. Each register is accessed by means of control signals, which are generated by the control unit of the CPU.

Registers are usually divided into two groups: general purpose and special purpose. *General purpose registers*, portrayed in Fig. 2-5 as registers B through G, are sometimes referred to as *GPRs*. GPRs are used in conjunction with the ALU to perform tasks such as mathematical operations and temporary data storage. Sometimes, one or more of the GPRs are called *accumulators*. *Special purpose registers*, such as the stack pointer (SP) and program counter (PC), store addresses that point to locations in memory.

The PC holds the address of the next instruction to be executed. After an instruction is fetched from memory, the PC is automatically incremented. The incrementation usually ranges from 1 to 6, since the length of instructions ranges from 1 to 6 bytes in length, although most instructions take no more than 3 bytes. Sometimes, however, the contents of the PC is changed by the programmer, as in the case of a jump instruction, which is comparable to a GOTO statement in BASIC or Pascal. In this case, since program control jumps to another part of the program, the contents of the PC must be changed (usually by more than 3) in order to access the next instruction to be executed.

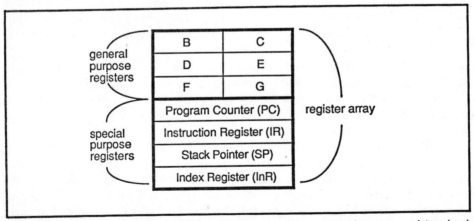

Fig. 2-5. Simplified register array: There are two kinds of registers, general purpose registers (such as B-G here) and special purpose registers such as the Program Counter (PC), Instruction Register (IR), Stack Pointer (SP) and Index Register (InR). The general purpose registers often are paired, for example, as double register BC, in order to double the number of bits that can be used to represent numbers.

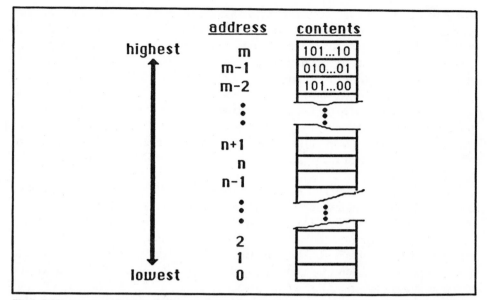

Fig. 2-6. Memory organization: Each memory location has two numbers associated with it, an address and contents. Each location has its own unique address, ranging from 0 to some maximum number m. Each location is a fixed number of bits wide—usually 8, 16, or 32. Memories that hold 8 bits in one location hold one byte, which is usually what is required to represent a single character such as the letter L. Memories are organized in numbers that are powers of 2. A *K* is a kilobyte or 1024 (2^{10}) bytes and is the most common measure of memory.

The instruction register (IR) contains the instruction to be executed and is used in the process of decoding the instruction in order to determine what operation is to be performed. Not shown in Fig. 2-5 is the *memory address register*, or MAR. The MAR, like the PC, stores the address of the next location in memory to be accessed. But it is the MAR that actually drives the memory address decoder in memory that determines the physical location of the memory location to be accessed. It gets its address either from the PC or the current instruction in order to access data that is stored in memory.

Figure 2-5 includes an index register (InR). One or more of these are used in micros to specify locations in memory. They are used with some instructions to specify the addresses of the memory locations that contain the data the instruction operates on. Instructions add the contents of one or more index registers to another number to determine the correct address of the data.

How a register is used depends on the machine instructions that are available. Sometimes specific instructions must be used with specific registers; other times registers can be used with a variety of instructions. Other registers are not directly associated with any particular instruction but are used by the CPU for a special purpose. See Chapter 6 for a more complete description of various registers.

Memory

Memory is where program instructions, data, and other information is stored. As illustrated in Fig. 2-6, memory is organized sequentially in locations numbered from

0 to some multiple of 1 K*, such as 64K, 128K or 512K. Each location is some number of bits wide, usually 4, 8, 16 or 32 bits, and is accessed by the address bus and is read from or written to by means of the data bus. Both program code and data are stored in the computer's memory—sometimes only in RAM, but often in RAM and external mass memory such as a disk drive.

The first electronic computers used *magnetic core* memory. This memory was *nonvolatile*—the contents were not lost when the power was turned off. Magnetic core memory is rarely used in contemporary computers because it is both expensive and slow. Instead, memory, as shown in the top right section of Fig. 2-2, consists primarily of what is called RAM and ROM. RAM is fast but volatile while ROM is fast and non-volatile.

RAM is an abbreviation for *Random Access Memory*, ROM for *Read Only Memory*. The term *random access* refers to the fact that all memory locations in RAM can be read from and written to it. RAM is also *volatile*—it preserves its contents only as long which is a more accurate description since RAM can have data and instructions both read from and written to it. RAM is also volatile—it preserves its contents only as long as the power is continuous, the computer is not turned off, and no new data is written to the locations containing the original data.

ROM is an alternate storage memory system that is used to store programs that are run many times or to store data that does not change—such as the operating system of the computer, an important application program, or perhaps a high level language interpreter. ROM is written to once in a special "burn" process and cannot have new data written to it—it is a read operation only memory. Since the program or data in ROM is burned in and doesn't depend on a constant power supply to sustain it, it is permanently stored in memory.

The difference between these two kinds of memory can be remembered easily with the help of an analogy. RAM is like a notebook in which information is stored using a pencil. Notes can be made in the notebook, erased, transferred or moved as one pleases. ROM is like a book in which all the pages are filled with permanent ink information. ROM can be read like a book, but no new information can be stored there.

There are several other types of memory that are widely used. For example, *PROM* (programmable read only memory) and *EEROM* (electronically erasable ROM), unlike regular ROM, can have data written to them by the programmer. EEPROM can have its contents erased electronically by ultraviolet light and new data can then be written to it; this gives PROM and EEPROM some of the capabilities of both ROM and RAM.

RAM and ROM are often referred to as the computer's *main memory* since it is accessed directly by the CPU. Another type of memory is shown in the lower right hand corner of Fig. 2-4. *External mass memory* refers to the variety of I/O systems that are used to store data and instructions on a more permanent basis than RAM but on a less permanent basis than ROM. Moreover, external mass memory is typically a mass storage system—it is capable of storing many times what can be stored in RAM or ROM. Examples of external mass storage devices include tape cassettes, floppy disk drives, rigid or *hard* disk drives, and reel-to-reel systems. Microcomputers usually use only the first three.

---

* K is an abbreviation for *kilo* and is short for 1000 in electronics, but in computer science it means 1024 because 1024 is the nearest power of 2 to 1000 (namely, 2^{10} or 1024).

External mass memory normally stores data electromagnetically on media such as tape or disks. Floppy disks, for example, are coated with iron oxide, which can be magnetized. Magnetization occurs when the spins of all the electrons in a region called a *domain* are aligned in the same direction. If the electrons in a domain are aligned in one direction, the read/write head of the storage device interprets it as a 1, if the other way, a 0. These two numbers comprise the binary number system, which is used to encode both data and instructions. Typical floppy disks can store up to a million or more 1s and 0s in this way. Rigid disks can store as much as 100 million or more 1s and 0s.

It is not important for the programmer to get too involved in the technical details of memory. The two important things to know about memory are how the contents of memory are accessed and how much memory, at any given time, is available for use for a program or the data it manipulates.

Input/Output

The input/output system provides a means of communication between the central processing unit and the external world, such as people and peripheral devices or sometimes other computers and electronic devices. These external devices are not connected directly to the CPU by means of the data or address bus. Instead, they are connected by means of an *interface adapter*. The reason for this is that the signals in the bus are unique to each type of microcomputer, and the signals required by the external device are unique to that kind of device—hence an interface is required to make the two compatible.

Another reason that the interface is needed is that the data is transferred over the bus much faster than the external devices can accept it. The interface adapter is a kind of converter and temporary *buffer*—a place where data can be stored temporarily and reformatted. Each interface adapter is assigned one or more address locations, which are called *ports*. The word *port* is used to distinguish between an I/O interface address and a memory address used in programs. One or more ports may be connected to a single external device. Some of these ports will be used for controlling various operations such as selecting options, while others will be used to "talk" to external devices.

On some micros, a memory address and a port address are distinguished by the operation being performed. Other computers do not distinguish explicitly between memory addresses and port addresses. Instead, they assign a group of memory addresses as I/O port addresses. This practice is referred to as *memory-mapped* I/O.

Although memory-mapped I/O offers greater flexibility in terms of how data is transferred to and from the I/O devices, it also restricts the amount of memory that can be used for other purposes. Since memory is always allocated in blocks of 256 bytes (or in multiples of 256 bytes), even if the I/O devices require only a few bytes, 256 bytes (or some multiple of 256) are allocated. In other words the greater flexibility and more attractive screen presentation of memory-mapped I/O is purchased at the price of using a sizeable chunk of the system's limited memory resources.

Generally, with high level languages, the programmer is unaware of the presence of the interface adapter. These HLL instructions are predefined in terms of how data can be sent and received from external devices. With assembly language, however, the programmer has the added advantage of being able to send control information to the interface adapters. This means that different formats can be used and a wide variety of external devices can be accessed.

There are many different types of external devices. Some interface adapters are designed for particular types of devices, such as video displays, printers, or disk drives. Others supply a standard interface such as the RS-232 interface, which can be connected to a variety of devices, including terminals, modems, and printers.

The details of how the interfaces work are beyond the scope of this text. For some programming tasks, however, the details are important to an AL programmer. We will simply observe that many micros contain a special set of instructions for communicating with I/O devices.

OTHER COMPONENTS

Computers include two other important parts: the busses and the power supply.

Busses

All instructions, data, control signals, and power are transferred from where they are generated to where they are needed by means of busses. A *bus*, sometimes known as a *trunk*, is a group of wires connecting two or more points.

As illustrated in Fig. 2-4, the two most important busses in the computer are the *data bus* and the *address bus*. Both the data and the address busses have internal and external parts. The internal (to the CPU) bus connects the ALU, the controller, and the registers. The external (to the CPU) bus connects the CPU to the memory and I/O devices. Data is transferred over the bus in parallel, one bit per wire. The number of wires determines the number of bits of data that can be transferred at one time. It is not uncommon for computers to have an external data bus that is less than the size of the internal data bus—i.e., an 8 bit external bus and a 16 bit internal bus is a common arrangement. This increases the amount of data that can be processed with one instruction and simplifies external hardware.

The external data bus is used to transfer instructions and data between the CPU and various external sources and destinations such as memory and I/O devices. The address bus, which usually has more wires than the data bus, selects which memory location or I/O device data will be used in data transfer. The number of wires in the address bus determines how much main memory a microcomputer can use, since one bit is sent in parallel on each wire. A 16 wire address bus can transmit a 16 bit address word, which can address 64K (65,536 since 1 "K" = 1024) locations of memory.

Some newer micros use what is called a *multiplexed* bus. In order to decrease the physical number of wires required, the same wires will be used for both the address bus and the data bus. For a brief period of time, the wires are used to transport an address, then for another brief period, to transport data.

Another bus, not shown in Fig. 2-4, is the *control bus*, which carries all the control and timing signals. The content of this bus varies drastically between the different micros. Some prefer to call it something other than a bus, using the term *group of signals*. Of concern to the programmer are the interrupt, reset, and other program-controlled signals. The interrupt signals are generated by the I/O devices to tell the CPU that they require attention. The reset signal returns the CPU to a state that is much like the state of the computer when first powered up. Sometimes this is called a *warm* boot. The program-controlled signals are used to set up certain external conditions or control a timer or counter if the micro contains one as part of its internal architecture or specific external devices.

Power Supply

Another part of the computer is the *power supply*. The electronic circuits of a microcomputer cannot use the high voltages or the alternating current (ac) of household or office electrical supply. A micro's power supply converts this high-voltage alternating current to a low voltage, direct current (dc). The power supply also suppresses electrical *noise* that would cause problems for the micro's circuits. Generally, the programmer need not be concerned with the power supply other than to know it is there and can cause problems of various kinds that may require the attention of technical service persons.

THE BASIC INSTRUCTION CYCLE

Computers execute programs by repeating small, usually quite simple, operations many thousands or millions of times. These operations include moving a piece of data from one location to another or comparing two pieces of data to see which is largest. Each of these small tasks is accomplished by the computer's *instruction cycle*. Each time the computer undertakes an operation, it must first *fetch* the next instruction. It does so by determining the address of the next instruction, which is contained in the program counter, or PC. The code for the instruction is copied from memory to the instruction register, or IR. At this point, the PC is incremented so that it contains the address of the next location in memory to be accessed. Then the instruction is decoded or translated into a series of control signals.

Next, any operands needed for the execution of the instruction are fetched from memory. With some operations, the data may already be stored in one of the registers. In this case, the data is immediately available for performing the operation and no additional memory fetches are required. For example, if the instruction is to sum two numbers stored in memory, a copy of each is fetched from memory. As the next step, the operation is actually executed. Last, any result from the operation—in the case of an add instruction, the sum of the addition—is stored in memory or in a register. If storage is to a memory location, it might be necessary to fetch the storage location address from memory.

Thus the execution of an instruction consists of a series of steps referred to as an *instruction cycle*. There are three basic parts to the cycle, memory fetch, execution, and memory store. As illustrated in Fig. 2-7, at least five parts can be distinguished in the cycle. Of course, the type and number of steps required to execute one instruction depends on the complexity of the instruction and the architecture of the micro.

With some computers, the instruction fetch, execution, and data store may overlap. The number of machine cycles depends on the complexity of the operation. For instance, moving (really copying) data from one location to another requires less work than multiplying two numbers. Additionally, how the actual address in memory of the operands and instructions is determined will affect the number of cycles required. Sometimes, determining addresses is simple, and sometimes it is quite complex. In the former

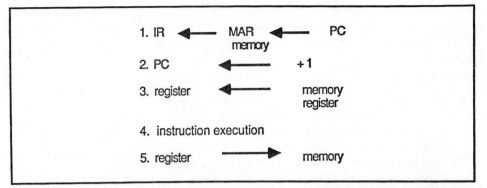

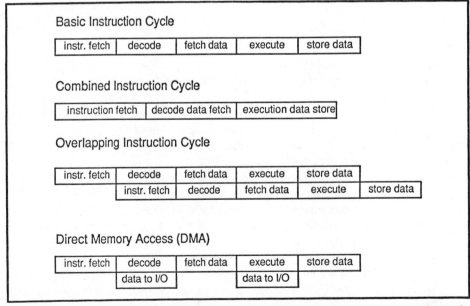

Fig. 2-7. The basic instruction cycle: Computers execute tasks by repeating a basic instruction cycle over and over: The first step is to locate the instruction. This is done by getting the instruction's address from the PC (Program Counter) to the MAR (Memory Address Register), which enables copying the instruction to the IR (instruction register). Second, the PC is updated by the number of bytes in the instruction, which ranges from 1 to 6, so that it points to the next instruction. Third, any needed operands are fetched from memory or another register. Fourth, execution takes place in a register that is often called the accumulator. Last, results are often stored in memory or another register.

case, obviously, fewer cycles are required. The basic operation of the computer is to repeat this cycle continuously. Even the simplest programs require thousands or millions of instruction cycles.

Fig. 2-8 illustrates the fact that there are variations on the basic instruction cycle.

Fig. 2-8. Variations on the basic instruction cycle: There are variations on the basic instruction cycle. In the combined instruction cycle, steps are combined from the basic instruction cycle so that there are just three steps in the cycle. Some computers will overlap the instruction cycles for an overlapped instruction cycle, or, as it is sometimes called, pipelined operation. Some computers use the time used to fetch instructions to perform operation such as I/O data transfers, commonly known as direct memory access.

The steps in the basic instruction cycle can be combined, for example, from five steps to three steps, so that the only steps are instruction fetch, decode data fetch, and execution data store. Instructions can be overlapped (sometimes called *pipelining*) since the decode and execute cycles do not require accessing main memory. As a result, this time can be used to fetch the next instruction or to store the results of previous instruction executions. This time can also be used on some computers to perform operations such as direct memory to I/O data transfers, a practice commonly known as *direct memory access*, or DMA.

FOR FURTHER READING

Kay, Alan. "Computer Software," in *Scientific American* (September, 1984).

Osborne, Adam. *An Introduction to Microcomputers: Volume 0 :The Beginner's Book.* (Berkeley, 1979).

Shore, John. *The Sachertorte Algorithm and Other Antidotes to Computer Anxiety.* (New York, 1985).

Walter, Russ. *The Secret Guide to Computers, Vol. 1: The Main Secrets.* (Boston, 1984).

Zaks, Rodney. *Microprocessors : From Chips to Systems.* (Sybex, 1980).

Chapter 3

Data Representation

Purpose of the Chapter. In this chapter, we discuss how various kinds of data (numbers and characters) are represented in a computer whose individual electronic circuits are capable of only two different states (1 and 0 or on and off). We cover binary, octal and hexadecimal representation, 2's complement, ASCII code (alphanumeric data), and real number representation. The chapter concludes by discussing several special coding and data compacting methods.

REPRESENTATION AND POSITIONAL NUMBER SYSTEMS

An understanding of the methods used to represent and process data is critical to an understanding of how computers perform the tasks we assign them. We must represent the problems we wish a computer to solve in terms that the computer can use. Specifically, a program is written using the concepts and procedures associated with the problem to be solved. For example, in preparing a payroll, we might use a list of names, pay scales, and hours worked and a procedure that multiplies the scales times the hours to determine the pay due the employees. Then the computer maps these concepts and procedures onto the data structures (ultimately, the 1s and 0s) and the instruction set of the computer. The result is that the computer becomes a general purpose problem solving system.

All instructions and data are stored internally in the computer as binary numbers, or to be more exact, as binary electronic states. For our benefit, the computer's electronic states are represented in various formats that we can understand more easily. For example, if the character C is entered at the computer terminal, it is represented in the computer as the binary number 01000011, which we can also represent decimally (our familiar base 10) as 67 or hexadecimally (base 16) as 43. Hence, the computer's eight electronic states, the binary number 01000011, the decimal number 67, and the hexadecimal number 43 are all different ways to represent C.

Most people have no difficulty understanding the number 555 as five hundred fifty-five. The value of this decimal representation is the value of the first five times one hundred, the value of the second five times ten, and the value of the third five times one. We know that the number that a digit represents stems from two factors: 1) the digit itself and 2) the place it has in the representation. Generally speaking, letting the d's represent digits and the B's bases, the value of a numeric representation is determined by this formula:

$$(d \times B^n) + ... + (d \times B^1) + (d \times B^0) . + (d \times B^{-1}) + (d \times B^{-2}) + ... + (d \times B^{-n})$$

Any representation in any base can be evaluated by sustituting its digits for the d 's and its bases for the B 's and then evaluating the resulting expression. The digit with the smallest value will be zero and the largest digit will be one less than the base of the system. For example, base 10 uses digits 0 through 9; base 2, 0 and 1; base 8, 0 through 7, and base 16, 0 through F (because letters A..F are pressed into service to represent 10 through 15).

In a positional number system, the value of a digit in a representation is a function of the value of digit times the value of the position the digit has in the representation. The digit furthest to the left is designated the *most significant digit*, or *MSD*, and the digit to the right is the *least significant digit*, or *LSD*. The MSD of 16, 338, for instance, is 1, and the LSD is 8.

Integer representations or the integer part of a real number can be evaluated by multiplying each digit times the base raised to a power that is one less than its position from the radix point. Evaluating the decimal representation 456, for example, means multiplying the 4 times 10^2 since the 4 is three places left of the radix (in this case the decimal) point; multiplying the 5 times 10^1; multiplying the 6 times 10^0; and summing the results—which, of course, yields four hundred fifty six:

distance from the radix point:	3	2	1
base raised to power:	10^2	10^1	10^0
representation:	4	5	6
evaluation:	$4*10^2 + 5*10^1 + 6*10^0 = 456$ decimal		

Fractional representations or the fractional part of a real number representation can be evaluated by raising each digit to the negative power of the number of places the digit is from the radix point. For example, suppose we wish to evaluate .456 decimal. Substituting from left to right, since the 4 is one place from the decimal or radix point, $4 \times 10^{-1} = 4 \times .1$ or four tenths; since the 5 is two places from the radix, $5 \times 10^{-2} = 5 \times .01$ or five hundredths; since the 6 is three places from the radix, $6 \times 10^{-3} = 6 \times .001$ or six thousandths.

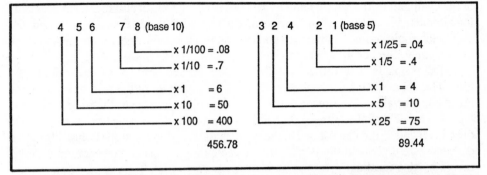

Fig. 3-1. *Value tables and base conversions:* In the first case, with base 10 or decimal, each digit is worth 1/10th the previous value of the digit to its immediate left and ten times the value of the digit to its right. In the second case, with base 5, each digit is worth 1/5th the previous value of the digit to its immediate left and five times the value of the digit to its right. A representation is evaluated by multiplying each digit times its fractional or integral value and then summing the results.

A less formal way to evaluate numeric representations is to use the value tables displayed in Fig. 3-1.

A general value table is shown in Fig. 3-2. It shows how to determine the value of any representation in any base.

THREE NUMERIC SYSTEMS: BINARY, OCTAL, AND HEX

Three numeric representation systems enjoy general use in computers. They are the binary, or base 2, the octal, or base 8, and the hexadecimal, or base 16, systems. We have explained how binary digits correspond exactly to the switches, the bits, of the computer. Binary is the principal numeric representation system. Octal and hexadecimal, or *hex*, are widely used in programming for two reasons. First, people find them much easier to use than binary and second, each digit in octal and hex represents 3 and 4 binary bits respectively—which makes them easily converted to and from binary.

The relation of octal and hex to binary is like the relation of paper money to coins in the same currency: conversions are easy to do and easy to remember how to do. The relation of decimal to binary, on the other hand, is like the relation of English pounds and shillings to American dollars and cents: relatively complicated and difficult to

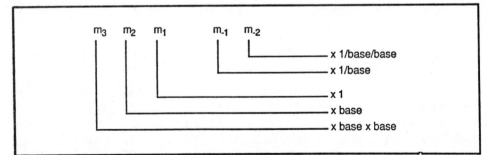

Fig. 3-2. *General value table:* To determine the decimal value of any representation, simply multiply each digit by the formula on the right and sum the results. The pattern repeats on each side of the radix point so, for example, the value of m_5 would be x base x base x base x base.

remember. It is simply a fact of assembly language life that programmers must become conversant with the binary, octal, and hexadecimal systems.

To distinguish between numbers of different bases in contexts where the base is not obvious, the mathematical convention is to use subscripts to denote the base. For example, 1011_2, is read "one-zero-one-one, base 2" and 1011_{10}, is read as the familiar "one thousand eleven." In decimal, we read the place value as well as the number—"one thousand eleven"—but in nondecimal representations, we simply read the numbers and indicate the base if there is any doubt about which base is being used. Some care should be used in representing bases since carelessness here is a common cause of programming error.

In most computers, however, bases are not denoted by subscripts since many line editors and printers don't support subscripting. Instead, if no base is indicated, as in 1010, decimal is the default or assumed value. Sometimes, the context will indicate which system is being used. Sometimes, a nondecimal base is indicated by a trailing character, as in 1010B, for 1010 binary. Some examples are:

105 = "one hundred five" (default for decimal)

10A = "one zero A hex" ("H" for hexadecimal)

107Q = "one zero seven octal" ("Q" for octal*)

1011B = "one zero one one binary" ("B" for binary)

(* "Q" instead of "O" so that it won't be mistaken for a zero)

Most assemblers will allow you to use hex, binary, octal or decimal, with decimal being the default representation on some compilers.

The Binary Number System

Since today's computers are nearly all digital machines with electronic switches for memory circuits, it makes sense to use a representational system that corresponds to the open-closed or "off-on" characteristics of the computer's memory circuits. In other words, we need a system with only two digits—0 and 1. Such a system is called the *binary* or base 2, number system.

The binary system possesses only two digits. As a result, with the exception of the numbers zero and one, it will always take more digits to represent a number in binary than it does in decimal. With larger numbers, binary representations require so many digits that they become difficult to understand, to read, and to copy without error. These difficulties are the reason why numeric systems that are easily converted to and from the binary system (which decimal is not), such as octal and hex, are widely used in programming. Since the binary system is the basic system for all computers (it is used to represent both instructions and data), each digit represents the smallest unit of information that is stored in the computer. Each digit is called a *bit*, which is a contraction of *binary digit*. Each bit is stored in the computer as an electronic or magnetic switch in one of two possible positions. The number 0110 contains four bits and 00101011 contains eight bits. As indicated earlier, representations in bases other than decimal are read as a string of digits: 0110, base two, is read as "binary zero one one zero."

One principal characteristic of a micro is the number of bits that are grouped together to form the next unit larger than a bit. A series of four bits is called a *half-byte* or *nibble*. An eight bit series is called a byte. Most computers store and manipulate information in locations that are a fixed number of bits—this fixed number is called a *word*. Microcomputers typically have either 8, 16, or 32 bit words. 16 bits are referred to as a *word*, and 32 bits as a *double word*.

The Octal and Hexadecimal Number Systems

The fewer the digits available for use, the more of them it will take to represent numbers and ideas. As a result, as the numbers represented become large, the number of binary digits required to represent them becomes unwieldy and error-prone. For example, compare the following binary and decimal representations of the same number:

binary: 0111111111111111   decimal: 32767

Information theorists tell us what our experience likely will confirm—that the greater the number of alphanumeric characters in a message, the greater the chance there is for error in the reading and transmission of that message. Binary requires a larger number of digits, as the above example illustrates; therefore, its potential for error is greater.

One way to address this problem is to use a representational scheme that is easily converted to binary and yet does not require as many digits to represent a given number or alphabetic character. Two possibilities are the octal (base 8) and hex (base 16) systems. The octal and hex systems are arithmetically related to the binary system since all three systems are powers of 2. This fact makes conversion between the three systems very simple.

The reason that octal was used early in the history of computers and has been steadily replaced by hex is historical. Octal was used exclusively on first generation computers and dominated second generation computers because the digital displays of these computers were not capable of displaying the alphabetic characters A through Z. Hence, hex could not be used, and since octal was close to decimal in terms of ease of use, it was used.

There are, however, difficulties with octal representations of 16 bit words. Figure 3-3 contrasts the awkwardness of octal representation with the straightforward way hex represents 16 bit words and underscores how hex is more easily converted to and from ASCII.

Bits are grouped from right to left, from the LSD to the MSD. In the octal representation, the first two octal digits take up six bits, counting from the right, of the first or lower byte. That means that two bits remain in the first byte. To get a third group of three bits (three since it takes three bits to make an octal digit), a bit must be taken from the first bit in the higher byte to complete the third octal digit. Using six more bits from the higher byte to form the next two octal digits leaves only one bit to represent the the MSD. The octal equivalent of the binary word 0101001101111010 turns out to be 51572. By taking the word as two bytes, however, the two bytes in octal represent 123 (high byte) and 172 (low byte). Since program listings often print out data by bytes rather than words, octal representation can become confusing.

By contrast, notice how simple hex is. Each of the four bits is equivalent to one

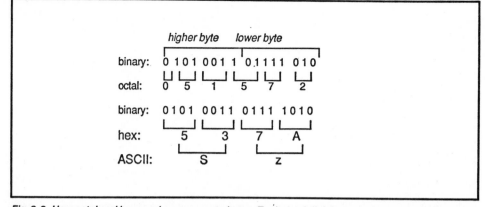

Fig. 3-3. *How octal and hex numbers map onto bytes:* Each octal digit is equivalent to three bits, working from right to left, from the lower to the higher byte of a 16 bit word, while each hex digit is equivalent to four bits. As a result, an octal number is awkwardly shoehorned into a 16 bit word, while a hex number maps naturally into a 16 bit word—to get the third bit required for the third octal digit, a bit must be taken from the higher byte. The hex digits neatly take four bits from each byte so that exactly two hex digits can be stored in each byte. The hex representation, in turn, is easily translated to and from ASCII.

hex digit. There is nothing left over, nothing to borrow, and the listings print out hex digits. Everything is quite straightforward. The hex representation above, therefore, is 537A with 53 stored in the higher byte and 7A in the lower byte. If alphabetic characters are stored in the two bytes, then 537A can easily be converted to its ASCII equivalent, Sz. The octal representation 51572 does not lend itself so easily to alphabetic representation.

In spite of the advantages of hex over octal, octal is still supported on many systems in order to maintain compatibility with older systems that still use octal. Octal is probably most widely used on minicomputers.

Converting from One Base to Another

We will suggest two methods for converting numeric representations to other bases. We suggest that you read and attempt to understand both and then use the method which you find the easiest to use and remember. At this point, we will deal with integers but not fractions. Later, fractions and real numbers will be discussed.

Table 3-1 compares the binary, octal and hex systems in terms of the values of their respective digits relative to their position in a representation.

The value of each next MSD in a representation is the previous position times the base. Each MSD position in base 2, for instance, is simply twice the last one—i.e., position 5, with a value of 16, is worth twice position 4, with a value of 8. Each larger position in octal or base 8 is worth eight times the last one—i.e., position 4 is worth eight times that of position 3.

Method 1: The Brute Force Method

Probably the easiest method of converting from decimal to some other base is to use Table 1 with the following procedure. Although it is not mathematically elegant,

	Octal (O)	Binary (B)	Hex (H)
(LSD)	1	1	1
		2	
		4	
	8	8	
		16	16
		32	
	64	64	
		128	
		256	256
	512	512	
		1024	
		2048	
	4096	4096	4096
		8192	
		16384	
	32768	32768	
(MSD)		65536	65536

Table 3-1. Position Values of the Octal, Binary and Hex Systems: The table is set up so that the arithmetic relationship between the three bases is illustrated. The LSD of all three is the value in 1s, the next most significant digit is 2 for binary, 8 for octal, and 16 for hex, the next 4 for binary, 64 for octal, and 256 for hex, and so on. The value of each digit is the base times the value of the next least significant digit—e.g., in the octal or base 8, column 3, 64, is 8 times the value of the next LSD, namely 8.

it is easy to remember since it can be recreated without being memorized:

1. From Table 1 identify the largest number in the target base column that is less than the decimal number.

2. Divide the decimal number by this number—the integral result of the division is the converted MSD, and the remainder is the number to use in successive divisions.

3. Use the next smallest number in the column of the target base as the new divisor.

4. Repeat steps 2 and 3 until the remainder is less than the target base—this last remainder becomes the LSD.

For example, suppose we wish to convert 942 decimal to its octal equivalent. Since octal is the target base, we consult the octal column in Table 1. We find that 512 is the largest number in the column that is less than 942 decimal. Dividing 942 by 512 yields 1 with a remainder of 430. As a result, 1 is the MSD of the octal equivalent, and 430 becomes our new dividend. Since 64 is the next smallest number in the octal column in the table, it is our next divisor. Dividing 430 by 64 yields 6 with a remainder of 46. As a result, 6 is the next most significant digit and 46 becomes our new dividend. Consulting the table again, we see that 8 is is the next smallest number in the octal column, so it is the new divisor. Dividing 46 by 8 yields 5 with a remainder of 6. The two least significant digits, therefore, are 5 and 6. Our answer, therefore, is 1656.

To convert to a decimal number from another base, follow this procedure:

---

1. From Table 1, find the position value of the MSD of the representation to be converted.

2. Multiply this value by the digit and save the result.

3. From Table 1, find the position value of the next digit to be converted and multiply this value by the digit and save the result.

4. Repeat step 3 for all remaining digits in the representation.

5. Add the saved results to determine the decimal equivalent.

For example, to convert 1656, base 8, to decimal, we do the following. Consulting Table 3-1, we see that the fourth MSD for octal has a value of 512 decimal. $1 \times 512 = 512$. The third MSD for octal equals 64 decimal. $6 \times 64 = 384$. The second MSD for octal is 8. $5 \times 8 = 40$. And $6 \times 1 = 6$. Summing, we get 942 decimal.

As suggested earlier, converting between binary and octal or binary and hex is very easy—that's one reason why octal and hex are used. Each octal digit represents three binary bits and each hex digit four bits. Practically, this means that to convert between binary and octal, we only need to convert each group of three bits in binary corresponding to one digit in octal; to convert between binary and hex, we convert each group of four binary bits to one hex digit.

Suppose we wish to convert the binary number 10101100 to octal and then back again. We group the bits in the binary representation by threes from the LSD or, as it is called with binary representations, the least significant bit (LSB). Each three bit grouping is converted to its octal equivalent and the resulting representation is the answer.

$$
\begin{array}{ccc}
10 & 101 & 110 \\
| & | & | \\
2 & 5 & 6
\end{array}
$$

If the leftmost group has only one or two bits, we imagine that it has leading zeros. Converting from octal to binary is a matter of reversing the process—replacing the 6 with its binary equivalent, 110, the 5 with 101, and so on. If Table 3-2 is handy or committed to memory, then with practice, conversions are straightforward.

Since hex is binary to the fourth power, to convert a binary number to hex, we group the binary representation from the LSB by fours and then convert to each grouping's hex equivalent.

Decimal	Binary	Octal	Hex
0	0	0	0
1	1	1	1
2	10	2	2
3	11	3	3
4	100	4	4
5	101	5	5
6	110	6	6
7	111	7	7
8	1000	10	8
9	1001	11	9
10	1010	12	A
11	1011	13	B
12	1100	14	C
13	1101	15	D
14	1110	16	E
15	1111	17	F

Table 3-2. Decimal, Binary, Octal and Hex Equivalents: This table illustrates the binary, octal and hex equivalents of 1-15 in decimal. It is through 15 decimal since this is the maximum value that can be stored in a half byte and the largest hex digit.

```
1010 1110
 ↓    ↓
 A    E
```

Converting from hex to binary is a matter of reversing the process:

```
 A    E
 ↓    ↓
1010 1110
```

It should be noted that, unlike octal, in converting from hex to binary, each hex digit will be equivalent to four bits.

Converting from octal to hex and vice versa is rarely required since a computer system, assembler, or compiler usually will primarily use either octal or hex but not both—even though both may be available to do this. Convert the source base representation to binary first; then convert it back to the target base, using the methods described above. As mentioned earlier, hex is used more often than octal in the newer computers.

Method 2: Arithmetic

The second method of converting between bases is mathematically more elegant but somewhat more difficult to remember and use, at least for those who are less mathematically inclined. Recall our formula for evaluating representations of numbers:

$$(d \times B^n) + ... + (d \times B^1) + (d \times B^0). + (d \times B^{-1}) + (d \times B^{-2}) ... (d \times B^{-n})$$

Let's denote that part of the representation that is on the left of the radix point, the integral part, with R_i. Let's denote that part of the representation that is on the right of the radix point the fractional part, with R_f.

If R_i is a decimal representation, converting it to its binary equivalent is simply a matter of repeated remainder division (or *mod* arithmetic). Suppose, for instance, that we wish to convert 30.65625 to its binary equivalent. Since $R_i = 30$, we repeatedly divide it by the target base, in this case, 2, noting the remainders, until the quotient equals zero:

Division	Quotients	Remainders	
30/2	15	0	(LSD)
15/2	7	1	↑
7/2	3	1	
3/2	1	1	↓
1/2	0	1	(MSD)

Note that 1) the quotient for each remainder division becomes the divisor for the next division; and 2) the remainder becomes the next LSD. Hence, 30, base 10, equals 11110, base 2.

To determine the binary fractional equivalent of 30.65625, we use repeated integral multiplication instead of repeated remainder division. Specifically, we multiply R_f, and each successive fractional part, by the target base, in this case, base 2, taking the integral part of the result as the next LSD of the new binary representation. We repeat this procedure until the fractional result is zero:

Multiplication	Product	Integral Part	
.65625 x 2	1.31250	1	(MSD)
.31250 x 2	.625	0	↑
.625 x 2	1.250	1	
.25 x 2	.5	0	↓
.5 x 2	1.00	1	(LSD)

With each multiplication, we get a product with either a one or a zero for the integral result. If the integral result is a one, we record the next LSD as a one, otherwise a zero. Hence, our binary R_f becomes .10101. Putting the two results together, we get 11110.10101. Of course, not all fractions will terminate as quickly as this when put through this routine.

NEGATIVE NUMBERS

We've maintained that everything in a digital computer is represented as bits. In the decimal system, we represent a negative number by prefixing a – in front of the numeric magnitude of the number, i.e., negative 8 is represented as – 8. But in binary we have only a 0 and a 1 to do all our representing; the machine has no direct way to represent negative values. One way to solve this problem is to use one of the bits to represent the sign of the number. Since, by convention, we prefix magnitudes with their signs, it is a natural convention to use the high order bit, the bit in the leftmost place of the binary number, as the sign bit:

sign bit (high order bit)

0 1 1 0 0 1 1 0

magnitude (bits 0 through 6, counting right to left)

(sign bit: 1 indicates a negative, 0 a positive value)

This mode of representation is called *signed magnitude* representation. A 1 in the MSB means that the number represented is negative, and a 0 means the number is positive. The magnitude then represents the distance from zero.

Zero Relative Magnitude

Signed magnitude is not the only way to represent negative values. Consider the fact that mathematicians sometimes speak of a number line that can be portrayed as follows:

-5 -4 -3 -2 -1   0   1   2   3   4   5

Zero marks the middle of the line and both positive and negative integers are represented as distances from zero. The notion of absolute value refers to the distance on the line that a number, positive or negative, is from zero. We could call the number line a *zero relative system* since a number's (positive or negative) absolute value is equivalent to its distance on the line from zero. Both 3 and −3, for example, are three units from zero on the number line.

Another zero relative system is a trip odometer since it tells a person how many miles—how far from zero—a car has gone. But suppose that you wished to represent negative numbers on a mileage odometer, which you could spin, like an unscrupulous used car dealer, in either direction. If the odometer reads, "0000," and if it were spun backwards one position, the odometer would read "9999." Spinning it forward, of course, would yield "0001." Provided that we were willing to restrict the settings "0000" up to "4999" for representing positive numbers, we could represent negative numbers by using the odometer's settings "9999" down to "5000." The price we pay for this new representational power is that now our system can no longer represent positive numbers 5000..9999. In other words, we trade some of our positive representations for some negative representations—without needing the signs + and −.

Where this kind of representation gets slightly tricky is that 9999, which represents −1, is a smaller negative number (in terms of absolute value) than 9998, which represents −2. We're accustomed to thinking that 9999 represents a larger value than 4999—but it does only on the usual interpretation. Moreover, 4999 represents a greater number than 5000 since the latter represents −5000. When we have spun the odometer backwards until it gets to 5000, we have represented the most negative number we can, and, when we have spun it up to 4999, we have represented the largest positive number we can.

As Fig. 3-4 portrays, the same relationships obtain in the binary system used in computers. An 8-bit binary number can represent 256 values. If we choose to represent only positive numbers, then an 8-bit word can represent 0 through 255. If, however, we choose to use the first bit as a *sign bit*, then we have chosen to use half of the representational power to represent negative numbers. In such a case, with the first bit used to represent the sign, 0 for positive and 1 for negative, we are left with 7 bits to represent the positive numbers 0..127 (00000000 to 01111111) and 7 bits to represent the negative numbers $-1..-128$ (111111111 to 10000000).

As Fig. 3-4 illustrated, the positive binary representations start with zero (00000000) and increase in absolute magnitude; negative representations start with -1 (11111111) and decrease in magnitude. Consequently, 01111111 is the largest representable number on the binary odometer and 10000000 is the smallest representable number—even though 10000000 interpreted the usual way is one larger than 01111111.

2's Complement Representation

To switch the value of a bit to its opposite value is to take its *complement*. The complement of a set of bits is its flip-flopped opposite. For example, the complement of 101 is 010. More specifically, in terms of arithmetic representation, this is called the 1's complement. The one's complement of a number is gotten by changing all its 1s to 0s and all its 0s to 1s.

The 2's complement of a number is just like its 1's complement except that 1 is added to the LSD. For example, since decimal 10 is 1010 in binary, its complement is 0101 and its 2's complement is 0110.

There are two reasons why complement representation is used in computers: (1) negative numbers can be represented and (2) subtraction becomes equivalent to addition.

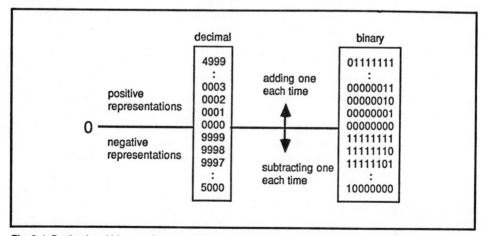

Fig. 3-4. Decimal and binary odometers: We can represent negative values in a system with no minus sign by trading some of the positive representational capability for some negative representational capability. On the decimal odometer, we interpret numbers 5000-99999 as negative values and on the binary odometer we interpret numbers 10000000-11111111 as negative values.

To convert a negative decimal number to 2's complement, do the following:

---

1. Convert the absolute value of the decimal number to its binary equivalent.

---

2. Depending on the word length of the machine in question, fill in on the left with as many leading 0's as necessary until the result is as many bits as the machine's word length—making sure that the MSD is 0, since we are dealing with absolute value.

---

3. Complement the result from step 2—change all 1s to 0s and all 0s to 1s.

---

4. Add 1 to the LSD (this last step converts the representation from 1s complement to 2s complement).

In order to convert a 2's complement representation to its decimal equivalent, simply reverse these steps. For example, suppose we wish to represent – 12 in 2's complement. The binary equivalent of 12 is 1100. Assuming that we are working with an 8-bit word, we fill out this result with leading zeroes, obtaining 00001100. Next, we complement this result to obtain 11110011, which gives us the 1's complement result. Last, we add one to the result to obtain "11110100." The 2s complement representation of a positive number is just that number in binary, with a zero in the MSB. Decimal 9, for instance, would be "00001001" in 2's complement form in an 8-bit word.

Note that 2's complement representation, by convention, uses the leftmost bit to indicate sign. As a result, if the leftmost bit is 0, the number represented is positive; if it is 1, the number represented is negative. Moreover, if the number represented is negative, it will be represented in 2's complement form.

One distinct disadvantage to using the MSB as the sign bit is that the maximum representable number is approximately halved. Suppose that we are working with an 8-bit system. With the leftmost bit used to represent the sign, we are left with seven bits to represent the magnitude. As a result, the maximum value that can be represented by an 8-bit word with one bit used for the sign is $2^7 - 1$ or 127 decimal and 01111111 binary. It is minus 1 because zero takes up the first bit pattern, which is considered positive. Conversely, the maximum negative value is -2^8 or – 128 decimal and 1000000 binary.

As a result, the range of integer representation on a computer with an 8-bit word is – 128 to + 127 decimal, or 1000000 to 01111111 binary. With a 16-bit word (most 8-bit machines are capable of pairing bytes to get a 16-bit word), the range of representation is – 32768 to + 32767. You can see how, just as in the case of the car's odometer representation, we sacrifice representation at the positive end in order to be able to represent negative numbers—without needing a – sign. It should be noted that the bits in the computer do not change—any more than the car's odometer physically changed in any way. We alter our *interpretation* to represent negative numbers by using the first bit as a sign bit. Only the interpretation of the digits changes.

Using 2's complement, subtraction proves quite straight forward. Suppose, for instance, that we wish to subtract 23 from 47. The solution is to convert the subtrahend (the number which is subtracted) to its 2's complement representation. The minuend (the other number in the subtraction) is left as is. Then we add as usual.

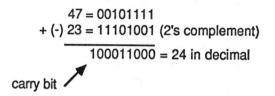

$$47 = 00101111$$
$$+ (-) \; 23 = 11101001 \;\text{(2's complement)}$$
$$\overline{100011000} = 24 \text{ in decimal}$$

carry bit

The addition of the two numbers is executed as usual. The exception is that the carry bit that results at the leftmost bit is ignored.

There is, however, an exception to this last statement. If the addition of two numbers with the same sign results in a number with a different sign, an error has occurred. Consider the following addition of "65" and "66":

$$.65 = 01000001$$
$$+ \; \underline{66 = 01000010}$$
$$10000011$$

The result is the representation of a negative number since a leading 1 means the number represented is negative. This is an overflow condition. The cause of the overflow is the attempt to represent a number that exceeds the largest representable positive integer in 8 bit 2's complement notation. The problem can be avoided by using more bits to represent numbers, but no matter how many bits are used, errors will occur if an arithmetic operation exceeds the representation limits of the computer. Most machines provide flags that can be tested to determine if the result of an arithmetic operation using 2's complement notation produces a result that is out of range. As a result, it is always a good idea to test for this condition after each arithmetic operation where 2's complement representation is used.

ASCII CODE

Binary code is used in many applications besides computers. One important use of binary code is in telecommunications. For many years, a widely used communications device has been the Teletype terminal, or *TTY* for short. It has been used for a variety of communications and was the predecessor of the CRT (cathode ray tube) or VDT (video display terminal). One of the earliest systems used was the 6-bit Baudot code. Since the earliest computers were only able to use paper tape and IBM cards for I/O, like the TTY, variations of the 6-bit Baudot code were adapted for use with computers. However, since six bits can only represent 64 distinct characters, which is too few for many programming tasks, the six bits were expanded to seven bits with an eighth bit for error checking. The *error* or *parity* bit, as it is commonly called, was assigned the most significant bit, while the other seven bits represented alphanumeric characters or control characters such as backspace or carriage return.

Using 7 bits for communication means that 128 different characters can be represented, which is more than adequate for most applications. The eighth parity bit was at first quite essential since early equipment was especially error prone. Today, however, with more reliable equipment, the parity bit is less often used or is used for other purposes.

The binary code now used with most computers has become known as the American Standard Code for Information Interchange or ASCII (pronounced "as-key"). The ASCII code is simply a way, like the old Morse Code, to encode messages using numbers. Morse Code was used because messages had to be encoded as dots and dashes in order to be sendable over telegraph lines. ASCII is used because computers utilize only 1s and 0s.

REAL NUMBERS

Many solutions to problems require the use of numbers between the integers 1, 2, 3, . . ., specifically, fractions such as .25 and mixed numbers such as 2.66. Numbers that contain a radix point are usually called *real* numbers. The two most common ways to represent real numbers is as an integer plus radix fraction or as a real number with an expansionary exponent. See Fig. 3-5.

In the examples in Fig. 3-5, *expansion* indicates an exponential expansion. The value indicates the the direction and magnitude of the expansion. For example, the scientific notation of the real number 93.271 would be 9.3271 E1 where the exponent 1 (positive is the default value) indicates that the decimal point is to moved to right one place in the equivalent real representation. Moving the decimal point to the right one place in 9.3271 yields 93.271. A negative exponent indicates the number of places to the left the decimal point is moved.

There are three generally used methods for storing real numbers, *implied decimal point, fixed point,* and *floating point* number storage. The last two methods are variations on the first.

Fixed Point and Floating Point

In *fixed point* representation, the radix point is fixed at a definite location in the binary word. All bits to the left of the radix point are given integer values, and all bits

	integer part	fractional part	expansion
integer	93	-	-
fixed	93	.271	-
scientific	9	.3271	x 10^1 (10^n)
floating point		.93271	E2 (En)

Fig. 3-5. Integers, fixed point, scientific notation, and floating point representation: **Fixed point numbers contain a fractional part but not an expansion. In scientific notation, the integral and fractional parts are expanded by some power of 10. In floating point notation, there is no integral part since the representation must be some number between 0 and 1 expanded by some exponent.**

to the right are given fractional values. Examples of fixed point representations include 0101.1001 binary and 93.271 decimal.

A *floating point* number is stored as two binary numbers, an integer portion and a fractional portion. The real number 2.5 decimal or 10.1 binary can be represented in floating point format in the following way. First, its representation is *normalized*—the binary point is moved so that 1) no 1s remain to its left and 2) the first bit after the point is a 1. (The number zero is allowed to violate this last part.) Normalized, 10.1 is .101. The fractional portion of the representation in memory holds this normalized number. The integer portion in memory holds the exponent that is needed to restore the normalized number to the original number or 10.1 This exponent turns out to be 2. In binary, of course, this is 10.

Often, floating point numbers will be stored in four bytes, with byte 1 storing the integer portion exponent and bytes 2—4 storing the (normalized) fractional portion number. As illustrated in Fig. 3-6, bit 7 of byte 2, because of normalization, will be a 1 except in the case where the number represented is zero. Figure 3-6 also displays how "2.5" would be stored in a computer that uses this floating point format.

The difference between floating point numbers and fixed point numbers is that in fixed point the decimal point is shifted after the number is converted into its decimal equivalent. Both the first and second numbers can be any number of bits and the radix point can be located anywhere within the first number. It is, however, customary for the first number, the relative value, to be a multiple of 8 bits (i.e., 8, 16 or 24 bits) and the second number, which locates the radix point, to be 8 bits or less. The radix point normally is located just before or just after the MSB.

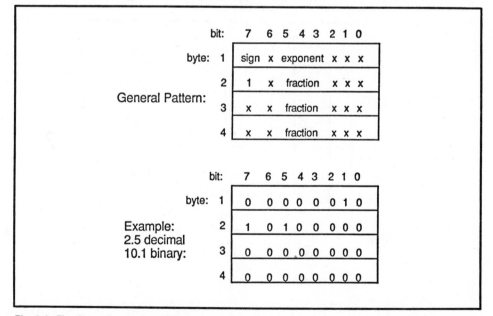

Fig. 3-6. Floating point representation: A common way to store floating point representations of real numbers is shown here. The first byte contains the exponent, the next three bytes the fractional part. The 1 in the general pattern (byte 2, bit 7) reflects the normalization of the representation. The sign of the exponent is stored in the high-order bit of the first byte.

Problems in Representing Real Numbers

A major problem in representing real numbers in computers is that absolute accuracy is not possible. This stems from the way a real number is represented in the binary system. Each bit to the right of the radix point is worth one half the value of the previous bit; for instance, the bit two places to the right of the radix point is worth .25D, while the bit one place to the right is worth .5D. Figure 3-7 displays the values of the bits closest to the radix or binary point.

The value of any fractional place is simply 1/2 raised to the power of the place. For instance, the fourth place to the right of the radix point is worth $(1/2)^4$ or .0625. The problem is that the value representable by the fractional part of a binary number can converge to but never equal 1. With many fractional places, the value can approach one, but even using multiple words (more than 32 bits), some fractional values simply cannot be represented. For example, with four bits reserved to represent the fractional part, the largest fractional value that can be represented is .1111 or .9375D; the fractional values between .9375 and 1 cannot be represented. The result is that, in many cases, binary representations can only approximate many decimal fractions.

For scientific applications, this does not constitute a serious problem since scientists and engineers work with approximate values—they realize that no measurement is absolutely accurate. As long as computer representations approach measurement tolerances, which they usually can, they can live with the problem.

For many business applications, however, this inability to represent values with precise accuracy becomes a serious difficulty. For example, an accounting program that uses values rounded of to the nearest fractional value, say hundredths, will probably be adequate for a limited number of executions. With a larger number of calcula-

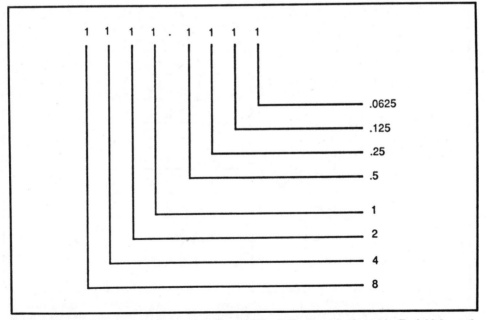

Fig. 3-7. Binary value table: This is just an instance of Fig. 3-2's general value table. Each bit is worth twice what the bit to its right is worth and one half what the bit to its left is worth.

tions, however, the truncated portion of the fraction will multiply repeatedly as the program is used. What starts out as a small statistical inaccuracy can become a large discrepancy—a development that business associates often will find unacceptable.

The standard convention used with better accounting systems is what is called *weighted* binary numbers. This method involves multiplying or dividing a real number by a factor of 10 so it appears as an integer when used by the computer. At output time, the process is reversed so that accuracy is restored. For example, suppose that an actual value was 7.91. The weighted binary representation, when multiplied by 100, is 791. The machine uses this weighted representation then, at output, divides by 100 so that the accurate value is restored. Using this technique means that relative accuracy is retained during calculations. This is effectively the same as a fixed point real number where the radix is positioned after the LSD so that there is no fractional part.

Although the bits required to represent very large or very small numbers in weighted binary form is often greater than would be needed with binary real representation, arithmetic operations performed on the weighted representation are actually faster. It should be noted that high level languages will normally only support real numbers or integers within a fairly small range. Only AL provides for weighted binary representation or the ability to store the value in a format that is best suited for an individual application.

ALTERNATE ENCODING METHODS

It has become standard throughout the computer industry to represent data in terms of the 8-bit binary numbers or in multiples of eight bits. This is due in part to the fact that most I/O devices are designed to operate with eight bits of data. It is not, however, always necessary to use eight bits of memory to store a piece of data when fewer bits can do the job just as well. Using fewer bits means that more data can be stored in the same amount of space. It is not always practical to convert data into its most compact binary format since the conversion process can be complicated.

As a result, various methods of code compacting have been developed. Two of the most popular methods are *binary coded decimal* (BCD), which is used extensively on calculators, and *packed binary*, which is sometimes referred to as *bit flags*. Other, more system-specific, methods are also used.

BCD

Binary coded decimal typically is used to store integer and real numbers. In the previous section, we showed how decimal numbers are converted into binary numbers for use in computers. This system allocated an entire word, a designated number of bits, to represent the number in binary format. Although the value was stored in a compact format, the method required that the decimal number be converted into the binary number for storage and back again for display purposes. Another method that simplifies the conversion process and stores the data in a relatively compact format is BCD. This method uses four bits for each decimal digit, which is what simplifies the conversion process.

```
X     X    decimal number
|     |
xxxx  xxxx  BCD bits
```

For example, 49 decimal would be represented as 0100 1001 in BCD. It should be noted that the 4 bit binary numbers 1010 through 1111 are meaningless in BCD. Also note that each digit is replaced by its complete, full 4-bit equivalent. Additionally, since the higher byte is always 0011, ASCII representations of numbers can be stored two per byte:

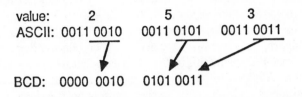

In this case, the first four bits are identical in all the bytes of the ASCII representation. As a result, the information in these bytes can be combined into each half byte in the BCD representation. When the ASCII representation is used, three bytes are required but when BCD is used only two are needed, a 33 percent savings in memory space with no loss of information.

Since there are six unused bit groups in BCD, specifically, 1010 to 1111, it takes more bytes to represent numbers in BCD than it does in regular binary. The advantage is that the conversion procedure is much simpler than with regular binary. Most computers include special math instructions that are designed to work with BCD numbers. As a result, BCD can be viewed as a compromise between the compact data storage and fast math—but complex conversion problems—of regular binary, and the inefficient storage and slower math—but easy conversion—of ASCII representation.

Packed Binary

Packed binary is very useful when only one or two bits are required to represent a condition or value. For example, a variable that specifies a day of the week requires only three bits for storage since three bits can represent 2^3 or 8 different numbers (including 0), which is all that is needed. Similarly, since 31 is the largest number of days in one month, all we need is five bits since five bits can represent 2^5 or 32 days (days 0 through 31). Rather than use two full, 8-bit bytes to store "Friday the 13th," this information can be stored in one single byte—all we need is eight bits total.

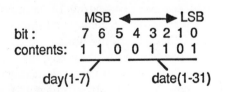

As a result of this compaction, memory requirements are exactly halved—we need one byte instead of the two we would otherwise need. Compacting code in this fashion will require additional program code and operation time since the compacted data will have to be expanded, but the pay-off is that much more data can be stored on external storage devices such as tapes or disk drives. Often, this kind of data is stored in large quantities, as in large data bases. The small price paid for this advantage in terms of additional program code and operating speed is often well worth the advantage in storage requirements since I/O devices are much slower than the computer itself.

The use of these kinds of techniques is the responsibility of the programmer. They are not automatically incorporated in any language. In fact, most high level languages do not permit the programmer to compact data in this way. Only assembly language allows the programmer to compact code and data in order to achieve the most efficient use of storage space and execution speed.

FOR FURTHER READING

Wirth, Niklaus, "Data Structures and Algorithms," in *Scientific American* (September, 1984).

Liffick, Blaise W., ed. *Numbers in Theory and Practice*. (BYTE Books, 1977).

Lipschutz, Seymour. *Essential Computer Mathematics*. (New York, 1982).

Chapter 4

Basic Computer Operations

Purpose of the Chapter: This chapter introduces many of the computer operations, specifically the arithmetic and logical operations, that most of today's microcomputers support. As the chapter explains these operations, it will illustrate some of the associated concepts as well. The chapter concludes with a short program in UAL for the 6502. The program will illustrate some of these basic computer operations at work and will begin to show how universal assembly language differs from conventional ALs such as 6502 AL.

To simplify learning AL instructions, it is important to understand a number of basic computer operations. Understanding the function and purpose of these basic operations makes it easier to understand AL instructions. The micro instruction set tables in the appendix list the instructions used with most currently available micros. As these tables illustrate, about 90 percent of the instructions are based on variations of these basic operations. The other 10 percent are unique to specific micros or perform special functions, some of which the typical programmer may rarely use.

For the sake of clarity, similar operations will be presented in groups, starting with the most basic and most frequently used operations. Each computer operation is displayed and described in the following way:

operation	*mnemonic, parameter(s)*

Description/Explanation

The operation is listed first, and the mnemonic with one or more parameters follow. A *parameter*, sometimes known as *control data*, refers to an item of information that is used to clarify the operation to be performed; it can be given a different value each time the instruction is used. The types of operations covered include data manipulation, math operations, program control, logical operations, bit operations, I/O operations, and multiple and special operations.

DATA MANIPULATION

Move	MOV *source, destination*

The most basic operation performed by a computer is to make a copy of a piece of data stored in one location and place that copy in another location. Data is moved from one location, a *source*, to a *destination*. Consider this example:

instruction	location(s)	contents	
		before	*after*
MOV LOC 30, LOC 75	30	00010010	00010010
	:	:	:
	75	11001101	00010010

The move instruction means copying the contents of location 30 and replacing whatever is in location 75 with this copy. The contents of location 30 are unaffected, and the original contents of location 75 are lost.

While the idea of a move is certainly obvious enough, there are enough locations in a computer and methods for specifying a location that can be used by move instructions (see Chapter 7 on addressing modes), that they can be confusing. Data is stored in two principal locations, *main memory* and *registers*. Data used by an instruction can also be stored in the instruction itself. When stored this way, it is referred to as *immediate data*. As a result, five combinations of operation source and destination are possible:

memory to register
register to memory
register to register
immediate to register
immediate to memory

Even though there are five types of data transfers here, the operation is essentially the same: data is copied from one location and replaces the data in another. In the last two instances, the data is stored as part of the instruction itself.

In a move operation, usually a byte (8 bits) or word (16 bits) or double word (32 bits) of data is moved. But there are exceptions. It is often necessary to move several bytes or words, a string of data, or occasionally, data from or to a special location. In order to perform these different kinds of moves, several different instruction mnemonics are used. The fact remains, however, that these various mnemonics represent move operations.

The move operation is sometimes referred to as a LOAD operation. This alternative name is commendable in one sense because move operations really are copy operations; a copy of the data in the source is loaded in the destination register or memory location. On the other hand, this name can be misleading when it is used with other types of data transfers.

Load Effective Address	LEA *source, destination*

This operation is similar to a move since a value is to be placed in a destination location. The difference is that the value is calculated rather than copied from a location. Usually the value that is calculated represents a memory location that is specified by the first parameter, *source*, using some form of addressing mode. The calculated address value is stored at the destination location, as shown in this example:

instruction	location(s)	contents	
		before	*after*
LEA X+10, loc 30	30	00010010	00111100
	:	:	:
(assuming that reg X	60	01001011	01001011
contains 50)			

The contents of register X at execution time, 50, are added to 10, producing 60. The value 60 is placed in location 30, destroying the original contents. The contents of location 60 are unaffected.

Exchange	XCHG *var, var*

The exchange operation is another variation on the move operation. Exchange can be understood as a double move. The values contained in the locations represented by the first and second parameters are exchanged.

instruction	location(s)	contents	
		before	after
XCHG loc 75, loc 30	30	00010010	11001101
	:	:	:
	70	11001101	00010010

Swap	SWAP *var*

The swap operation is a variation on the exchange operation. In the case of the swap operation, however, only one location is involved. The contents of the upper and lower portions of the location are exchanged. In an 8-bit location, for example, the four most significant bits are exchanged with the four least significant bits.

instruction	location(s)	contents	
		before	after
SWAP reg A	A	11110000	00001111

Clear	CLEAR *var*

The clear operation is another form of the move operation with the source defined to have value zero. Effectively, the location specified by the parameter is set equal to zero.

instruction	location(s)	contents	
		before	after
Clear reg A	A	00001111	00000000

Push Data Onto the Stack	PUSH *srce*

This is a form of the move operation in which the data is moved to a predefined location called the *stack* (see Chapter 6, which discusses the stack). The location in the stack that stores the needed data is pointed to by the *stack pointer register*, and the operation of storing data at this location is called a *push* operation. The value contained in the location specified by the parameter is pushed onto the stack and the stack pointer is adjusted so that it points to the next location to be accessed.

instruction	location(s)	contents	
		before	after
PUSH loc 30	30	11110010	11110010
(Stack Pointer = 90)	90	00011011	11110010

Pop Data from the Stack	POP *dest*

The reverse of PUSH is the POP operation. This can be visualized as a move in which the source is the location in the stack pointed to by the stack pointer. The contents of this location are removed from the stack and stored in the location specified as a parameter in the instruction. The stack register is then adjusted to point to the next location in the stack.

instruction	location(s)	contents	
		before	after
POP loc 30	30	10101010	00110011
(Stack Pointer = 90)	90	00110011	00110011

MATH OPERATIONS

Add	ADD *source, destination*
with carry	ADC

Addition is the simplest of the mathematical operations. The second number to be added, stored in the destination location, can be considered a subtotal since its value will be augmented by the value in the first location. The value in the source location is added to the value contained in the destination location, and the result is stored in

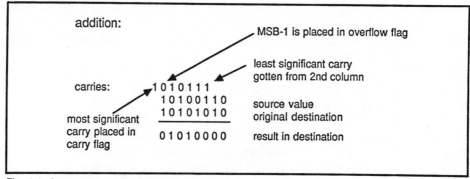

Fig. 4-1. An example of the addition operation.

the destination location. Of course, addition is performed using two binary numbers. The number of bits in the binary numbers depends on the word size of the micro. Consider the display of addition shown in Fig. 4-1.

The most significant carry is always placed in the *carry flag*. This flag is used to store the most significant carry bit during an add operation to indicate if the result is too large to be stored in the destination location. In effect, it represents an error condition that can be checked using other instructions. The carry from the MSB-1 bit is stored in the overflow flag. This flag is used when adding signed numbers to check for an error. Signed numbers use the MSB as a sign indicator. With signed numbers, the following conditions are possible:

carry	overflow	condition
0	0	normal
1	0	error
0	1	error
1	1	normal

On some computers, when adding 8-bit, or byte, values, the overflow resulting from adding the fourth bit is stored in the auxiliary carry flag. This is used when adding binary coded decimal numbers. In BCD, the most significant four bits and least significant four bits each represent an integer value ranging from zero to nine. When two BCD numbers are added together, the result must be adjusted. For example:

        28 in BCD = 00101000
        39 in BCD = 00111001

adding them together yields:

        0001000   auxiliary carry
        0111000   carry

        00101000 = 28 in BCD
        +00111001 = 39 in BCD
        01100001 which <> 67 in BCD; it equals 61

The auxiliary carry from the fourth bit position is set; this indicates that an adjustment is required. Combining the least significant four bits and the auxiliary carry yields 10001, which is 17, or 10111 in BCD. Consequently, the result is adjusted to 01100111, which is 67 in BCD.

Some computers have a special instruction or operating mode to make the necessary adjustments automatically. On other computers, the programmer has to check the auxiliary carry flag and provide for the necessary correction in the program.

The actual addition is performed either in the accumulator or another register or memory. As a result, the addition operation is limited to the word size of the micro. When multiple-byte word values (binary numbers containing a multiple of the word size) are added, it must be done a byte at a time. The carry that is generated when adding each byte must be added to the next significant byte. This operation is called *addition with carry* and consists of adding the carry flag to the new result.

```
carry 1 0 1 0 1 1 1 1
      1 0 1 0 0 1 1 0    with value
      1 0 1 0 1 0 0 1    current destination
                    1    current carry flag
      ─────────────────
      0 1 0 1 0 0 0 0    result in destination
```

The flags are set as described above.

```
┌─────────────────────────────────────────────────────────────┐
│ Increment                                         INC var     │
└─────────────────────────────────────────────────────────────┘
```

Another variation on the addition instruction is the *increment*. In this case, the first value is assumed to be simply 1. Hence, the second parameter's contents are incremented by 1.

```
┌─────────────────────────────────────────────────────────────┐
│ Add Carry Flag Only                      ADCF source, [dest]  │
└─────────────────────────────────────────────────────────────┘
```

This operation means add the carry flag to the contents of the location specified by the first parameter and store the result in the same location or that specified by the optional second parameter. This type of operation is often used when adding a single or multiple byte value to a value of more bytes. The carry, if there is one, must be added to the remaining MSBs of the total. Figure 4-2 shows an example of this process.

```
┌─────────────────────────────────────────────────────────────┐
│ Subtract                         SUB    source, destination   │
│         with borrow              SBB                          │
└─────────────────────────────────────────────────────────────┘
```

Subtraction is very similar to addition. As in the case of addition, the second value (the destination) can be considered a subtotal since the result will replace this value.

```
                example: add a single byte value 5H to a double byte value 7FDH.
                First add 5H to 80H, then add the carry to 07H

                                    location 31  location 30     in hex:
           ADD 5, loc 30            00000111    11111101         7FD
                                    00000111    00000101         +5
                                                00000010
           ADFC loc 31                      1 (carry)
                                    00001000    00000010         802
```

Fig. 4-2. An example of the add-carry-flag-only operation.

Historically, subtraction has been conceived as a two-step operation since it is implemented this way on many—particularly older—computers. First, the first parameter, the *subtrahend*, the number which is to be subtracted from the second parameter, or *minuend*, is converted into 2's complement form. Then this 2's complemented number is added to the minuend or subtotal since subtraction can be conceived as the addition of a positive and a 2's complemented number. On micros that do not have a distinct subtract operation, this method is implemented as two separate operations by the programmer. Figure 4-3 shows an example of this process. First, the subtrahend is changed to its 2's complement representation; then this representation is added to the value stored at the destination, and the result is stored at the destination.

Most current computers, in fact, support subtraction as a single operation. The subtraction operation is the operation we're all familiar with, except that it is done in binary and the borrowing can affect various flags, as shown in Fig. 4-4. The borrow required by the MSB, is stored in the *carry flag*. The carry flag is used to indicate whether the result in the destination of the subtract operation is correct. If it is not correct, the carry flag serves as an error indicator that can be checked by other instructions. In this case, the set carry flag indicates that the true result is less than the one saved as the result in the destination location.

The borrow required by the MSB-1 is stored in the overflow flag. This is used with signed numbers to indicate an error. Additionally, on some computers, if the fourth

```
    subtraction example: 105-53
    (1) change the subtrahend (number to be subtracted) to its 2's complement:
                 subtrahend:  0 0 1 1 0 1 0 1  (+53)
                 complement:  1 1 0 0 1 0 1 0
                 add 1                      1
                              1 1 0 0 1 0 1 1  (-53)
    (2) add as usual:
          original destination:  0 1 1 0 1 0 0 1     105 (decimal)
                                 1 1 0 0 1 0 1 1     -53 (decimal)

          final destination:     0 0 1 1 0 1 0 0     52
```

Fig. 4-3. An example of the subtract operation.

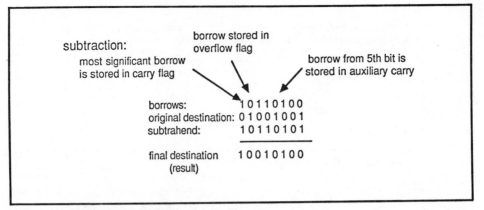

MSB requires a borrow, the auxiliary carry flag is set and used to adjust the result when using BCD numbers. For example,

```
  00100010 = 22 in BCD
- 00011001 = 19 in BCD
  00001001 <> 3 in BCD
```

Subtracting 110 from the erroneous answer 00001001 yields the correct result, namely, 0011 in BCD. This reason that this works is that one bit was borrowed from position 5, which represents a value of 16. But, in effect, we want to borrow a bit from the next significant BCD digit whose value is 10. So we subtract the difference, which is 6.

The actual subtraction is performed in the accumulator or another register, and consequently, the subtraction must be executed in the limits of the word size of the computer. When multiple-byte values are subtracted, it must be done a unit at a time. The borrow generated by subtracting each byte must be subtracted from the next significant unit. This is called *subtract with borrow (carry flag)*. This operation is identical to the one just described except that the current value of the carry flag is also subtracted from the result:

```
01001001  destination
10110101  value
       1  current carry flag
10010011  destination after operation
```

Decrement	DEC *var*

One special form of the subtract operation is the *decrement* instruction. The implied subtrahend in this case is 1. The minuend is diminished or decremented by one. Decrement instructions are commonly used with loops that repeat a procedure a number of times.

Subtract Carry Flag Only	SBCF *srce, [dest]*

This operation subtracts the carry flag only from the location specified by the first parameter and stores the result in the same location or in the location specified in the optional second parameter. This type of operation is often used when subtracting a single- or multiple-byte value from a value of one or more bytes. The borrow, if any, must be subtracted from the remaining MSBs of the result, as shown in Fig. 4-5.

Multiply	MUL *source, destination*
signed integer	IMUL

The multiply operation is merely a form of repeated addition. Not all micros support multiplication in their instruction sets. Of those that do, the values to be multiplied and the places they are to be stored vary from micro to micro. In most cases, the values must be stored in specific locations. As with conventional arithmetic, multiplication involves multiplying two numbers, the *multiplicand* and the *multiplier*. If we multiply 7 by 5, 7 is the multiplicand and 5 is the multiplier. It is mandatory to store the multiplicand in a memory location or register that is large enough to contain the product. As a result, the multiplicand often is represented in 16 bits, while the multiplier may be represented in only 8 bits. Other systems store the product in a third location, which must be as large as the two factors combined. If one factor is 16 bits and the other 8 bits, for instance, then the product requires a 24-bit location. This is also true when implementing a multiply operation in programming.

Each bit of the multiplier, the second number in the multiplication, is checked to see if it is a 1 or a 0. If it is a 1, then the multiplicand is added to a subtotal. In both cases, the multiplicand is shifted to the left one bit (see the shift instruction). This process is repeated for every bit in the multiplier. For example, suppose that we wished to multiply 00101011 by 00010110. We would do the following:

1. The LSB of the multiplier is zero so it can be ignored (if it were a 1, the initial product would be the multiplicand).
2. Shift the multiplicand one bit to the left, as in 00101011 - -> 01010110;
3. Check the second bit of the multiplier; this can be done by shifting the multiplier

example: subtract a single byte value 5H from a double byte value 702H. First subtract 5H from 02H, then subtract the borrow from 07H.

		location 31	location 30	hex:
sub 5, loc 30		00000111	00000010	702
			00000101	-5
		00000111	11111101	
SBCE loc 31		(borrow) 1		
		00000110	11111101	6FD

Fig. 4-5. An example of the subtract-carry-flag-only operation.

to the right by one bit and checking the carry flag—for example, 00001011 --> 00000101, carry = 1.

4. If the carry is 1, add the shifted multiplicand to the product (initially 0);
5. Repeat steps 1 through 4 for the number of bits contained in the multiplier.

For example, multiply 00101011 (43) by 00010110 (22):

```
    00101011
    00010110    (left shift 1 place, as in decimal, since LSB=0)
    00101011    (since 2nd bit is 1 add multiplier, left shifted 1)
   00101011     (since 3rd bit is 1 add multiplier, left shifted 1)
  00101011      (since 5th bit is 1 add multipler, left shifted 2)
00101011        (since 7th bit is 1 add multiplier, left shifted 2)
  1110110010    (= 946 decimal, which is correct)
```

Since the length in bits of the product may be as long as the sum of the bits of the multiplicand and multiplier (i.e., 11 * 11 = 1001), the storage location of the multiplicand, which will receive the product, must be large enough to hold both the multiplicand and the multiplier, if they were concatenated (11 concatenated with 11 is 1111).

When performed as a series of operations as just described, the multiplication operation will consume a fair amount of CPU time. As a result, many newer micros support multiplication instructions in hardware that take much less time. In some systems, mathematical operations such as multiply and divide are executed by a separate *coprocessor*. In this case, the two factors are supplied to the coprocessor and the result is returned.

Unlike the add and subtract operations, which set flags to indicate certain conditions, the multiply operation normally does not set any flags. The reason is that the destination must be large enough to hold the product—hence there can be no overflow errors. On other computers where an error is possible, either special flags are set or program execution may automatically be transferred to a predefined location. If signed numbers are supported, they are usually multiplied in a separate operation called *integer multiply*. Multiplication of BCD numbers is normally only performed by a separate coprocessor.

Divide	DIV *source, destination*
signed integer	IDIV

The divide operation is usually only supported on the larger micros. Of those that do support it, the values to be used and the dividend must be stored in specific locations, which varies from micro to micro. Typically, division is implemented on a separate math coprocessor. Division, of course, is the inverse of multiplication. In multiplication, repetitive addition is used; in division, repetitive subtraction is used. In the operation $6 \div 3 = 2$, 6 is the *dividend*, 3 the *divisor*, 2 the *quotient*. Since occasionally the quotient will require as many bits for its representation as the dividend (as in the example just cited), storage for the quotient must be as large as that for the dividend. Likewise, storage for the remainder must be as large as that for the divisor. Micros that do not support division by means of a divide instruction can perform division as follows. In this example, 00110110 (54) is divided by 00010101 (21):

1. Shift the divisor over to the left until the MSB is 1, remembering how many bits it was shifted; for example 00010101- ->10101000 has been shifted three bits.
2. Subtract this temporary number from the dividend: 100110110 − 10101000 = 10001110 with 1 borrowed. If this operation results in a borrow, then a zero is placed in the LSB of the quotient. If not, a 1 is placed in the LSB of the quotient.
3. Shift the temporary value to the right one bit.
4. Repeat steps 2 and 3 for as many times as the divisor was shifted to the left in step 1, each time shifting the result to the left one bit.

This method is a sequence of repetitive subtractions. The result, the quotient, either is stored in a new location or replaces the dividend. The remainder will either be stored in a new location or in place of the dividend.

Consider this example:

	result:	
00110110		
- 10101000	0	(MSB)
(result too small: less than 0)		
00110110		
- 01010110 (still less than 0)	0	
- 00101010 (large enough)	1	
00101101 (subtotal)		
- 00001100 (too small)	0	(LSB)

The result of the operation is 10 (2) with a remainder of 1100 (12).

Some microprocessors support a divide operation that is implemented in hardware in order to increase speed of execution. Other systems implement the divide operation on a math coprocessor that supports both BCD and real numbers. As is the case with multiplication, signed numbers are handled in a separate operation called *integer divide*, or *IDIV*.

Adjust decimal	DA
ASCII	AA

As mentioned in the description for add, subtract, multiply, and divide, mathematical operations in a computer are performed with binary numbers. For some programming tasks, however, it is more convenient to store the value as a packed or unpacked binary coded decimal (BCD). Binary, in fact, requires the least amount of space to store a given number. For example, the decimal number 153 takes 1 byte in its binary representation, 10011001, two bytes in its packed BCD representation, 00000001 01010011, and three bytes in its unpacked BCD representation, 00000001 00000101 00000011. The unpacked BCD is sometimes referred to as ASCII, but this is misleading. Although binary is the most compact, it is the most difficult to convert into a displayable format or to convert from ASCII to binary for storage purposes. Unpacked BCD is the easiest to work with in terms of I/O, but it takes the most memory and uses the most CPU time for math operations.

Since math functions can be performed on binary numbers only, the result must be converted to the proper format if a packed or unpacked BCD result is required. On some micros, for example the 6502, a special operating mode is available such that for packed BCD this adjustment is performed automatically after every math operation. Other micros, such as the 8086, provide a series of instructions that perform these adjustments for both packed and unpacked BCD, and it is left to the programmer to specify when an adjustment is needed.

Adjustments made on packed BCD numbers are called *decimal adjust*, and on unpacked BCD *ASCII adjust*. The operation performed depends on the value being adjusted and is the result of an add, subtract, multiply, or divide operation. On some computers, different instructions are used for each type of adjustment. On others, different flags are set by the add, subtract, multiply, and divide operations to indicate the proper type of adjustment.

Compare	CMP *source, value*

The compare instruction, as the name implies, is used to compare two values, to see if one is larger than the other. Compare instructions, in conjunction with a conditional JUMP, CALL, or RET instruction (see below) are usually used to determine which of several procedures are to be employed or which paths are to be followed. On the basis of the compare operation, one procedure can be invoked rather than another. Since the compare operation is integral to the decision making power of the computer, it is frequently used.

The compare operation is essentially a subtraction operation. The second value of the two values that are compared is subtracted from the first, just as in subtraction. But, in the case of a compare, the result is not saved. Instead, the operation sets a flag, depending on the result of the compare (subtraction). The flag is then checked by another instruction, such as a JUMP, CALL, or BRANCH, prior to execution. These instructions will execute only if the appropriate flag(s) is (are) set a certain way. See Fig. 4-6, Condition Flags, for a listing of some basic conditions and flags that are set and reset to represent the conditions.

For instance, we might have, "CMP A,B." If A = 25 and B = 9, the subtraction of B from A, since it is a positive result, would leave both the zero flag and the carry flag reset to 0. Some micros will only support the comparison of two binary numbers during subtraction operations. Some micros will also set other flags that will allow the comparison of two values in more detail. Some support the comparison of nonbinary data such as signed integers and BCD data. A series of compare instructions is sometimes available for checking both single bytes or words and a continuous string of bytes or words.

Change Sign	NEG *var*

This operation changes the value contained in the location specified by the parameter to its negative equivalent—to a negative value if the original value is positive, and to a positive value if the original value is negative. If the value of NUMBER were −2, the operation NEG NUMBER would result in the value of NUMBER being 2. This is equivalent to complementing the value and adding one or to taking the 2's complement of the number. This instruction is very useful with computers that do not have a subtract instruction.

Convert	CNV___ *var*

This operation converts the contents of the location specified from one type of value to another. Characters must be appended to the mnemonic to specify the type of conversion to be performed. For example:

BW: byte to word
WDW: word to double word
DWGW: double word to quad word

This operation is primarily used when moving signed binary values from one location to a larger location and it is necessary to extend the sign bit to all MSB of the destination. Figure 4-7 shows an example of this process.

PROGRAM CONTROL

Jump	JMP *location*

The jump operation is used to continue program execution at a location other than

Condition Flags

condition	flag(s)
A=B	zero set
A≠B	zero reset
A<B	carry set or zero reset
A>B	carry & zero reset
A≥B	carry reset or zero set
A≤B	carry set or zero set

Fig. 4-6. Condition flags: Most computers have several flags that are set to 1 or reset to 0 whenever certain conditions are generated as a result of an arithmetic operation. Suppose the instruction "CMP A,B" is executed, and the value of A is less than B. In this case, the carry flag would be set to 1 and the zero flag reset to 0.

```
                example: move the value -2 from a byte location to a word location

                                        │         location 30  location 31
        MOV BYTE, WORD                  │                       11111110
                                        │         00000000  11111110

        CNVBW NUMBER                    │         11111111  11111110
```

Fig. 4-7. An example of the convert operation.

the next instruction in the program. It replaces the contents of the program counter with the effective address of its own operand. Frequently, a jump instruction is used in tandem with a compare operation so that the jump depends on the comparison. If the condition specified, such as one value being greater than another is true, then program execution continues at the specified location; if the condition is not true, then the program execution continues with the next instruction. The conditions checked are the flags set or reset in previous operations. The flags themselves are unaffected by the execution of a jump instruction.

The condition can be expressed in terms of a specific flag (e.g., cc = carry clear) or in terms of what the flag or flags represent as a result of a compare, math, or logical operation. The following are some of the most common conditions:

condition	explanation
UN	under all conditions
EQ or Z	equal (zero flag set)
NE or NZ	not equal (zero flag clear)
PO	parity odd
PE	parity even
C	carry flag set
NC	carry flag clear

See the conditional expressions section of the AL standard for a more complete listing. If no condition is specified, this is called an *unconditional jump* operation and is sometimes considered a separate operation.

The location in the program where control is to be transferred if the condition is true can be expressed in two primary ways—either as a specific location or as a location relative to the location of the current instruction. The first way uses what is called *absolute addressing*, and the second *relative addressing* or *displacement*. In the second case, the address given in the instruction is the number of bytes or words from the current or next instruction that would normally have been execution. The advantage of relative addressing over absolute is that it requires fewer bytes of memory. However, the location jumped to must be within 255 bytes of the current instruction—which is why this is referred to as a *jump relative* operation (JMPR). Even more importantly, the section of code in which the instruction is used is position independent. It can be moved to a different memory location and still be valid.

Some of the larger micros use large amounts of memory, which is divided into segments of 64K (the largest value possible with 16 bits). If the location to be jumped to is a location in another segment of memory, two address values must be included in the jump instruction—the address of the segment and the location within the segment. This kind of jump operation is usually called a *jump other segment* (JMPOS) and is considered to be a separate routine. Figure 4-8 illustrates the three types of jumps.

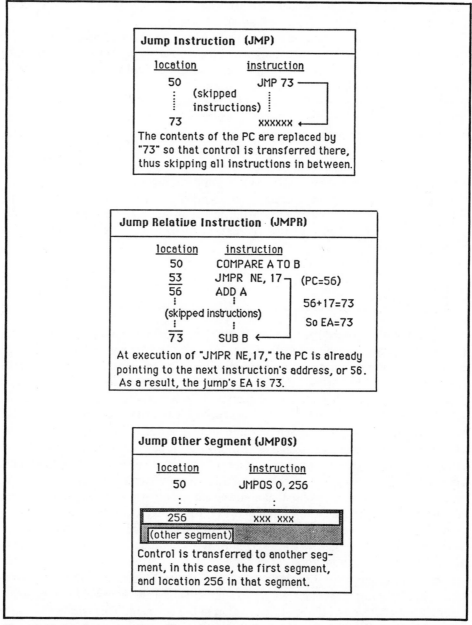

Fig. 4-8. Various jump operations: These three jump instructions work as described in each box.

Call Subroutine	CALL *condition, location*

Most programs consist of a number of short procedures that are repeated many times. Listing the entire procedure each time it is used in the source file is both time consuming and potentially error-prone. It is wiser, therefore, to define the procedure once and invoke or execute it whenever it is needed. Such a procedure is called a *subroutine*, and it is invoked by the *call* operation.

The call operation is similar to the jump instruction except that the contents of the PC are saved so that control can return to the next sequential instruction after the calling instruction. Upon a certain condition, program control will transfer to a location in the program other than the one whose address is contained in the PC. The difference is that the instruction which would have been executed next is saved on the stack. The address of the instruction in the PC is saved so that execution will resume at the conclusion of the subroutine at the location whose address is saved in the PC. This address is normally referred to as the *return address*. The operation to return to that location or main program is the return instruction. The conditions under which the subroutine is executed are the same as the jump instruction.

As in the case of a jump operation, the location of the subroutine may be in another segment of memory, in which case the operation is a *call other segment* operation. It can also be specified as a relative address, in which case it is called a *call relative* or *call displacement* operation.

Return	RET *condition*

This operation is used in conjunction with the call or interrupt operation to return to the next instruction that would have been executed had the subroutine or interrupt handling procedure not been invoked and executed. The principal difference from the jump instruction, which it resembles, is that the address to transfer control to is taken from the stack rather than the instruction itself. It is usually a one byte instruction, with its implied operands being taken from the stack and the PC. In other terms, the return is a jump operation in which the jump location is determined prior to the operation. Figure 4-9 shows an example of this process. A subroutine can be entered for several reasons besides the execution of a call instruction. For example, an I/O interrupt can invoke a subroutine. In this case, in addition to fetching the address from the stack and transferring control to that address, certain other predefined information is also fetched from the stack and stored in the registers, flags, or other predefined locations. This is called a *return from interrupt* operation or "RETI." The data transferred from the stack to the registers and the condition or operation that invoked the subroutine will vary between micros.

As with the jump operation, if the location of the next instruction, the return location, is in another segment of memory, two address values are retrieved from the stack, the segment address and the specific location in the segment. This is called a *return other segment* or RETOS.

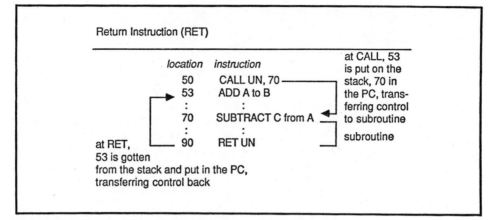

Fig. 4-9. An example of the call subroutine and return operation.

| Skip | SKIP *condition* |

The next instruction after the SKIP instruction is bypassed if the condition specified as a parameter evaluates as true. SKIP is similar to the relative jump except that the location to jump to is predefined as the next instruction after the one following this one.

Example:	*location*	*instruction*	
	23	:	
	24	SKIP NC	; skip, no carry
	25	INC A	
	26	MOV A, B	

If, when the SKIP instruction executes, the carry flag is not set, the increment instruction at location 25 will be skipped. If the carry flag is set, the increment instruction will be executed.

| Halt Computer Operation | HALT |

With this operation, the computer stops executing instructions; it resumes execution only if an interrupt or other external signal is received. This operation is normally used with real time operation systems or with instrument controllers in which certain conditions render further operation impossible or inadvisable. This operation suspends processing until conditions have changed or the operator intervenes.

Two special forms of the halt operation are the wait and break. In these cases, the computer waits for another processor, usually called a coprocessor or mathprocessor, to finish a task. Associated with this operation is the escape or ESC operation, which requests a coprocessor to perform a specific task.

No Operation	NOP

The computer performs no operation. This is an important instruction in writing and especially in debugging programs. When writing programs, it is used when the specific operation to be performed is not known or depends on a condition which is not easily tested using the conditional jump operation. For example, consider the fragment:

```
ADD  B,A
INC A
MOV  A, loc 5
```

Under some circumstances, it might be necessary to increment register A before storing it in location 5. Instead of checking the conditions, which may be relatively complicated, we can substitute a NOP for the INC A instruction when the INC A is not required. This practice is referred to as *run time alterable code* and is usually to be avoided—except in a case where it can reduce the size of the program and increase its execution speed.

In program debugging, the NOP is useful if it happens that an operation is not needed. In this case, the operation can be replaced by a NOP without reassembling the program. This practice is often referred to as *patching*.

Loop Until	LOOP *cond, [cnt], loc*
Repeat	REP *cond, [cnt]*

These two operations are available on some of the newer, more advanced computers. They enable an instruction to be executed or for a procedure to be repeated a number of times. They are similar to a while or repeat /until loop in Pascal. These instructions are most useful in decreasing the size of a program. These two instructions are not more widely used because they are not as well known to programmers as the compare, jump-if combination they replace.

The loop-until operation will cause a jump to the location specified by the second or last parameter if the condition specified by the first parameter is not true or for the number of times specified by the optional second parameter.

The repeat operation causes the following instruction to be repeated until the condition specified by the first parameter is reached or for the number of times specified in the second parameter.

Restart	RST *[type]*
Trap	TRAP *[cond], [type]*
Program Interrupt	SWI *[cond], [type]*

70

These operations are similar to the call subroutine operations with the exception that the subroutine to which control is passed is specified as a type rather than an address. For each type of transfer, a predefined location is used; the location either specifies the actual address or is the address. Additionally, the return address as well as other data is placed on the stack.

A restart operation is a call to one of several subroutines stored in a predefined area of memory. The parameter specifies which subroutine or predefined location is called. A trap operation, provided that the condition specified by the first parameter is true, performs a software interrupt of the type specified by the second parameter. If no parameters are specified, a software interrupt of the default type occurs.

LOGICAL OPERATIONS

Every computer operation, no matter how complex, can be thought of as a series of single bit operations. A binary number, for instance, is represented as a string of bits, each of which represents a single value. Many conditions, in fact, can be represented as a single bit since they take only one of two possible values, as in "yes" or "no" and "set" or "reset."

When several such items exist, it saves memory to include them in a single byte or word, with each bit representing a different item of information. For example, a single byte could include personnel items such as male/female, tenured/nontenured, married/unmarried, and so on. If an item had four possible combinations, two bits could be used, since two bits can assume a total of four different combinations—00, 01, 10, and 11.

When a byte or word represents multiple items, it is necessary to manipulate individual bits (this practice has the curious nickname of "bit twiddling"). These operations are categorized as *logical* operations. These operations perform a specific operation on each bit of a byte or word.

And		AND *source, destination*

The logical AND instruction compares two bits in the same location of two bytes or words. This operation is based on the logical *boolean* operation of AND. If they are both 1s, the result of the compare is 1, otherwise it is 0. The following table defines the boolean AND operation:

bit 1	bit 2	result
0	0	0
1	0	0
0	1	0
1	1	1

Letting & represent *and*, the sentence "Both Rich and Harry enjoy classical music" could be symbolized as "R & H." This sentence will be true, of course, only if it is true that Rich enjoys classical music (R = true or 1) and if it is also true that Harry enjoys classical music (H = true or 1). If either of these is false (= 0), or if both are false, then "R & H" will be false (= 0) since, to be true, both parts must be true. For a "bit sentence" of "bit & bit" to have the value 1, both bits must be 1. Any of the other three possible combinations (1&0, 0&1, 0&0) will yield 0. *Anding* the following two bytes yields:

```
11010101  first byte
00011100  "mask" byte
00010100  result
```

Only in those columns that have two 1s does a 1 appear in the result. The result is stored in the first byte or the second parameter. This operation is normally used to extract or save the values of specific bits. In this example, bits 2, 3, and 4 are transferred to the result. All other bits are set to zero. The second byte, 00011100, is sometimes called a *mask* since it will pass on whatever values happen to appear in the first byte in positions 2, 3, and 4. A 1 in a mask in a certain position guarantees that the bit in the first byte will appear in the result unchanged since anding with a 1 merely passes the bit along.

This operation will normally set the sign flag and the zero flag according to the result. Depending on the micro, other flags will be set as well. Thus the AND instruction is a convenient way of checking a variable for sign and other conditions by ANDing it with itself.

Test	TST *source, mask*

The TEST operation is similar to the AND operation except that the result is not saved—only the flags are affected. It is also similar to the compare operation, but instead of subtracting the second value from the first, the two values are ANDed. The test operation is used to check the value of certain bits in a variable byte or word and sets the flags accordingly. The conditional operation is then used to check the flag settings.

Alternate forms of the test operation test for a specific condition by performing a logical AND of the value contained in the location specified by the parameter with itself and setting the appropriate flags. Also, TST can be used to test all the bits selected by the second parameter or to mask for certain conditions, such as all the bits reset or set.

Logical Or	OR *source, destination*

The OR, which logicians define as the *inclusive* OR (see below for the exclusive OR), is similar in some respects to the logical AND. The difference is that there are three conditions that will produce a 1 in the result for a particular bit. If either bit is 1 or if both bits are 1, then the OR result will be a 1. As a result, the only combination bits that will yield a 0 in an OR operation is when both bits are 0.

bit 1	bit 2	result
0	0	0
1	0	1
0	1	1
1	1	1

A chain of men's clothiers, for instance, advertises that it caters to "BIG or TALL" men. What this means, of course, is that if you are tall, or big, or both, then they will have clothes which are likely to fit. Letting the "v" denote *or*, it could be symbolized as "B v T." If you could put a 1, for true, on either side of the v sign, or on both sides, they will clothe you. ORing two bytes is like the ANDing operation, except that the conditions for 1 in the result byte are as just described:

00101101 *source*

10100100 OR *destination*

10101101 *result*

In order for a 0 to appear in the result, both bits must be zero. Otherwise, a 1 appears. This operation is used to set specific bits within a variable to the value 1, or to assure that they are already 1.

Logical Exclusive Or	XOR *source, destination*

This operation is like a hybrid between the OR and AND instructions. XORing two bits is defined as follows:

bit 1	bit 2	result
0	0	0
1	0	1
0	1	1
1	1	0

An everyday illustration may help. If you are dating two persons, you may be thinking also of getting married. You would say to yourself, "I can marry X or I can marry Y." In this sense of or, given that polygamy is illegal, you are most likely using or in the exclusive sense. What the sentence really means is that "I can marry X or I can marry Y—but not both." This is exactly the sense of the exclusive or XOR as it is denoted. In terms of bits it means that, if either of the same bit in two bytes is 1, then its XOR result is 1 as well. If both bits are 1, then the result is 0—which accounts for the *exclusive* part of the exclusive or. Exclusive ORing two bytes will give this result:

10100011 *to*

11110000 *XOR with (mask)*

01010111 *result*

This operation is normally used to change or complement individual bits within a variable. In the example above, the most significant four bits had their values complemented from what they had been; the least significant four bits remained unchanged. In the case of an XOR mask, then, 0 bits in the mask byte (the second byte) pass on whatever was in the first byte initially; the 1 bits reverse the bit value of the first byte. XORing a variable by itself will reset it to zero since all 1 bits change to zero (1 XOR 1 = 0) and all zero bits remain unchanged.

Complement	CPL *var*

It is often necessary to invert a value or bit of data to its opposite value or *complement*. Complementing is simply reversing the value of that which is complemented—changing 1s to 0s and 0s to 1s. For instance, complementing 10110010 results in 01001101.

This operation is often associated with input and output routines. Owing to various hardware considerations, where a 1 can represent no and a 0 yes, it is often necessary to complement bytes from software which takes 1 to represent yes and 0 no. Complementing is used, as well, in generating 2's complement representations. In other instances, it is desirable to complement a flag or a variable to represent the opposite condition.

Rotate	RLxx *location, count*
	RRxx
Shift	SLxx
	SRxx

The most versatile operations in assembly language are the rotate and shift operations. Although they are relatively straightforward, their use can cause difficulties in some situations. Their primary use is mathematical operations in which processing individual bits in a variable is required. Both operations are similar with the exception of how the LSB and MSB are handled. Both the rotate and the shift operations move all the bits in a byte or word one bit to the left or one bit to the right. These operations could be characterized as the "musical chairs" of the micro world.

For example, shifting the byte 11110000 left results in 1110000x, where the x could be a 1 or 0. All the bits move to the next most significant bit, filling the LSB with a 1 or 0. Shifting or rotating it right would yield x01111000.

The difference between the two is what is done with the bit that is moved from the left or right and what value replaces the vacant bit at either end. An easy way to remember the difference between a shift and a rotate is that if the rotate operation is performed the proper number of times, all bits will end up in the same position that they started in—they are all moved through a circular loop. If a shift operation is performed a certain number of times, all bits will have the same value and the original data will be completely lost.

There are three kinds of rotate operations, *to carry, with carry,* and *without the carry.* In the *to carry,* the bit that is moved out is placed in the carry and the vacancy at the other end. In the with carry, the bit that is moved out is placed in the carry flag, and the old value of the carry is placed in the vacant position. In the without the carry, the bit moved out is put in the vacated position at the other end; the carry flag is not affected.

Rotating the byte 11110000 left would result in 11100001. In this case, the MSB becomes the LSB. It's as if the MSB is pushed out of the byte and, after all the other bits have moved up, the MSB recognizes that there is an opening in the now vacant LSB, and quickly assumes it. Rotating right is just the opposite: every bit moves down one spot and the LSB becomes the MSB.

Rotating *to* the carry left moves all the bits over 1 bit; the MSB is moved both to the carry flag and the LSB; rotating to the carry right moves the bits the other way. Rotating *with* the carry left causes the carry flag to move to the LSB and the MSB moves to the flag; all the other bits move left as usual. Rotating with the carry right moves the bits the other way.

The rotate to carry is normally used when the programmer wishes to process each bit individually. The rotate with carry has the dual capability of examining each bit in the variable and/or changing each bit.

Figure 4-10 illustrates the different types of rotate operations. In each case, the contents of the location specified by the first parameter is rotated left or right for the number of bits specified by the second parameter. The result is stored in the same location. If there is no second parameter, one is assumed.

The shift operation has two forms, arithmetic and logical. In both cases, the bit moved out is placed in the carry flag. In the logical shift, the vacated bit is replaced by a zero. In the arithmetic shift, the vacated bit retains the same value it had previously.

An arithmetic shift is normally used to multiply or divide a variable by two. Each time the variable is shifted to the left one bit, the value effectively is multiplied by two. Shifting the value to the right effectively divides it by two.

Figure 4-11 shows the different types of shift operations. In each case the contents of the location specified by the first parameter is shifted left or right for the number of bits specified by the second parameter. The result is stored in the same location. If there is not a second parameter, one is assumed.

The combination of shift instructions that are available on any micro will vary. Some micros allow the programmer to specify the number of bits to be shifted. Others will include special instructions that automatically shift a multiple number of bits in one operation. The most common of these is the 4- or 8-bit rotate instructions that are used when processing ASCII or BCD data in which each half of a byte or word contains an ASCII character or digit.

There are no definite rules as to when to use a shift or rotate instruction, or, in fact, which type to use. The programmer is left to his or her own devices in solving the task at hand. In many cases, either a rotate or a shift will produce equally useful results.

RLNC Rotate Left No Carry

operation:

example:

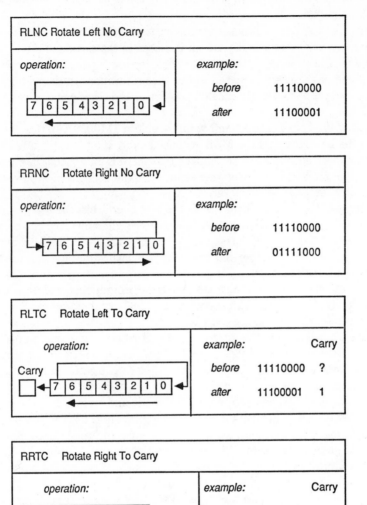

before   11110000

after   11100001

RRNC   Rotate Right No Carry

operation:

example:

before   11110000

after   01111000

RLTC   Rotate Left To Carry

operation:

example: Carry

before   11110000   ?

after   11100001   1

RRTC   Rotate Right To Carry

operation:

example: Carry

before   11110000   ?

after   01111000   0

RLWC   Rotate Left With Carry

operation:

example: Carry

before   11110000   0

after   11100000   1

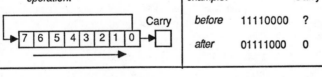

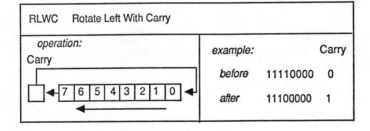

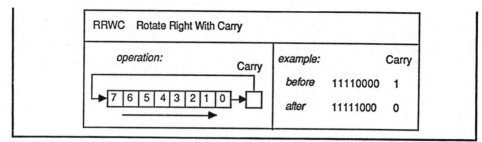

Fig. 4-10. The different type of rotate operations.

BIT OPERATIONS

| Set/Reset | Set *location* |
| | Reset *location* |

It is often necessary to access individual bits of a variable rather than the variable as a whole, since, as we have seen, each bit can represent a distinct item of informa-

---

SLA Shift Left Arithmetic
SLL Shift Left Logical

operation:

Carry

	example:		Carry
	before	11110000	?
	after	11100000	1

SRA Shift Right Arithmetic

operation:

Carry

	example:		Carry
	before	11110000	?
	after	11111000	0

SRL Shift Right Logical

operation:

Carry

	example:		Carry
	before	11110000	?
	after	01111000	0

Fig. 4-11. The different shift operations.

tion itself. This is especially true of the status register which contains the flag bits. When accessing individual bits, it is easier to think in terms of setting and resetting the bit rather than equating it to a value. As a result, most micros have operations that act on specific bits. The single bit to be changed is specified by the parameters of the instruction—reset will always set a bit to the value 0 and set will always set it to 1. For instance, if Register A contains 00000000, an instruction "SET Reg. A, bit 2" will change the byte to 00000100, with the LSB being bit 0.

In the case of flag bits that are located in the status register, they are assigned an abbreviation. Consequently, it is necessary only to specify the flag since its location is predefined. For example, "RESET carry flag" will set the carry flag bit in the status register to "0."

I/O OPERATIONS

Input	IN	*port, var*
Output	OUT	*srce, port*

Computers must be able to exchange data with peripheral devices such as keyboards and printers. Such a transfer is called an *input/output* operation. These operations are performed in either of two ways: *memory mapped* or *port address I/O*. In memory mapped I/O, a section of memory is dedicated to the external device. In other words, if memory locations xxx – yyy are dedicated for use by the CRT, an address of xxx + 1 may transfer data to the screen, while an address of xxx + 2 will accept data from the keyboard. This makes it possible to use the data move instructions to transfer data back and forth from an external device. The price paid for this advantage, of course, is decreased available memory. Since memory is normally allocated in blocks of 4K, even if only a few addresses are required for external devices, the total amount of memory must still be decreased by 4K.

In port addressed I/O, by contrast, a separate set of instructions is used for the I/O. Each external device is assigned a series of addresses that are separate from the memory addresses. An external device will normally use two or more addresses—one for data transfer, the others for the transfer of control information. An input operation receives data from an external device and the output instruction sends data to an external device. For instance, if port 5 is the address of a CRT, "INPUT port 5" will fetch one character from the keyboard. "Output port 5" will send one character to the display, as shown in Fig. 4-12. The input operation IN moves data from the port specified or external device, to a location in memory. The output operation OUT moves data from a location in the computer to the specified port or external device.

The input operation will also set certain flags, such as the parity flag, which indicates whether the input data has an even or odd number of 1 bits. Parity is a way of checking the validity of the data received. The MSB of an 8-bit byte representing an ASCII character will be set or reset so that the data will have an even or odd number of bits set to one.

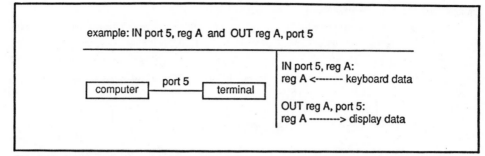

example: IN port 5, reg A and OUT reg A, port 5

```
                                    IN port 5, reg A:
                                    reg A <-------- keyboard data
            port 5
  computer -------- terminal        OUT reg A, port 5:
                                    reg A --------> display data
```

Fig. 4-12. An example of an input/output operation.

| Disable Interrupts | DI |
| Enable Interrupts | EI |

An interrupt is the way that an external device interrupts the usual flow of control, or execution, of a program, so a special procedure can be executed. This is often referred to as an interrupt handler. When an interrupt is received, the computer suspends the sequential flow of control and saves all necessary data in order to execute a specific interrupt handling subroutine. Analogously, if you are playing a good game of chess, the ringing of a telephone interrupts your "flow of control" and you execute a subroutine—you pick up the receiver and say "Hello." At the conclusion of the conversation, you resume the game of chess where you left it.

Two ways of controlling to interrupts are *disable* and *enable* interrupts, or DI and EI. The first defeats interrupt signals and the second makes it possible for them to interrupt the flow of control. Other instructions define which interrupts are permitted and how they will be answered. Some computers have other instructions to define which interrupts are permitted and how they are handled. On some micros, it is possible to force an interrupt from within the program. This is called a *software interrupt* or *break* operation.

MULTIPLE OPERATIONS

Some micros feature single instructions that perform more than one operation or allow an operation to be repeated a given number of times or until some condition exists. These instructions are not difficult to understand and use as long as each of the operations combined are understood.

SPECIAL OPERATIONS

Because of the uniqueness of each micro, distinct instructions are required to perform operations that are unique to a particular micro. These instructions typically are not used by an applications programmer—rather, they are used principally by systems programmers. These instructions require some knowledge of the internal architecture of the micro being programmed.

A SMALL PROGRAMMING EXAMPLE

A typical small programming exercise is to divide one number by another. Suppose that we wanted to write the program for the 6502 microprocessor. Using basic operations explained in this chapter and using the standard mnemonic set developed later in this book, we could write the program as follows. Comments explain the purpose of each instruction.

```
;   DIVIDE.MLS              TEST PROGRAM
;
    ORG 300H                ; start program at address 300 Hex
;
5              MOV # 2,A     ; move 2 to accumulator (divisor)
6              MOV A,PZ 10H  ; store this number in loc 10 Hex
7              MOV # 11,A    ; move 11 to accum (dividend)
8              MOV A,PZ 11H  ; store this in loc 11 Hex
9              MOV # 8,X     ; move 8 to X reg, (number of bits)
10             MOV # 0,A     ; move 0 to accum
11   NEXT      SLA PZ 11     ; shift dividend left -
12             RLWC A        ; into partial dividend
13             CMP A,PZ 10H  ; compare the two
14             JMPR NC,COUNT ; jump if divisor greater then count
15             SBB PZ 10H,A  ; if not, subtract divisor (again)
16             INC PZ 11H    ; and increment the dividend
17   COUNT DEC X            ; decrement the bit counter
18             JMPR NZ,NEXT  ; loop back, if not done
19             MOV A,PZ 12H  ; store remainder in loc 12
20   DONE  BRK
;
END
```

We can use this diagram to understand how the program performs division:

location 11 = dividend | 00001011 | (11) Δ = one step

location 10 = divisor | 00000010 | (2)   ¶ = separation between number and remainder

location 10	location 11	register A	register X
00000010	Δ 00001011	00000000	00001000
	Δ 0001011¶0	00000000	00000111
	Δ 001011¶00	00000000	00000110
	Δ 01011¶000	00000000	00000101
	Δ 1011¶0000	00000000	00000100
	Δ 011¶00000	00000001	00000011
	$\Delta\lceil$ 11¶000010	00000010	
	$\Delta\lfloor$ 11¶000001	00000000	00000010
	Δ 1¶0000010	00000001	00000001

$$\Delta \bigg[\quad 00000101 \qquad \begin{array}{l} 00000011 \\ 00000001 \end{array} \qquad 00000000$$

$$\text{result} = 5 \qquad \text{remainder} = 1$$

The dividend, the number to be divided, is stored in location 11 and the divisor is stored in location 10. Register X is set to 8 to since we have 8 bits in the word; this is decremented each cycle and will keep track of how long we have to keep subtracting to get the answer. We shift the number into the accumulator one bit at a time, shifting the result into location 11 at the same time. If the number in the accumulator is larger than the divisor, we subtract the divisor and add one to the result, the quotient. We repeat this process as long as register X is greater than zero.

An assembly listing such as this provides a great deal of information about the program. This is a good time to look at such a listing because we can use some of the concepts developed in this and other chapters.

The numbers on the extreme left are line numbers. These are supplied by the assembler and are not included by the programmer in the source code. They help locate instructions in the source file when the programmer is using an editor. Notice that, even though the first four lines are not numbered, they are counted; the first instruction in the program appears at line 5. A line that begins with a semicolon is a comment and is ignored by the assembler; hence comment lines need no memory in the program's memory locations and there are no address numbers to the left of the comments.

The four digit numbers on the left after the line numbers are addresses listed in hexadecimal. They start at 0300 since the first instruction, a directive to the assembler, specifies that the program is to begin at address 0300. That there is no memory address to the left of the ORGinate commands indicates that no program code is generated by the directive.

The number of bytes that each instruction takes is reflected in the addresses. At line 5, the address is 0300, at line 6 0302. Two bytes are needed by the instruction beginning at line 5, which is a move instruction. The first byte, the one stored at 0300, contains A9 which is the opcode for store the number which follows in the next byte in memory, in register A. As you might guess, "02" designates that the number to be stored in A is 2.

In the center of line 5, the mnemonic is followed by two parameters, sometimes called operands. The instruction, "MOV, #, 2, A", has a pound sign # in front of the 2 in order to signify that it is the number 2 that is to be moved and not the number that is stored at address 2. The A stands for the accumulator, the principal register in the 6502 microprocessor.

In line 6, the operands are more numerous because a PZ parameter must be added to signify that this is base page or *page zero* addressing. The 10H designates location 10 hexadecimal in memory. It is not interpreted as the number 10 hex because there is no pound sign preceding it. Some assemblers use the prefix $ instead of the suffix H to designate a hex number; instead of 10H, using this convention, we would have $10. The mnemonics differ between the 6502 assembler and the universal assembler, but the machine codes do not—both assemblers translate their equivalent mnemonics into the same machine codes.

Next look at the *label* in line 11. In many assemblers, labels must start in the first column of the source file, instructions in the second or later column. As this listing illustrates, often AL listings are printed so that the labels are quite distinct. Note that the instruction in line 12, RLWC A, requires only a single byte; the address of line 12 is 030E and the address of line 13 is 030F, and there are only 2 hex digits next to the address in line 12.

Labels can be used as operands. In line 14, the jump instruction specifies that control is to switch to the instruction whose label is COUNT if the carry bit equals 0. The opcode is 90, the operand 04. The 04 is the *offset*, the number needed to be added to the PC in order for it to contain the address associated with the label COUNT (0317). It might be thought that the operand, the offset, should be 06 since the difference between 0317 and 0311, the address of the jump instruction, is 06. But by the time the jump instruction is executed, the PC has been incremented so that its contents are 0313, the address of the instruction following the jump instruction. Hence 04 is the correct offset, because 0313 + 04 = 0317.

The next instruction of interest is the one on line 18. The opcode for a JMPR (NZ) is DO. The F2, which is the second byte of the instruction, is in 2's complement form. In binary, F2 equals 11110010. The leading 1 signifies a negative number. If the condition is satisfied, control is to be transferred to the location with the label NEXT. The address of NEXT is 030C, in binary, 00111100. If we add 11110010 (F2) to 31A, which is what the PC contains as the instruction is executed, we get this result:

```
            1 (carry)
   1111 1111  1111 0010    (F2 in 2's complement)
 + 0000 0011  00011010     (31A, number in PC, in binary)
   0000 0011  0000 1100
         3       0   C     (address of instruction with label NEXT)
```

3OC is the address of the instruction with the label NEXT, which is where control is to be transferred.

FOR FURTHER READING

Lister, Paul, ed., *Single-Chip Microcomputers*. (New York, 1984).

Chapter 5

Writing Assembly Language Programs

Purpose of the Chapter: This chapter discusses some general points to remember while writing programs. More specifically, it considers problem decomposition and structured programming, steps in successful program writing, program documentation, the pros and cons of compact code, subroutines, labels, and conditional assemblies. It concludes with a prime number generator program. The goal of the chapter is to provide the reader with a clear understanding of proper programming techniques in assembly language program writing.

PROGRAMMER'S POINTS TO REMEMBER

The difficulty of an assembly language program stems from two considerations: first, the relative difficulty of the programming task; and second, the soundness of the techniques the programmer uses. We maintain that if proper techniques are followed, assembly language programming, even with large programming tasks, can be a relatively straightforward undertaking. If poor techniques are employed, then as one should expect, assembly language programming almost always proves difficult if not impossible. We will now suggest several "programmer's points to remember," which should prove helpful to you as an AL programmer.

Point 1: the computer does exactly what its instructions, not your intentions, tell it to do.

This often quoted adage is resisted by some computer professionals, perhaps for the following reasons. In writing a program, a programmer does not write all of the instructions that drive the computer. For example, someone else probably wrote the assembler or compiler and operating system. The program depends on this other software and problems that appear could stem from problems in this software. But the fact remains that the computer's operation is directly a function of the instructions given it. If it does not perform as intended by the programmer, it is nearly always the fault of the programmer.

The exactness and specificity required by AL programming can surprise people who are accustomed to HLLs. The programmer who learns assembly language after learning a high level language, which is almost always the case today, brings with him or her an experience in programming that is procedure-instruction based. That is, high level language instructions such as PRINT or FOR/NEXT are really procedures since they are translated into as many as 20 or 30 machine level instructions. The implementation of these procedure-instructions is hidden from the programmer; they are implemented automatically or in terms of default values by the compiler. In assembly language, by contrast, little is automatic, or done by hidden default conditions, or accomplished by hidden procedures. In other words, the AL programmer has nearly complete control over the operations of the computer.

This control over the computer is a welcome freedom. But with this freedom comes a measure of responsibility: the programmer must specify exactly what is to be done by the machine. Every operation that the computer must do to accomplish its task must be explicitly defined in the assembly language program. In other words, the AL programmer bears nearly complete responsibility for everything that the machine does or fails to do.

Most programmers would like a language that offers complete control over the computer but provides, at the same time, the convenience of procedural instructions. But this is to ask the impossible. Compromise is therefore necessary. AL's compromise is the power of complete control of the computer at the price of sacrificing the convenience of procedure-instructions. High level languages compromise by offering the convenience of procedural instructions at the price of sacrificing nearly complete control.

The relationship between AL and HLL is much like that between manual and automatic transmissions in cars. Years ago, people complained about all the shifting they had to do with manual transmissions. With great fanfare automatic transmissions were introduced; it was thought that it was just a matter of time before all transmissions would be automatic. But it was eventually discovered that automatic transmissions isolate the driver from full control of the vehicle. The driver looses the "feel" of the machine. Then it was discovered that automatic transmissions were less fuel efficient than manual transmissions. The thrifty began to return to manual transmissions. Today, manual transmissions command a loyal following and a sizable share of the auto market because, for the price of a little extra work, they provide greater control over the vehicle and greater efficiency than automatic transmissions.

The relation between AL and HLL is much the same. When high level languages were first invented with great fanfare, it was thought they would replace the use of assembly language. It hasn't happened because, by compromising with a little extra work up front, AL offers numerous advantages over HLLs in terms of control, speed and efficiency.

Point 2: Make everything in the program completely explicit.

This second point really follows from the first-since the computer does exactly and only what the programmer tells it to do, every part of the programming task must be explicitly programmed. This is both the strength and the weakness of assembly language—it explains why many serious programming tasks are still done in assembly language and it explains why it was thought necessary to develop high level languages.

One advantage of this characteristic of assembly language is that there are far fewer rules and special conditions to remember with AL programming. With complete explicitness in programming comes a simplicity in terms of both understanding and using instructions. The disadvantage of this characteristic of assembly language is that the task must be made fully explicity, fully *decomposed*, before coding should begin. Complete explicitness in programming results in longer programs and increased possibility for errors. As a rule of thumb, longer programs (in the same language) prove more difficult to debug and maintain than shorter programs.

Point 3: Successful programming is not learned in the abstract, as in reading a book; it is acquired in the practice of actual programming.

A person can no more learn to program by reading a programming book than an athlete could learn to play baseball by reading *Sports Illustrated*. Programming requires practice—doing—as well as reading, since it is a skill that one acquires by doing it. Correct coding is only one part of programming. The way to learn programming, especially AL programming, is to do it by reading, programming, listening, programming, reading, and programming some more in an ongoing cycle of learning-by-doing.

Some writers emphasize the value of reading well-written programs, and there is a good deal to be said for this claim since we often learn by imitation. Writing and debugging programs, however, reinforces what is learning by reading and imitating. Programming activities such as decomposing a problem, tracing an executing module, and debugging a module that is not working properly remain the best way to grasp the art of writing good programs. Moreover, in writing and debugging programs, the programmer develops his or her own approach to programming, discovers which tactics work best, and learns which programming styles seem best to use in tackling various programming problems.

PROBLEM DECOMPOSITION AND STRUCTURED PROGRAMMING

One way to look at a computer program is to view it as algorithms operating on data structures. Ultimately, a computer's data structures are simply the 1s and 0s stored in memory, and its algorithms are the instruction set as implemented in the CPU. The programmer's task is to provide a way of translating the data structures and algorithms that are natural to the problem to be solved into the data structures and algorithms that the computer can understand. The term usually employed for this task is *problem decomposition*.

Very few problems that people undertake to solve involve data structures as simple as 1s and 0s, and algorithms as simple as the instruction set of a computer. On the contrary, we often are interested in data structures such as lists of names and tables of employee wage rates, and in algorithms such as determining who gets paid what on the 15th of the month. The task then is to translate such everyday data structures and algorithms into computer data structures and algorithms.

Since we don't handle large numbers of 1s and 0s very well, it is necessary to develop what Nicklaus Wirth has called a "hierarchy of abstractions" in order to solve a problem.* To write a program is to design an algorithm that captures the abstractions we work with, such as lists of names and pay scales, in terms that can be used by another program, in our case an assembler, that can translate the abstractions into the machine language a computer requires. Figure 5-1 illustrates the process of decomposing a problem from the terms we prefer to work with into the terms the computer must have.

The best method for solving any problem is the divide and conquer approach, which has been known by generals and engineers for centuries. In terms of programming, it means that we analyze the problem we have to solve, breaking it into its constituent components. That is, we divide the larger problem into a series of problems that together comprise the original, undecomposed problem. We keep dividing the problems in this fashion into increasingly simpler subproblems until we reach the point where the problems we face are rather straightforwardly capable of translation into understandable and manageable modules.

This approach results in a *top-down* structure, which greatly simplifies the writing of a program. Decomposing the problem this way, among other things, makes it easier to identify procedures that will be needed more than once. These procedures can be written as subroutines, which can be used as often as necessary. Rather than taking on the entire problem, which likely cannot be fully understood, we take on parts of the problem in small enough parts that the parts can be understood and written as programming modules.

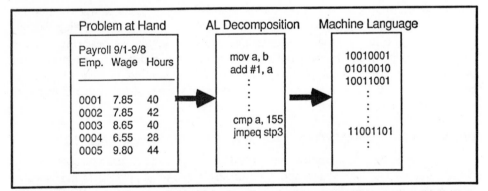

Fig. 5-1. *Problem Decomposition:* The programmer must decompose the problem at hand into terms which can be used by a language processor. Decomposition means starting with abstractions such as wages and hours worked and translating them into terms required by the assembler, such as MOV and ADD instructions. Since AL bears a closer relation to machine language than a HLL, the AL programmer must decompose the problem more completely than would be the case with a HLL. Then the assembler takes the decomposition (the AL program) and translates it into the terms the computer must have, data and instructions consisting of nothing other than 1's and 0s.

---

*"Data Structures and Algorithms," in *Scientific American* (September 1984).

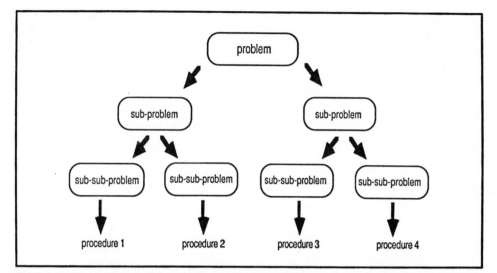

Fig. 5-2. Top-Down Problem Decomposition and Structured Programming: The best way to solve a programming problem is the venerable "divide and conquer" strategy. Problems are broken into subproblems, which are broken into sub-subproblems, and so on, until the resulting subproblems are simple enough to be easily understood and translated into an AL procedure. This method results in reduced programming time, especially in the debugging phase. As a result, the structure of the program reflects the solution path of the original problem. The procedures should be made as independent of each other as possible so that they are independently testable. This is the emphasis in a structured program.

In recent years, considerable interest in top-down decomposition and structured programming has developed. As illustrated in Fig. 5-2, the idea of top-down programming is to decompose larger problems into two or more subproblems which, in turn, are decomposed into additional subproblems, and so on, until the subproblems facing the programmer are simple enough to be understood well and written as separate procedures or routines. The main program is then comprised of a series of calls to the procedures. Another way to express this is to say that the resulting program mirrors the solution path of the problem's decomposition. For example, the main program might consist of only the following:

```
STRT CALL GET_EMPLOYEE_TABLE
CALL CALCULATE_PAY
CALL PRINT_LISTING
CALL PRINT_CHECKS
EXIT
```

Procedure PRINT_CHECK could call additional subroutines such as:

```
FORMAT_DATA
PRINT_INDIVIDUAL_CHECK
PRINT_EMPLOYEE_RECEIPT
```

As illustrated in Fig. 5-3, decomposing the payroll problem in a top-down fashion allows the programmer to identify which subtasks are needed and how they must interact in order to produce the desired results. Identified at the same time are the common procedures, such as output to the printer in a certain format, that will be used by several of the procedures. Each step, it is a matter of ascertaining "to do this task, what subtasks must be done?," until the problem is decomposed into manageable units such as calculating pay for one employee and getting the record of the next employee in the list. Each of the identified subtasks can be translated into the corresponding AL procedure. The resulting program should mirror what is called the *solution path* of the problem decomposition:

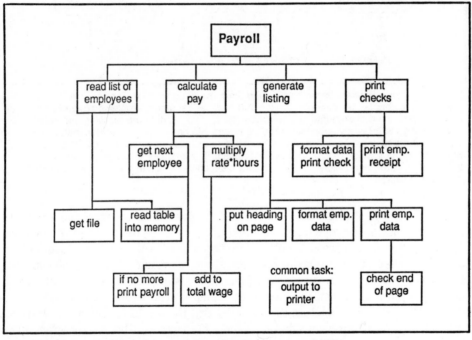

Fig. 5-3. The decomposition of the payroll problem in a top-down fashion.

Often associated with structured programming in a HLL are control structures such as IF/THEN/ELSE, REPEAT/UNTIL, and WHILE loops. These structures are used so that control of programming structures can be as clear as possible, and the extensive use of GOTO statements can be avoided. While GOTOs are sensible for certain tasks, it is often more advisable to use the control structures just mentioned, since the extensive use of GOTO statements tends to confound program logic and hence debugging and maintenance. Also associated with structured programming is the distinction between *global* and *local* variables. Global variables are declared at the program rather than the procedural level, and they are valid in all procedures. A local variable is declared at the procedure level and is not valid at the program level. This means that procedures modifying the value of a local variable cannot modify the value of a global variable at the same time. This aids in debugging programs, since unwanted side effects can be more easily avoided.

Assembly language is usually understood to be a nonstructured language. If written properly, however, AL programs can be structured in ways that parallel structured HLL programs. Top-down problem decomposition helps in writing an AL program in a structured manner. Procedures can be implemented as separately written and debugged subroutines that pass parameters as needed. If labels and jump instructions are used properly, AL programs can be structured logically by means of subroutines. In terms of local and global variables, the same effect can be achieved in AL by means of external subroutines that can only modify the variables that are passed to them as parameters or are designated for common use.

STEPS IN SUCCESSFUL PROGRAM WRITING

The average programmer today turns out just a few lines, on average about five to ten lines, of successful code per day.* This is because typical programming practice employs "fly by the seat of your pants" method; with a programming problem just handed him, the programmer sits down and begins typing in code. Coding should be the last or one of the last steps of programming. Lots of design work should be done prior to coding. The programmer should think in terms of the steps required to write a program. As illustrated in Fig. 5-4 and explained in the next two pages, we advocate an eight step process.

```
(1) identify the programming task
(2) design the input and output
(3) design the algorithm(s)
(4)  do some comparative analysis
(5) refine your design
(6) translate your pseudo-code to AL code
(7) test your procedures
(8) integrate the procedures, test and debug the program
```

Fig. 5-4. Eight Steps in the Development of a Program: Experience has shown that using sound methods results in more reliable programs written more quickly. Here is one method that works well. Note how relatively late in the program's development coding occurs. Programming by problem decomposition as opposed to programming by "fly by the seat of your pants" means that problem decomposition is mainly a matter of solving problems in English and pseudo-English rather than a computer language.

1. Identify the Programming Task. In English, write out what it is the program is supposed to do; identify the data that the program is supposed to take as input and the data it is supposed to produce as output. Describe the input and output data and procedures to be used so that it covers all conceivable cases. By writing everything out, you will think of many things that you otherwise would not have considered prior to writing. Remember the old adage, "You never fully understand something until you have explained it to someone else." Consider your design document the someone else in this case. Even if you were given the design specification by someone else,

---

Scientific American (August 1985).

rewrite it in your own words and see if your translation is acceptable to the person or person(s) who designed the original document.

2. Refine Your Design. Begin thinking about how to represent the kinds of data your program must handle. Choice of representation is critical since representation choices affect the kind of algorithms that will be required to operate on them. Always think of more general tasks first; then think in terms of more specific ways to accomplish these tasks. The movement of refinement should be from the completely abstract task to the completely concrete operation. That's why coding should come last. Think of single procedures accomplishing specific tasks. Keep the analysis in English or some kind of pseudocode as long as you can. Put together a list of all the procedures and data you'll need.

3. Design the Input/Output. In English, list the various types of data that the program will operate on—for instance, a list of names and addresses, perhaps a salary formula. For each data type, identify the operations that will need to be performed on it. For each, identify the range of acceptable values. Define how the program will get the data—i.e., keyboard, file, or mass storage. Then define the output data in terms of a file, CRT display, or printer listing and how it will be formatted.

4. Design the Algorithm(s). Write out (again in English or some form of pseudocode) the algorithms that are required to perform the operations in greater detail. Start with the ones that process the data and then do the ones that convert the data from its input to its output formats. Decompose each of the algorithms into their most basic operations. In working with the algorithms, you likely will discover additional input data or output formats that you had not identified initially.

5. Do Some Comparative Analysis. If you can, devise an alternative conception of the data types and algorithms devised in step 2. Then compare the two in terms of simplicity, clarity, and ease of translation into programming concepts and procedures. Often, the first solution to a problem is not elegant and a second pass at the problem will result in a superior solution. In general, think some more about the project—always in general concepts and general procedures (in English or some kind of pseudocode). Turn the problem over in your head a few times. As they say, "Sleep on it for a night or two."

This is also a good time to anticipate how the program may need to be expanded in the future and to consider ways to write the program so that such expansion is as easy as possible. In fact, most programs, no matter how well conceived and written, will need to be expanded and enhanced over time.

6. Translate Your Pseudocode to AL Code. Translate your pseudocoded procedures into assembly language code, again keeping procedures as independent of each other as possible. Some programmers find it best to start with the easiest procedures first. When designing a program, it is usually best to start at the top and work down but, when writing actual code, to work from the bottom up. That is, when decomposing the problem, work from the most abstract descriptions to the most concrete tasks, but when writing code, code the most basic procedures first and then build the program from these procedures, cumulatively adding new procedures to old, tested procedures until the entire program is written.

7. Test Your Procedures. If possible, test all procedures independently, revising them until they do their tasks flawlessly with the full range of data they'll be expected to handle. It is much easier to test a single procedure than an entire program. Writing a separate test routine for each procedure takes some time, but it will actually save time in terms of the total debugging effort, especially if some of the procedures are general purpose enough to be used in several programs. By verifying sections of a full program independently of each other, debugging efforts can be restricted to a smaller area of the program.

It is difficult to overemphasize the importance of testing procedures or routines independently. An error in even one instruction will often generate several seemingly unrelated errors, since other instructions depend on it. Moreover, a programming error in one subroutine might affect the operation of another subroutine. In this case, when you test the program, it will appear that one subroutine is not working properly, when in fact, the problem lies with another subroutine. Attempting to debug a properly working subroutine can unnecessarily consume a large amount of programming effort.

8. Integrate the Procedures, and Test and Debug the Program. Pull all the independent procedures together into one program. Test and debug this program. If problems seem to concentrate on one procedure, pull it out of the program and work on it independently until you're confident it's correctly coded. Begin with a simple set of input data that should yield a known set of output data. Then expand the test data to include a broader and broader range of possible data. When the procedure seems to be working well, make sure it is capable of handling erroneous data and reporting to the user that the data was erroneous. Testing a program with erroneous data is particularly important. Try to anticipate the wide variety of erroneous actions the user might take and make the program capable of handling such use. In other words, attempt to make the program as *user-friendly* as possible.

DOCUMENTATION

Good documentation is the heart of writing a program that can be maintained over a period of time. This is especially true of assembly language in which, first, individual instructions are not as self-documenting as instructions in high level languages such as Pascal; and second, AL instructions by themselves often do not indicate clearly what operation is being performed. Remember these two points about documentation:

First, the amount of documentation is important. Too much documentation can be as harmful as too little or no documentation. Too much documentation can obscure the code and constitute a maintenance program in its own right. Sparse or inconsistently detailed documentation, on the other hand, can mislead the reader of the source code file, giving a false sense of understanding. As the program is revised, documentation should also be revised. If the documentation is lengthy, it is tempting not to maintain the documentation because it is too much work. Additionally, source code files with too much documentation take longer to assemble, list and edit.

Second, it generally is not necessary to document every instruction since the operation of some instructions is obvious in any context. An instruction should be documented, however, if there is any doubt as to its operation and function to a person who did not write the program. Other instructions should contain enough documentation to help explain the operation of the procedure in which the instruction is located.

Two levels of documentation should be included in a program. First, the program should include a general description of what the program does. A description of typical inputs and outputs can be helpful. Second, the program should include detailed descriptions of how the various procedures and instructions perform their specific functions.

General Documentation

At the beginning of every program there should be a header that identifies the program, explains exactly what the program does, and explains how the user should use it. Many programmers also provide a sample listing of the input and output of the procedure. This facilitates complete testing.

The first line in the program or header should be an identification line that identifies the program. A single line identification is recommended for the sake of simplicity. It can include source file name, date written or last revised, revision number, system for which it was written, and the individual or organization by which it was developed. Consider this example:

WEATHER.ASM   11/24/86   Rev: 1.00   IBM-PC   V.O.C.S.

This example includes, in order, the source file name, "WEATHER.ASM," the date, the fact that this is revision 1.00 written for the IBM PC, and that it was developed by VOCS.

Follow the identification line with a description of the program. This should explain what the program does and how, generally, it does it. It should provide all the information needed to execute the program.

The organization of this information should depend on the type of program (or program segment) being described. If feasible, the documentation should be extractable from the source file so that it can be used as part of a manual or user's guide without changes. Some of the newer assemblers and software development systems include utilities for extracting documentation from the source file. Figure 5-5 outlines one possible format. Whatever format is used, use the same format for programs of the same type; this will make locating specific information much easier.

Many programmers maintain documentation separately rather than including it in the source file as we have suggested. This can result in two problems. First, separate documentation is easily misplaced, with the result that program development can continue without the documentation or it can be based on outdated versions of the documentation. Second, maintaining the documentation separately can result in the documentation not being maintained as the program is developed. It might also mean that someone other than the original programmer(s) maintains the documentation, which can result in inaccurate documentation, especially if there is some time lag between work on the program and the writing of the documentation. Including formal documentation as part of the program means that it will never get lost, the programmer(s) is reminded consistently that he, she, or they have the responsibility to maintain the documentation, and it is much more likely overall that the documentation will be maintained in a timely, accurate way.

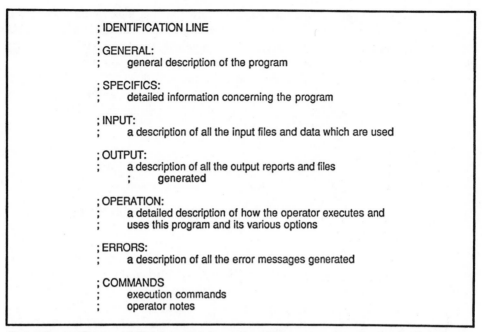

```
; IDENTIFICATION LINE
;
; GENERAL:
;       general description of the program

; SPECIFICS:
;       detailed information concerning the program

; INPUT:
;       a description of all the input files and data which are used

; OUTPUT:
;       a description of all the output reports and files
;           generated

; OPERATION:
;       a detailed description of how the operator executes and
;       uses this program and its various options

; ERRORS:
;       a description of all the error messages generated

; COMMANDS
;       execution commands
;       operator notes
```

Fig 5-5. General Documentation: A general description of the program precedes the detailed information. I/O is detailed and operation instructions are included. A description of error messages and their meanings and an explanation of the program's commands complete the general documentation.

In-Line Documentation

Included in the code at appropriate places should be enough documentation that a person who has not written the program can understand what the program is doing. In particular, variables and subroutines should be described fully.

For instance, suppose you are working on a program for a weather broadcaster. You could name the location in memory that stores the current temperature "CURTEMP." You could document the meaning of this variable in a variable section as follows:

CURTEMP   single byte   holds the value of the current
                          temperature in degrees Fahrenheit
                          valid range: -100 to +150

CURHUM   three bytes   holds the value of the current
                          humidity in percent as an ASCII string
                          valid range: 0 to 100

Variable names, as far as possible, should bear some resemblance to their meaning, but a well-chosen name is not enough. Documentation should include what it is that the memory location named CURTEMP holds and what its valid range of values is.

One characteristic of a well-written program is that it checks the validity of entered data. If the user enters 288 as the current temperature instead of 88, a good program would flag the 288 as an error. Documentation should identify error-checking routines and acceptable ranges of data input. If the reasons for the range of acceptable data is not obvious, the documentation should explain why the range is what it is. Note the close relationship here between good documentation and good programming.

As suggested above, each instruction does not necessarily need its own comment. The purpose of each section of code can be described with a statement, and instructions that are unusual or complicated can be individually documented. For example, consider this program fragment:

```
MOV  RATE, AX    ; calculate pay where pay = rate * hours
MOV  HOURS, BX
MUL  HOURS, RATE
CALL CONV        ; convert binary string to ASCII equivalent
JMP  NEXT
```

In this example, the first instruction's comment is a description of the function performed by this group of five instructions. The second, third, and fifth instructions are not documented since their operations are straightforward. The fourth instruction, however, is documented since it calls an external routine whose operation might not be clear.

Last, it is a good idea to use uppercase letters for instructions and lowercase letters for comments that follow instructions. This makes it easier to read programs and keep instructions distinct from comments.

COMPACT CODE: PROS AND CONS

Compact code is the practice of using as few instructions as possible to perform a programming task. The following justification is sometimes offered. A programmer must work with systems with limited memories. Since compact code takes up less space, for some tasks it is justifiable. Moreover, since shorter programs sometimes are easier to debug, compact code is sometimes desirable.

For most applications, however, compact, or condensed, code is actually more of a disadvantage than an advantage. The reason is that condensed code can conceal the operation of the program since it often means employing seldom-used instructions. Good programs are characteristically straightforward, readable and intelligible. This makes for easier debugging and maintenance. Unfortunately, even experienced programmers fall into the trap of trying to demonstrate their cleverness by writing cryptic, condensed code. One sign of a competent programmer is that he or she anticipates another programmer taking on the task of reworking an already written program. He or she makes it as easy for that programmer as possible.

The programmer must weigh the pros and cons of condensed coding. Let's consider some of the advantages and disadvantages of compact code.

Execution Time

Pro: Eliminating instructions that are not completely necessary decreases execution time, making the program faster.

Con: This argument has more validity in the case of high level languages than it does with assembly language. HLL instructions execute in the millisecond range, AL instructions in the microsecond range. Unless the eliminated instructions will execute thousands of times, their elimination will have no noticeable effect on execution times.

Memory Size

Pro: Condensed code obviously takes up less space, a useful factor when working with machines of limited memory.

Con: A smaller and smaller percentage of machines today have less than 64K of main memory. Saving a few hundred bytes by condensing a readable, straightforward program into an unreadable, condensed program will make little difference. Only if the program and its data will not fit into main memory is condensation worth considering.

Development Time

Pro: Shorter programs generally take less time to write and debug than longer programs.

Con: Shorter programs, if the brevity is gotten by means of condensing the code, don't necessarily take less time to write and debug. In fact, condensed programs will often take much longer to write and debug than straightforward programs simply because condensing is not unlike encryption. Instead of being a program to understand and master, the program becomes an encryption to decode.

Maintenance

Pro: Shorter programs are generally easier to maintain.

Con: Actually, compact code usually is considerably more difficult to modify and maintain. It's also much more difficult for other programmers to read and work with. Remember that it is the rule and not the exception that eventually somebody else will attempt to maintain—revise, update, upgrade—your program. Programs should be written so that they can be understood by a variety of people—not just the original programmer and the computer. As a result, use compact code only when it is the only way to solve a memory-availability problem or when there are distinct advantages to be gained that outweigh the disadvantages.

SUBROUTINES

The use of subroutines can greatly reduce the size of a program and the amount of time it takes to develop the program. As a result, they are a useful tool for the programmer. However, too much of a good thing is no longer a good thing; some programmers use too many subroutines, a practice that obscures and complicates the programming task.

There are two basic reasons for using a subroutine:

1. when a procedure that accomplishes one basic task is needed repeatedly (for example, an output procedure);

2. when a procedure that has become complicated could be divided in two or more parts.

Unfortunately, many programmers give in to the temptation to turn every procedure into a subroutine—regardless of the simplicity of the procedure's task or how many times it is used. Too many subroutines enlarges the program, complicates its logic, and therefore makes the program less readable and maintainable. There is a price to pay for converting a series of instructions into a subroutine. A call instruction is required to invoke the subroutine, and a return instruction is needed to return control to the calling block of code. Parameters may need to be passed back and forth. These require additional instructions, which consume additional computer time and memory. The subroutine will also require documentation. Consider the two following program fragments:

```
First                    Second
MOV  BUF, A              MOV  BUF, A
RLTC A                   CALL REV
RLTC A                   AND  0FH, A
RLTC A                        :
RLTC A                        :
AND  0FH, A          REV  RLTC A
                          RLTC A
                          RLTC A
                          RLTC A
                          RET
```

In the first fragment, the routine contained in the second fragment's subroutine is contained in line. This routine reverses the most significant and least significant four bits. In this case, the use of a subroutine to accomplish this task complicates the program and results in a longer program. The programmer who writes the second fragment doubtless understands what REV does in the second line, but the programmer maintaining the program would have to look for the subroutine or rely on documentation, which may or may not be present.

As this example illustrates, judgment is needed in terms of when to use a subroutine and when the code should be written in line. There is no magic formula, and programmers can disagree about these matters. This is the question that should be answered in the affirmative before using a subroutine: Is the price that I will pay for using a subroutine worth what it will save—in terms of development, debugging, and maintenance time? In short, will using a subroutine simplify these tasks or make them more complicated? If it will, then subroutines should be used. If not, they shouldn't.

COMPLEX MATH OPERATIONS

The use of complex mathematical equations should, for the majority of applications, be avoided. Operands should be kept simple and intelligible so that actual values of expressions can be determined by the reader. Since programs are written for people as well as for computers, complex equations generally should be avoided.

Suppose a program requires the relative location of a particular entry in a table.

ADD TABLE+ (((SIZE/ENTRIES)*10)+5), B

This expression is difficult for most persons to evaluate without the assistance of pencil and paper or calculator. Unless there is a definite reasons for using variable labels to represent constants, the practice should be avoided. In the example just cited, if the size of the table and the number of entries will vary each time the program is assembled, then the expression is justifiable. In such cases, it is advantageous to use labels to represent constants, setting the label to a specific value at the beginning of the program. This eliminates the need to calculate the constant everywhere it is used in the program. But if the label does represent an actual constant which does not change, such a practice is a likely source of errors. In such a case, it would be better to use:

```
ADD TABLE+255, B        ; 5th byte, 10th entry
```

Some assemblers will allow only the use of add, subtract, logical AND, and logical OR in parameters. Others support more complex operations, such as multiply and divide, and complicated equations, as illustrated above. The fact that many assemblers fail to support these more complex operations does not mean that they are inferior. Rather, it reflects programming preference. Many professional programmers consider the use of complex operations to be bad programming practice. In their minds, support of the more complex operations serves to encourage poor programming habits. To repeat a recurring theme of this text, shortcuts up-front, such as complex parameters, may cost more in the long run, in terms of development time, debugging, and maintenance, than they are worth.

LABELS

One of the principal advantages of assembly language over machine code is that it allows the use of labels instead of memory addresses to identify values. Remember that assembly language represents the binary data of the computer with symbols that are easier for people to use. A label such as MORTRATE can be used, and the assembler will determine what it means in terms of a binary value or a memory address.

Whenever possible, meaningful labels should be used. If we are working on a program that utilizes a mortage rate, it is obviously more meaningful to use MORTRATE than X or SUZY. Mathematicians or people with substantial math backgrounds often suppose that the kind of variables used in math, such as X and Y, should also be used in programming, but this is a mistake since part of the purpose of a good label is to identify what is held in the memory location. SUZY is good for a smile but is poor practice for the same reason. Labels should be chosen so that they document the data that is held in the memory location.

As a suggestion, consider correlating subroutines and labels. All the labels of one subroutine could begin with the same character and be distinguished by successive characters. Suppose we were writing an output routine. We might have the following labels: OUTCHAR, OUTC1, and OUTC2. The initial OUTC tips us off that the labels' home is an output routine. In fact, when using labels, it is sometimes better to use a label that reflects its location rather than its purpose. Consider the following alternatives:

Option 1	Option 2	
OUTPUTCS	OUTPUTCS	; output character string
OUTFSTCH	OUTC1	; output first character
OUTNXTCH	OUTC2	; output next character
OUTCRLF	OUTC3	; output CR, LF
OUTPUTRN	OUTC5	; return

Although the labels in the first column are more descriptive than the labels in the second column, the labels in the second column are just as effective since they better represent the relative location of the instruction and they provide some indication of what they represent—and the comments assist in understanding their purpose. Knowing the location of a label makes reading and debugging the program easier. Note that the first label in option 2 does provide a clear indication of the purpose of the routine.

Many assemblers permit a maximum of six or eight characters in a label. Other assemblers allow longer names, but only the first six or eight guarantee uniqueness. For instance, suppose we were working with two mortgage rates, one for 10 years and one for 25. With more than eight significant characters we could use MORTRATE-10 and MORTRATE-25 but this would generate errors if we had only eight significant characters since the first nine characters in both labels are identical. A way around that would be to integrate the numeric factor into the middle of the label, as in MORT-10-RATE and MORT-25-RATE. Uniqueness is preserved, and yet the label is significantly self-documenting.

One controversial question has to do with the size of labels and instruction mnemonics. Some newer assemblers and compilers allow up to 32 (and more) characters even though only the first eight or so characters are used to distinguish one label from another. We question the wisdom of using large labels. Consider the following labels:

8 characters	32 characters
COSTAPLS	COST_PER_APPLE_SOLD
COSTAPLP	COST_PER_APPLE_PURCHASED

We could use them in a program as follows:

```
COSTAPLS  DW ; unit cost per apple sold
COSTAPLP  DW ; unit cost per apple purchased

COST_PER_APPLE_SOLD          DW;unit cost per apple sold
COST_PER_APPLE_PURCHASED     DW;unit cost per apple purchased
```

We would argue that the first two labels, along with their comments, are as effective as the second two. Using labels which are eight bits in length results in more readable programs that can be written more quickly since it takes time to type in long labels. The programs are more readable because we have only about 80 characters in a line and using up to 32 characters for labels results in too little space for code and comments. Long labels can be a problem in label tables, which list labels and their locations, and other relevant information in columns with limited space. Additionally, since large AL programs use several hundred or thousand labels, consistently using long labels consumes a considerable amount of space in the source file.

ADVANCED ASSEMBLER FEATURES

An example of an advanced assembler feature is *conditional assembly*, which provides a way to control the code that gets assembled. Conditional assembly makes it possible to decrease the number of programs required to perform similar tasks. Rather than writing a separate program for each task, all the code that is required for all the tasks is put into one source file. Conditions are set up to select which portions of the source file are to be assembled. In this way, one source file can be reassembled several times to produce similar—yet not identical—programs. The form of a conditional assembly sequence is:

```
IF (expression)
   :
IF (expression)
   :
END
```

The dots signify the instructions that would be assembled, depending on whether the expression associated with the IF evaluates to true or false.

There are, however, some precautions that should be kept in mind. If a sizable section of program is to vary or the major part of a subroutine is to change, then a better programming choice is to use an external subroutine. The external subroutine can then be linked into the program. Managing several versions of an external subroutine is considerably easier than trying to analyze or debug a single program that is loaded with conditional commands. The problem, we should keep in mind, does not belong to the computer. As is usually the case, it is the programmer that must keep track of how the program does what it does. The golden rule of thumb here, as in many programming decisions, is to write the program in a way that is most readable and analyzable by human beings. As a result, use conditionals when just a few lines of code or a short segment will vary.

Additionally, it is generally wise to avoid imbedded or nested conditionals (conditionals inside of conditionals) unless their use is obvious. Some programming languages allow nesting up to twenty levels deep. Such a feature is sometimes claimed to an indication of a "powerful" language. But powerful for whom? The computer will have no problem with that kind of programming practice, but even the best programmer will find such programming hopelessly indecipherable—but then the best programmer won't need to demonstrate his or her cleverness by making his or her programs unreadable to all but him or herself. It is better to repeat sections of the code than to obscure program control and logic.

Generally, we believe that the same lesson holds for other advanced assembler features, such as macros and include files. Unless use of these features offers a definite advantage, it is usually better to keep programs as simple as possible.

A PROGRAMMING EXAMPLE: GENERATING PRIME NUMBERS

A widely used programming example is that of generating prime numbers. It is widely used because it is fairly simple and yet generates something of interest, namely prime numbers. In this programming example, we will decompose the problem from the very beginning and successively rework it until it is suited for translation into both a high level language and assembly language.

Preliminary Decomposition

Suppose that we decide to identify the numbers up to 100 which are prime. A prime number is a positive integer greater than 1 whose only integral factors are itself and 1. To ascertain if 7, for instance, is prime is to attempt to find two numbers other than 7 and 1, call them x and y, whose product is 7. In other words, is there a $x*y = 7$ where neither x nor $y = 7$ or 1, and x and y are integers? The answer is no. Hence, 7 is prime. If we try 6 for primeness, we find out that if x is assigned 3 and y 2, or vice versa, the product is 6. That is, there are integral factors other than the number itself and 1 whose product is 6. Therefore, 6 is not prime.

Decomposing the problem is a matter of breaking it down into its constituent parts and working with it until we understand the problem well enough to solve it, at least in principle, without the aid of a computer. As it happens, the first prime number is 2, which is even. All prime numbers greater than 2 must be odd since all even integers are evenly divisible by 2; this means that they are *not* prime. Hence, 2 is the only even prime number.

This means that, for prime number candidates greater than 2, we can assume that they will be odd. In identifying prime numbers, we can take 2 to be prime and all candidates for primeness to be $3 + n$ where n is a multiple of 2. This simply generates the series, 3, 5, 7, 9, . . . So these will be the numbers that we will test for primeness.

Our preliminary decomposition looks like this:

1. Set a variable named *number* to 3 (taking 2 to be prime already)
2. Repeat
   a. Test number to see if it is prime
   b. Print it if tests as prime
   c. Increment number by 2 (take next number in series 3,5,7 . . .) until number is greater than 100

Decomposing Further (Step 2a)

Additional considerations will help us solve the problem so that we can decompose step 2a, which is still an involved task. In the equation, $5 * 3 = 15$, mathematicians call 5 and 3 *factors*, since they produce 15 when multiplied together; 5 and 3 are factors for 15; 3 can be said to be the *cofactor* of 5 for the number 15, and 5 is the cofactor of 3 for 15. Now, if a number has a factor other than itself and 1, this means it also has a factor less than or equal to its own square root. For example, 16 has a factor, namely 8. This means that 16 has a factor less than or equal $\sqrt{16}$, or 4. In fact, 4 is a factor of 16 (e.g., let the other factor also be 4).

The reason that this is the case is that if both factors of a number are larger than the square root of a number, then the number would have to be larger than it is. In the case of 16, we couldn't have two factors larger than $\sqrt{16}$, since taking their product would result in a number greater than 16. The result is that we will only have to test odd numbers to see if they are factors for a number that is a candidate for primeness up to the square root of the candidate number.

As an example, suppose that we wish to know if 61 is prime. Since $\sqrt{61}$ is about 7.81, we will test 61 for primeness by dividing it by 3. 5, and 7 (the odd numbers between 3 and the integer portion of the square root of the number in question, namely 61). Since none of these divide 61 evenly, 61 is prime.

Our mature decomposition looks like this:

1. Set *number* equal to 3 {first number to look at}
2. Repeat these steps:
  a. See if *number* is prime:
      initialize *prime* to true
      initialize *factor* to 3 {first divisor to try}
      initialize *limit* to $\sqrt{\text{number}}$
      while *factor* is less than or equal to *limit* and
         prime is still true do this:
         if *number/factor* yields no remainder then
            set *prime* to false {number fails test, not prime}
         else increment *factor* by 2
         {number passed one test, try another to see if prime}
  b. If it is prime, print number {if *prime* = true, *number* is prime}
      output *number* as a prime
  c. Set *number* to *number* +2 {try next odd number for primeness}
until *number* > 100 {when it is, we are done}

We are now in a position to translate this decomposition fairly straightforwardly into a high level language, specifically Pascal. Here is what the Pascal program for generating prime numbers from 3 to 100 looks like:

```
program prime;

var
        number,
        factor,
        limit : integer;
        prime : boolean;

begin
        writeln('The prime numbers between');
        writeln('3 and 100 are:');
        number := 3;
        repeat
                prime := true;
                factor := 3;
                limit := trunc(sqrt(number));
```

```
        while (factor <= limit) and prime do
                if number mod factor = 0 then
                        prime := false
                else
                        factor := factor + 2;
        if prime then
                write(number : 3);
        number := number + 2
    until number > 100
end.
```

The logic of the program in AL is essentially the same as that in Pascal. We assume, however, that we don't have the square root, truncate, and mod (remainder division) functions available—although we might have them available as external subroutines in a library in actual practice. Consequently, we need to develop a subroutine that returns the integer part of the square root, plus 1, of the candidate for primeness. As explained in the program header, we will use some external routines that make dealing with output easier, and we will need a routine to convert integers to their ASCII equivalents so that they can be displayed—but other than these problems, the program logic is very similar to the Pascal program.

Even though there are more instructions in the AL program than in its Pascal counterpart and there is somewhat more work to do in order to get the functions we need, each AL instruction is simpler in terms of what it does and is therefore easier to understand. In particular, the while loop in the Pascal program compresses many steps into a few steps and is not as easy to comprehend as it could be.

Note particularly that the AL program exemplifies some of what we have maintained in this chapter in terms of labels and comments. In this case, we have put comments on nearly every line of code because this program is educational in purpose. We probably wouldn't do that in commercial programming where we could presuppose greater familiarity with assembly language. And we would have said more about the method if we didn't have the text we just saw. Here is the equivalent AL program, written in UAL for the 8086 microprocessor.

```
;   PRIME.MLS  2/17/86  Rev:1  UAL  EXAMPLE  VOCS
;
;   This program, written for an 8086 MS-DOS computer,
;   displays the prime numbers between 3 and 100.
;
; Uses external subroutines:
;
;   ^CNSLO—output to terminal with cr/lf
;   ^CNSLO—output to terminal
;   ^ITOA—convert integer to ASCII
;
; Uses procedural instructions:
;
;   ADDV—add value to variable
;   JMPIFV—jump if variable
;
```

```
STRT          ^CNSLCL MSG1,80              ; output message 1
              ^CNSLCL MSG2,80              ; output message 2
NXT           FILLB FACTOR,3              ; strating factor = 3
              MOV NUMBER,BH               ; bh = # to take square root of
              CALL SQRT                   ; return square root in reg dl
TST           MOVW NUMBER,AX              ; move number to reg ax
              DIV FACTOR,AL               ; reg al = ax/factor, ah = remainder
              AND AH,AH                   ; check if remainder = 0
              JMPR Z,NOTPRIME             ; jump if not prime
              MOV FACTOR,AL               ; otherwise advance factor
              ADD # 2,AL                  ; add 2 to factor
              MOV AL,FACTOR               ; save factor
              CMP AL,DL                   ; check if past upper limit
              JMPR M,TST                  ; go to tst if not
              ^ITOA NUMBER,BUF,4,ERR      ; convert prime number to ascii
              ^CNSLO BUF,3                ; output prime number
NOTPRIME
ADDVB
2,NUMBER      ; next candidate for prime
              JMPIFVB NUMBER,LT,101,NXT   ; if number less 4 101 keep looking
              STOP                        ; exit program
;
;     FIND INTEGER PART OF SQUARE ROOT + 1
;
; Input: reg BH = the number to take square root of
; Output: reg DL = integer part of square root + 1
;
SQRT          MOVW # 1, DX                ; set lowest possible number
SQRT1         MOVW DX,AX                  ; move reg dx to ax
              MUL DL,AL                   ; multiply number by itself
              CMP BH,AL                   ; compare with number to be
                                          ; square rooted
              JMPR C,SQRT2                ; return if above maximum
              INCW DX                     ; next possible number
JMPR
UN,SQRT1      ; repeat process
SQRT2         RET                         ; number found, return to main code
;
ERR           ^CNSLCL MSG4,80             ; number conversion error
              STOP
;
MSG1 DB 'The prime numbers between',0
MSG2 DB '3and 100 are: ',0
MSG4 DB 'Conversion error',0
BUF           DS 4                        ; prime number buffer
NUMBER        DW 3                        ; candadate for prime
FACTOR        DW 0                        ; division variable
;
END
```

Once the program is assembled using MOPI, we execute it and get the following result:

```
The prime numbers between
3 and 100 are:
5 7 11 13 17 19 23 29 31 37 41 43 47 53 59 61 67 71 73 79 83 89 97
```

FOR FURTHER READING

Thomas, Richard A. "Using Comments to Aid Program Maintenance, " *BYTE* (May 1984).

Maly, Kurt and Hanson, Allen R., *Fundamentals of the Computing Sciences* (Englewood Cliffs, 1978), ch. 3.

Chapter 6

Registers

Purpose of the Chapter: This chapter defines what a register is and explains the role registers play in program execution. It details general purpose registers, register files, index registers, special purpose registers, and registers and stacks. The last section illustrates the pivotal role that one register, the stack pointer (or SP), plays in a major data structure, the stack.

WHAT A REGISTER IS

Computer systems possess several ways to store information. In addition to a main internal memory and mass external (to the microprocessor) memory, computer systems contain one or more *registers*. A register is a distinct kind of memory location that, unlike main memory and mass external memory, is part of the CPU. Of the three kinds of memory storage locations, registers, main, and external memory, registers are easily the fastest and the most versatile for the manipulation of data.

Like a main memory location, registers typically have fixed widths, such as 8, 16, or 32 bits. Some registers use *flip-flops* to store data. Each flip-flop, as portrayed in Fig. 6-1, stores one bit of data and can be accessed individually. Unlike main memory locations, registers usually are capable of manipulating the data they contain on a bit by bit basis. For example, a register can be instructed to increment (increase by 1 or 2) or decrement (decrease by 1 or 2) its contents. Its bits can be shifted to the left or right, effectively doubling or halving the number represented. Its bits can also be augmented by some value or complemented (its 1s changed to 0s and its 0s to 1s).

It is often claimed, with some justification, that n bit processors have $2n$ bit han-

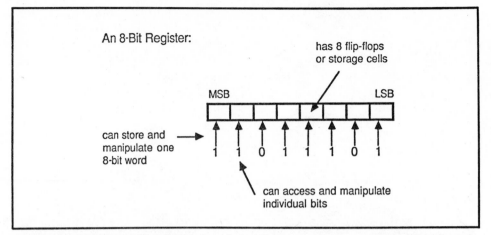

An 8-Bit Register:

has 8 flip-flops
or storage cells

MSB   LSB

can store and
manipulate one
8-bit word

1   1   0   1   1   1   0   1

can access and manipulate
individual bits

Fig. 6-1. An 8-bit register: The register is the principal data storage component in the CPU. Like main memory locations, it is used to store data, but it is much faster and is used, in math and logical operations, to alter data on a bit by bit basis. Bits are numbered right to left as 0 to 7.

dling capabilities. For instance, an 8-bit microprocessor such as the Z80 has only 8-bit general purpose registers, but they can be paired to handle 16 bits at a time. And microprocessors such as the Motorola 68000, which is either a 16-bit or 32-bit micro, depending on how you look at it, support 32-bit *long word* instructions and have 32-bit registers. The older 4-bit micros employed 4-bit registers and some 6-bit registers. Typically, on 8- and 16- bit micros, registers can hold 8 or 16 bits of data. The newer 16- and 32-bit microprocessors use 32-bit registers. Owing to its complexity, classifying micros in terms of bit size has become nearly a philosophical issue, but we adhere to the convention that the "size" of a microprocessor is a matter of the size of its registers and internal bus architecture—not the size of the words transferred between the microprocessor and external devices, such as mass memory or a printer.

Usually a part of the ALU, registers are used to store frequently used or intermediate data. Registers are also used to store data that the computer needs immediate access to, such as the memory address of the next instruction. Registers, rather than main memory, are used because of the speed of register accesses. As mentioned in ter 2, both programs and data are stored in the computer's main memory. Accessing the data in main memory is relatively slow, on the order of 300 to 600 nanoseconds (10^{-9} seconds) in MOS/LSI technology. By contrast, accessing data in a register often takes less than 100 nanoseconds. Obviously, if efficiency is important, data that is accessed a number of times is better stored in registers than in main memory.

Unlike main memory, which is accessed using address numbers that range from 0..64K (with a 16-bit address word) or 0..16M (with a 24-bit address word), each register is assigned a one or two character symbol that is an abbreviation for the type of data the register contains. For example, D0 names data register 0, while A7 names address register 7. As these names suggest, D0, as a data register, would be used to store data, while A7, as an address register, would be used to store the address of some location in main memory.

Microprocessor manufacturers classify registers according to their use or availability to the programmer. In this text, since we are discussing all microprocessors, we will adopt the convention that registers belong to one of three groups:

General Purpose registers can be used by the programmer for storing data such as intermediate results or counters. Sometimes a general purpose register is called an accumulator since it is used in most math and logical operations to save the result. Some of these registers may have special meaning with regard to certain instructions.

Index or Address registers are used to address locations in memory. Some kinds of instructions provide for modification or calculation of addresses accessed during program execution. Addressing modes that facilitate this kind of address calculation use these registers to determine which address is accessed. Address registers are sometimes called *index* registers since they are used to modify the effective addresses of instruction operands.

Special Purpose registers are assigned a particular function with respect to microprocessor operations. For example, the program counter or PC contains the address of the next instruction to be executed. The status register keeps track of the results of instruction execution—e.g., whether an addition instruction caused a register to overflow.

In the following sections, we will survey the registers found in currently available microprocessors and explain what they do.

GENERAL PURPOSE REGISTERS

General purpose registers are assigned permanent names, typically letters of the alphabet beginning with A. Register sizes, in terms of bits, range from 4 bits on the older 4-bit microprocessors, to 8 bits on a Z80, to 16 bits on an 8086/8088, to 32 bits on a Motorola 68000. As illustrated in Fig. 6-2, registers can sometimes be doubled up to form a larger register that can be addressed with one name. On the Z80, for example, registers H and L can be combined as register HL, and we could access the contents of HL as one word. The number of registers that may be combined in this fashion depends on the micro. Registers can also be divided into smaller units of data. On the 68000, for example, 32-bit registers D0 through D7 can be used as 8- or 16-bit registers, depending on the operation being executed.

One register is normally referred to as the *accumulator* and is given the label A or AX. The accumulator is the register that the microprocessor uses for most of the mathematical and logical operations. Often there is a separate set of commands that apply to the accumulator but not to the other registers. With many 4- and 8-bit micros, all data being transferred between the micro and external devices must be routed through the accumulator.

The other general purpose registers are used as temporary storage areas. If a value is to be used repeatedly, it is advantageous to store it in a general purpose register since, as noted above, accesses to registers are considerably faster than accesses to main memory. It is also possible to perform certain logical and mathematical operations on the contents of general purpose registers, which cannot be done if the data is stored in a main memory location.

As an example of using general purpose registers, consider the process of counting the number of 0 bits in an 8-bit binary value called JUNKY. We might use the fol-

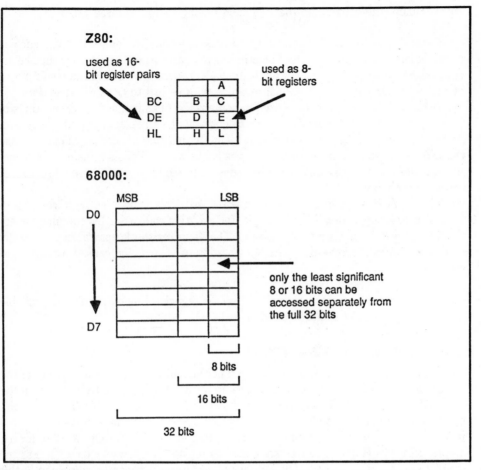

Fig. 6-2. The bits in a n bit register can vary from n: The registers of an n bit microprocessor are usually n bits wide; an 8-bit micro such as the Z80 has 8-bit registers and a 32-bit micro such as the 68000 has 32-bit registers. However, as in the case of the Z80, 8-bit registers can sometimes be combined to form a 16-bit register, and as in the case of the 68000, 8- and 16-bit segments can sometimes be accessed in 32-bit registers.

lowing procedure to accomplish this task:

    0. Set COUNT = 0   BITS = 8
    1. Check next bit of JUNKY
    2. If this bit is 0, then increment COUNT by 1
    3. Decrement BITS by 1
    4. If BITS > 0, then go to line 1

If we didn't use registers in this operation, the values of JUNKY, COUNT, and BITS would have to be read from main memory into the accumulator. Then the necessary operations, such as checking the next bit or incrementing COUNT, would be performed. Last, the result of the operation would have to be stored back into main memory—

during each execution of each step in the procedure. This repeated fetching and storing of data from main memory would consume relatively large amounts of CPU time.

Using registers instead of main memory speeds up the operation considerably. Storing JUNKY, COUNT, and BITS in registers means that the operations on them can be performed without time-consuming fetches and stores in main memory. The result is fewer instructions and much faster execution. Consider the following procedure, which performs the task mentioned earlier but now uses registers whenever possible. Note the explanatory comments after the semicolons; the slash indicates which program the comments refer to when the instructions differ.

	only one register		comments		several registers	
	MOV	#0, COUNT	; number of zeros found	;	MOV	#0, B
	MOV	#8, BITS	; number of BITS to use	;	MOV	#8, C
STP1	MOV	JUNKY, A	; load A with JUNKY	;	MOV	JUNKY, A
	RLWC	A	; rotate left with carry	; STP1	RLWC	A
	MOV	A, JUNKY	; store A/jump if clear	;	JMP	C, STP2
	JMP	C, STP2	; jump if clear/incr B	;	INC	B
	MOV	COUNT, A	; load A with COUNT/ decr C	; STP2	DEC	C
	INC	A	; incr A/jump if not zero	;	JMP	NZ, STP1
	MOV	A, COUNT	; store A in COUNT	;		
STP2	MOV	BITS, A	; load A with BITS	;		
	DEC	A	; decrement BITS	;		
	JMP	Z, STP3	; jump if result is zero	;		
	MOV	A, BITS	; store A in BITS	;		
	JMP	UN, STP1	; jump if not equal	;		
STP3	MOV	COUNT, B	; store COUNT in B	;		

REGISTER FILES

Although registers usually are part of the CPU and are not part of main or external memory, some computers have registers that are part of main or external memory. These are predefined locations in memory that start at a specified address and are used as registers. These locations are referred to as a *register file*. They are given a predefined label and may contain general information; they may serve as general purpose or special purpose registers. We can visualize the register file as shown in Fig. 6-3.

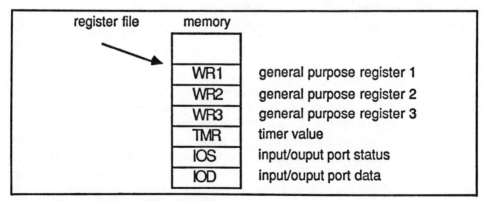

Fig. 6-3. A representation of the register file.

The advantage of a register file is that a micro can contain a larger number of registers that are used for special purposes. This is often necessary with microcomputers that contain circuitry that directly controls or communicates with external devices. Another advantage is that there can be multiple groups of the same registers. Each group is selected or pointed to by a base pointer or status flag. The programmer can preserve the contents of the registers by switching register files rather than saving them in memory or on a stack, which can be time consuming. This way, only the pointer to the desired set of registers needs to be changed when different sets of data are required.

INDEX REGISTERS

Index registers hold *address pointers*. A pointer in this case is a number, for example, 077540, that tells the computer where in main memory to find some piece of data. This number could be used in conjunction with the contents of other registers or other values to determine the address in main memory of the operand, the piece of data that is to be used or manipulated in some way.

Some index registers can also be used as general purpose registers to perform certain arithmetic operations. In some 8-bit micros the index register will be a combination of two or more general purpose registers. On the 8080, for example, H and L are each 8-bit registers. Together they can function as a 16-bit general purpose register or as index register HL. The size of an index register is either 8 or 16 bits. Which it is depends on the addressing modes that are used. They normally are given names that represent the type of indexing or special purpose they are used with.

Index registers are often specified in an instruction as part of the addressing mode. The data contained in the index registers can be manipulated (e.g., incremented or decremented) by other instructions. All of the newer microprocessors have at least one index register or a general purpose register that can be used as an index register. Some micros, however, do not designate a specific register as an index register—the register can be general purpose or index, and which it is will depend on the context in which it is used. Conversely, index registers can also be used as general purpose registers, which temporarily store data and perform mathematical operations.

Uses of Special Index Registers on the Various Micros

In the following sections, we will explain the use of some special index registers. Consult the microinstruction-set tables in the Appendix for those index registers that are available with specific micros.

Stack Pointer (SP). On some systems, the stack pointer is considered to be a special-purpose register since it serves a special function. The SP, however, is effectively an index register. See the section at the end of this chapter on how stacks are used.

Base Pointer (BP). The base pointer is an index register intended for use in locating a block of data in memory that normally contains predefined data. The base pointer is normally associated with specific instructions or addressing modes and need not be specified. As an example, consider a register file. Each location within the register file has a predefined label and position within the file but can be located anywhere in memory. WR3, for example, specifies the third location in the file, and the location of the file is specified by a base pointer; as shown in Fig. 6-4. With the instruction MOV #5, WR3, for example, the computer would move the value 5 to the location 3 plus the value in the base pointer, WR. The use of the base pointer is implied by the predefined label WR3.

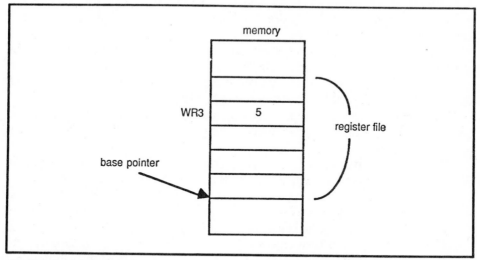

Fig. 6-4. The base pointer.

Segment Registers. Segment registers are used to specify the segments of a computer's total memory available for current use. The standard set of instructions can access a maximum of 64K of memory. Segment registers are used to indicate which 64K segment of memory is available for a specific application, as shown in Fig. 6-5. Each segment register is used for a different type of data and is associated with different instructions. For example, the *code segment* designates the segment of memory that contains the executable program. The *data segment* designates the segment of memory that contains the variable data used by a program.

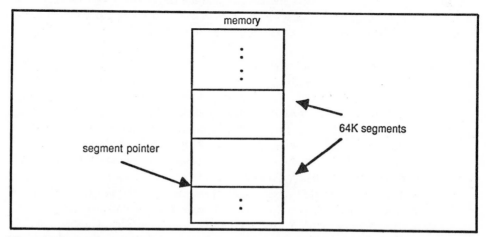

Fig. 6-5. The segment pointer.

SPECIAL PURPOSE REGISTERS

All microprocessors possess *dedicated registers*, that is, registers that are dedicated to a specific function or functions. Some dedicated registers appear in all micros, while others appear only in specific micros. Typically, these registers are 8, 16, or 32 bits, but they can be other sizes as well. While each of these registers is given a symbolic name for use in instructions, they are normally referred to by their function—what it is they do.

Although the data in these registers can be checked and modified by special instructions, they are usually modified by the micro as a result of the execution of certain instructions. These are the only registers that can be modified independent of any operator action. The other registers can only be changed by program instructions.

The special purpose registers of greatest interest are explained in the following sections. Consult the micro instruction set tables in the Appendix for the registers that apply to a specific micro.

Program Counter (PC). The PC register contains the address in memory of the next instruction or part of the current instruction. Most 8- and 16-bit microprocessors fetch instructions a byte at a time; as a result, the PC contains the address of the next byte. Some 16- and 32-bit micros fetch instructions a word at a time; in this case, the PC contains the address of the next (two byte) word. Whether a byte or a word is fetched depends on (1) how the instructions are organized and (2) the size of the data (8 or 16 bits) that can be fetched from memory in one cycle. The programmer usually does not access the PC directly, although there are instructions that will cause the PC to be changed. Usually the PC is updated or modified automatically by the micro—the programmer is not obligated to update this register.

Interrupt Vector Register. The Interrupt Vector register is used when the micro is processing certain types of interrupts. The interrupt vector is combined with a vector index, which is supplied by the interrupting device. These are combined to specify the address of the first instruction to jump to in order to process the interrupt.

Flag or Status (or Condition Code) Register. The Status or Flag register is unique because each of its individual bits or flags (sometimes called *flip-flops* since they flip back and forth after CPU operations), and not the entire word, are accessed. The contents and conditions under which each bit is changed varies greatly from micro to micro. Listed below are some of the most common:

carry contains the carry or borrow bit that results from math operations or logical operation such as bit shifts.

half carry contains the carry or borrow bit from the least significant 4 bits as a result of a math operation. Usually this is used with BCD numbers.

zero indicates whether or not the result of a math or logical operation is zero.

overflow indicates whether the result of a math operation was too large or small to be stored in the destination. Usually this is used with signed numbers, where the MSB indicates the sign and is not part of the number.

sign contains the same value as the MSB of the result of the last operation. It is used with signed numbers to indicate a positive or negative value.

parity is normally associated with I/O operations and indicates whether the data has odd or even parity (the number of 1 bits).

112

interrup enable specifies whether an external maskable interrupt is to be processed.

interrupt mask is used when processing interrupts—either to specify what procedure will be used to process them or which interrupts will be processed.

condition flags are normally associated with the compare instruction, but sometimes they are used with math and logical operations to indicate certain aspects of the result. With the compare instruction, they may indicate greater than, less than, equal to, and so on.

mode flags are used to indicate or select different operating modes within the CPU, such as binary/decimal emulation, and operations on the interface logic, such as the serial port and number of bits/parity/stop bits.

register file/bank select is used to select between two or more register files, memory banks, or alternate storage areas.

Special purpose registers are used to keep track of the state of the computer as it executes a program. Instruction execution generates results that are often recorded in the special purpose registers. For example, suppose the accumulator contains 40 and an instruction subtracts 45 from the number in the accumulator. The result will be less than zero. One flag, the S or sign flag, in the Flag Register, will be set after execution to indicate a less than zero condition. Other flags keep track of other conditions, such as whether a carry has occurred in addition and whether the contents of the accumulator equals zero. Based on conditions in the flags, decisions can be made in terms of which course of action to follow in the execution of the program's algorithm.

STACKS AND THE STACK POINTER REGISTER

In this section, we will look at one example of how one register, the stack pointer, is used with the data structure of stacks, which is an important concept in AL programming.

Historically, Burroughs popularized the use of stacks in the 1960s, and with the advent of mini and microcomputers, stacks became a widely used data structure because wise use of stacks conserves memory space. The stack is used to store temporary data in memory without having to specify an absolute location beforehand. As a result, the same locations can be used to store a much larger amount of data than would be needed if the stack were not used.

A stack is one kind of *ordered list*. In a stack, all the additions and deletions to a list are made at one end, which is designated as the *top*. By contrast, in a *queue*, which is another kind of ordered list, the additions are made at one end and the deletions are made at the other. As a result, a queue is like the line at a popular snack bar—first come, first served. A stack is more like a seniority system—last hired, first fired. The last item pushed on the top of the stack is the first to be popped off. As illustrated in Fig. 6-6, an often used analogy is that a stack is like a pushdown tray rack at a cafeteria—those pushed down on the mechanism last are the first to come off; to get to the tray pushed on first, one must first pop all the other trays off.

A stack will have a *pointer* that points to the current top of the stack. The bottom of a nonempty stack will contain the first item stored, and the top the last. Suppose that we add three items, *a, b,* and *c* to an empty stack (strictly speaking, a stack whose contents are unknown) with just three locations. Figure 6-7 shows a before and after look at the stack.

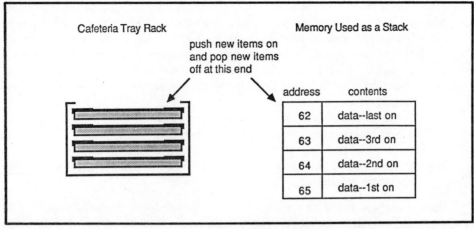

Fig. 6-6. A stack is like a cafeteria tray rack: In both a cafeteria tray rack and a stack, items are added by pushing them on the top. Items are removed by popping them off. The result is that both are first in, last out structures. In order to get to an item at the bottom, all of the items above would have to be popped first. Notice that, in terms of addresses in memory, the stack grows into lower memory, which means that the top of the stack will have the lowest address of all the items in the stack.

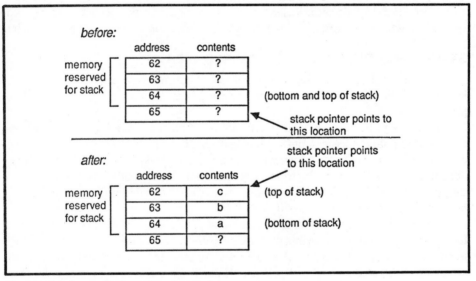

Fig. 6-7. A before and after look at the stack.

Usually, stacks are defined so that they "grow" into lower memory. This can be confusing since the top of the stack will possess the lowest memory address of the stack's filled locations. When the stack is empty, the pointer points at the address just above (in terms of address) the bottom of the stack. Initially, the stack pointer register or SP contains the number 65. To push an item onto the stack, the SP is decremented by 1 so that it points to the bottom-most location in the stack. Then item *a* is stored in the location pointed to by the SP, which is location 64. Items *b* and *c* are stored in a similar manner, with *b* stored in 63 and *a* in 62. As a result, the full stack looks like the "after" portrayal in the illustration. Popping the stack three times would yield first c, then b, then a, leaving the SP again pointing at location 65.

The bottom of the stack is usually located at the highest memory location so that the memory that is not used by the program can be used as the stack. Reversing the way we just visualized it, Fig. 6-8 will show the stack in memory with the lowest memory addresses at the bottom and the highest at the top.

To keep things simple and in order to control things better, many operating systems allocate a specific area of memory for use as a stack. Although this means that

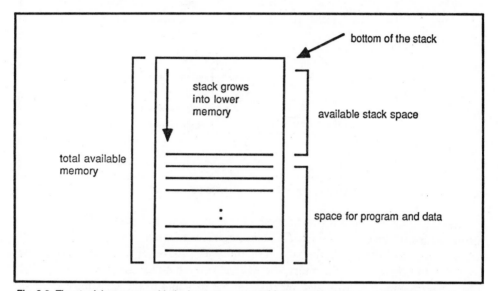

Fig. 6-8. The stack in memory with the lowest memory addresses at the bottom and the highest at the top.

the programmer does not have to define the location of the stack, it often restricts the number of items that can be stored at one time in the stack.

It should also be noted that with some computers the bottom of the stack will be the lowest address and the top will be the highest. As a result, to push items onto the stack, the SP is incremented rather than decremented. Also, many computers only allow the pushing of words (16 bits) or some other multiple of 8 bits of data onto the stack. Relatively few computers will allow the programmer to select the size of data, in terms of the number of bits, to be pushed or popped off the stack.

Some instructions, such as the call subroutine, automatically cause data to be put on the stack, while others, such as the return from subroutine, cause data to be popped off the stack.

Stacks and Subroutines

One principal use of stacks is to store addresses during repeated subroutine calls—a situation in which we want the last address stored to be the first one retrieved, the second address stored, the second one retrieved, and so on. Suppose that we have three subroutines, the first of which is called from the main program, and each of which, in turn, calls another subroutine. It can be visualized as shown in Fig. 6-9.

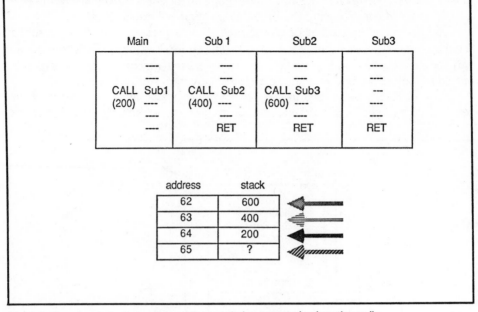

Fig. 6-9. The use of stacks to store addresses during repeated subroutine calls.

Let the dashes represent instructions; *CALL* means jump to subroutine and *RET* means return to the calling block. As Main begins executing, the SP points (slanted striped arrow) at location 65, the area in memory just above (in terms of address) the bottom of the stack. At CALL Sub1, the PC will contain 200, since after fetching the CALL instruction, the PC is incremented so that it points to the next instruction in the file.

When CALL Sub1 is executed, first the SP register is decremented by 1 so that it points to location 64 (solid black arrow). Then a copy of the number in the PC, or 200, is stored at the location in the stack pointed to by the SP, which is 64. This way, the computer will know what location contains the next instruction to execute, after the subroutine is finished executing. The address of Sub1 is then placed in the PC so that execution of subroutine Sub1 can begin. When control reaches a second subroutine call, CALL Sub2, 400 is stored in the stack at location 63 in a similar manner. Similarly, 600 is stored in the stack at location 62.

When control reaches RET at the end Sub3, it asks for the number at the top of the stack (the grey or top arrow). This number, 600, is popped off the stack and placed in the PC. Then the SP is incremented by 1 so that it points at the new top, which is now location 63 (lined arrow). The program then resumes execution of Sub2 until it reaches Sub2's RET instruction. It then branches to the instruction with address 400 to resume execution of Sub1. In a similar manner, control is returned to address 200 under Main.

As should be evident, a stack is one way to backtrack after repeated subroutine calls have transferred control repeatedly. This example illustrates well the crucial role the stack pointer register plays in the execution of programs.

FOR FURTHER READING

BYTE (April, 1983): issue on new microcomputer chips.

Fohl, Mark E., *An Assembly Language Course.* ch. 4, "The Instruction Set", especially pp. 61-81.

Lemone, Karen A., *Assembly Language & Systems Programming for the IBM PC and Compatibles.* (Boston, 1985), ch. 8, "Stacks and Procedures".

Lister, Paul, ed. *Single-Chip Microcomputers.* (New York, 1984).

Zaks, Rodney, *Microprocessors.* (Sybex, 1980).

Chapter 7

Addressing Modes

Purpose of the Chapter: This chapter introduces the concept of assembly language addressing modes. After introducing addressing mode syntax and memory addressing, it covers instruction specified, effective, and physical addresses. It then introduces basic elements of addressing modes before covering the more advanced addressing modes. To illustrate some of the addressing modes in use, the chapter concludes with a binary search program.

THE REASON FOR USING ADDRESSING MODES

A major portion of a computer's time is spent moving data from one location to another. As a result, many computer operations involve techniques whose purpose is to specify where data is to be stored in or retrieved from the computer's memory. These techniques are called *addressing modes*. The correct use of addressing modes (hereafter, *AM* for *addressing mode*) is traditionally considered one of the most difficult aspects of assembly language programming. Addressing modes will sometimes confuse even experienced programmers and their misuse will result in errors that are difficult to identify and correct. As is true with many components of AL that are judged difficult, the difficulty of learning and using addressing modes is often due more to the way they are explained and implemented than to any inherent difficulty in the addressing modes themselves.

In fact, the idea of AMs is sufficiently simple that everyday life provides a close parallel. For example, we could refer to the house at 805 Wilson Road as "805 Wilson Road." This is a *direct* reference to the actual address. If we lived in the neighborhood, we might refer to it as the "beige house with brown shutters." In explaining the location to a person from outside the neighborhood, we might say "it is two houses away from 801 Wilson, which is on the corner of Wilson and Eighth." In these last two situations, we refer to the house's location *indirectly*, that is, in "round about" ways, because it is more convenient or easier to understand, given the situation, than direct referencing. Addressing modes in assembly language instructions parallel the fact that often an explicit address is not the most convenient or efficient way to refer to a location, be it a house or a location in a computer's memory.

The way AMs are encoded in instructions differs greatly among the currently available assemblers. Most assemblers use common AM syntax, which represent the basic AM elements. Other assemblers, however, use special characters with no obvious relation to the AM they denote. Adding to the potential confusion, many assemblers use default AMs that depend on the instruction mnemonic and sometimes on various conditions, for example, how variables are defined in different parts of a program. All these factors contribute to the difficulty and confusion associated with AMs in AL programming.

Attempting to enumerate all of these variations in this text, we believe, would be neither possible nor valuable. Instead, we will explain each AM in terms of the most commonly used designation, which is employed in the universal AL instructions as listed in the tables in the Appendix.

AL Instruction Syntax

AL instructions consist of a mnemonic, which specifies what computer operation is to be performed, followed by one or more operands, which specify the source and destination of the data to be used in the operation. Optional fields include label and comments. The following displays an instruction using all four fields:

```
label   opcode mnemonic  operand(s)   comment
START           XXX       OP1, OP2    ; AL instruction
```

The optional label, which is not part of the assembled instruction, is used by the assembler to reference the location in memory where the instruction will eventually be located. The opcode mnemonic specifies the operation to be performed, and the operand(s) the data to be operated on. The comment is also not a part of the assembled instruction; it is used to explain the function of the instruction.

If the operand source or destination is a register or a predefined location, then the label for that register is used—e.g., R1 for Register 1. If an absolute memory address or value, that is, one that is not to be changed, then its value is entered directly as an operand—e.g., 0060H. For example:

```
MOV  #1, R1      ; store the number 1 in register 1
MOV  #1, 0060H   ; store the number 1 in hex location 60
```

Whenever the operand refers to a memory location and not a register, one of the AMs described later in the chapter must be used. For example, consider:

MOV A, (DE)   ; move register A to the address contained in DE

The address mode here is indirect and is explicit in the instruction; the parentheses around DE indicate indirection.

In some instructions, however, the AM and/or the operand are implied by the instruction mnemonic. Consider the 8080 AL instruction STAX DE. The source of the data, register A, and the AM of the destination, register indirect, are both implied by the instruction mnemonic. Moreover, this is really just a move operation—which also is not obvious. As you can probably see, the use of implied addressing can be quite confusing. Consider the universal AL alternative:

8080 AL	*Universal AL*
STAX DE	MOV A, (DE)

This means, make a copy of the contents of register A and move it to the location whose address is stored in the register pair DE. The Universal AL instruction is intuitively more straightforward and requires no special syntax rules. We believe that the Universal AL is easier to explain and to use. You should keep in mind, however, that this convention is not used in all of the currently available assemblers; the others are much more complicated. See the next chapter for an explanation of universal AL mnemonics.

Syntax refers to the rules that specify how the elements of a language may be used and put together; they are the rules that determine what constitutes well formed statements in a language. The English sentence, "This sentence no verb," for example, is not well-formed since it has no verb. The sentence, "This sentence has no verb" is well-formed even though it is false if it refers to itself. Addressing mode syntax refers to the formation of instructions so that they, and whatever AMs they encode, adhere to the rules governing correct AL statement syntax.

Two Principal Reasons for Using Addressing Modes

There are two principal reasons for using AMs. First, memory usage and speed can be increased if we include in the instruction only a portion of the actual physical address in memory we wish the instruction to reference. Second, instructions are more versatile, and therefore more powerful, when variable memory locations rather than specific memory locations are used.

It is a common practice to "squeeze" and "unsqueeze" information, using some kind of algorithm, so that information can be condensed into a smaller space for storage, and with the aid of the unsqueezing algorithm, it can be reconstructed without loss of data. In fact, many operating systems feature squeeze and unsqueeze utilities so that a maximum amount of data can be stored on diskettes. The price that must be paid for this efficiency is that the algorithm must be known by either a program or a programmer. As an analogy, learning shorthand takes some effort, but if you have ever watched two notetakers, one of whom uses shorthand while the other uses longhand, the advantage of squeezing schemes is obvious.

Whenever a location in memory is accessed, an addressing mode is used. Addressing modes are primarily used to specify a variable memory location while the program is executing. The memory location referenced by instructions can vary, depending on data that is external to the instruction. It is this variability that gives a computer much of its power. Hence, the variety and complexity of its AMs is one criterion used to measure a microprocessor's power.

Consider the following example:

```
MOV  TOTAL, A      ; move contents of location named TOTAL to Reg A
MOV  (HL), A       ; move contents of location whose address is stored
                   ; in  register HL to Reg A
```

In the first case, the location reserved in memory and named TOTAL is explicitly stated. As a result, the address of the location whose contents are to be moved is determined prior to execution at a fixed location in memory. In the second case, the address of the location whose contents are to be moved is dependent on whatever the contents of register HL happen to be at execution time. As a result, the address is determined during execution. Register HL is called a *pointer* or *index*, since it points to or names the address of the location to be referenced by the instruction.

As previously stated, much of the difficulty associated with the use of AMs stems not from their inherent complexity but from the way they have been implemented in various assembly languages. A large variety of addressing modes are used by various microprocessors, but typically, only a few basic elements are employed with any one micro. Hence, properly implemented AMs are relatively straightforward to learn and use.

One problem that causes considerable difficulty is that there are a number of different AM syntaxes used by various microprocessor manufacturers. The addressing mode syntax that is used for one addressing mode on one micro will often be quite different for the same AM on another micro. A related cause of confusion is the fact that AMs are sometimes implicit rather than explicit in the instruction mnemonic. As we argue in Chapter 8, we believe that our UAL eliminates this difficulty.

MEMORY ADDRESSING

To introduce addressing modes, a quick review of memory addressing might help. Recall that each memory location contains a unit of data that is some number of bits—8, 16, or 32 bits in most cases. Each location is identified by means of a unique address. Usually, it will take several locations to store a useful item of information. For example, the name JOHN could be stored in consecutive locations:

address:	contents:	ASCII:
0200	42H	J
0201	48H	O
0202	40H	H
0203	46H	N

In this case, four consecutive memory locations are used to store the name JOHN. Of course, what's actually stored in the locations is the binary representation of each character of the name JOHN.

Many micros specify memory locations using addresses to specify a memory location that are 16 bits long. This means that 2^{16} or 65,356 (64K) distinct locations can be addressed. With larger address words, of course, larger amounts of memory can be addressed. For example, some 16-bit micros provide 24 bit address words, this means that 2^{24} or 16,640,000 (16M) distinct locations can be addressed. Even with these larger address words, however, most instructions are still permitted to address at most 65,356 locations. Where the total available memory is greater than 64K, the total amount of available memory is divided into segments of 65,356 locations. As was explained earlier, a separate segment register specifies which segment of memory the instruction is to use. A computer with more than 64K of memory may have its memory divided into segments as illustrated in Fig. 7-1.

Many computer systems further divide memory into groups called *pages*. Machine code instructions consist of an instruction identifier and an optional address field, each of which may be one or more bytes:

operation :   *(1 or 2 byte addr field) :*

binary instruction: 01101101   01001110 10110010

The reason for using a 1-byte rather than a 2-byte address, of course, is that it requires less memory and executes faster. In special cases, especially on older computers, the address field of an instruction, instead of bytes, consists of 10, 9, or even 6 bits. In general, if the number of bits in the address field is less than 16, the amount of memory that can be addressed is called a page. With an 8-bit byte, this amounts to 256 locations.

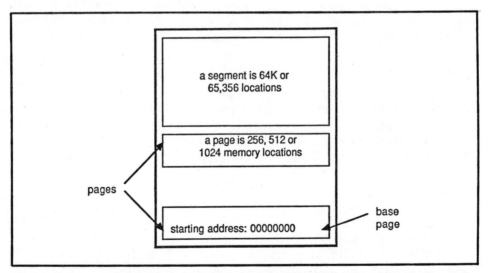

Fig. 7-1. Memory organization: The page starting at location 00000000 is referred to as the *base page*. Most instructions can directly address at most one segment of memory and often address as little as one page so that the address will fit in one byte of memory. This minimizes the amount of memory required by the instruction and maximizes its execution speed.

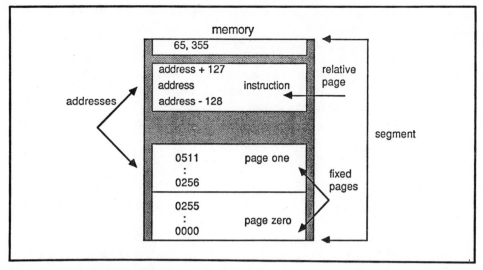

Fig. 7-2. Fixed and relative pages: Pages 0 through 255 of a segment are defined in terms of segment location 0000. A relative page, by contrast, is defined in terms of an instruction and can occur anywhere in the segment. The relative page extends 127 locations beyond the instruction and 128 locations preceding the instruction.

An increasing number of computers today have more than 64K of memory. If, for example, 5 Mbytes (5,000 K bytes) are available, the memory is divided into segments as illustrated in Fig. 7-1. Dividing segments further into pages results in shorter machine code instructions—a single byte can be used for the address field rather than two bytes. The newer 32-bit micros support a double word address (32 bits, which provides the ability to address up to 8,000 Mbytes). Even with these larger addresses, however, most instructions are still restricted to a 16-bit address field and permit 8-bit address fields.

To sum up, in the case of a 16-bit address field in an instruction, 64,536 locations can be addressed. This amount of memory is called a *segment*. If, however, the instruction field is only 8 bits long, then 256 locations can be addressed, and this is called a *page*. Likewise, if an instruction uses an unusual 9-bit or 10-bit address field, a 512 locations page or a 1024 locations page results.

In most computers, a segment can start at any location. A page can start anywhere within a segment, but it will normally start at a specific location or at a particular location relative to the instruction being executed. A page starting at location 0000, as noted above, is usually referred to as *page 0* or the *base page*. Pages starting at locations 256, 512, and so on, are called *page 1, page 2,* and so on. A page defined relative to the current instruction being executed is called a *relative page*. As shown in Fig. 7-2, the location of the current instruction will be the center of the page, with 128 bytes above and below.

With an 8-bit address field (and, consequently, a 256 byte page), for example, we could organize a 5-MB memory as illustrated in Fig. 7-2. As this figure illustrates, a relative page is defined relative to an instruction; it doesn't matter where in in the segment the instruction is. Fixed pages are defined in relation to segment location 0000. Finally, segments are located anywhere within available memory starting at main memory location 0000. The exact location is specified in a segment register. (Not surprisingly, segments are sometimes called *chapters*.)

Another form of page addressing occurs when the location of a page is specified by the most significant bits of the location of the instruction. The actual address is calculated by combining the MSB of the instruction's address with the address specified in the operand. This is called a *same page address*. The instruction can reference any location within the page that starts at the location specified by the MSB of the instruction address. The size of the the page depends on the number of bits in the operand address field, as illustrated in Fig.7-3.

Let's review:

1. Computer main memory consists of individual locations (4, 8, 16, or 32 bits in length), and each location is referenced by a unique address 0 .. to some number such as 64K or 5 M;
2. A group of consecutive locations in memory (between 256 and 1024 locations, depending on the instruction address field size) is called a *page*; such a page can be defined relative to an instruction, a segment, or physical memory;
3. A group of consecutive locations in memory 65,356 bytes long is called a *segment*. The starting address of the segment in terms of main memory is specified by the address in the segment register.

INSTRUCTION SPECIFIED, EFFECTIVE, AND PHYSICAL ADDRESSES

A set of related concepts important to understanding AMs are the *instruction specified address (ISA)*, the *effective address (EA)*, and the *physical address (PA)*. The ISA is the address value contained in an instruction, the EA is the location within a designated area of memory (normally 64K or a segment of memory) that is calculated based

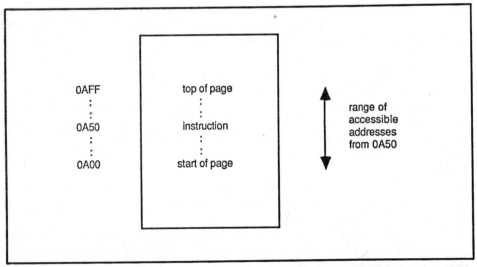

Fig. 7-3. Range of accessible addresses using 8 bits: If the instruction contains an 8-bit address field, the instruction at location OA5OH can reference the memory locations between OAOOH and OAFFH. The range of accessible addresses, using eight bits, will be OO to FF or one page.

on the addressing mode specified, and the PA is the name of an actual physical location in the machine's memory. As mentioned above, owing to considerations of memory space and execution speed, it is neither practical nor necessary to include the entire physical address in every instruction. For example, without using addressing modes in a computer with five MBytes of memory, 24 bits would be required in each instruction just to specify the address of the data to be referenced.

By restricting an instruction to directly addressing only 64K (16 bits) of memory, or only a segment or page of the total physical memory, we can reduce both the amount of memory that is required to store each instruction and the amount of time it takes to execute each instruction. Since fetching an instruction takes a finite amount of time, reducing the number of bytes in an instruction results in faster execution times. Specifically, the most significant portion of a 24-bit address, namely that which indicates the location of a segment, can be stored in a segment register or in other hardware. The segment location portion can then be combined with the ISA or EA to produce the full physical memory address.

Segment registers are normally found only in 16-bit and larger microprocessors or in newer 8-bit micros. Smaller micros such as 4- and 8-bit machines normally use an external hardware register to store the most significant bits of the address in order to activate segments of memory. This external register is normally part of an I/O port whose output is permanently connected to the memory address bus. Usually, this practice is called *bank* or *block* memory enable/disenable.

On larger micros (32 bit) and minicomputers, *virtual memory* is used. This storage method is beyond the scope of this text but we will say this much about it. Virtual memory simulates additional memory in the CPU by treating external disk storage as temporary main memory. Both programs and data are organized into *frames* that are transferred to and from disk memory on an as-needed basis. The size of a frame is often determined by the operating system; hence it is not under programming control. Since disk accessing is relatively slow with conventional diskettes, virtual memory systems are most commonly used with hard disks where access time is much faster.

To help clarify the differences between an ISA, an EA and a PA, consider the following. Suppose that you wished to send a memo to another person at work. Trusting the interoffice mail system, you could address the memo simply "John Johnson." Your secretary happens to know that the only John Johnson you do business with is in the Computer department so she adds "Computer Department" to the address. The mail room personnel determine that the Computer Dept. (there are several in the building, one on each floor) intended is the one on the second floor, and add "suite 2B." The complete address, then, would be:

```
John Johnson  (ISA)  ⎤
Computer Dept.        ⎥ EA ⎤
suite 2B              ⎦    ⎥ PA
                           ⎦
```

In terms of AMs, we could say that "John Johnson" is the ISA—it is the only address you specified to your secretary, and an ISA is the only address specified in an instruction. The operation performed by the secretary is similar to the processor applying

AM syntax to the address. Using predefined conditions or rules, the secretary expands the address so that it identifies a more specific location. Similarly, a computer using AM rules converts the ISA into a more specific address, the EA, based on the conditions specified for that addressing mode.

The operation of the mail room is similar to that performed by the processor, which uses the segment register to determine the exact physical address of the location to be accessed. The exact location in a segment of memory, like the specific suite in the department where John Johnson works, is determined when the PA is calculated.

The ISA, "John Johnson," contains enough information in it that other people can determine the EA, John Johnson in the Computer Room. Similarly, the address field of an instruction, the ISA, contains only enough information for the processor to to determine the EA, the logical address of the location that is to be accessed. The instruction specifies how the EA is calculated from the ISA with the assistance of the addressing mode. Like the mailroom personnel determining that the Computer Room intended is the one on the second floor, suite 2B, the processor then determines the PA, the exact physical location in memory, from the EA.

On micros that do not have a segment register or where the EA is large enough to address all of the physical memory, the EA is the PA. In buildings with just one floor and only one Computer Room, the EA of Computer Room would also be the PA, the Computer Room. On micros that have a segment register, calculating the physical address is a two step process. First, the effective address is calculated, and second, the effective address is applied to the contents of the appropriate segment register. Let's look at the second step first. The first step will be explained when we describe the various addressing modes.

There are three basic methods of applying the segment register to the EA: concatenation, addition, and addition with offset. *Concatenation* involves appending the EA, which represents the least significant bits, to the segment register, which represents the most significant bits. Concatenation is most often used when either the EA or segment register has less than 16 bits. As shown in Fig. 7-4, 16 bits from the EA are added to the 8 bits from the segment register to form the 24 bit physical address.

Addition involves adding the segment register to the EA. This is normally used when either or both the segment register and EA contain enough bits to access all of the computer's physical memory. As shown in Fig. 7-5, the contents of the segment register are added to the EA, which results in a 20-bit physical address.

Addition, with offset, uses the following method: segment registers are usually 16

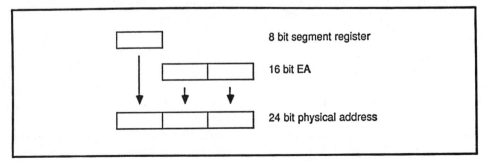

Fig. 7-4. The concatenation process used in determining the physical address.

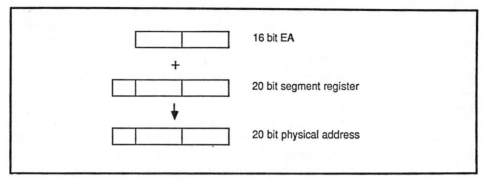

Fig. 7-5. The addition process used in determining the physical address.

bits long with an imaginary least-significant n bits set to zero, for a total of $16 + n$ bits. The effective address is combined with the appropriate segment register to form the physical address as shown in Fig. 7-6 (assuming n = 8 bits). In other words, the segment register is left shifted eight bits and added to the effective address to produce the 24-bit physical address. For example, we could combine the EA and segment registers in the following fashion to determine the PA:

```
          01011010 11011001   EA
00101100  00110000            segment register
_____
00101100  10001010 11011001   PA
```

The low-order byte of the EA becomes the low order byte of the PA; the high-order byte of the EA is added to the low-order byte of the segment register to form the PA's middle byte; and the high-order byte of the segment register becomes the high-order byte of the PA.

Each procedure is performed automatically whenever data is stored in or copied from memory. The programmer is restricted to setting the segment registers to the desired value, depending on which segment is desired and where a segment is located in the total available memory. Under most operating systems, segment registers are set to a specific value by the system software, and the programmer is advised not to change those values within an individual user program.

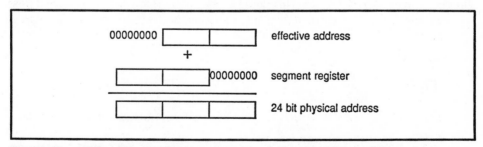

Fig. 7-6. The addition with offset process used in determining the physical address.

Most 16-bit and larger micros possess more than one segment register. Each is used for a specific type of data—for instance, program code, variable data, and the stack. The advantage of this practice is that it allows one program to occupy more than 64K of memory without changing the segment registers. By changing the value of a specific segment register (for instance, the data segment register) a program can access a completely different set of data without changing the program itself, or it can access more than 64k of data.

Now let's return to the first step of converting the instruction specified address (ISA), to the effective address (EA). Regardless of whether or not segment registers are used, all microcomputers must calculate the EA by means of addressing modes.

Virtually every AL instruction will access or store data in a register, predefined location, I/O port, or memory location. When accessing a register or predefined location, the ISA is the EA, and the location must be named explicitly. When referencing or storing data in memory or in an I/O port, an addressing mode algorithm is used to convert the address specified in the instruction to the effective address.

Remember that what is specified in an instruction as an address is contained in 16 or fewer bits; the AM algorithm is applied to this number to form an effective address within a 64K or larger memory segment or, on some micros, the address within physical memory. The actual AM algorithm to be used either depends on the type of instruction or is specified as part of the instruction's operand address field. The EA may or may not be the the actual physical address; if not, the full 16-bit (or more) address will be calculated automatically using a segment register or, on some 8-bit machines, a bank switching scheme.

BASIC ELEMENTS OF ADDRESSING MODES

First, we will explain the four basic elements of addressing modes and then we will deal with more complex addressing modes that are made up of these basic elements. How each is specified in an instruction will be discussed later. For the moment, it is important only to understand how each addressing mode functions.

In the following descriptions, if calculation from the instruction-specified address, or ISA, requires several steps, all intermediate address values will be called the *intermediate address*, or the *IA*.

The following four basic elements are used to form all of the more complex addressing modes. In other words, all of the more complex addressing modes are a combination of one or more of the following:

Direct: the ISA or IA is the EA. No additional calculations are required. The address we have calculated so far or which is contained in the instruction is the address of the data to be accessed.

EA = ISA
EA=IA

For example, in MOV A, 012H, the ISA, 0120H is the address of the data.

Indirect: the ISA or IA is the address of the location where the EA or next IA is stored.

That is, the data stored in the address specified in the instruction or calculated so far contains the address of the data to be referenced or next IA. For example, we can visualize MOV A, (0050H), as:

```
location:    contents:
  0050       0125
    :          :
  0125       xxxx
```

Location 50, the ISA, contains the effective address, 125, where the data to be referenced is stored.

$$EA = (ISA)$$
$$\text{or } EA = (IA)$$

The ( ) indicates the indirect addressing mode: e.g., (ISA) means that the address specified inside the parentheses points to the address of the data to be accessed.

Indexed: the ISA or IA is actually a value that is added to the contents of a register or previously calculated IA in order to determine the EA, the address where the data is located, or the next IA.

$$EA = ISA + Reg$$
$$EA = IA + value$$

For instance, in the instruction MOV A, (IX + 20), if the Index register IX contains 0070, and the instruction specifies an index of 20, then 20 is added to 0070 to form the effective address of 90.

```
          addr    contents   comment
IX --> 0070      | xxxx |    base location (addr)
          :
       0090      | 0050 |    effective address since 70 + 20 = 90
```

The plus sign between two or more values enclosed in parentheses indicates the indexed addressing mode. One value is considered the base address and the other an index or offset.

Consider an analogy to indexed addressing. Suppose we had a four drawer file cabinet, the third drawer of which was reserved for "Expenses," and we wished to store a receipt in the file folder labeled "Repairs," which we just happened to know was the fifth folder. The drawer numbered 3 is analogous to the base location; it gives us a general idea of where to look. The fifth folder, is like an index since "fifth" specifies precisely how far back in the drawer we will have to look to find the folder containing repair expense data. The number 0070 in register IX is like the drawer numbered 3 since both specify the basic area to look; the number 20 is like the number 5 since both give us the specific place to look, given the base location. Putting the two pieces of information together in each case allows us to find the data we need.

Autoincrement/decrement: this AM is a special form of indirect and indexed addressing. Here the contents of the location containing the variable pointer, index, or base address is automatically incremented or decremented as part of the computer operation. This mode is indicated by placing a plus or minus sign before or after the parentheses. Placing the plus or minus sign before the left parenthesis indicates that the value inside the parentheses is to be incremented or decremented *before* the operation is executed; placing it after the right parenthesis indicates that the incrementing or decrementing is to occur *after* the operation is performed. A double plus or minus sign may be used to signify incrementing or decrementing by more than one:

±*(location):* indirect with pre-autoincrement/decrement
(location)±1: indirect with post autoincrement/decrement
±*(location + value):* indexed, pre-autoincrement/decrement
(location + value)±: indexed, post autoincrement/decrement
(location + value)+ *amount:* indexed, post increment location by amount

For example: +(HL + 45)

The contents register HL are incremented; then they are added to 45 to calculate the address of the data to be referenced.

With double levels of indirect addressing, the location of the plus or minus sign indicates at what level autoincrement/decrement will take place and when.

For example: (R (R2))-

The register pointed to by R2 is post auto decremented.

SOME VARIATIONS ON THE BASIC MODES

All addressing modes are a combination of the basic elements that can be used alone or in combination. As a result, we are now in a position to present some of the addressing modes and addressing mode combinations used in the most common micros.

Immediate: the data contained in the instruction is not an address but is the actual data to be used by the instruction. Immediate data is entered as an operand, using the format for a numeric value, the pound sign, #.

For example: MOV #50, B

The #50 in the instruction is the data itself and not the address of the data to be moved. In this case, the value 50 (decimal) is placed in register B.

Predefined Location: this AM is used when a predefined location, such as a register or a flag, must be specified. It is entered as an operand. Normally registers and special memory locations are assigned an abbreviation by the manufacturer.

For example: PUSH BC ; store the contents of the BC
                    ; Reg on the stack

The destination of the data, the stack or address contained in the stack register, is implied by the instruction mnemonic—it does not have to be specified. The source of the data is the BC register, which is a predefined location represented by the abbreviation BC. Normally predefined locations are restricted to registers located internally in the micro and not externally in main memory. Some micros, however, contain registers or predefined locations that are a part of main memory.

Absolute: the simplest addressing mode, the address included in the AL and machine code instruction is the effective address. No addressing mode calculations are required. Depending on the micro or instruction for which code is being generated, this addressing mode is normally the default mode. Some instructions are of the type that only absolute is possible, thus no AM indicator is required.

For example: MOV AX, 0200H

Here, the EA = ISA, and the value 0200H is the actual address where the contents of the A register are stored.

Under other AL systems, this mode is indicated by parentheses or other special symbols. However, such practice causes confusion with other addressing modes.

There are seven special forms of absolute addressing: long, page zero, same page, relative, displacement, segmented, and vectored. Each is specified by the instruction mnemonic or the abbreviation preceding the absolute address, and each affects the range of address values that may be specified.

long: the address value specified is more than two bytes or 16 bits. Long addressing is specified by appending to the mnemonic or inserting before the absolute address the abbreviation LA.

For example: JMPLA   040AH

Here, the instruction is to transfer control to the location 040A hex.

page zero: the address specified must be in page 0. Only the least significant bits of the address are appended to the machine code instruction. The most significant bits are assumed to be 0. The numeric value of the address, therefore, must be between 0 and the maximum number permitted by the number of bits used.

For example: JMPPZ   LOC1

The location LOC1 must be in page zero of memory.

Register Indirect: the effective address is contained in one of the registers. The instruction contains the abbreviation for the desired register, which usually is enclosed in brackets to denote indirect addressing. The machine code instruction has the register included in the instruction.

EA = (Reg)—contents of the register

For example: MOV A, (HL)

The HL register contains the address of where the contents of the A register are to be moved.

Relative: the instruction contains the actual address (as in absolute addressing) except that the assembler converts the address into an 8-bit relative value. The signed value given in the machine code instruction is added to or subtracted from the program address register, the PC register, when the instruction is executed. This type of AM is normally only used with a jump or call instruction—which causes the program to continue execution somewhere other than the next sequential instruction. Since the relative value is only 8 bits, the location specified must be within ± 128 bytes of the current instruction.

EA = PC +/- ISA

This mode is normally implied by the operation being performed and therefore does not require a special indicator in the operand.

The PC registers contains the location of the currently executing instruction. Thus the next program instruction to be executed will be located relative to the current instruction rather than at a specific address. This means that the program can be relocated anywhere in memory without affecting the way it executes. Relative addressing in the universal AL system is always implied by the instruction mnemonic, which will normally end with an R, which designates relative addressing. The R is added to the mnemonic to remind the programmer that the specified address must be within ± 128 bytes.

For example: JUMPR STRT

The STRT here specifies that the location within the program to be jumped to; the assembler converts this to a value relative to the current instruction location, say 5. After (what amounts to) JUMPR +5 is fetched from memory, the P.C. is updated so that it contains the address of the next instruction to be executed. Hence, the effect of JUMPR +5 is to add 5 to the contents of the P.C. If the number in the P.C. is 30, the effective address of Jump +5 would be 35. Control is then transferred to location 35. As can be seen, the location jumped to is determined at execution time—the instruction is memory-location independent.

Displacement: this AM is identical to relative except that a 16-bit relative value is calculated rather than an 8-bit value. This means that the actual address specified can be within 32,655 rather than 128 bytes.

Reg Index: the values held in two or more registers are summed together with the index value contained in the instruction to get the EA. Usually, one register will be a general purpose register and the other an index register. This mode is normally valid for a restricted combination of registers.

EA = (Reg A) + (Reg B) + value

As with the indexed mode, a single + is used to indicate indexing. If the last character is not a +, it means that only the registers are added together; the instruction does not contain an index value.

For example: MOV A to (DI + BC)   MOV A to (DI + BC + 50)

This mode requires that both registers and the offset value be specified in the operand. As in the previous mode, the offset value can be preceded by an abbreviation indicating the addressing mode and registers to be used. Since some micros will allow the offset value to be either a single or double byte value (8 or 16 bits), the abbreviation can also specify which will follow the abbreviation:

(IX + BC + value) or (IX + BC++ value)

Although the first is most commonly used in assemblers designed for a single micro, the more general purpose assemblers will enclose the prefix in brackets and use a + or ++ to indicate a single or double byte value to follow.

The following addressing modes are normally only found in microprocessors that utilize a base page (sometimes called page zero), rather than registers. As explained above, the base page is a section of memory dedicated for uses such as storing intermediate data and address pointers.

Zero Page Addressing: the address given in the instruction is located in the base page location 0 through 255. The machine code instruction contains only the least significant eight bits. The most significant eight bits are always zero. This mode only allows for address 0 through 255 since only eight bits are used.

EA = 8 bit ISA

For example: MOV A to 120H

Zero Page Indexed: the value contained in the instruction is added to the index register specified to form an 8-bit value (the most significant eight bits are always zero. This addressing mode also only allows for address 0.. 255.

EA = 8 bit ISA + (Reg)

For example: MOV A to PZ (B+20)

In the universal AL a plus sign is used to indicate indexing and parentheses indirect addressing. With other assemblers, special characters are normally used.

A PROGRAMMING EXAMPLE: BINARY SEARCH

Looking through a set for one item is called *searching* the set. One search method is sequential search: we start at the beginning of a set and look for the element we are looking for until we find it. If the set is not ordered in some way and we have no idea where the element is located, sequential search is probably the best we can do in terms of search efficiency.

If, however, the set is ordered, then there is a more efficient search mechanism, namely *binary search*. Binary search is much like the method we use to locate numbers in a telephone book. The contents of the telephone book are ordered alphabetically. If we are looking for Jones, Mortimer, we probably open the book about half way. If the entry at the top of the page is Marson, we can discard the half after the name Marson since we know that Jones won't be in that half of the book. We now look about half way through the remaining part of the book and compare the results with Jones again. We continue this process until we find the page with the entry we are seeking. This discarding of half of the set or list we are searching each time we look at one location is the basis for calling this method *binary* search.

We can think of the elements of a list or set as being stored in an array. We can search the array by means of using the subscripts of the array in conjunction with the binary search technique. Suppose that we have five numbers, ordered in terms of magnitude and stored in an array, as shown in Fig. 7-7.

Suppose that we wish the program to determine the location of 21. Using binary search, we use the following algorithm: Take the smallest subscript, call it "first," set it equal to 1; take the largest subscript, call it "last," and set it equal to 5. Let "found" signify whether or not we have found the number—if we have not, leave it at 0, if we have, assign it 1.

We will keep searching either until we have found the location of 21 or until we have searched all the locations and discovered that it is not in the list. This means that each time we will look in the location that is in the middle of those locations we haven't looked in yet. After we look and we discover that the location does not contain 21,

location	contents
a[1]	2
a[2]	5
a[3]	9
a[4]	11
a[5]	21

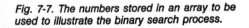

Fig. 7-7. The numbers stored in an array to be used to illustrate the binary search process.

we compare to see if 21 is in the upper half or lower half of the set of locations we just looked at. If it is in the lower half, we assign "last" the value of the location we just looked at, minus 1; otherwise, if it is in the upper half, we assign "first" this number, plus 1.

Here is our algorithm:

> let first = 1, last = subscript of largest element in list; found = 0
> while first is less than or equal to last and found = 0 do:
> > let sub = integer part of (first+last)/2
> > if a[sub] > number searched for then let last = sub -1
> > else if a[sub] < number searched for then let first = sub + 1
> > else if a[sub] = number searched for then let found = 1;
> if found = 0 then report number is not in list
> if found = 1 then report where in the list the number is

Executing our algorithm, if first, or 1, is less than or equal to last or 5, and found equals 0, we assign "sub," a new variable, the integer part of (first + last)/ 2, which yields 3. We test to see if a[sub], which is a[3], or 9, is greater than 21. It isn't, so now we test to see if a[3], or 9, is less than 21. It is, so we assign to first sub + 1 or 4. We run it again: if first, or 4, is less than or equal to last, or 5, and found still equals 0, we assign sub the integer part of (first + last/, 2 which yields 4. We test to see if a[sub], which is a[4], or 11, is greater than 21. It isn't, so now we test to see if a[4], or 11, is less than 21. It is, so we assign to first sub + 1, or 5.

We run it one last time: if first, or 5, is less than or equal equal to last, or 5, and found still equals 0, we assign sub the integer part of (first + last)/ 2, which yields 5. We test to see if a[sub], which is a[5], or 21, is greater than 21. It isn't. We test to see if a[sub], or 21, is less than 21. It isn't . This means the two are equal, so we , have found our number at location a[5], and we assign found 1 since the number is found and we use found = 1 to output the number and its location in the array.

Here is the program in UAL, for the 8086 microprocessor:

```
SQRT

MOVW

; SEARCH.MLS   3/25/86   Binary Search Program
;
; This program written for an 8086 MS-DOS computer performs a binary
; search for a number within a list of numbers. Both the list of
; numbers to be searched and the number to be searched for are input
; by the operator.
;
; Subroutines used:
;
;                 ^INPUT    - get input from the operator
;                 ^DSPFML  - display multiple lines of formatted
                             data
```

```
;              ^CNSLCL  - output message on the display
;
; Procedural instructions used:
;
;      MOVVB - move data byte in memory
;      DECJMPVB - decrement variable, jump if
;
;
;
  COMM EXBUF ; common data buffer
;
STRT       ^INPUT MSG1,2,ELEMENTS,FINI     ; get number of list elements
STRT1      MOVVB ELEMENTS,TEMP             ; move # elements to temporary location
STRT2      ^INPUT MSG2,2,VAL,FINI          ; get next list element
           MOV VAL,AL                      ; get element value
           MOVW INDEX,DI                   ; get list index
           MOV AL,(DI+ + ARRAY )           ; store value in list
           INCW DI                         ; increment list index
           MOVW DI,INDEX                   ; save list index
           DECJMPVB TEMP,NZ,STRT2          ; if more elements goto strt2
BEGIN      ^INPUT MSG3,2,VAL,FINI          ; input value to search for
           MOV # 0,AL                      ; reset bottom of range pointer
           MOV AL,SMALL
           MOVVB ELEMENTS,LARGE            ; reset top of range pointer
TEST       MOVW SMALL,BX                   ; get bottom of range pointer
           ADDW LARGE,BX                   ; add top of range pointer
           SRLW BX                         ; find middle of range
           MOV VAL,AL                      ; get value to search for
           CMP AL,(BX+ + ARRAY )           ; compare with middle of range element
           JMPR Z,FOUND                    ; jump if number found
           JMPR C,LOWER                    ; jump if lower
HIGHER     MOV BL,SMALL                    ; set new low end of range
           CMP BL,LARGE                    ; compare with high end of range
           JMPR Z,NOTFOUND                 ; if equal, number not found
           JMP TEST                        ; test next range of elements
LOWER      MOV BL,LARGE                    ; set new high end of range
           CMP BL,SMALL                    ; compare with low end of range
           JMPR Z,NOTFOUND                 ; if equal, number not found
           JMP TEST                        ; test next range of elements
FOUND      MOV BL,INDEX                    ; save index to element found
           ^DSPFML FORMAT,0,FINI           ; display number found
MSG1 DB 'Enter number of elements: ',0,0
MSG2 DB 'Enter next element: ',0,0
MSG3 DB 'Enter number to search for: ',0,0
MSG4 DB 'Number not found',0
;
FORMAT DB 'Number: ',0FFH,4
  DW VAL
  DB 4,' at index: ',0FFH,4
  DW INDEX
  DB 4,0,0
;
;
EXBUF DS 128
;
END
```

```
                    JMP BEGIN                   ; get next number to look for
NOTFOUND    ^CNSLCL MSG4,80            ; number not found
                    JMP BEGIN                   ; get next number to look for
FINI            STOP                         ; end of program
;
SMALL DW 0           ; low end of list range
LARGE DW 0           ; high end of list range
ELEMENTS DB 0        ; number of elements in list
INDEX DW 0           ; index to list elements
ARRAY DS 50          ; list array
VAL DB 0             ; number to look for
TEMP DW 0            ; temporary data
;
```

Chapter 8

Universal Assembly Language

Purpose of the Chapter: This chapter introduces the concept of universal assembly language and user-definable table-driven assemblers. It reviews briefly some of the problems of conventional, nonuniversal AL, and it explains how AL can be both universal and machine independent. It discusses how UAL is user-definable and variable from an AL that bears some resemblance to a conventional AL to an AL that bears considerable resemblance to HLLs. It compares program development in conventional and universal AL. The chapter concludes with an example of a small program in UAL in four different forms: first, written for the 8080; second, for the 8080 but using procedural instructions third, for the 8080 but using procedural instructions and external subroutines; and, finally, a version of the program that is completely machine independent.

PROBLEMS WITH CONVENTIONAL ASSEMBLY LANGUAGE

We have maintained that assembly language historically suffered from a number of deficiencies, some of which stemmed from the fact that there is no assembly language standard. The underlying problem is that the assembly language for every microprocessor uses a different set of instructions and instruction formats. Current assemblers often use different instruction mnemonics and formats for exactly the same operation; in fact, a single assembler will often use several mnemonics for the same basic operation.

Additional problems follow from the lack of a standard. First, it is more difficult to port AL programs from one computer to another than it should be. Second, learning conventional (nonuniversal) assembly language is unnecessarily difficult. And third, programming in conventional assembly language can be pretty tedious. Historically, the motivation for the development of high level languages was to address these AL deficiencies. Let's consider them in order.

The inability to port programs from one type of computer to another has been one of the strongest objections to the use of assembly language. The mnemonics and syntax for microprocessors as different as the 6502 and 8088 are so different that programs that do the same task will appear quite different.

Since the machine code instructions for different processors are different, and conventional AL is essentially a symbolic representation of the processors' machine code instructions, conventional AL exemplifies most clearly what it means to be nonportable. Consider the following two programs, one in 6502 and one in 8080, which do exactly the same thing—namely add a word variable in memory to another word variable in memory:

<pre>
        6502   8080

CLC   ; clear carry flag   LHLD LOC1 ; move LOC1 to reg HL
LDA   LOC1   ; move LOC1 to reg A   XCHG   ; exchange reg HL and DE
ADC   LOC2   ; add/c LOC2 to reg A   LHLD LOC2 ; move LOC2 to reg HL
STA   LOC2   ; move reg A to LOC2   DAD   D   ; add reg DE to HL
LDA   LOC1+1   ; add second byte   SHLD LOC2 ; move reg HL to LOC2
ADC   LOC2+1   ;
STA   LOC2+1   ;
</pre>

The important thing to notice here is that the instruction mnemonics are completely different, yet the task is the same. Consequently, translation of one program to another is unnecessarily complicated. Where 6502 uses four mnemonics and seven instructions for the operation, 8080 uses four different mnemonics and five instructions.

The result of these significant differences is not just poor portability. Learning AL when there are so many different dialects of AL is made needlessly complicated. If a person knew 6502 but not 8080 AL, for example, he or she might not recognize the fragment on the right as the same fragment, just in 8080 AL. As a result, learning a different AL once one knows one AL is more difficult than it should be.

Last, since conventional assembly language instructions perform one basic machine operation, such as adding a value in one location to a value stored in another, AL programming can be tedious. It can require quite a few instructions to perform even the simplest procedure, as the above example illustrates. Conversely, the largest advantage of a high level language over AL is that each instruction represents a procedure—a series of machine operations—rather than one operation. It follows from this that fewer instructions are required to write the same program than is the case in AL, and other things being equal, the program is easier to maintain. Macros as defined in conventional assemblers ease the tedium to some extent, but the fact remains that programming in conventional AL can be unnecessarily tedious.

HOW ASSEMBLY LANGUAGE CAN BE UNIVERSAL

Assembly language can be made universal in the sense that one basic set of mnemonics can be used to write programs for any microprocessor. Consider the routine in 6502 and 8080 AL illustrated above in a universal assembly language that is written for both the 6502 and 8080:

6502	8080	meaning
RES C	MOVW LOC1, HL	; move LOC1 to reg HL
MOV LOC1, A	XCHG HL, DE	; exchange reg HL and DE
ADC LOC2, A	MOVW LOC2, HL	; move LOC2 to reg HL
MOV A, LOC2	ADDW DE, HL	; add reg DE to HL
MOV LOC1+1, A	MOVW HL, LOC2	; move reg HL to LOC2
ADC LOC2+1, A		
MOV A, LOC1+1		

As is evident, using UAL in this case does not mean that identical source code can be used for both microprocessors. For one thing, AL instructions that are not procedural type instructions (and hence microprocessor independent—see next paragraph) must take account of the difference in registers between the two micros. Specifically, the 6502 has fewer registers available for programmer use than the 8080. But the fact remains that, in comparison with the conventional AL routines above, these two routines require fewer mnemonics. Most important is the fact that, with the exception of RES and XCHG, the mnemonics used are similar for both microprocessors.

With a UAL, however, we can go one step further. By using procedural type instructions as part of the AL instruction set that the programmer defines in a UAL, our example routine can be written as a single instruction:

6502	8080
ADDVVW LOC1, LOC2	ADDVVW LOC1, LOC2

This procedural type instruction is microprocessor independent. Now the same instruction can be used for both micros. We have the same degree of simplicity and portability as a HL language. Yet we are still programming in AL.

Using a standard or universal set of mnemonics and instruction formats results in a number of advantages. By using the same instruction mnemonics and format for all similar operations, there are fewer instructions to learn. And by using a single mnemonic to represent a series of machine code instructions, the number of AL instructions needed for any program can be decreased. Although it is impossible to avoid completely the differences in the machine code for each microprocessor, due to the differences in their respective architectures, the differences between the various ALs can be minimized. While, as we will see, UAL programs sometimes will be written with particular microprocessors in mind, one set of mnemonics can be used to write programs for quite different microprocessors, and UAL programs that are completely microprocessor independent can be written.

We have pointed out that current assemblers for the various micros use different instruction mnemonics for the same operation. In fact, a single assembler will often use several mnemonics for the same basic operation. This not only complicates porting a program from one computer to another, it makes learning assembly language needlessly difficult. By using a standard or universal set of mnemonics and instruction formats, AL is not only easier to learn and use, but it is simpler to transfer programs from one computer to another.

To illustrate this point, consider the following four instructions from the standard 8080 instruction set:

```
LDA   aa     ; load register A, absolute location
MOV   A,M    ; load register A, indirect register HL
LDAX B       ; load register A, indirect register BC
LDAX D       ; load register A, indirect register DE
```

These four instructions perform essentially the same operation—namely, moving a single byte of data from memory to the A register. The last three instructions are unique to the 8080 family. These four instructions can be replaced by a single mnemonic that uses a standard format, one that is common to all other computers and the other move data instructions of the 8080. Consider these four replacements:

```
MOV   aa, A      ; load register A, absolute location
MOV   (HL), A    ; load register BA, indirect register HL
MOV   (BC), A    ; load register A, indirect register BC
MOV   (DE), A    ; load register A, indirect register DE
```

These replacements eliminate both the use of two unnecessary mnemonics, specifically LDA and LDAX, and the need for special abbreviations, namely, M for HL, B for BC, and D for DE. More important is the fact that these instructions use a universal form of syntax. The parentheses indicate indirect addressing, or the location where the data is stored. The use of universal instruction mnemonics and format also makes it easier for someone who knows AL but who may not be familiar with 8080 AL to understand a program written for the 8080—or indeed, for any micro.

Table 8-1 compares some universal AL mnemonics with those used with three popular microprocessors, the 6502 (8 bit), 8086 (16 bit), and 68000 (32 bit). The universal mnemonics consist of a unique character string that indicates the basic type of operation. Characters that specify the particular operation within that basic type of operation are appended to the basic mnemonics. For example, consider:

```
JMP        jump
JMPR       jump relative
JMPOS      jump other segment
MOV        move
MOVW       move word
MOVDW      move double word
```

In the first three cases, the string in common is JMP. Clarifying characters R and OS are appended to indicate more specific operations in the cases of JMPR for jump relative and JMPOS for jump to other segment. Clarifying characters W and DW also specify the exact move operation to be performed in the cases of MOVW and MOVDW.

With some instructions, it could be argued that using fewer mnemonics that require more parameters rather than more mnemonics with fewer parameters unjustifiably complicates things. Consider this example:

```
LDA  LOC1        ; load register A with the contents of LOC1 (6502)
MOV  LOC1, A     ; move contents of LOC1 to register A        (UAL)
```

The 6502 LDA mnemonic, since it symbolizes, "load A," contains the destination (reg A) in the mnemonic itself. The UAL MOV mnemonic requires that register A be specified as a parameter. So there is at least the basis for an objection here. Yet, this is right only from the vantage point of a single micro. When considering a variety of micros, the simpler, more common mnemonic that uses parameters to specify specific operations is more descriptive and hence easier to learn and use.

Universal	6502 (8 bit)	8086 (16 bit)	68000 (32 bit)	description
CALL (OSR) CMP (W) CPL (F,W) JMP (R,OS, D)	JSR CMP, CPX, CPY JMP, BCC, BCS BEQ, BMI, BNE BPLS, BVC, BVS	CALL, CALLOS CMP NOT, CMC JMP, JMPOS, JE JL, JLE, JB, JBE JPE, JO, JS, JNE JNL, JNLE, JB, JBE JNBE, JOP, JNO JNS, JCXZ	BSR, JSR CMP, CMPI, CMPM NOT JMP BCC BRA	call subroutine (cond, loca) compare (var, with) invert, complement (to) jump (condition, location)
MOV (W,DW)	LDA, STA, LDX LSY, STX, STY TAX, TAY, TSX TXA, TXS, TYA	MOV, LAHF, SAHF LDS, LES, XLAT	MOVE, MOVEA MOVEQ, MOVEM MOVEP	move (from, to)
RET (OS, I, N) RLWC (W) SBB (W) SET (W) SRL (W) XCHG (W) XOR (W)	RTS, RTI ROL SBC SEC, SEC, EEI LSR EOR	RET, RETOS, RETI RCL SBB TC, STD, STI SHR XCHG XOR	RTS, RTE, RTR ROL, ROXL SUBX LSR EXG EOR, EORI	return from sub (cond, [val]) rotate left w/ carry (to, var) subtract w/borrow (value, var) set (loc, [bit]) shfit right logical (to, [cnt]) exchange (to, to) logical exclusive OR (to,with)

B=bit F=flag W=Word DW=double word I=interrupt N=non-masked interrupt D=displacement			
OS=other segment r=relative addressing ( )=parameters [ ]=optional parameter			

NE = not equal	VC = no overflow	CC = carry clear	GE = >=	LE = <=	MI = minus
PL = plus	VS = overflow	EQ = equal	GT = >	LS = < or same	
T = true	CC = condition	F = false	Hi = high	LT = <	

Table 8-1. A Comparison of Mnemonics: This table compares some UAL mnemonics with three of the more popular microprocessors, specifically the 6502, the 8086, and the 68000. Notice in particular that the instructions for each comparable operation are more numerous in the conventional ALs. This illustrates our claim that instruction sets in conventional ALs are often inflated beyond what is necessary. This can result in unnecessary difficulty, both in learning and using AL.

It might be argued that, in some cases at least, the UAL doesn't really reduce the number of instruction mnemonics since the clarifying characters in the UAL, when added to the basic instruction mnemonic, really amount to separate instructions:

	UAL	8086	68000
return	RET	RET	RTS
return, other segment	RETOS	RETOS	------
return, interrupt	RETI	RETI	------
return, exception	RETE	-------	RTE
return, reset status	RETC	-------	RTR

In fact, it is true that in the case of the universal instructions there is a total of five mnemonics, while there is a total of six different mnemonics for the 8086 and the 68000 (since RET and RTS are equivalent, the 8086 RETOS and RETI have no 68000 equivalents, and the 68000 RTE and RTR have no 8086 equivalents). Hence, it could be argued, there appears to be little advantage for UAL in terms of numbers of mnemonics.

We would respond that the UAL mnemonics are simpler since the five UAL mnemonics are comprised of a single basic mnemonic RET, which is easily recognized as return, supplemented by clarifying characters. In the case of the 68000, by contrast, RTE and RTR may not be easily recognized as return operations at all.

It might also be argued, against UAL, that in some cases we have simply shifted the complexity from the mnemonic to the parameter:

UAL	8086	6502
JMPR *cond, loc*	J*cc* *loc*	B*cc loc*

(*cond* or *cc* = condition, *loc* = location)

In other words, while it is true that the mnemonics are simpler in UAL, the simplicity is achieved at the cost of the added parameters that are more complicated in the case of the UAL than the 8086 and the 6502.

We would respond that the mnemonic JMPR is easily recognized while JLE or BCC, to choose examples from the 8086 and the 6502, are not easily identified. Including the condition as part of the mnemonic, as in B*cc*, instead of a parameter, as in JMPR *cond*, can lead to confusion in recognizing what operation the mnemonic represents. Moreover, the condition of the jump is clearly identified if, for every operation that is conditional, the condition is stated as a parameter, and the same abbreviations are used for each condition. More generally, we believe that the advantages of more complicated parameters outweigh the advantages of more complicated mnemonics. We believe the universal mnemonics to be simpler, in terms of ease of learning and use, and more explicit in terms of containing the information necessary to specify exactly what operation is represented.

In fact, this emphasis in UAL is consistent with the ideas of a growing number of computer scientists who argue that program instructions and identifiers should be as self-documenting as possible. The more self-documenting that instructions are, the less conventional documentation will have to accompany the source file. This makes for cleaner, more easily read programs. And self-documenting mnemonics need not be at the expense of ease of learning; in fact, they go hand in hand with it.

Consider another example. The manufacturer's instruction set for the 8086 and the 6502 use the mnemonics JS and BMI for the same operation, jump relative if the the preceding compare yields a minus result. Each requires only one parameter. By contrast, using a UAL common mnemonic requires a second parameter to indicate the condition of the jump. Moreover, relative addressing is implicit in the JS and BMI, mnemonic while in the UAL mnemonic JMPR, the R makes the relative addressing explicit:

```
8086    JS    LOC1      ; jump relative to LOC1 if compare result minus
6502    BMI   LOC1      ; branch to LOC1 if result of compare is minus
UAL     JMPR M, LOC1    ; jump relative to LOC1 if compare result minus
```

The advantage of the UAL approach to mnemonics is clear here. That the instruction is a jump instruction is apparent from the first three letters in the UAL mnemonic, but it is not clear in the other two. That it is a jump relative UAL instruction is indicated by the R. Finally, the condition on which control is to jump is indicated by the parameter M. In the case of the 6502, the minus condition is apparent, but the jump component is less obvious. In the case of the 8086 instruction, the jump component is arguably evident but the minus condition is not at all evident, from the mnemonic alone.

Additionally, most micros use different mnemonics for the same operation. Consider the rotate and shift instructions. Although some of them do not require parameters, the mnemonics by themselves often do not provide a clear picture of the operation to be performed. The UAL mnemonics eliminate this uncertainty. Consider this example:

```
ROL or RCL          ; manufacturers rotate reg. A left with carry, register
                    ; A implied (in 6502 and 8086 AL)
RLWC A              ; UAL rotate left with carry, register A explicit
```

The UAL's rotate left with carry explicitly identifies the type of rotate and names register A. Neither the ROL or RCL in 6502 and 8086 indicates the register explicitly since register A is implied. As a result, there may be uncertainty with regard to the meaning of the 6502 and 8086 mnemonic, while the UAL mnemonic is explicit in its meaning.

HOW ASSEMBLY LANGUAGE CAN BE MACHINE-INDEPENDENT

In addition to providing universal mnemonics, UAL makes it possible to write programs that are machine independent. What makes this possible, in part, is that a large portion of any program consists of a few basic procedures. Although the code that is required to perform these procedures may vary from computer to computer, the procedure performs the same task. As a result, a standard set of mnemonics can be used to represent those procedures that are common to all programming tasks. Contrary to usual assumption, this standard set of mnemonics can be developed in an AL, specifically a UAL, environment. The significant result is that AL can rival HLLs in terms of offering general purpose procedural instructions that can be executed on a wide variety of microprocessors.

For example, suppose that we wished to move a double byte of data from one memory location to another. 6502, 8080, 8086 and UAL would compare this way:

6502

```
LDA aa     ; load register A, first byte
STA bb+1 ; store first byte
LDA aa+1 ; load register A, second byte
STA bb+1 ; store second byte
```

8086

```
MOV AX, aa ; load register AX
MOV bb, AX ; store register AX
```

8080

```
LHLD aa  ; load reg. HL
SHLD bb ; store reg. HL
```

universal

```
MOVVW  from, to
```

Not only does UAL decrease the number of instructions required to write a program and therefore make understanding the program easier, it also uses the instruction MOVVW, which is microprocessor independent. *Procedural instructions*, such as MOVVW, can be reassembled for execution on any micro without changing the instruction itself.

We can now explain how this can be done. Although the machine code to perform these procedures is different for each microprocessor, the procedure itself is machine independent. Notice that the instruction consists of the basic mnemonic augmented by characters that indicate the specific operation:

```
MOVVW              ; move variable word to variable word
   |   L word
   |     variable
   |
   L_____ move
```

In this case, clarifying characters VVW appended to the basic mnemonic MOV explicitly specify the operation to be performed—the second V signifies that the move operation is a matter of moving one variable in memory to another; the W signifies that the variable involved is a 16-bit variable word.

In UAL, an assembler can convert a single procedural instruction into the equivalent machine code instructions. Not only can procedural instructions decrease the size of the program and hence clarify the program's logic, they can be made computer independent. Procedural instructions that simplify the programming task can be written—though this simplification comes at the price of relinquishing a measure of control over the system.

By implementing an AL standard that incorporates procedural instructions, a limited degree of portability can be achieved. If this ability is combined with the capability of converting almost any AL instruction into the machine code for virtually any microprocessor, then a degree of portability never before possible is the result. Table 8-2 suggests some possible procedural type instructions that could be used on a variety of different microprocessors.

145

Mnemonic	Description
ADDVB	add value to variable byte
ADDVVW	add variable word to variable word
DECJMPVB	decrement bye variable, jump on condition:
	zero, non-zero, positive, minus, carry, no-carry
DECJMPVW	decrement word variable, jump on condition: zero,
	non-zero
FILLS	fill string with value
FILLW	fill word with value
INCVW	increment variable word
JMPIFVB	jump if byte variable:
	equal, not-equal, less-than, not-less-than
JMPIFVS	jump if string variables: equal, not-equal
JMPTBL	jump via table entry
MOVVS	move variable string to variable string
MOVVW	move variable word to variable word
STOP	exit the program and return to the operating system
SYSTEM	execute an operating system function

Table 8-2. Some Procedural Type Instructions: By thinking in terms of procedures rather than specific operations, AL programs can be written so that they are potentially portable in application—they could run on a wide variety of microprocessors. Here are a number of precedural type instructions that could be implemented in a UAL.

More complicated procedures can be implemented by means of macros or external subroutines. For example, consider this instruction:

ATON buffer, # of chars, variable ;convert an ASCII string to a single
; byte value

This instruction, which converts an ASCII string to a single byte value, uses the same basic format as any other AL instruction and is computer independent. The code required to perform the procedure is written as a separate external relocatable subroutine or macro definition. With conventional assemblers, this procedure would be implemented as a macro instruction. During the assembly process, the macro instruction would be replaced by the sequence of instructions required to perform the procedure, the assembler would substitute the specified parameters for dummy parameters where necessary and then assemble the inserted instruction. The problem with this method is that the same instructions have to be reassembled and similar code generated each time the macro instruction procedure is used.

With a universal assembler, this procedure would be implemented as an external subroutine that is assembled once and saved in a relocatable load module. During the assembly process the external subroutine instruction is converted into a call subroutine instruction followed by the parameters. The external subroutine would be relocated and appended to the end of the executable code. As a result, a minimum of redundant code is generated, and the instructions comprising the procedure need to be assembled only once.

It is often argued that the advantage of a HLL compiler over an assembler is that they contain a set of fully tested procedures that work without any debugging, provided that they are used properly. But the same is largely true with AL. Once a subroutine has been written and debugged, it is available for repeated use. The major difference is that the compiler's procedures constitute an integral, largely nonmodifiable part of a HLL, while the assembler's procedures are external and user-definable in the case of UAL.

UAL AND CONVENTIONAL ASSEMBLERS

There are two features that distinguish a universal assembler from all conventional assemblers, namely a *user-definable instruction set* and a *standard set of instructions* that can be used for all microprocessors. Let's consider them in order.

User-Definable Instruction Set

Most assemblers are designed to generate machine code for a particular microprocessor or computer. The instructions and machine code that they represent cannot be changed by the user. If the user wishes to write programs for a different microprocessor, a different assembler, cross assembler, or cross compiler is required. Usually, this means using a different set of instruction mnemonics, control statements, and operating procedures. With a UAL, the AL instructions and the machine code that is generated are user-definable.

Additionally, a single instruction mnemonic, a procedural instruction, can be defined to represent a series of machine instructions, that reduces the number of instructions that are required. This is accomplished in one of three ways:

1. *instruction definition tables:* all single and multiple action AL instructions are defined in a set of tables. These tables can be changed by the user to define the required mnemonics, associated parameters and code to be generated. The UAL assembler itself contains the algorithms required to convert any defined instruction into the required machine code.

2. *external subroutines:* an external subroutine instruction, or *ESI*, is an instruction that is defined by writing a separately assembled subroutine. When an ESI is used, it is replaced by a call instruction to the requested subroutine. Required parameters are stored in memory after the call instruction where they can be accessed by the subroutine. The result of using ESIs is that less redundant code is generated. Since the number and type of parameters are defined when the subroutine is written, and their descriptions are saved in a table, ESIs can be checked for errors in the same way that AL instructions are checked.

3. *macro definitions:* macro instructions are defined by writing the AL instructions that will be substituted for the macro instructions, using dummy lables to represent the parameters that will be specified as part of the macro instruction. When used, the macro instruction is replaced by the designated sequence of instructions, replacing the specified parameters for the dummy labels, and then assembled. As a result, fewer instructions are required when the user is writing a program—although the same amount of code is generated as would be the case if all the instructions were included originally.

Standard Set of Instructions

A standard set of instruction mnemonics and addressing mode syntax is used for all instructions in UAL. With a conventional AL, the instruction mnemonics and addressing mode syntax is defined by the manufacturer of the micro and vary significantly from manufacturer to manufacturer.

When using macro instructions in a conventional AL, the mnemonics selected by the individual programmers often results in more inconsistencies. With a UAL, a standard set of mnemonics is used to represent similar computer operations. Clarifying characters are used to represent specific variations of the basic operations. Moreover, a standard addressing mode syntax is used for all parameters. This eliminates some of the confusion that currently exists as a result of all the different addressing modes that are used by manufacturers.

It might be thought that *user-definable* instructions and a UAL *standard* are incompatible with each other. After all, if the programmer is free to define his or her instructions as he or she wishes, it would seem to open the door to even more incompatibility. How can there be a standard if all instructions are user defined?

The answer lies in the fact that it is a matter of implementation. It is the responsibility of the programmer, when defining instructions, to observe the standard. Even if a user does not follow the standard initially, that is, even if he or she defines an instruction using a nonstandard variation of the standard mnemonics or a different addressing mode syntax, there is nothing from preventing others from defining and using the same instruction. What started out being a nonstandard instruction could become the standard instruction for that procedure.

Additionally, there will inevitably be a considerable amount of variation in any language. The large number of incompatibilities between different implementations of Pascal and BASIC is probably the most obvious example. Hence, UAL does not provide an absolute standardization, but a standardization that approaches that offered by HLLs such as Pascal and BASIC.

THE USER-DEFINABLE VARIABILITY OF UAL

It should be remembered that the instruction set of a UAL, although user definable, can conform to a standard We have been following the MOPI standard developed by VOCS of Minneapolis for use with their universal assembler MOPI for purposes of illustration, but there is, in principle, freedom on the part of the user to define the instruction set in the way that seems most appropriate for the task at hand. The obligation that the programmer defining a custom instruction set bears, of course, is to provide the required tables, subroutines and macros.

As illustrated in Fig. 8-1, the user has the freedom to customize the AL he or she is using in ways that allow it to vary from the simplicity of an AL that is much like a conventional, micro-specific AL (such as 8088 AL), which uses the manufacturer's mnemonics, to the convenience and portability of an AL that makes extensive use of macros, external subroutines, and procedural type instructions. This kind of AL bears as much resemblance to a conventional HLL, such as Pascal, as it does to a conventional AL.

The user is provided great versatility but must consider the trade-offs between absolute control over the computer and little portability on one hand, and limited control over the computer but increased portability on the other. Figure 8-2 portrays this

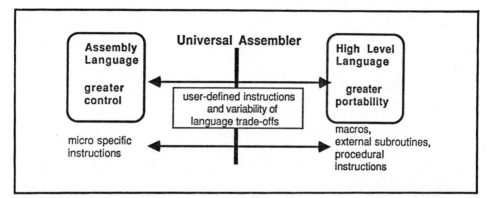

Fig. 8-1. The user-definable variability of UAL: In a table-driven UAL, the user decides how much like a traditional assembly language or a high level language he or she wants the language to be. For some applications, a language that is closer to the target microprocessor's language would enable greater control; for other applications, the speed in writing and portability of a language with macro and procedural instructions and external subroutines might be desirable. With a UAL, where on the spectrum the language appears is determined by the user. Neither traditional AL nor HLLs can claim such flexibility.

trade-off relationship and the fact that UAL has an advantage over conventional AL in this regard.

As UAL programs are made more portable by using procedural instructions, we increasingly lose control over the specific features of the microprocessor. Procedural instructions are general purpose routines that fail to take complete advantage of specific operations for specific tasks on particular micros. This results in less efficient programs that execute more slowly and require more memory. However, as illustrated in Fig. 8-2, with a universal assembler, since even specific computer-related instructions can be made semiportable, the loss in control and efficiency as portability increases is less

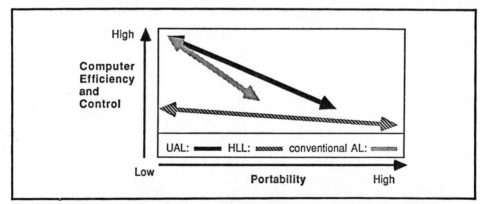

Fig. 8-2. The trade-off between efficiency/control and portability: In working with any language, there is a trade-off between computer efficiency and control on one hand, and portability on the other. Conventional AL programs can be quite efficient and yet are not very portable. High level language programs can be the most portable of all, but suffer in terms of efficiency and control when compared to either AL or UAL. A UAL program maintains more efficiency and control than a HLL even as it is made much more portable than a conventional AL program. Even for a UAL program, however, increased portability is purchased at the price of decreased efficiency in terms of code size and execution speed.

149

than it would be with a conventional AL or a HLL.

DEVELOPING A PROGRAM CONVENTIONALLY AND WITH A UAL

In order to understand how programs are developed using a UAL, it may help to review how programs are developed using a conventional AL. First, the microprocessor for which the programs are being written must be identified, since this determines the AL instructions that will be available. Next, a program specification is developed, the specification among other things, identifies the objectives of the program to be written. If the basic functions that each module must perform can be ascertained, then a common set of procedures or subroutines that can be used by one or more of the programs can be specified.

At this point, it becomes possible to examine the individual routines to see if they can be decomposed further into more basic routines. Particularly if the development task is a series of large programs, it is customary to divide the entire task into its simplest components and to build programs from these simpler components. Likewise, in writing and testing any program, it is best to start testing and debugging with the simplest subroutines, working up to the more complicated routines as the simpler routines are tested. Last, the entire program is put together and tested to see if the components work well together.

There is considerable variation to these practices with the exception that the choice of a particular microprocessor must be the first step. In many cases, the selection of a micro or computer may have been made already. If good programming practices are followed, documentation and reports are maintained throughout the process so as to maintain adequate control and ease of implementation and to allow for the almost inevitable changes in the initial design.

Developing a UAL program differs from the description just provided in several ways. First, an operational control table is set up; in it are the various options that must be included to achieve universality. It enables the programmer to select the desired options and to define the operational parameters that serve to control the development process. Then, depending on the microprocessor for which the programs are being written, the AL instruction tables are set up in order to define the AL machine dependent instructions that will be available for use. In most cases, predefined tables may be used.

If some of the subroutines that are needed in the program have already been written, they are used to establish a basic set of external subroutine instructions. The tables and subroutine source files, if written according to the standard so that they include the documentation related to the subroutine, can be used to begin a user's reference manual, which summarizes all the available instructions. The subroutine source files can also be used to start a manual describing the software being developed.

At this point, new external subroutines defining other external subroutine instructions can be written. As each subroutine is written and tested, it is automatically added to the macro instruction tables, and as a result, it becomes available as a new external subroutine instruction to be used by other subroutines and the final program. At the same time, data from each new subroutine source file may be extracted and used to update the User's Reference Manual and other documentation. Where practical, the relocatable modules containing the machine code for each subroutine can be combined into library files for easier control and system efficiency.

150

ONE IMPLEMENTATION OF A UAL

Although we wish to keep the text as generic as possible, in order to provide a clear picture of a UAL at work, we will describe some of the ideas behind the implementation of a UAL by using the example of MOPI (Macro Oriented Program Interpreter), a universal assembler developed by VOCS of Minneapolis. Though some of the particulars cited will specifically apply only to MOPI, much of what is said can apply, with just a few changes, to other universal assemblers.

As shown in Fig. 8-3 the MOPI system is a table-driven, two-pass relocatable macro assembler with an integrated linking loader and external linker/reformatter. Several support utilities simplify its operation and make it a complete software development system. The general operation of MOPI is controlled by what is called the *Operational Control Table* or *OCT*. The conversion of the source files into machine executable code is controlled by two additional sets of tables, namely the *Assembly Language (AL)* and *External Subroutine Instruction (ESIT) Tables*. Several MOPI functions and additional tables serve to support the maintenance of these three tables, generate reports, and supply documentation.

Using a predefined set of algorithms, MOPI is designed to generate machine code instructions for any 8-, 16- or 32-bit microprocessor. The user defines a set of tables or uses those supplied with the system; these tables control the conversion of the UAL instructions into specific machine code. The tables contain a complete description of each assembly language instruction, the format of the instruction, and the machine code to be generated. The tables are defined in a simple special-level language that is compiled by the utilities into a compact form of interpretive code. External subroutine instructions are defined by writing the required subroutines or using those provided with the system.

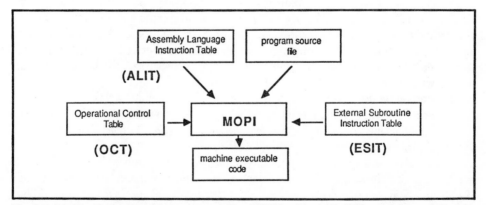

Fig. 8-3. A table-driven universal macro-assembler: MOPI implements a UAL as a two pass relocatable macro assembler and linking loader which is controlled by three tables. Overall operation is controlled by the Operational Control Table (OCT). The conversion of source files into machine executable code is controlled by the Assembly Language Instruction Table (ALIT) and the External Subroutine Instruction Table (ESIT).

When interpreted by the assembler, the tables cause a defined set of algorithms to be executed in the proper sequence. This results in the instruction's interpretation and the generation of the proper machine code instructions.

User Defined AL Instruction Tables

One primary objective of a universal assembler is the ability to generate machine code for any 8-, 16- or 32-bit microprocessor by means of a *user defined instruction set*. The process of interpreting machine-level AL instructions is controlled by a set of tables that is defined by the user or provided by the vendor. These tables must fully describe each assembly language instruction, specifically the format of the instruction parameters and the machine code to be generated. The tables themselves can be generated using a series of utility programs and a special instruction definition language. As interpreted by the assembler, the tables cause a defined set of procedures to be executed in the proper sequence so that the AL instruction is converted into the proper machine code.

Recall that AL instructions consist of an optional label, an instruction mnemonic, one or more (but usually two) parameters or operands, and an optional comment. Labels and comments are not usually considered part of the actual instruction:

label   *mnemonic*   *parameter(s) comment*

LBL1   MOV   A, B   ; move reg A to reg B

The label is used to reference the memory address where this instruction is stored. The mnemonic indicates the operation to be performed, while the parameters are used to clarify specifically what operation is to be performed; the mnemonic indicates only in general terms what operation is to be performed. The parameters or operands indicate which elements are to be operated on by the operation. Last, the comment, which explains the operation, is preceded by a ;.

All AL instructions use this same format, although sometimes the parameters differ in their ordering—some ALs use a destination-source order and some use a source-destination order. Here, we've adopted the source- destination convention. The number and type of instruction mnemonics, as well as the number and type of parameters associated with each instruction, depend on the microprocessor for which programs will be written.

Depending on the type of microprocessor for which they are written, the machine code instructions that are generated can be expressed in several formats. The three basic formats, as illustrated in Fig. 8-4, are *specific instruction, imbedded parameter*, and *appended parameter* instructions.

Specific instruction formatting is the simplest; the operation to be performed requires no parameters since it uses no data or the data is implied. Examples include HALT and NOP (no operation). *Imbedded parameter* formatting involves specific bits within the machine code that specifiy the data upon which the operation is to be performed. Examples include MOV and POP register(s) where the registers involved are specified by specific bits in the machine code instruction. *Appended parameter* formatting involves appending the data that is to be operated on to the machine code that specifies the operation to be performed. One example is CALL loc in which the address of the subroutine is appended to the machine code for a call subroutine operation. More complex formats use a combination of these three as shown in Fig. 8-5.

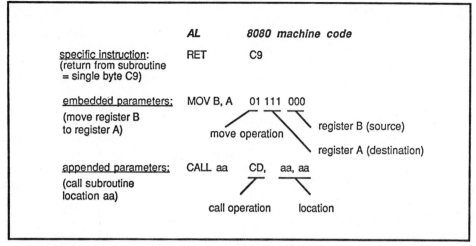

AL   8080 machine code

specific instruction: RET   C9
(return from subroutine
= single byte C9)

embedded parameters: MOV B, A   01 111 000
(move register B
to register A)   move operation   register B (source)
                                               register A (destination)

appended parameters: CALL aa   CD, aa, aa
(call subroutine
location aa)   call operation   location

Fig. 8-4. The three basic types of machine code: Here are the three basic types of instruction formatting as written for the 8080 microprocessor. The three types are specific, embedded parameter, and appended parameter. All three formats consist of a single or a multiple byte instruction, which is augmented by a modifier or appended data (parameters). The RET instruction is a single byte C9 in 8080 machine code. The MOV B, A instruction embeds the source and destination in the 6 LSBs, and the CALL aa appends the location code to the instruction as a parameter.

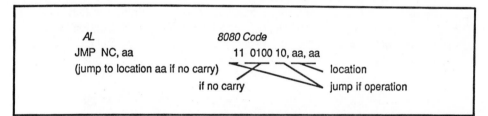

AL   8080 Code
JMP NC, aa   11 0100 10, aa, aa
(jump to location aa if no carry)   location
                    if no carry   jump if operation

Fig. 8-5. One complex format: Here is one possible combination of embedded and appended formats. It is a jump instruction conditional on the carry bit being clear. The equivalent 8080 machine code is also shown. The condition of the jump is embedded in the first byte by the four bits in the middle of the byte, the jump if operation is encoded in the other bits. The location to be jumped to is appended.

No matter what the format, a machine code instruction consists of a basic single or multiple-byte code to which some combination of modifiers and/or data are added, inserted, or appended. The modifiers are predefined values associated with specific parameters that are applied to the basic code to produce the actual machine code. The data is any variable value provided in the parameters to be used by the operation. When combined, the basic code and any modifiers and data value form a complete multiple byte machine code instruction. Consider these examples:

1)

40	basic machine code	(MOV data from, to in 8080)
+2	instruction modifier	(from reg. D)
+8	instruction modifier	(to reg. C)
4A	single byte instruction	(Mov D,C)

2)

	40		basic machine code	(MOV data from, to in Z80)
DD	06		instruction modifier	(from indexed register IX+)
		52	operation required data	(index value)
	08		instruction modifier	(to register C)
DD	4E	52	multiple byte instruction	(MOV (IX+ 82), C)

In example 1, an 8080 single byte instruction, the basic machine code is 40 hex. Two modifiers are added to the basic machine code to produce the final single byte instruction of 4A hex, which encodes the instruction "move a copy of the data in register D to register C." In example 2, an 8080 multiple byte instruction, the basic machine code is the same but the data to be moved is located by adding 52 hex (82 decimal) to the contents of the index register. This constitutes the effective address, and a copy of the data in that address is moved to register C.

Regardless of the format, any single or multiple byte machine code instruction can be generated by combing a basic code with the appropriate modifiers and data values. Likewise, any assembly language instruction can be converted into a machine code instruction by combining the code for the mnemonic with the modifier and data specified by the parameters in the proper sequence.

This is the method used in MOPI to convert assembly language instructions into microprocessor machine code instructions. The instruction mnemonic represents the basic operation and is converted into a basic single- or multiple-byte machine code. The parameters are then used to build the actual machine code instruction. The effect that each parameter has on the basic code depends on the basic operation, the mnemonic involved, and the micro machine code to be generated. Consider this 8080 instruction:

16 0C   MOV #12, D   ; move 12 to register D [8080]

The basic code for move immediate to register is 06, hex. The single byte number 12, 0C in hex, is appended to the basic code as a second byte. Finally, in order to designate the destination, in this case, register D, an instruction modifier, namely 10, must be added to the basic code . 10 and 06 sum to 16. As a result, the final 2-byte machine code instruction is 16 0C.

Regardless of the complexity of an instruction or the length of its format, for either a machine-code instruction or an AL instruction, it can still be interpreted as consisting of a basic code (mnemonic) to which one or more instruction modifiers and data bytes (parameters) are applied. Conversely, by applying the proper instruction modifiers and data bytes (parameters) to a basic machine instruction (mnemonic) in various ways, any AL instruction can be converted into the appropriate multiple byte machine code instruction.

This concept is essential, both in order to understand how MOPI operates and in order to be able to define new AL instructions. MOPI incorporates a series of algorithms, for examining the parameters and applying instruction modifiers and data values to a basic code or partially assembled instruction, that when executed, can convert any AL instruction into the machine code instructions for any currently available 8-, 16-

or 32-bit processor. The same concept is used with other assemblers with the exception that, instead of using a table, the sequence of procedures is hard coded into the assembler. This makes the instruction set difficult to modify, especially by the end user.

External Subroutine Instructions (ESI)

While a subroutine can be written as part of the program that uses it, it is often more convenient to write the subroutine as a separate subroutine program whose machine code can be relocated and appended to the programs that use it. Once a subroutine is defined, a single instruction can be used to call the subroutine as many times as needed. In MOPI, these instructions are called *External Subroutine Instructions* or *ESI*. The subroutines which define these instructions are written as external subroutine programs and are assembled into *Relocatable Load Modules* or *RLM*.

External subroutine instructions are defined by writing an external subroutine program. When assembled, the ESI(s) defined by the program are placed in the External Subroutine Instruction Tables (ESIT) so that they can be used and processed as AL instructions in other programs.

When an external subroutine is written, each ESI it defines is given a unique two to eight character instruction mnemonic; the first character must be the up-arrow or ^. The leading up-arrow signifies that it is an ESI. Just as labels should be meaningful if possible, the mnemonic for an ESI should be a meaningful abbreviation for the function the subroutine performs. If the subroutine performs a function that is similar to one or more of the AL instructions, the mnemonic should be an extension or combination of the AL mnemonics. When the subroutine is written, the quantity and type of data required by the subroutine are also specified. The actual values are specified as parameters when the EST instruction is used in a program.

For instance, the MOPI instruction ^ATON is an ESI that converts an ASCII string to a numeric value. The mnemonic begins with the requisite up-arrow and the mnemonic itself, ATON, is almost an acronym of "ASCII to numeric," and together with the up-arrow, it is less than the maximum eight characters permitted for all mnemonics. If we wished to convert an ASCII string stored in memory beginning at address labeled "LOC1", to its numeric equivalent and then store the value at address VAL, we would use this ESI:

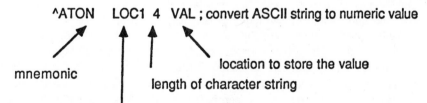

As should be apparent, an ESI has the same format and uses the same parameter syntax as any other UAL instruction. The difference is that an ESI is converted into the machine code for a call subroutine instruction, followed by the define data statements containing the parameters. For example:

```
^ATON       LOC1, 4, VAL
```

is equivalent to:

```
CALL    ^ATON
DW      LOC1
DB      4
DW      VAL
```

The subroutine itself is relocated and appended to the end of the executable code. While other methods of calling a subroutine are possible, of course, this way results in the least amount of redundant code.

Macro Instructions

Macros are a way to reduce the number of instructions in a source file by defining a single macro instruction to represent a series of instructions. When an MI is used in a program, the assembler substitues, for the single MI, the series of instructions that constitute the macro definition, replacing dummy labels with actual values; then it assembles each instruction.

Macro instructions are either defined within the file in which they are used or within an external library file. Each macro instruction is given an eight character mnemonic starting with a greater than sign (>):

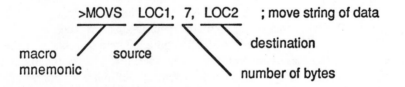

The macro mnemonic >MOVS is followed by the name of the location of the string to be moved, namely LOC1. This is followed by 7, which specifies the number of bytes in the string, and finally, by the name of the destination of the string.

There is a price to be paid for the convenience of reducing the number of instructions in the source file by using macros, namely, assembly time. First, the assembler has to locate the macro definition. Second, it must substitute the actual data for the dummy labels. Last, it must assemble each line. This three-step process must be repeated each time the program is assembled and the macro is used in the program.

This approach also results in all of the code representing the macro instruction being regenerated each time the macro appears. For simple procedures that require only a few instructions, this redundancy may be acceptable. For more complex procedures, the redundancy is often unacceptable, and subroutines should be used instead. Since embedded code will execute slightly faster than subroutines, it is a matter of judgment which course to follow—macros or subroutines.

Object Code

One of the most difficult decisions to make in designing a universal assembler is what kind of object code the assembler should generate. A binary file is the simplest—it contains the code exactly as it will be stored in memory. This is often called a *memory image file*. In the case of the MS-DOS and CP/M operating systems, it is called a *.COM* file.

Unfortunately, not all operating systems can execute this kind of file and some external devices will not accept it as input. Another type of file commonly used is a *hexadecimal file*, which is usually referred to as a *.HEX file*. In this case, the binary data is converted into a string of equivalent hexadecimal values and divided into a series of records that contain control information. Although standards that detail the format of .HEX files and the various record types used with .HEX files have been written, many different formats are used. Moreover, there are numerous other types of files used with different operating systems.

Most traditional assemblers and compilers are designed for use with a particular operating system or computer. As a result, the assembler's output only has to mesh with that specific system or computer. In the case of a universal assembler, however, provision must be made for a variety of operating systems and computers.

In addition to generating both .COM and .HEX files, MOPI also generates a form of relocatable file. While conventional assemblers generate relocatable files, they are formatted in order to be compatible with specific operating systems or linking loaders. A linking loader is a special program that combines individual relocatable modules into a complete program. A conventional assembler generates output that must be passed through a linking loader before it is executed. As stated above, MOPI contains an integral linking/loader routine so that it can generate executable programs directly. MOPI also incorporates an external linker reformatter that can be modified to generate the required file format for most operating systems.

The ideal would be for a universal assembler to generate output files that would be compatible with every computer system. Unfortunately, this is not practical. Even the adoption of a complete AL standard would probably not make it practical since, in many cases, the format required by an operating system or computer is dependent on its internal architecture. Changing the required format would mean compromising on the capabilities of the operating system. At this time, the only practical approach to this problem is for the assembler to generate a relocatable file with enough information so it can be passed through a linker/reformatter that can be modified by the user so it generates the required format.

A SAMPLE PROGRAM

To illustrate some of the principles we have advanced, we will look at a small program written in UAL. The program takes a string of characters as input, reverses the order of the string, and then outputs them in that reversed order. Table 8-3 includes the program in traditional 8080 AL and universal AL. It also includes listings of the program using simple procedural instructions, basic ESI and advanced ESI and macros. In this last form, it should be noted, the program is completely machine independent.

In Table 8-3, the first column indicates how this program may be written using

Table 8-3. A Comparison of a Conventional AL Program with Its Equivalent in Different Forms of UAL

Traditional			Universal			Simple Procedural			Using Basic ESI			Extended ESI		
STRT			STRT			STRT			STRT	^CNSLI	LOC1, 8	STRT	^CNSI	LOC1, 8
IN1	MVI	A,8 ; # char in	IN1	MOV	#8, A	IN1	FILL	CNT,8						
	LXI	H, LOC1 ; in buffer		MOVW	#LOC1, HL		MOVW	#LOC1, HL						
	PUSH	H ; save pointer		PUSH	HL		PUSH	HL						
	STA	CNT ; save count		MOV	A, CNT		SYSTEM	1						
	MVI	C,1 ; in char		MOV	#1, C									
	CALL	5H		CALL	5H									
	POP	H		POP	HL		POP	HL						
	MOV	M, A ; store char		MOV	A, (HL)		MOV	A, (HL)						
	INX	H		INCW	HL		INCW	HL						
	LDA	CNT		MOV	CNT, A									
	DCR	A ; more?		DEC	A		DEC.MPV	CNT, NZ, IN1						
	JNZ	IN1		JMP	NZ, IN1									
REV	MVI	B, 8 ; reverse	REV	MOV	#8, B	REV	MOV	#8, B	REV	MOV	#8, B	REV	>REVS	LOC1, 8, LOC2
	LXI	H, LOC1		MOVW	#LOC1, HL		MOVW	#LOC1, HL		MOVW	#LOC1, HL			
	LXI	D, LOC2+8		MOVW	#LOC2+8, DE		MOVW	#LOC2+8, DE		MOVW	#LOC2+8, DE			
REV1	MOV	A, M	REV1	MOV	(HL), A	REV1	MOV	(HL), A	REV1	MOV	(HL), A			
	STAX	D		MOV	A, (DE)		MOV	A, (DE)		INCW	HL			
	INX	H		INCW	HL		INCW	HL		DECW	DE			
	DCX	D		DECW	DE		DECW	DE		DEC	B			
	DCR	B		DEC	B		DEC	B		JMP	NZ, REV1			
	JNZ	REV1		JMP	NZ, REV1		JMP	NZ, REV1						
OUT	MVI	A, 8 ; ouput char	OUT	MOV	#8, A	OUT	FILL	CNT, 8	OUT	^CNSLO	LOC2, 8	OUT	^CNSLO	LOC2,8
	LXI	H, LOC2		MOVW	#LOC2, HL		MOVW	#LOC2, HL						
OUT1	PUSH	H ; out char	OUT1	PUSH	HL	OUT1	PUSH	HL						
	STA	CNT		MOV	A, CNT		MOV	(HL), E						
	MOV	E, M		MOV	(HL), E		SYSTEM	2						
	MVI	C, 2		MOV	#2, C									
	CALL	5H		CALL	5H									
	POP	H		POP	HL		POP	HL						
	INX	H		INCW	HL		INCW	HL						
	LDA	CNT		MOV	CNT, A									
	DCR	A		DEC	A		DEC.MPV	CNT, NZ, OUT1						
	JNZ	OUT1		JMP	NZ, OUT1									
FINI	MVI	C, 0 ; exit	FINI	MOV	#0, C	FINI	STOP		FINI	STOP		FINI	STOP	
LOC1	DS	8 ; 8 byte buffer	LOC1	DS	8	LOC1	DS	8	LOC1	DS	8	LOC1	DS	8
LOC2	DS	8 ; 8 byte buffer	LOC2	DS	8	LOC2	DS	8	LOC2	DS	8	LOC2	DS	8
CNT	DB	0 ; counter	CNT	DB	0	CNT	DB	0	CNT	DB	0	CNT	DB	0
END			END			END			END			END		

Table 8-3. A Comparison of a Conventional AL Program with Its Equivalent in Different Forms of UAL: This program inputs and reverses a string of eight characters, and then outputs the reversed character string. In conventional assembly language, it is written for the 8080 microprocessor and CP/M operating system. Notice that the universal AL program takes fewer mnemonics than the conventional 8080 AL. Using simple procedural instructions, not only are there fewer mnemonics, there is a decrease in the number of instructions overall. Using Basic ESI (see text), the number of instructions decreases further still. Using Basic ESI and macros or extended ESI, we get a program that is completely machine independent.

standard assembly language, in this case in 8080 AL. The second column shows the same sequence of instructions but using the UAL mnemonics and syntax. Although the same number of instructions is required, the program is easier to read and understand since there are fewer mnemonics used. A detailed knowledge of 8080 AL would not be required to understand the UAL version while, of course, it would be for the 8080 version.

The third column of Table 8-3 shows the same program using procedural instructions.

```
MOV  #X, C       is equivalent to    SYSTEM X
CALL UN, 5H

MOV  CNT, A      is equivalent to    DECJMPV  CNT, NZ, IN1
DEC  A
JMP  NZ, IN1

MOV  #8, A       is equivalent to    FILL   CNT, 8
MOV  A, CNT
```

Using procedural instructions means that we have reduced the number of instructions from 35 to 27, or about 20 percent. Moreover, the logic of the program is easier to understand—a fact that should result in easier debugging.

The fourth column shows the same program using basic ESI to perform the input/output procedures. At this point, the program is not only simpler to write, it is partially machine independent. The two ESI (^CNSLI and ^CNSLO) perform simple procedures; the input and output of data to the console. This sort of I/O is common to virtually every computer program.

The last column illustrates the same program written exclusively with procedural instructions. If the procedure to reverse the sequence of characters were to be used in several programs, it would be worth while to define it as a macro instruction or expanded ESI. Writing the program this way, we have written the program with just four instructions. Moreover, the program is machine independent since it can be assembled for execution on any computer under any operating system. In other words, we have progressed from a program that uses machine specific instructions and is written for a specific operating system, column 1, to completely machine independent instructions written for any operating system. This program offers most of the advantages of a high level language, namely simplicity, portability, and ease of writing, yet we are still working in an assembly language environment with all the advantages such an environment has to offer, namely, speed, compactness of code, and so on.

Some programmers might argue that what we have just done could be done using a conventional macro assembler. With the simple example we have used, there is considerable truth to this objection. But programs are usually more complicated than this example. The advantages of procedural AL and ESI increase dramatically as the size and complexity of the program increase. As programs grow in size, therefore, the advantages of a UAL over a conventional macro assembler grow as well.

Others might argue that although the listing on the right has only four instructions, the macro and ESI instructions still have to be written and debugged, and that the parallel between this form of assembly language and a HLL such as Pascal, where procedural instructions do not have to be debugged, is misleading. But this is not necessarily true. The macro and ESI instructions often will be used many times in a program. They only have to be written and debugged once. Additionally, libraries of such instructions are available or can be developed; each programmer does not have to write and debug a macro or ESI instruction whenever it is used.

PROPOSED
ASSEMBLY LANGUAGE
STANDARD

Version 2.0   March 15, 1986
As developed by
V.O.C.S.

Appendix A

Proposed Assembly Language Standard

This document describes a proposed standard for Assembly Language Programming as developed by VOCS for use with the Universal Assembler, MOPI. As yet it is not a universally accepted standard and open for criticism, additions, and modifications.

The purpose of this standard is not only to standardize AL but also introduce new concepts that make AL easier to learn and use.

The scope of this standard is currently limited to microprocessors, but eventually it will be expanded to encompass all aspects of AL. In this version we have concentrated on those areas of most importance and those from which a more extensive standard can be developed.

It must be recognized that the versatility, varied use, and past implementations of assembly language makes development of a complete standard difficult.

Parts of this standard may seem related to certain microprocessors, computers, and assemblers; however, it is intended to be general, combining the best, most logical features of them all. The concepts contained in this standard may be adapted to any computer system. Tables in Appendix G demonstrate how this standard can be applied to most currently available microprocessors.

It may be asked "By what authority does VOCS propose such a standard?" The answer is simply "By default." Although assembly language has been used since the introduction of the first electronic computers, no other organization has, to our knowledge, made a serious attempt to standardize assembly language and provide the software to implement that standard.

As with any other standard, it will take a few years for this standard to be perfected and universally accepted. However, for anything to become a reality someone must take the first step, and an Assembly Language Standard is long overdue.

VOCS solicits input and support from all interested individuals and organizations to help make this an effective and universally accepted standard.

Write to: VOCS
P.O. Box 3816
Minneapolis, MN 55403

SECTION 1: BACKGROUND

Until now the assembly language (AL) for every microprocessor has been different, with only limited similarities in certain cases. This has resulted in AL being:

Non-portable
Difficult to learn
Hard to document

The overall result is that AL has become known as a last resort language, to be used only when absolutely necessary. AL by its very nature may not be a very elegant sophisticated language. AL was however the first symbolic language used to program computers and is still widely used. For a number of years, in fact, it was the only language other than machine language. The development of FORTRAN in the 1950s was followed by many other languages that often took advantage of new technology and better understanding of programming. Little, however, was done to improve AL.

There will always be a need for AL. In fact for many application, AL is the only language that can be used. Most high level languages (HL) being developed today are for use with a particular operating system. Yet many microprocessor applications do not require, nor can they support, a sophisticated operating system, rendering the language useless for many applications. Also, HL languages are developed for particular types of applications and are not well-suited for applications other than those for which they were designed. AL is the only language that can be used for any application, under all conditions.

AL has some very important qualities that need to be expanded upon:

Versatility
Efficiency
Simplicity

Unfortunately during the past several years the negative aspects of AL have been overly exaggerated by supporters of the newer standardized HL languages, with little attention being given to the many advantages of AL or its improvement.

Most of AL's deficiencies can be overcome by the implementation of a standard, as exists for most other languages. A standard would make AL easier to learn and use,

164

offer a degree of portability, and enhance its many other advantages.

The reasons for not implementing a standard in the past are numerous and rather complex. In part it has always been assumed that since AL is a direct representation of the machine code for a particular computer and every computer is different, no standard was possible. An underlying fact is that in the past the AL instruction set for each computer was defined by the manufacturer, and it was to their advantage to make the instruction set different. Another major factor is that in the past the number of different computers was relatively small and each took years to develop. Individuals were trained on a specific computer or a compatible family of computers and not required to be retrained on another. The need for learning more then one version of AL was rare and thus a standard was deemed unnecessary.

Conditions have now changed. The number and types of computers, especially microprocessors, is increasing at a phenomenal rate. Many are designed for special applications with a limited life cycle. Additionally, the more sophisticated computers of today use multiple processors, each performing a specific function. The result is that today, and more so in the future, individuals will be required to work on many different types of computers, often more than one at the same time. The time required to learn a new language or version of AL, and the ability to become proficient in several languages simultaneously are matters of immediate concern. Since it is not economical or practical to redevelop similar software for different computers, portability between computers is an absolute requirement. The only way for AL to meet the needs of the future is through the implementation of an AL standard, a universal form of assembly language.

SECTION 2: CONCEPTS

Five widely known concepts and six relatively new concepts have been used as a basis for this proposed standard.

Fundamental Concepts

This proposed standard is based on five fundamental concepts.

1. The source code for an AL program is contained in a sequential ASCII text file, with a maximum of 80 characters per line or record. Three types of lines are permitted.

    Comments
    Instructions
    Assembler commands

2. Each assembly language instruction explicitly defines the computer operation or procedure to be performed, exclusive of any rules or assumptions unique to a particular assembler. Thus a programmer will know exactly what a single instruction or sequence of instructions does without having to know the peculiarities of a particular assembler or the computer for which it was written.

    Example: `JMP    UN,location`
             `JMPR   UN,location`

A jump absolute and jump relative operation is explicitly specified by the instruction mnemonic. It is not left for the assembler to determine which is to be used and the programmer to remember the rules under which each will be selected.

3. Every assembly language instruction has the same format: an optional label, instruction mnemonic, one or more parameters, and an optional comment. Each parameter consists of one or more elements separated by an operator.

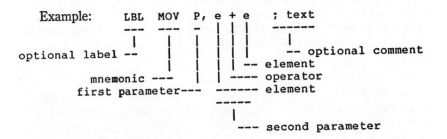

```
Example:    LBL  MOV  P, e + e   ; text
            ---  ---  - | | |    ------
             |    |   | | | |       |
optional label --  |  | | | |       -- optional comment
                   |  | | | |
                   |  | | | |-- element
      mnemonic ---  |  | |---- operator
      first parameter---  ------ element
                       ------
                          |
                          --- second parameter
```

4. All similar computer operations use the same basic mnemonic. Characters are appended to the basic mnemonic to identify individual operations.

```
Example: MOV    move data byte
         MOVW   move data word
         MOVS   move string
         MOVWR  move word repeat
         ---
          | --
          | |
          | --- appended characters
          --- basic mnemonic
```

5. All the data used by the instruction is explicitly identified by parameters and not implied by the instruction mnemonic.

```
Example: MOVS  from,to,count  ; move string
    not  LDS                  ; location and count assumed
```

New Concepts

In order to simplify the overall development of AL programs, six relatively new concepts are presented as part of this standard.

1. The most important new concept is that a single AL instruction may be assembled into a sequence of machine code instructions rather than just one. This permits the definition of machine independent procedural type instructions.

```
Example: ADDVVW  loc,loc  ; add the first variable to the
                            second variable in memory
```

Although a computer may not have a single machine code instruction to add a word variable in memory to a word variable in memory, a series of machine code instructions can be generated to perform the procedure.

The inclusion of procedural type instructions, which follow the AL instruction format, improves programming efficiency and offers a limited degree of portability, without the need for special rules and complex instruction formats.

2. This standard also introduces the concept of External Subroutine Instructions (ESI). An ESI is defined as a call to an external, separately assembled subroutine. The ESI is converted into a call subroutine instruction followed by the data (parameters) to be used by the subroutine. The relocatable subroutine is appended to the end of the program as part of the assembly process.

3. An executable load module is produced by the assembler, eliminating the need for a separate linking loader. As part of the assembly process, all external subroutines and defined data should be identified and appended to the program. Although with some systems or applications a separate linking loader may be required, for many applications it has become obsolete.

4. Comment type parameters may be inserted within an instruction or command to clarify the procedure being performed or the data to be used. These parameters are identified by the presence of a period as the first character. They are not processed by the assembler; instead, they are included in the listings as a comment is. The use of comment type parameters will make AL instructions more readable.

Example: `MOVS .message LOC1 .to .buffer LOC2 .length N`

The parameters .message, .to .buffer and .length are inserted to clarify the content of each parameter.

5. Documentation relating to the program is included as part of the program source file. Utility routines extract the appropriate data and generate the desired reports and manuals. This will help eliminate the traditional problems involved with maintaining documentation separate from the program. Although for large programs a separate system for maintaining documentation may be desirable, documentation for commonly used modules can best be maintained as part of the source code.

6. Variable data may be inserted while a program is being assembled. This is intended for use during the writing of programs that must be assembled several times with different values for certain parameters or data. The operator is prompted to enter the desired value as the program is being assembled. This eliminates the need to edit the source file each time.

SECTION 3: SOURCE CODE FILES

Source code for an assembly language program is stored in a sequential ASCII file, which may be generated using any standard editor. Each line, or record, is a maximum of 80 characters terminated by a carriage return / line feed and contains one complete instruction, assembler command, and/or comment. File names should use the .ASM extension to identify the file as containing source code for an assembly language program.

Types of Lines

There are basically three types of source code lines: comment, instruction, and assembler command.

Comment lines are used for documentation. They are not processed by the assembler other than being included on the assembled program listing. Utility routines are used to extract designated comment lines for use in generating a manual, user's reference guide, and other formal documentation.

Instructions specify the operations and procedures to be performed when the program or subroutine is executed. When processed by the assembler, an instruction is converted into a single machine code instruction, a series of machine code instructions, or a call to an external relocatable subroutine.

Assembler commands control the assembly process. They are used to instruct the assembler to perform a specific function, select the type of output to be generated, set certain variables, or define data for use by the program.

Recommended Format

The following format is recommended for use when writing AL programs. Following this format will not only make AL programs easier to read, but allows for the inclusion of associated documentation.

In general, every source file should consist of the following:

```
Identification Line
Assembler Control Block
Documentation Section
Program Source Code
END command
```

Identification Line. Every program source file should begin with an identification line that acts as a program or file identifier and is used for control purposes. Although a complex multiple-line identification block may be used, a simple one-line format is recommended. The identification line is a comment and is not processed by the assembler. It only appears on the assembled program listing. It is suggested that the following items be included:

Source file name
Date written and/or last updated
Revision number
System for which it was written
Individual or organization where developed

Assembler Control Block. The identification line should be followed by an assembler control block. This consists of all the assembler commands that are used to describe the type of program to be assembled, input/output requirements, and other preliminary procedures to be performed. Because of their function, these commands must come before any instructions or other commands that generate machine code or data. They are grouped together and placed at the beginning of the source file for quick reference. The following commands are typical of those that should be included in the assembler control block. If used, they should be used in the sequence indicated. Each is described in detail in section 12.

	NAME	—	The program name that will appear on all output listings and be used as a title in the documentation.
**	SUBR	—	Macro instruction subroutine.
**	SGMT	—	Program overlay segment.
**	MAIN	—	Main segment of a program with overlays.
**	HEX	—	Produce a .HEX compatible load module file.
	LBLTBL	—	Load a previously generated Label or Load Map Table into the current Label Table.
*	COMM	—	Data that may be referenced by other programs.
*	EXT	—	Externally defined data required by this program.
*	LOAD	—	Force load a relocatable module.
	ORG	—	Set start address of the program.
	ORGD	—	Set the start address of the data area.
	ORGDS	—	Set the data segment address.
	ORGCS	—	Set the code segment address.

* May be used as many times as required.
** Only one is permitted, if none are used an executable program is assumed.

Documentation Section. Next in the program source file is a description of the program for documentation purposes and future reference. This section should explain what the program does and provide all the information required to execute or use the program.

Although the organization and type of information will differ, depending on the type of program and purpose for which the documentation is being produced, the following general format applies.

```
;
;   documentation text
;
 TEXT  - Start of manual text
;
;   documentation text
;
 URMT  - Start of user reference guide text
;
;   documentation text
;
 SKIP
```

The TEXT and URMT commands are used to identify the start of that portion of the documentation section to be used in formal documentation as explained in Chapter 5.

The SKIP command is used to indicate the end of the documentation section. Although any instruction or command can be used, the SKIP command is best because it also separates the documentation from the actual program code on the assembled program listing.

Program Code. Following the documentation section is the actual program code. The program code consists of any combination of assembler commands, single action and/or procedural assembly language instructions, external subroutine and/or macro instructions, and comments that will cause the desired executable machine code to be generated.

Enough comments should be included to allow any programmer to understand the purpose and operation of each section of code and any unique instructions. The SKIP command should be used to separate logical sections of the program.

END Command. The last line of the source code to be assembled must be the END command. The END command does not have to be the last record in the source file; comment lines or any other code that is not to be assembled may follow the END command.

Sample

```
; SAMPLE.ASM   3/21/85  Rev:0    Sample      VOCS
;
  Assembler Control Block -------------------| NAME
;                                            | SUBR,SGMT,MAIN,HEX
  Documentation section --|Text              | LBLTBL
;                         |    Comments       | COMM
 SKIP                     |URMT              | EXT
;                         |    Comments       | LOAD
;                                            | ORG
  Program source code --|AL instructions    | ORGD
;                       |ES instructions    | ORGDS
;                       |Macro instructions | ORGCS
 END                    |Assembler commands
                        |Comments
```

General Rules

Some general rules regarding a source code file are:
1. Certain assembler commands, if used, must be used in a certain sequence.
2. Tabs and other special characters that are used in word processing to format data are not permitted. When generating the reports and listings, the utility routines provided with the assembler will format the data properly, without the use of tabs or other special characters. This stipulation is included because not all computer systems recognize or interpret a tab and other special characters in the same way.

SECTION 4: COMMENT LINES

Comment lines are used for documentation. They are not processed by the assembler other than being included on the assembled program listing. Comment lines start in the first character position with a comment line identifier. The rest of the line is the text of the comment.

```
Format: ;  line of text
        *  text not for use in a manual
        !  text not for use in a User's Reference Guide
        #  text not for use in any formal documentation
        -  -----------------------------------------------
        | |                      |
        | -- space          -- text
        -- comment line indicator
```

Four different comment line indicators have been defined providing three levels of documentation as follows:

1. A manual or other formal documentation.
2. A user's reference guide.
3. Detailed description of the source code and program execution.

The different comment line indicators are used by utility routines to generate documentation and special reports as follows.

; This is the standard indicator for a comment line. It contains no special meaning when generating reports. It is also used with instructions and commands to indicate that the rest of the input line is a comment and not part of the instruction or command.

* This indicates that the comment line contains text that should not be included when generating a manual, but should be included in a user's reference guide.

! This indicates that the comment line contains text that should not be included in the user's reference guide, but may be used in other documentation.

This indicates that the comment line contains text that should not be included in either the user's reference guide or any other formal documentation.

Documentation

Comment lines are extracted from the source file for use in documentation as follows.

The TEXT and URMT commands are used to specify which comment lines are to be extracted from the source file documentation section for use in a manual or user's reference guide. The TEXT command indicates that all comment lines following this command, up to the next noncomment line, except for the * and # comment lines or URMT command, are to be extracted for use in a manual. Likewise, the URMT command indicates that all comment lines following this command, up to the next noncomment line, except for the ! and # comment lines, are to be extracted for use in a user's reference guide. The *, !, and # comment line indicators are used to distinguish between the text that is to be included either in a manual or user's reference guide, but not in both, and the text that is to be included in both.

The parameter for each command (TEXT, URMT) specifies what section of the manual or User's Guide this text is to be part of. In this way text from various programs can be grouped together.

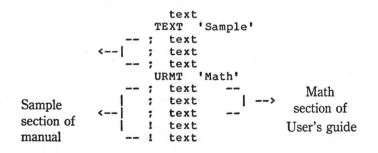

```
          *  text    --
          *  text        | -->
          *  text    --
          #  text
          #  text
     --  ;  text    --
  <--|    ;  text        | -->
     --  ;  text    --
             SKIP
```

The SKIP command is normally used to indicate the end of the documentation section and comment lines to be extracted.

Formatting Characters. Two special format control characters have been defined to format the documentation.

1. If the first character after the comment line indicator is an ampersand (&), this indicates that the next line should be printed at the top of the next page. It has the same effect as the SKIP command when printing the Assembled Program Listing. The SKIP command, however, cannot be used since that would indicate the end of the documentation section, as described above.

Example: ;&
```
        ; This line printed at the top of the next page.
```

2. If the first character after the comment line indicator is an up-arrow (^), this indicates that the next line should be printed over the current line. This is intended for underlining or over-printing lines.

Example:
```
      Comment lines            Printed
      -------------            -------
        ;^ text                 text
        ;  ____
```

SECTION 5: INSTRUCTION/COMMAND FORMAT

An instruction or assembler command consists of an optional label, mnemonic, one or more parameters, and an optional comment. The label, instruction mnemonic, and parameters are separated by spaces. Individual parameters are separated by a comma and optional spaces. The comment is separated from the parameters by spaces and a semicolon (;). The semicolon indicates that the rest of the line is a comment.

```
Format: [label] mnemonic parameters  [; comment]
               ^        ^         ^   ----
               |        |         |   |
        spaces --       |         |   -- spaces and semicolon
                 spaces --   -- comma between parameters

[] = optional
```

Label

A label is used to reference the location of the machine code generated by the instruction or data generated by a command. A label is one to eight characters with the first character being an alphabetic or symbol (A-Z, a-z, ^[ ). The other characters can be alphabetic or numeric (A-Z, a-z, 0-9). Although lower case alphabetic characters are permitted, it is recommended that only capital alphabetic and numeric characters be used. If a label is present it must start in the first character position on the line.

Special symbols are permitted as the first character to identify special locations or data items within a program.

```
Example: ^XXXXX mnemonic parameters
         |
         -- subroutine entry point

         <XXXXXX mnemonic parameters
         |
         -- local or dummy labels
```

Mnemonic

The mnemonic is the one to eight character abbreviation representing the command or instruction. The mnemonic can start in any character position on the line except the first, which is used to indicate a label or comment. To help distinguish external subroutine or macro instructions from other instructions and commands, the following rule applies. If the first character is a capital alphabetic, it is an AL instruction or assembler command. If the first character is an up-arrow (^), it is an external subroutine instruction. If it is a right arrow (>), it is a macro instruction.

```
Example: label AAA parameters
               |
               -- instruction or command

         label ^XXX parameters
               |
               -- external subroutine instruction
         label >XX parameters
               |
               -- macro instruction
```

Parameters

Parameters either clarify the conditions under which the operation specified by the mnemonic is to be performed or specifies the data upon which the operation will be performed. The number and type of parameters depend on the instruction or command. Each parameter is separated by a comma and optional spaces.

Most instructions will require two or more parameters. The first parameter specifies the source of the data or condition under which the operation will be performed. The second parameter is used to specify the destination of the data. A third parameter is often used to specify the number of times to repeat the operation or length of the data.

In some cases it may be desirable to have the first parameter specify the destination and the second parameter the source, which is traditional with many of the older micros. If this is the case, an equals sign (=) should be used instead of a comma to separate the first and second parameters. This will eliminate the confusion that exists as to which parameter is the source and which is the destination.

```
Example: MOV   A,B      ; move register A to register B
         MOV   B = A    ; move A to B
```

Comment

A semicolon (;) is used to indicate that the rest of the line is a comment and is not part of the actual instruction or command. No action is taken with respect to the comment, except that it is included on the assembled program listing. It is recommended that all lowercase letters (not capitals) be used in the comment. This will make it easier to spot comments in the program by differentiating them from the instructions and commands, which should contain all capitals.

SECTION 6: MNEMONICS

Mnemonics are one- to eight-character abbreviations representing the operation to be performed or machine code to be generated. There are four groups of mnemonics.

1. Assembly language instructions
2. External subroutine instructions
3. Macro instructions
4. Assembler commands

All characters used in the mnemonic should be capital alphabetics (A-Z) or numerics (0-9), except for the first character as explained below for external subroutine and macro instructions.

AL Instructions

AL instructions represent a single, or a series of, machine code instructions that perform a specific operation or procedure. The mnemonic consists of a basic abbreviation or mnemonic to which clarifying characters may be appended.

```
Format: xxxxcccc
            ----
    ----     |
     |     -- clarifying characters
     -- basic abbreviation
```

The basic abbreviation, or mnemonic, represents those basic operations that are common to most computers. The clarifying characters are used to describe specific variations of these basic operations. The currently defined basic mnemonics are described in Section 7 and the clarifying characters in Section 8. Instructions that are unique to a specific computer will be assigned a unique basic mnemonic that does not conflict with any previously defined mnemonics; they will use the same clarifiers where possible.

In the case of machine independent procedural type AL instructions, a combination of the basic mnemonics and clarifying characters that best describes the procedure should be used. A description of some standard procedural instructions is given in Section 10.

EXTERNAL SUBROUTINE INSTRUCTIONS

External subroutine instructions represent procedures performed by external, previously assembled subroutines contained in relocatable load modules. To help distinguish these instructions from other AL instructions and commands the first character of the mnemonic should be an up arrow (^).

The mnemonic should be a meaningful descriptive abbreviation of the procedure being performed. When possible, a combination of the basic mnemonics (Section 7) and clarifying characters (Section 8) as described for AL instructions should be used. A list of some basic subroutines common to most programming tasks is given in Section 12.

Macro Instructions

Macro instructions represent sequences of previously written AL instructions that are to be inserted into the program, replacing dummy labels with the parameters specified, then assembling the inserted instructions. To distinguish macro instructions from other AL instructions and commands, the first character of the mnemonic should be a greater than sign (>).

When possible, the mnemonic should be a meaningful descriptive abbreviation of the procedure or purpose of the code being inserted.

Assembler Commands

Assembler commands represent special procedures, or functions, to be performed by the assembler. They may or may not generate machine code or data to be included as part of the program. Each is given a unique mnemonic that describes its purpose or function. A basic set of assembler commands is defined in Section 11.

SECTION 7: PARAMETERS

The parameter portion of an instruction or command either clarifies the operation to be performed or specifies the data upon which the operation will be performed. There are four types of parameters:

Specific value
Character string
Numeric value
Comment

The number and type of parameters permitted with each instruction or command depends on the information the instruction requires, which is specified by the instruction definition.

Each parameter within an instruction or command is separated by a comma or equals sign and optional spaces.

```
Example: A,B   A,  B      Parameters A and B
         A = B             Parameters A and B when A is the
                           destination
```

Although a comma and multiple spaces are permitted, just a comma is recommended.

Specific Value

A specific value parameter is used when one of several predefined character strings is required. The characters are not enclosed in quotes, and therefore cannot include any of the special characters defined later in this section. The instruction definition determines what character strings are permitted. This type is normally used to specify a register or addressing mode, or clarify the operation to be performed.

```
Example: MOV D,HL   ; move reg to reg
             - --
             |  |
             |  -- to register
             -- from register
```

The from and to registers must be specified using predefined abbreviations.

Character String

A character string parameter is used when an unknown number of alphanumeric characters is expected. The character string is enclosed in single quotes and may contain any printable character except a single quote (').

```
Example: TITLE 'Test Program'
               ------------
                    |
                    -- character string
```

Numeric Value

A numeric value is used when the parameter is to be converted into a binary value or address. The parameter may consist of a single element, using one of the basic formats below, or may be complex consisting of several elements each separated by an operator indicating how the elements are to be combined. The maximum value of the parameter depends on the number of bits used to store the value as part of the machine code instruction.

Basic Numeric Formats

Constant. A series of numeric digits followed by an optional base indicator (H, B, O, Q, I) and preceded by an optional sign indicator (+, −).

```
                                  Range
Indicator     Valid Digits   1-byte  2-bytes        Examples
---------     ------------   ---------------        --------
H = Hex        0-9, A-F      0-FF    0-FFFF      1EH     0A52BH  *
```

176

```
B = Binary        0, 1      8 Bits   Invalid    01101B   Invalid
O,Q = Octal       0 - 7     0-377    0-177777   2070     173426Q
I = Integer       0 - 9     +-127    +-32678    +23I     -897I
                         or 0-255    0-65536    250I (unsigned)
none = Integer    0 - 9     +-127    +-32678    -23      -31000
                         or 0-255    0-65536    254 (unsigned)
```

* A hexadecimal number must start with a numeric.

Label. A string of one to eight alphanumeric characters, representing a memory location or value as defined in the program. The first character must be an alphabetic character or symbol. Although the other characters can be any printable character, only capital alphabetics should be used. None of the special characters (+ − @ & | / * : $?) may be used.

Example: `LBL1     ^BY     S9T5    >DIV`

Character Value. An ASCII character string, beginning and ending with a single quote ('), is equated to a single or multiple byte value. Any printable character may be used except a single quote. The first character is the low-order byte, and the last character is the high-order byte. Unused high-order bytes are set to zero.

Example: `'ab' = 6261H    'B' = 0042H`

External Subroutine Instruction Parameter. An ESI is used to access or reference the parameters given as part of an external subroutine instruction. It has the following format.

Format: `:Xlabel`

```
where :  =    ESI parameter indicator
      X  =    parameter number (first parameter = 1)
   label  =   label specifying where the instruction is located
```

Example: `MOV A,:2LPTZ1`   ; Replace the value of the   second
                             parameter of the ESI at location
                             LPTZ1 with the contents of reg A.
```
LPTZ1 ^CNSLO  MSG1 50  ; The   second   parameter initially
------    ---- --        contains the value 50.
      |      |   |
      |      |   -- 2nd parameter
      |      -- 1st parameter
      -- macro instruction mnemonic
```

The programmer must be sure that the operation being performed (instruction) is appropriate for the parameter being referenced. An instruction that references a two-byte variable should not be used with a single-byte parameter. In the above example we moved a single byte value to a single byte parameter.

Current Instruction Address. A special single-character label ($) is provided to indicate that the current value of the program counter should be used. The program counter contains the address of the first byte of the instruction currently being assembled.

```
Example: MOVW $+5,HL   ; the address  of  this instruction
                         plus 5  is  loaded  into  the  HL
                         register.
```

This should only be used with single-action AL instructions or commands. Using it with a procedural type instruction might cause undesirable results, unless the programmer is familiar with the sequence of code being generated.

Operator Input Value. The special two-character label (?x) is used to indicate that the value will be entered by the operator when the program is assembled. A maximum of ten values may be selected by the second character, an integer of 0-9. The first time the label (?0 thru ?9) is used, the operator is requested to enter the actual value. After that, the same value is used each time the label appears in the program.

```
Format: ?x
Where: x indicates one of ten individual values (0-9)
Example: ADD ?2,A
         MOV ?2,A
```

In the first instruction the operator is requested to enter the value for ?2. In the second instruction the same value is used.

Complex Format

Each of the basic formats (parameter elements) may be combined to form a complex parameter. Each element is separated by an operator with no spaces or commas. The value of each basic element is calculated and combined with the total value calculated so far in accordance with the operator.

The valid operators and their meanings are as follows.

Operator	Meaning
+	Add
–	Subtract
*	Multiply
/	Divide
@	Logical OR
&	Logical AND

```
Example: 125+LPT1-'B' ; Add 125 to the value of the  label  LPT1
                        then Subtract the ASCII character B.

         40H&LPT@13H  ; AND 40H with the value of  LPT  then  OR
                        the result with 13H. H = hexadecimal.
```

Comment Parameters

A comment parameter is any parameter or parameter element that starts with a period (.). This special type of parameter can be used with any instruction or command to clarify the meaning of either the instruction or a parameter. It is not treated as part of the instruction or command but as a comment inserted between the parameters, similar to a comment appended at the end of the instruction. When the source code, line is searched for the next parameter (element), dummy parameters are skipped over. They can be thought of as a single-word comment within an instruction.

```
Example: MOV   A,B                           ; as defined
         MOV   .byte_from_reg A .to_reg B    ; with dummy parameters
```

SECTION 8: ADDRESSING MODES

The term *addressing modes* refers to the methods of specifying a location in memory or the method to be used by an instruction to locate the source or destination of the data being processed. It may consist of either a specific value, character string, numeric value, or combination thereof as described in Section 5. The specific formats depend on the addressing modes available with each instruction for the computer being programmed. There are seven basic types of addressing modes.

> Immediate
> Predefined location
> Bit
> Absolute
> Indirect
> Indexed
> Auto increment/decrement

These basic addressing modes may be combined to form more complex addressing modes as indicated in the definitions below. Appendix C contains a list of the addressing modes used with most of the currently available micros.

Immediate Data

The immediate data type is used when the actual data, or numeric value, to be used by the instruction is included as part of the instruction. Immediate data is entered as a parameter using the format for a numeric value, as specified in Section 5, preceded by a pound sign (#). The pound sign is used to distinguish the numeric value as immediate data and not another form of address mode. For some instructions, such as number of bytes in a string, an immediate value may be the only form of addressing mode permitted. In these cases the pound sign (#) is not required but may be used in order to maintain consistency with those instructions in which some form of identification is required.

```
Format: # numeric_value
Example: MOV # 25,A              ; the value 25 is immediate data
         MOVS LOC1,LOC2,20       ; the number of bytes  to  move
                                   must be an immediate value.
```

Predefined Location

A predefined location type is used when a predefined location, such as a register or flag, must be specified. It is entered as a parameter using the format for a specific value as defined in Section 5. No special identification symbols are used. Normally registers and special memory locations are assigned an abbreviation by the manufacturer.

```
Format: specific_value
Example: MOV # 25,A   ; register A is a predefined location.
```

Bit

The bit form is used when an individual bit rather than the entire contents of a memory location is to be specified. With most instructions the bit location is specified as two separate parameters, a memory location and bit number, using the format for a numeric value described in Section 5. The location of a bit can also be specified using a single parameter. The location is entered first, followed by the bit number, separated by the vertical bar symbol (|). Bit addressing is specified by appending a B to the instruction mnemonic or by preceding the above format with the abbreviation "BIT."

```
Format: BIT numeric_value,numeric_value   ; location, bit
        BIT numeric_value|numeric_value   ; location, bit
Example: CPLB LOC1,3    ; bit operation specified by mnemonic
         CPL BIT LOC1|3   ; specified in parameter
```

Absolute

The absolute type is used when the actual memory location or location of the data to be used by the instruction is specified. It is entered as a parameter using the format for a numeric value, as specified in Section 5. No special identification symbol is used. This is similar to a predefined location except that the location is defined in the program.

```
Format: numeric_value
Example: MOV  AX,TOTAL   ; the absolute memory location named
                           TOTAL is defined in the program.
```

There are seven special forms of absolute addressing: long, page zero, same page, relative, displacement, segmented, and vectored. Each is specified by appending characters to the instruction mnemonic or by an abbreviation preceding the absolute address, and affects the range of address values that may be specified.

Long. The long form is used when the address value specified is more than the normal two bytes or 16-bits. With most 32-bit micros, long addressing is assumed and need not be specified.

```
Format: LA numeric_value
Example: JMPL numeric_value     ; specified by mnemonic
         JMP  LA numeric_value  ; specified by parameter
```

Page Zero. This form is used when the address specified must be in page 0. Only the least significant bits of the address are appended to the machine code instruction. The most significant bits by definition are equal to zero. Thus the address value must be between 0 and the maximum permitted by the number of bits in the machine code address field.

```
Format: PZ numeric_value
Example: JMPPZ  LOC1   ; specified by mnemonic
         JMP  PZ LOC1  ; specified by parameter
```

Same Page. This form is used when the address specified must be within the same page as the current instruction. The least significant bits of the address specified are combined with the most significant bits of the address of the current instruction. The number of least and most significant bits will vary between computers. The most significant bits of the numeric value, or address, specified must be the same as the most significant bits of the instruction address.

```
Format: SP numeric_value
Example: JMPSP  LOC1   ; specified by mnemonic
         JMP  SP LOC1  ; specified by parameter
```

Relative Address. This form is used when the address specified must be within a specific range of the current instruction, normally + − 125 bytes. The difference between the address specified and the address of the next instruction (contents of the program counter) is appended to the machine code instruction. This difference value, or range, is limited by the number of bits in the machine code address field.

```
Format: RA numeric_value
Example: JMPR   LOC1   ; specified by mnemonic
         JMP RA LOC1   ; specified by parameter
```

Displacement Address. This form is similar to a relative address except that the range is larger, normally + − 32K. In this case the difference value appended to the instruction is normally 16-bits, limiting the numeric value, or address, specified in the parameter to within 32K of the current instruction, which for most micros is anywhere within the addressable memory or the program-accessible segment of memory.

```
Format: DA numeric_value
Example: JMPD   LOC1   ; specified by mnemonic
         JMP  DA LOC1  ; specified by parameter
```

Segmented. This form is similar to long addressing except the address is specified as two separate values; a segment location and an address value within that segment. The maximum value of each and the method of combining the two values varies between computers. Both values are entered using the format for a numeric value separated by the vertical bar sign (|). Different abbreviations are used to indicate segmented addressing depending on the number of bits (the maximum value permitted for both the segment and address).

```
Format: OS numeric_value|numeric_value   ; other segment
        SS numeric_value|numeric_value   ; segmented short
        SL numeric_value|numeric_value   ; segmented long
Example: JMP  OS SEG1|LOC1  ; 16-bit seg, 16-bit loc
         JMP  SS SEG1|LOC1  ; 7-bit seg, 8-bit loc
         JMP  SL SEG1|LOC1  ; 7-bit seg, 16-bit loc
         JMPOS   SEG1|LOC1. ; implied by mnemonic
         JMPSS   SEG1|LOC1  ; implied by mnemonic
         JMPSL   SEG1|LOC1  ; implied by mnemonic
```

Vectored. This form is a variation of same-page mode with the exception that both the least significant bits and the location containing the most significant bits of the address are specified. The most significant bits are stored in a predefined location specified using the specific value format. The least significant bits are specified as a numeric value. Both are separated by the vertical bar symbol (|). The most significant bits contained in the location specified are combined with the least significant bits, value specified, to form the complete address. Vectored addressing is specified by the letters VA.

```
Format: VA specific_value|numeric_value
Example: JMP VA R2|25   ; most significant bits in reg R2,
                          least significant bits = 25.
         JMPV   R2|25   ; implied by mnemonic
```

Indirect

The indirect type of addressing is used to specify the location in which the actual memory address to be used by the operation is stored. It consists of a specific value or numeric value, as described in Section 5, enclosed within parentheses.

```
Format: (specific_value)
        (numeric_value)
```

Parentheses are always used to indicate some type of indirect or indexed addressing. The location indicated in parenthesis contains the address of the data, not the actual data. A specific value is used to indicate a predefined location, and a numeric value is used to indicate a memory location.

Double parentheses are used to indicate two levels of indirect addressing.

```
Example: ( (DX) )   ; register DX contains the address of a
                      location in memory which contains the
                      actual memory address to be used.
```

The parentheses may be preceded by one of the absolute addressing mode prefixes to specify the type of address contained in the location specified.

```
Example: SP(R2)      ; reg R2 contains the   same   page   address
                       value to be used by the instruction.
         LA(LOC1)    ; location LOC1 contains a'long,  3  byte,
                       address value.
```

Indexed

The Index type is used when the actual memory address is the total of the values contained in one or more registers or memory locations and an optional specified value. The register(s), memory location(s), and/or value to be added are enclosed in parentheses.

```
Format: (XX+YY)                  ; 2 or more registers
        (XX+ numeric_value )     ; 1 register and a single
                                   byte value
        (XX++ numeric_value )    ; 1 register and a double
                                   byte value
```

The specification for each location whose contents are to be added together is separated by a plus sign. The final plus sign(s) indicates whether a single or double byte value is to be added to the total of the value(s) contained in those location(s). The numeric value is separated from the location specifications and the right parentheses by a space to explicitly distinguish it as a numeric value. If the spaces were not included, a one or two character label used to represent the numeric value might be misinterpreted as a predefined location whose content is to be added.

One of the absolute addressing mode prefixes may be used after the final plus sign to indicate special types of numeric values.

```
Example: (R2+SS seg|adr )   ; add contents of reg R2 and the
                              short segmented address value.
```

The locations whose contents are to be added may be specified using indirect addressing.

```
Example: ((PZ x )+R2)   ; the contents of page zero address x
                          and reg r2 are added together.
```

Auto Increment/Decrement

This mode is a special form of indirect and indexed addressing; the content of the location specified is automatically incremented or decremented as part of the computer operation. This is indicated by placing a plus or minus sign outside the parentheses. Placing the plus or minus sign before the left parenthesis indicates pre-auto increment/decrement. Placing the sign after the right parenthesis indicates post auto-increment/decrement. A double plus or minus sign means increment or decrement by two rather than one. Post auto-increment/decrement may be followed by a numeric value by which to increment or decrement the contents of the location specified.

```
Format: +(location)   ; indirect with pre- auto increment
```

```
-(location)      ; indirect with pre- auto decrement
(location)+      ; indirect with post auto increment
(location)-      ; indirect with post auto decrement
+(location+ value )   ; indexed, pre- auto increment
-(location+ value )   ; indexed, pre- auto decrement
(location+ value )+   ; indexed, post auto increment
(location+ value )-   ; indexed, post auto decrement
(location+ value)+amnt ; indexed, post increment
                        location by amnt
```

Where; location is a register or memory location that is incremented or decremented, as defined above.

Example: +(HL+ 45) ; The contents of register HL is first incremented then used to calculate the address of the data.

With double levels of indirect addressing, the location of the plus or minus sign indicates at what level auto increment/decrement will take place and when.

Example: (R(R2)+) ; register R2 is auto post incremented.
(R(R2))- ; the register pointed to by R2 is auto post decremented

SECTION 9: BASIC INSTRUCTION MNEMONICS

Following is a description of the basic instruction mnemonics that are common to most computers. Others will be added to this standard as they are identified. Mnemonics that are peculiar to specific computers or perform a complex function that requires specific knowledge of the computer with which they are used, are not listed.

Each mnemonic is described using the following format:

Mnemonic   Short description   parameters,[optional]

    Detailed description

    SO: secondary operations that augment the operation performed by this basic instruction.   (parameters,[optional])

The parameters normally used with each mnemonic are indicated at the right or following the secondary operation description if different parameters are required. Optional parameters are enclosed in brackets.

The Basic Instruction Mnemonics Table of Appendix A lists the mnemonic clarifying characters and parameters used with each variation of the basic mnemonics. The clarifying characters are defined in the next section

AA   ASCII adjust   [type],var

Adjust the value contained in the location specified to the proper ASCII value. Since math operations are performed on binary data, the result has to be modified if the data is of another type, in this case ASCII. The optional first parameter specifies the type

184

of math operation for which adjustment is being made: addition, subtraction, multiplication, or division.

ABS Absolute value var

The contents of the location specified is converted to an absolute value. A negative value is changed to a positive value; positive values are not effected.

ADC Add with carry srce,dest

Add the value or contents of the location specified by the first parameter to the contents of the location specified by the second parameter together with the carry flag and store the result in the location specified by the second parameter.

ADCF Add carry flag only srce,[dest]

Add the carry flag to the contents of the location specified by the first parameter and store the result in the same location or that specified by the optional second parameter.

ADD Add srce,dest

Add the value or contents of the location specified by the first parameter to the contents of the location specified by the second parameter and store the result in the location specified by the second parameter.

SNC — skip the next instruction if the addition does not result in the carry flag being set.

ADHC Add half carry flag only srce,[dest]

Add the half or auxiliary carry flag to the contents of the location specified by the first parameter and store the result in the same location or that specified by the second parameter.

AND Logical AND srce,dest

Logically AND the value or contents of the location specified by the first parameter with the contents of the location specified by the second parameter. Store the result back in the location specified by the second parameter.

IO — the destination specified is an I/O port.

BOUND Check address within bounds loc,range

The address value specified by the first parameter is checked against the range of permissible values specified by the second parameter. This test is performed to verify that the location is accessible by the program.

BRK   Break

Suspend execution of the program until a predefined operation is complete, or signal an external device that an operation has been completed.

CALL   Call subroutine   [cond],loc

If the condition specified by the first parameter is true, store the address of the next sequential instruction on the stack or other specified location, and go to the address specified by the second parameter. If no condition is specified, unconditional is assumed.

TBL — the second parameter specifies the location of a table that contains the addresses to go to.

CLR   Clear   var

The location specified by the parameter is set equal to zero.

MOV — clear the location specified by the second parameter; then move the contents of the location specified by the first parameter to that location. Normally the destination location is larger than the source.

(srce,dest)

CMP   Compare   srce,var

Compare the value or contents of the location specified by the second parameter against the contents of the location specified by the first parameter. The second parameter is subtracted from the first, setting the flags but not saving the result.

JIF — after performing the compare, if the condition specified is true, go to the location specified.   (srce,cond,var,loc)
JNZ — jump to the location specified by the third parameter if the result is not zero.   (srce,var,loc)
SKP — ater performing the compare, if the condition specified is true, skip the next instruction.   (srce,cond,var)

CNV_____   Convert   var

Convert the contents of the location specified from one type of value to another. Characters must be appended to the mnemonic to specify the type of conversion to be performed.

186

BW	—	byte to word.
WDW	—	word to double word.
DWGW	—	double word to quad word.
ST	—	convert the string of values specified based on the contents of the table specified. (str,tbl,lth-str)
TST	—	convert the values specified and then check for a predefined condition. (srce,var,[cnt])

CPL   Complement   var

Logically complement the contents of the location specified by the parameter and store the result in the same location.

DA   Decimal adjust   [type],loc

Adjust the value contained in the location specified to the proper BCD value. The optional first parameter specifies if this is for an add, subtract, multiply, or divide.

DC   Disable counter/timer

Interrupts and/or operation of the counter/timer are turned off.

DEC   Decrement   var,[cnt]

The contents of the location specified by the first parameter is decremented by one, or amount specified by the second parameter.

JNZ	—	jump to the location specified by the second parameter if the result is not zero. (var,loc)
JIF	—	jump to the location specified if the condition specified is true. (var,cond,loc)
SZ	—	skip the next instruction if the result is zero.
SNZ	—	skip the next instruction if the result is not zero.

DI   Disable interrupts

External interrupts are turned off.

DIV   Divide, unsigned   srce,dest

Divide the contents of the location specified by the second parameter by the value or contents of the location specified by the first parameter and store the result in the location specified by the second parameter. Normally the location specified by the second parameter, the destination, will be twice as large as the source, the first parameter, and will contain both the result and remainder.

EC   Enable counter

Interrupts and/or operation of the counter are turned on.

EI   Enable interrupts

External interrupts are enabled.

ENTER   Enter procedure   var,lth,loc

Store the address of the next sequential instruction on the stack, or other specified location, together with the location and length of the data to be used by the procedure, as specified by the first and second parameters; then go to the address specified by the third parameter.

ESC   Escape to coprocessor   dev,inst,var

The coprocessor specified by the first parameter is requested to execute the procedure specified by the second parameter using data contained in the location specified by the third parameter.

EXEC   Execute instruction at   loc

The single instruction stored in the location specified is executed.

HALT   Halt computer operation

The computer stops executing any more instructions until an interrupt or other external signal is received.

IDIV   Divide, signed integer   srce,dest

Divide the contents of the location specified by the second parameter by the value or contents of the location specified by the first parameter. Store the result and remainder in the location specified by the second parameter. Normally the destination, second parameter, is twice as large as the source.

IMUL   Multiply, signed integer   srce,var,[dest]

Multiply the value or contents of the location specified by the first parameter with the contents of the location specified by the second parameter. Store the result in the location specified by the second parameter, or third parameter if given.

ADD   —   after performing the multiplication add the result to the initial contents of the destination.

IN   Input   port,var

An item of data is received from an external device through the port specified by the first parameter and stored in the location specified by the second parameter.

AD   —   the input port is an analog to digital converter.

INC   Increment   var,[cnt]

The contents of the location specified by the first parameter is incremented by one, or amount specified by the second parameter.

JNZ   —   jump to the location specified by the second parameter if the result is not zero.   (var,loc)

SZ   —   skip the next instruction if the result is zero.

JMP   Jump   [cond],loc

If the condition specified by the first parameter is true, go to the location specified by the second parameter.

CLR   —   if the condition is true, set the location specified by the second parameter equal to zero; then go to the location specified by the third parameter.   (cond,var,loc)

DEC   —   if true, decrement the contents of the location specified by the second parameter.   (cond,var,loc)

MOV   —   if the condition is true, also move the data specified.

LEA   Load effective address   adr,var

The address value specified by the first parameter is stored in the location specified by the second parameter.

LEAVE   Leave procedure

Leave a procedure entered using the ENTER instruction and continue execution.

LOOP   Loop until   cond,[cnt],loc

Jump to the location specified by the second parameter if the the condition specified by the first parameter is not true or for the number of times specified by the optional second parameter.

MOV   Move   srce,dest

Move the value, or contents of the location specified by the first parameter to the location specified by the second parameter.

BW	—	byte to word.
ADD	—	after moving the data, add the value specified.
CLR	—	and set the source location to zero.
DEC	—	decrement the value after being moved.
INC	—	increment the value after being moved.
SUB	—	after moving the data, subtract the value specified.

MUL   Multiply, unsigned   srce,var,[dest]

Multiply the value or contents of the location specified by the first parameter with the contents of the location specified by the second parameter. Store the result in the location specified by the second parameter. Normally the destination, the second parameter, is twice as large as the source.

ADD — add the result of the multiplication to the initial value of the location specified by the second parameter.

NEG   Change sign   var

Change the value contained in the location specified by the parameter to its negative equivalent (or positive equivalent if initially negative). This is equivalent to complementing the value and adding one.

NOP   No operation

The computer performs no operation.

NORM   Normalize   var

The contents of the location specified is shifted to the left, filling the least significant bits with zeros, until the most significant bit is a one.

OR   Logical OR   srce,dest

Logically OR the value or contents of the location specified by the first parameter with the contents of the location specified by the second parameter and store the result in the location specified by the second parameter.

HALT	—	then wait for an interrupt.
IO	—	the destination is an I/O port.

OUT   Output   srce,port

The contents of the location specified by the first parameter is sent to an external device via the port specified by the second parameter.

CLR — then set the source, first parameter location, to zero.

POP   Pop data from the stack   dest

The next data element is removed from the stack and stored in the location specified by the parameter; the stack register is adjusted accordingly.

PUSH   Push data onto the stack   srce

The data element contained in the location specified by the parameter is stored on the stack, and the stack register is adjusted accordingly.

MOV   —   then move the predefined data.

REP   Repeat   [cond],[cnt]

Repeat the following instruction until the condition or for the number of times specified by the parameter.

RES   Reset   var,[bit]

Set the location specified by the parameter to a value of one.

IO   —   reset the I/O port or data contained in the I/O port.

RET   Return from subroutine   [cond],[value]

If the condition specified by the first parameter is true, go to the location specified by the top element on the stack or as contained in another predefined location. If a second parameter is given, stored the value specified on the stack or other predefined location.

I   —   return from interrupt; other predefined values are removed from the stack and stored in the appropriate locations.
NMI   —   return nonmaskable interrupt; other predefined values are removed from the stack and stored in appropriate locations.
ID   —   return with interrupts disabled
IE   —   return with interrupts enabled
MOV   —   return and move predefined data
OFF   —   return to a location offset from the normal location by the amount specified by the second parameter.

RIM   Read interrupt mask   var

Move the contents of the interrupt mask status bits into the location specified. All of the interrupt mask bits may not be initially stored in the same location and need to be combined into a single data item.

RLBCD   Rotate left BCD   var,var,[cnt]

Rotate left the contents of the locations specified by the first and second parameters by the number of BCD digits specified by the third parameter and store the result in the same locations. The locations specified are normally registers.

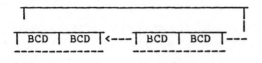

RLNC   Rotate left no carry   var,[cnt]

Rotate left the contents of the location specified by the first parameter for the number of bits specified by the second parameter and store the result in the same location. If there is no second parameter one is assumed.

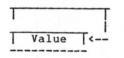

RLTC   Rotate left to carry   var,[cnt]

Rotate left to carry the contents of the location specified by the first parameter for the number of bits specified by the second parameter and store the result in the same location. If there is no second parameter one is assumed.

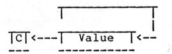

RLWC   Rotate left with carry   var,[cnt]

Rotate left with carry the contents of the location specified by the first parameter for the number of bits specified by the second parameter and store the result in the same location. If there is no second parameter one is assumed.

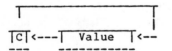

RLWR   Rotate left with register   var,reg,[cnt]

Rotate left the contents of the location specified by the first parameter with the contents of the register specified by the second parameter for the number of bits specified by the third parameter and store the result in the same location and register.

192

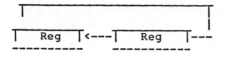

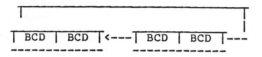

RRBCD   Rotate right BCD   var,var,[cnt]

Rotate right the contents of the locations specified by the first and second parameters by the number of BCD digits specified by the third parameter and store the result in the same locations.

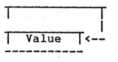

RRNC   Rotate right no carry   var,[cnt]

Rotate right the contents of the location specified by the first parameter for the number of bits specified by the second parameter and store the result in the same location. If there is no second parameter one is assumed.

RRTC   Rotate right to carry   var,[cnt]

Rotate right to carry the contents of the location specified by the first parameter for the number of bits specified by the second parameter and store the result in the same location. If there is no second parameter one is assumed.

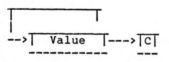

RRWC   Rotate right with carry   var,[cnt]

Rotate right with carry the contents of the location specified by the first parameter for the number of bits specified by the second parameter and store the result in the same location. If there is no second parameter one is assumed.

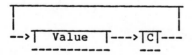

RRWR   Rotate right with register   var,reg,[cnt]

Rotate right the contents of the location specified by the first parameter with the contents of the register specified by the second parameter for the number of bits specified by the third parameter and store the result in the same location and register.

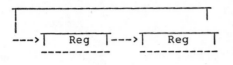

RST   . Restart   [type]

A call to one of several subroutines stored in predefined areas of memory. The parameter specifies which subroutine or predefined location.

SBB   Subtract with borrow   srce,dest

Subtract the value or contents of the location specified by the first parameter, and the carry flag, from the contents of the location specified by the second parameter and store the result in the location specified by the second parameter.

SBCF   Subtract carry flag only   srce,[dest]

Subtract the carry flag only from the location specified by the first parameter and store the result in the same location or the location specified by the second parameter.

SBHC   Subtract half carry only   srce,[dest]

Subtract the half carry flag only from the location specified by the first parameter and store the result in the same location or the location specified by the second parameter.

SCAN   Search for value   str,val,cnt

Starting at the location specified by the first parameter, check the number of elements specified by the third parameter for the value specified by the second parameter.

SEL   Select   opt,[val]

Select the option or operating mode specified by the first and second parameters. The valid values for both parameters depends on the options and modes available.

SET   Set   var,[bit],[val]

Set the location or bit specified by the first parameters to a value of all ones or the value specified by the last parameter.

IF   —   if the condition specified is true.   (cond,var,[bit])

194

IO   —   I/O port or bit.

SHIFTA   Shift arithmetic   var,dir-cnt

Shift arithmetic the contents of the location specified by the first parameter for the number of bits and direction specified by the second parameter and store the result in the same location.

```
 ┌───┬─┐
 │   │
 ──->│ Value │<── 0
     └──────────┘
```

SHIFTL   Shift logical   var,dir-cnt

Shift logical the contents of the location specified by the first parameter for the number of bits and direction specified by the second parameter and store the result in the same location.

```
0 ──>│ Value │<── 0
     └──────────┘
```

SKIP   Skip   cond

If the condition specified is true, skip the next instruction or byte.

CLR   —   and clear the location specified.   (cond,var)

SLA   Shift left arithmetic   var,[cnt]

Shift left arithmetic the contents of the location specified by the first parameter for the number of bits specified by the second parameter and store the result in the same location. If there is no second parameter, one is assumed.

```
│C│<───│ Value │<─── 0
└─┘     └──────────┘
```

SC   —   skip the next instruction if the carry flag is set.

SLEEP   Sleep

The computer is put in a low power mode of operation. Some or all processing is suspended until a predefined condition is met or external signal received.

SLL   Shift left logical   var,[cnt]

Shift left logical the contents of the location specified by the first parameter for the number of bits specified by the second parameter and store the result in the same location. If there is no second parameter, one is assumed.

```
 |C|<---|   Value   |<--- 0
 ---     -----------
```

SRA   Shift right arithmetic   var,[cnt]

Shift right arithmetic the contents of the location specified by the first parameter for the number of bits specified by the second parameter and store the result in the same location. If there is no second parameter one is assumed.

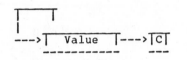

SRL   Shift right logical   var,[cnt]

Shift right logical the contents of the location specified by the first parameter for the number of bits specified by the second parameter and store the result in the same location. If there is no second parameter one is assumed.

```
 0 -->|   Value   |--->|C|
       -----------      ---
```

SC   —   skip the next instruction if the carry flag is set.

START   Start device   dev

The internal or external device specified is started.

STOP   Stop device   dev

The internal or external device specified is stopped.

SUB   Subtract   srce,dest

Subtract the value or contents of the location specified by the second parameter from the contents of the location specified by the first parameter and store the result in the location specified by the second parameter.

IF   —   if the condition specified by the first parameter is true, subtract the contents of the location specified by the second parameter from the third and store the result in the third parameter location.
                                              (cond,srce,dest)

SNC   —   skip the next instruction if the carry flag is reset.

196

SWAP   Swap   var

The contents of the upper and lower portions of the location specified are exchanged.

SWI   Program interrupt   [cond],[type]

If the condition specified by the first parameter is true, a software interrupt of the type specified by the second parameter is performed.

TEST   Logical AND to flags only   srce,[var]

Logically AND the value contained in the location specified by the first parameter with itself or the contents of the location specified by the second parameter. The appropriate flags are set but the value is not stored.

TRAP   Trap   [cond],[type]

If the condition specified by the first parameter is true, perform a software interrupt of the type specified by the second parameter. If no parameters are specified, perform a software interrupt of the default type.

TST____   Test for condition   srce,[var]

Test for a specific condition by performing a logical AND of the value contained in the location(s) specified by the parameters, with itself or other specified data, setting the appropriate flags and performing any additional operations specified. This mnemonic requires that characters be appended to specify the condition or other actions to be performed.

ABR	—	test if all bits specified by the mask, first parameter, are reset in the location specified by the second parameter.
ABS	—	test if all bits specified by the mask, first parameter, are set in the location specified by the second parameter.
AND	—	test the contents of the location specified by the first parameter and then logically AND it with the contents of the location specified by the second parameter saving the result in the location specified by the second parameter.
B	—	test the bit location specified.
BCHG	—	test the bit location specified and complement its value.
BCLR	—	test the bit location specified and set its value to zero.
BSET	—	test the bit location specified and set its value to one.
BSR	—	test the bit location specified and skip if reset.
CLR	—	test the location specified by the first parameter; then set the location to zero.
CHG	—	test the location specified by the first parameter; then change the contents as specified by the other parameters.

CPL	—	test the location specified by the first parameter; then complement the contents of that location.
IO	—	the location specified for testing is an I/O port.
JMP	—	test the value or contents of the location specified by the first parameter against the contents of the location specified by the third parameter for the condition specified by the second parameter and if true, jump to the location specified by the last parameter.
JNZ	—	test the first parameter value with the second parameter or itself, jump to the location specified by the last parameter if the result is not zero. ([val],var,loc)
JZ	—	test the first parameter value with the second parameter or itself, jump to the location specified by the last parameter if the result is zero. ([val],var,loc)
RES	—	test the location specified then reset the location to zero.
FSR	—	if the flag specified is set, skip the next instruction and reset the flag to zero.
SET	—	test the location specified, then set all bits to one.
SKP	—	test the value or contents of the location specified by the first parameter against the contents of the location specified by the third parameter for the condition specified by the second parameter, if true skip the next instruction. (val,cond,var)
SKPC	—	test the location specified by the second parameter, and if the condition specified by the first parameter is true, set all bits of the location to zero. (cond,var)

WAIT   Wait

The CPU temporarily stops executing any more instructions until a signal is received from a coprocessor indicating that the coprocessor has completed the last request.

XCHG   Exchange   var,var

The values contained in the locations specified by the first and second parameters are exchanged.

XOR   Logical exclusive OR   srce,dest

Logically Exclusive OR the contents of the location specified by the second parameter with the value or contents of the location specified by the second parameter and store the result in the location specified by the second parameter.

IO   — the destination is an I/O port.

SECTION 10: CLARIFYING CHARACTERS
The following is a description of the clarifying characters that may be appended

to the basic mnemonics defined in Section 7. The Basic Instruction Mnemonics Table, Appendix B, indicates which clarifying character strings are normally used with each of the basic mnemonics.

A   All, all possible source/destination locations are processed.

B   Bit, the operation is performed on a single bit of data.

BCD   Binary coded decimal, the operation is performed on a binary coded decimal string.

BS   Bit string, the data processed by this operation is in the form of a bit string.

C   Code segment, the location specified as a source or destination is located in the program code area of memory.

D   Displacement, the memory location specified is appended to the machine code as a displacement value.

DW   Double word, the operation is performed on a double word (four bytes) of data.

EA   Effective address, the data processed by this operation is the address of the location specified by the parameter, not the contents of that location.

F   Flag, the operation is performed on a single bit flag, normally part of the status register.

FP   Floating point, the operation is performed on a floating point real number.

L   Long, the machine code or data contains an extra byte.

LL   Double long, the machine code or data contains two extra bytes.

MB   Multiple bytes, the operation is performed on the number of bytes specified by the last parameter.

MW   Multiple words, the operation is performed on the number of words specified by the last parameter.

N   Nibble, the operation is performed on a nibble or four bits, of data.

OS   Other segment, used with instructions that change the instruction address register to indicate that the program segment register and program counter are changed.

QW   Quad word, the operation is performed on four words, or eight bytes, of data.

R   Relative, the memory location specified by the parameter is appended to the machine code as a relative address value.

RL   Relative long, the memory location specified is appended to the machine code as an 11-bit relative address value.

RS   Relative short, the memory location specified is appended to the machine code as a 6-bit relative address value.

S   String, the operation is performed on a string (multiple bytes) of data, but executed only for one byte.

SP   Same page, the memory location specified by the parameter is appended to the machine code using the same page addressing mode.

SR   String repeat, the operation is performed on a string (multiple bytes) of data for the number of bytes indicated.

SW   Shifted word, the source data is shifted the specified number of bits before being applied to the destination.

W   Word, the operation is performed on a word (two bytes) of data.

WS   Word string, the operation is performed on a string (multiple words) of data, but executed for only one word.

WSR   Word string repeat, the operation is performed on multiple words, a string, of data for the number of words indicated.

X   External memory, the location specified as the destination or source is located in external memory.

:   This symbol is used to indicate that processor unique or optional clarifying characters are appended to this mnemonic. Check the instruction set listings in the appendix for a description.

Note: Unless otherwise specified, a byte type operation is assumed.

SECTION 11: CONDITIONAL EXPRESSIONS

The following is a list of the conditional expressions used with most instructions. Others are permitted to test for special conditions or flags unique to a particular computer.

Abreviation	Flags Checked	Meaning
AZ		Amount zero, both values equal zero
ANZ		Amount not zero, both values not equal zero
BS		Bit set
BR		Bit reset
C	$C = 1$	Carry set, binary less than
EQ	$Z = 1$	CMP - binary equal
F		False
GE	$C = 0$	CMP - binary value, greater than or equal
GE	$Z = 1$ or $C = 0$	CMP - binary value, greater than or equal
GEZ		VAL - greater than or equal zero
GT	$C \& Z = 0$	CMP - binary value, greater than
GZ		VAL - greater than zero
H		CHAR - high
HC	$HC = 1$	Half carry flag set
HS		CHAR - high or same
ID		Interrupts disabled
IE		Interrupts enabled
L		CHAR - low
LE	C or $Z = 1$	CMP - binary value, less than or equal
LEZ	$S = 1 \& Z = 1$	VAL - less than or equal zero
LS		CHAR - low or same
LT	$C = 1$	CMP - binary value, less than
LZ		VAL - less than zero
M	$S = 1$	VAL - minus
MZ		VAL - minus or zero
NC	$C = 0$	Carry reset, binary greater than or equal

NE	Z=0	CMP - not equal
NHC	HC = 0	Half carry flag reset
NS	S = 0	The sign flag is reset, binary plus
NV	V = 0	The overflow flag is reset.
NZ	Z=0	VAL - not equal zero
N___		Condition not true
P	S = 0	VAL - positive
PE	P = 1	Even parity
PL		VAL - plus
PO	P = 1	Odd parity
PZ		VAL - plus or zero
S	S = 1	The sign flag is set
SGE	S XOR V = 0 or Z = 1	CMP - signed value, greater than or equal
SGT	(S XOR V) = 0 and Z = 0	CMP - signed value, greater than
SLE	S XOR V = 1 or Z = 1	CMP - signed value, less than or equal
SLT	S XOR V = 1	CMP - signed value, less than
T		True
T___		Condition true
UN		Unconditionally
V	V = 1	The overflow flag is set
Z	Z=1	VAL - equal zero, CMP - binary equal

Note: Not all computers will check for a particular condition using the same flags or in the same manner. Also, the meaning of a particular condition may vary depending on the procedure in which it is used.

If you are checking the result of a compare, the first value (parameter) is compared to the second value (parameter).

If no condition is specified, unconditional is the default.

SECTION 12: MACHINE INDEPENDENT PROCEDURAL INSTRUCTIONS

The following is a description of those machine independent procedural type assembly-language instructions that have been defined. Others will be added as they are identified. Although some of these procedures are implemented as a single instruction on some computers, they normally require a sequence of instructions. The assembler should be set up to convert these instructions into the appropriate sequence of machine-code instructions for the computer being programmed.

Each is described using the same format as for the basic mnemonics in Section 7. The applicable clarifying characters for each are enclosed in parenthesis after the mnemonic.

ADDV (B,W)   Add value to variable   val,var

Add the value specified by the first parameter to the contents of the memory location specified by the second parameter.

ADDVV (B,W)   Add variable to variable   var,var

Add the contents of the memory location specified by the first parameter to the contents of the memory location specified by the second parameter and store the result in the second location.

DECJMPV (B,W)   Decrement variable, jump if   var,cond,loc

Decrement the contents of the memory location specified by the first parameter; if the condition specified by the second parameter is true, go to the location specified by the third parameter.

FILL (B,W,S)   Fill variable with value   var,[cnt],val

Fill the memory location specified by the first parameter with the value given in the last parameter. If all elements of a string are to be filled with the value, the number of elements is given in the second parameter.

INCV (B,W)   Increment variable   var

Increment the contents of the memory location specified by the parameter.

JMPIFV (B,W,S)   Jump if variable   var,[cnt],cond,val,loc

The contents of the memory location specified by the first parameter is compared against the value specified by the last – 1 parameter, and if the condition specified by the last – 2 parameter is met go to the location specified by the last parameter. If all elements of a string are to be compared, the second parameter indicates the number of elements.

JMPTBL   Jump via table   tbl,var

The first parameter specifies the location of a table, or list, of address values. The second parameter specifies the location of a variable containing the desired table entry number. Go to the address contained in the table entry specified by the variable.

MOVV (B,W,S)   Move variable to variable   var,var,[cnt]

Move the contents of the memory location specified by the first parameter to the memory location specified by the second parameter. If all elements of a string are to be moved, the third parameter contains the number of elements.

POPA   Pop all registers

Pop all or all significant register values from the stack.

PUSHA   Push all registers

Push all or all significant registers onto the stack.

RETERR   Return error

This instruction is intended for use with external subroutine instructions in which the last parameter is the location to return to if an error condition exists. If there is an error, the subroutine will return to the indicated address.

RETGD   Return good

This instruction is intended for use with external subroutine instructions in which the last parameter is the location to return to if an error condition exists. If there is no error, the subroutine will return to the next instruction following the macro instruction that invoked the subroutine.

REVHL   Reverse 4 bits

The most significant four bits of the accumulator are exchanged with the least significant four bits. This is the same as executing a rotate instruction four times.

STOP   Exit program

This instruction is used to exit a program and return to the operating system.

SUBV (B,W)   Subtract value from
variable   val,var

The value specified in the first parameter is subtracted from the memory location specified by the second parameter; the result is stored in the second parameter location.

SYSTEM   Call to operating system   func,val

This instruction is used to execute operating system functions. The first parameter specifies the function to be executed, and the second parameter, a value to be passed to the system. If more than one value is required, additional parameters can be used.

SECTION 13: ASSEMBLER COMMANDS

Following is a description of the assembler commands used to control the assembly process, designate the type of program and output to be generated, and define data items used in the program.

The commands are defined in groups according to the function they perform.

Type of Program
Memory Location of Assembled Code
Define Data or Labels
Assembly Control
Macro Definition
Listings

Each command is described using the following format:

mnemonic description of what the command does

        Format: label mnemonic parameters

                                      └ required and optional.

            └ if a label is not indicated, none is permitted.

        Ex: example included if necessary

Type of Program

These commands indicate the type of program being assembled and the type of machine code file to be generated. If used, they must be among the first commands in the source file; only comment lines may precede them. If none are used, an executable program is assumed, and a memory image load module file is produced.

HEX   Indicates that when assembling this program a .HEX compatible load module file will be produced.

        Format: HEX

MAIN   Indicates that this is the main segment of a program which is separated into overlay segments. The load map must be saved in a file using the source file name and .TBL extension so it can be used when assembling the overlay segments.

        Format: MAIN

SGMT   Indicates that the program being assembled is an overlay segment. An overlay formatted load module file, .OLY, will be produced. The Load Map file designated by the parameter, which was generated when the main segment was assembled, is read into the current Label Table so that common data and routines can be referenced. The main program segment, of which this overlay segment is a part, must be assembled first.

```
Format: SGMT   prog-name
                 |
                 -- previously assembled main segment
```

SUBR Indicates that this source file is an external subroutine that defines the indicated external subroutine instruction (ESI) and that a relocatable load module (.RLM) will be produced. One SUBR command is used for each ESI defined by the source file, all of which are placed in the same relocatable load module. The same label used with this command must be used to identify the first executable instruction of the subroutine, or entry point. The parameters specify the number and type of parameters which must be given as part of the external subroutine instruction. Up to eight may be specified.

```
Format: label SUBR p1,p2,p3,p4,p5,p6,p7,p8
```

```
where: label  - macro instruction mnemonic
       p1 - p8 - are the parameter specifiers
                 SB    - single-byte value
                 DB    - double-byte value
                 ADR   - absolute address value
                 ASCII - ASCII string, location and length
```

```
Ex: XXX SUBR ADR,SB
      {        }
      }        {
    XXX   subroutine code
      {        }
```

Defines the external subroutine instruction XXX, which requires two parameters, a memory address, and a single byte value.

Memory Location of the Assembled Code

These commands specify the starting address of the machine code and data for the program being assembled. These commands are not permitted with a relocatable external subroutine, since they must start at location 0. Each command may be used anywhere in a program as many times as required, provided the address values specified increase. If omitted, default values are assumed.

ORG   Specifies the starting address of the program, or address where the next instruction or data item is to be stored.

```
Format: ORG   adr-value
```

ORGD Specifies the starting address of the data portion of the program, or the address of the next item to be stored in the data segment. This command is only meaningful if the code and data are to be separated into different areas, or segments, of memory.

Format: `ORGD  address-value`

ORGCS Specifies the location of the code area, or segment, within physical memory.

Format: `ORGCS  address-value`

ORGDS Specifies the location of the data area, or segment, within physical memory.

Format: `ORGDS  address-value`

Define Data or Labels

These commands define data items (labels) to be used in the program. Unless otherwise stated, these commands can be used anywhere in a program, as many times as required.

COMM Indicates that the labels listed as parameters may be referenced by other program segments or external subroutines. For external relocatable subroutines, these labels are listed in the RLM header records as common data entry points. If this command is used, it must follow the type of program commands or be the first command. Each label specified must be defined within the program.

```
Format: COMM  labels
Ex:     COMM  Vall,VAL2
              {        }
              }        {
      VAL1 DB   xx
           {        {
      VAL2 DS   yy
           {        {
```

VAL1 and VAL2 may be referenced by an external subroutine or overlay.

DB Defines a series of single-byte data items. Any number of parameters may be given, each representing a one byte value in memory. If a parameter is enclosed in quotes, it represents an ASCII character string with a maximum of 74 characters, one byte per character not including the quotes.

```
Format: label  DB  parameters

Ex: DB  23      ; a single byte of vale 23
    DB  0,5,14  ; three consecutive bytes of value 0, 5 & 14
    DB  'Test'  ; four  consecutive  bytes  containing   the
                  ASCII values for 'T', 'e', 's' and 't'.
```

DW Defines a series of double-byte (word) data items. Any number of parameters may be given, each representing a double-byte value in memory. If a parameter is enclosed in quotes, it represents an ASCII string with a maximum of two characters; the first character is placed in the first byte, the second character in the second byte.

```
Format: label DW  parameters
Ex: DW 512      ; a single double byte value of 512.
    DW 600,0,410 ; three consecutive double  byte  values
                   of 600, 0, and 410.
    DW 'TE'     ; a single double byte value, the  first
                  byte contains 'T' and the second 'E'.
```

DDW   Defines a series of double-word (32-bit) data items. Any number of parameters may be given, each representing a double-word value in memory. If a parameter is enclosed in quotes, it represents an ASCII string with a maximum of four characters. The first character is placed in the first byte, the second character in the second byte.

```
Format: label DDW  parameters
Ex: DDW 512      ; a single double word value of 512.
    DDW 600,0,410 ; three consecutive double  word values
                    of 600, 0, and 410.
    DDW 'STOP'   ; a single double word value, the first
                   byte contains 'S' and the last 'P'.
```

DS   Defines an area of memory within the program to be reserved for storing data. The parameter indicates the amount of memory, in bytes, to be reserved. The reserved area of memory is filled with zeroes. If a large amount of memory is required, it is best to designate an area of memory outside the program so the Executable Load Module will be smaller. This is done using the EQU command and checking the load map for the start address of an available area of memory.

```
Format: label  DS  bytes
Ex:        {  }
    XXX  DS  30  ; reserves 30 bytes of memory referenced
         }  {    ; by the label  XXX.
```

EQU   Specifies that the indicated label should be assigned the value represented by the parameter. Although this command can be used anywhere within a program, it should only be used as part of the header. All labels are equated to double-word values; they can, however, be used to represent a single- or double-byte value.

```
Format: label  EQU  value
Ex:        {   }
    XXX  EQU  40  ; the label XXX is assigned the value 40.
         }   {
```

EXT   Indicates that the label specified is defined in another program or external subroutine. The parameter indicates where the label is defined.

If you are dealing with an external subroutine and the parameter is 'PROG', the label is defined in the program that uses the subroutine. Otherwise, the parameter must be a valid ESI mnemonic that is used to identify the subroutine in which the label is defined.

If you are using an overlay segment, this command is not required for labels defined in the main segment.

This command, if used, must be placed before any instructions or commands that generate machine code. One command is used for each externally defined label. If several externally defined labels are defined in the same external subroutine, the LOAD command can be used to reference all the labels.

```
Format:   label EXT  where-defined
Ex: YYY   SUBR                    XXX   EXT   WWW
      {   }
    XXX   EXT   PROG
      }   {
```

The label XXX must be defined in the program where the subroutine is used, as below.

The label XXX is defined in the subroutine WWW, as below.

```
  {    }
COMM   XXX
  }    {
XXX  inst
  {    }
```

```
WWW    SUBR
  {    }
     COMM   XXX
  }    {
XXX  inst
```

LBL-
TBL   Specifies that the previously generated Label Table or Load Map stored in the file indicated by the parameter should be loaded into the current Label Table before assembling the program. This command is intended for use with programs or computers that contain common predefined memory locations to eliminate having to redefine the locations in each program.

Format: `LBLTBL  file-name`

LOAD   Specifies that the RLM for the external subroutine instruction specified by the parameter contains common data items to be used by this program or subroutine. The RLM is located, and all data entry points are added to the Label Table as externally defined. This command, if used, must be before any instructions or commands that generate machine code. One command is used for each RLM to be loaded. This command is used in place of the EXT command when a single RLM has several common data items that are to be used.

Format: `LOAD macro-inst-mnemonic`

Ex: `Subroutine XXX defines the common labels YYY and ZZZ.`

```
XXX  SUBR
 {    }
COMM  YYY,ZZZ
```

A program can reference the common data items YYY and ZZZ by;

```
 {    }                   YYY  EXT  XXX
LOAD  XXX      or         ZZZ  EXT  XXX
 }    {                    {    }
```

S.N.   Defines an 8-byte block of data into which is stored a serial number using some form of coding algorithm.

Format: `S.N.`

USER   This command allows the operator to enter text data into the program as it is being assembled. It is intended for use in programs where each copy or version contains a different text message. Rather than edit the source file each time to change the message, the USER command allows the operator to enter the text of the message when the program is assembled. The parameter specifies the maximum number of text characters that may be entered. If the actual number of characters entered is less, the remaining characters are filled with spaces.

Format: `USER  max-number-characters`
Ex:
```
 {    }
USER  8   ; during the second  pass  the operator  is
 }    {      requested to enter 8 characters of text.
```

Assembly Control

These commands are used to control the assembly process.

DMOC   Defines a message to be displayed on the console during the first or second pass through the assembly process. The first parameter indicates which pass (1 or 2). The second parameter is the message to be displayed. No quotes are required; the message is assumed to be everything after the comma following the first parameter. This command is intended to be used in conjunction with the USER command to prompt the operator as to what text should be entered.

Format: `DMOC pass, message`
Ex: `DMOC 1,message ; the message is displayed on the console`
`                      during the first pass.`

END   Indicates the end of the source code file. This command must be the last line of the source file to be assembled. Anything in the source file after this command will be ignored during the assembly process.

```
Format: END
Ex: {      }
      END         ; end of the code to be assembled.
      }    {      ; rest of source file is not assembled.
```

IF   Indicates the start of a conditionally assembled portion of the program source file. The conditional expression represented by the parameters is evaluated. If the expression is not true, all source code following this command, until the associated NOIF command, will be excluded from the current assembly of this program. If the condition is true, the source code following this command is included.

    The conditional expression consists of three parameters; The first and third parameters specify the values to be compared. The second parameter represents the relationship that the first parameter value must have in respect to the third parameter value.

```
Format: IF   value,condition,value
where condition is: =  equal       >  greater than
                    ~  not equal   <  less than
Ex: {     }
      IF   Y  ~  Q
      }       {  --
      {       }     | -- If Y is not equal Q, the enclosed source
      }       {  --    file lines are included in the assembly.
      NOIF             If Y is equal Q, they are not included.
      {     }
```

NOIF   Indicates the end of a conditionally assembled portion of the program source file. This command must be used in conjunction with the IF command.

```
Format: NOIF
Ex: See IF above
```

INSERT   The contents of the source file specified by the parameter should be inserted into the program being assembled at this point. This command is intended for use when the same sequence of code or defined data is required in several different programs. Rather than actually include the required instructions and commands in each source file, they are saved in a separate file. In this way only one file has to be edited if the common section of a program is changed, rather than each individual file. Every line of the file to be inserted is assembled as if it were a part of the program being assembled.

```
Format: INSERT   file-name
Ex: {      }               --
      }    {               | File XXX.MLS is inserted at
      INSERT   XXX   <--  this point and assembled as
```

{   } | part of the program.
                        --

STRTD   Indicates that the code generated by the following instructions and com-
            mands will be placed in the data area. The area of memory to be used for
            the data is specified by the ORGD command. If used with a program gener-
            ating a memory image executable load module, blank data will be inserted
            between the end of the code area and beginning of the data area.

Format: STRTD
Ex: | {   }
                        <-|--   }   {
placed in   STRTD
code area   '   {   }   --|-->   placed in
                            }   {   --| data area
                            ENDD
                        <-|--   {   }
                            |

ENDD   Indicates the end of that portion of the program to be placed in the data
            area. This command must be preceded by the STRTD command. All in-
            structions and commands following this command up to the next STRTD
            command will be assembled into the code area.

Format: ENDD
Ex: See the STRTD command above

Macro Definition

The following commands are used to define macro instruction.

DEFM   Identifies the macro instruction to be defined and parameter that may be
            specified as part of the macro instruction. The label specifies the mnemonic
            for this macro instruction. The parameters identify dummy labels that are
            replaced with the values given as parameters when the macro instruction
            is used. All instructions and commands following this command up to the
            ENDM command are part of the macro definition. Dummy labels should
            start with the less than sign, <, for easy identification. Local labels that
            are replaced by assembler generated labels should start with a percent sign,
            %, for identification.

Format: macro-instruction-mnemonic DEFM   dummy-labels
Ex: >SQUARE DEFM <SRCE,<DEST   ; defines the macro   square
    ;   requiring two parameters.
            MOVW <SRCE,AX
            MULW AX,AX
            MOVW AX,<DEST
            ENDM
    ;
        >SQUARE   AMT,SQAMT   ; square contents of AMT and
                               store result in SQAMT

ENDM Indicates the end of a macro instruction definition. This command must be used in conjunction with the DEFM command.

Format: `ENDM`

Listings

These commands do not affect the assembly process. They are only used by the utility routines.

NAME Specifies the name or title that should appear on all output listings associated with this source file. The title specified by the parameter must be 50 characters or less. Although this command may be used anywhere in the program, it should be one of the first lines in the source file. This is the only command that may precede the type of program commands.

Format: `NAME    'title'`

SKIP This command indicates a skip to top of next page on the assembled program listing. It is used to separate sections of the program for easy identification.

Format: `SKIP`

TEXT
URMT These two commands are used to indicate the comment lines in the header of the source file that are to be used for documentation. The parameter specifies the category or section title to be used when combining these comment lines with those from other programs. These commands should only be used as part of the header, and each can be used only once.

Format: `TEXT 'category'`
`       URMT 'category'`
Ex: See the documentation part of Section 4.

SECTION 14: EXTERNAL SUBROUTINE INSTRUCTIONS

External subroutine instructions are used to access previously written external subroutines that perform commonly used functions or procedures. When used, these instructions are converted by the assembler to a call subroutine instruction followed by the parameters (data) to be used by the subroutine.

```
Example: ^CNSLO TEXT,LTH   ; output message to the console
equivalent code: CALL    ^CNSLO   ; call subroutine
                 DW      TEXT     ; define word
                 DB      LTH      ; define byte
```

The machine code for each subroutine is contained in a relocatable load module

(RLM), which is automatically relocated and appended to the program executable load module as part of the assembly process. Each RLM may contain more then one subroutine, and each subroutine may have more than one entry point. Groups of related RLM are saved in a library file.

The ESI mnemonic, representing the entry point into a subroutine, should be a descriptive abbreviation of the procedure being performed. When possible, a combination of the basic mnemonics (Section 7) and clarifying characters (Section 8) as defined for AL instructions should be used. To help distinguish an ESI from other AL instructions and commands, the first character of the mnemonic should be an up-arrow (^).

External Subroutine Instructions are primarily user defined. An ESI can be defined for any procedure that can be written as an external subroutine. Described in this section are a group of ESI that perform commonly used procedures. Others will be added as they are identified. Including a set of predefined ESI as part of this standard will help maintain a certain degree of compatibility. Each is described using the same format as for the basic AL instructions. The instructions are described in groups based on the type of procedure they perform.

Console I/O	Operator input
Data conversions	Printer I/O
Disk I/O	Reports and displays
Formatting data	Table processing

Console I/O

These instructions perform basic console input/output functions.

CNSLI   Console input   buf,m__lth,L__adr

Input a line of text from the console. Store the text in the buffer specified by the first parameter and the number of characters input in the location specified by the third parameter. The second parameter specifies the maximum number of characters to be entered.

CNSLO   Console output   text,lth

Output a line of text to the console. The first parameter specifies the location of the text and the second parameter the number of characters. Output stops at the number of characters specified or when a zero byte is detected.

CNSLCL   Console output w/CR-LF   text,lth

Same as CNSLO above except a carriage return/line feed is appended to the end of the text.

CLEAR   Clear screen

Clear the screen and return the cursor to the upper left corner of the screen.

Data Conversions

These instructions convert data from one format to another.

ATOI   ASCII to integer   buf,lth,var,err

Convert an integer character string into a double-byte signed binary value.

ITOA   Integer to ASCII   var,buf,m__lth,
                                                        l__adr,err

Convert a double-byte signed binary value into an integer character string.

BTOA   Binary to ASCII   var,buf

Convert a single-byte binary value into a binary character string of eight characters.

ATOB   ASCII to binary   buf,lth,var,err

Convert a binary character string into a single-byte binary value.

HTOA   Hex to ASCII   var,bytes,buf

Convert a one or two byte binary value into a hexadecimal character string of two or four characters.

ATOH   ASCII to Hex   buf,lth,var,bytes,err

Convert a hexadecimal character string into a one or two byte binary value.

OTOA   Octal to ASCII   var,buf

Convert a single-byte binary value into an octal character string of three characters.

ATOO   ASCII to Octal   buf,lth,var,err

Convert an octal character string into a single-byte binary value.

ATON   ASCII to numeric   buf,lth,var,err

Convert an integer character string into a single-byte binary value.

NTOA   Numeric to ASCII   var,buf

Convert a single-byte signed binary value into an integer character string.

UNTOA   Unsigned numeric to ASCII   var,buf

Convert a single-byte unsigned binary value into an integer character string.

BCDTOA   BCD to ASCII   var,bytes,buf

Convert a binary-coded-decimal value of the indicated number of bytes into an integer character string. The maximum length of the character string is twice the number of bytes.

ATOBCD   ASCII to BCD   buf,lth,var,bytes,
                                                     err

Convert an integer character string into a binary-coded-decimal value of the number of bytes indicated.

FNDTS   ASCII to File name   buf,lth,var,err

Convert a file name from displayable to storable format.

FNSTD   File name to ASCII   var,buf

Convert a file name from its stored format to a displayable ASCII string.

Disk I/O

The following operations perform disk input/output operations.

OPEN   Open file   fcb,new,err

Prepare the file indicated in the file control block specified by the first parameter for input/output operations. If a new file is created, go to the address specified by the second parameter.

CLOSE   Close file   fcb,err

Close the file indicated in the FCB and update the disk directory.

DELETE   Delete file   fcb,err

Delete the file indicated in the FCB from the disk.

RDREC   Read a record   fcb,buf,m-lth,L_adr,
                                                     end,err

Read the next logical record from the file indicated in the FCB into the buffer specified. The end of a logical record is indicated by a carriage return/line feed.

WTREC   Write a record   fcb,buf,lth,err

A carriage return/line feed is appended to the data contained in the buffer, and the logical record written to the file indicated in the FCB.

RRAF   Read random access file   fcb,num,err

Read the random access record specified by the second parameter from the file indicated in the FCB into memory at the location specified in the FCB.

WTRAF   Write random access file   fcb,num,err

Write the random access record specified by the second parameter to the file indicated in the FCB from memory starting at the location specified in the FCB.

RNSPR   Read next physical record   fcb,err

Read the next sequential physical or random access record of the file indicated in the FCB into memory starting at the location specified in the FCB.

OVLYRD   Overlay read   f__name,c__adr,
                                              blks,d__adr,blks,
                                              err

Store the code and data contained in the file specified by the first parameter into memory starting at the addresses indicated by the second and fourth parameters. If the file contains more data or code than the number of 128 byte blocks indicated by the third and fifth parameters, go to the error address indicated by the last parameter.

OVLYWT   Overlay write   f__name,c__adr,
                                              blks,d__adr,blks,
                                              err

Write the number of 128 byte blocks of data and code specified starting at the addresses specified into the overlay file specified.

TBLRD   Table read   f__name,table,err

Store the table contained in the file indicated by the first parameter at the address specified by the second parameter.

TBLWT   Table write   f__name,table,err

216

Write the table located at the address specified by the second parameter into the file specified by the first parameter.

Formatting

FORMAT   Format data for output   frmt,buf,loc,err

Data stored at the location specified by the third parameter is formatted in accordance with the format specification string located at the address specified by the first parameter and stored in the buffer indicated by the second parameter. The format specification string contains a combination of ASCII text and variable fields. A variable field is indicated using a five byte variable field specifier as follows:

VARIABLE FIELD SPECIFIER:

1 BYTE	FFH variable field indicator.
1 BYTE	Number of characters in the variable field.
2 BYTES	Actual address or relative location of the variable with respect to the location specified in the instruction.
1 BYTE	Type of conversion (negative if relative loc).

CONVERSION TYPES:

1	=	Single-byte numeric, right justified
2	=	Single-byte numeric, left justified
3	=	Unsigned single-byte numeric, right justified
4	=	Unsigned single-byte numeric, left justified
5	=	Double-byte integer, right justified
6	=	Double-byte integer, left justified
7	=	Single-byte Hex value
8	=	Double-byte Hex value
9	=	Logical, 1 = Yes 0 = No
10	=	File Name
11	=	ASCII String, No Conversion
12	=	Fill variable field with character in third byte
20-29	=	Special external procedures

Operator Input

These instructions request, accept, and process data input by the operator.

GETCMD   Get command line   prmpt,help,buf,m__
                                             lth,none

Display the prompt message specified by the first parameter and store the line of text, consisting of multiple data items input by the operator, at the location specified by the third parameter. If a question mark (?) is entered, display the help message specified by the second parameter. If no data is input, go to the location specified by the last parameter.

PRGCMD   Get program parameters   none

Get the parameters input as part of the program execution command line and prepare it for processing by the CMDPAR, CMDVAL CMDNXT instructions.

CMDPAR   Extract parameter   tbl,err

Extract the next element in the operator input command line (GETCMD) or program execution command line (PRGCMD), find out if it is a parameter indicator (first character a colon ':'), and compare the second character against those codes listed in the table specified by the first parameter. If it is in the table, go to the address indicated in the table for that code. If it is not in the table, the next element is not a parameter, or there are no more parameters, go to the address specified by the second parameter.

TABLE: 1 byte = Parameter Code Character
       2 bytes = Routine Address

CMDVAL   Extract value   type,var,err,none

Extract the next element in the operator input or program execution command line, convert it to the type of value indicated, and store the value in the location specified. If a conversion error is detected or there are no more parameters, go to the location specified.

TYPE: 1 = File Name
      2 = Single-byte Numeric
      3 = Single-byte Hex
      4 = Double-byte Hex
      5 = Jump to specific routine via a table
     −N = ASCII String of N characters

CMDNXT   Extract next element   none

Extract the next element in the operator input or program execution command line. Save the address of the first character, last character and number of characters in the common variables CMDFST, CMDLST and CMDLTH. If there are no more elements, go to the location specified.

INPUT   Get operator input   prmpt,type,var,

Prompt the operator to input the type of value specified, convert it into the proper format, and store it in the location specified. If nothing is input, go to the location specified by the last parameter.

INPUT-TYPE: 1 = File name
                2 = Single-byte Numeric
                3 = Double-byte Integer
                4 = Single-byte Hex
                5 = Double-byte Hex
          -N = ASCII string of N characters

GETYN   Get yes/no response   prmpt,if_yes

Prompt the operator to respond with a yes or no. If yes is entered, go to the location specified.

GETREQ   Get operator request   prmpt,tbl,help

Prompt the operator to select one of several possible options and go to the address specified in the table for that option. If a question mark is entered, output the help display. If nothing is input return to the next instruction.

TABLE: 1 byte - Selection char, last entry = 0
           2 bytes - Routine address

Printer I/O

Theses instructions are used for printing data. They are intended to be used as a group and interact with each other. The end of a print line is indicated by a zero byte; the end of multiple lines, by two zero bytes.

PRINT   Print a line   text,lth

Print a single line of text. Printing stops when a zero byte is detected or the number of characters specified is printed.

PRTHDR   Print header   text

Print the multiple line header specified by the parameter at the top of the next page.

PRTTR   Print trailer   text

Print the multiple line trailer specified by the parameter at the bottom of the current page.

PRTDHT   Specify header/trailer   header,trailer,page-#

Specify the header and trailer to be automatically printed at the top and bottom of each page and the location of the page number to be automatically incremented. The first and second parameters specify the address of a multiple line header and trailer. The third parameter specifies the location in the header or trailer of the page number.

PRTCTL   Define printer variables   loc

Set the value of control variables to be used in printing data.

CONTROL VARIABLES: LPP - lines between pages
                       LBP - lines per page
                       TOF - top of form control sequence
                       CR-LF - use both or CR only flag

PRTSKP   Skip lines   num

Skip the specified number of lines.

Reports/Displays

These instructions are used to display or print multiple lines of text and data on the console or printer. The end of each line to be displayed or printed is indicated by a zero byte; the end of the multiple line buffer is indicated by two zero bytes.

DSPML   Display multiple lines   text

Display multiple lines of text on the console.

DSPRPT   Display report   frmt,loc,offset,repeat,err

Using the format specified by the first parameter, display the data starting at the address specified by the second parameter. Then advance the data location by the amount specified by the third parameter and repeat the procedure the number of times indicated by the fourth parameter. See the FORMAT instruction for details on how to format the data.

DSPFML   Display formatted m/lines   frmt,loc,err

Using the format specified, display the data stored at the location specified as a multiple line display.

PRTFML   Print lines w/formatting   frmt,loc,err

Same as DSPFML above except the data is output to the printer.

| **PRTRPT** | Print report | frmt,loc,off-
set,repeat,err |

Same as DSPRPT above except the data is output to the printer.

Table Functions

These instructions are used when processing tables of data. They are intended to be used as a group and interact with each other. One possible way to define a table is:

```
TABLE FORMAT:       DB 0 ; Maximum number of entries (255 MAX)
                    DW 0 ; Address next new entry
                    DW 0 ; Address entry last found by STFE
                    DB 0 ; Number entries not searched by STFE
                    DB 0 ; Number entries (255 MAX)
                    DB 0 ; Bytes / Entry (255 MAX)
              TBL DS N ; N= Bytes/Entry * Max-#-Entries
```

| **TBLDEL** | Delete entry | tbl |

Delete the entry last found by the STFE instruction.

| **TBLADD** | Append entry | loc,tbl,err |

Add the data stored at the location specified by the first parameter to the end of the table as a new entry.

| **STFE** | Search for entry | loc,bytes,tbl,
offset,none |

Search the indicated table for an entry containing the desired data. Each entry starting at the byte position indicated by the fourth parameter is compared against the data contained in the location specified by the first parameter for the number of bytes specified by the second parameter. If a match is found, the entry location is saved for use by the other table-related instructions.

| **TBLCHG** | Change entry | loc,tbl |

Change the entry last found by the STFE instruction to the data stored in the location specified.

| **TBLINS** | insert entry | loc,tbl,err |

Insert the data stored in the location specified by the first parameter as a new entry before the entry last found by the STFE instruction.

Appendix B

Basic Instruction
Mnemonics Table

```
-- Basic mnemonic
 |   -- Secondary operation
 |    |    -- Clarifying characters
 |    |     |           Description                    Parameters
 --  ---  ------        -----------                    ----------
```

Basic mnemonic	Secondary operation	Clarifying characters	Description	Parameters
AA			ASCII adjust	[type],loc
ABS	W		Absolute value	var
ADC	W		Add, with carry	srce,dest
ADCF			carry flag only	var,[dest]
ADD	B,W,		Add,	srce,dest
	FP,:			
	SW,QW			
	BCD			srce,dest,[cnt]
SNC	W		then skip if no carry	srce,dest
ADHC			Add half carry flag only	var,[dest]
AND	W,SW,N		Logical AND,	srce,dest
IO	B,W		to I/O port	srce,port
BOUND			Check address within boundary	loc,range
BRK			Break	
CALL	R,D,OS		Call subroutine	[cond],loc
	RS,SP			
	RL			
TBL			Call via table of values	tbl
CLR	W,DW		Clear	var
	B,F			loc
MOV	W		Clear dest, then move	srce,dest
CMP	W,DW,SW		Compare (1st par to 2nd par)	srce,var
	S,SR			srce,var,[cnt]
	BCD			srce,var,cnt
JIF			Compare and jump if	srce,cond,var,loc
JNZ			jump if not zero	srce,var,loc
SKP			skip if	srce,cond,var
CNVBW			Convert byte to word	var
WDW			word to double word	
DWQW			double word to quad word	
ST			string with table	str,tbl,lth-str
TST	S,SR		and test	srce,var,[cnt]
CPL	W		Invert, complement	var
	F,B			var,[bit]
DA			Decimal adjust	[type],var
DC			Disable counter/timer	
DEC	W		Decrement,	var,[cnt]
JNZ	W,R		jump not zero	var,loc
JIF	W,R		jump if condition	var,cond,loc
SZ			skip if zero	var
SNZ			skip if not zero	var
DI			Disable interrupts	
DIV	W,FP		Divide, unsigned	srce,dest
EC			Enable, counter/timer	
EI			interrupts	
ENTER			Enter procedure, with data	var,lth,loc
ESC			Escape to coprocessor	dev,inst,var
EXEC			Execute instruction at	loc
HALT			Halt program till interrupt	[status]
IDIV	W,DW		Divide, signed integer	srce,dest
IMUL	W		Multiply, signed integer	srce,var,[dest]

```
    ADD | W       |               signed int and add       | srce,dest
 IN     | W,      | Input,                                   | port,var
        | S,SR,BS |                                          | port,var,cnt
    AD  |         |           analog/digital port            | port,var
 INC    | W,:     | Increment                                | var,[cnt]
    JNZ | R       |               jump not zero              | var,loc
    SZ  |         |               skip if zero               | var
 JMP    | R,OS,SP | Jump, to location if                     | [cond],loc
        | RS,D,RL |                                          | [cond],loc
        |         |     [cond=bit set/reset (BS, BR)]        | cond,var,bit,loc
    CLR |         |        and clear variable if             | cond,var,loc
    DEC |         |        and decrement if                  | cond,var,loc
    MOV |         |        and move data if                  | cond,loc
 LEA    |         | Load effective address                   | adr,var
 LEAVE  |         | Leave procedure                          |
 LOOP   | R,D     | Loop to location until condition         | cond,[cnt],loc
 MOV    | W,DW,N  | Move,                                    | srce,dest
        | B,C,X,: |                                          | srce,dest
        | MW,SW   |                                          | srce,dest,cnt
        | S,WS,SR |                                          | srce,dest,cnt
        | WSR     |                                          |
        | BS      |                        | frm[:bit],to[:bit],cnt
    BW  | S       |         byte to word                     | srce,dest
    ADD | W       |         and add                          | srce,dest
    CLR | W       |         and clear source                 | srce,dest
    DEC | W       |         and decrement                    | srce,dest
    INC | W       |         and increment                    | srce,dest
    SUB | SW      |         and subtract                     | srce,dest
 MUL    | W       | Unsigned multiply,                       | srce,var,[dest]
    ADD | W       |                    and add               | srce,var,[dest]
 NEG    | W       | Change sign                              | var
 NOP    | L,LL    | No operation                             |
 NORM   | W,DW    | Normalize                                | var
 OR     | W,B     | Logical OR,                              | srce,dest
    HALT|         |            and wait for interrupt        | srce,dest
    IO  | W       |               to port                    | srce,port
 OUT    | W,      | Output to port,                          | srce,port
        | S,SR,BS |                                          | srce,port,cnt
    CLR |         |               and clear source           | srce,port
 POP    | W       | Pop data from the stack                  | dest
        | A       |                                          |
 PUSH   | W,EA,A  | Push data onto the stack,                | srce
    MOV | W       |         and move predefined data         | srce
 REP    |         | Repeat until condition, count            | [cond],[cnt]
 RES    | F,B     | Reset,                                   | var,[bit]
    IO  | B       |         I/O                              | port,[bit]
 RESET  |         | Reset system                             |
 RET    | OS,L    | Return from subroutine                   | [cond],[val]
    I   |         |         from interrupt                   | [cond],[val]
    NMI |         |         from non-maskable interrupt      | [cond],[val]
    ID  |         |         with interrupts disabled         | [cond]
    IE  |         |         with interrupts enabled          | [cond]
    MOV |         |         and move data                    | [cond]
    OFF |         |         with offset                      | [cond],val
 RIM    |         | Read interrupt mask                      | var
 RLBCD  |         | Rotate left bcd                          | var,var,[cnt]
    NC  | W       |               no carry                   | var,[cnt]
```

TC	W	to carry	var,[cnt]
WC	W	with carry	var,[cnt]
WR		with register	var,reg,cnt
RRBCD		Rotate right bcd	var,var,[cnt]
NC	W	no carry [wrd]	var,[cnt]
TC	W	to carry [wrd]	var,[cnt]
WC	W	with carry [wrd]	var,[cnt]
WR		with register	var,var,cnt
RST		Restart	[type]
SBB	W,BCD	Subtract with borrow	srce,dest,[cnt]
SBCF	W	Subtract carry flaf only	srce,[dest]
SBHC	W	Subtract half carry only	srce,[dest]
SCAN		Search string for value	str,val,cnt
SEL		Select operating mode or option	opt,[val]
SET	F,B	Set to one's	var,[bit]
	W	to predefined value	var, val
IF	B	if condition	cond,var,[bit]
IO	B	I/O port	port,[bit]
SHIFTA	W	Shift arithmetic	var,dir-cnt
SHIFTL	W	logical	var,dir-cnt
SKIP	W	Skip next instruction if	cond
CLR		and clear	cond,var
SLA	W,DW	Shift left arithmetic,	var,[cnt]
SC		then skip if carry	var
SLEEP		Low power operation	
SLL	W,DW	Shift left logical	var,[cnt]
SRA	W,DW	Shift right arithmetic	var,[cnt]
SRL	W,DW	Shift right logical,	var,[cnt]
SC		skip if carry	var
START		Start device	dev
STOP		Stop device	dev
SUB	W,,FP,:	Subtract	srce,dest
	SW,QW		
	BCD		srce,dest,cnt
IF	W	if	cond,srce,dest
SNC	W	then skip if no carry	srce,dest
SWAP	N,W	Swap	var
SWI		Software interrupt	[cond],[type]
TEST	W,DW	Logical AND to flags only	var,[var]
TRAP		Trap, program interrupt	[cond],[type]
TSTAND		Test, then AND with destination	srce,dest
ABR	W	all bits reset	mask,var
ABS	W	all bits set	mask,var
B		if bit set	var,bit
BCHG		bit and complement	var,bit
BCLR		bit and clear	var,bit
BSET		bit and set	var,bit
BSR		bit and skip if reset	var,bit
CLR	W	and clear	var
CHG	W	and change	var
CPL		value then complement	srce,dest
IO		port	val,port
	B	I/O bit	port,bit
JMP		jump if	val,cond,var,loc
JNZ	R	jump if not zero	[val],var,loc
JZ	B,R	jump if zero	var,loc
RES		and reset	var

```
    FSR   |       |     flag, skip and reset    | var
    SET   | DW    |     and set                 | var
    SKP   | B     |     skip if true            | var,cond,var
    SKPC  |       |     skip if true and clear  | cond,var
WAIT      |       | Wait for external device    |
XCHG      | N,W,F | Exchange                    | var,var
          | MB,MW |                             | vars,vars
XOR       | W,F   | Logical exclusive OR,       | srec,dest
          | SW    |                             | srce,cnt,dest
    IO    |       | Logical exclusive OR to port| val,port
          |
```

PARAMETERS

```
bit       location of a specific bit
cnt       number, of elements or times to repeat the operation
cond      condition upon which operation is performed
dest      destination address
dev       external device identifier
dir-cnt   direction and number of bits to shift an item of data
inst      location of or instruction to be executed
loc       location to jump to or memory address value
lth       length of a string variable or data
mask      mask used to select individual bits
opt       option identifier
port      address of I/O port or external device
range     location specifying range of permitted values
srce      location of the source or immediate data value
str       location of a string variable or data
tbl       location of a table of values
type      type of operation to be performed
val       location of data or immediate data
var       location of variable data
[]        optional parameter
```

Appendix C

Addressing Modes

Immediate
#n	– immediate data, 8-bits
#nn	– immediate data, 16-bits
#M nn	– immediate data, MSB of 16-bit value
#L nn	– immediate data, LSB of 16-bit value
m	– bit mask, 8-bits

Specific Location
ACx	– accumulator register
ARx	– auxiliary register
Rr	– register within RAM memory
WRr	– working register
XX	– specific register, one or two capital alphabetic characters

Bit
b	– bit number
aa|b	– bit address, memory location + pit number
BIT b	– bit number, when not implied by mnemonic
BIT aa|b	– bit address, memory location + bit number, if not implied

Absolute
a	– page zero address, 8-bits LSB, MSB = 0
PZ a	– page zero address, not implied
aa	– absolute address, 16-bits
LA aaaa	– absolute long address, 24 or 32-bits
r	– relative address, 8-bits or less
rr	– relative long address, 9 to 15 bits
dd	– displacement address value, 16-bit relative
RA r	– relative address vale, not implied by mnemonic
SR r	– stack pointer relative
p	– port address, 8-bits or less
pp	– port address, 16-bits
P p	– port address, not implied by mnemonic
s	– same page address, 8-bits LSB, MSB from inst adr
ss	– same page address, 9-bits or more
SP s	– same page address, not implied by mnemonic
ss|dd	– segmented address, 16-bit segment and displacement
SS s|a	– segmented short address, 7-bit seg, 8-bit LSB adr, MSB = 0
SL s|aa	– segmented long address, 7-bit seg, 16-bit adr
Rx|a	– vectored address, MSB in register, LSB value a

Indirect
(aa)	– absolute indirect
(RA r)	– relative address indirect
(Rr)	– register indirect
(PZ a)	– page zero indirect
(SP a)	– same page indirect
L(PZ a)	– page zero long indirect, page zero loc contains 3-byte adr
L(aa)	– absolute long indirect, location contains 3-byte address
(R(RX))	– indirect register indirect
SP(X)	– same page register indirect
Pp(X)	– page p register indirect

Indexed
EA =
(Rx+Rx)	– total one or more registers
(Rx+N d)	– reg + less then 8-bit value
(Rx+ d)	– reg + 8-bit value

228

```
(Rx++ dd )      - reg + 16-bit value
(Rx+++ aaa )    - reg + 24-bit value
(Rx+Rx+ d )     - multiple registers plus 8-bit value
(Rx+Rx++ dd )   - multiple registers plus 16-bit value
(Rx+SS s|aa )   - reg + segmented short address
(Rx+SL s|aa )   - reg + segmented long address
((Rx+ d ))      - indirect, reg + 8-bit value
((Rx++ dd ))    - indirect, reg + 16-bit value
(PZ(Rx+ d ))    - indirect, page zero loc ( reg + 8-bit value)
((PZ a )+Rx)    - contents of 2-byte pz loc + reg
((SR r )+Rx)    - contents of stack relative location + reg
(L(PZ a )+Rx)   - contents 3-byte page zero loc + reg
```

Auto Increment/Decrement

```
-XX             - register auto decrement
(Rx)+           - register indirect with post auto incrementing
(Rx)++          - register indirect with post auto incrementing by 2
+(Rx)           - register indirect with pre- auto incrementing
++(Rx)          - register indirect with pre- auto incrementing by 2
+(PZ a)         - page zero indirect with pre- auto increment
(Rx)-           - register indirect with post auto decrementing
-(Rx)           - register indirect with pre- auto decrementing
--(Rx)          - register indirect with pre- auto decrementing by 2
(Rx)+Rc         - register indirect with post auto increment by register
(Rx)-Rc         - register indirect with post auto decrement by register
((Rx)+)         - indirect indirect with post auto increment
(-(Rx))         - indirect indirect with pre- auto decrement
(R(Rx))+        - indirect register indirect with post auto increment
(R(Rx))-        - indirect register indirect with post auto decrement
```

Appendix D

Procedural Instructions Table

```
ADDV    (B,W)     Add value to variable         value,var
ADDVV   (B,W)     Add variable to variable      var,var
DECJMPV (B,W)     Decrement variable, jump if   var,cond,loc
FILL    (B,W,S)   Fill variable with value      var,[cnt],val
INCV    (B,W)     Increment variable            var
JMPIFV  (B,W,S)   Jump if variable              var,[cnt],cond,val,loc
JMPTBL            Jump via table                tbl,var
MOVV    (B,W,S)   Move variable to variable     var,[cnt],var
POPA              Pop all registers
PUSHA             Push all registers
RETERR            Return error
RETGD             Return good
REVHL             Reverse 4 bits
STOP              Exit program
SUBV    (B,W)     Subtract value from variable  var,val
SYSTEM            Call to operating system      func,val
```

Appendix E

Assembler
Commands Table

```
Type of Program:
-----------------

HEX     Generate a .HEX load module
MAIN    Main segment of a program with overlays
SGMT    Overlay segment
SUBR    Macro instruction subroutine

Machine Code Location
---------------------

ORG     Start address of the program code
ORGD    Start address of the data portion of the program
ORGCS   Location of the code segment in physical memory
ORGDS   Location of the data segment in physical memory.

Define Data or Labels
---------------------

COMM    Labels usable by external subroutines and overlays
DB      Defines a series of single-byte data items
DDW     Defines a series of double-word (32-bit) data items
DW      Defines a series of double-byte (word) data items
DS      Defines an area of memory to be reserved for use in the program
EQU     Equate label to value
EXT     Externally defined label
LBLTBL  Read into memory a previously generated load map or label table
LOAD    Force load a relocatable load module
S.N.    Enter an 8-byte coded serial number
USER    Text data input by the operator at assembly time

Assembly Control
----------------

DMOC    Display message on the console
END     End of the source code file to be assembled
IF      Start of a conditionally assembled portion of the program
NOIF    End of a conditionally assembled portion of the program
INSERT  Insert another the source file
STRTD   Assemble the following instructions into the data segment
ENDD    End assembly to data segment

Macro Definition
----------------

DEFM    Define macro instruction
ENDM    End macro instruction definition

Output Listings
---------------

NAME    Name of the program
SKIP    Skip to top of next page
TEXT    Documentation to be used in a manual
URMT    Documentation to be used in a user's reference guide
```

External Subroutine Instructions Table

CONSOLE I/O

^CNSLI	Console input	BUF,M_LTH,L_ADR
^CNSLO	Console output	TEXT,LTH
^CNSLCL	Console output w/CR-LF	TEXT,LTH
^CLEAR	Clear screen	

DATA CONVERSIONS

^ATOI	ASCII to integer	BUF,LTH,VAR,ERR
^ITOA	Integer to ASCII	VAR,BUF,M_LTH,L_ADR,ERR
^BTOA	Binary to ASCII	VAR,BUF
^ATOB	ASCII to binary	BUF,LTH,VAR,ERR
^HTOA	Hex to ASCII	VAR,BYTES,BUF
^ATOH	ASCII to Hex	BUF,LTH,VAR,BYTES,ERR
^OTOA	Octal to ASCII	VAR,BUF
^ATOO	ASCII to Octal	BUF,LTH,VAR,ERR
^ATON	ASCII to numeric	BUF,LTH,VAR,ERR
^NTOA	Numeric to ASCII	VAR,BUF
^UNTOA	Unsigned numeric to ASCII	VAR,BUF
^BCDTOA	BCD to ASCII	VAR,BYTES,BUF
^ATOBCD	ASCII to BCD	BUF,LTH,VAR,BYTES,ERR
^FNDTS	ASCII to File name	BUF,LTH,VAR,ERR
^FNSTD	File name to ASCII	VAR,BUF

DISK I/O

^OPEN	Open file	FCB,NEW,ERR
^CLOSE	Close file	FCB,ERR
^DELETE	Delete file	FCB,ERR
^RDREC	Read a record	FCB,BUF,M-LTH,L_ADR,END,ERR
^WTREC	Write a record	FCB,BUF,LTH,ERR
^RRAF	Read random access file	FCB,NUM,ERR
^WTRAF	Write random access file	FCB,NUM,ERR
^RNSPR	Read next physical record	FCB,ERR
^OVLYRD	Overlay read	F_NAME,C_ADR,BLKS,D_ADR,BLKS,ERR
^OVLYWT	Overlay write	F_NAME,C_ADR,BLKS,D_ADR,BLKS,ERR
^TBLRD	Table read	F_NAME,TBL,ERR
^TBLWT	Table write	F_NAME,TBL,ERR

FORMATTING

^FORMAT	Format data for output	FRMT,BUF,LOC,ERR

OPERATOR INPUT

^GETCMD	Get command line	PRMPT,HELP,BUF,M_LTH,NONE
^PRGCMD	Get program parameters	NONE
^CMDPAR	Extract parameter	TBL,ERR
^CMDVAL	Extract value	TYPE,VAR,ERR,NONE
^CMDNXT	Extract next element	NONE

```
^INPUT          Get operator input        PRMPT,TYPE,VAR,NONE
^GETYN          Get yes/no response       PRMPT,IF_YES
^GETREQ         Get operator request      PRMPT,TBL,HELP

Printer I/O
-----------

^PRINT          Print a line              TEXT,LTH
^PRTHDR         Print header              TEXT
^PRTTR          Print trailer             TEXT
^PRTDHT         Define header/trailer     HEADER,TRAILER,PAGE-#
^PRTCTL         Define printer variables  LOC
^PRTSKP         Skip lines                NUM

REPORTS / DISPLAYS
------------------

^DSPML          Display multiple lines    TEXT
^DSPRPT         Display report            FRMAT,LOC,OFFSET,REPEAT,ERR
^DSPFML         Display formatted m/lines FRMT,LOC,ERR
^PRTFML         Print lines w/formatting  FRMT,LOC,ERR
^PRTRPT         Print report              FRMT,LOC,OFFSET,REPEAT,ERR

TABLE FUNCTIONS
---------------

^TBLDEL         Delete entry              TBL
^TBLADD         Append entry              LOC,TBL,ERR
^STFE           Search for entry          LOC,BYTES,TBL,OFFSET,NONE
^TBLCHG         Change entry              LOC,TBL
^TBLINS         Insert entry              LOC,TBL,ERR
```

Appendix G

Microprocessor
Instruction Set Tables

These tables describe the instruction set for most of the currently available microprocessors and microcomputers. This data was compiled from the manufacturer's specification sheets, product descriptions and user manuals. Although every attempt has been made to assure that the tables are accurate, discrepancies may exist—caused mainly by the limited information supplied to us by the manufacturer and the fact that minor differences may exist between different versions of the same processor or operational capabilities may be implementation dependent.

These tables are not intended to describe all the programming and operational characteristics of each micro. They are intended only as a reference, to describe the instruction set and the implementation of this standard, and provide data necessary to understanding the operation of the instructions. For details of how to program each device, consult the manufacturer's programming reference manual or other books written explicity for the micro.

Each table contains the following information.

List of micros
Instructions
    data move
    math operations
    logical operations
    bit operations
    string operations

program control
I/O operations
Description
   registers
   flags
   addressing modes
   instruction expansion
   special memory locations
   notes

THE LIST OF MICROS

Listed are most of the micros that use each set of instructions. If certain micros include additional instructions or capabilities, they are separated into groups and assigned numbers to identifying the data associated with that group. In the instructions and description sections of the table, those portions that pertain only to specific micros are identified by an asterisk and the same numeric identifier, as shown in this example:

```
ex:    (1) 8641, 8042
       (2) 8048, 8049
       (2,3) NS80CX48

  *  EMI    EN I  . . . . . . . . .  (1)
  *  ORIO   ORL   . . . . . . . . .  (2)
  *  EFC    ENFCR . . . . . . . . .  (3)

  instruction  EMI  is for the 8641 and 8042 only
               ORIO      both 8048, 8049 and NS80CX48
               EFC       the NS80CX48 only
```

INSTRUCTIONS

Here are descriptions of all the instructions available for use with the micros listed. Each instruction is described using the following format:

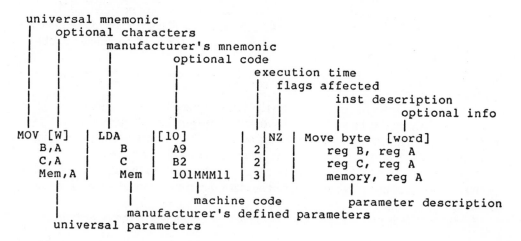

237

Universal Mnemonic: the mnemonic used to identify this instruction as defined in this proposed AL standard.

Universal Parameters: the parameters used to clarify the operation to be performed or identify the data to be used and/or result stored. Capital letters are used to indicate specific parameters, such as a register, condition code, or addressing mode indicator, that must be used. Lowercase letters are used to specify variable data, such as an address or numeric value, or a table of parameters defined in the Instruction Expansion portion of the Description section. If there are more than one parameter, the first parameter is normally the source and the second or last parameter the destination.

Manufacturer's Mnemonic: the mnemonics suggested by the manufacturer to identify this computer operation.

Manufacturer's Parameter: these are the parameters as defined by the manufacturer. For many instructions the parameters may be implied by the instruction mnemonic, rather than being explicitly stated. Therefore, the number of parameters required by the manufacturer's defined mnemonics may be less than with the universal mnemonics. Also the sequence of parameters may differ. With the universal mnemonics, the first parameter is normally the source. With the manufacturer's mnemonics, the first parameter may be the source or destination.

Machine Code: the machine code for each instruction is expressed as one or more bytes or words depending on the processor involved. Two alphanumeric characters followed by a space or comma represent a specific hexadecimal value (one byte). A string of eight or more characters represent a binary type or word with variable elements. The variable portion is represented by alphabetic characters and defined in the Instruction Expansion portion of the table.

Execution Times: these numbers represent the relative execution time of each instruction, normally expressed in terms of machine cycles. The actual execution time of an instruction depends on several factors, primarily addressing mode, clock frequency, interrupts, and memory of I/O device speed. If the number is on the same line as an instruction mnemonic, it applies to all parameter combinations for that instruction. If the number is followed by a plus sign, it indicates that this is a base value; the actual value depends on the parameters specified.

Flags Affected: this column indicates the flags that are affected by the instruction. If proceeded by a minus sign, it indicates those flags that are not affected. Each flag is represented by a single character as defined in the Flags portion of the table. If it is on the same line as an instruction mnemonic, it applies to all parameter combinations for that instruction.

Inst Description: this is a short description of the operation being performed by the instruction.

Parameter Description: describes the purpose and meaning of the parameters in the same sequence as listed for the universal parameters (source destination). The manufacturer's parameters may be reversed or implied by the instruction mnemonic.

Optional: optional parts of an instruction are enclosed in brackets.

Optional Characters: characters that may be appended to the basic mnemonic to clarify the operation being performed. The clarifying characters are defined in section 8 of this standard.

Optional Code: data to be added, inserted, or appended to the basic machine code if the optional characters are specified. If only a few bits are affected by the use of an optional character, the affected bits are indicated by an alphabetic character in the machine code. The position of the optional code above the basic code indicates if it is to be inserted before or appended to the end of the basic code. A plus or minus sign indicates that the value should be subtracted or added from/to the byte above which it is placed, as shown in this example:

```
MOV   [W]   |[10]        insert 10 as first byte if
            |  28,19     W is specified.

MOV   [W]   | [+10]      add 10 to the first byte if
            |  28,19     W is specified.

MOV   [W]   |      [10]  append 10 after last byte if
            |  28,19     W is specified.
```

Optional Info: short description of the optional fields.

The instructions are separated into the following groups based on the type of operation they perform.

Data Move: instructions that move data from one location to another without changing the data except for possibly extending the sign or filling a portion of the destination with a predefined value.

Math Operations: instructions that perform mathematical operations such as add or subtract, or otherwise modify the data based on some mathematical equation.

Logical Operations: instructions that perform some sort of logical operation on the data, such as logical AND or shift.

Bit Operations: instructions that affect specific bits of a variable or the status flags and condition codes.

String Operations: instructions intended for use with strings (multiple bytes or words) of data. They may perform data move or mathematical type operations.

Program Control: instructions that affect the sequence in which the instructions are to be executed or change the mode of operation in which the processor will execute instructions.

I/O Operation: instructions that transfer data to/from an external device other than main memory, and control the transfer of data or the operation of specific signals connected to external devices.

Micro Unique: instructions that are unique to a particular processor or perform some function that does not fit into any of the other categories. These instructions are not defined as part of this standard.

DESCRIPTION

This section contains all the information needed to understand the operation of the instructions, the meaning of any special symbols and abbreviations used to describe the instructions, and other information.

Registers: a description of the registers and how they are organized.

Flags: a list of flags that are under program control.

Addressing Modes: a description of the addressing modes available and the method of specifying each.

Instruction Expansion: this may consist of several tables depending on the complexity of the instructions being defined. They describe how instructions with variable elements or tables of valid parameters are to be expanded into each individual instruction. In order to keep the instruction tables relatively short, parameters that are common to several instructions are put in a table and the table identifier place in the parameter field. This eliminates having to list every individual instruction. This portion also defines any special symbols that may have been used. An example is shown below:

```
MOV     |            | Move data byte
   Rs,Rd| 10SSSDDD   |    source, destination

        Registers
    Rs/Rd    SSS/DDD
    -------  -------
      A       001
      B       010
      C       100
```

Register A, B, or C may be used as the source and destination; the indicated value is substituted for SSS and DDD in the machine code. For the instruction MOV C,A the machine code is 10100001.

Special Memory Locations: this describes how the memory is organized and identifies any memory locations that are assigned special usage that is important in understanding the instructions. This data may vary greatly depending on the application for which the processor is being used.

Notes: this contains any additional information that is considered important and not clearly explained in any of the above.

ABBREVIATIONS

Following is a list of abbreviation used in the tables.

abs	the actual address of a location in memory.
dec	decrement the contents of a memory location or register.
disp	displacement address, the difference between the actual memory address and some predefined location.
immed	immediate data included as part of an instruction.
inc	increment the contents of a memory location or register.
ind	indirect addressing mode.
loc	memory location, specified as part of the instruction.
port	the address used to access an external device.
prog	program, that portion of memory used to store a program.
pz	page zero, a memory location in the lower portion of memory.
RAM	random access memory or read/write memory.
reg	register, one of the predefined locations used to store data.

rel   relative address, difference between the actual memory location and some predefined location.

ROM   read only memory, used to store a program or permanent data.

SP   same page, a location in memory within a specified range with respect to the location of the current instruction.

uncond the unconditional execution of an instruction.

1650

PIC1650A, PIC1650XT, PIC1654, PIC1655A, PIC1655XT (1,2) PIC16C55, PIC16C63

Data Move

```
MOV         :              :                    :   :   : Move byte
   W,Rr     : MOVWF  Rr     : 0000001RRRRR  :   :   :    W, to reg
   Rr,W     : MOVF   Rr,0   : 0010000RRRRR  :   :Z  :    reg, to W (MOVFW)
   Rs,Rd    :        Rr,1   : 0010001RRRRR  :   :Z  :    reg to itself (TEST)
   n,W      : MOVLW  n       : 1100NNNNNNNN  :   :   :    immed, to W
   Rs,W     : MOVFW  Rr      : 0010000RRRRR  :   :Z  :    reg, to W
CLR         :              :                    :   :   : Clear
   W        : CLRW          : 000001000000  :   :Z  :    W = 0
   Rr       : CLRF   Rr      : 0000011RRRRR  :   :Z  :    reg = 0
```

Math Operations

```
ADD        : ADDWF    :                  :CDZ: Add
   Rr,W    :    Rr,0  : 0001110RRRRR  :   :     reg to W
   W,Rr    :    Rr,1  : 0001111RRRRR  :   :     W to reg
ADDCF      : ADDCF    :                  :Z  : Add carry
   Rr,W    :    Rr,0  : 011000000011  :   :     skip no carry
           :          : 0010100RRRRR  :   :     W = reg +1
   Rr      :    Rr,1  : 011000000011  :   :     skip no carry
           :          : 0010101RRRRR  :   :     reg = reg + 1
ADDHC      : ADDDCF   :                  :Z  : Add half carry
   Rr,W    :    Rr,0  : 011000100011  :   :     skip no half carry
           :          : 0010100RRRRR  :   :     W = reg +1
   Rr      :    Rr,1  : 011000100011  :   :     skip no half carry
           :          : 0010101RRRRR  :   :     inc reg
INC        : INCF     :                  :Z  : Increment
   Rr,W    :    Rr,0  : 0010100RRRRR  :   :     W = reg + 1
   Rr      :    Rr,1  : 0010101RRRRR  :   :     reg
SUB        : SUBWF    :                  :CDZ: Subtract
   W,Rr,W  :    Rr,0  : 0000100RRRRR  :   :     W = Reg - W
   W,Rr    :    Rr,1  : 0000101RRRRR  :   :     Reg = Reg - W
SUBCF      : SUBCF    :                  :Z  : Subtract carry
   Rr,W    :    Rr,0  : 011000000011  :   :     skip if no carry
           :          : 0000110RRRRR  :   :     W = Reg - 1
   Rr      :    Rr,1  : 011000000011  :   :     skip if no carry
           :          : 0000111RRRRR  :   :     dec reg
SUBHC      : SUBDCF   :                  :Z  : Subtract half carry
   Rr,W    :    Rr,0  : 011000100011  :   :     skip if no half carry
           :          : 0000110RRRRR  :   :     W = Reg - 1
   Rr      :    Rr,1  : 011000100011  :   :     skip if no half carry
           :          : 0000111RRRRR  :   :     dec reg
```

```
DEC       ! DECF       !                   ! !Z ! Decrement
   Rr,W   !    Rr,0    ! 0000110RRRRR !   !   !    reg store in W
   Rr     !    Rr,1    ! 0000111RRRRR !   !   !    Reg

NEG       ! NEGF       !                   ! !Z ! Change to negative equiv
   Rr,W   !    Rr,0    ! 0010011RRRRR !   !   !    reg = cpl reg
          !            ! 0010100RRRRR !   !   !    W = reg + 1
   Rr     !    Rr,1    ! 0010011RRRRR !   !   !    reg = cpl reg
```

(C) Copyrigh' '985: VOCS, Mpls, MN.

```
          !            ! 0010101RRRRR !   !   !    reg = reg + 1
```

Bit Operations

```
RESF      !            !                   ! ! ! Reset flag
   C      ! CLRC       ! 010000000011 !   !   !    carry
   D      ! CLRDC      ! 010000100011 !   !   !    half carry
   Z      ! CLRZ       ! 010001000011 !   !   !    zero
SETF      !            !                   ! ! ! Set flag
   C      ! SETC       ! 010100000011 !   !   !    carry
   D      ! SETDC      ! 010100100011 !   !   !    half carry
   Z      ! SETZ       ! 010101000011 !   !   !    zero
RESB      ! BCF        !                   ! ! ! Reset bit
   Rr,b   !    Rr,b    ! 0100BBBRRRRR !   !   !    reg, bit
SETB      ! BSF        !                   ! ! ! Set bit
   Rr,b   !    Rr,b    ! 0101BBBRRRRR !   !   !    reg, bit
```

I/O Operations

```
* TRIS  p ! TRIS  p    ! 0000000PPPPP !   !   ! Tristate port F6 or F7 (1)
          !            !                   !   !   !    W to tristate status
```

Logical Operations

```
AND       ! ANDWF      !                   ! !Z ! Logical AND
   Rr,W   !    Rr,0    ! 0001010RRRRR !   !   !    reg, W
   W,Rr   !    Rr,1    ! 0001011RRRRR !   !   !    W, reg
   #n,W   ! ANDLW  n   ! 1110NNNNNNNN !   !   !    immed, W
OR        ! IORWF      !                   ! !Z ! Logical OR
   Rr,W   !    Rr,0    ! 0001000RRRRR !   !   !    reg, W
   W,Rr   !    Rr,1    ! 0001001RRRRR !   !   !    W, reg
   #n,W   ! IORLW  n   ! 1101NNNNNNNN !   !   !    immed, W
XOR       ! XORWF      !                   ! !Z ! Logical Exclusive OR
   Rr,W   !    Rr,0    ! 0001100RRRRR !   !   !    reg, W
   W,Rr   !    Rr,1    ! 0001101RRRRR !   !   !    W, reg
   #n,W   ! XORLW  n   ! 1111NNNNNNNN !   !   !    immed, W
CPL       ! COMF       !                   ! !Z ! Complement
   Rr,W   !    Rr,0    ! 0010010RRRRR !   !   !    reg, store in W
   Rr     !    Rr,1    ! 0010011RRRRR !   !   !    reg
RRWC      ! RRF        !                   ! !C ! Rotate right w/carry
   Rr,W   !    Rr,0    ! 0011000RRRRR !   !   !    reg, 1 bit, save in W
   Rr     !    Rr,1    ! 0011001RRRRR !   !   !    reg, 1 bit
RLWC      ! RLF        !                   ! !C ! Rotate left w/carry
   Rr,W   !    Rr,0    ! 0011010RRRRR !   !   !    reg, 1 bit, save in W
   Rr     !    Rr,1    ! 0011011RRRRR !   !   !    reg, 1 bit
SWAP      ! SWAPF      !                   ! ! ! Swap half bytes
   Rr,W   !    Rr,0    ! 0011100RRRRR !   !   !    reg into W
   Rr     !    Rr,1    ! 0011101RRRRR !   !   !    reg
```

242

```
TEST      | TSTF   |                  | |Z | Test byte
   Rr     |   Rr   | 0010001RRRRR |  | |    reg
```

Program Control

```
CALL      | CALL   |              |  |  | Call subroutine
   aa     |   aa   | 1001AAAAAAAA |  |  |    uncond, loc aa
RET       | RETLW  |              |  |  | Return from subroutine
   #n,W   |   n    | 1000NNNNNNNN |  |  |    uncond, W = n
* RETI    | RETURN |              |  |  | Return from interrupt (2)
          |        | 000000000010 |  |  |    uncond, PC from stack
JMP       | GOTO   |              |  |  | Jump if
   UN,aa  |     aa | 101AAAAAAAAA |  |  |    uncond, loc aa
   UN,aa  | B   aa | 101AAAAAAAAA |  |  |    uncond, loc aa (JMP)
   C,aa   | BC  aa | 011000000011 |  |  |    carry,  skip on carry
          |        | 101AAAAAAAAA |  |  |           jump loc aa
   NC,aa  | BNC aa | 011100000011 |  |  |    no carry; skip no carry
          |        | 101AAAAAAAAA |  |  |           jump loc aa
   HC,aa  | BDC aa | 011100100011 |  |  |    half carry, skip
          |        | 101AAAAAAAAA |  |  |           jump loc aa
   NHC,aa | BNDC aa| 011001000011 |  |  |    no half carry,  skip
          |        | 101AAAAAAAAA |  |  |           jump loc aa
   Z,aa   | BZ  aa | 011101000011 |  |  |    zero,  skip if zero
          |        | 101AAAAAAAAA |  |  |           jump loc aa
   NZ,aa  | BNZ aa | 011101000011 |  |  |    not zero,  skip
          |        | 101AAAAAAAAA |  |  |           jump loc aa
INCSIZ    | INCFSZ |              |  |  | Increment and skip if zero
   Rr,W   |   Rr,0 | 0011110RRRRR |  |  |    reg, store in W
   Rr     |   Rr,1 | 0011111RRRRR |  |  |    reg
DECSIZ    | DECFSZ |              |  |  | Decrement and skip if zero
   Rr,W   |   Rr,0 | 0010110RRRRR |  |  |    reg, store in W
   Rr     |   Rr,1 | 0010111RRRRR |  |  |    reg
TSTSIZB   | BTFSC  |              |  |  | Test bit skip if zero
   Rr,b   |   Rr,b | 0110BBBRRRRR |  |  |    reg, bit
          | BTFSS  |              |  |  |
   Rr,b,NZ|   Rr,b | 0111BBBRRRRR |  |  |    reg, bit, not zero
SKIP      |        |              |  |  | Skip next inst if
   C      | SKPC   | 011100000011 |  |  |    carry
   NC     | SKPNC  | 011000000011 |  |  |    no carry
   HC     | SKPDC  | 011100100011 |  |  |    half carry
   NHC    | SKPNDC | 011000100011 |  |  |    no half carry
   Z      | SKPZ   | 011101000011 |  |  |    zero
   NZ     | SKPNZ  | 011001000011 |  |  |    not zero
NOP       | NOP    | 000000000000 |  |  | No operation
```

Registers

```
          8        1
        ---------
   F1 | RTCC | Real time clock/counter
        ---------
   F2 |  PC  | Prog counter (9 bits)
        ---------
   F3 |11111ZDC| Status word
        ---------
   F4 |111 FSR | File select reg (5 bits)
        ---------
   F5 |        | I/O Reg A, micro dependent
        ---------
   F6 |        | I/O Reg B, micro dependent
        ---------
   F7 |        | I/O Reg C, micro dependent
        ---------
```

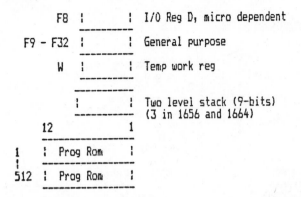

```
        F8  :        :  I/O Reg D, micro dependent
             ----------
   F9 - F32  :        :  General purpose
             ----------
        W    :        :  Temp work reg
             ----------

             :        :  Two level stack (9-bits)
             ----------  (3 in 1656 and 1664)
        12            1
             ----------------
    1    :  Prog Rom  :
    :                 :
   512   :  Prog Rom  :
             ----------------
```

Flags

```
   C = carry flag
   D = half carry from bit 3
   Z = zero
```

```
                              1656 & 1664
                              -----------
            BIT 3  IE   interrupt enable
                4  RTCE real time clock enable
                5  IR   interrupt request
                6  RTCR real time clock int req
                7  CNT  count select
```

Addressing Modes

```
   Univ  Manuf
   ----  -----

   #n    #n - immediate, 8-bits
   Rr    Rr - register
   aa    aa - absolute, 8 or 9-bits as indicated by inst
   (F4)  F0 - indirect, low order 5-bits of F4
   b     b  - bit number
```

Instruction Expansion

```
   Rr  Register    RRRRR = F0 - F32   F0 is indirect F4
   #n  immediate   NNNNNNNN = 8 bit data
   aa  address     AAAAAAAAA = 8 or 9 bit address
   b   bit number  BBB = 0 - 7
```

Special Memory Locations

Notes

1670

PIC1670   **(1) PIC1665**

Data Move

```
MOV     :           :               : :  : Move byte
   W,Rr :  MOVWF Rr : 0000001RRRRRR  : :  :   W, reg
   #n,W :  MOVLW n  : 10010NNNNNNNN  : :  :   immed, W
   Rr,W :  MOVFW Rr : 1000000RRRRRR  : :Z :   reg, W
```

```
CLR          :             :                  : :  : Clear
    Reg      : CLRF  Rr     : 1000001RRRRRRR  : :Z : Reg = 0
```

Math Operations

```
ADD          : ADDWF        :                  : :VCDZ: Add
    Rr,W     :     Rr,0     : 0001110RRRRRRR  : :    : reg, W
    W,Rr     :     Rr,1     : 0001111RRRRRRR  : :    : W, reg
    #n,W     : ADDLW  nn    : 10011NNNNNNNN   : :    : immed, W
ADC          : ADCWF        :                  : :VCDZ: Add w/carry
    Rr,W     :     Rr,0     : 0010000RRRRRRR  : :    : reg, W
    W,Rr     :     Rr,1     : 0010001RRRRRRR  : :    : W, reg
INC          : INCF         :                  : :VCDZ: Increment
    Rr,W     :     Rr,0     : 0010100RRRRRRR  : :    : W = reg + 1
    Rr       :     Rr,1     : 0010101RRRRRRR  : :    : reg
SUB          : SUBWF        :                  : :VCDZ: Subtract
    W,Rr,W   :     Rr,0     : 0000100RRRRRRR  : :    : W = Reg - W
    W,Rr     :     Rr,1     : 0000101RRRRRRR  : :    : Reg = Reg - W
SUBC         : SUBBWF       :                  : :VCDZ: Subtract w/carry
    W,Rr,W   :     Rr,0     : 0000010RRRRRRR  : :    : W = reg - W - C
    W,Rr     :     Rr,1     : 0000011RRRRRRR  : :    : reg = reg - W - C
DEC          : DECF         :                  : :VCDZ: Decrement
    Rr,W     :     Rr,0     : 0000110RRRRRRR  : :    : W = Reg -1
    Rr       :     Rr,1     : 0000111RRRRRRR  : :    : Reg
DA  W        : DAW          : 0000000000100   : :C : Decimal adjust reg W
TEST         : TSTF         :                  : :Z : Test byte
    Rr       :     Rr       : 1000111RRRRRRR  : :  : reg
```

Bit Operations

```
RESB         : BCF          :                  : :  : Reset bit
    Rr,b     :     Rr,b     : 0100BBBRRRRRRR  : :  : reg, bit
SETB         : BSF          :                  : :  : Set bit
    Rr,b     :     Rr,b     : 0101BBBRRRRRRR  : :  : reg, bit
```

Logical Operations

```
AND          : ANDWF        :                  : :Z : Logical AND
    Rr,W     :     Rr,0     : 0001010RRRRRRR  : :  : reg with W
    W,Rr     :     Rr,1     : 0001011RRRRRRR  : :  : W with reg
    #n,W     : ANDLW  n     : 10101NNNNNNNN   : :  : immed with W
OR           : IORWF        :                  : :Z : Logical OR
    Rr,W     :     Rr,0     : 0001000RRRRRRR  : :  : reg with W
    W,Rr     :     Rr,1     : 0001001RRRRRRR  : :  : W with reg
    #n,W     : IORLW  n     : 10100NNNNNNNN   : :  : immed with W
XOR          : XORWF        :                  : :Z : Logical Exclusive OR
    Rr,W     :     Rr,0     : 0001100RRRRRRR  : :  : reg with W
    W,Rr     :     Rr,1     : 0001101RRRRRRR  : :  : W with reg
    #n,W     : XORLW  n     : 10110NNNNNNNN   : :  : immed with W
CPL          : COMPF        :                  : :Z : Complement
    Rr,W     :     Rr,0     : 0010010RRRRRRR  : :  : reg, store in W
    Rr       :     Rr,1     : 0010011RRRRRRR  : :  : reg
RRWC         : RRCF         :                  : :C : Rotate right w/carry
    Rr,W     :     Rr,0     : 0011000RRRRRRR  : :  : reg, save in W
    Rr       :     Rr,1     : 0011001RRRRRRR  : :  : reg,
RLWC         : RLCF         :                  : :C : Rotate left w/carry
    Rr,W     :     Rr,0     : 0011010RRRRRRR  : :  : reg, save in W
    Rr       :     Rr,1     : 0011011RRRRRRR  : :  : reg,
RRNC         : RRNCF        :                  : :  : Rotate right no carry
    Rr       :     Rr       : 1000010RRRRRRR  : :  : reg,
RLNC         : RLNCF        :                  : :  : Rotate left no carry
    Rr       :     Rr       : 1000011RRRRRRR  : :  : reg,
```

```
SWAP         ! SWAPF   !                  ! !   ! Swap half bytes
   Rr,W      !   Rr,0  ! 0011100RRRRRRR ! !   !    reg into W
   Rr        !   Rr,1  ! 0011101RRRRRRR ! !   !    reg
```

Program Control

```
CALL        ! CALL    !                  ! !   ! Call subroutine
   aa       !   aa    ! 111AAAAAAAAAA  ! !   !    uncond, loc aa
RET         ! RETFS   !                  ! !   ! Return from subroutine
            !         ! 0000000000011  ! !   !    uncond
   #n,W     ! RETLW n ! 10111NNNNNNNN  ! !   !    uncond, W = n
* RETI      ! RETFI   !                  ! !   ! Return from interrupt
            !         ! 0000000000010  ! !   !    uncond, (1)
JMP         ! GOTO    !                  ! !   ! Jump if
   aa       !   aa    ! 110AAAAAAAAAA  ! !   !    uncond, loc aa
INCSZ       ! INCFSZ  !                  ! !   ! Increment, skip if zero
   Rr,W     !   Rr,0  ! 0011110RRRRRRR ! !   !    reg, store in W
   Rr       !   Rr,1  ! 0011111RRRRRRR ! !   !    reg,
DECSZ       ! DECFSZ  !                  ! !   ! Decrement, skip if zero
   Rr,W     !   Rr,0  ! 0010110RRRRRRR ! !   !    reg, store in W
   Rr       !   Rr,1  ! 0010111RRRRRRR ! !   !    reg,
CMPSKP      !         !                  ! !   ! Compare and skip if
   Rr,LT,W  ! CPFSLT Rr ! 1000100RRRRRRR ! !   !    Reg less then W
   Rr,EQ,W  ! CPFSEQ Rr ! 1000101RRRRRRR ! !   !    Reg equal W
   Rr,GT,W  ! CPFSGT Rr ! 1000110RRRRRRR ! !   !    Reg greater then W

TSTSKPB     ! BTFSC   !                  ! !   ! Test bit skip if zero
   Rr,b     !   Rr,b  ! 0110BBBRRRRRRR ! !   !    reg, bit
            ! BTFSS   !                  ! !   !
   Rr,b,NZ  !   Rr,b  ! 0111BBBRRRRRRR ! !   !    reg, bit, not zero
NOP         ! NOP     ! 0000000000000  ! !   ! No operation
* HALT      ! HALT    ! 0000000000001  ! !   ! Halt in   (1)
```

Registers

```
        8     1
      ---------
F1    !   W   !  Work register
      ---------
F2    !  PC   !  Prog counter (8 bits, 2 MSB in F3)
      ---------
F3    !0X98VZDC!  Status register
      ---------
F4    !11  FSR !  File select reg (6 bits)
      ---------
F5    !XCACRXRX!  Interrupt status reg
      ! EBSIREE!
      ---------
F6    ! RTCCA !  Real Time Clock Counter A
      ---------
F7    ! RTCCB !  Real Time Clock Counter B
      ---------
F8    !       !  I/O Reg Port A
      ---------
F9    !       !  I/O Pins Port A
      ---------
F10   !       !  I/O Reg Port B
      ---------
F11   !       !  I/O Pins Port B
      ---------
```

246

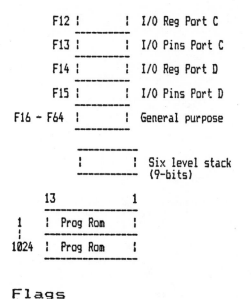

```
   F12 |         |  I/O Reg Port C
       -----------
   F13 |         |  I/O Pins Port C
       -----------
   F14 |         |  I/O Reg Port D
       -----------
   F15 |         |  I/O Pins Port D
       -----------
F16 - F64 |      |  General purpose
       -----------


          -----------
       |            |  Six level stack
          -----------  (9-bits)

      13            1
      -----------------
   1  |  Prog Rom    |
   :  -----------------
 1024 |  Prog Rom    |
      -----------------
```

Flags

```
  C = carry flag
  D = half carry from bit 3
  Z = zero
  V = overflow
  8 = 9th bit of the PC
  9 = 10th bit of the PC

       Interrupt Flags
       ---------------
  XE  interrupt enable
  RE  real time clock enable
  XR  interrupt request
  RR  real time clock requist
  CS  clock source
  AB  clock A/B
  CE  count enable
  X
```

Addressing Modes

```
  Univ   Manuf
  ----   -----

  #n     n      - immediate
  Rr     Rr     - register
  aa     aa     - absolute
  (R4)   R0     - indirect
  W      W      - temp register
```

Instruction Expansion

```
  Rr   Register     RRRRRR = F0 - F64,  F0 is use for reg R4 indirect
  #n   immediate    NNNNNNNN = 8 bit data
  aa   address      AAAAAAAAAA = 10 bit address
  b    bit number   BBB = 0 - 7
```

Special Memory Locations

1802

1802C, CDP1802, CDP1802C   (1) CDP1804, CDP1804C

Data Move

```
MOV         ¦        ¦          ¦2¦ ¦ Move byte
  (Rr),D    ¦ LDN r  ¦ 0000RRRR ¦ ¦ ¦    ind reg, reg D : except R0
  (Rr)+,D   ¦ LDA r  ¦ 1000RRRR ¦ ¦ ¦    ind_inc reg,reg D
  (R(X)),D  ¦ LDX    ¦ F0       ¦ ¦ ¦    ind_ind X, reg D
  (R(X))+,D ¦ LDXA   ¦ 72       ¦ ¦ ¦    ind_ind_inc X, reg D
  (R(P))+,D ¦ LDI    ¦ F8       ¦ ¦ ¦    ind_ind_inc P, reg D
  #n,D      ¦        ¦ F8,nn    ¦ ¦ ¦    imed, reg D
  #Mn,D     ¦        ¦ F8,nn    ¦ ¦ ¦    imed MSB, reg D
  D,(Rr)    ¦ STR r  ¦ 0101RRRR ¦ ¦ ¦    reg D,ind reg
  D,(R(X))- ¦ STXD   ¦ 73       ¦ ¦ ¦    reg D,ind_ind_dec X
  Lr,D      ¦ GLO r  ¦ 1000RRRR ¦ ¦ ¦    reg LSB, reg D
  D,Lr      ¦ PLO r  ¦ 1010RRRR ¦ ¦ ¦    reg D, reg LSB
  Hr,D      ¦ GHI r  ¦ 1001RRRR ¦ ¦ ¦    reg MSB, reg D
  D,Hr      ¦ PHI r  ¦ 1011RRRR ¦ ¦ ¦    reg D,reg MSB
  #n,P      ¦ SEP r  ¦ 1101RRRR ¦ ¦ ¦    immed (0-15), reg P
  #n,X      ¦ SEX r  ¦ 1110RRRR ¦ ¦ ¦    immed (0-15), reg X
  T,(R(X))  ¦ SAV    ¦ 78       ¦ ¦ ¦    reg T, ind_ind X
* MOVW       ¦        ¦          ¦ ¦ ¦ Move word (1)
  (R(X))+,Rr ¦ RLXA r ¦ 68,     ¦ ¦ ¦    ind_ind_inc X, reg
             ¦        ¦ 0110RRRR ¦ ¦ ¦
  #nn,Rr    ¦ RLDI   ¦ 68,      ¦ ¦ ¦    immed, reg
            ¦   r,nn ¦ 1100RRRR ¦ ¦ ¦
  Rr,(R(X))- ¦ RSXD r ¦ 68,     ¦ ¦ ¦    reg, ind_ind_dec X
             ¦        ¦ 1010RRRR ¦ ¦ ¦
  Rr,R(X)   ¦ RNX  r ¦ 68,      ¦ ¦ ¦    reg, reg_ind X
            ¦        ¦ 1011RRRR ¦ ¦ ¦    reg, reg ind X
  D,CTR     ¦ LDC    ¦ 68,06    ¦ ¦ ¦    reg D, counter
  CTR,D     ¦ GEC    ¦ 68,08    ¦ ¦ ¦    counter, reg D
PUSH+       ¦        ¦          ¦2¦ ¦ Push byte onto stack and
  XP        ¦ MARK   ¦ 79       ¦ ¦ ¦    move X & P to T then ind R2
            ¦        ¦          ¦ ¦ ¦    move P to X then Dec R2
```

Math Operations

```
ADD         ¦        ¦          ¦2¦ ¦ Add byte
  (R(X)),D  ¦ ADD    ¦ F4       ¦ ¦C¦    ind_ind X, reg D
  (R(P))+,D ¦ ADI    ¦ FC       ¦ ¦C¦    ind_ind_inc P, reg D
  #n,D      ¦        ¦ FC,nn    ¦ ¦ ¦    imed, reg D
  #Mn,D     ¦        ¦ FC,nn    ¦ ¦ ¦    imed MSB, reg D
ADC         ¦        ¦          ¦2¦ ¦ Add byte w/c
  (R(X)),D  ¦ ADC    ¦ 74       ¦ ¦C¦    ind_ind X, reg D
  (R(P))+,D ¦ ADCI   ¦ 7C       ¦ ¦C¦    ind_ind_inc P, reg D
  #n,D      ¦        ¦ 7C,nn    ¦ ¦ ¦    imed, reg D
  #Mn,D     ¦        ¦ 7C,nn    ¦ ¦ ¦    imed MSB, reg D
INCW        ¦        ¦          ¦2¦ ¦ Increment word
  Rr        ¦ INC r  ¦ 0001RRRR ¦ ¦ ¦    reg
  R(X)      ¦ IRX    ¦ 60       ¦ ¦ ¦    reg ind X
SUB         ¦        ¦          ¦2¦ ¦ Subtract byte  (result reg D)
  D,(R(X)),D ¦ SD    ¦ F5       ¦ ¦C¦    ind_ind X - reg D
  D,(R(P))+,D¦ SDI   ¦ FD       ¦ ¦C¦    ind_ind_inc P - reg D
```

```
        D,#n,D       !         ! FD,nn  ! ! !  imed - reg D, reg D
        D,#Mn,D      !         ! FD,nn  ! ! !  imed MSB - reg D, reg D
        (R(X)),D     ! SM      ! F7     ! !C!  reg D - ind_ind X
        (R(P))+,D    ! SMI     ! FF     ! !C!  reg D - ind_ind_inc P
        #n,D         !         ! FF,nn  ! ! !  imed, reg D
        #Mn,D        !         ! FF,nn  ! ! !  imed MSB, reg D
     SBB             !         !        !2! !  Sub byte w/c  (result reg D)
        D,(R(X)),D   ! SDB     ! 75     ! !C!  ind_ind X - reg D
        D,(R(P))+,D  ! SDBI    ! 7D     ! !C!  ind_ind_inc P - reg D
        D,#n,D       !         ! 7D,nn  ! ! !  imed - reg D, reg D
        D,#Mn,D      !         ! 7D,nn  ! ! !  imed MSB - reg D, reg D
        (R(X)),D     ! SMB     ! 77     ! !C!  reg D - ind_ind X
        (R(P))+,D    ! SMBI    ! 7F     ! !C!  reg D - ind_ind_inc P
        #n,D         !         ! 7F,nn  ! ! !  imed, reg D
        #Mn,D        !         ! 7F,nn  ! ! !  imed MSB, reg D
     DECW            !         !        !2! !  Decrement word
        Rr           ! DEC r   ! 0010RRRR ! !  reg
   *    CTR          ! DTC     ! 68,01  !3! !  counter  (1)
```

Logical Operations

```
     AND             !         !        !2! !  Logical AND byte
        (R(X)),D     ! AND     ! F2     ! ! !  ind_ind X, reg D
        (R(P))+,D    ! ANI     ! FA     ! ! !  ind_ind_inc P, reg D
        #n,D         !         ! FA,nn  ! ! !  imed, reg D
        #Mn,D        !         ! FA,nn  ! ! !  imed MSB, reg D
     OR              !         !        !2! !  Logical OR byte
        (R(X)),D     ! OR      ! F1     ! ! !  ind_ind X, reg D
        (R(P))+,D    ! ORI     ! F9     ! ! !  ind_ind_inc P, reg D
        #n,D         !         ! F9,nn  ! ! !  imed, reg D
        #Mn,D        !         ! F9,nn  ! ! !  imed MSB, reg D
     XOR             !         !        !2!    Logical Exclusive OR byte
        (R(X)),D     ! XOR     ! F3     ! ! !  ind_ind X, reg D
        (R(P))+,D    ! XRI     ! FB     ! ! !  ind_ind_inc P, reg D
        #n,D         !         ! FB,nn  ! ! !  imed, reg D
        #Mn,D        !         ! FB,nn  ! ! !  imed MSB, reg D
     RLWC            ! SHLC    !        !2!C!  Rotate byte w/c left
        D            ! RSHL    ! 7E     ! !C!  reg D
     RRWC            ! SHRC    !        !2!C!  Rotate byte w/c right
        D            ! RSHR    ! 76     ! !C!  reg D
     SLA             !         !        !2!C!  Shift left arithmetic
        D            ! SHL     ! FE     ! !C!  reg D
     SRL             !         !        !2!C!  Shift right logical
        D            ! SHR     ! F6     ! !C!  reg D
```

Bit Operations

```
     RESF            !         !        !2! !  Reset flag
        Q            ! REQ     ! 7A     ! !Q!    Q flip flop
     SETF            !         !        !2! !  Set flag
        Q            ! SEQ     ! 7B     ! !Q!    Q flip flop
```

Program Control

```
   * CALL            ! SCAL    !        ! ! !  Call subroutine  (1)
        aa,Rr        ! r,aa    ! 68,    !9! !    using reg
                     !         ! 1000RRRR ! !    using reg
   * RET             ! SRET    !        ! ! !  Return from subr  (1)
        Rr           ! r       ! 68     !8! !    using reg
                     !         ! 1001RRRR ! !    using reg
     JMP             !         !        !3! !  Jump to location
```

UN,aa	LBR aa	C0	| |	uncond
Z,aa	LBZ aa	C2	| |	zero
NZ,aa	LBNZ aa	CA	| |	not zero
C,aa	LBDF aa	C3	| |	carry
NC,aa	LBNF aa	CB	| |	no carry
Q,aa	LBQ aa	C1	| |	flag Q = 1
NQ,aa	LBNQ aa	C9	| |	flag Q = 0
JMPSP			|2|	Branch, same page
UN,s	BR a	30	| |	uncond
NZ,s	BNZ a	3A	| |	not zero
C,s	BDF a	33	| |	carry
	BPZ a	33	| |	pos or zero
NC,s	BNF a	3B	| |	no carry
	BM a	3B	| |	minus
	BL a	3B	| |	less
Q,s	BQ a	31	| |	flag Q = 1
NQ,s	BNQ a	39	| |	flag Q = 0
IO1,s	B1 a	34	| |	I/O EF1 = 1
NIO1,s	BN1 a	3C	| |	I/O EF1 = 0
IO2,s	B2 a	35	| |	I/O EF2 = 1
NIO2,s	BN2 a	3D	| |	I/O EF2 = 0
IO3,s	B3 a	36	| |	I/O EF3 = 1
NIO3,s	BN3 a	3E	| |	I/O EF3 = 0
IO4,s	B4 a	37	| |	I/O EF4 = 1
NIO4,s	BN4 a	3F	| |	I/O EF4 = 0
* CI,s	BCI a	68,3E	|3|	counter int (1)
* EI,s	BXI a	68,3F	|3|	external int (1)
SKIP			|2|	Skip byte
UN	NBR	38	| |	uncond
	SKP	38	| |	uncond
SKIPW			|3|	Skip word
UN	NLBR	C8	| |	uncond
	LSKP	C8	| |	uncond
Z	LSZ	CE	| |	zero
NZ	LSNZ	C6	| |	not zero
C	LSDF	CF	| |	carry
NC	LSNF	C7	| |	no carry
Q	LSQ	CD	| |	flag Q = 1
NQ	LSNQ	C5	| |	flag Q = 0
IE	LSIE	CC	| |	flag IE = 1
HALT	IDL	00	|2|	Stop till interrupt or DMA
NOP	NOP	C4	|3|	No operation
RETIE	RET	70	|2|	Move (R(X)) to X & P, inc R(X) and set IE = 1
RETID	DIS	71	|2|	Move (R(X)) to X & P, inc R(X) and set IE = 0
* STOP C	STPC	68,00	|3|	Stop counter clock (1)
* SEL			|3|	Select (1)
TM	STM	68,07	| |	timer mode
CM1	SCM1	68,05	| |	counter mode 1
CM2	SCM2	68,03	| |	counter mode 2
PM1	SPM1	68,04	| |	pulse width mode 1
PM2	SPM2	68,02	| |	pulse width mode 2

I/O Operations

IN	INP		|2|	Input from port, 1 thru 7
p,(R(X))	P	01101PPP	| |	port, ind_ind X and reg D
OUT	OUT		|2|	Output to port, 1 thru 7
(R(X))+,p	P	01100PPP	| |	ind_ind_inc X, port
EI	XIE	68,0A	|2|	Enable external interrupts
DI	XID	68,0B	|2|	Disable external interrupts

```
EC          ¦ CIE    ¦ 68,0C   ¦2¦ ¦ Enable counter interrupts
DC          ¦ CID    ¦ 68,0D   ¦2¦ ¦ Disable counter interrupts
```

Registers

```
      8    5¦4    0
      ----------------
      ¦  I  ¦  N  ¦    Instruction
      ----------------
            ¦  P  ¦    Inst adr pointer
            -------
            ¦  X  ¦    Data adr pointer
      ----------------
      ¦     T     ¦    Temp data
      ----------------
      ¦     D     ¦    Temp data, accum
      ----------------
```

Memory Address Registers

```
       16    8¦7     0
       -----------------
  R0  ¦  H0  ¦  L0  ¦
       -----------------
  R1  ¦  H1  ¦  L1  ¦
       -----------------
  R2  ¦  H2  ¦  L2  ¦
       -----------------
Rreg    Hreg    Lreg
       -----------------
  RF  ¦  HF  ¦  LF  ¦
       -----------------
```

```
   R0 - Inst adr after reset
        and during DMA
   R1 - Inst adr when interrupt
   R2 - Stack pointer
```

Flags

```
   DF = carry
   IE = interrupt enable
   Q  = flip flop
```

Addressing Modes

```
Univ    Manuf
----    -----
Rr       r     - register
aa       aa    - absolute (16-bit)
(Rr)     r     - register indirect
s        a     - same page (8-bit)
# nn     nn    - immediate data
#L n           - immediate data, LSB of word value
#M n           - immediate data, MSB of word value
(R(X))         - indirect reg pointed to by reg X
(Rr)+    r     - indirect reg post auto increment
(R(X))+        - indirect reg pointed to by reg X or P post auto inc
(R(X))-        - indirect reg pointed to by reg X or P post auto dec
```

p   p   - port address (3-bits)

Instruction Expansion

```
                   Rr Mr Lr
                   --------

  r    RRRR    r    RRRR    r    RRRR    r    RRRR
 ---   ----   ---   ----   ---   ----   ---   ----
  0    0000    4    0100    8    1000    C    1100
  1    0001    5    0101    9    1001    D    1101
  2    0010    6    0110    A    1010    E    1110
  3    0011    7    0111    B    1011    F    1111
```

    Rr = 16 bit register
    Mr = MSB register
    Lr = LSB register

s   - same page adr 8-bit value appended to inst
aa - absolute adr 16-bit value appended to inst, MSB first
#nn - immediate value appended to inst, MSB first
#n - immediate single byte value appended to inst
#L n - immediate LSB of double byte value appended to inst
#M n - immediate MSB of double byte value appended to inst

Special Memory Locations

Notes

2650 Incomplete

2650A   **(1) 2650B**

Data Move

```
MOV             :             :           : :   : Move byte
     Rr,R0      : LODZ  r     : 000000RR   : 2:cc :   reg, reg 0
     #n,Rr      : LODI  r,n   : 000001RR   : 2:cc :   immed, reg
     RA a,Rr    : LODR  r,a   : 000010RR   : 3:cc :   relative, reg
     aa,Rr      : LODA  r,aa  : 000011RR   : 4:cc :   abs, reg
     R0,Rr      : STRZ  r     : 110000RR   : 2:cc :   reg 0, reg
     Rr,RA a    : STRR  a,r   : 110010RR   : 3:  :   reg, relative
     Rr,aa      : STRA  aa,r  : 110011RR   : 4:  :   reg, abs
     R0,PSU     : LPSU        : 92         : 2:all:   reg 0, prg sts upper
     R0,PSL     : LPSL        : 93         : 2:all:   reg 0, prg sts lower
     PSU,R0     : SPSU        : 12         : 2:cc :   prg sts upper, reg 0
     PSL,R0     : SPSL        : 13         : 2:cc :   prg sts lower, reg 0
*    aa,PSL     : LDPL  aa    : 10         : 4:all:   abs, prg sts lower  (1)
*    PSL,aa     : STPL  aa    : 11         : 4:  :   prg sts lower, abs  (1)
```

Math Operations

```
ADD             :             :           : :all: Add  w/wo carry
     Rr,R0      : ADDZ  r     : 100000RR   : 2:  :   reg, reg 0
     #n,Rr      : ADDI  r,n   : 100001RR   : 3:  :   immed,reg
```

252

```
      RA a,Rr  ! ADDR r,a  ! 100010RR ! 3!    !  relative, reg
      aa,Rr    ! ADDA r,aa ! 100011RR ! 4!    !  abs, reg
SUB            !           !          !  !all! Subtract w/wo carry
      Rr,R0    ! SUBZ  r   ! 101000RR ! 2!    !  reg, reg 0
      #n,Rr    ! SUBI r,n  ! 101001RR ! 2!    !  immed, reg
      RA a,Rr  ! SUBR r,a  ! 101010RR ! 3!    !  relative, reg
      aa,Rr    ! SUBA r,aa ! 101011RR ! 4!    !  abs, reg
DA    Rr       ! DAR  r    ! 100101RR ! 3!    ! Decimal adjust register
CMP            !           !          !  !cc ! Compare arith/logical
      Rr,R0    ! COMZ  r   ! 111000RR ! 2!    !  reg, reg 0
      #n,Rr    ! COMI r,n  ! 111001RR ! 3!    !  immed, reg
      RA a,Rr  ! COMR r,a  ! 111010RR ! 3!    !  relative, reg
      aa,Rr    ! COMA r,aa ! 111011RR ! 4!    !  abs, reg
```

Logical Operations

```
AND            !           !          !  !cc ! Logical AND
      Rr,R0    ! ANDZ  r   ! 010000RR ! 2!    !  reg, reg 0
      #n,Rr    ! ANDI r,n  ! 010001RR ! 3!    !  immed, reg
      RA a,Rr  ! ANDR r,a  ! 010010RR ! 3!    !  relative, reg
      aa,Rr    ! ANDA r,aa ! 010011RR ! 4!    !  abs, reg
OR             !           !          !  !cc ! Logical OR
      Rr,R0    ! IORZ  r   ! 011000RR ! 2!    !  reg, reg 0
      #n,Rr    ! IORI r,n  ! 011001RR ! 3!    !  immed, reg
      RA a,Rr  ! IORR r,a  ! 011010RR ! 3!    !  relative, reg
      aa,Rr    ! IORA r,aa ! 011011RR ! 4!    !  abs, reg
XOR            !           !          !  !cc ! Logical Exclusive OR
      Rr,R0    ! EORZ  r   ! 001000RR ! 2!    !  reg, reg 0
      #n,Rr    ! EORI r,n  ! 001001RR ! 3!    !  immed, reg
      RA a,Rr  ! EORR r,a  ! 001010RR ! 3!    !  relative, reg
      aa,Rr    ! EORA r,aa ! 001011RR ! 4!    !  abs, reg
TEST           ! TMI       !          !  !   ! Test logical AND set flags
      #n,Rr    !       r,n ! 111101RR ! 3!CC !  immed, reg
RRNC           ! RRR       !          !  !   ! Rotate right w/wo carry
      Rr       !       r   ! 010100RR ! 2!all!  reg
RLNC           ! RRL       !          !  !   ! Rotate left w/wo carry
      Rr       !       r   ! 110100RR ! 2!all!  reg
```

Bit Operations

```
TESTB          !           !          !  !   ! Test bits
      PSU,m    ! TPSU  m   ! B4       ! 3!cc !  prg sts upper, mask
      PSL,m    ! TPSL  m   ! B5       ! 3!cc !  prg sts lower, mask
RESB           !           !          !  !   ! Reset bits
      PSU,m    ! CPSU  m   ! 74       ! 3!all!  prg sts upper, mask
      PSL,m    ! CPSL  m   ! 75       ! 3!all!  prg sts lower, mask
SETB           !           !          !  !   ! Set bits
      PSU,m    ! PPSU  m   ! 76       ! 3!all!  prg sts upper, mask
      PSL,m    ! PPSL  m   ! 77       ! 3!all!  prg sts lower, mask
```

Program Control

```
CALL           !           !          !  !   ! Call subroutine if
      CC,aa    ! BSTA  CC,aa! 001111CC ! 3!   !  cond true, abs
      NCC,aa   ! BSFA  CC,aa! 101111CC ! 3!   !  cond false, abs
      RNZ,Rr,aa! BSNA r,aa ! 011111RR ! 3!   !  reg not zero, reg, abs
      UN,aa    ! BSXA  aa  ! 10111111 ! 3!   !  uncond, index abs
CALLR          !           !          !  !   ! Call subroutine if
      CC,r     ! BSTR  CC,r! 001110CC ! 3!   !  cond true, relative
      NCC,r    ! BSFR  CC,r! 101110CC ! 3!   !  cond false, relative
      RNZ,Rr,r ! BSNR  r,a ! 011110RR ! 3!   !  reg not zero, reg, rel
      UN,r     ! ZBSR  a   ! 10111011 ! 3!   !  uncond, rel
```

```
RET    CC    | RETC  CC    | 000101CC | 3| | Return from subr, if
RETIE  CC    | RETE  CC    | 001101CC | 3| | Return from subr EI, if
JMP          |             |          | | | Jump if
    CC,aa    | BCTA  CC,aa | 000111CC | 3| |   cond true, abs
    NCC,aa   | BCFA  CC,aa | 100111CC | 3| |   cond false, abs
    UN,aa    | BXA   aa    | 10011111 | 3| |   uncond, indexed abs
JMPR         |             |          | | | Jump if
    CC,a     | BCTR  CC,r  | 000110CC | 3| |   cond true, relative
    NCC,a    | BCFR  CC,r  | 100110CC | 3| |   cond false, relative
    UN,a     | ZBRR  r     | 10011011 | 3| |   uncond, relative
INCJNZ       |             |          | | | Increment and jmp not zero
    Rr,RA a  | BIRR  r,a   | 110110RR | 3| |   reg, relative
    Rr,aa    | BIRA  r,aa  | 110111RR | 3| |   reg, abs
DECJNZ       |             |          | | | Decrement and jmp not zero
    Rr,RA a  | BDRR  r,a   | 111110RR | 3| |   reg,.relative
    Rr,aa    | BDRA  r,aa  | 111111RR | 3| |   reg, abs
TSTJNZ       |             |          | | | Test jump if not zero
    Rr,RA a  | BRNR  r,a   | 010110RR | 3| |   reg, relative
    Rr,aa    | BRNA  r,aa  | 010111RR | 3| |   reg, abs
NOP          | NOP         | 11000000 | 1| | No operation
HALT         | HALT        | 01000000 | 1| | Enter wait state
```

I/O   Operations

```
OUT          |             |          | 2| | Output data
    Rr,P     | WRTD  r     | 111100RR | | |     to port from reg
    Rr,C     | WRTC  r     | 101100RR | | |     to control from reg
    Rr,E     | WRTE  r     | 110101RR | 3| |     to extended from reg
IN           |             |          | 2|CC| Input data
    P,Rr     | REDD  r     | 011100RR | | |     to reg from port
    C,Rr     | REDC  r     | 001100RR | | |     to reg, from control
    E,Rr     | REDE  r     | 010101RR | 3| |     to reg, from extended
```

Registers

```
    15      7      0
            ---------
            |  R0  |
            ---------      ---
            |  R1  |
            ---------
            |  R2  |  Two banks of 3 registers (R1 - R3)
            ---------
            |  R3  |
    -------------------    ---
    |                 |  8 Stack registers
    -------------------
    |       PC        |  Prog adr reg
    -------------------
    | PSU  |   PSL    |  Prog status word
    -------------------
```

Flags

```
              PSU                    PSL
              ---                    ---
    bit 0 - carry/borrow      stack pointer bit 0
        1 - logical/arithmetic compare   stack pointer bit 1
        2 - overflow          stack pointer bit 2
```

3 - with/without carry
4 - register bank select
5 - half carry from bit 3
6 - condition code LSB
7 - condition code MSB

```
3 - with/without carry        *  user flag 2    (1)
4 - register bank select      *  user flag 1    (1)
5 - half carry from bit 3        interrupt inhibit
6 - condition code LSB           flag output
7 - condition code MSB           sense input
```

```
Condition code CC = 00   zero, equal, all selected bits are 1
                    01   positive, R0 > r, r > V
                    10   negative, R0 < r, r < V, all selected bits not = 1
                    11   uncoditional branch
```

Addressing Modes

```
Univ  Manuf
----  -----
#n    n   - immediate
Rr    r   - register
aa    aa  - absolute, 16-bit adr, see below
RA a  a   - relative adr, 8-bit adr, see below
```

Instruction Expansion

```
Rr    register      RR = R0 - R3, 00 - 11 respectively
CC    condition     CC = see above
#n    immediate     8 bit data appended to instruction
aa    abs adr       16 bit address appended to instruction
                    non-jump-inst = bit 0 - 12  address
                                         13-14  index indicator
                                               00 = no   01 = index inc
                                               11 = index 10 = index dec
                                          15  indirect
                    jump inst or PSL bit 0 - 12  address
                                        13-14  page
                                         15    indirect
r     rel address   7 bit rel value appended to inst, MSB indirect indicator
m     mask          8 bit mask appended to inst
```

Special Memory Locations

32K bytes organized as 8 pages of 192 bytes

Notes

32000

TMS32010, TMS320M10, SMJ32010   (*) TMS32020

Data Move

```
MOVB      !         !       !                   ! !  ! Move single bit value
  v,ARP   ! LARP  v ! 0110100010000000V  !1!  !   immed, reg ARP
  v       ! MAR  *,v ! 0110100000000000V  !1!  !   ARP to (AC),n to ARP
  Mem,DP  ! LDP  Mem ! 01101111MMMMMMMM  !1!  !   memory, reg DP
  v,DP    ! LDPK  v ! 0110111100000000V  !1!  !   immed, reg DP
  Mem,SR  ! LST  Mem ! 01111011MMMMMMMM  !1!  !   memory, status reg
  SR,Mem  ! SST  Mem ! 01111100MMMMMMMM  !1!  !   status reg, memory
* #n,PM   ! SPM  n   ! 11001110000010nn  !1!  !   immed, reg PM sft mode
```

```
*  Mem,b,TC   | BIT  Mem,b  | 1001bbbbMMMMMMMM |1|TC|  memory,bit, TC
*  Mem,T,TC   | BITT Mem    | 01010111MMMMMMMM |1|TC|  memory,bit T, reg TC
MOV           |             |                  | | | Move byte
   #n,AC      | LACK n      | 01111110nnnnnnnn |1| |   immed, accum
   #n,ARr     | LARK n      | 0111000Rnnnnnnnn |1| |   immed, aux reg [1]
*  Mem,PH     | LPH  Mem    | 01010011MMMMMMMM |1| |   memory, reg PH
MOVW          |             |                  | | | Move word
   Mem,ARr    | LAR  ARr,Mem| 0011100RMMMMMMMM |1| |   memory, aux reg
*  #nn,ARr    | LRLK ARr,n  | 11010RRR00000000 |1| |   immed, aux reg
   ARr,Mem    | SAR  ARr,Mem| 0011000RMMMMMMMM |1| |   aux reg, memory [2]
   Mem,+1     | DMOV Mem    | 01101001MMMMMMMM |1| |   memory,memory+1
   Mem,T      | LT   Mem    | 01101010MMMMMMMM |1| |   memory, reg T
   AC,Mem     | SACL Mem    | 01010000MMMMMMMM |1| |   accum LSW, memory
   (AC),Mem   | TBLR Mem    | 01100111MMMMMMMM |3| |   ind accum, memory
              |             |                  | | |   prog mem to data mem
   Mem,(AC)   | TBLW Mem    | 01111101MMMMMMMM |3| |   memory, ind accum
              |             |                  | | |   data mem to prog mem
*  Mem,ST1    | LST1 Mem    | 01010001MMMMMMMM |1| |   memory, status reg 1
*  ST1,MEM    | SST1 Mem    | 01111001MMMMMMMM |1| |   status reg 1, memory
MOVDW         |             |                  | | | Move double word
   P,AC       | PAC         | 0111111110001110 |1| |   reg P, accum
MOVSLW        |             |                  | | | Move shifted word
   Mem,s,AC   | LAC  Mem,s  | 0010SSSSMMMMMMMM |1| |   srce, bits, accum
*  Mem,T,AC   | LACT Mem    | 01000010MMMMMMMM |1| |   srce,reg T,accum
*  #nn,s,AC   | LALK nn,s   | 1101SSSS00000001 |2| |   immed,bits,accum
MOVHSLW       | SACH        |                  | | | Shift left move MSW
   AC,s,Mem   |      Mem,s  | 01011SSSMMMMMMMM |1| |   accum, bits, memory
              |             |                  | | |   shift can be 0,1,4 bit
MOVADD        | LTA         |                  | | | Move and add words
   Mem,T,P,AC |      Mem    | 01101100MMMMMMMM |1|OV|  move memory to reg T
              |             |                  | | |   add reg P to accum
MOVSUBSW      | LTS         |                  | | | Move, sub shifted wrd
*  Mem,T,P,PM |      Mem    | 01011011MMMMMMMM |1|OV|  move memory to reg T
   Ac         |             |                  | | |   sub P,Pm bits, accum
MOVAM         | LTD         |                  | | | Move add move words
   Mem,T,P,AC |      Mem    | 01101011MMMMMMMM |1|OV|  move memory to reg T
   +1         |             |                  | | |   add reg P to accum
              |             |                  | | |   move memory to memory+1
MOVMOVSW      | LTP         |                  | | | Move, move shifted word
*  Mem,T,P,   |      Mem    | 00111110MMMMMMMM |1| |   move mem to reg T
   PM,AC      |             |                  | | |   reg P,PM bits, accum
POP           |             |                  | | | Pop 12-bit word from stk
   ACL        | POP         | 0111111110011101 |2| |   accum
*  Mem        | POPD        | 01111010MMMMMMMM |2| |   memory
PUSH          |             |                  | | | Push 12-bits on stack
   ACL        | PUSH        | 0111111110011100 |2| |   accum
*  Mem        | PSHD Mem    | 01010100MMMMMMMM |2| |   memory
CLRDW         | ZAC         |                  | | | Clear double word
   AC         |             | 0111111110001001 |1| |   accum
CLRMOV        |             |                  | | | Clear dword, move word
   Mem,ACH    | ZALH Mem    | 01100101MMMMMMMM |1| |   memory, accum MSW
   Mem, ACL   | ZALS Mem    | 01100110MMMMMMMM |1| |   memory, accum LSW
```

Logical Operations

```
ANDW          | AND         |                  | | | Logical AND word
   Mem,AC     |      Mem    | 01111001MMMMMMMM |1| |   scre, accum
ANDSW         | ANDK        |                  | | | Logical AND shifted word
*  #nn,s,AC   |      nn,s   | 1101SSSS00000100 |2| |   immed,bits,accum
ORW           | OR          |                  | | | Logical OR, word
   Mem,AC     |      Mem    | 01111010MMMMMMMM |1| |   srce, accum
ORSW          | ORK         |                  | | | Logical OR shifted word
```

```
*  #nn,s,AC  ¦   nn,s      ¦ 1101SSSS00000101 ¦2¦ ¦   immed,bits,accum
XORW         ¦ XOR         ¦                  ¦ ¦ ¦ Exclusive OR word
   Mem,AC    ¦   Mem       ¦ 01111000MMMMMMMM ¦1¦ ¦   source, accum
XORSW        ¦ XORK        ¦                  ¦ ¦ ¦ Exclusive OR shifted word
*  #nn,s,AC  ¦   nn,s      ¦ 1101SSSS00000110 ¦2¦ ¦   immed,bits,accum
CMPDW        ¦ CMPL        ¦                  ¦ ¦ ¦ Complement dword
*  AC        ¦             ¦ 1100111000100111 ¦1¦ ¦   accum
SLLDW        ¦ SFL         ¦                  ¦ ¦ ¦ Shift left logical dword
*  AC        ¦             ¦ 1100111000011000 ¦1¦ ¦   accum
SRLDW        ¦ SFR         ¦                  ¦ ¦ ¦ Shift right logical dword
*  AC        ¦             ¦ 1100111000011001 ¦1¦ ¦   accum
```

Bit Operations

```
RESF         ¦             ¦                  ¦ ¦ ¦ Reset flag
   OVM       ¦ ROVM        ¦ 0111111110001010 ¦1¦ ¦   overflow mode
*  CNF       ¦ CNFD        ¦ 1100111000000100 ¦1¦ ¦   configure B0 RAM
*  SXM       ¦ RSXM        ¦ 1100111000000110 ¦1¦ ¦   sign extension mode
*  XF        ¦ RXF         ¦ 1100111000001100 ¦1¦ ¦   external flag
SETF         ¦             ¦                  ¦ ¦ ¦ Set flag
   OVM       ¦ SOVM        ¦ 0111111110001011 ¦1¦ ¦   overflow mode
*  CMF       ¦ CNFP        ¦ 1100111000000101 ¦1¦ ¦   config B0 prg mem
*  SXM       ¦ SSXM        ¦ 1100111000000111 ¦1¦ ¦   sign extension mode
*  XF        ¦ SXF         ¦ 1100111000001101 ¦1¦ ¦   external flag
REP          ¦             ¦                  ¦ ¦ ¦ Repeat following inst
*  Mem       ¦ RPT  Mem    ¦ 01001011MMMMMMMM ¦1¦ ¦   repeat count in mem
*  #n        ¦ RPTK n      ¦ 11001011nnnnnnnn ¦1¦ ¦   count
MOVSW        ¦ BLKD        ¦                  ¦ ¦ ¦ Move string of words
*  aa,Mem    ¦   aa,Mem    ¦ 11111101MMMMMMMM ¦3¦ ¦   data aa, memory
*  aa,Mem    ¦ BLKP aa,Mem ¦ 11111100MMMMMMMM ¦3¦ ¦   prg aa,memory
```

Math Operations

```
ADDSW        ¦             ¦                  ¦ ¦  ¦ Add shifted word
   Mem,s,AC  ¦ ADD  Mem,s  ¦ 0000SSSSMMMMMMMM ¦1¦OV¦   srce,bits,accum
*  Mem,T,AC  ¦ ADDT  Mem   ¦ 01001010MMMMMMMM ¦1¦OV¦   srce,reg T,accum
*  #nn,s,AC  ¦ ADLK  nn,s  ¦ 1101SSSS00000010 ¦2¦OV¦   immed,bits,accum
ADDSWQW      ¦ SQRA        ¦                  ¦ ¦  ¦ Add sft wrd, mov sqr
*  P,PM,AC,  ¦   Mem       ¦ 00111001MMMMMMMM ¦1¦OV¦   regP,PM bits,accum
   Mem,P     ¦             ¦                  ¦ ¦  ¦   regP= mem squared
ADDHW        ¦ ADDH        ¦                  ¦ ¦  ¦ Add word to MSW of Accum
   Mem,AC    ¦   Mem       ¦ 000000100010RRRR ¦1¦OV¦   srce, accum
ADDW         ¦ ADDS        ¦                  ¦ ¦  ¦ Add word no sign extend
   Mem,AC    ¦   Mem       ¦ 01100001MMMMMMMM ¦1¦OV¦   srce, accum
ADDDW        ¦ APAC        ¦                  ¦ ¦  ¦ Add double word
   P,AC      ¦             ¦ 0111111110001111 ¦1¦OV¦   reg P, accum
INCW         ¦             ¦                  ¦ ¦  ¦ Increment word
   AR        ¦ MAR  *+     ¦ 0110100010101000 ¦1¦  ¦   current aux reg
   AR,v      ¦ MAR  *+,v   ¦ 011010001010000V ¦1¦  ¦   aux reg, set ARP = n
SUBW         ¦             ¦                  ¦ ¦  ¦ Subtract word
   Mem,ACH   ¦ SUBH  Mem   ¦ 01100010MMMMMMMM ¦1¦OV¦   memory, accum MSW
   Mem,ACL   ¦ SUBS  Mem   ¦ 01100011MMMMMMMM ¦1¦OV¦   memory, accum LSW
SUBDW        ¦ SPAC        ¦                  ¦ ¦  ¦ Subtract double word
   P,AC      ¦             ¦ 0111111110010000 ¦1¦OV¦   reg P, accum
SUBSW        ¦             ¦                  ¦ ¦  ¦ Subtract shifted word
   Mem,s,AC  ¦ SUB  Mem,s  ¦ 0001SSSSMMMMMMMM ¦1¦OV¦   memory, bits, accum
*  #nn,s,AC  ¦ SBLK  nn,s  ¦ 1101SSSS00000011 ¦2¦OV¦   immed,bits,accum
*  Mem,T,AC  ¦ SUBT  Mem   ¦ 01000110MMMMMMMM ¦1¦OV¦   srce,reg T,accum
SUBSWQW      ¦ SQRS        ¦                  ¦ ¦  ¦ Sub sft wrd, mov sqr
*  P,PM,Ac,  ¦   Mem       ¦ 01011010MMMMMMMM ¦1¦OV¦   regP,PM bits,accum
   Mem,P     ¦             ¦                  ¦ ¦  ¦   regP= mem squared
SUBIF        ¦ SUBC        ¦                  ¦ ¦  ¦ Conditional subtract
```

```
       Mem,AC   !     Mem    ! 01100100MMMMMMMM !1!OV!    see micro manual
DECW             !            !                  !  !   ! Decrement word
     AR          ! MAR  *-    ! 0110100010011000 !1!   !    current aux reg
     AR,v        ! MAR  *-,v  ! 011010001001000V !1!   !    aux reg, set ARP = v
MULW             ! MPY        !                  !  !   ! Multiply words
     Mem,T,P     ! MPY   Mem  ! 0110110111MMMMMMMM !1!  !    reg P=srce x reg T
     #nn,T,P     ! MPYX  nn   ! 100nnnnnnnnnnnnn !1!   !    reg P=immed x reg T
MULADDW          ! MAC        !                  !  !   ! Multiply and add
*  Mem,aa,P      !   aa,Mem   ! 01011101MMMMMMMM !3!OV!    reg P=memory x prg adr
     P,s,Ac      !            !                  !  !   !    add reg P,PM bits, acum
MULADMVW         ! MACD       !                  !  !   ! Multiply, add, move word
*  Mem,aa,P      !   aa,Mem   ! 01011100MMMMMMMM !3!OV!    reg P=mem x prg adr
     P,s,AC,+1   !            !                  !  !   !    add P,PM bits,accum
                 !            !                  !  !   !    move mem to mem+1
ABS   AC         ! ABS        ! 0111111110001000 !1!OV! Change to absolute value
* NEGW AC        ! NEG        ! 1100111000100011 !1!OV! Negate word, accum
NROMW            ! NORM       !                  !  !   ! If 2 MSBs = 0 or 1
*   AC,AR        !            ! 1100111000100010 !1!TC!    shift accum left
                 !            !                  !  !   !    and inc aux reg
CMPW             ! CMPR       !                  !  !   ! Compare words
*  AR,ARr        !    ARr     ! 110011100101000RR !1!TC!    aux reg, cur aux reg
```

Program Control
```
CALL             !            !                  !  !   ! Call subroutine
     (AC)        ! CALA       ! 0111111110001100 !2!   !    uncond, ind accum
     aa          ! CALL PRGaa ! 1111100000000000 !2!   !    uncond, loc
RET              ! RET        ! 0111111110001101 !2!   ! Return from subroutine
JMP              ! B          !                  !  !   ! Jump if
     aa          !      PRGaa ! 1111100100000000 !2!   !    uncond, loc
     (AC)        ! BACC       ! 1100111000100101 !2!   !    uncond, ind accum
JMPDEC           ! BANZ       !                  !  !   ! Jump if and decrement
     AR,NZ,aa    !      PRGaa ! 1111010000000000 !2!   !    AR LSB not 0, loc
JMP              !            !                  !  !   ! Jump if accum
     GEZ,aa      ! BGEZ PRGaa ! 1111111010000000 !2!   !    > or = 0
     GT,aa       ! BGZ  PRGaa ! 1111110000000000 !2!   !    > 0
     NIO,aa      ! BIOZ PRGaa ! 1111011000000000 !2!   !    I/O status = 0
     LEZ,aa      ! BLEZ PRGaa ! 1111101100000000 !2!   !    < or = 0
     LZ,aa       ! BLZ  PRGaa ! 1111101000000000 !2!   !    minus
     NZ,aa       ! BNZ  PRGaa ! 1111111000000000 !2!   !    <> 0
     V,aa        ! BV   PRGaa ! 1111010100000000 !2!   !    overflow
     Z,aa        ! BZ   PRGaa ! 1111111100000000 !2!   !    = 0
JMPMOD           ! BBNZ       !                  !  !   ! Jump if and modify
*   BS,aa,Mem    !   aa,Mem   ! 11111001MMMMMMMM !2!   !    if TC=1 jump
                 !            !                  !  !   !    modify AR and ARP
*   BR,aa,Mem    ! BBZ  aa,Mem! 11111000MMMMMMMM !2!   !    if TC=0 jump
*   V,aa,Mem     ! BNV  aa,Mem! 11110111MMMMMMMM !2!   !    if OV=0 jump
NOP              ! NOP        ! 0111111110000000 !1!   ! No operation
WAIT             ! IDLE       ! 1100111000011111 !2!   ! Wait till interrupt
* TRAP           ! TRAP       ! 1100111000011110 !2!   ! Software interrupt
```

I/O Operations
```
IN               ! IN         !                  !  !   ! Input word
     P,Mem       ! Mem,PAp    ! 01000PPPMMMMMMMM !2!   !    memory, port
OUT              ! OUT        !                  !  !   ! Output word
     Mem,p       ! Mem,PAp    ! 01001PPPMMMMMMMM !2!   !    source,# bits,to CRU
DI               ! DINT       ! 0111111110000001 !1!   ! Disable interrupts
EI               ! EINT       ! 0111111110000010 !1!   ! Enable interrupts
* FRMT           ! FORT       !                  !  !   ! Format serial I/O port
     v           !   v        ! 110011100000111V !1!   !    0=16 bit; 1=8 bit
```

```
* SPXMT    : RTXM    : 1100111000100000 :1: : Serial port xmt mode =0
* STXM     : STXM    : 1100111000100001 :1: : Serial port xmt mode =1
```

REGISTERS

32010

```
        32             15            0
      ----------------------------------
ACC   :    ACCH     :     ACCL     :    Accumulator
      ----------------------------------
ARØ                 :               :    9 LSB bidirectional counter
                    -------------------  8 LSB used for indirect RAM adr
AR1                 :               :
      ----------------------------------
T                   : Multiplicand :
      ----------------------------------
P     :    Multiply product        :
      ----------------------------------
PC              :   12-bit    :         Program counter
                -------------
                :  4 x 12     :         Stack registers
                -------------
                      : 5-bit :         Status register
                      ---------
```

32020

```
        32             15            0
      ----------------------------------
ACC   :    ACCH     :     ACCL     :    Accumulator
      ----------------------------------
                    :  ARØ - AR4   :    Auxilary registers
                    ----------------
                          : ARP:         3-bit auxiliary reg pointer
                          ------
                          : ARB:         3-bit aux reg pointer buffer
                          ------
                    :  DP  :              9-bit data page pointer
                    --------                (512, 128 word pages)
      ----------------------------------
TR                  : Multiplicand :    Temporary register
      ----------------------------------
P     :    PH       :     PL       :    Multiply product
      ----------------------------------
PC                  :    16-bit    :    Program counter
                    ----------------
                    :    4 x 16    :    Stack registers
                    ----------------
                    :    2 x 16    :    Status registers
                    ----------------
```

Flags

32010

```
   SR  Mem
   --  ---
bit 1   8    ARP = auxiliary register pointer, selects ARØ or AR1 for use in
             indirct addressing.
```

```
    0   0   DP  = data memory page pointer, 0 = loc 0 - 127
                                            1 = loc 128 - 144
    2   13  INTM = interrupt mode
    4   15  OV  = overflow
    3   14  OVM = overflow mode
```

INTF = interrupt flag, not part of status register

32020
-----
status reg 0
```
bit 15-13   ARP = auxiliary register pointer, selects AR0 to AR4 for use in
                  indirct addressing.
    8-0     DP  = data memory page pointer, MSB of data address
    9       INTM = interrupt mode
    12      OV  = overflow
    11      OVM = overflow mode
```

status reg 1
```
bit 0    PM = P reg shift mode  00 - no shift
                                01 - left shift 1 bit, zero filled
                                10 - left shift 4 bits, zero filled
                                11 - right shift 6 bits, sign extended
    1-2     TXM = transmit mode
    3       F0 = serial port format
    4       XF = external flag
    10      SXM = sign extension mode
    11      TC = test/control bit flag
    12      CNF = RAM configuration control
    13-15   ARB = auxiliary register pointer buffer
```

Addressing Modes
---------- -----

```
Univ    Manuf
----    -----
#n      n      - immediate data
XX      XX     - register or flag
ARx     ARx    - auxiliary register
aa      PRGaa  - absolute address, program
a       DATa   - absolute address, data
(AR)    *      - register indirect, AR or AC
(AR)+   *+     - indirect post auto increment, by 1
(AR)-   *-     - indirect post auto decrement, by 1
(AR)-AR0 *0-   - indirect post auto decrement by AR0
(AR)+AR0 *0+   - indirect post auto increment by AR0
P       PAp    - port address
```

Instruction Expansion

```
                 (Mem)
Univ    Man      Mode           MMMMMMMM
----    ---      ----           --------
a       DATa     data adr       0aaaaaaa   * adr = reg DP + a  (1)
(AR)    *        AR  indirect   1000YYYY
(AR)+   *+       AR ind_inc by 1 1010YYYY
(AR)-   *-       AR ind_dec by 1 1001YYYY
* (AR)-AR0 *0-   AR ind_dec by AR0 1101YYYY  (1)
* (AR)+AR0 *0+   AR ind_inc by AR0 1110YYYY  (1)
```

AR = current aux register as specified in ARP

```
                     Univ   Mam                         YYYY
                     ----   ---                         ----
if the parameter     AR0     0   is appended to the inst 0000
                     AR1     1                           0001
*                    AR2     2                           0010  (1)
*                    AR3     3                           0011  (1)
*                    AR4     4                           0100  (1)
                     niether                             1000
```

the indicated number 0 - 4 is put in the ARP and the new AR is
        incremented or decremented is indicated by the addressing mode.

[1] auto inc/dec although permitted as an operand is not performed
[2] if the same AR is stored as is used for indirect addressing the
        value stored will be inc or dec.

aa = address, 12-bit program address appended to inst
v = immediate data, single pit value part of inst
n = immediate data, 8-bit value part of inst
                     or 16-bit value appended to inst
s = number of bits to shift, 4-bits part of inst
p = port adr, 3-bits part of inst

Special Memory Locations

32010
-----

144 x 16 on chip RAM
1536 x 16 on chip ROM, TMS320M10 only
maximum external RAM is 4K x 16

loc 0 = reset first word
    1 = reset scond word
    2 = interrupt

32020
-----

544 x 16 on chip RAM organized as   block B0   256 words data or prog memory
                                          B1   256   data memory
                                          B2   32   data memory

Maximum of 64K data memory and 64K program memory
        data memory devided into 512 128 word pages
Maximum of 15 external I/O addresses

```
   Program Memory              Data Memory
   --------------              -----------

0-31    Interrupts     0-5    mem maped reg  ------- 0  DRR serial port rcvr
32-65K  External       6-95   reserved               1  DXR serial port xmtr
                       96-127 on chip block B2        2  TIM timer
                      128-511 reserved                3  PRD period
                      512-767 on chip block B0        4  IMR 5-bit inter mask
                     768-1023 on chip block B1        5  GREG global memory
                     1024-65K external                   allocation reg
```

the CNFP instruction deactivates data memory 512-767, on chip block B0
        and assigns program memory 65280-65535 as block B0

261

6100

HM6100, IM6100   **(1) HD6120**

Data Move

```
* MOVN                                   Move nible   (1)
*    #n,DF     | CDF  n    | 110010nnn001 |  6|   immed,DF flag
*    #n,IF     | CIF  n    | 110010nnn010 |  6|   immed, IF flag
*    #n,DFIF   | CDF CIF n | 110010nnn011 |  6|   immed, DF & IF flags
*    DF,AC     | RDF       | 110010001100 |  6|   DF flag, reg AC bits 6-8
*    IF,AC     | RIF       | 110010010100 |  6|   IF flag, reg AC bits 6-8
*    ISFDSF,AC | RIB       | 110010011100 |  6|   ISF flag, reg AC bits 6-8
                                                   DSF flag,         9-11
*  IBDF,ISFDSF | RMF       | 110010100100 |   |   IB to ISF & DF to DSF
MOV                                      Move
     SW,AC     | LAS       | 111110000100 |15|    switch reg, reg AC
     MQ,AC     | ACL       | 111111000001 |10|    MQ reg, reg AC
     FLGS,AC   | GTF       | 110000000100 |10|    flags, reg AC
     AC,FLGS   | RTF       | 110000000101 |10|    reg AC, to flags
*    SP1,AC    | RSP1      | 110010000111 |  |    SP 1, reg AC  (1)
*    SP2,AC    | RSP2      | 110010010111 |  |    SP 2, reg AC  (1)
*    STS,AC    | GCF       | 110010101110 |  |    status, reg AC (1)
MOVCLR                                   Move and clear
     AC,Mem1   | DCA  Mem1 | 011IPAAAAAAA |11|    AC to memory, AC = 0
     L,AC      | GLK       | 111010000100 |15L    L to reg AC, L = 0
     AC,MQ     | MQL       | 111100010000 |10|    AC to MQ, AC = 0
     MQ,AC     | CLA SWP   | 111111010001 |10|    MQ to AC, MQ = 0
*    AC,SP1    | LSP1      | 110010001111 |  |    AC to SP1, AC = 0 (1)
*    AC,SP2    | LSP2      | 110010011111 |  |    AC to SP2, AC = 0 (1)
CLR  AC        | CLA       | 111010000000 |10|  Clear,  AC = 0
     AC        | CLA       | 111110000001 |10|    AC = 0, alternate inst
     ACMQ      | CAM       | 111110010001 |10|    AC = 0, MQ = 0
SET                                      Set
     AC,FFFH   | STA       | 111010100000 |10|    AC=FFF
     AC,0      | CLA CLL   | 111011000000 |10L    =0
     AC,1      | CLA IAC   | 111010000001 |10|    =1
     AC,1      | NL0001    | 111011000001 |10L    =1
     AC,2      | NL0002    | 111011000101 |15L    =2
     AC,3      | NL0003    | 111011010101 |15L    =3
     AC,4      | NL0004    | 111011000111 |15L    =4
     AC,6      | NL0006    | 111011010111 |15L    =6
     AC,64     | NL0100    | 111011000011 |15L    =64
     AC,1024   | NL2000    | 111011011010 |15L    =1024
     AC,2047   | NL3777    | 111011101000 |15L    =2047
     AC,-0     | NL4000    | 111011011000 |15L    =-0
     AC,-1025  | NL5777    | 111011101010 |15L    =-1025
     AC,-1024  | NL6000    | 111011011011 |15L    =-1024
     AC,-3     | NL7775    | 111011100110 |15L    =-3
     AC,-2     | NL7776    | 111011100100 |15L    =-2
     AC,-1     | NL7777    | 111011100000 |10L    =-1
XCHGW                                    Exchange words
     AC,MQ     | SWP       | 111101010001 |10|    AC and MQ
SWAP AC        | BSW       | 111000000010 |15|  Swap 6-bits,  reg AC
* PUSH                                   Push onto the stack (1)
*    PC,1      | PPC1      | 110010000101 |  |    PC onto stack 1
```

```
*   PC,2    | PPC2  | 110010100101 | | | PC onto stack 2
*   AC,1    | PAC1  | 110010001101 | | | AC onto stack 1
*   AC,2    | PAC2  | 110010101101 | | | AC onto stack 2
*   POP     |       |              | | | Pop from the stack  (1)
*   AC,1    | POP1  | 110010011101 | | | AC from stack 1
*   AC,2    | POP2  | 110010111101 | | | AC from stack 2
```

Math Operations

```
ADD         | TAD   |              |10|L| Add
    Mem,AC  |   Mem | 001IPAAAAAAA | | |    memory, reg AC
INC  AC     | IAC   | 111000000001 |10|L| Increment, reg AC
NEG         |       |              | |L| Change to negative equiv
    AC      | CIA   | 111000100001 |10| |    reg AC
MUL         |       |              | |L| Multiply
    2,AC    | CLL RAL | 111001000100 |15| |   reg AC x 2
    4,AC    | CLL RTL | 111001000110 |15| |   reg AC x 4
DIV         |       |              | |L| Divide
    2,AC    | CLL RAR | 111001001000 |15| |   reg AC / 2
    4,AC    | CLL RTR | 111001001010 |15| |   reg AC / 4
```

Micro Unique Operations

```
*  PR       |       |              | | | Panel control  (1)
*    0      | PR0   | 110010000110 | 6| |   see the manual
*    1      | PR1   | 110010001110 | 6| |
*    2      | PR2   | 110010010110 | 6| |
*    3      | PR3   | 110010011110 | 6| |
```

Logical Operations

```
AND         | AND   |              |10| | Logical AND
    Mem,AC  |   Mem | 000IPAAAAAAA | | |    memory, reg AC
OR          |       |              | | | Logical OR
    SW,AC   | OSR   | 111100000100 |15| |    reg SW, reg AC
    MQ,AC   | MQA   | 111101000001 |10| |    reg MQ, reg AC
CPL         |       |              | | | Complement
    AC      | CMA   | 111000100000 |10| |    reg AC
RRWC        |       |              | |L| Rotate right w/carry
    AC      | RAR   | 111000001000 |15| |    AC, 1 bit
    AC,2    | RTR   | 111000001010 |15| |    AC, 2 bits
RLWC        |       |              | |L| Rotate left w/carry
    AC      | RAL   | 111000000100 |15| |    AC, 1 bit
    AC,2    | RTL   | 111000000110 |15| |    AC, 2 bits
*  RLNC     |       |              | | | Rotate left no carry
*   AC,3    | R3L   | 111000001100 | 8| |    AC, 3 bits  (1)
```

Bit Operations

```
RESF        |       |              | | | Reset flag
    L       | CLL   | 111001000000 |10|    link
    ALL     | CAF   | 110000000111 |10|    flags and AC
*  HLT      | PG0   | 110000000011 | 6| |    HLTFLG flip flop (1)
*  PD       | CPD   | 110010110110 | 5| |    panel data flip flop (1)
SETF        |       |              | | | Set flag
    L       | STL   | 111001010000 |10|    link
*   PD      | SPD   | 110010111110 | 5| |    panel data flip flop (1)
CPLF L      | CML   | 111000010000 |10| | Complement flag,  link
```

Program Control

CALL	JMS		11	Call subroutine
Mem	Mem	100IPAAAAAAA		PC to memory, memory+1 to PC
* RETI				Return int (1)
* 1	RTN1	110010010101		using SP 1
* 2	RTN2	110010110101		using SP 2
JMP	JMP		10	Jump if
Mem	Mem	101IPAAAAAAA		uncond, memory
INCSZ	ISZ		16	Increment and skip if
Mem	Mem	010IPAAAAAAA		zero
SKIP				Skip next inst if
UN	SKP	111100001000	10	unconditionally
L	SNL	111100010000	10	L = 1
NL	SZL	111100011000	10	L = 0
Z	SZA	111100100000	10	AC = 0
NZ	SNA	111100101000	10	AC not 0
M	SMA	111101000000	10	AC minus
P	SPA	111101001000	10	AC plus
ZL	SZA SNL	111100110000	10	AC = 0 or L = 1
NZNL	SNA SZL	111100111000	10	AC not 0 and L = 0
LZL'	SMA SNL	111101010000	10	AC < 0 or L = 1
GEZNL	SPA SZL	111101011000	10	AC >= 0 and L = 0
LEZ	SMA SZA	111101100000	10	AC <= 0
GZ	SPA SNA	111101101000	10	AC > 0
LEZL	SMA SZA SNL	111101110000	10	AC <= 0 or L = 1
GZNL	SPA SNA SZL	111101111000	10	AC > 0 and L = 0
ION	SKON	110000000000	10	interrupt on
IR	SRQ	110000000011	10	interrupt request
EX	SGT	110000000110	10	external > flag
* SKPCLR				Skip if then clear (1)
* Z,AC	SZA CLA	111110100000	7	AC = 0, then AC = 0
* NZ,AC	SNA CLA	111110101000	7	AC not 0, then AC = 0
* M,AC	SMA CLA	111111000000	7	AC minus, then AC = 0
* P,AC	SPA CLA	111111001000	7	AC plus, then AC = 0
NOP	NOP	111000000000	10	No operation
	NOP	111100000000	10	alternate NOP
	NOP	111100000001	10	alternate NOP
HALT	HLT	111100000010	10	Stop till interrupt
* PEX	PEX	110000000100	6	Exit panel mode (1)

I/O Operations

IOT	IOT		17	Input/Output transfer
d,c		110dddddccc		d and c are user defined
				for PDP-8 d = device
				c = operation
EI	ION	110000000001	10	Interrupts on
DI	IOF	110000000010	10	Interrupts off
* OUTCLR				Output data & clear (1)
* AC,SW	WSR	110010100110	7	AC to SW reg, AC = 0
* IN				Input data (1)
* PS,AC	PRS	110000000000	8	panel status, reg AC

Registers

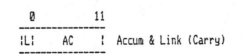

```
    0        11
   -----------------
   |L|   AC   |    Accum & Link (Carry)
   -----------------
```

```
!    PC    !   Prog Counter
-----------------
!    MQ    !   Temporary register
-----------------
!    SP1   !   Stack Pointer 1 (1)
-----------------
!    SP2   !   Stack Pointer 2 (1)
-----------------
!    SW    !   I/O switch register
-----------------
```

6120 Memory Control Registers

```
Each is 3 bits and contains a memory field number
    IF   instructions & operands
    IB   instruction buffer
    ISF  save IF during interrupt
    DF   indirect adr and data
    DSF  save DF during interrupt
```

Flags

```
bit 0  link
    1  greater than flag *     4  interrupt enable  *
    2  INT req bus  *          5  user flag  *
    3  interrupt inhibit *     6-11 save field reg  *

  *  indicates externally set  (1)
```

6120 FLAGS

```
bit 0  link
    1  greater than flag *     4  = 1
    2  INT req bus  *          5  = 0
    3  power on flag           6-8  ISF field
                               9-11 DSF field
```

6120 Status Fields

```
bit 0  link               5  not used
    1  GT flag            6-8  IF field
    2  int req line       9-11 DF field
    3  PWRON flag
    4  int enable
```

Addressing Modes

Univ	Manuf	
#n	n	- immediate data, 3-bits
PZ a	RP a	- absolute, zero page
SP a	MP a	- absolute, current page
(PZ a)	@RP a	- indirect, zero page
(SP a)	@MP a	- indirect, current page
* (PZ a)	@RP a	- indirect, zero page loc 8-F pre auto increment (1)

265
```
```

Instruction Expansion

		Mem			
Univ	Man	Def	I	P	AAAAAAA
----	---	---	-	-	-------
PZ a	RP a	page zero adr	0	0	7-bit loc
SP a	MP a	same page adr	0	1	7-bit loc
(PZ a)	a RP a	indirect PZ	1	0	7-bit loc
(SP a)	a MP a	indirect SP	1	1	7-bit loc

d = 6 bit external device code, part of inst
c = 3 bit device operation, part of inst
#n = immediate data, 3-bits, part of inst

* PZ adr 08 - 0F are pre auto increment (1)

Memory Organization

        organized into 4096 12-bit words   adr 000 - FFF
        subdevided into 32 pages of 128 words
        memory- bit 11-7 = page number
                    6-0 = page address
        page 0 is the register page

            HD6120 Memory Expansion
            ----
        organized into 8 fields of 4096 words
        and 2 blocks 32k, main memory and panel memory

Notes

Cycle times are for the 6100, the 6120 is faster

6502

R6502, R6503, R6504, R6505, R6506, R6507, R6512, R6513, R6514, R6515, R6500, R6501, R65001E, R6501EB, R6501EAB

(1, 5) G65SC02, G65SC03, G65SC04, G65SC05, G65SC06, G65SC07, G65SC12, G65SC13, G65SC14, G65SC15, G65SC102, G65SC103, G65SC104, G65SC105, G65SC106, G65SC107, G65SC112, G65SC115, G65SC150, G65SC151

(2,6) R6511, R6512, R6513, R6541, R6542, R6543, R6501Q, R6511Q, R6511Q, R6541Q, R65F11, R65F12 R6511EB, R6511EAB, R6541EB, R6541EAB

(1, 2, 3, 5, 6) R65C21, R65C29

(1, 4, 5, 6) R65C02, R65C102, R65C112, W65SC02, W65C02, W65SC01, W65SC03, W65SC04, W65SC05, W65SC06, W65SC07, W65SC12, W65SC13, W65SC14, W65SC15, W65SC102, W65SC103, W65SC104, W65SC105, W65SC106, W65SC107, W65WSC112, W65SC115

Data Move

```
MOV            !          !        ! !    ! Move byte
    #n,A       ! LDA #n    ! A9     !2!NZ  !    immed, reg A
    Mem1,A     !     Mem1  ! 101MMM01 ! !  !    memory, reg A
    A,Mem1     ! STA Mem1  ! 100MMM01 ! !  !    reg A, memory
    #n,X       ! LDX #n    ! A2     !2!NZ  !    immed, reg X
    aa,X       !     aa    ! AE     !4!    !    abs, reg X
    PZ a,X     !     a     ! A6     !3!    !    pz, reg X
    (Y+a),X    !     a,Y   ! B6     !4!    !    index Y, reg X
    (Y++aa),X  !     aa,Y  ! BE     !4!    !    index Y, reg X
    #n,Y       ! LDY #n    ! A0     !2!NZ  !    immed, reg Y
    Mem2,Y     !     Mem2  ! 101MMM00 ! !  !    memory, reg Y
    X,aa       ! STX aa    ! 8E     !4!    !    reg X, abs
    X,PZ a     !     a     ! 86     !3!    !    reg X, pz
    X,(Y+a)    !     a,Y   ! 96     !4!    !    reg X, index Y
    Y,aa       ! STY aa    ! 8C     !4!    !    reg Y, abs
    Y,PZ a     !     a     ! 84     !3!    !    reg Y, pz
    Y,(X+a)    !     a,X   ! 94     !4!    !    reg Y, index X
    A,X        ! TAX       ! AA     !2!NZ  !    reg A, reg X
    A,Y        ! TAY       ! A8     !2!NZ  !    reg A, reg Y
    S,X        ! TSX       ! BA     !2!NZ  !    reg S, reg X
    X,A        ! TXA       ! 8A     !2!NZ  !    reg X, reg A
    X,S        ! TXS       ! 9A     !2!    !    reg X, reg S
    Y,A        ! TYA       ! 98     !2!NZ  !    reg Y, reg A
*   (PZ a),A   ! LDA (a)   ! B2     !5!    !    pz_ind, reg A
*   A,(PZ a)   ! STA (a)   ! 92     !5!    !    reg A, pz_ind (4)
PUSH           !           !        ! !    ! Push word onto the stack
    A          ! PHA       ! 48     !3!    !    reg A
    F          ! PHP       ! 08     !3!    !    reg F
*   X          ! PHX       ! DA     !3!    !    reg X    (5)
*   Y          ! PHY       ! 5A     !3!    !    reg Y    (5)
POP            !           !        ! !    ! Pop word from the stack
    A          ! PLA       ! 68     !4!NZ  !    reg A
    F          ! PLP       ! 28     !4!all !    reg F
*   X          ! PLX       ! FA     !4!NZ  !    reg X    (5)
*   Y          ! PLY       ! 7A     !4!NZ  !    reg Y    (5)
*   CLR        ! STZ       !        ! !    ! Clear byte    (1)
*     aa       !     aa    ! 9C     !4!    !    absolute   (1)
*     PZ a     !     a     ! 64     !3!    !    page zero  (1)
*     (X+a)    !     a,X   ! 74     !4!    !    index X    (1)
*     (X++aa)  !     aa,X  ! 9E     !5!    !    abs_index X    (1)
```

Math Operations

```
ADC            ! ADC       !        ! !NVZC! Add byte w/c
    #n,A       !     #n    ! 69     !2!    !    immed, reg A
    Mem1,A     !     Mem1  ! 011MMM01 ! !  !    memory, reg A
*   (PZ a),A   !     (a)   ! 72     !2!    !    pz_ind, reg A  (4)
INC            ! INC       !        ! !NZ  ! Increment byte
    Mem2       !     Mem2  ! 111MMM10 ! !  !    memory
    X          ! INX       ! E8     !2!NZ  !    reg X
    Y          ! INY       ! C8     !2!NZ  !    reg Y
*   A          ! INC A     ! 1A     !2!NZ  !    reg A    (4)
SBB            ! SBC       !        ! !NVZC! Subtract byte w/c
    #n,A       !     #n    ! E9     !2!    !    immed, reg A
    Mem1,A     !     Mem1  ! 111MMM01 ! !  !    memory, reg A
*   (PZ a),A   !     (a)   ! F2     !5!    !    pz_ind, reg A  (4)
DEC            ! DEC       !        ! !NZ  ! Decrement byte
    Mem2       !     Mem2  ! 110MMM10 ! !  !    memory
    X          ! DEX       ! CA     !2!NZ  !    reg X
```

267

```
      Y          | DEY    | 88    |2|NZ  |  reg Y
*     A          | DEC A  | 3A    |2|NZ  |  reg A  (4)
CMP              | CMP    |       | |NZC | Compare byte
      A,#n       | #n     | C9    |2|    |  reg A, immed
      A,Mem1     | Mem1   | 110MMM01 | | |  reg A, memory
*     A,(PZ a)   | (a)    | D2    |5|    |  reg A, pz_ind  (4)
      X,#n       | CPX #n | E0    |2|NZC |  reg X, immed
      X,aa       | aa     | EC    |4|    |  reg X, abs
      X,PZ a     | a      | E4    |3|    |  reg X, pz
      Y,#n       | CPY #n | C0    |2|NZC |  reg Y, immed
      Y,aa       | aa     | CC    |4|    |  reg Y, abs
      Y,PZ a     | a      | C4    |3|    |  reg Y, pz
* MUL            | MUL    |       | |    | Multiply  (3)
      Y,A,AY     |        | 02    |9|    |  reg A x reg Y = reg AY
```

Logical Operations

```
AND              | AND    |       | |NZ  | Logical AND byte
      #n,A       | #n     | 29    |2|    |  immed, reg A
      Mem1,A     | Mem1   | 001MMM01 | | |  memory, reg A
*     (PZ a),A   | (a)    | 32    |5|    |  pz_ind, reg A  (4)
TEST             | BIT    |       | |NVZ | Logical AND, set flags
      aa,A       | aa     | 2C    |4|    |  reg A, abs
      PZ a,A     | a      | 24    |3|    |  reg A, pz
*     #n,A       | #n     | 89    |2|    |  reg A, immed  (4)
*     (X+a),A    | a,X    | 34    |4|    |  reg A, indexed  (4)
*     (X++aa),A  | aa,X   | 3C    |4|    |  reg A, indexed  (4)
OR               | ORA    |       | |NZ  | Logical OR byte
      #n,A       | #n     | 09    |2|    |  immed, reg A
      Mem1,A     | Mem1   | 000MMM01 | | |  memory, reg A
*     (PZ a),A   | (a)    | 12    |5|    |  pz_ind, reg A  (4)
XOR              | EOR    |       | |NZ  | Logical Exclusive OR byte
      #n,A       | #n     | 49    |2|    |  immed, reg A
      Mem1,A     | Mem1   | 010MMM01 | | |  memory, reg A
*     (PZ a),A   | (a)    | 52    |5|    |  pz_ind, reg A  (4)
RLWC             | ROL    |       | |NZC | Rotate byte w/c left
      A          | A      | 2A    |2|    |  reg A
      Mem2       | Mem2   | 001MMM10 | | |  memory
RRWC             | ROR    |       | |NZC | Rotate byte w/c right
      A          | A      | 6A    |2|    |  reg A
      Mem2       | Mem2   | 011MMM10 | | |  memory
SLA              | ASL    |       | |NZC | Shift left arithmetic
      A          | A      | 0A    |2|    |  reg A
      Mem2       | Mem2   | 000MMM10 | | |  memory
SRL              | LSR    |       | |NZC | Shift right logical
      A          | A      | 4A    |2|    |  reg A
      Mem2       | Mem2   | 010MMM10 | | |  memory
* TSTRES         | TRB    |       | |Z   | Test and reset bits  (1)
*     aa         | aa     | 1C    |6|    |  absolute  (1)
*     PZ a       | a      | 14    |5|    |  page zero  (1)
* TSTSET         | TSB    |       | |Z   | Test and set bits  (1)
*     aa         | aa     | 0C    |6|    |  absolute  (1)
*     PZ a       | a      | 04    |5|    |  page zero  (1)
```

Bit Operations

```
RESF             |        |       | |    | Reset flag
      C          | CLC    | 18    |2|C   |  carry
      D          | CLD    | D8    |2|D   |  decimal mode
      V          | CLV    | B8    |2|V   |  overflow
SETF             |        |       | |    | Set flag
      C          | SEC    | 38    |2|C   |  carry
```

```
   D          | SED   | F8    |2|D | decimal mode
 * SETB       | SMB   |       | | | Set bit (6)
   PZ a,b     | #b,a  | 1bbb0111 | | | pz a, bit b
 * RESB       | BBR   |       | | | Reset bit (6)
   PZ a,b     | #b,a  | 0bbb0111 | | | pz a, bit b
```

Program Control

```
CALL          | JSR   |       | | | Call subroutine
   aa         | aa    | 20    |6| | uncond, abs
RET           | RTS   | 60    |6| | Return from subroutine
RETI          | RTI   | 40    | |all| Return from interrupt
JMP           | JMP   |       | | | Jump to location
   aa         | aa    | 4C    |3| | uncond, abs
   (aa)       | (aa)  | 6C    |3| | uncond, ind_abs  (except 4)
 * (PZ a)     | (a)   | 6C    |6| | pz_ind  (4)
 * ((X+aa))   | (aa,X)| 7C    |6| | ind_index abs  (4)
JMPR          |       |       | | | Jump relative
   NC,r       | BCC r | 90    |2| | no carry
   C,r        | BCS r | B0    |2| | carry
   V,r        | BVS r | 70    |2| | overflow
   NV,r       | BVC r | 50    |2| | no overflow
   NZ,r       | BNE r | D0    |2| | not zero
   Z,r        | BEQ r | F0    |2| | zero
   M,r        | BMI r | 30    |2| | minus
   P,r        | BPL r | 10    |2| | positive
 * UN,r       | BRA r | 80    |2| | uncondtionally (5)
 * BS  PZ a,  | BBS   |       | | | Jump relative if bit set (6)
        b,r   | #b,a,r| 1bbb1111 | | | pz a, bit b, adr rel
              |       | aa,rr | | |
 * BR  PZ a,  | BBR   |       | | | Jump relative if bit reset (6)
        b,r   | #b,a,r| 0bbb1111 | | | pz a, bit b, adr rel
              |       | aa,rr | | |
BRK           | BRK   | 00    |7|BI| Break
HALT          | BRK   | 00    |7| | Stop till interrupt
NOP           | NOP   | EA    |2| | No operation
```

I/O Operations

```
DI            | CLI   | 58    |2|I | Disable interrupts
EI            | SEI   | 78    |2|I | Enable interrupts
```

Registers

```
    16      8|7      0
           ---------
           |   A   |
           ---------
           |   Y   |  Index
           ---------
           |   X   |  Index
  ---------------------
  | Program Counter   |
  ---------------------
           |1|  S   |  Stack pointer
           ---------
         P |NV BDIZC|  Flags
           ---------
```

Flags

    N = sign of result
    Z = zero result
    V = overflow
    C = carry
    B = break
    D = decimal mode
    I = interrupt disable

Addressing Modes

Univ	Manuf	
#n	#n	- immediate
XX	XX	- register
aa	aa	- absolute address
(aa)	(aa)	- absolute adr indirect
PZ a	a	- page zero address, loc 0 - 256
(X+a)	a,X	- indexed, page zero loc X+a
(X++aa)	aa,X	- indexed, memory loc X+aa or Y+aa
r	r	- relative address
(PZ(X+a))	(a,X)	- indexed indirect, page zero loc X+a contains adr
((X++aa))	(aa,X)	- indexed indirect, memory loc X+aa contains adr
((PZ a)+Y)	(a),Y	- indirect_indexed, reg Y added to contents of page 0 adr

Instruction Expansion

Univ	Manuf	Mem1	Mem2	MMM	Type	Cyc
		memory				
aa	aa	x	x	011	absolute	4
PZ a	a	x	x	001	page zero	3
(PZ(X+a))	(a,X)	x		000	index_ind	6
((PZ a)+Y)	(a),Y	x		100	ind_index	5
(X+a)	a,X	x	x	101	indexed	4
(X++aa)	aa,X	x	x	111	indexed	4
(Y++aa)	aa,Y	x		110	indexed	4

    #n   immediate data, 8-bits appended to inst
    aa   absolute address, 16-bits appended to inst
    a   page zero address, 8-bits appended to inst
    b   bit number, 3-bits part of inst
    r   relative adr, 8-bits appended to inst

Special Memory Locations

    loc FFFA   non masked interrupts
        FFFE   interrupt request
        FFFC   restart

Notes

    Stack starts at loc 01FF, top of page one

65816

W65SC816, W65SC802, W65SC902, W65C802, W65C816

Data Move

MOV					Move byte
#n,A	LDA #n	A9	2	NZ	immed, reg A
Mem1,A	Mem1	101MMM01			memory, reg A
(PZ a),A	(a)	B2	5		pz_ind, reg A
Mem3,A	Mem3	101MMM11			memory, reg A
A,Mem1	STA Mem1	100MMM01			reg A, memory
A,(PZ a)	(a)	92	5		reg A, pz_ind
A,Mem3	Mem3	100MMM11			reg A, memory
#n,X	LDX #n	A2	2	NZ	immed, reg X
ABS aa,X	aa	AE	4		abs, reg X
PZ a,X	a	A6	3		pz, reg X
(Y+a),X	a,Y	D6	4		reg Y, index X
(Y++aa),X	aa,Y	DE	4		reg Y, index X
#n,Y	LDY #n	A0	2	NZ	immed, reg Y
Mem2,Y	Mem2	101MMM00			reg Y, memory, reg Y
X,aa	STX aa	8E	4		reg X, abs
X,PZ a	a	86	3		reg X, pz
X,(Y+a)	a,Y	96	4		reg Y, index Y
Y,aa	STY aa	8C	4		reg Y, abs
Y,PZ a	a	84	3		reg Y, pz
Y,(X+a)	a,X	94	4		index Y, reg X
A,X	TAX	AA	2	NZ	reg A, reg X
A,Y	TAY	AB	2	NZ	reg A, reg Y
S,X	TSX	BA	2	NZ	reg S, reg X
X,A	TXA	8A	2	NZ	reg X, reg A
X,S	TXS	9A	2		reg X, reg S
Y,A	TYA	98	2	NZ	reg Y, reg A
Y,X	TYX	BB	2		reg Y to X
X,Y	TXY	9B	2		reg X to Y
MOVW					Move word
C,D	TCD	5B	2		reg C to D
D,C	TDC	7B	2		reg D to C
C,SR	TCS	1B	2		reg C to SR
SR,C	TSC	3B	2		reg SR to C
XCHG					Exchange bytes
B,A	XBA				reg B and A
PUSH					Push word onto the stack
A	PHA	48	3		reg A
F	PHP	08	3		reg F
X	PHX	DA	3		reg X
Y	PHY	5A	3		reg Y
#nn	PEA	F4	5		immed
PZ a	PEI	D4	6		pz adr
(PC+rr)	PER	62	6		PC relative
DBR	PHB	8B	3		data bank register
DR	PHD	0B	4		direct register
PBR	PHK	4B	3		program bank register
POP					Pop word from the stack
A	PLA	68	4	NZ	reg A
F	PLP	28	4	all	reg F
X	PLX	FA	4	NZ	reg X
Y	PLY	7A	4	NZ	reg Y
DBR	PLB	AB	4		data bank reg
DR	PLD	2B	5		direct register
CLR	STZ				Clear byte

```
aa              | aa   | 9C      |4|    | absolute
PZ a            | a    | 64      |3|    | page zero
(X+d)           | d,X  | 74      |4|    | index X    (1,4)
(X++dd)         | dd,X | 9E      |5|    | abs_index X   (1,4)
```

Math Operations
_____

```
ADC             | ADC  |         | |NVZC| Add byte w/c
  #n,A          | #n   | 69      |2|    |   immed, reg A
  Mem1,A        | Mem1 | 011MMM01| |    |   memory, reg A
  (PZ a),A      | (a)  | 72      |2|    |   pz_ind, reg A
  Mem3,A        | Mem3 | 011MMM11| |    |   memory, reg A
INC             | INC  |         | |NZ  | Increment byte
  Mem2          | Mem2 | 111MMM10| |    |   memory
  X             | INX  | E8      |2|NZ  |   reg X
  Y             | INY  | C8      |2|NZ  |   reg Y
  A             | INC A| 1A      |2|NZ  |   reg A
SBB             | SBC  |         | |NVZC| Subtract byte w/c
  #n,A          | #n   | E9      |2|    |   immed, reg A
  Mem1,A        | Mem1 | 111MMM01| |    |   memory, reg A
  (PZ a),A      | (a)  | F2      |5|    |   pz_ind, reg A
  Mem3,A        | Mem3 | 111MMM11| |    |   memory, reg A
DEC             | DEC  |         | |NZ  | Decrement byte
  Mem2          | Mem2 | 110MMM10| |    |   memory
  X             | DEX  | CA      |2|NZ  |   reg X
  Y             | DEY  | 88      |2|NZ  |   reg Y
  A             | DEC A| 3A      |2|NZ  |   reg A
CMP             | CMP  |         | |NZC | Compare byte
  A,#n          | #n   | C9      |2|    |   reg A, immed
  A,Mem1        | Mem1 | 110MMM01| |    |   reg A, memory
  A,(PZ a)      | (a)  | D2      |5|    |   reg A, pz_ind
  A,Mem3        | Mem3 | 110MMM11| |    |   reg A, memory
  X,#n          | CPX #n| E0     |2|NZC |   reg X, immed
  X,aa          | aa   | EC      |4|    |   reg X, abs
  X,PZ a        | a    | E4      |3|    |   reg X, pz
  Y,#n          | CPY #n| C0     |2|NZC |   reg Y, immed
  Y,aa          | aa   | CC      |4|    |   reg Y, abs
  Y,PZ a        | a    | C4      |3|    |   reg Y, pz
```

Logical Operations
_____

```
AND             | AND  |         | |NZ  | Logical AND byte
  #n,A          | #n   | 29      |2|    |   immed, reg A
  Mem1,A        | Mem1 | 001MMM01| |    |   memory, reg A
  (PZ a),A      | (a)  | 32      |5|    |   pz_ind, reg A
  Mem3,A        | Mem3 | 001MMM11| |    |   memory, reg A
TEST            | BIT  |         | |NVZ | Logical AND, set flags
  ABS aa,A      | aa   | 2C      |4|    |   abs, reg A
  PZ a,A        | a    | 24      |3|    |   pz, reg A
  #n,A          | #n   | 89      |2|    |   immed, reg A
  (X+d),A       | d,X  | 34      |4|    |   indexed, reg A
  (X++dd),A     | dd,X | 3C      |4|    |   indexed, reg A
OR              | ORA  |         | |NZ  | Logical OR byte
  #n,A          | #n   | 09      |2|    |   immed, reg A
  Mem1,A        | Mem1 | 000MMM01| |    |   memory, reg A
  (PZ a),A      | (a)  | 12      |5|    |   pz_ind, reg A
  Mem3,A        | Mem3 | 000MMM11| |    |   memory, reg A
XOR             | EOR  |         | |NZ  | Logical Exclusive OR byte
  #n,A          | #n   | 49      |2|    |   immed, reg A
  Mem1,A        | Mem1 | 010MMM01| |    |   memory, reg A
  (PZ a),A      | (a)  | 52      |5|    |   pz_ind, reg A
  Mem3,A        | Mem3 | 010MMM11| |    |   memory, reg A
```

				flags	
RLWC	ROL			NZC	Rotate byte w/c left
A	A	2A	2		reg A
Mem2	Mem2	001MMM10			memory
RRWC	ROR			NZC	Rotate byte w/c right
A	A	6A	2		reg A
Mem2	Mem2	011MMM10			memory
SLA	ASL			NZC	Shift left arithmetic
A	A	0A	2		reg A
Mem2	Mem2	000MMM10			memory
SRL	LSR			NZC	Shift right logical
A	A	4A	2		reg A
Mem2	Mem2	010MMM10			memory
TSTRES	TRB			Z	Test and reset bits
aa	aa	1C	6		absolute
PZ a	a	14	5		page zero
TSTSET	TSB			Z	Test and set bits
aa	aa	0C	6		absolute
PZ a	a	04	5		page zero

Bit Operations
----

				flags	
RESF					Reset flag
C	CLC	18	2	C	carry
D	CLD	D8	2	D	decimal mode
V	CLV	B8	2	V	overflow
m	REP m	C2	3		immed mask
SETF					Set flag
C	SEC	38	2	C	carry
D	SED	F8	2	D	decimal mode
m	SEP m	E2	3		immed mask
XCNGF C,E	XCE	FB	2		Exchange flags C and E

String Operations

MOVS					Move string
Y+,X+,C	MVN	54,dd,ss	7		ind inc Y to X, for C
s,d	s,d				srce bank adr,dest bank adr
Y-,X-,C	MVP	44,dd,ss	7		ind dec Y to X, for C
s,d	s,d				srce bank adr,dest bank adr

Program Control
----

				flags	
CALL	CALL				Call subroutine
aa	aa	20	6		uncond, abs
L aaa	JSL aaa	22	8		abs long
((X+a))	JSR (a,X)	FC	6		abs indexed indirect
RET	RTS	60	6		Return from subroutine
RETI	RTI	40	7	all	Return from interrupt
RETL	RTL	6B	6		Return for subr long
JMP	JMP				Jump to location
aa	aa	4C	3		uncond, abs
(aa)	(aa)	6C	3		uncond, ind_abs
((X++aa))	(aa,X)	7C	6		ind_index abs
L(aa)	JML (aa)	DC	6		indirect long
L aaa	JMP aaa	5C	4		absolute long
JMPR					Jump relative
NC,r	BCC r	90	2		no carry
C,r	BCS r	B0	2		carry
V,r	BVS r	70	2		overflow
NV,r	BVC r	50	2		no overflow
NZ,r	BNE r	D0	2		not zero
Z,r	BEQ r	F0	2		zero

```
      M,r         | BMI r  | 30  |2|  |   minus
      P,r         | BPL r  | 10  |2|  |   positive
     UN,r         | BRA r  | 80  |2|  |   uncondtionally
JMPD     rr       | BRL rr | 82  |3|  | Jump relative long
BRK               | BRK    | 00  |7|BI| Break
STOP              | STP    | DB  |3|  | Stop the clock
HALT              | WAI    | CB  |3|  | Wait for interrupt
NOP               | NOP    | E6  |2|  | No operation
ESC  n            | COP n  | 02  |8|  | Co processor operation
```

I/O   Operations

```
DI                | CLI    | 58  |2|I | Disable interrupts
EI                | SEI    | 78  |2|I | Enable interrupts
                  |        |     | | |
```

Registers

```
       16      8|7      0
             ------------------
  C  |   B   |   A   |  Accumulator
             ------------------
  Y  |  YH   |  YL   |  Index
             ------------------
  X  |  XH   |  XL   |  Index
             ------------------
  PC |  PCH  |  PCL  |  Program counter
             ------------------
  S  |  SH   |  SL   |  Stack pointer
             ------------------
  D  |  DH   |  DL   |  Direct register
             ------------------

          |  DBR  |  Data bank reg, used with X and Y index reg
          ---------
          |  PBR  |  Program bank reg, used with PC
          ---------
     P  |NVMXDIZC|E|  Flags
          ---------
```

Addressing Modes
----------- ------

```
Univ      Manuf
----      -----
#n        n      - immediate (8 or 16-bits)
XX        XX     - register
PZ a      a      - page zero (location a + D reg)
aa        aa     - absolute (16-bit adr appended to DBR)
LA aaa    aaa    - absolute long (24-bit adr)
(aa)      (aa)   - indirect abs (contents of bank 0 loc aa into PC)
L(aa)     (aal)  - indirect long (contents of bank 0 loc aa into PC,
                         third byte into PBR)
(PZ a)    (a)    - page zero  indirect (location a + D reg,
                         2-byte value appended to DBR)
L(PZ a)   (al)   - page zero long indirect (location a + D reg,
                         3-byte value = long address)
(X+d)     d,X    - indexed (d added to D and X or Y reg)
(X++aa)   aa,X   - indexed absolute (aa added to X or Y reg
                         and appended to DBR)
(X+++aaa) aaa,X  - indexed long  (aaa added to X reg)
r         r      - relative  (r added to PC, +128 -127)
```
```
274
```

```
rr          rr      - displacement (rr added to PC, +32768 -32767)
((X+d))     (d,x)   - indexed indirect (location d + D and X reg,
                        2-byte value appended to DBR)
((PZ a)+Y)  (a),Y   - indirect indexed (location a + D reg,
                        2-byte value added to Y and append to DBR)
(L(PZ a)+Y) (dl),Y  - indirect long indexed (location a + D reg,
                        3-byte value added to Y)
(S)         s       - stack indirect (reg S, bank always zero)
SR r        sr      - stack relative (r added to reg S, always bank 0)
((SR r)+Y)  (sr),y  - stack relative indirect indexed (location r + reg S,
                        2-bye contents added to Y and appended to DBR)
((X++aa))   (aa,x)  - absolute indexed indirect (location aa + X reg,
                        2-byte contents into PC)
xyc         xyc     - block move (srce reg X appended to 2nd byte of inst,
                        destination reg Y appended to 3rd byte of inst,
                        number of bytes is in reg C )
```

Flags

```
N = sign of result
Z = zero result
V = overflow
C = carry
D = decimal mode
I = interrupt disable
M = memory select, 1=8-bit 0=16-bit
X = index reg select, 1=8-bit 0=16-bit
E = 6502 emulation
```

Instruction Expansion

		memory				
Univ	Manuf	Mem1	Mem2	MMM	Type	Cyc
aa	aa	x	x	011	absolute	4
PZ a	a	x	x	001	page zero	3
((X+d))	(d,X)	x		000	index_ind	6
((PZ a)+Y)	(a),Y	x		100	ind_index	5
(X+d)	d,X	x	x	101	indexed	4
(X++dd)	dd,X	x	x	111	indexed	4
(Y++dd)	dd,Y	x		110	indexed	4

		Mem3	
Univ	Manuf	MM	Cyc
(L(PZ a)+Y)	(dl),Y	101	6
L(PZ a)	(dl)	001	6
SR r	sr	000	4
((SR r)+Y)	(sr),Y	100	7
LA aaa	aaa	011	5
(X+++aaa)	aaa,X	111	5

```
n    immediate data, 8-bits appended to inst
a    page zero adr, 8-bits appended to inst
aa   absolute adr, 16-bits appended to inst
aaa  long adr, 24-bits appended to inst
r    relative adr value, 8-bits appended to inst
rr   displacement value, 16-bits appended to inst
```

d   index value, 8-bits appended to inst
dd index value, 16-bits appended to inst

Special Memory Locations (vectors)
----

    loc FFF4   COP software int
        FFF6   BRK software int
        FFF8   ABORT hardware int
        FFFA   non masked interrupts
        FFFC   restart hardware int
        FFFE   IRQ/BRK hardware int

Addressable Memory
----

memory devided into 256 65K banks
direct register puts page zero anywhere in first 64K

Notes

    Stack starts at loc 01FF, top of page one

6800

HD6800, HD68A00, HD68B00, HG6802, HD6802W MC6800, MC68A00, MC68B00, MC6802, MC6802N2, MC6808

(1) HD6801S0, HD6801S5, HD6801V0, HD6801V5, HD6803, HD68P01V07, HD68P01M0, MC6801, MC6803 (E), MC6801U4, MC68HC01, MC6803U4, MC68701, MC68701U4, MC68A702, MC68B701, MC68120

(1,2) HD6301V1, HD63A01, HD63B01V1, HD630X0, HD64A01X0, HD63B01X0, HD6303R, HD63A03R, HD63B03R, HD6303X, HD63A03X, HD63B03X, HD6303Y, HD63A03Y, HD63B03Y, HD63P01M1, HD63PA01m1[4] HD63PB0M1, HD6301X0

Data Move

MOV						Move byte	
#n,A	LDAA n	86	2	NZV		immed, reg A	
Mem,A	Mem	10MM0110	0+			memory, reg A	
#n,B	LDAB n	C6	2	NZV		immed, reg B	
Mem,B	Mem	11MM0110	0+			memory, reg B	
A,Mem	STAA	10MM0111	0+	NZV		reg A, memory	
B,Mem	STAB	11MM0111	0+	NZV		reg B, memory	
A,B	TAB	16	2	NZV		reg A, reg B	
B,A	TBA	17	2	NZV		reg B, reg A	
A,CCR	TAP	06	2	all		reg A, flags	
CCR,A	TPA	07	2			flags, reg A	
MOVW						Move word	
#nn,X	LDX nn	CE	3	NZV		immed, reg X	
Mem,X	Mem	11MM1110	1+			memory, reg X	
#nn,SP	LDS nn	8E	3	NZV		immed, reg SP	
Mem,SP	Mem	10MM1110	1+			memory, reg SP	
X,Mem	STX Mem	11MM1111	1+	NZV		reg X, memory	
SP,Mem	STS Mem	10MM1111	1+	NZV		reg SP, memory	
* #nn,D	LDD nn	CC	3	NZV		immed, reg D	(1)
* Mem,D	Mem	11MM1100	1+	NZV		memory, reg D	(1)
* D,Mem	STD Mem	11MM1101	1+	NZV		reg D, memory	(1)

```
* XCHG  A,X  ! XGDX  ! 18       ! 2!    ! Exchange reg A and X  (2)
CLR          !       !          ! !    ! Clear byte
    (X+d)    ! CLR d ! 6F       ! 3!NZVC!    indexed
     aa      !   aa  ! 7F       ! 4!    !    abs
     A       ! CLRA  ! 4F       ! 2!NZVC!    reg A
     B       ! CLRB  ! 5F       ! 2!NZVC!    reg B
PUSH         !       !          ! !    ! Push byte onto the stack
     A       ! PSHA  ! 36       ! 3!    !    reg A
     B       ! PSHB  ! 37       ! 3!    !    reg B
*    X       ! PSHX  ! 3C       ! 4!    !    reg X    (1)
POP          !       !          ! !    ! Pop byte from the stack
     A       ! PULA  ! 32       ! 4!    !    reg A
     B       ! PULB  ! 33       ! 4!    !    reg B
*    X       ! PULX  ! 38       ! 5!    !    reg X    (1)
MOVDEC       !       !          ! !    !
    X,SP     ! TXS   ! 35       ! 4!    ! Move reg X - 1 to reg SP
MOVINC       !       !          ! !    !
    SP,X     ! TSX   ! 30       ! 4!    ! Move reg SP + 1 to reg X
```

Math Operations

```
ADD          !       !          ! !    ! Add byte
    #n,A     ! ADDA n! 8B       ! 2!-I  !    immed, reg A
    Mem,A    !  Mem  ! 10MM1011  !0+!    !    memory, reg A
    #n,B     ! ADDB n! CB       ! 2!-I  !    immed, reg B
    Mem,B    !  Mem  ! 11MM1011  !0+!    !    memory, reg B
    B,A      ! ABA   ! 1B       ! 2!-I  !    reg B, reg A
ADC          !       !          ! !    ! Add byte w/c
    #n,A     ! ADCA n! 89       ! 2!-I  !    immed, reg A
    Mem,A    !  Mem  ! 10MM1001  !0+!    !    memory, reg A
    #n,B     ! ADCB n! C9       ! 2!-I  !    immed, reg B
    Mem,B    !  Mem  ! 11MM1001  !0+!    !    memory, reg B
* ADDW       ! ADDD  !          ! !    ! Add word     (1)
    #nn,D    !  nn   ! C3       ! 4!ZVC !    immed, reg D
    Mem,D    !  Mem  ! 11MM0011  !1+!ZVC !    memory, reg D
    B,X      ! ABX   ! 3A       ! 3!    !    reg B, reg X
INC          !       !          ! !    ! Increment byte
    (X+d)    ! INC d ! 6C       ! 7!NZV !    indexed
     aa      !   aa  ! 7C       ! 6!    !    abs
     A       ! INCA  ! 4C       ! 2!NZV !    reg A
     B       ! INCB  ! 5C       ! 2!NZV !    reg B
INCW         !       !          ! !    ! Increment word
     X       ! INX   ! 08       ! 4!Z   !    reg X
     SP      ! INS   ! 31       ! 4!    !    reg SP
SUB          !       !          ! !    ! Subtract byte
    #n,A     ! SUBA n! 80       ! 2!NZVC!    immed, reg A
    Mem,A    !  Mem  ! 10MM0000  !0+!    !    memory, reg A
    #n,B     ! SUBB n! C0       ! 2!NZVC!    immed, reg B
    Mem,B    !  Mem  ! 11MM0000  !0+!    !    memory, reg B
    B,A      ! SBA   ! 10       ! 2!NZVC!    reg B, reg A
* SUBW       ! SUBD  !          ! !NZVC! Subtract word  (1)
    #nn,D    !  nn   ! 83       ! 4!    !    immed, reg D
    Mem,D    !  Mem  ! 10MM0011  !1+!    !    memory, reg D
SBB          !       !          ! !    ! Subtract byte w/c
    #n,A     ! SBCA n! 82       ! 2!NZVC!    immed, reg A
    Mem,A    !  Mem  ! 10MM0010  !0+!    !    memory, reg A
    #n,B     ! SBCB n! C2       ! 2!NZVC!    immed, reg B
    Mem,B    !  Mem  ! 11MM0010  !0+!    !    memory, reg B
DEC          !       !          ! !    ! Decrement byte
    (X+d)    ! DEC n ! 6A       ! 7!NZV !    indexed
     aa      !   aa  ! 7A       ! 6!    !    abs
     A       ! DECA  ! 4A       ! 2!NZV !    reg A
```

B	DECB	5A	2	NZV	reg B
DECW					Decrement word
X	DEX	09	4	Z	reg X
SP	DES	34	4		reg SP
NEG					Change to negative
(X+d)	NEG d	60	7	NZVC	indexed
aa	aa	70	6		abs
A	NEGA	40	2	NZVC	reg A
B	NEGB	50	2	NZVC	reg B
DA A	DAA	19	2	NZVC	Decimal adjust reg A
* MUL				C	Multiply bytes (1)
A,B,D	MUL	3D	10		reg D = reg A x reg B
CMP					Compare byte
A,#n	CMPA n	81	2	NZVC	reg A, immed
A,Mem	Mem	10MM0001	0+		reg A, memory
B,#n	CMPB n	C1	2	NZVC	reg B, immed
B,Mem	Mem	11MM0001	0+		reg B, memory
A,B	CBA	11	2	NZVC	reg A, reg B
CMPW					Compare word
X,#nn	CPX nn	8C	3	NZV	reg X, immed
X,Mem	Mem	10MM1100	1+		reg X, memory

Logical Operations

AND					Logical AND byte
#n,A	ANDA n	84	2	NZV	immed, reg A
Mem,A	Mem	10MM0100	0+		memory, reg A
#n,B	ANDB n	C4	2	NZV	immed, reg B
Mem,B	Mem	11MM0100	0+		memory, reg B
* #n,PZ a	AIM a,n	71	6	NZV	immed, page zero (2)
* #n,(X+d)	d,n	61	7		immed, indexed (2)
TEST					Logical AND, set flags
#n,A	BITA n	85	2	NZV	immed, reg A
Mem,A	Mem	10MM0101	0+		memory, reg A
#n,B	BITB n	C5	2	NZV	immed, reg B
Mem,B	Mem	11MM0101	0+		memory, reg B
00,(X+d)	TST d	6D	2	NZVC	00, indexed
00,aa	aa	7D	6		00, absolute
00,A	TSTA	4D	2	NZVC	00, reg A
00,B	TSTB	5D	2	NZVC	00, reg B
* #n,PZ a	TIM a,n	7B	4	NZV	immed, page zero (2)
* #n,(X+d)	d,n	6B	5		immed, indexed (2)
OR					Logical OR byte
#n,A	ORAA n	8A	2	NZV	immed, reg A
Mem,A	Mem	10MM1010	0+		memory, reg A
#n,B	ORAB n	CA	2	NZV	immed, reg B
Mem,B	Mem	11MM1010	0+		memory, reg B
* #n,PZ a	OIM a,n	72	6	NZV	immed, page zero (2)
* #n,(X+d)	d,n	62	7		immed, indexed (2)
XOR					Logical Exclusive OR byte
#n,A	EORA n	88	2	NZV	immed, reg A
Mem,A	Mem	10MM1000	0+		memory, reg A
#n,B	EORB n	C8	2	NZV	immed, reg B
Mem,B	Mem	11MM1000	0+		memory, reg B
* #n,PZ a	EIM a,n	75	6	NZV	immed, page zero (2)
* #n,(X+d)	d,n	65	7		immed, indexed (2)
CPL					Complement byte
(X+d)	COM d	63	7	NZVC	indexed
aa	aa	73	6		abs
A	COMA	43	2	NZVC	reg A
B	COMB	53	2	NZVC	reg B

RLWC					Rotate byte w/c left
(X+d)	ROL d	69	7	NZVC	indexed
aa	aa	79	6		abs
A	ROLA	49	2	NZVC	reg A
B	ROLB	59	2	NZVC	reg B
RRWC					Rotate byte w/c right
(X+d)	ROR d	66	7	NZVC	indexed
aa	aa	76	6		abs
A	RORA	46	2	NZVC	reg A
B	RORB	56	2	NZVC	reg B
SLA					Shift left arithmetic
(X+d)	ASL d	68	7	NZVC	indexed
aa	aa	78	6		abs
A	ASLA	48	2	NZVC	reg A
B	ASLB	58	2	NZVC	reg B
* SLAW				NZVC	Shift left arith word (1)
D	ASLD	05	3		reg D
SRA					Shift right arithmetic
(X+d)	ASR d	67	7	NZVC	indexed
aa	aa	77	6		abs
A	ASRA	47	2	NZVC	reg A
B	ASRB	57	2	NZVC	reg B
SRL					Shift right logical
(X+d)	LSR d	64	7	NZVC	indexed
aa	aa	74	6		abs
A	LSRA	44	2	NZVC	reg A
B	LSRB	54	2	NZVC	reg B
* SRLW				NZVC	Shift right logical word (1)
D	LSRD	04	3		reg D

Bit Operations

RESF					Reset flag
C	CLC	0C	2	C	carry
V	CLV	0A	2	V	overflow
SETF					Set flag
C	SEC	0D	2	C	carry
V	SEV	0B	2	V	overflow

Program Control

CALL					Call subroutine
aa	JSR aa	BD	9		uncond, abs
(X+d)	d	AD	8		uncond, indexed
PZ a	a	9D			uncond, page zero
CALLR					Call subroutine relative
r	BSR r	BD	8		uncond
RET	RTS	39	5		Return from subroutine
RETI	RTI	38	10	all	Return from interrupt
JMP	JMP				Jump to location
(X+d)	d	6E	4		uncond, indexed
aa	aa	7E	3		uncond, abs
JMPR					Jump relative
UN,r	BRA r	20	4		uncond
NC,r	BCC r	24	4		no carry
C,r	BCS r	25	4		carry
Z,r	BEQ r	27	4		zero
NZ,r	BGE r	2C	4		not zero
GZ,r	BGT r	2E	4		greater then zero
GT,r	BHI r	22	4		if higher
LT,r	BLE r	2F	4		LT
LE,r	BLS r	23	4		lowwer or same

```
   LZ,r   | BLT r | 2D   | 4|   | less then zero
   M,r    | BMI r | 2B   | 4|   | if minus
   NZ,r   | BNE r | 26   | 4|   | not zero
   NV,r   | BVC r | 28   | 4|   | v = 0
   V,r    | BVS r | 29   | 4|   | overfolw
   P,r    | BPL r | 2A   | 4|   | if plus
HALT      | WAI   | 3E   | 9|I | Stop till interrupt
NOP       | NOP   | 01   | 2|   | No operation
*  NOPL   | BRN   | 21,0 | 3|   | No operation, 2 bytes  (1)
SWI       | SWI   | 3F   |12|   | Software Interrupt
SLEEP     | SLP   | 1A   | 4|   | Enter sleep mode
```

I/O   Operations

```
DI        | CLI   | 0E   | 2|I | Disable interrupts
EI        | SEI   | 0F   | 2|I | Enable interrupts
          |       |      | |   |
```

Registers

```
    16      8|7     0
            ---------
            |  A  |
            ---------
            |  B  |
    ---------------------
    |       X       |  Index
    ---------------------
    | Program Counter |
    ---------------------
    |  Stack pointer  |
    ---------------------
        CCR  |11HINZVC|  Flags
```

* Reg A and B may be used as a single 16-bit reg D   (1)
* with reg A as MSB, and reg B as LSB   (1)

Flags

```
N = sign of result
Z = zero result
V = overflow
C = carry, bit 7
H = half carry, bit 3
I = interrupt
```


Addressing Modes

```
Univ  Manuf
----  -----

#n    n   - immediate
XX    XX  - register
aa    aa  -  absolute address
(X+d) d   - indexed, memory loc X+d
PZ a  a   - page zero address
r     r   - relative address value
```

Instruction Expansion

Univ	Mamuf	Memory MM	Type	Cyc
aa	aa	11	absolute	4
PZ a	a	01	page zero	3
(X+d)	d	10	indexed	5

#n   immediate data, 8-bits appended to inst
#nn immediate data, 16-bits appended to inst, MSB first
d   index value, 8-bits appended to inst
aa   absolute adr, 16-bits appended to inst, MSB first
a   page zero adr, 8-bits appended to inst
r   relative adr, 8-bits appended to inst

* immediate data is the 2nd byte and address value the 3rd byte (2)

Special Memory Locations

        Varies between each micro

Notes

    Data is stored MSB first then LSB

68000

HD68000, HD6800Y, HD68000Z, R68000, MC68008, MC68000, MC68C000

Data Move

MOV [W,DW]	MOVE			-X	Move byte,wrd,dwrd
Mem,MemDA	Mem,MemDA	00ssDDDDDDSSSSSS			srce, dest
MOVW				all	Move word
MemD,CCR	MemD,CCR	0100010011AAAAAA			memory, cond codes
MemD,SR	MemD,SR	0100011011AAAAAA			memory, status reg
SR,MemDA	SR,MemDA	0100000011AAAAAA			status reg, memory
MOVDW					Move double word
An,USP	An,USP	0100111001100RRR			An to USP
USP,An	USP,An	0100111001101RRR			USP to An
MOVW [DW]	MOVEA				Move wrd dwrd
Mem,An	Mem,An	00ssRRR001AAAAAA			memory to An
MOVMRW [DW]	MOVEM				Move multible registers
regs,MemCA	regs,MemC	010010001LAAAAAA			registers to memory
		0123456701234567			register list Dn,An
regs,-(An)	regs,-(An)	010010001LAAAAAA			registers to inddecAn
		0123456701234567			register list Dn,An
MemCA,regs	MemC,regs	010011001LAAAAAA			memory to registers
		7654321076543210			reg list An,Dn
(An)+,regs	(An)+,regs	010011001LAAAAAA			indincAn to registers
		7654321076543210			reg list An,Dn
MOVWB	MOVEP				Move by byte to lsb/wrd
(An++d),Dn	d(An),Dn	0000RRR100001AAA			indexed An to Dn
		dddddddddddddddd			
Dn,(An++dd)	Dn,d(An)	0000RRR110001AAA			Dn to indexed An
		dddddddddddddddd			

```
MOVDWB                                                         !!   ! Move by byte to msb/wrd
     (An++d),Dn    !  d(An),Dn   ! 0000RRR101001AAA ! !    !   indexed An to Dn
                   !             ! dddddddddddddddd ! !    !
     Dn,(An++dd)   !  Dn,d(An)   ! 0000RRR111001AAA ! !    !     Dn to indexed An
                   !             ! dddddddddddddddd ! !    !
MOVBDW             ! MOVEQ       !                  ! !    ! Move byte to dword
     #n,Dn         !  #n,Dn      ! 0111RRR0nnnnnnnn ! !-X  !   immed to Dn
CLR [W,DW]         ! CLR         !                  ! !-X  ! Move 0 to byte,wrd,dwrd
     MemDA         !  MemD       ! 01000010LWAAAAAA ! !    !   memory
PUSHEA             ! PEA         !                  ! !    ! Push adr onto the stack
     MemC          !  MemC       ! 0100100001AAAAAA ! !    !   efective long adr
XCHGDW             ! EXG         !                  ! !    ! Exchange dword
     Dn,Dn         !  Dn,Dn      ! 1100RRR101000RRR ! !    !   reg Dn and reg Dn
     An,An         !  An,An      ! 1100RRR101001RRR ! !    !   reg An and reg An
     Dn,An         !  Dn,An      ! 1100DDD110001AAA ! !    !   reg Dn and reg An
LEA                ! LEA         !                  ! !    ! Load efective address
     MemC,An       !  MemC,An    ! 0100RRR111AAAAAA ! !    !   location, reg An
LINK               ! LINK        !                  ! !    ! Link, put An on stack
     An,#nn        !  An,#nn     ! 0100111001010RRR ! !    !   move SP to An
                   !             ! nnnnnnnnnnnnnnnn ! !    !   add nn to SP
UNLK               ! UNLK        !                  ! !    ! Unlink,
     An            !  An         ! 0100111001011RRR ! !    !     An to SP, pop An
SETIF              ! Scc         !                  ! !    ! If cond, =FF else =00
     cc,MemDA      !  MemD       ! 0101CCCC11AAAAAA ! !    !   cond, memory
TSTSET   MemDA     ! TAS MemDA   ! 0100101011AAAAAA ! !-X  ! Test byte, set MSB
SWAPW Dn           ! SWAP Dn     ! 0100100001000RRR ! !-X  ! Swap words in dword
```

Math Operations

```
ADD [W,DW]         ! ADD         !                  ! !all! Add byte, wrd, dwrd
     Ds,MemMA      !  Ds,MemA    ! 1101RRR1LWAAAAAA ! !    !   Ds, memory
     Mem,Dd        !  Mem,Dd     ! 1101RRR0LWAAAAAA ! !    !   memory, Dd
     #nn,MemDA     ! ADDI #n,Mem ! 00000110LWAAAAAA ! !    !   immed, memory
ADDNB [W,DW]       !             !                  ! !    ! Add nible to byte,wrd
     #nn,MemA      ! ADDQ #n,Mem ! 0101nnn0LWAAAAAA ! !    !   immen 3-bits, memory
ADDW [DW]          ! ADDA        !                  ! !    ! Add word dword
     Mem,Ad        !  Mem,Ad     ! 1101DDDL11AAAAAA ! !    !   memory, reg An
ADC [W,DW]         ! ADDX        !                  ! !all! Add byte wrd dwrd w/x
     Ds,Dd         !  Ds,Dd      ! 1101DDD1LW000SSS ! !    !   reg Ds, reg Dd
     -(As),-(Ad)   !  -(As),-(Ad)! 1101DDD1LW001SSS ! !    !   ind-dec regs An
ADDBCD             ! ABCD        !                  ! !XZC! Add BCD w/x
     Ds,Dd         !  Ds,Dn      ! 1100DDD100000SSS ! !XZC!   reg Ds,reg Dd
     -(As),-(Ad)   !  -(As),-(Ad)! 1100DDD100001SSS ! !    !   ind_dec As, Ad
SUB [W,DW]         ! SUB         !                  ! !all! Sub byte, wrd, dwrd
     Ds,MemMA      !  Ds,MemA    ! 1001RRR1LWAAAAAA ! !    !   Ds, memory
     Mem,Dd        !  Mem,Dd     ! 1001RRR0LWAAAAAA ! !    !   memory, Dd
     #nn,MemDA     ! SUBI #n,Mem ! 00000100LWAAAAAA ! !    !   immed, memory
SUBNB [W,DW]       !             !                  ! !    ! Sub nible from
     #n,MemA       ! SUBQ #n,Mem ! 0101nnn1LWAAAAAA ! !    !   immen 3-bits, memory
SUBW [DW]          ! SUBA        !                  ! !    ! Sub word dword
     Mem,Ad        !  Mem,Ad     ! 1001DDDL11AAAAAA ! !    !   memory, Ad
SBB [W,DW]         ! SUBX        !                  ! !all! Sub byte wrd dwrd w/x
     Ds,Dd         !  Ds,Dd      ! 1001DDD1LW000SSS ! !    !   reg Ds, reg Dd
     -(As),-(Ad)   !  -(As),-(Ad)! 1001DDD1LW001SSS ! !    !   ind-dec regs An
SUBBCD             ! SBCD        !                  ! !all! Sub BCD w/x
     Ds,Dd         !  Ds,Dn      ! 1000DDD100000SSS ! !    !   reg Ds, reg Dd
     -(As),-(Ad)   !  -(As),-(Ad)! 1000DDD100001SSS ! !    !   ind_dec As, Ad
NEG [W,DW]         ! NEG         !                  ! !all! Change sign byte [word]
     MemDA         !  MemA       ! 01000100LWAAAAAA ! !    !   memory
NEGX [W,DW]        ! NEGX        !                  ! !all! Sub w/X from 0
     MemDA         !  MemD       ! 01000000LWAAAAAA ! !    !   memory
NEGBCD   MemDA     ! NBCD MemDA  ! 0100100000AAAAAA ! !all! Sub BCD byte & X frm 0
```

```
CNVBW  Dn      ! EXT  Dn      ! 0100100010000RRR ! !    ! Convert byte to word
CNVWDW Dn      !      Dn      ! 0100100011000RRR ! !    ! Convert word to d-word
CMP [W,DW]     ! CMP          !                  ! !-X  ! Compare byte,wrd,dwrd
   Dd,Mem      !      Mem,Dd  ! 1011RRR0LWAAAAAA ! !    !    Dd, memory
   MemDA,#nn   ! CMPI #n,Mem  ! 00001100LWAAAAAA ! !    !    memory, immed
               ! CMPM         !                  ! !    !
   (Ad)+,(As)+ ! (As)+,(Ad)+  ! 1011DDD1LW001SSS ! !    !    ind_inc Ad, As
CMPW [DW]      ! CMPA         !                  ! !-X  ! Compare wrd,dwrd
   Ad,Mem      !      Mem,An  ! 1011RRRL11AAAAAA ! !    !    Ad, memory
IMULW          ! MULS         !                  ! !-X  ! Multiply word by word
   MemD,Dn     !      MemD,Dn ! 1100RRR111AAAAAA ! !    !    Memory x Dn = Dn
MULW           ! MULU         !                  ! !-X  ! Multiply word by word
   MemD,Dn     !      MemD,Dn ! 1100RRR011AAAAAA ! !    !    memory x Dn = Dn
DIVW           ! DIVU         !                  ! !-X  ! Devide dword by word
   MemD,Dn     !      MemD,Dn ! 1000RRR011AAAAAA ! !    !    Dn/mem = LSW Dn
               !              !                  ! !    !    remainder = MSW Dn
IDIVW          ! DIVS         !                  ! !-X  ! Devide dword by word
   MemD,Dn     !      MemD,Dn ! 1000RRR111AAAAAA ! !    !    Dn/mem = LSW Dn
               !              !                  ! !    !    remainder = MSW Dn
```

I/O Operations

```
RESIO          ! RESET        ! 0100111001110000 ! !    ! Reset external dev
               !              !                  ! !    !
```

Logical Operations

```
AND [W,DW]     ! AND          !                  ! !-X  ! Log AND byte,wrd,dwrd
   Ds,MemMA    !      Ds,MemA ! 1100RRR1LWAAAAAA ! !    !    Ds, memory
   MemD,Dd     !      MemD,Dd ! 1100RRR0LWAAAAAA ! !    !    memory, Dd
   #nn,MemDA   ! ANDI #n,Mem  ! 00000010LWAAAAAA ! !    !    immed, memory
AND  #nn,SR    !      #n,SR   ! 0000001000111100 ! !    !    immed, status reg
ANDW #nn,CCR   !      #n,CCR  ! 0000001001111100 ! !    !    immed, status reg
OR [W,DW]      ! OR           !                  ! !-X  ! Logical OR byte/word
   Ds,MemMA    !      Ds,MemA ! 1000RRR1LWAAAAAA ! !    !    Ds, memory
   MemD,Dd     !      MemD,Dd ! 1000RRR0LWAAAAAA ! !    !    memory, Dd
   #nn,MemDA   ! ORI #n,MemA  ! 00000000LWAAAAAA ! !    !    immed, memory
OR  #nn,SR     !      #n,SR   ! 0000000000111100 ! !    !    immed, status reg
ORW #nn,CCR    !      #n,CCR  ! 0000000001111100 ! !    !    immed, status reg
TEST [W,DW]    ! TST          !                  ! !-X  ! Test logical OR w/0
   MemDA       !      MemA    ! 01001010LWAAAAAA ! !    !    memory
XOR [W,DW]     ! EOR          !                  ! !-X  ! Ex OR byte,wrd,dwrd
   Ds,MemDA    !      Ds,MemA ! 1011RRR1LWAAAAAA ! !    !    Ds, memory
   #nn,MemDA   ! EORI #n,Mem  ! 00001010LWAAAAAA ! !    !    immed, memory
XOR  #nn,SR    !      #n,SR   ! 0000101000111100 ! !    !    immed, status reg
XORW #nn,CCR   !      #n,CCR  ! 0000101001111100 ! !    !    immed, status reg
CPL [W,DW]     ! NOT          !                  ! !-X  ! Complement byte/word
   MemDA       !      MemA    ! 01000110LWAAAAAA ! !    !    memory
RLTC [W,DW]    ! ROL          !                  ! !-X  ! Rotate left to c
   Dd,Dn       !      Dd,Dn   ! 1110CCC1LW111RRR ! !    !    reg Dn, # bits Dn
   Dd,#b       !      Dd,#b   ! 1110bbb1LW011RRR ! !    !    reg Dn, b bits +1
RLTCW   MemMA  !      MemMA   ! 1110011111AAAAAA ! !-X  !    word, 1 bit
RRTC [W,DW]    ! ROR          !                  ! !-X  ! Rotate right to c
   Dd,Dn       !      Dd,Dn   ! 1110CCC0LW111RRR ! !    !    reg Dn, # bits Dn
   Dd,#b       !      Dd,#b   ! 1110bbb0LW011RRR ! !    !    reg Dn, b bits +1
RRTCW   MemMA  !      MemMA   ! 1110011011AAAAAA ! !-X  !    word, 1 bit
RLTCX [W,DW]   ! ROXL         !                  ! !all ! Rotate left to c and x
   Dd,Dn       !      Dd,Dn   ! 1110CCC1LW110RRR ! !    !    reg Dn, # bits Dn
   Dd,#b       !      Dd,#b   ! 1110bbb1LW010RRR ! !    !    reg Dn, b bits +1
RLTCXW  MemMA  !      MemMA   ! 1110010111AAAAAA ! !all !    word, 1 bit
RRTCX [W,DW]   ! ROXR         !                  ! !all ! Rotate right to c and x
   Dd,Dn       !      Dd,Dn   ! 1110CCC0LW110RRR ! !    !    reg Dn, # bits Dn
```

```
    Dd,#b       |    Dd,#b    | 1110bbb0LW010RRR |     |    reg·Dn, b bits +1
RRTCXW  MemMA   |    MemMA    | 1110010011AAAAAA | |all| word, 1 bit
SLA [W,DW]      | ASL         |                  | |all| Shift arith left,n bits
    Dd,Dn       |    Dd,Dn    | 1110CCC1LW100RRR |     |    reg Dn, # bits Dn
    Dd,#b       |    Dd,#b    | 1110bbb1LW000RRR |     |    reg Dn, b bits +1
SLAW  MemMA     |    MemMA    | 1110000111AAAAAA | |all| word, 1 bit
SRA [W,DW]      | ASR         |                  | |all| Shift arith left,n bits
    Dd,Dn       |    Dd,Dn    | 1110CCC0LW100RRR |     |    reg Dn, # bits Dn
    Dd,#b       |    Dd,#b    | 1110bbb0LW000RRR |     |    reg Dn, b bits +1
SRAW  MemMA     |    MemMA    | 1110000011AAAAAA | |all| word, 1 bit
SLL [W,DW]      | LSL         |                  | |all| Shift log left,n bits
    Dd,Dn       |    Dd,Dn    | 1110CCC1LW101RRR |     |    reg Dn, # bits Dn
    Dd,#b       |    Dd,#b    | 1110bbb1LW001RRR |     |    reg Dn, b bits +1
SLLW  MemMA     |    MemMA    | 1110001111AAAAAA | |all| word, 1 bit
SRL [W,DW]      | LSR         |                  | |all| Shift log right,n bits
    Dd,Dn       |    Dd,Dn    | 1110CCC0LW101RRR |     |    reg Dn, # bits Dn
    Dd,#b       |    Dd,#b    | 1110bbb0LW001RRR |     |    reg Dn, b bits +1
SRLW  MemMA     |    MemMA    | 1110001011AAAAAA | |all| word, 1 bit
```

Bit Operations

```
TSTBCHG         | BCHG        |                  | |Z | Test & chg bit, byte
    MemMA,Db    |    Db,MemA  | 0000BBB101AAAAAA | |  |    bit Dn,memory loc
    MemMA,#b    |    #b,MemA  | 0000100001AAAAAA | |  |    bit b, memory loc
                |             | 00000000bbbbbbbb | |  |
                |             |                  | |Z | Test & chg bit, dword
    Dn,Db       |    Db,Dn    | 0000BBB101AAAAAA | |  |    bit Dn, reg Dn
    Dn,#b       |    #b,Dn    | 0000100001AAAAAA | |  |    bit b, reg Dn
                |             | 00000000bbbbbbbb | |  |
TSTBCLR         | BCLR        |                  | |Z | Test & clr bit, byte
    MemMA,Db    |    Dn,MemA  | 0000BBB110AAAAAA | |  |    bit Dn,memory loc
    MemMA,#B    |    #b,MemA  | 0000100010AAAAAA | |  |    bit b, memory loc
                |             | 00000000bbbbbbbb | |  |
                |             |                  | |Z | Test & clr bit, dword
    Dn,Db       |    Db,Dn    | 0000BBB110AAAAAA | |  |    bit Db, reg Dn
    Dn,#b       |    #b,Dn    | 0000100010AAAAAA | |  |    bit b, reg Dn
                |             | 00000000bbbbbbbb | |  |
TSTBSET         | BSET        |                  | |Z | Test & set bit, byte
    MemMA,Db    |    Db,MemA  | 0000BBB111AAAAAA | |  |    bit Db,memory loc
    MemMA,#b    |    #b,MemA  | 0000100011AAAAAA | |  |    bit b, memory loc
                |             | 00000000bbbbbbbb | |  |
                |             |                  | |Z | Test & set bit, dword
    Dn,Db       |    Db,Dn    | 0000BBB111AAAAAA | |  |    bit Db, reg Dn
    Dn,#b       |    #b,Dn    | 0000100011AAAAAA | |  |    bit b, reg Dn
                |             | 00000000bbbbbbbb | |  |
TSTB            | BTST        |                  | |Z | Test bit in byte
    MemD,Db     |    Db,MemD  | 0000BBB100AAAAAA | |  |    bit Db,memory loc
    MemD,#b     |    #b,MemD  | 0000100000AAAAAA | |  |    bit b, memory loc
                |             | 00000000bbbbbbbb | |  |
                |             |                  | |Z | Test bit in dword
    Dn,Db       |    Db,Dn    | 0000BBB100AAAAAA | |  |    bit Db, reg Dn
    Dn,#b       |    #b,Dn    | 0000100000AAAAAA | |  |    bit b, reg Dn
                |             | 00000000bbbbbbbb | |  |
```

Program Control

```
CALL  MemC      | JSR  MemC   | 0100111010AAAAAA | |  | Call subr location
CALLD  dd       | BSR  dd     | 0110000100000000 | |  | Call subr displacement
                |             | dddddddddddddddd | |  |
CALLR  r        |       r     | 01100001rrrrrrrr | |  | Call subr relative
RET             | RTS         | 0100111001110101 | |  | Return from subr
RETE            | RTE         | 0100111001110011 | |all| Return from exception
```

284

```
RETRCC      ! RTR        ! 0100111001110111 ! !all! Return & restore CC
JMP  MemC   ! JMP  MemC   ! 0100111011AAAAAA ! !   ! Jump to loc
JMPD        ! Bcc        !                  ! !   ! Jump displacement if
     CC,dd  !      dd    ! 0110cccc00000000 ! !   !   cond cc, disp
            !            ! dddddddddddddddd ! !   !
     UN,dd  ! BRA  dd    ! 0110000000000000 ! !   !   uncond, disp
            !            ! dddddddddddddddd ! !   !
JMPR        ! Bcc        !                  ! !   ! Jump relative
     CC,r   !      r     ! 0110ccccrrrrrrrr ! !   !   cond cc, rel
     UN,r   ! BRA  r     ! 0110000rrrrrrrr ! !   !   uncond, rel
LOOPD       ! DBcc       !                  ! !   ! If not dec jump <> -1
     cc,Dn,dd !   Dn,dd  ! 0101cccc11001RRR ! !   !   cond, dec Dn, disp
            !            ! dddddddddddddddd ! !   !
TRAP        ! TRAP       !                  ! !   ! Trap
     UN,#n  !      #n    ! 010011100100nnnn ! !   !     vector n
     V      ! TRAPV      ! 0100111001110110 ! !   !     on overflow
BOUND       ! CHK        !                  ! !-X ! Check bounds, trap if
     MemD,Dn !    MemD,Dn ! 0100RRR110AAAAAA ! !   !   reg Dn =0 or >memory
HALT        ! STOP       ! 0100111001110010 ! !all! Stop till interrupt
     #nn    !      #nn   ! nnnnnnnnnnnnnnnn ! !   !   CC = nn
NOP         ! NOP        ! 0100111001110001 ! !   ! No operation
```

REGISTERS

```
        31              16 15     8 7       0
   D0  !               !         !         !
       -----------------------------------
   D1  !               !         !         !
       -----------------------------------
   D2  !               !         !         !
       -----------------------------------
   D3  !               !         !         !
       -----------------------------------
   D4  !               !         !         !
       -----------------------------------
   D5  !               !         !         !
       -----------------------------------
   D6  !               !         !         !
       -----------------------------------
   D7  !               !         !         !
       -----------------------------------
   A0  !               !                   !
       -----------------------------------
   A1  !               !                   !
       -----------------------------------
   A2  !               !                   !
       -----------------------------------
   A3  !               !                   !
       -----------------------------------
   A4  !               !                   !
       -----------------------------------
   A5  !               !                   !
       -----------------------------------
   A6  !               !                   !
       -----------------------------------
   A7  !    User Stack Pointer    (USP)   !
       -----------------------------------     SP
   A7' ! Supervisor Stack Pointer  (SSP)  !
       -----------------------------------
```

```
PC |              Program Counter            |
   ---------------------------------------------
SR                       |T S III|  XNZVC|  Flags (CCR)
                         ---------------------
```

FLAGS

```
C = carry                X = extended
V = overflow           III = interrupt mask
Z = zero                 S = subervisor state
N = negative             T = trace mode
```

ADDRESSING MODES

Univ	Manuf	
Rx	Rx	- register, Dx ,Ax, WDx or WAx
#nn	#nn	- immediate data, 8- 16- or 32-bits
SE aa	aa	- sign extended address, 16-bits
aaaa	aaaa	- absolute address, 32-bits
(Ax)	(Ax)	- reg indirect
(Ax++nn)	nn(Ax)	- indexed, adr reg + 16-bit signed value
(Ax+Rx+n)	n(Ax,Rx)	- indexed, two reg + 8-bit signed value
r	r	- relative address value
dd	PC dd	- displacement address value
(PC+Rx+n)	n(PC,Rx)	- indexed, PC + reg + 8-bit signed value
-(Ax)	-(Ax)	- indirect auto pre decrement by 1, 2 or 4
(Ax)+	(Ax)+	- indirect auto post increment by 1, 2 or 4d

Special Memory Locations

Data Types

word	16-bits	must start on wrd boundry even adr
byte	8-bits	any address
bit	8-bits	any address
integer	4-bytes	start on word boundry even adr MSB
long word	32 bits	start on word boundry even adr MSB
address	32 bits	word boundry even adr MSB
BCD	2 /byte	word boundry

Notes

All instructions and word data must start at an even adr.(wrd boundry).
Word and double word data is stored MSB first (low adr) LSB last.

```
         -----------------
Byte    |  00  |  byte  |             -----------------
         -----------------    Double | MSB  |       |
                               Word    -----------------
                                      |       |  LSB  |
         -----------------             -----------------
Word    |  MSB  |  LSB  |
         -----------------
```

Instruction Expansion

```
     Register
    Dx   Ax    RRR
    --   --    ---
    D0   A0    000
    D1   A1    001
    D2   A2    010
    D3   A3    011
    D4   A4    100
    D5   A5    101
    D6   A6    110
    D7   A7    111
```

                    Memory

```
   Mem                            MMMRRR
  D M C A   Univ       Manuf      AAAAAA    Append
  -------   ---------  -----      -------   ------
  x     x   Dn         Dn         000RRR
        x   An         An         001RRR    except byte operations
  x x x x   SE aa      aa         111000    16-bit signed adr
  x x x x   aaaa       aaaa       111001    32-bit adr (MSW / LSW)
  x x   x   (An)       (An)       010RRR
  x x   x   (An)+      (An)+      011RRR
  x x   x   -(An)      -(An)      100RRR
  x x x x   (An++dd)   dd(An)     101RRR    16-bit displacement
  x x x x   (An+WRn+d) d(An,Rn.W) 110RRR    see below, W=0
  x x x x   (An+Rn+d)  d(An,Rn.L) 110RRR    see below, W=1
  x x   x   DA aa      PC rel     111010    16-bit displacement
  x x   x   (PC+WRn+d) PC rel +Rn.W 111011  see below, W=0
  x x   x   (PC+Rn+d)  PC rel +Rn.L 111011  see below, W=1
  x x       #nn        #nn        111100    1 or 2 words
```

Mem=all, MemD=data, MemM=memory, MemC=control, MemA=alterable
        MemDA=data alterable, MemMA=memory alt, MemCA=control alt

```
for MOV    ss = word size, 01 byte, 11 word, 10 dword
-------     DDDDDD = destination,   RRRMMM see table above
            SSSSSS = source         MMMRRR see table above
```

for: reg+reg+disp

```
    ARRRW000dddddddd
    !---! --------
    ! ! !        !
    ! ! !        -- 8-bit signed
    ! ! -- index reg size, =0 word sign extended, =1 double word
    ! -- index reg
    -- =1 adr reg, =0 data reg
```

n = immediate data, 8-bits part of inst
              or 8-bits appended to inst followed by a zero byte
              or 16-bits appended to inst
              or 32-bits appended to inst
b = number of bits, 3-bits part of the inst.
    or bit number, 8-bits part of inst
dd = displacement adr, 16-bits appended to inst
r = relative address, 8-bits part of inst

287

pp = port address, 16-bits appended to the inst

PSW = program status words, Pc and FCW.
DW = double word indicator
W   = word indicator
L   = long double word

Condition Codes

Sym	Def		CCCC	Sym	Def		CCCC
T	true	1	0000	GT	high	C and Z = 0	0010
F	false	0	0001	LE	low or same	C or Z = 1	0011
NC	no carry	C=0	0100	SGE	> or =	N and V = 1 or 0	1100
C	carry	C=1	0101	SLT	<	N xor V = 1	1101
NE	not equald	Z=0	0110	SGT	>	N and V = 1, Z = 0	1110
EQ	equal	Z=1	0111			or N and V and Z = 0	
NV	no overflow	V=0	1000	SLE	< or =	Z or (N xor V) = 1	1111
V	overflow	V=1	1001				
P	plus	N=0	1010				
M	minus	N=1	1011				

Instruction Formats

word 1 - operation and modes
     2 - immediate data, 1 or 2 words
     3 - source address extension, 1 or 2 words
     4 - destination address extension, 1 or 2 words

6804

MC6804J2, MC6804P2, MC68HC04P2, MC68HC04P3

Data Move

MOV						Move byte
#n,A	LDA n	E8	4		immed, reg A
Mem,A	Mem	111MM000	4		memory, reg A
Dir,A	Dir	101011RR	4		direct, reg A
#n,X	LDXI n	B0,80	4		immed, reg X
#n,Y	LDYI n	B0,81	4		immed, reg Y
A,Mem	STA Mem	111MM001	4		reg A, memory
A,Dir	Dir	101111RR	4		reg A, direct
#n,Ra	MVI $a,n	B0,aa,nn	4		immed, data memory
A,X	TAX	BC	4		reg A, reg X
A,Y	TAY	BD	4		reg A, reg Y
X,A	TXA	AC	4		reg X, reg A
Y,A	TYA	AD	4		reg Y, reg A
CLR					Clear byte
A	CLRA	FB,FF	4		reg A
X	CLRX	FB,80	4		reg X
Y	CLRY	FB,81	4		reg Y

Math Operations

ADD						Add byte
#n,A	ADD n	EA	4		immed, reg A

```
    Mem,A    |    Mem   | 111MM010  | 4|     |   memory, reg A
INC          | INC      |           |  |     | Increment
    Mem      |    Mem   | 111MM110  | 4|     |   memory
    Dir      |    Dir   | 101010RR  | 4|     |   direct data loc
    A        | INCA     | FE,FF     | 4|     |   reg A
    X        | INCX     | A8        | 4|     |   reg X
    Y        | INCY     | A9        | 4|     |   reg Y
SUB          |          |           |  |     | Subtract byte
    #n,A     | SUB  n   | EB        | 4|     |   immed, reg A
    Mem,A    |    Mem   | 111MM011  | 4|     |   memory, reg A
DEC          | DEC      |           |  |     | Decrement
    Mem      |    Mem   | 111MM111  | 4|     |   memory
    Dir      |    Dir   | 101110RR  | 4|     |   direct data loc
    A        | DECA     | FF,FF     | 4|     |   reg A
    X        | DECX     | B8        | 4|     |   reg X
    Y        | DECY     | B9        | 4|     |   reg Y
CMP          |          |           |  |     | Compare byte
    A,#n     | CMP  n   | EC        | 4|     |   reg A, immed
    A,Mem    |    Mem   | 111MM100  | 4|     |   reg A, memory
```

Logical Operations

```
AND          |          |           |  |     | Logical AND byte
    #n,A     | AND  n   | ED        | 4|     |   immed, reg A
    Mem,A    |    Mem   | 111MM101  | 4|     |   memory, reg A
CPL          |          |           |  |     | Complement byte
    A        | COMA     | B4        | 4|     |   reg A
RLWC         |          |           |  |     | Rotate byte w/c left
    A        | ROLA     | B5        | 4|     |   reg A
SLA          |          |           |  |     | Shift left arithmetic
    A        | ASLA     | FA,FF     | 4|     |   reg A
```

Bit Operations

```
SETB         | BSET     |           |  |     | Set bit
    A,b      |    b     | 11011bbb  | 4|     |   reg A, bit b
RESB         | BCLR     |           |  |     | Reset bit
    A,b      |    b     | 11010bbb  | 4|     |   reg A, bit b
```

Program Control

```
CALL         |          |           |  |     | Call subroutine
    aa       | JSR aa   | 1000aaaa  | 4|     |   uncond, abs
             |          | aaaaaaaa  |  |     |
RET          | RTS      | 83        | 2|     | Return from subroutine
RETI         | RTI      | 82        | 2|all! | Return from interrupt
JMP          | JMP      |           |  |     | Jump to location
    aa       |    aa    | 1001aaaa  | 4|     |   uncond, abs
             |          | aaaaaaaa  |  |     |
JMPR         |          |           |  |     | Jump relative
    UN,r     | BRA  r   | 20        | 4|     |   uncond
    NC,r     | BCC  r   | 010rrrrr  | 2|     |   no carry
    C,r      | BCS  r   | 011rrrrr  | 2|     |   carry
    Z,r      | BEQ  r   | 001rrrrr  | 4|     |   zero
    LT,r     | BLO  r   | 011rrrrr  | 2|     |   if lower
    GT,r     | BHS  r   | 010rrrrr  | 2|     |   if higher
    NZ,r     | BNE  r   | 000rrrrr  | 2|     |   not zero
             | BRSET    |           |  |     | Jump rel if bit set
    BS,A,b,r |    b,r   | 11001bbb  | 5|     |   reg A, bit b, relative adr
             | BRCLR    |           |  |     | Jump rel if bit clear
    BR,A,b,r |    b,r   | 11000bbb  | 5|     |   reg A, bit b, relative adr
```

Registers

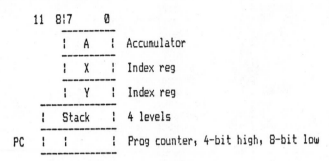

```
    11  8:7       0
                _____
                :   A   :   Accumulator
                _____
                :   X   :   Index reg
                _____
                :   Y   :   Index reg
           _____
           :    Stack   :   4 levels
           _____
    PC     :  :         :   Prog counter, 4-bit high, 8-bit low
           _____
```

Registers A, X, Y are part of RAM memory

RAM memory (256-bytes) is addressed as R0 - RFF or $0 - $FF

Flags

Z = zero result
C = carry, bit 7

Addressing Modes

Univ	Manuf	
#n	n	- immediate
XX		- register
Ra	$a	- register, data loc a
aa	aa	- absolute memory address
bit		- individual bits
r	r	- relative memory address
(X)	(X)	- indirect register X or Y

Instruction Expansion

	Memory				Direct		
Univ	Man	MM	Type		Mem	RR	Type
---	---	---	---		---	---	---
(X)	XP	00	indirect X		X	00	data loc 80
(Y)	YP	10	indirect Y		Y	01	81
Ra	$a	11	data address		R82	10	82
			(append 8-bit adr)		R83	11	83

#n immediate, 8-bits appended to inst
a   absolute data address, 8-bits appended to inst
b   bit number, 3-bits part of inst
aa absolute memory adr, MSB 4-bits part of inst, LSB 8-bits appended
r   relative memory adr, 5-bits part of inst, or 8-bits appended

Special Memory Locations

Prog ROM			Data Memory	
loc 000 - ADF	Reserved		loc 00 - 06	Port registers
AE0 - C0F	Self test		07 - 08	not used

C10 - FF7	User prog	
FF8 - FFF	Vectors	

09	Timer status
0A - 1F	future use
20 - 5F	Data ROM
60 - 7F	future use
80	Register X
81	Register Y
82 - 9F	Data RAM
A0 - FC	future use
FD - FE	Timer registers
FF	Register A

Notes

6805

MD6805S1, HD6805S6, HD6805U1, HD6805V1, HD6805T2, HD6805W1, HD63L05F1, HD63L05E0, HD68P05V07, HD68P05W0

MC6805P2, MC6805K2, MC6805P4, MC6805K3, MC6805P6 MC6805T2, MC68705P3, MC68705P5

(1) MC6805R2, MC6805R3, MC6805U2, MC6805U3, MCT8705R3, MC68705U3, MC68705R5, MC68705U5, MC680582, MC146805, MC68YHC05C4, MC1468705F2, MC1468705G2, MD14680532, MC146805E3, MC146805F2, MC146805G2, MC146805H2, CDPT805E2, CD6805E3, CDP6805G2

(1,2) HD6305X0, HD63A05X0, HD63B05X0, HD6305U0, HD63A05U0, HD63B05U0, HD305V0, HD63A05V0, HD63B05V0, HD630FX1, HD63A05X1, HD63B05X1, HD6305X2, HD63A05X2, HD63B05X2, HD6305Y0, HD63A05Y0, HD63B05Y0, HD6305Y1, HD63A05Y1, HD63B05Y1, HD6305Y2, HD63A05Y2, HD63B05Y2, HD63P05Y0, HD63PA05Y0, HD63PB05Y0

Data Move

MOV						Move byte
#n,A	LDA n	A6	2	NZ		immed reg A
Mem,A	Mem	1MMM0110	0+			memory, reg A
#n,X	LDX n	AE	2	NZ		immed, reg B
Mem,X	Mem	1MMM0110	0+			memory, reg B
A,Mem	STA Mem	1MMM0111	1+	NZ		reg A, memory
X,Mem	STX Mem	1MMM1111	1+	NZ		reg B, memory
A,X	TAX	97	2			reg A, reg X
X,A	TXA	9F	2			reg X, reg A
CLR	CLR			NZ		Clear byte
(X+a)	d	6F	7			indexed
(X)	(X)	7F	6			ind
PZ a	a	3F	6			page zero
A	A	4F	4	ZV		reg A
X	X	5F	4	ZV		reg B
RES	RSP		2			Reset byte to predefined value
SP		9C				stack pointer set to 07F

Math Operations

ADD						Add byte
#n,A	ADD n	AB	2	-I		immed, reg A
Mem,A	Mem	1MMM1011	0+			memory, reg A

```
ADC               !          !          ! 2!-I ! Add byte w/c
    #n,A          ! ADC  n   ! A9       ! 2!-I !    immed, reg A
    Mem,A         !    Mem   ! 1MMM1001 ! 0+!    !    memory, reg A
INC               ! INC      !          !  !NZ ! Increment byte
    (X+a)         !    d     ! 6C       ! 7!    !    indexed
    (X)           !    (X)   ! 7C       ! 6!    !    ind
    PZ a          !    a     ! 3C       ! 6!    !    page zero
    A             !    A     ! 4C       ! 4!    !    reg A
    X             !    X     ! 5C       ! 4!    !    reg B
SUB               ! SUB      !          !  !    ! Subtract byte
    #n,A          ! SUB  n   ! A0       ! 2!NZC!    immed, reg A
    Mem,A         !    Mem   ! 1MMM0000 ! 0+!    !    memory, reg A
SBB               ! SBC      !          !  !    ! Subtract byte w/c
    #n,A          ! SBC  n   ! A2       ! 2!NZC!    immed, reg A
    Mem,A         !    Mem   ! 1MMM0010 ! 0+!    !    memory, reg A
DEC               ! DEC      !          !  !NZ ! Decrement byte
    (X+a)         !    d     ! 6A       ! 7!    !    indexed
    (X)           !    (X)   ! 7A       ! 6!    !    ind
    PZ a          !    a     ! 3A       ! 6!    !    page zero
    A             !    A     ! 4A       ! 4!    !    reg A
    X             !    X     ! 5A       ! 4!    !    reg B
NEG               ! NEG      !          !  !NZC! Change to negative
    (X+a)         !    d     ! 60       ! 7!    !    indexed
    (X)           !    (X)   ! 70       ! 6!    !    ind
    PZ a          !    a     ! 30       ! 6!    !    page zero
    A             !    A     ! 40       ! 4!    !    reg A
    X             !    X     ! 50       ! 4!    !    reg B
CMP               !          !          !  !    ! Compare byte
    A,#n          ! CMP  n   ! A1       ! 2!NZC!    reg A, immed
    A,Mem         !    Mem   ! 1MMM0001 ! 0+!    !    reg A, memory
    X,#n          ! CPX  n   ! A3       ! 2!NZC!    reg X, immed
    X,Mem         !    Mem   ! 1MMM0011 ! 0+!    !    reg X, memory
    (X+a),00      ! TST d    ! 6D       ! 7!NZ !    indexed, 00
    (X),00        !    (X)   ! 7D       ! 6!    !    ind, 00
    PZ a,00       !    a     ! 3D       ! 6!    !    page zero, 00
    A,00          !    A     ! 4D       ! 4!    !    reg A, 00
    X,00          !    X     ! 5D       ! 4!    !    reg X, 00
* DA A            ! DAA      ! 8D       ! 2!NZC! Decimal adjust  (2)
```

Bit Operations
```
RESF              !          !          !  !    ! Reset flag
    C             ! CLC      ! 98       ! 2!C  !    carry
SETF              !          !          !  !    ! Set flag
    C             ! SEC      ! 99       ! 2!C  !    carry
SETB              ! BSET     !          ! 7!    ! Set bit
    A,b           !    b     ! 0001BBBB !  !    !    reg A, BBBB= 2 x b
RESB              ! BCLR     !          ! 7!    ! Reset bit
    A,b           !    b     ! 0001BBBB !  !    !    reg A, BBBB= (2 x b) + 1
```

I/O Operations
```
DI                ! CLI      ! 9A       ! 2!I  ! Disable interrupts
EI                ! SEI      ! 9B       ! 2!I  ! Enable interrupts
SWI               ! SWI      ! 83       !11!    ! Software Interrupt
```

Logical Operations
```
AND               !          !          !  !    ! Logical AND byte
    #n,A          ! AND  n   ! A4       ! 2!NZC!    immed, reg A
    Mem,A         !    Mem   ! 1MMM0100 ! 0+!    !    memory, reg A
TEST              !          !          !  !    ! Logical AND, set flags
```

```
     #n,A        | BIT  n  | A5        |  2|NZ |     immed, reg A
     Mem,A       |    Mem  | 1MMM0101  | 0+|   |     memory, reg A
OR                |         |           |   |   | Logical OR byte
     #n,A        | ORA  n  | AA        |  2|NZ |     immed, reg A
     Mem,A       |    Mem  | 1MMM1010  | 0+|   |     memory, reg A
XOR               |         |           |   |   | Logical Exclusive OR byte
     #n,A        | EOR  n  | A8        |  2|NZ |     immed, reg A
     Mem,A       |    Mem  | 1MMM1000  | 0+|   |     memory, reg A
CPL               | COM     |           |   |NZC| Complement byte
     (X+a)       |    d    | 63        |  7|   |     indexed
     (X)         |   (X)   | 73        |  6|   |     ind
     PZ a        |    a    | 33        |  6|   |     page zero
     A           |    A    | 43        |  4|   |     reg A
     X           |    X    | 53        |  4|   |     reg B
RLWC              | ROL     |           |   |NZC| Rotate byte w/c left
     (X+a)       |    d    | 69        |  7|   |     indexed
     (X)         |   (X)   | 79        |  6|   |     ind
     PZ a        |    a    | 39        |  6|   |     page zero
     A           |    A    | 49        |  4|   |     reg A
     X           |    X    | 59        |  4|   |     reg B
RRWC              | ROR     |           |   |NZC| Rotate byte w/c right
     (X+a)       |    d    | 66        |  7|   |     indexed
     (X)         |   (X)   | 76        |  6|   |     ind
     PZ a        |    a    | 36        |  6|   |     page zero
     A           |    A    | 46        |  4|   |     reg A
     X           |    X    | 56        |  4|   |     reg B
SLL               | LSL     |           |   |NZC| Shift left logical
     (X+a)       |    d    | 68        |  7|   |     indexed
     (X)         |   (X)   | 78        |  6|   |     ind
     PZ a        |    a    | 38        |  6|   |     page zero
     A           |    A    | 48        |  4|   |     reg A
     X           |    X    | 58        |  4|   |     reg B
SLA               | ASL     |           |   |NZC| Shift left arithmetic
     (X+a)       |    d    | 68        |  7|   |     indexed
     (X)         |   (X)   | 78        |  6|   |     ind
     PZ a        |    a    | 38        |  6|   |     page zero
     A           |    A    | 48        |  4|   |     reg A
     X           |    X    | 58        |  4|   |     reg B
SRA               | ASR     |           |   |NZC| Shift right arithmetic
     (X+a)       |    d    | 67        |  7|   |     indexed
     (X)         |   (X)   | 77        |  6|   |     ind
     PZ a        |    a    | 37        |  6|   |     page zero
     A           |    A    | 47        |  4|   |     reg A
     X           |    X    | 57        |  4|   |     reg B
SRL               | LSR     |           |   |NZC| Shift right logical
     (X+a)       |    d    | 64        |  7|   |     indexed
     (X)         |   (X)   | 74        |  6|   |     ind
     PZ a        |    a    | 34        |  6|   |     page zero
     A           |    A    | 44        |  4|   |     reg A
     X           |    X    | 54        |  4|   |     reg B
```

Program Control

```
CALL              |         |           |   |   | Call subroutine
     Mem         | JSR Mem | 1MMM1101  | 3+|   |     uncond, abs
CALLR             |         |           |   |   | Call subroutine relative
     r           |    a    | AD        |   |   |     uncond, relative
RET               | RTS     | 81        |  6|   | Return from subroutine
RETI              | RTI     | 80        |  9|all| Return from interrupt
JMP               | JMP     |           |   |   | Jump to location
     Mem         |    Mem  | 1MMM1100  | -1|   |     uncond, indexed
JMPR              |         |           |   |   | Jump relative
```

UN,r	BRA r	20	4		uncond
NC,r	BCC r	24	4		no carry
C,r	BCS r	25	4		carry
Z,r	BEQ r	27	4		zero
NI,r	BMC r	2C	4		no interrupts
IL,r	BIL r	2E	4		interrupt line low
GT,r	BHI r	22	4		if higher
IH,r	BIH r	2F	4		interrupt line high
LE,r	BLS r	23	4		lower or same
IE,r	BMS r	2D	4		interrupts enabled
M,r	BMI r	2B	4		if minus
NZ,r	BNE r	26	4		not zero
NHC,r	BHCC r	28	4		h = 0
HC,r	BHCS r	29	4		h = 1
P,r	BPL r	2A	4		if plus
	BRSET		10		Jump rel if bit set
BS,A,b,r	n,r	0000BBBB			reg A, BBBB = 2 x b
	BRCLR		10		Jump rel if bit clear
BR,A,b,r	n,r	0000BBBB			reg A, BBBB = (2 x b) + 1
NOP	NOP	9D	2		No operation
NOPL	BRN	21,0	3		No operation, 2 bytes
* HALT	STOP	8E	4		Stop mode (1)
* WAIT	WAIT	8F	4		Wait mode (1)

Registers

```
10  8 7     0
    ---------
    :  A  :
    ---------
      :  X  :   Index
    ---------
    :   PC    :
    ---------

10    5 4    0
    ---------
    :000011: SP  :
    ---------

       ------
    CCR   :HINZC:  Flags
       ------
```

Flags

N = sign of result
Z = zero result
C = carry, bit 7
H = half carry, bit 3
I = interrupt

Addressing Modes

Univ	Manuf	
#n	n	- immediate
XX	XX	- register
aa	aa	- absolute address
(X+a)	d	- indexed page zero, loc X+a
(X++aa)		- indexed absolute, loc X+aa

```
PZ a    a   - page zero address
r       r   - relative address
(X)     (X) - indirect reg X
```

Instruction Expansion

```
                    Mem
                    ---

    Mem     MM   Type        Cyc
    ---     --   ----        ---
    aa      100  absolute     5
    PZ a    011  page zero    4
    (X)     111  indirect     4
    (X+a)   110  indexed      5
    (X++aa) 101               6


    aa   absolute adr, 10-bits appended to inst MSB first
    a    page zero adr, 8-bits appended to inst
    r    relative addr, 8-bits appended to inst
    n    immediate data, 8-bits appended to inst
    b    bit number, 4-bits part of inst = 2 x b or (2 x b) + 1
```

Special Memory Locations

Notes

    Data is stored MSB first then LSB

6809

HD6809, HD68A09, HD68B09, HD6309, HD63093, HD6809E, HD68A09E, HD68B09E, HD6309E, MC6809, M6809E, MC68A09, MC68A09E, MC68B09, MC68B09E, MC68HC09E

Data Move

```
MOV    !          !          !   !NZV! Move byte
  #n,A     ! LDAA n  ! 86 !  2!    !     immed, reg A
  PZ a,A   !    <a   ! 96 !  4!    !     page zero, reg A
  aa,A     !    aa   ! B6 !  5!    !     abs, reg A
  Mem,A    !    Mem  ! A6 ! 4+!    !     memory, reg A
  #n,B     ! LDAB n  ! C6 !  2!    !     immed, reg B
  PZ a,B   !    <a   ! D6 !  4!    !     page zero, reg B
  aa,B     !    aa   ! F6 !  5!    !     abs, reg B
  Mem,B    !    Mem  ! E6 ! 4+!    !     memory, reg B
  A,PZ a   ! STA <a  ! 97 !  4!    !     reg A, pz
  A,aa     !    aa   ! B7 !  5!    !     reg A, abs
  A,Mem    !    Mem  ! A7 ! 4+!    !     reg A, memory
  B,PZ a   ! STB <a  ! D7 !  4!    !     reg A, pz
  B,aa     !    aa   ! F7 !  5!    !     reg A, abs
  B,Mem    !    Mem  ! E7 ! 4+!    !     reg A, memory
  Rs,Rd    ! TFR     ! 1F, !  6!all!    srce, dest
           ! Rd,Rs! SSSSDDDD !   !   !
MOVW   !          !          !   !NZV! Move word
  D,PZ a   ! STD <a  ! DD !  5!    !     reg D, page zero
  D,aa     !    aa   ! FD !  6!    !     reg D, abs
```

```
   D,Mem    !     Mem ! ED   !5+!   ! reg D, memory
   S,PZ a   ! STS <a ! 10,DF ! 6!   ! reg S, page zero
   S,aa     !     aa ! 10,FF ! 7!   ! reg S, abs
   S,Mem    !    Mem ! 10,EF !6+!   ! reg S, memory
   U,PZ a   ! STU <a ! DF   ! 5!   ! reg U, page zero
   U,aa     !     aa ! FF   ! 6!   ! reg U, abs
   U,Mem    !    Mem ! EF   !5+!   ! reg U, memory
   X,PZ a   ! STX <a ! 9F   ! 5!   ! reg X, page zero
   X,aa     !     aa ! BF   ! 6!   ! reg X, abs
   X,Mem    !    Mem ! AF   !5+!   ! reg X, memory
   Y,PZ a   ! STY <a ! 10,9F ! 6!   ! reg Y, page zero
   Y,aa     !     aa ! 10,BF ! 7!   ! reg Y, abs
   Y,Mem    !    Mem ! 10,AF !6+!   ! reg Y, memory
   #nn,D    ! LDD nn ! CC   ! 3!   ! immed, reg D
   PZ a,D   !     <a ! DC   ! 5!   ! pz, reg D
   aa,D     !     aa ! FC   ! 6!   ! abs, reg D
   Mem,D    !    Mem ! EC   !5+!   ! memory, reg D
   #nn,S    ! LDS nn ! 10,CE ! 4!   ! immed, reg S
   PZ a,S   !     <a ! 10,DE ! 6!   ! pz, reg S
   aa,S     !     aa ! 10,FE ! 7!   ! abs, reg S
   Mem,S    !    Mem ! 10,EE !6+!   ! memory, reg S
   #nn,U    ! LDU nn ! CE   ! 3!   ! immed, reg U
   PZ a,U   !     <a ! DE   ! 5!   ! pz, reg U
   aa,U     !     aa ! FE   ! 6!   ! abs, reg U
   Mem,U    !    Mem ! EE   !5+!   ! memory, reg U
   #nn,X    ! LDX nn ! 8E   ! 3!   ! immed, reg X
   PZ a,X   !     <a ! 9E   ! 5!   ! pz, reg X
   aa,X     !     aa ! BE   ! 6!   ! abs, reg X
   Mem,X    !    Mem ! AE   !5+!   ! memory, reg X
   #nn,Y    ! LDY nn ! 10,8E ! 4!   ! immed, reg Y
   PZ a,Y   !     <a ! 10,9E ! 6!   ! pz, reg Y
   aa,Y     !     aa ! 10,BE ! 7!   ! abs, reg Y
   Mem,Y    !    Mem ! 10,AE !6+!   ! memory, reg Y
CLR        !        !      !  !-H ! Clear byte
   PZ a     ! CLR <a ! 0F   ! 6!   ! page zero
   aa       !     aa ! 7F   ! 7!   ! abs
   Mem      !    Mem ! 6F   !6+!   ! memory
   A        ! CLRA   ! 4F   ! 2!   ! reg A
   B        ! CLRB   ! 5F   ! 2!   ! reg B
LEA        !        !      !4+!   ! Load efective address
   Mem,S    ! LEAS Mem! 32  !  !   ! reg S
   Mem,U    ! LEAU Mem! 33  !  !   ! reg U
   Mem,X    ! LEAX Mem! 30  !  !   ! reg X
   Mem,Y    ! LEAY Mem! 31  !  !   ! reg Y
PUSH       !        !      !  !   ! Push reg onto the stack
   Rr,S     ! PSHS   ! 34   !5+!   ! reg on S stack, see below
   Rr,U     ! PSHU   ! 36   !5+!   ! reg on U stack, see below
POP        !        !      !  !   ! Pop reg from the stack
   S,Rr     ! PULS   ! 35   !5+!   ! reg from S stack, see below
   U,Rr     ! PULU   ! 37   !5+!   ! reg from U stack, see below
XCHG       ! EXG    !      !  !   ! Exchange words
   Rs,Rd    !  Rd,Rs ! 1E   ! 7!all! reg,reg
           !        ! SSSSDDDD !  !   !
```

Math Operations

```
ADD        !        !      !  !   ! Add byte
   PZ a,A   ! ADDA <a! 9B   ! 4!   ! page zero, reg A
   aa,A     !     aa ! B9   ! 5!   ! abs, reg A
   #n,A     !      n ! 8B   ! 2!   ! immed, reg A
   Mem,A    !    Mem ! AB   !4+!   ! memory, reg A
   PZ a,B   ! ADDB <a! DB   ! 4!   ! page zero, reg B
```

```
    aa,B    !     aa   ! FB  ! 5!   !     abs, reg B
    #n,B    !     n    ! CB  ! 2!   !     immed, reg B
    Mem,B   !     Mem  ! EB  !4+!all!     memory, reg B
ADC         !          !     !  !all! Add byte w/c
    PZ a,A  ! ADCA <a  ! 99  ! 4!   !     page zero, reg A
    aa,A    !     aa   ! B9  ! 5!   !     abs, reg A
    #n,A    !     n    ! 89  ! 2!   !     immed, reg A
    Mem,A   !     Mem  ! A9  !4+!   !     memory, reg A
    PZ a,B  ! ADCB <a  ! D9  ! 4!   !     page zero, reg B
    aa,B    !     aa   ! F9  ! 5!   !     abs, reg B
    #n,B    !     n    ! C9  ! 2!   !     immed, reg B
    Mem,B   !     Mem  ! E9  !4+!   !     memory, reg B
ADDW        !          !     !  !   ! Add word
    B,X     ! ABX      ! 3A  ! 3!   !     reg B, reg X
    PZ a,D  ! ADDD <a  ! D3  ! 6!-H !     page zero, reg D
    aa,D    !     aa   ! F3  ! 7!   !     abs, reg D
    #nn,D   !     n    ! C3  ! 4!   !     immed, reg D
    Mem,D   !     Mem  ! E3  !6+!   !     memory, reg D
INC         !          !     !  !NZV! Increment byte
    PZ a    ! INC <a   ! 0C  ! 6!   !     page zero
    aa      !     aa   ! 7C  ! 7!   !     abs
    Mem     !     Mem  ! 6C  !6+!   !     memory
    A       ! INCA     ! 4C  ! 2!   !     reg A
    B       ! INCB     ! 5C  ! 2!   !     reg B
SUB         !          !     !  !all! Subtract byte
    PZ a,A  ! SUBA <a  ! 90  ! 4!   !     page zero, reg A
    aa,A    !     aa   ! B0  ! 5!   !     abs, reg A
    #n,A    !     n    ! 80  ! 2!   !     immed, reg A
    Mem,A   !     Mem  ! A0  !4+!   !     memory, reg A
    PZ a,B  ! SUBB <a  ! D0  ! 4!   !     page zero, reg B
    aa,B    !     aa   ! F0  ! 5!   !     abs, reg B
    #n,B    !     n    ! C0  ! 2!   !     immed, reg B
    Mem,B   !     Mem  ! E0  !4+!   !     memory, reg B
SUBW        !          !     !  !-H ! Subtract word  (1)
    PZ a,D  ! SUBD <a  ! 93  ! 6!   !     page zero, reg D
    aa,D    !     aa   ! B3  ! 7!   !     abs, reg D
    #nn,D   !     n    ! 83  ! 4!   !     immed, reg D
    Mem,D   !     Mem  ! A3  !6+!   !     memory, reg D
SBB         !          !     !  !all! Subtract byte w/c
    PZ a,A  ! SBCA <a  ! 92  ! 4!   !     page zero, reg A
    aa,A    !     aa   ! B2  ! 5!   !     abs, reg A
    #n,A    !     n    ! 82  ! 2!   !     immed, reg A
    Mem,A   !     Mem  ! A2  !4+!   !     memory, reg A
    PZ a,B  ! SBCB <a  ! D2  ! 4!   !     page zero, reg B
    aa,B    !     aa   ! F2  ! 5!   !     abs, reg B
    #n,B    !     n    ! C2  ! 2!   !     immed, reg B
    Mem,B   !     Mem  ! E2  !4+!   !     memory, reg B
DEC         !          !     !  !NZV! Decrement byte
    PZ a    ! DEC <a   ! 0A  ! 6!   !     page zero
    aa      !     aa   ! 7A  ! 7!   !     abs
    Mem     !     Mem  ! 6A  !6+!   !     memory
    A       ! DECA     ! 4A  ! 2!   !     reg A
    B       ! DECB     ! 5A  ! 2!   !     reg B
NEG         !          !     !  !-H ! Change to negative
    PZ a    ! NEG <a   ! 00  ! 6!   !     page zero
    aa      !     aa   ! 70  ! 7!   !     abs
    Mem     !     Mem  ! 60  !6+!   !     memory
    A       ! NEGA     ! 40  ! 2!   !     reg A
    B       ! NEGB     ! 50  ! 2!   !     reg B
DA A        ! DAA      ! 19  ! 2!-H ! Decimal adjust reg A
MUL         !          !     !  !ZC ! Multiply bytes
    A,B,D   ! MUL      ! 3D  !11!   !     reg D = reg A x reg B
```

CMP					all	Compare byte
A,#n	CMPA n		81	2		reg A, immed
A,PZ a	<a		91	4		reg A, page zero
A,aa	aa		B1	5		reg A, abs
A,Mem	Mem		A1	4+		reg A, memory
B,#n	CMPB n		C1	2		reg B, immed
B,PZ a	<a		D1	4		reg B, page zero
B,aa	aa		F1	5		reg B, abs
B,Mem	Mem		E1	4+		reg B, memory
CMPW					-H	Compare word
D,#nn	CMPD n		10,83	5		reg D, immed
D,PZ a	<a		10,93	7		reg D, page zero
D,aa	aa		10,B3	8		reg D, abs
D,Mem	Mem		10,A3	7+		reg D, memory
S,#nn	CMPS n		11,8C	5		reg S, immed
S,PZ a	<a		11,9C	7		reg S, page zero
S,aa	aa		11,BC	8		reg S, abs
S,Mem	Mem		11,AC	7+		reg S, memory
U,#nn	CMPU n		11,83	5		reg U, immed
U,PZ a	<a		11,93	7		reg U, page zero
U,aa	aa		11,B3	8		reg U, abs
U,Mem	Mem		11,A3	7+		reg U, memory
X,#nn	CMPX n		8C	4		reg X, immed
X,PZ a	<a		9C	6		reg X, page zero
X,aa	aa		BC	7		reg X, abs
X,Mem	Mem		AC	6+		reg X, memory
Y,#nn	CMPY n		10,8C	5		reg Y, immed
Y,PZ a	<a		10,9C	7		reg Y, page zero
Y,aa	aa		10,BC	8		reg Y, abs
Y,Mem	Mem		10,AC	7+		reg Y, memory
CNVBW	SEX					Convert byte to word
D			1D	2	NZ	reg D

Logical Operations

AND					NZV	Logical AND byte
PZ a,A	ANDA <a		94	4		page zero, reg A
aa,A	aa		B4	5		abs, reg A
#n,A	n		84	2		immed, reg A
Mem,A	Mem		A4	4+		memory, reg A
PZ a,B	ANDB <a		D4	4		page zero, reg B
aa,B	aa		F4	5		abs, reg B
#n,B	n		C4	2		immed, reg B
Mem,B	Mem		E4	4+		memory, reg B
#n,CC	ANDCC n		1C	3	all	immed, flags
TEST					NZV	Logical AND, set flags
#n,A	BITA n		85	2		immed, reg A
PZ a,A	<a		95	4		page zero, reg A
aa,A	aa		B5	5		abs, reg A
Mem,A	Mem		A5	4+		memory, reg A
#n,B	BITB n		C5	2		immed, reg B
PZ a,B	<a		D5	4		page zero, reg B
aa,B	aa		F5	5		abs, reg B
Mem,B	Mem		E5	4+		memory, reg B
00,A	TSTA		4D	2	NZV	zero, reg A
00,B	TSTB		5D	2	NZV	zero, reg B
00,PZ a	TST <a		0D	6	NZV	zero, pz
00,aa	aa		7D	7		zero, abs
00,Mem	Mem		6D	6+		zero, memory
OR						Logical OR byte

PZ a,A	ORA <a	9A	4		page zero, reg A
aa,A	aa	BA	5		abs, reg A
#n,A	n	8A	2		immed, reg A
Mem,A	Mem	AA	4+		memory, reg A
PZ a,B	ORB <a	DA	4		page zero, reg B
aa,B	aa	FA	5		abs, reg B
#n,B	n	CA	2		immed, reg B
Mem,B	Mem	EA	4+		memory, reg B
#n,CC	ANDCC n	1A	3	all	immed, flags
XOR					Logical Exclusive OR byte
PZ a,A	EORA <a	98	4		page zero, reg A
aa,A	aa	B8	5		abs, reg A
#n,A	n	88	2		immed, reg A
Mem,A	Mem	A8	4+		memory, reg A
PZ a,B	EORB <a	D8	4		page zero, reg B
aa,B	aa	F8	5		abs, reg B
#n,B	n	C8	2		immed, reg B
Mem,B	Mem	E8	4+		memory, reg B
CPL				-H	Complement byte
PZ a	COM <a	03	6		page zero
aa	aa	73	7		abs
Mem	Mem	63	6+		memory
A	COMA	43	2		reg A
B	COMB	53	2		reg B
RLWC					Rotate byte w/c left
PZ a	ROL <a	09	6		page zero
aa	aa	79	7		abs
Mem	Mem	69	6+		memory
A	ROLA	49	2		reg A
B	ROLB	59	2		reg B
RRWC					Rotate byte w/c right
PZ a	ROR <a	06	6		page zero
aa	aa	76	7		abs
Mem	Mem	66	6+		memory
A	RORA	46	2		reg A
B	RORB	56	2		reg B
SLA				all	Shift left arithmetic
PZ a	ASL <a	08	6		page zero
aa	aa	78	7		abs
Mem	Mem	68	6+		memory
A	ASLA	48	2		reg A
B	ASLB	58	2		reg B
SLL				-H	Shift left logical
PZ a	ASL <a	08	6		page zero'
aa	aa	78	7		abs
Mem	Mem	68	6+		memory
A	LSLA	48	2		reg A
B	LSLB	58	2		reg B
SRA				-V	Shift right arithmetic
PZ a	ASR <a	07	6		page zero
aa	aa	77	7		abs
Mem	Mem	67	6+		memory
A	ASRA	47	2		reg A
B	ASRB	57	2		reg B
SRL				NZC	Shift right logical
PZ a	LSR <a	04	6		page zero
aa	aa	74	7		abs
Mem	Mem	64	6+		memory
A	LSRA	44	2		reg A
B	LSRB	54	2		reg B

Program Control

CALL					Call subroutine
aa	JSR aa	BD	8		uncond, abs
PZ a	<a	9D	7		uncond, page zero
Mem	Mem	AD	7+		uncond, memory
CALLR					Call subroutine relative
r	BSR r	8D	7		uncond.
CALLD					Call subroutine displacement
rr	LBSR rr	17	9		uncond
RET	RTS	39	5		Return from subroutine
RETI	RTI	3B	15	all	Return from interrupt
JMP	JMP				Jump to location
PZ a	<a	0E	3		uncond, page zero
aa	aa	7E	4		uncond, abs
Mem	Mem	6E	3+		uncond, memory
JMPR [D]	[L]	[10],			Jump relative [displacement]
UN,rr	BRA r	20	3		uncond
NC,rr	BCC r	24	3		no carry
C,rr	BCS r	25	3		carry
Z,rr	BEQ r	27	3		zero
SGE,rr	BGE r	2C	3		N xor V = 0
SGT,rr	BGT r	2E	3		Z or (N xor V) = 0
GT,rr	BHI r	22	3		C or Z = 0
SLE,rr	BLE r	2F	3		Z or (N xor V) = 1
LE,rr	BLS r	23	3		C or Z = 1
SLT,rr	BLT r	2D	3		N xor V = 1
M,rr	BMI r	2B	3		N = 1
NZ,rr	BNE r	26	3		Z = 0
NV,rr	BVC r	28	3		V = 0
V,rr	BVS r	29	3		V = 1
P,rr	BPL r	2A	3		N = 0
HALT	SYNC	13	2+		Stop till interrupt
ORHLT					Logical OR and wait for int
#n,CCR	CWAI n	3C	20	all	immed, reg CCR
NOP	NOP	12	2		No operation
NOPL	BRN	21	3		No operation, 2 bytes
NOPLL	LBRN	10,21	5		No operation, 4 bytes

I/O Operations

SWI					Software Interrupt
1	SWI	3F	19		type 1
2	SWI2	10,3F	20		type 2
3	SWI3	11,3F	20		type 3

Registers

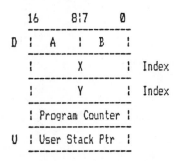

```
       16      8:7      0
       ------------------
  D :   A   :   B    :
       ------------------
       :       X      :   Index
       ------------------
       :       Y      :   Index
       ------------------
       : Program Counter :
       ------------------
  U  : User Stack Ptr  :
       ------------------
```

```
S  ! Hardware Stk Ptr!
   -------------------
              !  DP  ! Direct page Register
              ---------
     CCR  !EFHINZVC!  Flags
          ---------
```

Flags

```
N = sign of result
Z = zero result
V = overflow
C = carry, bit 7
H = half carry, bit 3
I = IRQ enable
F = FIRQ enable  (fast interrupt)
E = all reg put on stack
```

Addressing Modes

Univ	Manuf	
#n	n	- immediate data
R	R	- register, Rs source reg Rd destination reg
aa	aa	- absolute address
(R+Nd)	d,R	- indexed, 5-bit value d added to register R
(R+d)	d,R	- indexed, 8-bit value d added to register R
(R++dd)	aa,R	- indexed, 16-bit value dd added to register R
PZ a	<a	- page zero
r	r	- relative address
dd	r	- displacement address
(R)	R	- indirect, register R
(R)+	R+	- indirect post auto increment
(R)++	R++	- indirect post auto increment by 2
-(R)	-R	- indirect pre auto decrement
--(R)	--R	- indirect pre auto decrement by 2

Special Memory Locations

Varies between each micro

Instruction Expansion

Mem

Parameter			Normal		Indirect	
Univ	Manuf	Type	Append	Cyc	Append	Cyc
(R)	R	reg ind	1RR00100	0	1RR10100	3
(R+Nd)	n,R	index 5-bit	0RRnnnnn	1		
(R+d)	n,R	index 8-bit	1RR01000	1	1RR11000	4
(R++dd)	n,R	index 16-bit	1RR01001	4	1RR11001	7
(A+R)	A,R	index reg A	1RR00110	1	1RR10110	4
(B+R)	B,R	index reg B	1RR00101	1	1RR10101	4
(D,R)	D,R	index reg D	1RR01011	4	1RR11011	7
(R)+	R+	ind_inc 1	1RR00000	2		
(R)++	R++	ind_inc 2	1RR00001	3	1RR10001	6
-(R)	-R	ind_dec 1	1RR00010	2		
--(R)	--R	ind_dec 2	1RR00011	3	1RR10011	6
(PC+d)	n,PCR	index 8-bit	1..01100	1	1..11100	4
(PC++dd)	n,PCR	index 16-bit	1..01101	5	1..11101	8
aa	aa	absolute			10011111	5

```
  -------      -----
  ¦           ¦
  ¦           ¦     -- for indirect enclose in [ ],   ex [n,PCR]
  ¦     -- for indirect enclose in ( ),  ex ((PC+)d)
```

#n - immediate data, 8-bits appended to inst
#nn - immediate data, 16-bits appended to inst, MSB first
Nd - index value, 5-bit signed value part of inst
d   - index value, 8-bits signed value appended to inst
dd - index value, 16-bits signed value appended to inst, MSB first
a   - page zero adr, 8-bits appended to inst
aa - absolute adr, 16-bits appended to inst, MSB first

```
        Registers                 TFR and EXG Inst Registers
        ---------                 --------------------------
     R      RR          Rs/d  SSSS/DDDD       Rs/d  SSS/DDD
    ---     --          ----  ---------       ----  -------
     X      00           D     0000            PC    0101
     Y      01           X     0001            A     1000
     U      10           Y     0010            B     1001
     S      11           U     0011            CC    1010
                         S     0100            DP    1011
```

For PUSH and POP inst second byte indicates registers to be used
       bit 0 - CC   bit 4 - X
           1 - A   5 - Y
           2 - B   6 - S/U
           3 - DP   7 - PC

* immediate data is the second byte and address value the third byte (2)

Notes

    Data is stored MSB first then LSB

6811

MC68HC11A4, MC68HC11A8

Data Move

```
MOV      ¦          ¦          ¦  ¦ ¦  ¦ Move byte
   #n,A  ¦ LDAA n   ¦ 86       ¦ 2¦ ¦  ¦    immed, reg A
   Mem,A ¦    Mem   ¦ 10MM0110 ¦2+¦ ¦  ¦    memory, reg A
   #n,B  ¦ LDAB n   ¦ C6       ¦ 2¦ ¦  ¦    immed, reg B
   Mem,A ¦     Mem  ¦ 11MM0110 ¦2+¦ ¦  ¦    memory, reg B
   A,Mem ¦ STAA Mem ¦ 10MM0111 ¦ 3¦ ¦  ¦    reg A, memory
   B,Mem ¦ STAB Mem ¦ 11MM0111 ¦ 3¦ ¦  ¦    reg B, memory
   A,B   ¦ TAB      ¦ 16       ¦ 2¦ ¦  ¦    reg A, reg B
   B,A   ¦ TBA      ¦ 17       ¦ 2¦ ¦  ¦    reg B, reg A
MOVW     ¦          ¦          ¦  ¦ ¦  ¦ Move word
   D,Mem ¦ STD  Mem ¦ 11MM1101 ¦ 4¦ ¦  ¦    reg D, memory
   S,Mem ¦ STS  Mem ¦ 10MM1111 ¦ 4¦ ¦  ¦    reg S, memory
   IX,Mem¦ STX  Mem ¦ 11MM1111 ¦ 4¦ ¦  ¦    reg X, memory
   IY,Mem¦ STY  Mem ¦ 18,11MM1111¦5¦ ¦  ¦    reg Y, memory
   #nn,D ¦ LDD nn   ¦ CC       ¦ 3¦ ¦  ¦    immed, reg D
   Mem,D ¦      Mem ¦ 11MM1100 ¦3+¦ ¦  ¦    memory, reg D
```

#nn,S	LDS nn	8E	3	immed, reg S
Mem,S	Mem	10MM1110	3+	memory, reg S
#nn,X	LDX nn	CE	3	immed, reg X
Mem,X	Mem	11MM1110	4+	memory, reg X
#nn,Y	LDY nn	18,CE	4	immed, reg Y
Mem,Y	Mem	18,11MM1110	4+	memory, reg Y
S,X	TSX	30	3	reg S, reg X
S,Y	TSY	18,30	4	reg S, reg Y
X,S	TXS	35	3	reg X, reg S
Y,S	TYS	18,35	4	reg Y, reg S
CLR	CLR			Clear byte
aa	$aa	7F	6	abs
(X+d)	d,X	6F	6	index X
(Y+d)	d,Y	18,6F	7	index Y
A	CLRA	4F	2	reg A
B	CLRB	5F	2	reg B
PUSH	PSHA			Push reg onto the stack
A	PSHA	36	3	reg A
B	PSHB	37	3	reg B
X	PSHX	3C	4	reg X
Y	PSHY	18,3C	5	reg Y
POP				Pop reg from the stack
A	PULA	32	4	reg A
B	PULB	33	4	reg B
X	PULX	38	5	reg X
Y	PULY	18,38	6	reg Y
XCHG				Exchange words
D,X	XGDX	8F	3	reg D, reg X
D,Y	XGDY	18,8F	4	reg D, reg Y

Math Operations

ADD				Add byte
#n,A	ADDA n	8B	2	immed, reg A
Mem,A	Mem	10MM1011	2+	memory, reg A
#n,B	ADDB n	CB	2	immed, reg B
Mem,B	Mem	11MM1011	2+	memory, reg B
ADC				Add byte w/c
#n,A	ADCA n	89	2	immed, reg A
Mem,A	Mem	10MM1001	2+	memory, reg A
#n,B	ADCB n	C9	2	immed, reg B
Mem,A	Mem	11MM1001	2+	memory, reg B
ADDW				Add word
#nn,D	ADDD nn	C3	3	immed, reg D
Mem,D	Mem	11MM0011	2+	memory, reg D
INC				Increment byte
ABS aa	INC $aa	7C	6	abs
(X+d)	d,X	6C	6	index X
(Y+d)	d,Y	18,6C	7	index Y
A	INCA	4C	2	reg A
B	INCB	5C	2	reg B
INCW				Increment word
S	INS	31	3	reg S
X	INX	08	3	reg X
Y	INY	18,08	4	reg Y
SUB				Subtract byte
B,A	SBA	10	2	reg B, reg A
#n,A	SUBA n	80	2	immed, reg A
Mem,A	Mem	10MM0000	2+	memory, reg A
#n,B	SUBB n	C0	2	immed, reg B
Mem,B	Mem	11MM0000	2+	memory, reg B

```
SUBW            ¦         ¦          ¦   ¦ ¦ Subtract word
    #n,D        ¦ SUBD n  ¦ 83       ¦  4¦ ¦     immed, reg D
    Mem,D       ¦   Mem   ¦ 93       ¦  5¦ ¦     memory, reg D
SBB             ¦         ¦          ¦   ¦ ¦ Subtract byte w/c
    #n,A        ¦ SBCA n  ¦ 82       ¦  2¦ ¦     immed, reg A
    Mem,A       ¦   Mem   ¦ 10MM0010 ¦2+ ¦ ¦     memory, reg A
    #n,B        ¦ SBCB n  ¦ C2       ¦  2¦ ¦     immed, reg B
    Mem,B       ¦   Mem   ¦ 11MM0010 ¦2+ ¦ ¦     memory, reg B
DEC             ¦         ¦          ¦   ¦ ¦ Decrement byte
    aa          ¦ DEC $aa ¦ 7A       ¦  6¦ ¦     abs
    (X+d)       ¦   d,X   ¦ 6A       ¦  6¦ ¦     index X
    (Y+d)       ¦   d,Y   ¦ 18,6A    ¦  7¦ ¦     index Y
    A           ¦ DECA    ¦ 4A       ¦  2¦ ¦     reg A
    B           ¦ DECB    ¦ 5A       ¦  2¦ ¦     reg B
DECW            ¦         ¦          ¦   ¦ ¦ Decrement word
    S           ¦ DES     ¦ 34       ¦  3¦ ¦     reg S
    X           ¦ DEX     ¦ 09       ¦  3¦ ¦     reg X
    Y           ¦ DEY     ¦ 18,09    ¦  4¦ ¦     reg Y
NEG             ¦         ¦          ¦   ¦ ¦ Change to negative
    ABS aa      ¦ NEG $aa ¦ 70       ¦  6¦ ¦     abs
    (X+d)       ¦   d,X   ¦ 60       ¦  6¦ ¦     index X
    (Y+d)       ¦   d,Y   ¦ 18,60    ¦  7¦ ¦     index Y
    A           ¦ NEGA    ¦ 40       ¦  2¦ ¦     reg A
    B           ¦ NEGB    ¦ 50       ¦  2¦ ¦     reg B
DA A            ¦ DAA     ¦ 19       ¦  2¦ ¦ Decimal adjust reg A
MUL             ¦         ¦          ¦   ¦ ¦ Multiply bytes
    A,B,D       ¦ MUL     ¦ 3D       ¦ 10¦ ¦     reg D = reg A x reg B
DIVFP           ¦ FDIV    ¦ 03       ¦ 41¦ ¦ Devide
IDIV            ¦ IDIV    ¦ 02       ¦ 41¦ ¦ Devide
CMP             ¦         ¦          ¦   ¦ ¦ Compare byte
    A,#n        ¦ CMPA n  ¦ 81       ¦  2¦ ¦     reg A, immed
    A,Mem       ¦   Mem   ¦ 10MM0001 ¦2+ ¦ ¦     reg A, memory
    B,#n        ¦ CMPB n  ¦ C1       ¦  2¦ ¦     reg B, immed
    B,Mem       ¦   Mem   ¦ 11MM0001 ¦2+ ¦ ¦     reg B, memory
CMPW            ¦         ¦          ¦   ¦ ¦ Compare word
    D,#n        ¦ CPD nn  ¦ 1A,83    ¦  5¦ ¦     reg D, immed
    D,Mem       ¦   Mem   ¦ 1A,10MM0011 ¦5+ ¦ ¦     reg D, memory
    X,#n        ¦ CPX nn  ¦ 8C       ¦  4¦ ¦     reg X, immed
    X,Mem       ¦   Mem   ¦ 10MM1100 ¦4+ ¦ ¦     reg X, memory
    Y,#n        ¦ CPY nn  ¦ 18,8C    ¦  5¦ ¦     reg Y, immed
    Y,Mem       ¦   Mem   ¦ 18,10MM1100 ¦5+ ¦ ¦     reg Y, memory
CNVBW           ¦ SEX     ¦          ¦   ¦ ¦ Convert byte to word
    D           ¦         ¦ 1D       ¦  2¦ ¦     reg D
```

I/O Operations

```
SWI             ¦ SWI     ¦ 3F       ¦ 14¦ ¦ Software Interrupt
DI              ¦ CLI     ¦ 0E       ¦  2¦ ¦ Disable interrupts
EI              ¦ SEI     ¦ 0F       ¦  2¦ ¦ Enable interrupts
```

Micro Unique Operations

```
TEST            ¦ TEST    ¦ 00       ¦   ¦ ¦ Test, continue till reset
TPA             ¦ TPA     ¦ 07       ¦  2¦ ¦ Not clearly defined
```

Logical Operations

```
AND             ¦         ¦          ¦   ¦ ¦ Logical AND byte
    #n,A        ¦ ANDA n  ¦ 84       ¦  2¦ ¦     immed, reg A
    Mem,A       ¦   Mem   ¦ 10MM0100 ¦2+ ¦ ¦     memory, reg A
    #n,B        ¦ ANDB n  ¦ C4       ¦  2¦ ¦     immed, reg B
    Mem,B       ¦   Mem   ¦ 11MM0100 ¦2+ ¦ ¦     memory, reg B
```

TEST				Logical AND, set flags
#n,A	BITA n	85	2	immed, reg A
Mem,A	Mem	10MM0101	2+	memory, reg A
#n,B	BITB n	C5	2	immed, reg B
Mem,B	Mem	11MM0101	2+	memory, reg B
00,aa	TST $aa	7D	6	00, abs
00,(X+d)	d,X	6D	6	00, index X
00,(Y+d)	d,Y	18,6D	7	00, index Y
00,A	TSTA	4D	2	00, reg A
00,B	TSTB	5D	2	00, reg B
OR				Logical OR byte
#n,A	ORAA n	8A	2	immed, reg A
Mem,A	Mem	10MM1010	2+	memory, reg A
#n,B	ORAB n	CA	2	immed, reg B
Mem,B	Mem	11MM1010	2+	memory, reg B
XOR				Logical Exclusive OR byte
#n,A	EORA n	88	2	immed, reg A
Mem,A	Mem	10MM1000	2+	memory, reg A
#n,B	EORB n	C8	2	immed, reg B
Mem,B	Mem	11MM1000	2+	memory, reg B
CPL				Complement byte
aa	COM $aa	73	6	abs
(X+d)	d,X	63	6	index X
(Y+d)	d,Y	18,63	7	index Y
A	COMA	43	2	reg A
B	COMB	53	2	reg B
RLWC				Rotate byte w/c left
aa	ROL $aa	79	6	abs
(X+d)	d,X	69	6	ind X
(Y+d)	d,Y	18,69	7	ind Y
A	ROLA	49	2	reg A
B	ROLB	59	2	reg B
RRWC				Rotate byte w/c right
aa	ROR $aa	76	6	abs
(X+d)	d,X	66	6	ind X
(Y+d)	d,Y	18,66	7	ind Y
A	RORA	46	2	reg A
B	RORB	56	2	reg B
SLA				Shift left arithmetic
aa	ASL $aa	78	6	abs
(X+d)	d,X	68	6	index X
(Y+d)	d,Y	18,68	7	index Y
A	ASLA	48	2	reg A
B	ASLB	58	2	reg B
SLAW D	ASLD	05	3	Shift left arith word, reg D
SLL				Shift left logical
aa	LSL $aa	78	6	abs
(X+d)	d,X	68	6	index X
(Y+d)	d,Y	18,68	7	index Y
A	LSLA	48	2	reg A
B	LSLB	58	2	reg B
SLLW D	LSLD	05	3	Shift left logical word, reg D
SRA				Shift right arithmetic
aa	ASR $aa	77	6	page zero
(X+d)	d,X	67	6	abs
(Y+d)	d,Y	18,67	7	memory
A	ASRA	47	2	reg A
B	ASRB	57	2	reg B
SRL				Shift right logical
aa	LSR $aa	74	6	abs
(X+d)	d,X	64	6	index X
(Y+d)	d,Y	18,64	7	index Y

```
     A        | LSRA   | 44      | 2|  | reg A
     B        | LSRB   | 54      | 2|  | reg B
SRLW  D        | LSRD   | 04      | 3|  | Shift right logical word, reg D
```

Bit Operations

```
RESF         |        |         |  |  | Reset flag
    C        | CLC    | 0C      | 2|  |    carry
    V        | CLV    | 0A      | 2|  |    overflow
    X        | TAP    | 06      | 2|  |    interrupt mask X
SETF         |        |         |  |  | Reset flag
    C        | SEC    | 0D      | 2|  |    carry
    V        | SEV    | 0B      | 2|  |    overflow
RESB         | BCLR   |         |  |  | Reset bit
    PZ a,m   |   $a,m | 15,aa,mm| 6|  |    adr, mask
    (X+d),m  |  d,X,m | 1D,dd,mm| 7|  |    index X, mask
    (Y+d),m  |  d,Y,m | 18,1D,dd,| 8| |    index Y, mask
             |        |    mm   |  |  |
SETB         | BSET   |         |  |  | Set bit
    PZ a,m   |   $a,m | 14,aa,mm| 6|  |    adr, mask
    (X+d),m  |  d,X,m | 1C,dd,mm| 7|  |    index X, mask
    (Y+d),m  |  d,Y,m | 18,1C,dd,| 8| |    index Y, mask
             |        |    mm   |  |  |
```

Program Control

```
CALL         | JSR    |         |  |  | Call subroutine
    Mem      | Mem    | 10MM1101| 5|  |    uncond, memory
CALLR        |        |         |  |  | Call subroutine relative
    r        | BSR r  | 8D      | 7|  |    uncond
CALLD        |        |         |  |  | Call subroutine displacement
    rr       | LBSR rr| 17      | 9|  |    uncond
RET          | RTS    | 39      | 5|  | Return from subroutine
RETI         | RTI    | 3B      |12|  | Return from interrupt
JMP          | JMP    |         |  |  | Jump to location
    aa       | $aa    | 7E      | 3|  |    uncond, abs
    (X+d)    | d,X    | 6E      | 3|  |    uncond, index X
    (Y+d)    | d,Y    | 18,6E   | 4|  |    uncond, index Y
JMPR         |        |         |  |  | Jump relative
    UN,r     | BRA r  | 20      | 3|  |    uncond
    NC,r     | BCC r  | 24      | 3|  |    no carry
    C,r      | BCS r  | 25      | 3|  |    carry
    Z,r      | BEQ r  | 27      | 3|  |    zero
    NZ,r     | BGE r  | 2C      | 3|  |    N xor V = 0
    SGT,r    | BGT r  | 2E      | 3|  |    Z or (N xor V) = 0
    GT,r     | BHI r  | 22      | 3|  |    C or Z = 0
    SLE,r    | BLE r  | 2F      | 3|  |    Z or (N xor V) = 1
    LE,r     | BLS r  | 23      | 3|  |    C or Z = 1
    SLT,r    | BLT r  | 2D      | 3|  |    N xor V = 1
    M,r      | BMI r  | 2B      | 3|  |    N = 1
    NZ,r     | BNE r  | 26      | 3|  |    Z = 0
    NV,r     | BVC r  | 28      | 3|  |    V = 0
    V,r      | BVS r  | 29      | 3|  |    V = 1
    P,r      | BPL r  | 2A      | 3|  |    N = 0
             | BRCLR  |         |  |  | Jump rel if bits reset
 BR,PZ a,    |  $a,m,r| 13,aa,mm| 6|  |   pz a, mask, rel
    m,r      |        |   rr    |  |  |
 BR,(X+d),   | d,X,m, | 1F,dd,mm,| 7| |   index X, mask, rel
    m,r      |   r    |   rr    |  |  |
 BR,(Y+d),   | d,Y,m, | 18,1F,aa| 8|  |   index Y, mask, rel
    m,r      |   r    | mm,rr   |  |  |
             | BRSET  |         |  |  | Jump rel if bits set
```

```
BS,PZ a,   ¦  $a,m,  ¦ 12,aa,mm  ¦  6¦  ¦  abs, mask, rel
    m,r    ¦    r    ¦ rr        ¦   ¦  ¦
BS,(X+d),  ¦  d,X,m, ¦ 1E,aa,mm, ¦  7¦  ¦  index X, mask, rel
    m,r    ¦    r    ¦ rr        ¦   ¦  ¦
BS,(Y+d),  ¦  d,Y,m, ¦ 18,1E,aa  ¦  8¦  ¦  index Y, mask, rel
    m,r    ¦    r    ¦ mm,rr     ¦   ¦  ¦
HALT       ¦ STOP    ¦ CF        ¦  2¦  ¦ Stop till interrupt
SLEEP    n ¦ WAI   n ¦ 3E        ¦ 14¦  ¦ Low power wait mode = n
NOP        ¦ NOP     ¦ 01        ¦  2¦  ¦ No operation
NOPL       ¦ BRN     ¦ 21        ¦  3¦  ¦ No operation, 2 bytes
NOPLL      ¦ LBRN    ¦ 10,21     ¦  5¦  ¦ No operation, 4 bytes
           ¦         ¦           ¦   ¦  ¦
```

Registers

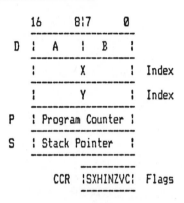

```
        16      8¦7      0
      -------------------
D   ¦   A   ¦   B   ¦
      -------------------
    ¦       X       ¦  Index
      -------------------
    ¦       Y       ¦  Index
      -------------------
P   ¦ Program Counter ¦
      -------------------
S   ¦ Stack Pointer   ¦
      -------------------

              ---------
     CCR   ¦SXHINZVC¦  Flags
              ---------
```

Flags

```
N = sign of result
Z = zero result
V = overflow
C = carry, bit 7
H = half carry, bit 3
I = interrupt mask
S = stop disable
X = X interrupt mask
```

Addressing Modes

```
Univ  Manuf
----  -----
#nn    nn    - immediate data
X      X     - register
aa     $aa   -  absolute address
(X+d)  d,X   - indexed, loc = X+d or Y+d
PZ a   $a    -  page zero address
r      r     - relative address value
dd     rr    - displacement address value
```

Instruction Expansion

		Mem		
Univ	Manuf	Type	MM	Append
PZ a	$a	direct	01	adr byte

```
aa          $aa     absolute     11     adr MSB, LSB
(X+ d )     d,X     index 8-bit  10     unsigned 8-bit value
(Y+ d )     d,Y     index 8-bit  10     unsigned 8-bit value (note 1)
```

note 1:
```
        insert 18 as first byte, except for
                        CPD - change first byte to CD
            STX, LDX, CPX - insert CD
            STY, LDY, CPY - leave first byte as 18
```

```
n  - immediate data, 8-bits appended to the inst
nn - immediate data, 16-bits appended to inst, MSB first
aa - absolute adr, 16-bits appended to inst, MSB first
a  - page zero adr, 8-bits appended to inst
d  - index displacement, 8-bits appended to inst
m  - bit mask, 8-bits appended to inst
r  - relative address, 8-bits appended to inst
dd - displacement address, 16-bits appended to inst, MSB first
m  - bit mask, 8-bits appended to inst
```

* immediate data is the second byte and address value the third byte (2)

Special Memory Locations

```
256 bytes RAM    starting at loc 0000
512 bytes EEPROM starting at loc B600
4K  bytes ROM    starting at loc F000
```

other memory within 65K limit is external

special memory locations for interrupts vectors and register blocks will
vary between each micro

Notes

Data is stored MSB first then LSB

7000

**TMS7020, TMS7040, TMS70120, TMS7001, TMS7041, TMS70P161, TMS70C00,
TMS70C20, TMS70C40, TMS7042, TMS7002, TMS7742**

* Instructions might be changed in microcode

Data Move

MOV	MOV		CNZ	Move byte
Tbll	Tbll	MMMM0010		srce, to dest
A,B	A,B	C0	6	reg A, reg B
A,Rn	A,Rn	D0	8	reg A, reg n
B,Rn	B,Rn	D1	7	reg B, reg n
Mem,A	LDA Mem	10AA1010	7 CNZ	memory, reg a
B,SP	LDSP	0D	13	reg B, stack pointer
SP,B	STSP	09	13	stack pointer, reg B
A,Mem	STA Mem	10AA1011	5 CNZ	reg A, memory
* MOVW	MOVD		CNZ	Move word, reg pair
#vv,Rn	@vv,Rn	98	15	immed to reg n = LSB
Rs,Rd	Rs,Rd	98	14	srce to dest n-1 = MSB

(B++aa),Rn	@aa(B),Rn	A8	17		indexed reg B to reg
POP				CNZ	Pop byte
Reg	POP Reg	MMMM1001	6		reg
ST	POPST	08	6		status
PUSH				CNZ	Push byte
Reg	PUSH Reg	MMMM1000	6		reg
ST	PUSHST	0E	6		status
CLR	CLR			CNZ	Clear
Reg	Reg	MMMM0101	7		Reg
* SWAPN	SWAP			CNZ	Swap register halves
Reg	Reg	MMMM0111	9		reg
* XCHG	XCHB			CNZ	Exchange bytes
B,Reg	Reg	MMMM0110	8		reg B with reg

Math Operations

ADD	ADD			CNZ	Add
Tbl1	Tbl1	MMMM1000	10		source to dest
ADC	ADC			CNZ	Add w/carry
Tbl1	Tbl1	MMMM1001	10		source to dest
* ADBCDC	DAC			CNZ	Add BCD w/carry
Tbl1	Tbl1	MMMM1110	12		source to dest
INC	INC			CNZ	Increment
Reg	Reg	MMMM0011	7		reg
SUB	SUB			CNZ	Subtract
Tbl1	Tbl1	MMMM1010	8		source from dest
SBB	SBB			CNZ	Subtract w/borrow
Tbl1	Tbl1	MMMM1011	8		source from dest
DEC	DEC			CNZ	Decrement
Reg	Reg	MMMM0010	7		reg
* DECW	DECD			CNZ	Decrement register pair
Reg	Reg	MMMM1011	11		reg LSB, reg-1 = MSB
* SBBBCD	DSB			CNZ	Subtract BCD w/borrow
Tbl1	Tbl1	MMMM1111	12		source from dest
CMP	CMP			CNZ	Compare
Tbl1 (rev)	Tbl1	MMMM1101	10		source with dest
* A,Mem	CMPA Mem	1MMM1101	14	CNZ	reg A with memory
* MUL	MPY			CNZ	Multiply
Tbl1	Tbl1	MMMM1100	49		reg AB = srce x dest

Logical Operations

AND	AND			CNZ	Logical AND
Tbl1	Tbl1	MMMM0011	10		source, with dest
OR	ORL			CNZ	Logical OR
Tbl1	Tbl1	MMMM0100	10		source with dest
XOR	XRL			CNZ	Logical Exclusive OR
Tbl1	Tbl1	MMMM0101	10		source, with dest
TEST					Test
A,A	TSTA	B0	5		reg A
B,B	TSTB	C1	6		reg B
CPL	INV			CNZ	Complement
Reg	Reg	MMMM0100	7		reg
RRWC	RRC			CNZ	Rotate right w/carry
Reg	Reg	MMMM1101	7		reg
RLWC	RLC			CNZ	Rotate left w/carry
Reg	Reg	MMMM1111	7		reg
RLNC	RL			CNZ	Rotate left no carry
Reg	Reg	MMMM1110	7		reg
RRNC	RR			CNZ	Rotate right no carry
Reg	Reg	MMMM1100	7		reg

Bit Operations

```
RESF       | CLR    |          |    |      | Reset flag
  C        |   C    | B0       | 7  | CNZ  |   carry        NZ set from reg A
SETF       |        |          |    |      | Set flag
  C        | SETC   | 07       | 5  | CNZ  |   carry        N = 0, Z = 1
```

Program Control

```
CALL       | CALL   |          |    |      | Call subroutine
  Mem      |   Mem  | 10MM1110 | 12 |      |   uncond, memory
RET        |        |          |    |      | Return from subroutine
           | RETS   | 0A       | 7  |      |   uncond
RETI       |        |          |    | all  | Return from interrupt
           | RETI   | 0B       | 9  |      |   uncond
JMP        | BR     |          |    |      | Jump if
  Mem      |   Mem  | MMMM1100 | 12 |      |   uncond, memory
JMPR       |        |          |    |      | Jump relative if
  UN,r     | JMP  r | E0       | 7  |      |   uncond
  M,r      | JN   r | E1       | 7  |      |   minus
  LT,r     | JLT  r | E1       | 7  |      |   <
  Z,r      | JZ   r | E2       | 7  |      |   zero
  EQ,r     | JEQ  r | E2       | 7  |      |   equal
  C,r      | JC   r | E3       | 7  |      |   carry
  HS,r     | JHS  r | E3       | 7  |      |   higher or same
  P,r      | JP   r | E4       | 7  |      |   plus
  GT,r     | JGT  r | E4       | 7  |      |   >
  GEZ,r    | JPZ  r | E5       | 7  |      |   plus or zero
  GE,r     | JGE  r | E5       | 7  |      |   > or =
  NZ,r     | JNZ  r | E6       | 7  |      |   not zero
  NE,r     | JNE  r | E6       | 7  |      |   not =
  NC,r     | JNC  r | E7       | 7  |      |   no carry
  L,r      | JL   r | E7       | 7  |      |   lower
TSTJNZR    | BTJO   |          |    | CNZ  | Test jmpr if <> 0
  Tbl1,r   |   Tbl1,r| MMMM0110 | 12 |      |   table1, rel
*          | BTJOP  |          |    | CNZ  |
*  A,Pp,r  |   A,Pp,r | 86      | 11 |      |   reg A, port p, rel
*  B,Pp,r  |   B,Pp,r | 96      | 11 |      |   reg B, port p, rel
*  #n,Pp,r |   @n,Pp,r| A6      | 11 |      |   immed, port p, rel
TSTJZR     | BTJZ   |          |    | CNZ  | Test jmpr if = 0
  Tbl1,r   |   Tbl1,r| MMMM0111 | 12 |      |   table1, rel
*          | BTJZP  |          |    | CNZ  |
*  A,Pp,r  |   A,Pp,r | 87      | 11 |      |   reg A, port p, relative
*  B,Pp,r  |   B,Pp,r | 97      | 11 |      |   reg B, port p, relative
*  #n,Pp,r |   @n,Pp,r| A7      | 11 |      |   immed, port p, relative
DECJNZR    | DJNZ   |          |    |      | Decrement and jump if not 0
  Rn,r     |   Rn,r | DA       | 9  |      |   reg n, rel
  A,r      |   A,r  | BA       | 9  |      |   reg A, rel
  B,r      |   B,r  | CA       | 9  |      |   reg B, rel
TRAP       | TRAP   |          |    |      | Trap
  n        |   n    | 11111NNN | 8  |      |   n = 0 - 7, NNN = 7 - n
*  n       |   n    | 111NNNNN | 8  |      |   n = 8 - 23
NOP        | NOP    | 00       | 5  |      | No operation
HALT       | IDLE   | 01       | 5  |      | Idel
```

I/O Operations

```
* OUT      | MOVP   |          |    | CNZ  | Output data to port
  A,Pp     |   A,Pp | 82       | 9  |      |   reg A, port p
  B,Pp     |   B,Pp | 92       | 9  |      |   reg B, port p
  #v,Pp    |   @v,Pp| A2       | 11 |      |   immed, port p
```

```
* IN       | MOVP      |    |   |CNZ | Input data from port
    Pp,A   |    Pp,A   | 80 | 8|    |     port p, reg A
    Pp,B   |    Pp,B   | 91 | 8|    |     port p, reg B
DI         | DINT      | 06 | 5|all | Disable interrupts
EI         | EINT      | 05 | 5|all | Enable interrupts
* ANDIO    | ANDP      |    |   |CNZ | Logical AND port
    A,Pp   |    A,Pp   | 83 | 9|    |     reg A, port p
    B,Pp   |    B,Pp   | 93 | 9|    |     reg B, port p
    #v,Pp  |    ∂v,Pp  | A3 |11|    |     immed, port p
* ORIO     | ORP       |    |   |CNZ | Logical OR port
    A,Pp   |    A,Pp   | 84 | 9|    |     reg A, port p
    B,Pp   |    B,Pp   | 94 | 9|    |     reg B, port p
    #v,Pp  |    ∂v,Pp  | A4 |11|    |     immed, port p
* XORIO    | XORP      |    |   |CNZ | Logical Exclusive OR port
    A,Pp   |    A,Pp   | 85 | 9|    |     reg A, port p
    B,Pp   |    B,Pp   | 95 | 9|    |     reg B, port p
    #n,Pp  |    ∂n,Pp  | A5 |11|    |     immed, port p
```

Registers
----

    128 bytes RAM register file
which includes the following special function registers.

    R0   A register   loc 0000
    R1   B register   0001
    R2 - R127 general purpose   0002 - 007F
    P0 - P255 peripherial file 0100 - 01FF

    SP   8-bit stack pointer, initialized to 0001 on reset
    ST   8-bit status register
    PC   16-bit program counter
              implemented as two 8-bit registers, PCH and PCL

 PA,PB,PC,PD = on chip general purpose I/O ports,
              usage depends on memory mode selected

Flags

    C = carry   bit 7
    N = sing   6
    Z = zero   5
    I = interrupt enable   4

Addressing Modes
----------- -----

    Univ   Manuf
    ----   -----
    #v   ∂v   - immediate data, 8 or 16-bits
    Rn   Rn   - register, Rs = source, Rd = destination
    aa   ∂aa   - absolute address, 16-bits
    r   r   - relative address, 8-bits
    Pp   Pp   - port address
    (Rn)   *Rn   - register indirect
    (B++aa) ∂aa(B) - indexed, reg B + aa, 16-bit value

Instruction Expansion
----------- ---------

            tbl1   Reg
            ----   ---

Param MMMM Append   Disc   Param MMMM Append Disc
----- ---- ------   ----   ----- ---- ------ ----

Rn,A 0001 nn   reg n, reg A   A 1011   reg A

```
#v,A    0010   vv      immed, reg A          B   1100              reg B
Rn,B    0011   nn      reg n, reg B          Rn  1101      nn      reg n
Rs,Rd   0100   ss,dd   reg s, reg d
#v,B    0101   vv      immed, reg B
B,A     0110           reg B, reg A
#v,Rn   0111   vv,nn   immed, reg n

                       Mem
                       ---
Univ     Param   MMM    Append    Disc
----     -----   ---    ------    ----
aa       @aa     000    aa,aa     direct
(Rn)     *Rn     001              indirect
(B++aa)  @aa(B)  010    aa,aa     indexed


aa   abs adr    16 bit address appended to instruction, MSB first
r    rel adr    8 bit relative address appended to instruction
p    port       8 bit port address appended to inst
v    immediate  8-bit value appended to inst
vv   immediate  16-bit value appended to inst, MSB first
Rn   register   8-bit reg location appended to inst

address modifiers are appended last
source modifier appended before destination modifier
```

Special Memory Locations

```
loc 0000 - 007F = 128 byte RAM register file, on chip
    0080 - 00FF = reserved for future expansion
    0010 - 010B = on chip I/O
    010C - 01FF = 256 byte peripherial expansion file
    0200 - xxxx = not available or memory expansion
    xxxx - FFFF = on chip ROM or external memory
```

Notes

16-bit data and address values are stored MSB first LSB second

7800   (Incomplete)

uPD7800, uPD7801, uPD7802, uPD78C06, uPD78C05
(*) uPD7810, uPD7811, uPD7809, uPD7807, uPD78P09

Data Move

```
MOV       ! MOV      !             ! !  ! Move byte, from to
  A, r1   !   r1, A  ! 00011RRR    ! 4!  !   reg A, r1
  r1, A   !   A, r1  ! 00001RRR    ! 4!  !   r1, reg A
  A, sr   !   sr, A  ! 4D,110RRRRR !10!  !   reg A, sr
  sr1, A  !   A, sr1 ! 4C,11RRRRRR !10!  !   sr1, reg A
  aa, r0  !   r0,(aa)! 70,01101RRR !17!  !   abs, r0
  r0, aa  !  (aa),r0 ! 70,01111RRR !17!  !   r0, abs
  #n,r0   ! MVI r0,n ! 01101RRR    ! 7!  !   immed, r0
* #n, sr2 !   sr2,n  ! 64,R0000RRR !14!  !   immed, sr2
  #n,(V+d)! MVIW d,n ! 71          !13!  !   immed, abs reg V disp
  #n, rpa1! MVIX rpa1,n! 010010AA  !10!  !   immed, rpa1
  A,(V,d) ! STAW d   ! 63          !10!  !   reg A, abs reg V disp
  (V,d),A ! LDAW d   ! 01          !10!  !   abs reg V disp, reg A
```

```
    A,rpa2      | STAX   rpa2 | A0111AAA   |13| |   reg A, rpa2
    rpa2,A      | LDAX   rpa2 | A0101AAA   |13| |   rpa2, reg A
  MOVW          | DMOV        |            |  | | Move word
*   EA,rp3      |       rp3,EA| 101101RR   | 4| |   reg EA, rp3
*   rp3,EA      |       EA,rp3| 101001RR   | 4| |   rp3, reg EA
*   EA,sr3      |       sr3,EA| 48,1101001R|14| |   reg EA, sr3
*   sr4,EA      |       EA,sr4| 48,110000RR|14| |   sr4, reg EA
    BC,aa       | SBCD  (aa)  | 70,1E      |20| |   reg BC, abs
    DE,aa       | SDED  (aa)  | 70,2E      |20| |   reg DE, abs
    HL,aa       | SHLD  (aa)  | 70,3E      |20| |   reg HL, abs
    SP,aa       | SSPD  (aa)  | 70,0E      |20| |   reg SP, abs
*   EA,rpa3     | STEAX  rpa3 | 48,1001AAAA|20| |   reg EA, rpa3
    aa,BC       | LBCD  (aa)  | 70,1F      |20| |   abs, reg BC
    aa,DE       | LDED  (aa)  | 70,2F      |20| |   abs, reg DE
    aa,HL       | LHLD  (aa)  | 70,3F      |20| |   abs, reg HL
    aa,SP       | LSPD  (aa)  | 70,0F      |20| |   abs, reg SP
*   rpa3,EA     | LDEAX  rpa3 | 48,1000AAAA|20| |   rpa3, reg EA
    #nn,rp2     | LXI  rp2,nn | 0RRR0100   |10| |   immed, rp2
    (PC+3+A),BC | TABLE       | 48,A8      |17| |   ind PC+3+regA, reg BC
  PUSH          | PUSH        |            |  | | Push word onto the stack
    rp1         |        rp1  | 10110RRR   |13| |   rp1
  POP           | POP         |            |  | | Pop word from the stack
    rp1         |        rp1  | 10100RRR   |10| |   rp1
  XCHMW         |             |            |  | | Exchange multiple words
*   VAEA,VAEA'  | EXA         | 48,AC      | 8| |   reg VAEA & VAEA'
  XCHGW         |             |            |  | | Exchange words
    HL,HL'      | EXH         | 48,AE      | 8| |   reg HL & HL'
  XCHMB         |             |            |  | | Echange multiple bytes
*   BCDEHL,BCDEHL'| EXX       | 48,AF      | 8| |   reg BCDEHL & BCDEHL'
```

Math Operations

```
ADD           | ADD         |            |  |CZ| Add byte
    r0,A      |       A,r0  | 60,11000RRR| 8| |   reg r0 to reg A
    A,r0      |       r0,A  | 60,01000RRR| 8| |   reg A to reg r0
    rpa,A     | ADDX  rpa   | 70,11000AAA|11| |   memory rpa, reg A
    #n,A      | ADI   A,n   | 46         | 7|CZ|   immed, reg A
    #n,r0     |       r0,n  | 74,01000RRR|11| |   immed, reg r0
    #n,sr2    |       sr2,n | 60,R1000RRR|20| |   immed, reg sr2
    (V,d),A   | ADDW  d     | 74,C0      |14|CZ|   ind reg V disp, reg A
ADDW          |             |            |  |CZ| Add word
*   r2,EA     | EADD  EA,r2 | 70,010000RR|11| |   reg r2, reg EA
*   rp3,EA    | DADD  EA,rp3| 74,110001RR|11| |   reg rp3, reg EA
ADC           | ADC         |            |  |CZ| Add byte w/c
    r0,A      |       A,r0  | 60,11010RRR| 8| |   reg r0 to reg A
    A,r0      |       r0,A  | 60,01010RRR| 8| |   reg A to reg r0
    rpa,A     | ADCX  rpa   | 70,11010AAA|11| |   memory rpa, reg A
    #n,A      | ACI   A,n   | 56         | 7|CZ|   immed, reg A
    #n,r0     |       r0,n  | 74,01010RRR|11| |   immed, reg r0
    #n,sr2    |       sr2,n | 60,R1010RRR|20| |   immed, reg sr2
    (V,d),A   | ADCW  d     | 74,D0      |14|CZ|   ind reg V disp, reg Av
ADCW          |             |            |  |CZ| Add word w/c
*   rp3,EA    | DADC  EA,rp3| 74,110101RR|11| |   reg rp3, reg EA
ADDSNC        | ADDNC       |            |  |CZ| Add byte skip if no carry
    r0,A      |       A,r0  | 60,10100RRR| 8| |   reg r0, to reg A
    A,r0      |       r0,A  | 60,00100RRR| 8| |   reg A, to reg r0
    rpa,A     | ADDNCX rpa  | 70,10100AAA|11| |   memory rpa to reg A
    #n,A      | ADINC A,n   | 26         | 7|CZ|   immed, reg A
    #n,r0     |       r0,n  | 74,00100RRR|11| |   immed, reg r0
    #n,sr2    |       sr2,n | 60,R0100RRR|20| |   immed, reg sr2
    (V,d),A   | ADDNCW d    | 74,A0      |14|CZ|   ind reg V disp, reg A
ADDSNCW       | DADDNC      |            |  |CZ| Add word skip if no carry
```

```
*  rp3,EA      !      EA,rp3 ! 74,101001RR !11!     reg rp3, reg EA
INC            ! INR         !             !  !CZ ! Increment byte
   r2          !      r2     ! 010000RR    ! 4!     reg r2
   (V,d)       ! INRW d      ! 20          !16!Z    ind reg V disp
INCW           ! INX         !             !  !CZ ! Increment word
   rp          !      rp     ! 00RR0010    ! 7!     Reg rp
*  EA          !      EA     ! A8          ! 7!     reg EA
SUB            ! SUB         !             !  !CZ ! Subtract byte
   r0,A        !      A,r0   ! 60,11100RRR ! 8!     reg r0, from reg A
   A,r0        !      r0,A   ! 60,01100RRR ! 8!     reg A, from reg r0
   rpa,A       ! SUBX rpa    ! 70,11100AAA !11!     memory rpa, from reg A
   #n,A        ! SUI  A,n    ! 66          ! 7!CZ   immed, reg A
   #n,r0       !      r0,n   ! 74,01100RRR !11!     immed, reg r0
   #n,sr2      !      sr2,n  ! 60,R1100RRR !20!     immed, reg sr2
   (V,d),A     ! SUBW d      ! 74,E0       !14!CZ   ind reg V disp, reg A
SUBW           ! ESUB        !             !  !CZ ! Subtract word
*  r2,EA       !      EA,r2  ! 70,011000RR !11!     reg r2, reg EA
*  rp3,EA      ! DSUB EA,rp3 ! 74,111001RR !11!     reg rp3, reg EA
SBB            ! SBB         !             !  !CZ ! Subtract byte w/c
   r0,A        !      A,r0   ! 60,11110RRR ! 8!     reg r0, reg A
   A,r0        !      r0,A   ! 60,01110RRR ! 8!     reg A, from reg r0
   rpa,A       ! SBBX rpa    ! 70,11110AAA !11!     memory rpa, from reg A
   #n,A        ! SBI  A,n    ! 76          ! 7!CZ   immed, reg A
   #n,r0       !      r0,n   ! 74,01110RRR !11!     immed, reg r0
   #n,sr2      !      sr2,n  ! 60,R1110RRR !20!     immed, reg sr2
   (V,d),A     ! SBBW d      ! 74,F0       !14!CZ   ind reg V disp, reg A
SBBW           ! DSBB        !             !  !CZ ! Subtract word w/c
*  rp3,EA      !      EA,rp3 ! 74,111101RR !11!     reg rp3, reg EA
SUBSNC         ! SUBNB       !             !  !CZ ! Subtract, skip if no borrow
   r0,A        !      A,r0   ! 60,10110RRR ! 8!     reg r0, from reg A
   A,r0        !      r0,A   ! 60,00110RRR ! 8!     reg A, from reg r0
   rpa,A       ! SUBNBX rpa  ! 70,10110AAA !11!     memory rpa, from reg A
   #n,A        ! SUINB A,n   ! 36          ! 7!CZ   immed, reg A
   #n,r0       !      r0,n   ! 74,00110RRR !11!     immed, reg r0
   #n,sr2      !      sr2,n  ! 60,R0110RRR !20!     immed, reg sr2
   (V,d),A     ! SUBNBW d    ! 74,B0       !14!CZ   ind reg V disp, reg A
SUBSNCW        ! DSUBNB      !             !  !CZ ! Sub word, skip if no borrow
*  rp3,EA      !      EA,rp3 ! 74,101101RR !11!     reg rp3, reg EA
DA             ! DAA         !             !  !CZ ! Decimal adjust Accum
   A           !             ! 61          ! 4!
DEC            !             !             !  !CZ ! Decrement byte
   r2          ! DCR  r2     ! 010100RR    ! 4!Z    Reg r2
   (V,d)       ! DCRW d      ! 30          !16!Z    ind reg V disp
DECW           !             !             !  !CZ ! Decrement word
   rp          ! DCX  rp     ! 00RR0011    ! 7!     reg rp
*  EA          !      EA     ! A9          ! 7!     reg EA
NEG            !             !             !  !CZ ! Change sign
*  A           ! NEGA        ! 48,3A       ! 8!     reg A
MULT           ! MLT         !             !  !CZ ! Multiply
*  A,r2,EA     !      r2     ! 48,001011RR !32!     EA = reg A x reg r2
DIV            ! DIV         !             !  !CZ ! Devide
*  r2,EA       !      r2     ! 48,001111RR !59!     EA = EA/r2, r2=remain
```

String Operations

```
MOVWSR         ! BLOCK       !             !  !   ! Move word string repeat
   (HL)+,(DE)+,C! D+         ! 10          !13!     ind_inc HL, DE, for C
*  (HL)-,(DE)-,C! D-         ! 11          !13!     ind_dec HL, DE, for C
```

Bit Operations

```
RESF           !             !             !  !   ! Reset bit
```

C	CLC	48,2A	8	C	carry
CPLF					Complement flag
* C	CMC	48,AA	8	C	carry
SETF					Set flag
C	STC	48,2B	8	C	carry

Logical Operations

AND	ANA			C	Logical AND byte
r0,A	A,r0	60,10001RRR	8		reg r0, Reg A
A,r0	r0,A	60,00001RRR	8		reg A, reg r0
rpa,A	ANAX rpa	70,10001AAA	11		memory rpa, reg A
#n,A	ANI A,n	07	7	CZ	immed, reg A
#n,r0	r0,n	74,00001RRR	11		immed, reg r0
#n,sr2	sr2,n	60,R0001RRR	20		immed, reg sr2
(V,d),A	ANAW d	74,88	14	Z	ind reg V disp, reg A
#n,(V,d)	ANIW d,n	05	19	Z	immed, ind reg V disp
ANDW	DAN			C	Logical AND word
* rp3,EA	EA,rp3	74,100011RR	11		reg rp3, reg EA
OR	ORA			C	Logical OR byte
r0,A	A,r0	60,10011RRR	8		reg r0, Reg A
A,r0	r0,A	60,00011RRR	8		reg A, reg r0
rpa,A	ORAX rpa	70,10011AAA	11		memory rpa, reg A
#n,A	ORI A,n	17	7	C	immed, reg A
#n,r0	r0,n	74,00011RRR	11		immed, reg r0
#n,sr2	sr2,n	60,R0011RRR	20		immed, reg sr2
(V,d),A	ORAW d	74,98	14	Z	ind reg V disp, reg A
#n,(V,d)	ORIW d,n	15	19	Z	immed, ind reg V disp
ORW	DOR			C	Logical OR word
* rp3,EA	EA,rp3	74,100111RR	11		reg rp3, reg EA
XOR	XRA			C	Logical Exclusive OR byte
r0,A	A,r0	60,10010RRR	8		reg r0, Reg A
A,r0	r0,A	60,00010RRR	8		reg A, reg r0
rpa,A	XRAX rpa	70,10010AAA	11		memory rpa, reg A
#n,A	XRI A,n	16	7	Z	immed, reg A
#n,r0	r0,n	74,00010RRR	11		immed, reg r0
#n,sr2	sr2,n	60,R0010RRR	20		immed, reg sr2
(V,d),A	XRAW d	74,90	14	Z	ind reg V disp, reg A
XORW	DXR			C	Logical Exclusive OR word
* rp3,EA	EA,rp3	74,100101RR	11		reg rp3, reg EA
RLWC	RLL			C	Rotate byte w/c left
r3	r3	48,001101RR	8		reg r2
RLWCW	DRLL			C	Rotate word w/c left
* EA	EA	48,B4	8		reg EA
RRWC	RR			C	Rotate byte w/c right
r3	r3	48,001100RR	8		reg r2
RRWCW	DRLR			C	Rotate word w/c right
* EA	EA	48,B0	8		reg EA
RLWR	RLD				Rotate left w/reg n bits
A,HL,4		48,38	17		reg A, reg HL, 4 bits
RRWR	RRD				Rotate right w/reg n bits
A,HL,4		48,39	17		reg A, reg HL, 4 bits
SLA	SLL			C	Shift left arithmetic
r3	r3	48,001001RR	8		reg r2
SLAW	DSLL			C	Shift left arith word
* EA	EA	48,A4	8		reg EA
SLASC	SLLC			C	Shift left arith, skip C
* r3	r3	48,000001RR	8		reg r2
SRAW	DSLR			C	Shift right arith word
* EA	EA	48,A0	8		reg EA
SRL	SLR			C	Shift right logical
r3	r3	48,001011RR	8		reg r2

```
SRLSC          ! SLRC      !              ! !C ! Shift right log, skip C
* r3           !    r3     ! 48,000000RR ! 8!   !   reg r2

Program Control
---------------

CALL           !           !             ! !   ! Call subroutine
    aa         ! CALL  aa  ! 40          !16!   !   uncond, abs
    (PC)       ! CALB      ! 48,29       !17!   !   zero, abs
CALLS          !           !             ! !   !   not zero, abs
    aa         ! CALF  aa  ! 01111aaa    !13!   ! Call short
               !           ! aaaaaaaa    ! !   !
CALLTBL        ! CALT      !             ! !   ! Call table
    aa         !       aa  ! 100aaaaa    !16!   !   uncon, ind PC + 2x aa
RET            ! RET       ! B8          !10!   ! Return from subroutine
RETI           ! RETI      ! 62          !13!   ! Return from interrupt
RETS           ! RETS      ! B9          !10!   ! Return from subr w/offset
SKIP           !           !             ! !   ! Skip if
    flag       ! SK   flag ! 48,00001FFF ! 8!   !   flag set
    Nflag      ! SKN  flag ! 48,00011FFF ! 8!   !   flag reset
TSTSKPRS       ! SKIT      !             ! !   ! Test, skip and reset
    iflag      !     iflag ! 010iiiiii   ! 8!   !   int flag
               ! SKNIT     !             ! !   !
    iflag      !     iflag ! 011iiiiii   ! 8!   !
CMPSKP         !           !             ! !   ! Test and skip if true
    A,GT,r0    ! GTA  A,r0 ! 60,10101RRR ! 8!CZ !   reg A > reg r0
    r0,GT,A    !      r0,A ! 60,00101RRR ! 8!   !   reg r0 > reg A
    A,LT,r0    ! LTA  A,r0 ! 60,10111RRR ! 8!CZ !   reg A < reg r0
    r0,LT,A    !      r0,A ! 60,00111RRR ! 8!   !   reg r0 < reg A
    r0,NE,A    ! NEA  A,r0 ! 60,11101RRR ! 8!CZ !   reg r0 <> reg A
    A,NE,r0    !      r0,A ! 60,01101RRR ! 8!   !   reg A <> reg r0
    A,EQ,r0    ! EQA  A,r0 ! 60,11111RRR ! 8!CZ !   reg r0 = reg A
    r0,EQ,A    !      r0,A ! 60,01111RRR ! 8!   !   reg A = reg r0
    A,GT,rpa   ! GTAX rpa  ! 70,10101AAA !11!CZ !   reg A > memory rpa
    A,LT,rpa   ! LTAX rpa  ! 70,10111AAA !11!CZ !   reg A < memory rpa
    A,NE,rpa   ! NEAX rpa  ! 70,11101AAA !11!CZ !   reg A <> memory rpa
    A,EQ,rpa   ! EQAX rpa  ! 70,11111AAA !11!CZ !   reg A = memory rpa
    A,GT,#n    ! GTI   A,n ! 27          ! 7!CZ !   reg A > immed
    r0,GT,#n   !      r0,n ! 74,00101RRR !11!   !   reg r0 > immed
    sr2,GT,#n  !      sr2,n ! 60,R0101RRR !14!   !   reg sr2 > immed
    A,LT,#n    ! LTI   A,n ! 37          ! 7!CZ !   reg A < immed
    r0,LT,#n   !      r0,n ! 74,00111RRR !11!   !   reg r0 < immed
    sr2,LT,#n  !      sr2,n ! 60,R0111RRR !14!   !   reg sr2 < immed
    A,NE,#n    ! NEI   A,n ! 67          ! 7!CZ !   reg A <> immed
    r0,NE,#n   !      r0,n ! 74,01101RRR !11!   !   reg r0 <> immed
    sr2,NE,#n  !      sr2,n ! 60,R1101RRR !14!   !   reg sr2 <> immed
    A,EQ,#n    ! EQI   A,n ! 77          ! 7!CZ !   reg A = immed
    r0,EQ,#n   !      r0,n ! 74,01111RRR !11!   !   reg r0 = immed
    sr2,EQ,#n  !      sr2,n ! 60,R1111RRR !14!   !   reg sr2 = immed
    A,GT,(V,d) ! GTAW d    ! 74,A8       !14!CZ !   reg A > ind reg V disp
    A,LT,(V,d) ! LTAW d    ! 74,B0       !14!CZ !   reg A < ind reg V disp
    A,NE,(V,d) ! NEAW d    ! 74,E0       !14!CZ !   reg A <> ind reg V disp
    A,EQ,(V,d) ! EQAW d    ! 74,F0       !14!CZ !   reg A = ind reg V disp
    (V,d),GT,#n! GTIW d,n  ! 25          !13!CZ !   ind reg V disp > immed
    (V,d),LT,#n! LTIW d,n  ! 35          !13!CZ !   ind reg V disp < immed
    (V,d),NE,#n! NEIW d,n  ! 65          !13!CZ !   ind reg V disp <> immed
    (V,d),EQ,#n! EQIW d,n  ! 75          !13!CZ !   ind reg V disp = immed
*   EA,GT,rp3  ! DGT  EA,rp3! 74,101011RR !11!   !   reg EA > reg rp3
*   EA,LT,rp3  ! DLT  EA,rp3! 74,101111RR !11!   !   reg EA < reg rp3
*   EA,NE,rp3  ! DNE  EA,rp3! 74,111011RR !11!   !   reg EA <> reg rp3
*   EA,EQ,rp3  ! DEQ  EA,rp3! 74,111111RR !11!   !   reg EA = reg rp3
TSTSKP         !           !             ! !   ! Test and skip if =0
```

316

```
    r0,AND,A     | ONA   A,r0  | 60,11001RRR | 8|Z | reg r0 AND reg A not 0
    r0,NAND,A    | OFFA  A,r0  | 60,11011RRR | 8|Z | reg r0 AND reg A = 0
    A,AND,rpa    | ONAX  rpa   | 70,11001AAA |11|Z | reg A AND mem rpa <> 0
    A,NAND,rpa   | OFFAX rpa   | 70,11011AAA |11|Z | reg A AND mem rpa = 0
    A,AND,#n     | ONI   A,n   | 47         | 7|Z | reg A AND immed <> 0
    r0,AND,#n    |             | 74,01001RRR |11| | reg r0 AND immed <> 0
    sr2,AND,#n   |       sr2,n | 60,R1001RRR |14| | reg sr2 AND immed <> 0
    A,AND,#n     | OFFI  A,n   | 57         | 7|Z | reg A AND immed = 0
    r0,AND,#n    |       r0,n  | 74,01011RRR |11| | reg r0 AND immed = 0
    sr2,AND,#n   |       sr2,n | 60,R1011RRR |14| | reg sr2 AND immed = 0
    A,AND,(V,d)  | ONAW  d     | 74,C0      |14|Z | A AND ind V disp <> 0
    A,NAND,(V,d) | OFFAW d     | 74,D0      |14|Z | A AND ind V disp = 0
    (V,d),AND,#n | ONIW  d,n   | 45         |13|Z | ind V disp AND immed <>0
    (V,d),NAND,#n| OFFIW d,n   | 55         |13|Z | ind V disp AND immed =0
*   EA,AND,rp3   | DON   EA,rp3| 74,110011RR |11| | reg EA AND reg rp3 <> 0
*   EA,NAND,rp3  | DOFF  EA,rp3| 74,110111RR |11| | reg EA AND reg rp3 = 0
TSTSKPB          | BIT         |            | | | Test bit and skip if =0
    (V,d),bit    |       bit,d | 01011bbb   |10| |   ind reg V disp, bit
JMP              |             |            | | | Jump
    UN,aa        | JMP   aa    | 54         |10| |   uncond, abs
    UN,(BC)      | JB          | 21         | 4| |   uncond, ind BC
*   UN,(EA)      | JEA         | 48,28      | 8| |   uncond, ind EA
JMPRS            |             | 30         | | | Jump relative short
    UN,r         | JR    r     | 11rrrrrr   |10| |   uncond, rel
JMPR             |             |            | | | Jump relative
    UN,r         | JRE   r     | 47         |10| |   uncond,rel
HALT             | HALT        | 48,3B      |11| | Stop till interrupt
NOP              | NOP         | 00         | 4| | No operation
```

I/O   Operations

```
DI            | DI     | BA  | 4| | Disable interrupts
EI            | EI     | AA  | 4| | Enable interrupts
SWI           | SOFTI  | 72  |16| | Software interrupt
START   SIO   | SIO    |     | 4| | Start serial I/O
START   T     | STM    |     | 4| | Start timer
IN            | IN     |     |10| | Input from port
OUT           | OUT    |     |10| | Output to port
```

Micro Unique

```
PEX           | PEX    |     |11| | BC to PE
PEN           | PEN    |     |11| | B (7-4) to PE (15-12)
PER           | PER    |     |11| | Port E AB mode
```

Registers

```
        16    8|7      0        16    8|7      0
        -----------------       -----------------
   VA | V   |   A   |      VA' | V'  |   A'  |
        -----------------       -----------------
   BC | B   |   C   |      BC' | B'  |   C'  |
        -----------------       -----------------
   DE | D   |   E   |      DE' | D'  |   E'  |
        -----------------       -----------------
   HL | H   |   L   |      HL' | H'  |   L'  |
        -----------------       -----------------
*  EA | Extended Accum|    EA' | Extended Accum|
        -----------------       -----------------

   SP | Stack Pointer |
```

317

```
            -------------------
PC   !Program Counter!
            -------------------
              !  PSW  !
              ---------
```

Special Registers

PA - Port A	MM - Memory mapping	ANM - A/D channel mode
PB - Port B	TM0 - Timer reg 0	CR0 - A/D result 0
PC - Port C	TM1 - Timer reg 1	CR1 - A/D result 1
PD - Port D	TMM - Timer mode	CR2 - A/D result 2
PF - Port F	ETM0 - T/C reg 0	CR3 - A/D result 3
MA - Mode A	ETM1 - T/C reg 1	TXB - Tx buffer
MB - Mode B	ECNT - T/C upcounter	RXB - Rx buffer
MC - Mode C	ECPT - T/C capture	SMH - Serial mode high
MCC - Mode control C	ETMM - T/C mode	SML - Serial mode low
MF - Mode F	EOM - T/C output mode	
MKH - Mask high	MKL - Mask low	

Flags

```
    Z = zero result
*   HC = half carry from bit 3
    C = carry
```

Interrupt Flags

```
F0  -  int 0      FT - timer
F1  -  int 1      FS - serial port
F2  -  int 2
```

(*)

```
FNMI -nmi       FE0  - counter 0    FST - serial xmt    AN6 - A/D 6
FT0 - timer 0   FE1  - counter 1    ER  - Error         AN7 - A/D 7
FT1 - timer 1   FEIN - sig cl t0    OV  - Overflow      SB  - Standby
F1  - int 1     FAD  - a/d          AN4 - A/D 4
F2  - int 2     FSR  - serial rcvr  AN5 - A/D 5
```

Addressing Modes

Univ	Manuf	
#n	n	- immediate data, 8 or 16-bits
XX	X	- register
aa	aa	- absolute address
r	r	- relative address
V:d	d	- vectroed address, MSB in reg V, LSB immediate data
(XX)	X	- indirect address
(XX+XX)	X+X	- indexed address
-(X)	X-	- indirect pre auto decrement by one
+(X)	X+	- indirect pre auto increment by one
* ++(X)	X++	- indirect pre auto increment by two

Instruction Expansion

r0	r1	rp1	rp2	RRR	sr	RRRRR	sr1	RRRRRR	sr2	RRRR
V	* EAH	VA	SP	000	PA	00000	PA	000000	PA	0000

```
A  * EAL  BC   BC   001      PB   00001     PB   000001     PB   0001
B    B    DE   DE   010      PC   00010     PC   000010     PC   0010
C    C    HL   HL   011    * PD   00011   * PD   000011   * PD   0011
D    D   *EA  *EA   100    * PF   00100   * PF   000100   * PF   0100
E    E                       MKH  00101     MKH  000101     MKH  0101
H    H                       MKL  00110     MKL  000110     MKL  0110
L    L                     * ANM  00111   * ANM  000111   * ANM  0111
                           * SMH  01000   * SMH  001000   * SMH  1000
                           * SML  01001   * EOM  001001   * EOM  1001
r2  *rp3 *sr4   rp   RR     * EOM  01010   * TMM  001010   * TMM  1010
--- ---  ---    --   --     * ETMM 01011   * RXB  001011
A    BC   ECNT  SP   00     * TMM  01100   * CR0  001100
B    DE   ECPT  BC   01     * MM   01101   * CR1  001101   * sr3    R
C    HL         DE   10     * MCC  01110   * CR2  001110     ---    -
                HL   11     * MA   01111   * CR3  001111     ETM0   0
                             MB   10000                      ETM1   1
                             MC   10001
r3  RR                     * MF   10010
--  --                     * TBX  10011
A   00                       TM0  10100
*B  01                       TM1  10101
C   10
```

Memory

```
rpa   AAA    rpa1  AA    rpa2     *rpa3     AAAA
---   ---    ----  --    ----     -----     ----
(BC)  001    (BC)  00    (BC)     (DE)      0000
(DE)  010    (DE)  01    (DE)     (HL)      0001
(HL)  011    (HL)  10    (HL)     ++(DE)    0010
(+DE) 100                +(DE)    ++(HL)    0011
(+HL) 101                +(HL)    (DE+d)    0100
(-DE) 110                -(DE)    (HL+A)    0101
(-HL) 111                -(HL)    (HL+B)    0110
                       * (DE+d)   (HL+EA)   0111
                       * (HL+A)   (HL+d)    1000
                       * (HL+B)             1001
                       * (HL+EA)            1010
                       * (HL+d)             1011
```

Flags

```
flag  FFF    * iflag  IIIII   * iflag  IIIII   * iflag  IIIII
----  ---      -----  -----     -----  -----     -----  -----
CY    000      FNMI   00000     FE1    00110     OV     01100
* HC  001      FT0    00001     FEIN   00111     AN4    01101
Z     010      FT1    00010     FAD    01000     AN5    01110
               F1     00011     FSR    01001     AN6    01111
               F2     00100     FST    01010     AN7    10000
               FE0    00101     ER     01011     SB     10001

iflag  IIIII
-----  -----
F0     00000
F1     00001
F2     00010
FT     00011
FS     00100
```

#n - immediate data, 8-bits appended to inst
#nn - immediate data, 16-bits appended to inst

aa - absolute adr, 16-bits appended to inst
r   - relative adr, 6-bits part og inst or 8-bits appended to inst
d   - LSB vectored adr, 8-bits appended to inst
bit - bit number, 3-bits part of inst

address data is appended before immediate

Special Memory Locations

```
LOC 0000 - 0FFF   Internal ROM, loc 00 - FF contain int vectors.
    1000 - FEFF   External memory
    FF00 - FFFF   Internal RAM
```

memory allowcation varies between micros.

Notes

Each processor has a dirferent combination of interrupt flags, special
registers and instructions. For simplicity we have merely separated them
into two groups. Consult the manufacturers specification sheets for
an exact listing of each.

8020   Incomplete

(1) 8021, uPD8021   **(2) 8022, 8022H**

Data Move

MOV	MOV					Move byte
Rr,A	A,Rr	11111RRR	1			reg, reg A
(Rr),A	A,∂Rr	1111000R	1			ind reg 0 or 1, reg A
#n,A	A,#n	23	2			immed, reg A
A,Rr	Rr,A	10101RRR	1			reg A, reg
A,(Rr)	∂Rr,A	1010000R	1			reg A, ind reg
#n,Rr	Rr,#n	10111RRR	2			immed, reg
#n,(Rr)	∂Rr,#n	1011000R	2			immed, ind reg
T,A	A,T	42	1			timer/counter, reg A
A,T	T,A	62	1			reg A, timer/counter
(A),A	MOVP A,∂A	A3	2			current page, reg A
						prog ROM
CLR	CLR					Clear
A	A	27	1			Reg A
SWAPN	SWAP					Swap 4-bit halfs
A	A	47	1			in reg A
XCHG	XCH					Exchange bytes
Rr,A	A,Rr	00101RRR	1			reg, reg A
(Rr),A	A,∂Rr	0010000R	1			ind reg, reg A
XCHGN	XCHD					Exchange lower 4 bits
(Rr),A	A,∂Rr	0011000R	1			ind reg, reg A

Math Operations

ADD	ADDWF				C	Add
Rr,A	A,Rr	01101RRR	1			reg, reg A
(Rr),A	A,∂Rr	0110000R	1			ind Reg 0 or 1, reg A
#n,A	A,#n	03	2			immed, reg A
ADC	ADC				C	Add w/carry

320

```
    Rr,A      |    A,Rr    | 01111RRR | 1|       |   reg, reg A
    (Rr),A    |    A,@Rr   | 0111000R |  |       |   ind reg 0 or 1, reg A
    #n,A      |    A,#n    | 13       | 2|       |   immed, reg A
INC           | INC        |          |  |       | Increment
    A         |    A       | 17       | 1|       |   reg A
    Rr        |    Rr      | 00011RRR | 1|       |   reg
    (Rr)      |    @Rr     | 0001000R | 1|       |   ind reg 0 or 1
DEC           | DEC        |          |  |       | Decrement
    A         |    A       | 07       | 1|       |   reg A
DA  A         | DA  A      | 57       | 1|C      | Decimal adjust reg A
```

Logical Operations

```
AND           | ANL        |          |  |       | Logical AND
    Rr,A      |    A,Rr    | 01011RRR | 2|       |   reg, reg A
    (Rr),A    |    A,@Rr   | 0101000R | 2|       |   ind reg 0 or 1, reg A
    #n,A      |    A,#n    | 53       | 2|       |   immed, reg A
OR            | ORL        |          |  |       | Logical OR
    Rr,A      |    A,Rr    | 01001RRR | 1|       |   reg, reg A
    (Rr),A    |    A,@Rr   | 0100000R | 1|       |   ind reg 0 or 1, reg A
    #n,A      |    A,#n    | 43       | 2|       |   immed, reg A
XOR           | XRL        |          |  |       | Logical Exclusive OR
    Rr,A      |    A,Rr    | 11011RRR | 1|       |   reg, reg A
    (Rr),A    |    A,@Rr   | 1101000R | 1|       |   ind reg 0 or 1, reg A
    #n,A      |    A,#n    | D3       | 2|       |   immed, reg A
CPL           | CPL        |          |  |       | Complement
    A         |    A       | 37       | 1|       |   reg A
RRWC          | RRC        |          |  |C      | Rotate right w/carry
    A         |    A       | 67       | 1|       |   reg A
RLWC          | RLC        |          |  |C      | Rotate left w/carry
    A         |    A       | F7       | 1|       |   reg A
RLTC          | RL         |          |  |C      | Rotate left to carry
    A         |    A       | E7       | 1|       |   reg A
RRTC          | RR         |          |  |C      | Rotate right to carry
    A         |    A       | 77       | 1|       |   reg A
```

Bit Operations

```
RESF          | CLR        |          |  |       | Reset flag
    C         |    C       | 97       | 1|       |   carry
CPLF          | CPL        |          |  |       | Complement flag
    C         |    C       | A7       | 1|       |   carry
```

Program Control

```
CALL          | CALL       |          |  |       | Call subroutine
    UN,aa     |    aa      | AAA10100 |  |       |   uncond, loc aa
              |            | AAAAAAAA |  |       |
RET           | RET        |          |  |       | Return from subroutine
    UN        |            | 83       |  |       |   uncond
* RETI        | RETI       |          |  |       | Return from interrupt (2)
    UN        |            | 93       |  |       |   uncond
JMP           | JMP        |          |  |       | Jump if
    UN,aa     |    aa      | AAA00100 | 2|       |   uncond, 11 bit adr
              |            | AAAAAAAA |  |       |
JMPSP         |            |          |  |       | Jump same page if
    UN,(A)    | JMPP   @A  | B3       | 2|       |   uncond, ind reg A
    C,a       | JC     a   | F6       | 2|       |   carry, abs  8-bit adr
    NC,a      | JNC    a   | E6       | 2|       |   no carry, abs
    Z,a       | JZ     a   | C6       | 2|       |   A=0, abs
    NZ,a      | JNZ    a   | 96       | 2|       |   A not zero, abs
*   T0,a      | JT0    a   | 36       | 2|       |   test 0 = 1, abs  (2)
```

* NT0,a	JNT0 a	26	2	test 0 = 0, abs (2)
T1,a	JT1 a	56	2	test 1 = 1, abs
NT1,a	JNT1 a	46	2	test 1 = 0, abs
TF,a	JTF a	16	2	timer flag, abs
DECSNZ	DJNZ			Decrement and skip if not 0
Rr,a	Rr,a	11101RRR	2	reg, 8-bit adr
NOP	NOP	00000000		No operation
START	STRT			Start
T	T	55	1	timer
CNT	CNT	45	1	counter
STOP	STOP			Stop
TCNT	TCNT	65	1	timer/counter
* SEL	SEL			Select input (1)
AN0	AN0	85	1	analog chan 0
AN1	AN1	95	1	analog chan 1

I/O   Operation

IN	IN			Input from port
1,A	A,1	08	2	port 1, reg A
2,A	A,2	09	2	port 2, reg A
* p,A	A,p	000010pp	2	port 1 thru 2, reg A (1)
* Ep,A	MOVD A,p	000011pp	2	exp port 4-7, reg A (1)
OUT	OUTL			Output to port
A,1	1,A	90	2	reg A, port 1
A,2	2,A	39	2	reg A, port 2
* A,p	p,A	001110pp	2	reg A, port 1 thru 2 (1)
* A,Ep	MOVD p,A	001111pp	2	reg A, exp port 4-7 (1)
ANDIO	ANLD			Logical AND to port
* A,Ep	p,A	100111pp	2	reg A, expander port (1)
ORIO	ORLD			Logical OR to port
* A,Ep	p,A	100011pp	2	reg A, expander port (1)
* EI	EN I	05	1	Enable external interrupts (2)
* EC	EN TCNTI	25	1	counter/timer interrupts (2)
* DI	DIS I	15	1	Disable external interrupts (2)
* DC	DIS TCNTI	35	1	counter/timer interrupts (2)
* INAD	RAD	80	2	Input A/D to reg A (2)

Registers

```
                8     1
              ---------
    12   9  !  A  !  Accumulator
       -----  ---------
PC  !  !  !  !  PC  !  Prog counter (12 bits)
    -----  ---------
      PSW  !        !  Prog status word
           ---------
        !        !  Flags
           ---------
```

Resident data RAM

```
        ---------
        !  R0  !  indirect RAM adr
        ---------
        !  R1  !  indirect RAM adr
        ---------
        !  R2  !
        ---------
        !  R3  !
        ---------
```

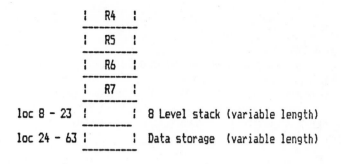

```
        !   R4   !
        -----------
        !   R5   !
        -----------
        !   R6   !
        -----------
        !   R7   !
        -----------
loc 8 - 23 !        !   8 Level stack (variable length)
        -----------
loc 24 - 63 !        !   Data storage  (variable length)
        -----------


        -----------
        !Prog Rom!  1 or 2 k
        -----------
```

Flags

```
   C = carry flag
   Z = zero
   T0 = test 0
   T1 = test 1
   TF = timer flag
```

Addressing Modes

```
Univ  Manuf
----  -----

#n    n     - immediate
Rn    Rn    - register
aa    aa    - absolute
a     a     - same page address
(Rn)  əRn   - indirect register R0 or R1
```

Instruction Expansion

```
Rn   Register, RRR = 0 - 7   for R0 to R7 respctively
n    immediate, 8-bit value appended to instruction
aa   address, 11 bit address  8 bits appended to instruction
                        most significant 3 bit part of inst code
a    same page address, 8-bits appended to inst
r    relative adr, 8 bits appended to inst
p    port number, 2-bits part of inst
```

Special Memory Locations

Notes

Information on these processors was limited and may not be absolutely correct.

(1,2)   port 0 is used to communicate with an external I/O expander which contains ports 4 thru 7. Ports 1 and 2 are for general use.

8048

(1) 8651, 8741, 8042, 8742, uPD8041A, uPD8741A
(2) 8048, 8049, 8039, 8658, 8035, INS8048, INS8049, INS8050, 89748H, 8749H, 8048AH,
    8050AH, 8035AHL, 8039AHL, 8040AHL, 8039H, 8035H, 8243, 80C49, 80C39,
    80C48, 80C35, 8739, uPD80C49, uPD80C39, uPD8049H, uPD8749H, uPD8039HL,
    uPD8048H, uPD8035HL, uPD8748, uPD80C48, uPD80C35, NS8050U, NS8040U,
    NS87P50, TMP8048, TMP8049, TMP80C48, TMP80C49, TMP80C50
(2,3) NS80CX48, NS80CX35

Data Move

```
MOV       | MOV          |          | |  | Move byte
   Rr,A   |    A,Rr      | 11111RRR |1|  |    reg, reg A
   (Rr),A |    A,aRr     | 1111000R |1|  |    ind reg, reg A
   #n,A   |    A,#n      | 23       |2|  |    immed, reg A
   A,Rr   |    Rr,A      | 10101RRR |1|  |    reg A, reg
   A,(Rr) |    aRr,A     | 1010000R |1|  |    reg A, ind reg
   #n,Rr  |    Rr,#n     | 10111RRR |2|  |    immed, reg
   #n,(Rr)|    aRr,#n    | 1011000R |2|  |    immed, ind reg
   T,A    |    A,T       | 42       |1|  |    timer/counter, reg A
   A,T    |    T,A       | 62       |1|  |    reg A, timer/counter
   SP(A),A| MOVP  A,aA   | A3       |2|  |    same page, reg A
   PSW,A  | MOV   A,PSW  | C7       |1|  |    prog status wrd, reg A
   A,PSW  | MOV   PSW,A  | D7       |1|  |    reg A, prog status wrd
   P3(A),A| MOVP3 A,aA   | E3       |2|  |    page 3 ind A, reg A
* MOVN    | MOV          |          | |  | Move upper 4 bits  (1)
   A,STS  |    STS,A     | 90       |1|  |    reg A, status reg
* MOVX    | MOVX         |          | |  | Move external data memory  (2)
   (Rr),A |    A,aRr     | 1000000R |2|  |    ind reg, reg A
   A,(Rr) |    aRr,A     | 1001000R |2|  |    reg A, ind reg
CLR       | CLR          |          | |  | Clear
   A      |    A         | 27       |1|  |    reg A
SWAPN     | SWAP         |          | |  | Swap 4-bit halves
   A      |    A         | 47       |1|  |    reg A
XCHG      | XCH          |          | |  | Exchange bytes
   Rr,A   |    A,Rr      | 00101RRR |1|  |    reg, reg A
   (Rr),A |    A,aRr     | 0010000R |1|  |    ind reg, reg A
XCHGN     | XCHD         |          | |  | Exchange lower 4 bits
   (Rr),A |    A,aRr     | 0011000R |1|  |    ind reg, reg A
```

Math Operations

```
ADD       | ADD          |          | |C | Add
   Rr,A   |    A,Rr      | 01101RRR |1|  |    reg, reg A
   (Rr),A |    A,aRr     | 0110000R |1|  |    ind reg, reg A
   #n,A   |    A,#n      | 03       |2|  |    immed, reg A
ADC       | ADDC         |          | |C | Add w/carry
   Rr,A   |    A,Rr      | 01111RRR |1|  |    reg, reg A
   (Rr),A |    A,aRr     | 0111000R |1|  |    ind reg, reg A
   #n,A   |    A,#n      | 13       |2|  |    immed, reg A
INC       | INC          |          | |  | Increment
   A      |    A         | 17       |1|  |    reg A
   Rr     |    Rr        | 00011RRR |1|  |    reg
   (Rr)   |    aRr       | 0001000R |1|  |    ind reg
DEC       | DEC          |          | |  | Decrement
   A      |    A         | 07       |1|  |    reg A
```

```
     Rr          :     Rr      : 11001RRR :1:      :   reg
 DA  A          : DA  A        : 57       :1: C    : Decimal adjust reg A
```

Logical Operations

```
 AND            : ANL          :          : :      : Logical AND
     Rr,A       :     A,Rr     : 01011RRR :1:      :    reg, reg A
     (Rr),A     :     A,aRr    : 0101000R :1:      :    ind reg, reg A
     #n,A       :     A,#n     : 53       :2:      :    immed, reg A
 OR             : ORL          :          : :      : Logical OR
     Rr,A       :     A,Rr     : 01001RRR :1:      :    reg, reg A
     (Rr),A     :     A,aRr    : 0100000R :1:      :    ind reg, reg A
     #n,A       :     A,#n     : 43       :2:      :    immed, reg A
 XOR            : XRL          :          : :      : Logical Exclusive OR
     Rr,A       :     A,Rr     : 11011RRR :1:      :    reg, reg A
     (Rr),A     :     A,aRr    : 1101000R :1:      :    ind reg, reg A
     #n,A       :     A,#n     : D3       :2:      :    immed, reg A
 CPL            : CPL          :          : :      : Complement
     A          :     A        : 37       :1:      :    reg A
 RRWC           : RRC          :          : : C    : Rotate right w/carry
     A          :     A        : 67       :1:      :    reg A
 RLWC           : RLC          :          : : C    : Rotate left w/carry
     A          :     A        : F7       :1:      :    reg A
 RLNC           : RL           :          : :      : Rotate left no carry
     A          :     A        : E7       :1:      :    reg A
 RRNC           : RR           :          : :      : Rotate right no carry
     A          :     A        : 77       :1:      :    reg A
```

Bit Operations

```
 RESF           : CLR          :          :1:      : Reset flag
     C          :     C        : 97       : : C    :    carry
     F1         :     F1       : A5       : :      :    flag 1
     F0         :     F0       : 85       : :      :    flag 0
 CPLF           : CPL          :          :1:      : Complement flag
     C          :     C        : A7       : : C    :    carry
     F0         :     F0       : 95       : :      :    flag 0
     F1         :     F1       : B5       : :      :    flag 1
```

Program Control

```
 CALL           : CALL         :          :2:      : Call subroutine
     aa         :     aa       : AAA10100 : :      :    uncond, loc aa
                :              : AAAAAAAA : :      :
 RET            : RET          :          :2:      : Return from subroutine
                :              : 83       : :      :    uncond
 RETR           : RETR         :          :2:      : Return from subr w/PSW
                :              : 93       : :      :    uncond
 JMP            : JMP          :          :2:      : Jump if
     aa         :     aa       : AAA00100 : :      :    uncond, 11 bit adr
                :              : AAAAAAAA : :      :
 JMPSP          :              :          :2:      : Jump same page if
     UN,(A)     : JMPP    aA   : B3       : :      :    uncond, ind reg A
     C,a        : JC     a     : F6       : :      :    carry
     NC,a       : JNC    aa    : E6       : :      :    no carry
     Z,a        : JZ     a     : C6       : :      :    A=0
     NZ,a       : JNZ    a     : 96       : :      :    A not zero
     F0,a       : JF0    a     : B6       : :      :    flag 0 = 1
     F1,a       : JF1    a     : 76       : :      :    flag 1 = 1
     NT0,a      : JNT0   a     : 26       : :      :    test 0 = 0
     T0,a       : JT0    a     : 36       : :      :    test 0 = 1
     NT1,a      : JNT1   a     : 46       : :      :    test 1 = 0
```

```
     T1,a      | JT1    a  | 56        | |  |   test 1 = 1
     TF,a      | JTF    a  | 16        | |  |   timer flag
  *  NIBF,a     | JNIBF  a  | D3        | |  |   IBF flag = 0  (1)
  *  OBF,a     | JOBF   a  | 83        | |  |   OBF flag = 1  (1)
  *  NI, a     | JNI    a  | 86        | |  |   no interrupt  (2)
     BS,A,b,a   | JBb    a  | bbb10010  | |  |   bit set, reg A, bit b
DECJNZ       | DJNZ      |           |2|  | Decrement and jump if not 0
     Rr,SP a    |    Rr,aa  | 11101RRR  | |  |   reg, same page adr
NOP          | NOP       | 00000000  |1|  | No operation
```

I/O   Operations

```
IN           | IN        |           |2|  | Input from port
     1,A       |    A,1    | 08        | |  |   port 1, reg A
     2,A       |    A,2    | 09        | |  |   port 2, reg A
     p,A       | MOVD A,Pp | 000011pp  | |  |   port 4 - 7, reg A
     DBB,A     | INS A,DBB | 08        | |  |   BUS port, reg A
OUT          | OUTL      |           |2|  | Output to port
     A,1       |    1,A    | 39        | |  |   reg A, port 1
     A,2       |    2,A    | 3A        | |  |   reg A, port 2
     A,p       |    Pp,A   | 001111pp  | |  |   reg A, port 4 - 7
     A,DBB     |    DBB,A  | 02        | |  |   reg A, BUS port
ANDIO        | ANL       |           |2|  | Logical AND to I/O
     #n,DBB    |    BUS,#n | 98        | |  |   immed, BUS port

     #n,p      |    Pp,#n  | 100110pp  | |  |   immed, port (1,2)
     A,p       | ANLD Pp,A | 100111pp  | |  |   reg A (bits 0-3), port 4 - 7
             |           |           | |  |     port 4 = 0, port 7 = 3
             |           |           | |  |
ORIO         |           |           |2|  | Logical OR port
     #n,Pp     | ORL  Pp,#n| 100010pp  | |  |   immed, port 1 or 2
  *  #n,DBB    |    BUS,n  | 88        | |  |   immed, BUS port  (2)
     A,Pp      | ORLD Pp,A | 100011pp  | |  |   reg A, port 4-7
EI           | EN   I    | 05        |1|  | Enable external interrupts
EC           | EN   TCNTI| 25        |1|  |   counter/timer interrupts
  *  EDMA     | EN   DMA  | F5        |1|  |   dma lines  (1)
  *  EMI      | EN   FLAGS| E5        |1|  |   master interrupts  (1)
  *  ETO      | ENTO CLK  | 75        |1|  |   clock output  (2)
  *  EFC      | ENFCR     |           | |  |   feature control reg  (3)
DI           | DIS  I    | 15        |1|  | Disable external interrupts
DC           | DIS  TCNTI| 35        |1|  |   counter/timer interrupts
```

Micro Unique Operations

```
STRT         | STRT      |           |1|  | Start
     T         |    T      | 55        | |  |   timer
     CNT       |    CNT    | 45        | |  |   counter
STOP         | STOP      |           |1|  | Stop
     TCNT      |    TCNT   | 65        | |  |   timer/counter
SEL          | SEL       |           |1|  | Select
     RB0       |    RB0    | C5        | |  |   register bank 0
     RB1       |    RB1    | D5        | |  |   register bank 1
  *  MB0      |    MB0    | E5        | |  |   memory bank 0  (2)
  *  MB1      |    MB1    | F5        | |  |   memory bank 1  (2)
             |           |           | |  |
```

Registers

```
                8    1
                ----------
        12  9 | A  |  Accumulator
        ----- ----------
  PC  |   |   | PC  |  Prog counter  (12 bits)
```

```
       ------  --------
  PSW  !      !   Prog status word
       --------
       !      !   Flags
       --------
       !  T   !   Timer/Counter
       --------
```

Resident data RAM
```
       --------
       !  R0  !   indirect RAM adr
       --------
       !  R1  !   indirect RAM adr
       --------
       !  R2  !
       --------
       !  R3  !
       --------
       !  R4  !
       --------
       !  R5  !
       --------
       !  R6  !
       --------
       !  R7  !
       --------
loc 8 - 23 !   !   8 Level stack (variable length)
       --------
       !      !   Optional second register bank
       --------
       !      !   Data storage (variable length)
       --------
```

Flags

```
  C = carry flag
  Z = zero
 T0 = test 0
 T1 = test 1
 TF = timer flag
 F0 = flag 0
 F1 = flag 1
```

Addressing Modes

Univ	Manuf	
#n	n	- immediate
Rr	r	- register
aa	aa	- absolute address
(Rr)	@Rr	- indirect register R0 or R1
SP(A)	@A	- same/current page indirect reg A
P3(A)	@A	- page 3 indirect reg A
b	b	- bit position
SP a	a	- same page address

Instruction Expansion

```
Rr   Register, RRR = 0 - 7   for R0 to R7 respctively
n    immediate, 8-bit value appended to instruction
aa   address, 11-bit address  8 bits appended to instruction
                    most significant 3 bit part of inst code
```

a   same page, 8-bit address appended to inst
d   bit number, 3-bits part of inst
p   port number, 2-bits part of inst

Special Memory Locations

Notes

8051

8031, 8751H, 80C51, 80C31, 8052, 8031AH, 8051
SAB801, SAB8051
(1) 8044, 8044AH, 8344AH, 8744H
AH, 8032AH, 8052AH, 80C51BH, 80C31BH, 80C59, AM9761H,

Data Move

```
MOV        | MOV         |            |12|  | Move byte
   Rr,A    |    A,Rr     | 11101RRR   |  |  |    reg, reg A
   PZ a,A  |    A,a      | E5         |  |  |    8-bit data adr, reg A
   (Ri),A  |    A,aRi    | 1110011R   |  |  |    ind reg, reg A
   #n,A    |    A,#n     | 34         |  |  |    immed, reg A
   A,Rr    |    Rr,A     | 11111RRR   |  |  |    reg A, reg
   PZ a,Rr |    Rr,a     | 10101RRR   |24|  |    8-bit adr, reg
   A,(Ri)  |    aRi,A    | 1111011R   |  |  |    reg A, ind reg
   PZ a,(Rr)|   aRi,a    | 1010011R   |24|  |    8-bit adr, ind reg
   A,PZ a  |    a,A      | F5         |  |  |    reg A, 8-bit adr
   Rr,PZ a |    a,Rr     | 10001RRR   |24|  |    reg, 8-bit adr
   PZ a,PZ a|   a,a      |85,src,dst  |24|  |    srce, dest  8-bit adr
   (Rr),PZ a|   a,aRi    | 1000011R   |24|  |    ind reg, 8-bit adr
   #n,PZ a |    a,#n     | 75         |24|  |    immed, 8-bit adr
   #n,Rr   |    Rr,#n    | 01111RRR   |  |  |    immed, reg
   #n,(Ri) |    aRi,#n   | 0111011R   |  |  |    immed, ind reg
MOVX       | MOVX        |            |24|  | Move external data memory
   (R),A   |    A,aR     | 1110000R   |  |  |    ind reg, reg A
   (DPTR),A|    A,aDPTR  | E0         |  |  |    ind DPTR, reg A
   A,(Ri)  |    aRi,A    | 1111001R   |  |  |    reg A, ind reg
   A,(DPTR)|    aDPTR,A  | F0         |  |  |    reg A, ind DPTR
MOVC       | MOVC        |            |24|  | Move code segment
   (A+DPTR),A|  A,aA+DPTR| 93         |  |  |    indexed A+DPTR, reg A
   (A+PC),A|    A,aA+PC  | 83         |  |  |    indexed A+PC, reg A
MOVB       | MOV         |            |12|  | Move bit
   bit,C   |    C,bit    | A2,bit_adr |  |C|    bit, carry flag
   C,bit   |    bit,C    | 92,bit_adr |  |  |    carry flag, bit
MOVW       | MOV         |            |  |  | Move word
   #nn,DPTR|    DPTR,#nn | 90         |24|  |    immed, reg DPTR
POP        | POP         |            |24|  | Pop byte
   PZ a    |    a        | D0         |  |  |    8-bit data adr
PUSH       | PUSH        |            |24|  | Push byte
   PZ a    |    a        | C0         |  |  |    8-bit data adr
CLR        | CLR         |            |12|  | Clear
   A       |    A        | E4         |  |  |    Reg A
SWAPN      | SWAP        |            |12|  | Swap 4-bit halves
   A       |    A        | C4         |  |  |    in reg A
XCHG       | XCH         |            |12|  | Exchange bytes
   Rr,A    |    A,Rr     | 11001RRR   |  |  |    reg, reg A
   PZ a,A  |    A,a      | C5         |  |  |    8-bit adr, reg A
```

```
        (Ri),A   !    A,aRi  ! 1100011R !   !   !  ind reg, reg A
XCHGN            ! XCHD      !          !12!   !  Exchange lower 4 bits
        (Ri),A   !    A,aRi  ! 1101011R !   !   !  ind reg, reg A
```

Math Operations

```
ADD              ! ADD       !          !12!COA!  Add
        Rr,A     !    A,Rr   ! 00101RRR !   !   !  reg, reg A
        PZ a,A   !    A,a    ! 25       !   !   !  8-bit data adr, reg A
        (Ri),A   !    A,aRi  ! 0010011i !   !   !  ind reg R0 or R1, reg A
        #n,A     !    A,#n   ! 24       !   !   !  immed, reg A
ADC              ! ADC       !          !12!COA!  Add w/carry
        Rr,A     !    A,Rr   ! 00111RRR !   !   !  reg, reg A
        PZ a,A   !    A,a    ! 35       !   !   !  8-bit data adr, reg A
        (Ri),A   !    A,aRi  ! 0011011R !   !   !  ind reg R0 or R1, reg A
        #n,A     !    A,#n   ! 34       !   !   !  immed, reg A
INC              ! INC       !          !12!   !  Increment
        A        !    A      ! 04       !   !   !  reg A
        Rr       !    Rr     ! 00001RRR !   !   !  reg
        PZ a     !    a      ! 05       !   !   !  8-bit data adr
        (Ri)     !    aRi    ! 0000011i !   !   !  ind reg R0 or R1
INCW    DPTR     ! DPTR      ! A3       !24!   !  Increment word   DPTR
SBB              ! SUBB      !          !12!COA!  Subtract w/borrow
        Rr,A     !    A,Rr   ! 10011RRR !   !   !  reg, reg A
        PZ a,A   !    A,a    ! 95       !   !   !  8-bit data adr, reg A
        (Ri),A   !    A,aRi  ! 1001011i !   !   !  ind reg R0 or R1, reg A
        #n,A     !    A,#n   ! 94       !   !   !  immed, reg A
DEC              ! DEC       !          !12!   !  Decrement
        A        !    A      ! 14       !   !   !  reg A
        Rr       !    Rr     ! 00011RRR !   !   !  reg
        PZ a     !    a      ! 15       !   !   !  8-bit data adr
        (Ri)     !    aRi    ! 0001011i !   !   !  ind reg R0 or R1
DA  A            ! DA  A     ! D4       !12!C  !  Decimal adjust reg A
DIV              ! DIV       !          !48!CO !  Devide
        A,B      !    AB     ! 84       !   !   !  A/B,  A=val  B=remainder
MUL              ! MUL       !          !48!CO !  Multiply
        A,B      !    AB     ! A4       !   !   !  A x B, A=LSB B=MSB
```

Bit Operations

```
RESF             ! CLR       !          !12!   !  Reset flag
        C        !    C      ! C3       !   !C  !  carry
RESB    bit      !    bit    ! C2       !   !   !  Reset bit
SETF             ! SETB      !          !12!   !  Set flag
        C        !    C      ! D3       !   !C  !  carry
SETB    bit      !    bit    ! D2       !   !   !  Set bit
CPLF             ! CPL       !          !12!   !  Complement flag
        C        !    C      ! B3       !   !C  !  carry
CPLB    bit      !    bit    ! B2       !   !   !  Complement bit
ANDB             ! ANL       !          !24!C  !  Logical AND bit
        bit,C    !    C,bit  ! 82       !   !   !  bit, C flag
        /bit,C   !    C,/bit ! B0       !   !   !  not bit, C flag
ORB              ! ORL       !          !24!C  !  Logical OR bit
        bit,C    !    C,bit  ! 72       !   !   !  bit, C flag
        /bit,C   !    C,/bit ! A0       !   !   !  not bit, C flag
```

Logical Operations

```
AND              ! ANL       !          !12!   !  Logical AND
        Rr,A     !    A,Rr   ! 01011RRR !   !   !  reg, reg A
        PZ a,A   !    A,a    ! 55       !   !   !  8-bit data adr, reg A
        (Ri),A   !    A,aRi  ! 0101011R !   !   !  ind reg R0 or R1, reg A
```

#n,A	A,#n	54			immed, reg A
A,PZ a	a,A	52			reg A, 8-bit adr
#n,PZ a	a,#n	53	|24|	immed, 8-bit adr
OR	ORL		|12|	Logical OR
Rr,A	A,Rr	01001RRR			reg, reg A
PZ a,A	A,a	45			8-bit data adr, reg A
(Ri),A	A,@Ri	0100011R			ind reg R0 or R1, reg A
#n,A	A,#n	44			immed, reg A
A,PZ a	a,A	42			reg A, 8-bit adr
#n,PZ a	a,#n	43	|24|	immed, 8-bit adr
XOR	XRL		|12|	Logical Exclusive OR
Rr,A	A,Rr	01101RRR			reg, reg A
PZ a,A	A,a	65			8-bit data adr, reg A
(Ri),A	A,@Ri	0110011R			ind reg R0 or R1, reg A
#n,A	A,#n	64			immed, reg A
A,PZ a	a,A	62			reg A, 8-bit adr
#n,PZ a	a,#n	63	|24|	immed, 8-bit adr
CPL	CPL		|12|	Complement
A	A	F4			reg A
RRWC	RRC		|12|C	Rotate right w/carry
A	A	13			reg A
RLWC	RLC		|12|C	Rotate left w/carry
A	A	33			reg A
RLNC	RL		|12|	Rotate left no carry
A	A	23			reg A
RRNC	RR		|12|	Rotate right no carry
A	A	03			reg A

Program Control

CALLSP			|24|	Call subroutine, same page
ss	ACALL ss	AAA10001			uncond, page adr
		AAAAAAAA			
CALL			|24|	Call subroutine, absolute
aa	LCALL aa	12			uncond, abs adr
RET	RET		|24|	Return from subroutine
		22			uncond
RETI	RETI	32	|24|	Return from interrupt
		93			uncond
JMPSP			|24|	Jump same page if
ss	AJMP ss	AAA00001			uncond, page adr
		AAAAAAAA			
JMP			|24|	Jump if
aa	LJMP aa	02			uncond, abs adr
(A+DPTR)	JMP @A+DPTR	73			uncond, indexed A + DPTR)
JMPR			|24|	Jump relative if
UN,r	SJMP r	80			uncond
C,r	JC r	40			carry
NC,r	JNC r	50			no carry
Z,r	JZ r	60			A=0
NZ,r	JNZ r	70			A not zero
BS,bit,r	JB bit,r	20			bit set
BR,bit,r	JNB bit,r	30			bit reset
JMPCLR	JBC		|24|	Jump if bit set and clear
BS,bit,r	bit,r	10			bit, rel adr
DECJNZ	DJNZ		|24|	Decrement and skip if not 0
Rn,r	Rn,r	11011RRR			reg, rel adr
PZ a,r	a,r	D5			8-bit adr, rel adr
CMPJMP			|24|	Compare and jump if
A,NE,PZ a,r	CJNE A,a,r	B5		C	A, <>,8-bit adr,rel adr
A,NE,#n,r	A,n,r	B4			A, not =,immed, rel adr
Rn,NE,#n,r	Rn,#n,r	10111RRR			reg, not =,immed, rel adr

```
     (Ri),NE,n,r|   @Ri,#n,r| 1011011i |  |    | ind_reg, <>,immed, rel adr
   NOP          | NOP        | 00000000 |12|    | No operation
                |            |          |  |    |
```

Registers

     128 bytes RAM, 256 bytes for 8052 and 8032
which includes the following special function registers.

```
     A        accumulator      loc E0  $
     B        register             F0  $
     PSW      prog status wrd      D0  $
     SP       stack pointer       81      initialized to 07
     DPTR     data pointer        82,83   16-bit adr
     P0       port 0  latch       80  $
     P1       port 1  latch       90  $
     P2       port 2  latch       A0  $
     P3       port 3  latch       B0  $
     IP       interrupt priority  B8  $
     IE       interrupt enable    A8  $
     TMOD     timer/counter mode  89

     TCON     timer/counter ctrl  88  $
  *  T2CON    timer/counter 2 ctrl C8    (8052)
     TH0      t/c 0 high byte     8C
     TL0      t/c 0 low byte      8A
     TH1      t/c 1 high byte     8D
     TL1      t/c 1 low byte      8B
  *  TH2      t/c 2 high byte     CD    (8052)
  *  TL2      t/c 2 low byte      CC    (8052)
  *  RCAP2H   t/c capture high byte CB   (8052)
  *  RCAP2L   t/c capture low byte CA    (8052)
  *  SCON     serial control      98  $ (not 8044)
  *  SBUF     serial data buffer  99    (not 8044)
     PCON     power control       87
  *  SMD      serial mode         C9    (1)
  *  STS      status command      C8  $ (1)
  *  NSNR     send/receive count  D8  $ (1)
  *  STAD     station address     CE    (1)
  *  TBS      xmt buffer address  DC    (1)
  *  TBL      xmt buffer length   DB    (1)
  *  TCB      xmt control byte    DA    (1)
  *  RBS      rcv buffer address  CC    (1)
  *  RBL      rcv buffer length   CB    (1)
  *  RFL      received field length CD   (1)
  *  RCB      received control byte CA    (1)
  *  DMACNT   dma count           CF    (1)
  *  FIFO     fifo, three bytes   DD-DF (1)
  *  SIUST    siu state counter   D9    (1)
```

$ = bit addressable locations,   address = loc + bit number

The above will vary between micros.

Special Memory Locations

Separate 64K address space for program and data

Flags

  CY = carry flag   bit 7

```
AC = auxilary carry          6
F0 = flag 0                  5
RS1= register bank select    4
RS0= register bank select    3
         RS1 RS0  registers
          0   0    00-07
          0   1    08-0F
          1   0    10-17
          1   1    18-1F
OV = overflow                2
P  = parity                  0
```

Addressing Modes

```
Univ  Manuf
----  -----

#n    n       - immediate
Rn    Rn      - register
PZ a  a       - absolute 8-bit data address
ss    ss      - same page address, 11-bits, +-2K page
aa    aa      - absolute 16-bit program address
r     r       - relative address
(Ri)  @Ri     - indirect register, 8-bit address
(DPTR) @DPTR  - indirect register pair, 16-bit address
(A+XX) @A+XX  - indexed, register A + register PC or DPTR
aa:b  bit     - bit address, register location + bit number
```

Instruction Expansion

```
Rn    Register   RRR = 0 - 7  corresponding to R0 thru R7 respectively
Ri    ind reg    I = 0 for reg R0, = 1 for reg R1
n     immediate  8-bit value appended to instruction
nn    immediate  16-bit value appended to inst, MSB first
a     data adr   8-bit data address appended to instruction
aa    prog adr   16-bit address appended to instruction, MSB first
ss    page adr   11 bit address, most significant 3-bit part of inst
                         least significant 8-bits appended
r     rel adr    8 bit relative address appended to instruction
aa:b  bit adr    8 bit address appended to inst (reg loc + bit number)

address value (a) is appended before immediate data
                   or before rel address (r)
immediate data appended before rel address (r)
bit address is appended before rel address
```

Notes

```
16 bit data and addresses are stored MSB first, LSB second
```

8080

INS8080A   ,) 8085, HS80C85RH, uPD8085A, TMP8085

Data Move

```
MOV    !       !        !        ! !  ! Move byte
   aa,A  ! LDA aa   ! 3A   !13!  !    abs, reg A
   (BC),A ! LDAX B  ! 0A   ! 7!  !    ind BC, reg A
   (DE),A !    D    ! 1A   ! 7!  !    ind DE, reg A
```

(HL),Reg	MOV Reg,M	01RRR110	7		ind HL, Reg
Reg,Reg	Reg,Reg	01DDDSSS	5		srce, dest
Reg,(HL)	M,Reg	01110RRR	7		Reg, ind HL
#n,Reg	MVI Reg,n	00RRR110	7		immed, Reg
#n,(HL)	M,n	36	10		immed, ind HL
A,aa	STA aa	32	13		reg A, abs
A,(BC)	STAX B	02	7		reg A, ind BC
A,(DE)	D	12	7		reg A, ind D
MOVW					Move word
aa,HL	LHLD aa	2A	16		abs, reg HL
HL,aa	SHLD aa	22	16		reg HL, abs
#nn,Reg	LXI Reg,nn	00RR0001	10		immed, Reg
HL,SP	SPHL	F9	5		reg HL, reg SP
PUSH	PUSH				Push word onto the stack
BC	B	C5	11		reg BC
DE	D	D5	11		reg DE
HL	H	E5	11		reg HL
PSW	PSW	F5	11		reg PSW
POP	POP				Pop word from the stack
BC	B	C1	11		reg BC
DE	D	D1	11		reg DE
HL	H	E1	11		reg HL
PSW	PSW	F1	11	all	reg PSW
XCHGW					Exchange words
DE,HL	XCHG	EB	4		reg DE & reg HL
HL,(SP)	XTHL	E3	18		reg HL & ind SP

Math Operations

ADD	ADD			all	Add byte
Reg,A	Reg	10000RRR	4		Reg, reg A
(HL),A	M	86	7		ind HL, reg A
#n,A	ADI	C6	7	all	immed, reg A
ADDW	DAD			C	Add word
Reg,HL	Reg	00RR1001	10		Reg, reg HL
ADC	ADC			all	Add byte w/c,
Reg,A	Reg	10001RRR	4		Reg, reg A
(HL),A	M	8E	7		ind HL, reg A
#n,A	ACI	CE	7	all	immed, reg A
INC	INR			-C	Increment byte
Reg	Reg	00RRR100	5		Reg
(HL)	M	34	10		ind HL
INCW	INX				Increment word
Reg	Reg	00RR0011	5		Reg
SUB	SUB			all	Subtract byte
Reg,A	Reg	10010RRR	4		Reg, reg A
(HL),A	M	96	7		ind HL, reg A
#n,A	SUI	D6	7	all	immed, reg A
SBB	SBB			all	Subtract byte w/c
Reg,A	Reg	10011RRR	4		Reg, reg A
(HL),A	M	9E	7		ind HL, reg A
#n,A	SBI	DE	7	all	immed, reg A
DA	DAA			all	Decimal adjust Accum
A		27	4		
DEC	DCR			-C	Decrement byte
Reg	Reg	00RRR101	5		Reg
(HL)	M	35	10		ind HL
DECW	DCX				Decrement word
Reg	Reg	00RR1011	5		Reg
CMP	CMP			all	Compare byte
A,Reg	Reg	10111RRR	4		Reg, reg A
A,(HL)	M	BE	7		ind HL, reg A

```
     A,#n      ! CPI     !         ! FE    ! 7!all!   immed, reg A
```

Bit Operations

```
CPLF        ! CMC     !         !       ! !C ! Complement flag
   C        !         !         ! 3F    ! 4! !    Carry
SETF        ! STC     !         !       ! ! ! Set flag
   C        !         !         ! 37    ! 4!C !    Carry
```

Logical Operations

```
AND         ! ANA     !         !       ! !all! Logical AND byte
   Reg,A    !    Reg  ! 10100RRR ! 4!  !    Reg, reg A
   (HL),A   !    M    ! A6      !       ! 7! !    ind HL, reg A
   #n,A     ! ANI n   ! E6      !       ! 7!all!    immed, reg A
OR          ! ORA     !         !       ! !all! Logical OR byte
   Reg,A    !    Reg  ! 10110RRR ! 4!  !    Reg, reg A
   (HL),A   !    M    ! B6      !       ! 7! !    ind HL, reg A
   #n,A     ! ORI n   ! F6      !       ! 7!all!    immed, reg A
XOR         ! XRA     !         !       ! !all! Logical Exclusive OR byte
   Reg,A    !    Reg  ! 10101RRR ! 4!  !    Reg, reg A
   (HL),A   !    M    ! AE      !       ! 7! !    ind HL, reg A
   #n,A     ! XRI n   ! EE      !       ! 7!all!    immed, reg A
CPL         ! CMA     !         !       ! ! ! Complement byte
   A        !         !         ! 2F    ! 4! !    reg A
RLWC        ! RAL     !         !       ! !C ! Rotate byte w/c left
   A        !         !         ! 17    ! 4! !    reg A
RRWC        ! RAR     !         !       ! !C ! Rotate byte w/c right
   A        !         !         ! 1F    ! 4! !    reg A
RLTC        ! RLC     !         !       ! !C ! Rotate byte left to/c
   A        !         !         ! 07    ! 4! !    reg A
RRTC        ! RRC     !         !       ! !C ! Rotate byte right to/c
   A        !         !         ! 0F    ! 4! !    reg A
```

Program Control

```
CALL        ! CALL    !         !       ! 9! ! Call subroutine
   UN,aa    !    aa   !         ! CD    !18! !    uncond, abs
   Z,aa     ! CZ aa   !         ! CC    !18! !    zero, abs
   NZ,aa    ! CNZ aa  !         ! C4    !18! !    not zero, abs
   P,aa     ! CP aa   !         ! F4    !18! !    positive, abs
   M,aa     ! CM aa   !         ! FC    !18! !    minus, abs
   C,aa     ! CC aa   !         ! DC    !18! !    carry set, abs
   NC,aa    ! CNC aa  !         ! D4    !18! !    carry reset, abs
   PE,aa    ! CPE aa  !         ! EC    !18! !    parity even, abs
   PO,aa    ! CPO aa  !         ! E4    !18! !    parity odd, abs
RET         ! RET     !         !       ! 6! ! Return from subroutine
   UN       !         !         ! C9    !10! !    uncond
   Z        ! RZ      !         ! C8    !12! !    zero
   NZ       ! RNZ     !         ! C0    !12! !    not zero
   P        ! RP      !         ! F0    !12! !    plus
   M        ! RM      !         ! F8    !12! !    minus
   C        ! RC      !         ! D8    !12! !    carry set
   NC       ! RNC     !         ! D0    !12! !    carry reset
   PE       ! RPE     !         ! E8    !12! !    parity even
   PO       ! RPO     !         ! E0    !12! !    parity odd
JMP         ! JMP     !         !       ! 7! ! Jump to location
   UN,aa    !    aa   !         ! C3    !10! !    uncond, abs
   Z,aa     ! JZ aa   !         ! CA    !10! !    zero, abs
   NZ,aa    ! JNZ aa  !         ! C2    !10! !    not zero, abs
   P,aa     ! JP aa   !         ! F2    !10! !    positive, abs
   M,aa     ! JM aa   !         ! FA    !10! !    minus, abs
```

```
       C,aa    | JC  aa  | DA       |10|  |  carry set, abs
       NC,aa   | JNC aa  | D2       |10|  |  no carry, abs
       PE,aa   | JPE aa  | EA       |10|  |  parity even, abs
       PO,aa   | JPO aa  | E2       |10|  |  parity odd, abs
       UN,(HL) | PCHL    | E9       | 5|  |  uncond, ind HL
RST            | RST     |          |  |  |  Restart at location
       t       |    t    | 11TTT111 |11|  |    t = 0 (00H) to 7 (38H)
HALT           | HALT    | 76       | 7|  |  Stop till interrupt
NOP            | NOP     | 00       | 4|  |  No operation
```

I/O Operations

```
IN             | IN      |          |  |  |  Input byte
       P,A     |      P  | DB       |10|  |    reg A, port p
OUT            | OUT     |          |  |  |  Output byte
       A,p     |      P  | D3       |10|  |    port p, reg A
DI             | DI      | F3       | 4|  |  Disable interrupts
EI             | EI      | FB       | 4|  |  Enable interrupts
* RIM          |RIM      | 20       | 4|  |  Read interrupt mask   (1)
* SETIM        |SIM      | 30       | 4|  |  Set interrup mask     (1)
```

Registers

```
          16      8|7      0
          -------------------
PSW  |    A    |  Flags  |
          -------------------
BC   |    B    |    C    |
          -------------------
DE   |    D    |    E    |
          -------------------
HL   |    H    |    L    |
          -------------------

          -------------------
SP   |   Stack Pointer   |
          -------------------
PC   |  Program Counter  |
          -------------------
```

Addressing Modes

```
Univ  Manuf
----  -----
#n    n    - immediate data
XX    XX   - register
aa    aa   - absolute address
(HL)  M    - indirect register HL
(SP)       - indirect register SP
```

Notes

    None

Flags

    S = sign of result
    Z = zero result
    A = auxilary carry from bit 3
    P = parity
    C = carry

Instruction Expansion

```
              Reg
              ---
   Byte  RRR     Word  RR
   ----  ---     ----  --
    A    111     BC    00
    B    000     DE    01
    C    001     HL    10
    D    010     SP    11
    E    011
    H    100     DDD = to register
    L    101     SSS = from register
```

```
n    immediate data, 8-bits appended to inst
nn   immediate data, 16-bits appended to inst
t    restart number, 3-bits part of inst
p    port address, 8-bits appended to inst
aa   absolute adr, 16-bits appended to inst
```

Special Memory Locations

```
     None
```

8086

8088, 80C86, 80C88, iAPX86, iAPX88, SAB8086, SAB8088
(1) 80186 (AMD), iAPX186, iAPX188
(1,2) 80286, iAPX286, SAB80286   (3) uPD70116, uPD70108

Data Move

```
MOV            !            !                   ! !  !Move byte
  FF,AH        ! LAHF       ! 9F                ! !  !   reg FF, reg AH
  AH,FF        ! SAHF       ! 9E                ! !J!   reg AH, reg FF
  (BX+AL),AL!  XLAT        ! D7                ! !  !   ind BX+AL, reg AL
MOV [W]        ! MOV        !                   ! !  !Move
  Reg,Reg      ! Reg,Reg    ! 1000100W 11FFFTTT ! 2!  !   Reg, Reg
  Mem,Reg      ! Reg,Mem    ! 1000101W DDRRRMMM ! 8+! !   memory, reg
  Reg,Mem      ! Mem,Reg    ! 1000100W DDRRRMMM ! 9+! !   reg, memory
  #n,Mem       ! Mem,n      ! 1100011W DD000MMM !10+! !   immed, memory
  #n,Reg       ! Reg,n      ! 1011WRRR          ! 4!  !   immed, reg
  aa,A         ! A,aa       ! 1010000W          !10!  !   abs, reg A
  A,aa         ! aa,A       ! 1010001W          !10!  !   reg A, abs
MOVW           !            !                   ! !  !Move word
  Reg,Seg      ! Seg,Reg    ! 8E,110SSRRR       ! 2!  !   reg, seg
  Mem,Seg      ! Seg,Mem    ! 8E,DD0SSMMM       ! 8+! !   memory, seg
  Seg,Reg      ! Reg,Seg    ! 8C,110SSRRR       ! 2!  !   seg, reg
  Seg,Mem      ! Mem,Seg    ! 8C,DD0SSMMM       ! 9+! !   seg, memory
MOVD           !            !                   ! !  !Move 2 words, from to to
  Mem,DS,Reg! LDS Reg,Mem!  C5,DDRRRMMM        !16+! !   memory, reg DS, Reg
  Mem,ES,Reg! LES Reg,Mem!  C4,DDRRRMMM        !16+! !   memory, reg ES, Reg
* MOVBS        ! INS        !                   ! !  !Move bits  (3)
  A,(DS+IY):!   Rb,Rc      ! 0F,31,11RRRRRR     !67+! !   Rc bits, from bit 0
  Rb,Rc        !            !                   ! !  !   A to (DS+IY) bit Rb
  A,(DS+IY):!   Rb,n       ! 0F,31,11000RRR     !67+! !   n bits, from bit 0
  Rb,#n        !            !                   ! !  !   A to (DS+IY) bit Rb
```

(DS+IY):Rb	Ext Rb,Rc	0F,33,11RRRRRR	67+		Rc bits, to bit 0 of A
A,Rc					from (DS+IX) bit Rb
(DS+IY):Rb	Rb,n	0F,33,11000RRR	67+		n bits, to bit 0 reg A
A,#n					from (DS+IX) bit Rb
PUSH	PUSH				Push word onto the stack
Mem	Mem	FF,DD110MMM	16+		memory
Reg	Reg	01010RRR	8		Reg
Seg	Seg	000SS110	10		Seg
* [S]nn	nn	011010S1	10		immed (1,3)
FF	PUSHF	9C	10		reg FF
*PUSHA	PUSHA	60	36		all (1,3)
POP	POP				Pop word from the stack
Mem	Mem	8F,DD000MMM	17+		memory
Reg	Reg	01011RRR	8		Reg
Seg	Seg	000SS111	8		Seg
FF	POPF	9D	8	E	reg FF
*POPA	POPA	61	51	E	all (1,3)
XCHG [W]	XCHG				Exchange
Reg,Reg	Reg,Reg	1000011W 11TTTFFF	4		Reg, Reg
Reg,Mem	Reg,Mem	1000011W DDRRRMMM	17+		Reg, memory
XCHGW					Exchange word
AX,Reg	Reg,AX	10010RRR	3		Reg, reg AX
LEA	LEA				Load efective address
Mem,Reg	Reg,Mem	8D,DDRRRMMM	3		memory, reg

Math Operations

ADD [W]	ADD			C	Add
Reg,Reg	Reg,Reg	0000000W 11FFFTTT	3		Reg, Reg
Mem,Reg	Reg,Mem	0000001W DDRRRMMM	9+		memory, Reg
Reg,Mem	Mem,Reg	0000000W DDRRRMMM	16+		reg, memory
[S]#nn,Reg	Reg,n	100000SW 11000RRR	4		immed, Reg
[S]#nn,Mem	Mem,n	100000SW DD000MMM	17+		immed, memory
#nn,Acc	Acc,n	0000010W			immed, accum
ADC [W]	ADC			C	Add w/c
Reg,Reg	Reg,Reg	0001000W 11FFFTTT	3		Reg, Reg
Mem,Reg	Reg,Mem	0001001W DDRRRMMM	9+		memory, Reg
Reg,Mem	Mem,Reg	0001000W DDRRRMMM	16+		reg, memory
[S]#nn,Reg	Reg,n	100000SW 11010RRR	4		immed, Reg
[S]#nn,Mem	Mem,n	100000SW DD010MMM	17+		immed, memory
#nn,Acc	Acc,n	0001010W	4		immed, accum
* ADDBCD	ADD4S				Add BCD string (3)
(IX),(IY),CL		0F,20	19+		ind IX to ind IY for CL
INC	INC			G	Increment byte
Reg	Reg	FE,11000RRR	3		Reg
INC [W]					Increment
Mem	Mem	1111111W DD000MMM	15+		memory
INCW					Increment word
Reg	Reg	01000RRR	3		Reg
SUB [W]	SUB			C	Subtract
Reg,Reg	Reg,Reg	0010100W 11FFFTTT	3		Reg, Reg
Mem,Reg	Reg,Mem	0010101W DDRRRMMM	9+		memory, Reg
Reg,Mem	Mem,Reg	0010100W DDRRRMMM	16+		reg, memory
[S]#nn,Reg	Reg,n	100000SW 11101RRR	4		immed, Reg
[S]#nn,Mem	Mem,n	100000SW DD101MMM	17+		immed, memory
#nn,Acc	Acc,n	0010110W			immed, accum
SBB [W]	SBB			C	Subtract w/c
Reg,Reg	Reg,Reg	0001100W 11FFFTTT	3		Reg, Reg
Mem,Reg	Reg,Mem	0001101W DDRRRMMM	9+		memory, Reg
Reg,Mem	Mem,Reg	0001100W DDRRRMMM	16+		reg, memory
[S]#nn,Reg	Reg,n	100000SW 11011RRR	4		immed, Reg
[S]#nn,Mem	Mem,n	100000SW DD011MMM	17+		immed, memory

```
          #nn,Acc   |    Acc,n    | 0001110W          |  4|  |   immed, accum
  * SUBBCD           | SUB4S       |                   |   |  |:Sub BCD string  (3)
    (IX),(IY),CL:    |             |    0F,22          |19+|  |   ind IX frm ind IY for CL
AA                   |             |                   |   |  |:ASCII adjust for
    A                | AAA         | 37                |  8|A|   add
    S                | AAS         | 3F                |  8|A|   subtract
    M                | AAM         | D4,0A             | 83|B|   multiply
    D                | AAD         | D5,0A             | 60|B|   devide
DA                   |             |                   |   |  |:Decimal adjust Accum
    A                | DAA         | 27                |  4|M|   add
    S                | DAS         | 2F                |  4|M|   subtract
DEC                  | DEC         |                   |   |G|:Decrement byte
    Reg              |    Reg      | FE,11001RRR       |  3|  |   Reg
DEC [W]              |             |                   |   |  |:Decrement
    Mem              |    Mem      | 1111111W DD001MMM |15+|  |   memory
DECW                 |             |                   |   |  |:Decrement word
    Reg              |    Reg      | 01001RRR          |  3|  |   Reg
NEG [W]              | NEG         |                   |   |C|:Change sign
    Reg              |    Reg      | 1111011W 11011RRR |  3|  |   Reg
    Mem              |    Mem      | 1111011W DD011MMM |16+|  |   memory
MUL [W]              | MUL         |                   |   |L|:Binary Multiply
    Reg,Acc          |    Reg      | 1111011W 11100RRR |70+|  |   reg, accum
    Mem,Acc          |    Mem      | 1111011W DD100MMM |76+|  |   memory, accum
IMUL [W]             | IMUL        |                   |   |L|:Integer Multiply
    Reg,Acc          |    Reg      | 1111011W 11101RRR |80+|  |   Reg, accum
    Mem,Acc          |    Mem      | 1111011W DD101MMM |86+|  |   memory, accum
IMULW                |             |                   |   |  |
  * [S]nn,Reg        |    Reg,nn   | 011010S1 11101RRR |22+|  |   immed, reg (1)
  * [S]nn,Mem        |    Mem,nn   | 011010S1 DD101MMM |22+|  |   immed, mem (1)
  * [S]nn,Reg,Reg!   | Reg,Reg,nn  | 011010S1 11RRRRRR |34+|  |   Reg = Reg x immed (3)
  * [S]nn,Reg,Mem!   | Reg,Mem,nn  | 011010S1 DDRRRMMM |34+|  |   Reg = Mem x immed (3)
DIV [W]              | DIV         |                   |   |K|:Binary Devide
    Reg,Acc          |    Reg      | 1111011W 11110RRR |80+|  |   Reg, accum
    Mem,Acc          |    Mem      | 1111011W DD110MMM |86+|  |   memory, accum
IDIV [W]             | IDIV        |                   |   |K|:Integer Devide
    Reg,Acc          |    Reg      | 1111011W 11111RRR |101|  |   reg, accum
    Mem,Acc          |    Mem      | 1111011W DD111RRR |107|  |   memory, accum
CMP [W]              | CMP         |                   |   |C|:Compare
    Reg,Reg          | Reg,Reg     | 0011101W 11FFFTTT |  3|  |   Reg, Reg
    Reg,Mem          | Reg,Mem     | 0011101W DDRRRMMM |  9+|  |   reg, memory
    Mem,Reg          | Mem,Reg     | 0011100W DDRRRMMM |  9+|  |   reg, memory
    Reg,[S]n         | Reg,n       | 100000SW 11111RRR |  4|  |   reg, immed
    Mem,[S]n         | Mum,n       | 100000SW DD111MMM |10+|  |   memory, immed
    Acc,#nn          | Acc,n       | 0011110W          |  4|  |   accum, immed
  * CMPBCD           | CMP4S       |                   |   |  |:Compare BCD string  (3)
    (IX),(IY),CL:    |             |    0F,26          |19+|  |   ind IX, ind IY for CL
CNVBW    AX          | CBW         | 98                |  2|  |:Convert, byte to word
CNVWDW   DXAX        | CWD         | 99                |  5|  |          wrd to dble wrd

Logical Operations
------------------

AND [W]              | AND         |                   |   |D|:Logical AND
    Reg,Reg          | Reg,Reg     | 0010000W 11FFFTTT |  3|  |   Reg, Reg
    Mem,Reg          | Reg,Mem     | 0010001W DDRRRMMM |  9+|  |   memory, reg
    Reg,Mem          | Mem,Reg     | 0010000W DDRRRMMM |16+|  |   reg, memory
    #nn,Reg          | Reg,n       | 1000000W 11100RRR |  4|  |   immed, reg
    #nn,Mem          | Mem,n       | 1000000W DD100MMM |17+|  |   immed, memory
    #nn,Acc          | Acc,n       | 0010010W          |  4|  |   immed, accum
TEST [W]             | TEST        |                   |   |D|:Logical AND to flags only
    Reg,Reg          | Reg,Reg     | 1000010W 11FFFTTT |  3|  |   Reg, Reg
    Mem,Reg          | Reg,Mem     | 1000010W DDRRRMMM |  9+|  |   memory, reg
```

```
    #nn,Reg     |   Reg,n    | 1111011W 11000RRR |  5| |  immed, reg
    #nn,Mem     |   Mem,n    | 1111011W DD000MMM |11+| |  immed, memory
    #nn,Acc     |   Acc,n    | 1010100W          |   | |  immed, accum
 OR [W]         | OR         |                   |  D|Logical OR
    Reg,Reg     |   Reg,Reg  | 0000100W 11FFFTTT |  3| |  Reg, Reg
    Mem,Reg     |   Reg,Mem  | 0000101W DDRRRMMM |  9+| |  memory, reg
    Reg,Mem     |   Mem,Reg  | 0000100W DDRRRMMM |16+| |  reg, memory
    #nn,Reg     |   Reg,n    | 1000000W 11001RRR |  4| |  immed, reg
    #nn,Mem     |   Mem,n    | 1000000W DD001MMM |17+| |  immed, memory
    #nn,Acc     |   Acc,n    | 0000110W          |  4| |  immed, accum
 XOR (W)        | XOR        |                   |  D|Logical Exclusive OR
    Reg,Reg     |   Reg,Reg  | 0011000W 11FFFTTT |  3| |  Reg, Reg
    Mem,Reg     |   Reg,Mem  | 0011001W DDRRRMMM |  9+| |  memory, reg
    Reg,Mem     |   Mem,Reg  | 0011000W DDRRRMMM |16+| |  reg, memory
    #nn,Reg     |   Reg,n    | 1000000W 11110RRR |  4| |  immed, reg
    #nn,Mem     |   Mem,n    | 1000000W DD110MMM |17+| |  immed, memory
    #nn,Acc     |   Acc,n    | 0011010W          |   | |  immed, accum
 CPL (W)        | NOT        |                   |   | |Complement
    Reg         |   Reg      | 1111011W 11010RRR |  3| |  Reg
    Mem         |   Mem      | 1111011W DD010MMM |16+| |  memory
 RLWC (W)       | RCL        |                   |   |H|Rotate w/c left
    Reg,[CL]    |   Reg,[CL] | 110100VW 11010RRR |  2+| |  Reg, [reg CL]
    Mem,[CL]    |   Mem,[CL] | 110100VW DD010MMM | 15| |  memory, [reg CL]
 *  Reg,#n      |   Reg,n    | 1100000W 11010RRR |  2+| |  Reg, count (1,3)
 *  Mem,#n      |   Mem,n    | 1100000W DD010MMM | 15| |  memory, count (1,3)
 RRWC [W]       | RCR        |                   |   |H|Rotate w/c right
    Reg,[CL]    |   Reg,[CL] | 110100VW 11011RRR |  2+| |  Reg, [reg CL]
    Mem,[CL]    |   Mem,[CL] | 110100VW DD011MMM | 15+| |  memory, [reg CL]
 *  Reg,#n      |   Reg,n    | 1100000W 11011RRR |  2+| |  Reg, count (1,3)
 *  Mem,#n      |   Mem,n    | 1100000W DD011MMM | 15+| |  memory, count (1,3)
 RLTC (W)       | ROL        |                   |   |H|Rotate left to/c
    Reg,[CL]    |   Reg,[CL] | 110100VW 11000RRR |  2+| |  Reg, [reg CL]
    Mem,[CL]    |   Mem,[CL] | 110100VW DD000MMM | 15+| |  memory, [reg CL]
 *  Reg,#n      |   Reg,n    | 1100000W 11000RRR |  2+| |  Reg, count (1,3)
 *  Mem,#n      |   Mem,n    | 1100000W DD000MMM | 15+| |  memory, count (1,3)
 RRTC (W)       | ROR        |                   |   |H|Rotate right to/c
    Reg,[CL]    |   Reg,[CL] | 110100VW 11001RRR |  2+| |  Reg, [reg CL]
    Mem,[CL]    |   Mem,[CL] | 110100VW DD001MMM | 15+| |  memory, [reg CL]
 *  Reg,#n      |   Reg,n    | 1100000W 11001RRR |  2+| |  Reg, count (1,3)
 *  Mem,#n      |   Mem,n    | 1100000W DD001MMM | 15+| |  memory, count (1,3)
 SLL (W)        | SHL/SAL    |                   |  D|Shift left arithmetic
    Reg,[CL]    |   Reg,[CL] | 110100VW 11100RRR |  2| |  Reg, [reg CL]
    Mem,[CL]    |   Mem,[CL] | 110100VW DD100MMM | 15+| |  memory, [reg CL]
 *  Reg,#n      |   Reg,n    | 1100000W 11100RRR |  2| |  Reg, count (1,3)
 *  Mem,#n      |   Mem,n    | 1100000W DD100MMM | 15+| |  memory, count (1,3)
 SRA (W)        | SAR        |                   |  D|Shift right arithmetic
    Reg,[CL]    |   Reg,[CL] | 110100VW 11111RRR |  2+| |  Reg, [reg CL]
    Mem,[CL]    |   Mem,[CL] | 110100VW DD111MMM | 15| |  memory, [reg CL]
 *  Reg,#n      |   Reg,n    | 1100000W 11111RRR |  2+| |  Reg, count (1,3)
 *  Mem,#n      |   Mem,n    | 1100000W DD111MMM | 15| |  memory, count (1,3)
 SRL (W)        | SHR        |                   |  D|Shift right logical
    Reg,[CL]    |   Reg,[CL] | 110100VW 11101RRR |  2+| |  Reg, [reg CL]
    Mem,[CL]    |   Mem,[CL] | 110100VW DD101MMM | 15+| |  memory, [reg CL]
 *  Reg,#n      |   Reg,n    | 1100000W 11101RRR |  2+| |  Reg, count (1,3)
 *  Mem,#n      |   Mem,n    | 1100000W DD101MMM | 15+| |  memory, count (1,3)
 * RLBCD        | ROL4       |                   |   |Rotate BCD left   (3)
    Reg,AL      |   Reg      | 0F,28,11000RRR    | 25| |  AL 4-bits and reg
    Mem,AL      |   Mem      | 0F,28,DD000MMM    | 28| |  AL 4-bits and memory
 * RRBCD        | ROR4       |                   |   |Rotate BCD right (3)
    Reg,AL      |   Reg      | 0F,2A,11000RRR    | 29| |  AL 4-bits and reg
    Mem,AL      |   Mem      | 0F,2A,DD000MMM    | 33| |  AL 4-bits and memory
```

339

String Operations

```
REP              :           :           :   :  :Repeat while
    Z            : REPZ      : F3        : 2:  :   zero
    NZ           : REPNZ     : F2        : 2:  :   non-zero
*   C            : REPC      : 65        : 2:  :   carry set    (3)
*   NC           : REPNC     : 64        : 2:  :   carry reset  (3)
MOVS [W]         : MOVS      :           :   :  :Move string
    (+SI),(+DI),CX:         : 1010010W  :18+:  :   ind DS SI,ind ES DI,CX
    (+SI),Acc    : LODS      : 1010110W  :12+:  :   ind SI, Accum
    Acc,(+DI)    : STOS      : 1010101W  :11 :  :   accum, ind SI
CMPS [W]         : CMPS      :           :   :C:Compare string
    (+DI),(+SI),CX:         : 1010011W  :22+:  :   ind DS SI,ind ES DI,CX
SCAN [W]         : SCAS      :           :   :C:Scan string
    (+SI),Acc,CX :          : 1010111W  :15+:  :   ind SI,Accum, reg CX
```

Bit Operations

```
CPLF             :           :           :   :  :Complement flag
    C            : CMC       : F5        : 2:F:   carry
RESF             :           :           :   :  :Reset flag
    C            : CLC       : F8        : 2:F:   carry
    D            : CLD       : FC        : 2:F:   direction
*   t            : CTS       : 0F,06     : 2:  :   task switch
SETF             :           :           :   :  :Set flag
    C            : STC       : F9        : 2:F:   carry
    D            : STD       : FD        : 2:F:   direction
* TESTB [W]      : TEST1     : 0F,       :   :  : Test bit   (3)
    Reg,CL       :   Reg,CL  : 0001000W,11000RRR  : 3:  :   reg, bit CL
    Mem,CL       :   Mem,CL  : 0001000W,DD000MMM  :12:  :   memory, bit CL
    Reg,#nn      :   Reg,nn  : 0001100W,11000RRR  : 4:  :   reg, bit immed
    Mem,#nn      :   Mem,CL  : 0001100W,DD000MMM  :13:  :   memory, bit immed
* CPLB  [W]      : NOT1      : 0F,       :   :  : Complement bit  (3)
    Reg,CL       :   Reg,CL  : 0001011W,11000RRR  : 4:  :   reg, bit CL
    Mem,CL       :   Mem,CL  : 0001011W,DD000MMM  :18:  :   memory, bit CL
    Reg,#nn      :   Reg,nn  : 0001111W,11000RRR  : 5:  :   reg, bit immed
    Mem,#nn      :   Mem,CL  : 0001111W,DD000MMM  :19:  :   memory, bit immed
* RESB  [W]      : CLR1      : 0F,       :   :  : Reset bit   (3)
    Reg,CL       :   Reg,CL  : 0001001W,11000RRR  : 5:  :   reg, bit CL
    Mem,CL       :   Mem,CL  : 0001001W,DD000MMM  :14:  :   memory, bit CL
    Reg,#nn      :   Reg,nn  : 0001101W,11000RRR  : 6:  :   reg, bit immed
    Mem,#nn      :   Mem,CL  : 0001101W,DD000MMM  :15:  :   memory, bit immed
* SETB  [W]      : SET1      : 0F,       :   :  : Set bit   (3)
    Reg,CL       :   Reg,CL  : 0001010W,11000RRR  : 4:  :   reg, bit CL
    Mem,CL       :   Mem,CL  : 0001010W,DD000MMM  :13:  :   memory, bit CL
    Reg,#nn      :   Reg,nn  : 0001110W,11000RRR  : 5:  :   reg, bit immed
    Mem,#nn      :   Mem,CL  : 0001110W,DD000MMM  :14:  :   memory, bit immed
```

Program Control

```
CALL         : CALL      :           :   :  :Call subroutine
    dd       :     dd    : E8        :19 :  :   uncond, disp
    (Mem)    :     (Mem) : FF,DD010MMM:21+:  :   uncond, memory
    (Reg)    :     (Reg) : FF,11010RRR:16 :  :   uncond, ind Reg
CALLOS       : CALLOS    :           :   :  :Call subr other seg
    dd ss    :     dd ss : 9A        :28 :  :   uncond, abs
    (Mem)    :     (Mem) : FF,DD011MMM:37+:  :   uncond, ind memory
    (Reg)    :     (Reg) : FF,11011RRR:37+:  :   uncond, ind Reg
RET          : RET       :           : 5 :  :Return from subroutine
             :           : C3        :16 :  :   uncond
    #nn      :     nn    : C2        :20 :  :   uncond, add immed SP
RETOS        : RETOS     :           :   :  :Return frm subr other seg
```

```
                          | CB        | 26| | uncond
  #nn        | nn         | CA        | 25| | uncond, add immed SP
RETI         | RETI       |           |   | |Return from interrupt
             |            | CF        | 32| | uncond
JMP          | JMP        |           |   | |Jump to location
   dd        | dd         | E9        | 15| | uncond, disp
   (Mem)     | (Mem)      | FF,DD100MMM|18+| | uncond, ind memory
   (Reg)     | (Reg)      | FF,11100RRR| 11| | uncond, ind Reg
JMPOS        | JMPOS      |           |   | |Jump other seg
   aa ss     | aa ss      | EA        | 15| | uncond, abs
   (Mem)     | (Mem)      | FF,DD101MMM|24+| | uncond, ind memory
   (Reg)     | (Reg)      | FF,11101RRR|24+| | uncond, ind Reg
JMPR         |            |           |  4| |Jump relative
   UN,r      | r          | EB        | 11| | uncond
   EQ,r      | JE r       | 74        | 16| | =
   SLT,r     | JL r       | 7C        | 16| | <
   SLE,r     | JLE r      | 7E        | 16| | < or =
   LT,r      | JB r       | 72        | 16| | below
   LE,r      | JBE r      | 76        | 16| | below or =
   PE,r      | JPE r      | 7A        | 16| | parity even
   V,r       | JO r       | 70        | 16| | overflow
   M,r       | JS r       | 78        | 16| | sign minus
   NE,r      | JNE r      | 75        | 16| | not =
   SGE,r     | JNL r      | 7D        | 16| | not <
   SGT,r     | JNLE r     | 7F        | 16| | not < or =
   GE,r      | JNB r      | 73        | 16| | not below
   GT,r      | JN BE r    | 77        | 16| | not below or =
   PO,r      | JPO r      | 7B        | 16| | parity odd
   NV,r      | JNO r      | 71        | 16| | no overflow
   P,r       | JNS r      | 79        | 16| | no sign
   CXZ,r     | JCXZ r     | E3        | 16| | reg CX = 0
SWI          | INT        |           | I|Software interrupt
   UN,t      | t          | CD        | 51| | uncond, type t
   UN,3      |            | CC        | 52| | uncond, type 3
   V         | INTO       | CE        | 52| | on overflow
   NZ,r      | NZ,r       | 20,xx     | 12| | not zero, rel
LOOPR        |            |           |   | |Loop on condition to
   CX,r      | LOOP r     | E2        | 5+| | reg CX times, rel
   Z,r       | LOOPZ r    | E1        | 5+| | while zero, rel
   NZ,r      | LOOPNZ r   | E0        | 5+| | while not zero, rel
HALT         | HLT        | F4        |  2| |Stop till interrupt
NOP          | NOP        | 90        |  3| |No operation
WAIT         | WAIT       | 9B        | 4+| |Wait for external device
ESC          | ESC        |           |   | |Call to external device
   xx,yy,Mem | DD,II,Mem  | 11011XXX DDYYYMMM | 8+| | device, inst, data loc
* ESC2       | ESC2       |           |   | | (3)
   xx,yy,Mem | DD,II,Mem  | 0110011X DDYYYMMM | 8+| | device, inst, data loc
LOCK         | LOCK       | F0        |  2| |Buss lock prefix
SEL          | SEG        |           |   | |Select segment to be used
   CS        | CS         | 2E        |  2| | code
   DS         | DS         | 3E        |  2| | data
   ES        | ES         | 26        |  2| | extra
   SS        | SS         | 36        |  2| | stack
```

I/O Operations

```
IN [W]       | IN         |           |   | |Input
   p,Acc     | p          | 1110010W  | 10| | port p, accum
   (DX),Acc  |            | 1110110W  |  8| | ind DX, accum
*INS [W]      | INS        |           |   | |Input string (1)
*  (SX),+(DI)|            | 0110110W  |  8| | inc SX;ind_inc DX (3)
   (SX),+(DI),CX|          | F2,0110110W| 8+| | inc SX;ind_inc Dx,CX
```

```
OUT [W]        ! OUT      !              !    ! !Output
   Acc,p       !   p      ! 1110011W     ! 10! !   accum, port p
   Acc,(DX)    !          ! 1110111W     !  8! !   accum, ind DX
*OUTS [W]      ! OUTS     !              !    ! !Output string (1)
*  +(SI),(DX)! !          ! 0110111W     !  8! !   ind_inc SI,ind DX (3)
   +(SI),(DX),CX!         ! F2,0110111W  ! 8+! !   ind_inc SI,ind DX,CX
DI             ! CLI      ! FA           !  2!F!Clear interrupt
EI             ! STI      ! FB           !  2!F!Set interrupt
```

Micro Unique Operations
————————————————————————————

```
(1,3)
———
ENTER          ! ENTER    !              !15+! !Enter procedure
   aa.l        !   aa,l   ! C8           !   ! !   data adr,length
               !          !              !   ! !   prepare new stack fram
LEAVE          ! LEAVE    ! C9           !  8! !Leave procedure
               !          !              !   ! !   release stack fram
   BOUND       ! BOUND    !              !   ! !Detect value out of range
      Reg,Mem  !    Reg,Mem ! 62,DDRRRMMM !33+! !   Reg > memory
               !          !              !   ! !         < memory + 2
               !          !              !   ! !   if not jump (loc 5)

(2)
———
LGDT           ! LGDT     !              ! 11! !Load global discriptor
   Reg         !   Reg    ! 0F,01,11010RRR !  ! !   table register
   Mem         !   Mem    ! 0F,01,DD010MMM !  ! !
SGDT           ! SGDT     !              ! 11! !Store global discriptor
   Reg         !   Reg    ! 0F,01,11000RRR !  ! !   table register
   Mem         !   Mem    ! 0F,01,DD000MMM !  ! !
LIDT           ! LIDT     !              ! 12! !Load interrupt discriptor
   Reg         !   Reg    ! 0F,01,11011RRR !  ! !   table register
   Mem         !   Mem    ! 0F,01,DD011MMM !  ! !
SIDT           ! SIDT     !              ! 12! !Store int discriptor
   Reg         !   Reg    ! 0F,01,11001RRR !  ! !   table register
   Mem         !   Mem    ! 0F,01,DD001MMM !  ! !
LLDT           ! LLDT     !              ! 11! !Load local discriptor
   Reg         !   Reg    ! 0F,00,11010RRR !  ! !   table register
   Mem         !   Mem    ! 0F,00,DD010MMM !  ! !
SLDT           ! SLDT     !              ! 11! !Store local discriptor
   Reg         !   Reg    ! 0F,00,11000RRR !  ! !   table register
   Mem         !   Mem    ! 0F,00,DD000MMM !  ! !
LTR            ! LTR      !              ! 19! !Load task register
   Reg         !   Reg    ! 0F,00,11011RRR !  ! !
   Mem         !   Mem    ! 0F,00,DD011MMM !  ! !
STR            ! STR      !              !  3! !Store task register
   Reg         !   Reg    ! 0F,00,11001RRR !  ! !
   Mem         !   Mem    ! 0F,00,DD001MMM !  ! !
LMSW           ! LMSW     !              !  6! !Load machine status
   Reg         !   Reg    ! 0F,01,11110RRR !  ! !
   Mem         !   Mem    ! 0F,01,DD110MMM !  ! !
SMSW           ! SMSW     !              !  3! !Store machine status
   Reg         !   Reg    ! 0F,01,11100RRR !  ! !
   Mem         !   Mem    ! 0F,01,DD100MMM !  ! !
LAR            ! LAR      !              ! 16! !Load access rights
   Reg         !   Reg    ! 0F,02,11xxxRRR !  ! !
   Mem         !   Mem    ! 0F,02,DDxxxMMM !  ! !
LSL            ! LSL      !              ! 16! !Load segment limits
   Reg         !   Reg    ! 0F,03,11xxxRRR !  ! !
   Mem         !   Mem    ! 0F,03,DDxxxMMM !  ! !
ARPL           ! ARPL     !              ! 11! !Adjust requested
   Reg         !   Reg    ! 63,11xxxRRR  !   ! !   privilege level
```

```
    Mem    !    Mem    ! 63,DDxxxMMM    !   !  !
VERR       ! VERR      !                ! 16! !Verify read access
    Reg    !    Reg    ! 0F,00,11100RRR !   !  !
    Mem    !    Mem    ! 0F,00,DD100MMM !   !  !
VERW       ! VERW      !                ! 16! !Verify write access
    Reg    !    Reg    ! 0F,00,11101RRR !   !  !
    Mem    !    Mem    ! 0F,00,DD101MMM !   !  !
(3)
---
SEL  EM,#n ! BRKEM  n  ! 0F,FF,nn       !38+! !Enter 8080 emulation
SEL  NM    ! RETEM     !                !27+! !Exit emulation mode
CALLN  #n  ! CALLN  n  ! ED,ED,nn       !38+! !Call native mode routine
           !           !                !   !  !
```

Registers

```
         16      8!7      0      16                 0
        ---------------------   ---------------------
  AX  !   AH   !   AL   !   CS  !   Code Segment   !
        ---------------------   ---------------------
  BX  !   BH   !   BL   !   DS  !   Data Segment   !
        ---------------------   ---------------------
  CX  !   CH   !   CL   !   SS  !   Stack Segment  !
        ---------------------   ---------------------
  DX  !   DH   !   DL   !   ES  !   Extra Segment  !
        ---------------------   ---------------------

        ---------------------   ---------------------
  SP  !   Stack Pointer   !   FF  !.n11ODITSZ.A.P.C!  Flags
        ---------------------   ---------------------
  BP  !   Base Pointer    !       !  Program Counter!
        ---------------------   ---------------------
  SI  !   Source Index    !  * MSW !............temp!  Status  (2)
        ---------------------   ---------------------
  DI  !     To Index      !
        ---------------------
```

Flags

Flags	Flag set code
S = sign of result	A = A C OU PU SU ZU
Z = zero result	B = AU CU OU P S Z
A = auxilary carry from bit 3	C = A C O P S Z
P = parity	D = AU C O P S Z
O = overflow	E = all flags
C = carry	F = no others
T = test (single step)	G = A O P S Z
I = interrupt enable	H = C O
D = direction	I = I T
* ll = I/O privalege level (2)	J = A C P S Z
* n = nested task flag (2)	K = AU CU OU PU SU ZU
* t = task switch (2)	L = AU C O PU SU ZU
* e = processor extension emulated (2)	M = A C OU P S Z
* m = monitor processor extension (2)	
* p = protection enable (2)	

Addressing Modes

Univ	Manuf	
#nn	nn	- immediate data, 8 or 16-bits
S#n	nn	- sign extended immediate value

```
XX          XX          - register
aa          aa          - absolute address
(XX)        (XX)        - indirect, register or memory
r           r           - relative address value
dd          dd          - displacement address value
ss:dd       dd ss       - displacement address and segment address
(XX+XX)     (XX+XX)     - indexed, one or more registers
(XX+n)      (XX+n)      - indexed, one or more registers and 8-bit value
(XX++nn)    (XX+nn)     - indexed, one or more registers and 16-bit value
+(XX)                   - indirect auto incremented
```

Efective Address

```
------------------
|              | |   Address specfied in the instruction
------------------  is added to the
|             |  |   Segment register shifted left 4 bits
------------------
|             |  |   20 bit physical address
------------------
```

*   For the 80286 (2)

```
------------------------------------
| Segment Reg   | Inst spec adr  |   32 bit physical address
------------------------------------
```

Instruction Expansion

Reg, Rb, Rc

Byte	Word	RRR		Seg	RR
AL	AX	000		ES	00
CL	CX	001		CS	01
DL	DX	010		SS	10
BL	BX	011		DS	11
AH	SP	100			
CH	BP	101			
DH	SI	110			
BH	DI	111			

```
TTT = to register
FFF = from register
CCC = bit count register
```

Mem

Mode	DD MMM	Mode	DD MMM	Mode	DD MMM	Mode	DD MMM
(BX)	00 111	(DI)	00 101	(BP+SI)	00 010	(BX+SI)	00 000
(BX+n)	01 111	(DI+n)	01 101	(BP+SI+n)	01 010	(BX+SI+n)	01 000
(BX++nn)	10 111	(DI++nn)	10 101	(BP+SI++nn)	10 010	(BX+SI++nn)	10 000
abs adr	00 110	(SI)	00 100	(BP+DI)	00 011	(BX+DI)	00 001
(BP+n)	01 110	(SI+n)	01 100	(BP+DI+n)	01 011	(BX+DI+n)	01 001
(BP++nn)	10 110	(SI++nn)	10 100	(BP+DI++nn)	10 011	(BX+DI++nn)	10 001

Manufacturer's equivalent of above modes is (XX+n),(XX+nn),(XX+XX+n)

```
n   - immediate data, 8-bits appended to inst
nn  - immediate data, 16-bits appended to inst
S n - immediate data, 8-bits appended to inst, sign extended
Acc - accumulator, AX for word, AL for byte
dd  - displacement adr, 16-bits appended to inst
ss  - segment adr, 16-bits appended to inst
r   - relative adr, 8-bits appended to inst
t   - operation type, 8-bits appended to inst
p   - port adr, 8-bits appended to inst
```

immediate data appended after addressing mode variables

Modifiers

```
DD,XXX = external device number
II,YYY = external device instruction code
W      = 1 if word data, 0 if byte data
S      = 0 immediate data is 16 bits
         1 immediate data is 8 bits sign
           extended to form 16 bits
V      = 0 shift or rotate one bit
         1 number of bits is in reg CL
```

Special Memory locations

```
    00000-00003  type 0 int, divide error
    00004-00007  type 1 int, single step
    00008-0000B  type 2 int, NMI
    0000C-0000F  type 3 int, INT, break
    00010-00013  type 4 int, INTO, overflow
    00014-0007F  type 5 thru 31 int, INTEL USE
*   00014-00017  type 5 int, BOUND array bounds (1)
    00018-0001B  type 6 int, undefined inst
    0001C-0001F  type 7 int, ESC
    00020-00023  type 8 int, Timer 0
    00024-00027  type 9 int, reserved
    00028-0002B  type 10 int, DMA 0
    0002C-0002F  type 11 int, DMA 1
    00030-00033  type 12 int, INT 0
    00034-00037  type 13 int, INT 1
    00038-0003B  type 14 int, INT 2
    0003C-0003F  type 15 int, INT 3
    00040-00043  type 16 int, Timer 1
    00044-00047  type 17 int, Timer 2
  00080-003FF    type 32 thru 255 int, or general use
  00400-FFFEF    main memory space
  FFFF0-FFFFB    reset jump location
  FFFFC-FFFFF    reserved intel products
```

Notes

8096

8094, 8396, 8394, 8097, 8095, 8397, 8395

Data Move

MOV						Move byte
Mem,Rd	LDB Rd,Mem	101100MM	4			memory, reg

```
     Rs,Mem  |  STB Rs,Mem  | 110001MM  |  4|     |      reg, memory
MOVBW        |  LDBSE       |           |   |     | Move byte to word
     S,Mem,Rd|     Rd,Mem   | 101111MM  |  4|     |      memory sign extended, reg
             |  LDBZE       |           |   |     |
     Mem,Rd  |     Rd,Mem   | 101011MM  |  4|     |      memory, reg
MOVW         |              |           |   |     | Move word
     Mem,Rd  |  LD Rd,Mem   | 101000MM  |  4|     |      memory, reg
     Rs,Mem  |  ST Rs,Mem   | 110000MM  |  4|     |      reg, memory
POP          |  POP         |           |   |     | Pop word
     Mem     |     Mem      | 110011MM  | 14|     |      memory
     PSW     |  POPF        | F3        | 13| all | flags
PUSH         |  PUSH        |           |   |     | Push word
     Mem     |     Mem      | 110010MM  | 12|     |      memory
     PSW     |  PUSHF       | F2        | 12|     | flags
CLR          |  CLR         |           |   | ZNCV| Clear
     Rn      |     Rn       | 11        |  4|     |      Reg
CLRW         |  CLR         |           |   | ZNCV| Clear word
     Rn      |     Rn       | 01        |  4|     |      Reg
```

Math Operations

```
ADD          |  ADDB        |           |   |-ST  | Add
     Mem,Rd  |     Rd,Mem   | 011101MM  |  4|     |      memory, reg
     Rs,Mem,Rd|    Rd,Rs,Mem| 010101MM  |  5|     |      reg+memory, reg
ADDW         |  ADD         |           |   |-ST  | Add words
     Mem,Rd  |     Rd,Mem   | 011001MM  |  4|     |      memory, reg
     Rs,Mem,Rd|    Rd,Rs,Mem| 010001MM  |  5|     |      reg+memory, reg
ADC          |  ADDCB       |           |   |-ST  | Add w/carry
     Mem,Rd  |     RD,Mem    | 101101MM  |  4|     |      memory, reg
ADCW         |  ADDC        |           |   |-ST  | Add words w/carry
     Mem,Rd  |     Rd,Mem   | 101001MM  |  4|     |      memory, reg
INC    Rn    |  INCB Rn     | 17        |  4|-ST  | Increment
INCW   Rn    |  INC  Rn     | 07        |  4|-ST  | Increment word
SUB          |  SUBB        |           |   |-ST  | Subtract
     Mem,Rd  |     Rd,Mem   | 011110MM  |  4|     |      memory, reg
     Rs,Mem,Rd|    Rd,Rs,Mem| 010110MM  |  5|     |      reg-memory, reg
SUBW         |  SUB         |           |   |-ST  | Subtract words
     Mem,Rd  |     Rd,Mem   | 011010MM  |  4|     |      memory, reg
     Rs,Mem,Rd|    Rd,Rs,Mem| 010010MM  |  5|     |      reg-memory, reg
SBB          |  SUBCB       |           |   |-ST  | Subtract w/borrow
     Mem,Rd  |     Rd,Mem   | 101110MM  |  4|     |      memory, reg
SBBW         |  SUBC        |           |   |-ST  | Subtract word w/borrow
     Mem,Rd  |     Rd,Mem   | 101010MM  |  4|     |      memory, reg
DEC          |  DECB        |           |   |-ST  | Decrement
     Rn      |     Rn       | 15        |  4|     |      reg
DECW         |  DEC         |           |   |-ST  | Decrement word
     Rn      |     Rn       | 05        |  4|     |      reg
DIVW         |  DIVUB       |           |   | VVT | Devide word by byte
     Mem,Rd  |     Rd,Mem   | 100111MM  | 17|     |      reg = reg/memory
             |              |           |   |     |      LSB=value, MSB=remainder
DIVDW        |  DIVU        |           |   | VVT | Devide dword by word
     Mem,Rd  |     Rd,Mem   |100011MM   | 25|     |      reg = reg/memory
             |              |           |   |     |      LSW=value, MSW=remainder
IDIVW        |  DIVB        |           |   | VVT | Int Devide word by byte
     Mem,Rd  |     Rd,Mem   |FE,100111MM| 21|     |      reg = reg/memory
             |              |           |   |     |      LSB=value, MSB=remainder
IDIVDW       |  DIV         |           |   | VVT | Int Devide dword by word
     Mem,Rd  |     Rd,Mem   |FE,100011MM| 29|     |      reg = reg/memory
             |              |           |   |     |      LSW=value, MSW=remainder
MUL          |  MULUB       |           |   |     | Multiply
     Mem,Rd  |     Rd,Mem   | 011111MM  | 17|     |      wrd reg = reg x Mem
     Rs,Mem,Rd|    Rd,Rs,Mem| 010111MM  | 18|     |      wrd reg = byte reg x memory
```

346

```
MULW       ! MULU        !            ! !    ! Multiply words
   Mem,Rd  !    Rd,Mem   ! 011011MM !25!    !    dwrd reg = reg x memory
   Rs,Mem,Rd !  Rd,Rs,Mem ! 010011MM !26!    !    dwrd reg = wrd reg x memory
IMUL       ! MULB        !            ! !    ! Int multiply
   Mem,Rd  !    Rd,Mem   !FE,011111MM!21!    !    wrd reg = reg x Mem
   Rs,Mem,Rd !  Rd,Rs,Mem !FE,010111MM!22!    !    wrd reg = byte reg x memory
IMULW      ! MUL         !            ! !    ! Int Multiply words
   Mem,Rd  !    Rd,Mem   !FE,011011MM!29!    !    dwrd reg = reg x memory
   Rs,Mem,Rd !  Rd,Rs,Mem !FE,010011MM!30!    !    dwrd reg = wrd reg x memory
CMP        ! CMPB        !            ! !-ST ! Compare
   Rd,Mem  !    Rd,Mem   ! 100110MM ! 4!    !    reg, memory
CMPW       ! CMP         !            ! !-ST ! Compare words
   Rd,Mem  !    Rd,Mem   ! 100010MM ! 4!    !    reg, memory
CNVWDW Rn  ! EXT  Rn     ! 06         ! 4!ZNCV! Sign extend word to dword
CNVBW  Rn  ! EXTB Rn     ! 16         ! 4!ZNCV! Sign extend byte to word
NEG    Rn  ! NEGB Rn     ! 13         ! 4!-ST ! Negate
NEGW   Rn  ! NEG  Rn     ! 03         ! 4!-ST ! Negate word
NORMDW     ! NORML       !            ! !ZNC ! Shift dword left till MSB=1
   Rn,Rc   !    Rn,Rc    ! 0F         ! 8!    !    reg, save count
```

Bit Operations

```
RESF       !             !            ! !    ! Reset flag
   C       ! CLRC        ! F8         ! 4!C  !    carry
   VT      ! CLRVT       ! FC         ! 4!VT !    overflow trap
SETF       !             !            ! !    ! Set flag
   C       ! SETC        ! F9         ! 4!C  !    carry
```

Logical Operations

```
AND        ! ANDB        !            ! !ZNCV! Logical AND
   Mem,Rd  !    Rd,Mem   ! 011100MM ! 4!    !    memory, reg
   Rs,Mem,Rd !  Rd,Rs,Mem! 010100MM ! 5!    !    reg = reg AND memory
ANDW       ! AND         !            ! !ZNCV! Logical AND words
   Mem,Rd  !    Rd,Mem   ! 011000MM ! 4!    !    memory, reg
   Rs,Mem,Rd !  Rd,Rs,Mem! 010000MM ! 5!    !    reg = reg AND memory
OR         ! ORB         !            ! !ZNCV! Logical OR
   Mem,Rd  !    Rd,Mem   ! 100100MM ! 4!    !    memory, reg
ORW        ! OR          !            ! !ZNCV! Logical OR word
   Mem,Rd  !    Rd,Mem   ! 100000MM ! 4!    !    memory, reg
XOR        ! XORB        !            ! !ZNCV! Logical Exclusive OR
   Mem,Rd  !    Rd,Mem   ! 100101MM ! 4!    !    memory, reg
XORW       ! XOR         !            ! !ZNCV! Logical Exclusive OR word
   Mem,Rd  !    Rd,Mem   ! 100001MM ! 4!    !    memory, reg
CPL        ! NOTB        !            ! !ZNCV! Complement
   Rn      !    Rn       ! 12         ! 4!    !    reg
CPLW       ! NOT         !            ! !ZNCV! Complement word
   Rn      !    Rn       ! 02         ! 4!    !    reg
SLL        ! SHLB        !            ! !-ST ! Shift logical left
   Rd,#n   !    Rd,#n    ! 19         ! 7!    !    reg;count immed
   Rd,Rc   !    Rd,Rc    ! 19         ! 7!    !    reg;count in reg
SLLW       ! SHL         !            ! !-ST ! Shift logical left word
   Rd,#n   !    Rd,#n    ! 09         ! 7!    !    reg;count immed
   Rd,Rc   !    Rd,Rc    ! 09         ! 7!    !    reg;count in reg
SLLDW      ! SHLL        !            ! !-ST ! Shift logical left dword
   Rd,#n   !    Rd,#n    ! 0D         ! 7!    !    reg;count immed
   Rd,Rc   !    Rd,Rc    ! 0D         ! 7!    !    reg;count in reg
SRL        ! SHRB        !            ! !-ST ! Shift logical right
   Rd,#n   !    Rd,#n    ! 18         ! 7!    !    reg;count immed
   Rd,Rc   !    Rd,Rc    ! 18         ! 7!    !    reg;count in reg
SRLW       ! SHR         !            ! !-ST ! Shift logical right word
   Rd,#n   !    Rd,#n    ! 08         ! 7!    !    reg;count immed
   Rd,Rc   !    Rd,Rc    ! 08         ! 7!    !    reg;count in reg
```

347

```
SRLDW        : SHRL      :      :  : :-ST : Shift logical right dword
   Rd,#n     :    Rd,#n  : 0C   : 7: :     :    reg,count immed
   Rd,Rc     :    Rd,Rc  : 0C   : 7: :     :    reg,count in reg
SRA          : SHRAB     :      :  : :-ST : Shift arith right
   Rd,#n     :    Rd,#n  : 1A   : 7: :     :    reg,count immed
   Rd,Rc     :    Rd,Rc  : 1A   : 7: :     :    reg,count in reg
SRAW         : SHRA      :      :  : :-ST : Shift arith right word
   Rd,#n     :    Rd,#n  : 0A   : 7: :     :    reg,count immed
   Rd,Rc     :    Rd,Rc  : 0A   : 7: :     :    reg,count in reg
SRADW        : SHRAL     :      :  : :-ST : Shift arith right dword
   Rd,#n     :    Rd,#n  : 0E   : 7: :     :    reg,count immed
   Rd,Rc     :    Rd,Rc  : 0E   : 7: :     :    reg,count in reg
```

Program Control

```
CALL         :          :        :   : : Call subroutine
   dd        : LCALL dd  : EF     :16 : :    uncond, 16 bit displacement
CALLLR       :          :        :   : :
   rr        : SCALL rr  : 00101rrr :16 : :    uncond, 11 bit relative
             :          : rrrrrrrr :   : :
RET          : RET      :        :   : : Return from subroutine
             :          : F0     :16 : :    uncond
JMP          :          :        :   : : Jump if
   (Rn)      : BR  Rn   : E3     : 8 : :    uncond, reg ind
   dd        : LJMP dd  : E7     :   : :    uncond, 16-bit displacement
JMPLR        :          :        :   : : Jump long relative if
   rr        : SJMP rr  : 00100rrr :   : :    uncond, 11-bit relative
             :          : rrrrrrrr :   : :
JMPR         :          :        :   : : Jump relative if
   EQ,r      : JE   r   : DF     :   : :    Z=1
   C,r       : JC   r   : DB     :   : :    C=1
   GZ,r      : JGT  r   : D2     :   : :    N=0 and Z=0
   P,r       : JGE  r   : D6     :   : :    N=0
   LT,r      : JH   r   : D9     :   : :    C=1 and Z=0
   LEZ,r     : JLE  r   : DA     :   : :    N=1 or Z=1
   M,r       : JLT  r   : DE     :   : :    N=1
   NC,r      : JNC  r   : D3     :   : :    C=0
   NE,r      : JNE  r   : D7     :   : :    Z=0
   GE,r      : JNH  r   : D1     :   : :    C=0 or Z=1
   NST,r     : JNST r   : D0     :   : :    ST=0
   NV,r      : JNV  r   : D5     :   : :    V=0
   NVT,r     : JNVT r   : D4     :   : :    VT=0
   ST,r      : JST  r   : D8     :   : :    ST=1
   V,r       : JV   r   : DD     :   : :    V=1
   VT,r      : JVT  r   : DC     :   : :    VT=1
   BS,Rn,b,r : JBS  Rn,b,r: 00111bbb : 9 : :    bit set, reg, bit
   BR,Rn,b,r : JBC  Rn,b,r: 00110bbb : 9 : :    bit reset,  reg, bit
DECJNZ       : DJNZ     :        :   : : Decrement and jump if not 0
   Rn,r      :    Rn,r  : E0     : 9 : :    reg, rel adr
SKIP         : SKIP     : 00,xx  : 4 : : No operation, 2 bytes
NOP          : NOP      : FD     : 4 : : No operation
RESET        : RST      : FF     :16 :all : Reset system
TRAP         : TRAP     : F7     :24 : : Interrupt call thru loc 2010
```

I/O Operations

```
DI           : DI       : FA     : 4 : : Disable interrupts
EI           : EI       : FB     : 4 : : Enable interrupts
             :          :        :   : :
```

Registers

128 bytes RAM, 256 bytes for 8052 ans 8032
which includes the following special function registers.

	Read operation	Write operation
loc 00	R0 (LO)	R0 (LO)
01	R0 (HI)	R0 (HI)
02	AD-Result (LO)	AD-command
03	AD-Result (HI)	HSI-Mode
04	HSI-Time (LO)	HS0-Time (LO)
05	HSI-Time (HI)	HS0-Time (HI)
06	HSI-Status	HS0-Command
07	SBUF (rcvr)	SBUF (xmt)
08	INT-Mask	INT-Mask
09	INT-Pending	INT-Pending
0A	TIMER1 (LO)	WATCHDOG
0B	TIMER1 (HI)	reserved
0C	TIMER2 (LO)	reserved
0D	TIMER2 (HI)	reserved
0E	I/O port 0	BAUD-RATE
0F	I/O port 1	I/O port 1
10	I/O port 2	I/O port 2
11	SP-Status	SP-CON
12	reserved	reserved
13	reserved	reserved
14	reserved	reserved
15	IOS0	IOC0
16	IOS1	IOC1
17		PWM-Control
18	stack pointer (LO)	stack pointer (LO)
19	stack pointer (HI)	stack pointer (HI)
1A-EF	general use	
F0-FF	power down ram	

Registers may be used as bytes
                words, starting at even locations
                double words, starting at even locations

Flags

Z =	zero	bit 15
N =	negative	14
V =	overflow	13
VT =	overflow trap	12
C =	carry flag	11
I =	interrupt	9
ST =	shift from carry	8
IMR =	int mask reg	7-0

Notes

16-bit data and adedresses stored MSB first LSB second

Addressing Modes

Univ	Manuf	
#n	n	- immediate data
Rx	Rx	- register; Rd destination, Rs source
dd	dd	- displacement address, 16-bits

```
rr       rr       - long relative address, 11-bits
r        r        - relative address, 8-bits
(Rx)     [Rx]     - indirect, word register
(Rx+d)   d[Rx]    - indexed, register + d, 8-bit value
(Rx++dd) dd[Rx]   - indexed, register + dd, 16-bit value
(Rx)+    [Rx]+    - indirect post auto increment, word register
```

Instruction Expansion

Univ	Manuf	Memory desc	MM	Appended
Rn	label	register (word or byte)	00	reg adr
n	#n	immediate	01	value
(Rn)	[label]	word register indirect	10	reg adr LSB=0
(Rn)+	[label]+	indirect auto inc	10	reg adr LSB=1
(Rn+d)	n[label]	indexed by 8-bit value	11	reg adr LSB=0 8-bit value
(Rn++dd)	nn[label]	indexed by 16-bit value	11	reg adr LSB=1 16-bit value

```
memory appended first
source register appended before destination
register appended before relative address value
number of bits to shift appended before register
```

```
n    bits to shift, 8-bits appended to inst,
                if < 16 number of bits to shift
                if 16 - 255 loc of reg containing number of bits
a    address    8 bits data address appended to instruction
dd   disp adr   16-bits appended to instruction, MSB first
r    rel adr    8-bits appended to instruction
rr   long rel   most significant 3-bits part of inst, other 8-bits appended
Rx   register   8-bit location appended to inst
```

Special Memory Locations

```
Loc  0000 - 00FF   internal RAM register file see above
     0100 - 1FFD   external memory or I/O
     1FFE - 1FFF   port 3 and 4
     2000 - 2011   interrupt vectors 0 thru 8
     2012 - 207F   factory test code
     2080 - 3FFF   internal program storage ROM
     4000 - FFFF   external memory or I/O
```

9900   Incomplete

TMS9995, TMS99105A, SBP9989, TMS9981, TMS9980A, TMS9900-40
(1) TMS99110A   (2) TMS9940

Data Move

MOV [W]	MOV [B]		3	Move word/byte
tbl,tbl	tbl,tbl	110WDDDDDDSSSSSS	[0-2]	source,destination
MOVW	LI		3	Move word
#nn,Rr	#nn,Rr	0000000100000RRRR	[0-2]	immed, reg r
#nn,WP	LWPI nn	0000001011100000	4	immed, WP

350

ST,Rr	STST Rr	000000101100RRRR	3		ST, reg r
Rr,ST	LST Rr	000000001000RRRR	5	all	reg r, ST
WP,Rr	STWP Rr	000000101010RRRR	3		WP, reg r
Rr,WP	LWP Rr	000000001001RRRR	4		reg r, WP
MOVN	LIMI		5		Move nible
#n,IM	n	0000001100000000			immed bits 12-15, IM
CLRW	CLR		3		Clear word
tbl	tbl	0000010011DDDDDD			location
SETW	SETO		3		Set word to all 1s
tbl	tbl	0000011100DDDDDD			location
SWAP	SWPB		13		Swap bytes in word
tbl	tbl	0000011011DDDDDD			location

Math Operations

ADD [W]	A [B]		4		Add word/byte
tbl,tbl	tbl,tbl	101WDDDDDDSSSSSS		0-5	source,destination
ADDW	AI		4		Add word
#nn,Rr	#nn,Rr	000000100010RRRR		0-4	immed, reg r
CMP [W]	C [B]		4		Compare word/byte
tbl,tbl	tbl,tbl	100WDDDDDDSSSSSS		0-2	source,destination
CMPW	CI		4		Compare word
#nn,Rr	#nn,Rr	000000101000RRRR		0-2	immed, reg r
INCW	INC		3		Increment word
tbl	tbl	0000010110DDDDDD		0-4	location
INCW	INCT		3		Increment word by 2
tbl,2	tbl	0000010111DDDDDD		0-4	location
SUB [W]	S [B]		4		Subtract word/byte
tbl,tbl	tbl,tbl	100WDDDDDDSSSSSS		0-5	source,destination
DECW	DEC		3		Decrement word
tbl	tbl	0000011000DDDDDD		0-4	location
DECW	DECT		3		Decrement word by 2
tbl,2	tbl	0000011001DDDDDD		0-4	location
MULW	MPY		23		Multiply words
tbl,Rn	tbl,Rn	001110NNNNSSSSSS			reg N:N+1=srce x reg n
IMULW	MPYS		25		Multiply signed words
tbl,R0	tbl	0000000111SSSSSS		0-2	reg 0:1=reg 0 x srce
DIVW	DIV		6		Divide word
tbl,Rn	tbl,Rn	001111NNNNSSSSSS		4	reg n=reg n:n+1/src
					reg n+1=remainder
IDIVW	DIVS		10		Signed Divide word
tbl,R0	tbl	0000000110SSSSSS			reg 0=reg 0:1/srce
					reg 1=remainder

Logical Operations

ANDW	ANDI		4		Logical AND word
#nn,Rr	#nn,Rr	000000100100RRRR		0-2	immed, reg r
OR [W]	SOC [B]		4		Logical OR, word/byte
tbl,tbl	tbl,tbl	111WDDDDDDSSSSSS		0-2	source,destination
ORW	ORI		4		Logical OR word
#nn,Rr	#nn,Rr	000000100110RRRR		0-2	immed, reg r
XORW	XOR		4		Exclusive OR word
tbl,Rn	tbl,Rn	001010NNNNSSSSSS		0-2	source, reg
NEGW	NEG		3		Change to negative value
tbl	tbl	0000010100DDDDDD		0-4	location
ABSW	ABS		3		Change to absolute value
tbl	tbl	0000011101DDDDDD		0-4	location
CPLW	INV		3		Complement word
tbl	tbl	0000010101DDDDDD		0-2	location
RRNC	SRC		7		Rotate right no carry
Rr,#c	Rr,c	00001011ccccRRRR		0-3	reg r, bits
SRLW	SRL		7		Shift logical right

Rr,#c	Rr,c	00001001ccccRRRR	|0-3|	reg r, bits
SRAW	SRA		7|	Shift arith right
Rr,#c	Rr,c	00001000ccccRRRR	|0-3|	reg r, bits
SLAW	SLAD		7|	Shift arith left
Rr,#c	Rr,c	00001010ccccRRRR	|0-4|	reg r, bits

Bit Operations

RESF	RSET	0000000110110000	7|	Reset flags 12-15
RESB [W]	SZC [B]		4|	Reset indicated bits
tbl,tbl	tbl,tbl	010WDDDDDDSSSSSS	|0-2|	source,destination
TESTBSW	COC		4|	Test if bits set
tbl,Rn	tbl,Rn	001000NNNNSSSSSS	|2	mask, reg
TESTBRW	CZC		4|	Test if bits reset
tbl,Rn	tbl,Rn	001001NNNNSSSSSS	|2	mask, reg

Program Control

CALL	BL		5|	Call subroutine
tbl	tbl	0000011010SSSSSS		uncond, memory
				reg 11=PC
RET	RTWP		6|	Return from subroutine
		0000001110000000		ST=reg 15,PC=reg 14
				WP=reg 13
JMP	B		3|	Jump if
tbl	tbl	0000010001SSSSSS		uncond, memory
JMPMOV	BLWP		|11|	Jump and load WP
tbl	tbl	0000010000SSSSSS		uncond,memory
				WP=(mem),PC=(mem+2)
				new reg 13=old WP
				14= PC
				15= ST
JMPR				Jump relative if
EQ,r	JEQ r	00010011rrrrrrrr	3|	equal
GT,r	JGT r	00010101rrrrrrrr	3|	>
SGT,r	JH r	00011011rrrrrrrr	3|	high
SLT,r	JL r	00011010rrrrrrrr	3|	low
SLE,r	JLE r	00010010rrrrrrrr	3|	low or =
LT,r	JLT r	00010001rrrrrrrr	3|	<
UN,r	JMP r	00010000rrrrrrrr	3|	uncond
NC,r	JNC r	00010111rrrrrrrr	3|	no carry
NE,r	JNE r	00010110rrrrrrrr	3|	not =
NV,r	JNO r	00011001rrrrrrrr	3|	no overflow
C,r	JOC r	00011000rrrrrrrr	3|	carry
PO,r	JOP r	00011100rrrrrrrr	3|	odd parity
HALT	IDLE	0000001101000000	|21|	Wait for interrupt
EXEC	X		2|	Execute instruction at
tbl	tbl	0000010010DDDDDD		location

I/O Operations

TSTIOB	TB		8|	Test I/O bit in CRU
CRU,b	b	00011111bbbbbbbb	|2	bit = reg 12 + b
RSTIOB	SBZ		8|	Reset I/O bit in CRU
CRU,b	b	00011110bbbbbbbb		bit = reg 12 + b
SETIOB	SBO		8|	Set I/O bit in CRU
CRU,b	b	00011101bbbbbbbb		bit = reg 12 + b
INBS	STCR		|43|	Input bits
CRU,tbl,#c	tbl,c	001101ccccDDDDDD	|0-2|	from CRU,dest,# bits
OUTBS	LDCR		|41|	Output bits
tbl,#c,CRU	tbl,c	001100ccccSSSSSS	|0-2|	source,# bits,to CRU

Micro Unique Operations

XOP tbl,#n	XOP tbl,#n	001011nnnnSSSSSS	15	Expanded operation WP = (40H +4n) PC = (42H +4n) new reg 11 = SA 13 = old WP 14 = PC 15 = ST
CKOF	CKOF	0000001111000000	7	User defined
CKON	CKON	0000001110100000	7	User defined
LREX	LREX	0000001111100000	7	User defined
* LDD	LDD			Incomplete info (1)
* LDS	LDS			Incomplete info (1)
* DCA	DCA			Incomplete info (2)
* DCS	DCS			Incomplete info (2)

Registers

```
          0               15
          -----------------
PC        | Prog Counter  |
          -----------------
WP        | Work Space Ptr|
          -----------------
ST        | Status Word   |
          -----------------
```

Workspace Registers

```
reg 0 - shift count, MSW mul, div result
    1 - LSW mul, div remainder
   11 - return adr, effective adr
   12 - CRU bus adr
   13 - saved WP reg
   14 - saved PC reg
   15 - saved ST reg

 1-15 - can be used for index addressing
```

each register is 2 byte, MSB at even adr, LSB subsequent odd address byte type instructions use the MSB of the register only, LSB must be accessed directly as a memory location.

Flags

```
bit  0 = L>  logical greater than
     1 = A>  arithmetic greater than
     2 = EQ  equal / TB indicator
     3 = C   carry
     4 = OV  overflow
     5 = OP  odd parity
     6 = X   XOP in progress
    10 = EN  overflow interrupt enable
 12-15 = IM  interrupt mask
```

Notes

16 bit data and address values stored in consecutive 8-bit bytes
        MSB must be an even address
        LSB is next odd address

Addressing Modes

Univ	Manuf	
#nn	#nn	- immediate data, 16-bits
Rx	Rx	- register, R0 - R15
aa	∂aa	- absolute address, 16-bits
r	r	- relative address, 8-bits
(Rx)	*Rx	- register indirect
(Rx++aa)	∂aa(Rx)	- indexed, register + 16-bit address
(Rx)+	*Rx+	- register indirect auto increment

Instruction Expansion

tbl

			SSSSSS/DDDDDD		
Univ	Man	Mode	MM	RRRR	Append
Rx	Rx	register	00	0-15	
(Rx)	*Rx	reg indirect	01	0-15	
aa	∂aa	absolute	10	0	address
(Rx++aa)	∂aa(Rx)	indexed	10	1-15	address
(Rx+)	*Rx+	ind_increment	11	0-15	

if both source and destination are indexed
    the source address is appended first

#nn	immediate data, 16-bits appendet to inst, MSB first
#n	immediate data, appended as 16-bit value, MSB first or part of inst
#c	number of bits, 4-bits part of inst
r	relative adr, 8-bits part of inst
b	bit number, 8-bits part of inst

Special Memory Locations

loc 0000-EFFF - External memory
                loc 0000-0013   level 1 thru 4 interrupt vectors
                    0014-003F   general use
                    0040-007F   XOPO 1 thru 15 software interrupt vectors
                    0080-EFFF   general use
    F000-F0FB   On chip RAM, general use
    F0FC-FFF9   External general use memory
    FFFA-FFFB   decrementor, internal memory maped I/O
    FFFC-FFFF   non masked interrupt vector

F8

MC3870

Data Move

```
MOV             !              !          !   !     ! Move byte
    #n,A        ! LI  n        ! 20       ! 2!     !     immed, reg A
    (+DC),A     ! LM           ! 16       ! 3!     !     ind inc DC, reg A
    A,(+DC)     ! ST           ! 17       ! 3!     !     reg A, ind inc DC
    Ram,A       ! LR A,Ram     ! 0100rrrr ! 1!     !     ram loc, reg A
    KU,A        !    A,KU      ! 00       ! 1!     !     ram loc 12, reg A
    KL,A        !    A,KL      ! 01       ! 1!     !     ram loc 13, reg A
    QU,A        !    A,QU      ! 02       ! 1!     !     ram loc 14, reg A
    QL,A        !    A,QL      ! 03       ! 1!     !     ram loc 15, reg A
    A,Ram       !    Ram,A     ! 0101rrrr ! 1!     !     reg A, ram loc
    A,KU        !    KU,A      ! 04       ! 1!     !     reg A, ram loc 12
    A,KL        !    KL,A      ! 05       ! 1!     !     reg A, ram loc 13
    A,QU        !    QU,A      ! 06       ! 1!     !     reg A, ram loc 14
    A,QL        !    QL,A      ! 07       ! 1!     !     reg A, ram loc 15
    A,ISAR      !    IS,A      ! 0B       ! 1!     !     reg A, reg ISAR
MOVW            !              !          !   !     ! Move 11-bits
    Q,DC        ! LR  DC,Q     ! 0F       ! 4!     !     ram loc 14, reg DC
    H,DC        !     DC,H     ! 10       ! 4!     !     ram loc 10, reg DC
    #nn,DC      ! DCI  aa      ! 2A       ! 6!     !     immed, reg DC
    K,P         ! LR  P,K      ! 09       ! 4!     !     ram loc 12, stack reg
    DC,Q        !     Q,DC     ! 0E       ! 4!     !     reg DC, ram loc 14
    DC,H        !     H,DC     ! 11       ! 4!     !     reg DC, ram loc 10
    P,K         !     K,P      ! 08       ! 4!     !     stack reg, ram loc 12
MOVN            !              !          !   !     ! Move 4-bits
    #n,A        ! LIS  n       ! 0111nnnn ! 1!     !     immed, reg A
    #n,ISARL    ! LISL n       ! 11010nnn ! 1!     !     immed, lower 3-bits ISAR
    #n,ISARU    ! LISU n       ! 01100nnn ! 1!     !     immed, upper 3-bits ISAR
    J,SR        ! LR  W,J      ! 1D       ! 2!all !     ram loc 9, flags
    ISAR,A      !    A,IS      ! 0A       ! 1!     !     reg ISAR, reg A
    SR,J        !    J,W       ! 1E       ! 1!     !     flags, ram loc 9
XCHG  DC,DC1    ! XDC          ! 2C       ! 2!     ! Exchange reg DC and DC1
CLR             !              !          !   !     ! Clear byte
    A           ! CLR          ! 70       ! 1!     !     reg A
```

Math Operations

```
ADD             !              !          !   !     ! Add byte
    #n,A        ! AI  n        ! 24       ! 2!all !     immed, reg A
    (+DC),A     ! AM           ! 88       ! 3!all !     ind inc DC, reg A
    A,DC        ! ADC          ! 8E       ! 3!     !     reg A, reg DC
    Ram,A       ! AS  Ram      ! 1100rrrr ! 1!all !     ram loc, reg A
ADC             !              !          !   !     ! Add carry
    A           ! LNK          ! 19       ! 1!all !     reg A
ADDBCD          !              !          !   !     ! Decimal add byte
    (+DC),A     ! AMD          ! 89       ! 3!all !     ind inc DC, reg A
    Ram,A       ! ASD  Ram     ! 1101rrrr ! 2!all !     ram loc, reg A
INC             !              !          !   !     ! Increment byte
    A           ! INC          ! 1F       ! 1!all !     reg A
DEC             !              !          !   !     ! Decrement byte
    Ram         ! DS  Ram      ! 0011rrrr ! 2!all !     ram loc
CMP             !              !          !   !     ! Compare byte
    A,#n        ! CI  n        ! 25       ! 2!all !     reg A, immed
    A,(+DC)     ! CM           ! BD       ! 3!all !     reg A, ind inc DC
```

Logical Operations

AND					Logical AND byte
#n,A	NI n	21	2	all	immed, reg A
(+DC),A	NM	8A	3	all	ind inc DC, reg A
Ram,A	NS Ram	1111rrrr	1	all	ram loc, reg A
OR					Logical OR byte
#n,A	OI n	22	2	all	immed, reg A
(+DC),A	OM	8B	3	all	ind inc DC, reg A
XOR					Logical Exclusive OR byte
#n,A	XI n	23	2	all	immed, reg A
(+DC),A	XM	8C	3	all	ind inc DC, reg A
Ram,A	XS Ram	1110rrrr	1	all	ram loc, reg A
CPL					Complement byte
A	COM	18	1	all	reg A
SLA	SL				Shift left arithmetic
A	1	13	1	all	reg A
A,4	4	15	1	all	reg A, 4 bits
SRA	SR				Shift right arithmetic
A	1	12	1	all	reg A
A,4	4	14	1	all	reg A, 4 bits

Program Control

CALL					Call subroutine
(R12)	PK	0C	4		uncond, ind ram loc 12
aa	PI aa	28	7		uncond, abs
RET	POP	1C	2		Return from subroutine
JMP	JMP				Jump to location
aa	aa	29	5		uncond, abs
(R14)	LR P0,Q	0D	4		uncond, ind ram loc 14
JMPR					Jump relative
UN,r	BR a	90	4		uncond
NC,r	BNC a	92	3		no carry
C,r	BC a	82	3		carry
Z,r	BZ a	84	3		zero
T[ZCS],r	BT [ZCS],a	10000ZCS	3		if indicated flags set
NV,r	BNO a	98	3		no overflow
M,r	BM a	91	3		if minus
NZ,r	BNZ a	94	3		not zero
ISAR7,r	BR7 a	8F	3		if ISAR bits 0-2 not = 7
P,r	BP a	81	3		if plus
N[OZCS],r	BF [OZCS]a	10010ZCS	3		if indicated flags not set
NOP	NOP	2B	1		No operation

I/O Operations

DI	DI	1A	2	I	Disable interrupts
EI	EI	1B	2	I	Enable interrupts
IN					Input from port
p,A	IN p	26	4	all	port p,reg A
Pp,A	INS p	1010pppp	4	all	port Pp, reg A
OUT					Output to port
A,p	OUT p	27	4		reg A, port aa
A,Pp	OUTS p	1011pppp	4		reg A, port a

Registers

```
    10  7  5     0
              ---------
              ! ISAR !   RAM address, two 3-bit elements
              ---------
           !  A   !      Accumulator
        ---------------
        !     DC     !   Data counter  (auto inc) (ROM adr)
        ---------------
        !    DC1     !   Aux data counter
        ---------------
        !    PO      !   Prog counter
        ---------------
        !     P      !   Single element stack reg
        ---------------
           SR  !IOZCS!   Flags
               -------
```

RAM locations 9 - F are called J, HU, HL, KU, KL, QU, QL respectively

Flags

```
S = sign of result
Z = zero result
O = overflow
C = carry, bit 7
I = interrupt
```


Notes

Data is stored MSB first then LSB

Addressing Modes
-------------- -----

```
#n    n  - immediate data, (11, 8, 4 or 3-bits)
reg    - register
aa    aa - absolute 11-bit address
r     a  - relative, 8-bit relative address value
p     p  - port address
(ISAR)   - indirect reg ISAR
(Rxx)    - indirect reg xx
+(DC)    - indirect reg DC auto increment, points to ROM location
+(ISAR)  - indirect reg ISAR auto increment
-(ISAR)  - indirect reg ISAR auto decrement
```


Instruction Expansion

| | | RAM | |
Univ	Manuf	Mode	rrrr
Rr	r	RAM loc 0-11	0 - B
(ISAR)		ind reg ISAR	C
+(ISAR)		ind inc ISAR	D
-(ISAR)		ind dec ISAR	E

F9445

Data Move

```
MOV            :               :                  : : : Move byte
    Mem,ACn    : LDB ACn,Mem:   011AAMMMDDDDDDDD :24:     LSB accum = memory
               :               :                  : :       MSB accum = 0
    ACn,Mem    : STB ACn,Mem:   011AAMMMDDDDDDDD :26:     accum to memory
MOVW           :               :                  : : : Move word
    Mem,ACn    : LDA ACn,Mem:   001AAMMMDDDDDDDD :12:     memory, accum
    ACn,Mem    : STA ACn,MEM:   010AAMMMDDDDDDDD :12:     accum, memory
    (SP),ACn   : TOPR ACn   :   011AA01111000001 :16:     top of stack, accum
    ACn,(SP)   : TOPW ACn   :   011AA01101000001 :16:     accum, top of stack
    ACn,SP     : MTSP ACn   :   011AA01000000001 : 6:     accum, stack pointer
    SP,ACn     : MFSP ACn   :   011AA01010000001 : 6:     stack pointer, accum
    ACn,FP     : MTFP ACn   :   011AA00000000001 : 6:     accum, frame pointer
    FP,ACn     : MFFP ACn   :   011AA00010000001 : 6:     frmae pointer, accum
MOVW [Inst1]   : MOV [Inst1]:                     : 6: Move word shift,skip
    Par1       :     Par1   :   1SSDD010SSCCLPPP : : :    see Inst1, Par1
PUSH           :               :                  : : : Push word on the stack
    ACn        : PSHA ACn   :   011AA01100000001 :16:     accum
    PSW        : PSHF       :   0111010101000001 :16:     flags
    AC2        : PSHR       :   0111010111000001 :16:     return address
POP            :               :                  : : : Pop word from stack
    ACn        : POPA ACn   :   011AA01110000001 :16:     accum
    PSW        : POPF       :   0111010100000001 :16:     flags
PUSHMOV        : SAV        :                     :42: Push AC0-AC1,AC2,FP,C &
               :               :   0110010100000001 : : :  AC3 or PC, on stack
               :               :                  : : :   movw SP to FP,AC3
```

Math Operations

```
ADDW [Inst1]   : ADD [Inst1]:                     : 6:CV: Add word, shift,skip
    Par1       :     Par1   :   1SSDD110SSCCLPPP : : :    see Inst1, Par1
ADM [Inst1]    : ADC [Inst1]:                     : 6:CV: Add complement,shift,skip
    Par1       :     Par1   :   1SSDD100SSCCLPPP : : :    see Inst1, Par1
INCW [Inst1]   : INC [Inst1]:                     : 6:CV: Increment word,shift,skip
    Par1       :     Par1   :   1SSDD011SSCCLPPP : : :    see Inst1, Par1
SUBW [Inst1]   : SUB [Inst1]:                     : 6:CV: Subtract word,shift,skip
    Par1       :     Par1   :   1SSDD101SSCCLPPP : : :    see Inst1, Par1
DECW           : DSP        :                     : 6: Decrement word
    SP         :               :   0111011010000001 : : :    stack pointer
MULWA          : MUL        :                     :16: Multiply word and add
  .AC1,AC2,AC0:               :   0111011011000001 : : :    AC0,AC1=AC0+(AC1xAC2)
IMULWA         : MULS       :                     :16: Multiply signed word,add
   AC1,AC2,AC0:               :   0111101000010RRR : : :    AC0,AC1=AC0+(AC1xAC2)
DIVW           : DIV        :                     :26:CV: Divide word
    AC2,AC0    :               :   0111011001000001 : : :    AC0,AC1/AC2
               :               :                  : : :    AC1=result,AC0=remain
IDIVW          : DIVS       :                     :32:CV: Signed Divide word
    AC2,AC0    :               :   0111111000000001 : : :    AC0,AC1/AC2
               :               :                  : : :    AC1=result,AC0=remain
NORMDW         : NORM       :                     :10:V: Normalize d-word
    AC2,AC0    :               :   0110011011000001 : : :    shift AC0,AC1 till
               :               :                  : : :    MSB=1,AC2=AC2-# bits
```

Logical Operations

```
ANDW [Inst1]   : AND [Inst1]:                     : 6: : Logical AND, Shift,Skip
    Par1       :     Par1   :   1SSDD111SSCCLPPP : : :    see Inst1, Par1 below
ORW            : OR         :                     : 6: : Logical OR, Shift,Skip
```

ACs,ACd	ACs,ACd	011SS111DD000001			reg,reg
NEG [Inst1]	NEG [Inst1]		6	CV	Change to negative value
Par1	Par1	1FFTT001SSCCLPPP			see Inst1 and Par1
CPL [Inst1]	COM [Inst1]		6		Complement [see Inst1]
Par1	Par1	1FFTT000SSCCLPPP			see table below
SLLDW	SLLD		10		Shift logical left d-word
AC0,AC2		0110011000000001			AC0,AC1 # bits in AC2
SRLDW	SLRD		10		Shift logical right d-wrd
AC0,AC2		0110011010000001			AC0,AC1, # bits in AC2
SRADW	SARD		10		Shift arith right d-wrd
AC0,AC2		0110011001000001			AC0,AC1, # bits in AC2
SLADW	SALD		10		Shift arith left d-word
AC0,AC2		0111011000000001			AC0,AC1, # bits in AC2

Bit Operations

RESF					Reset flag
T	DTRP	0111111011000001	10		trap
64K	D64K	0110111010000001	10		64K mode
SETF					Set flag
T	ETRP	0111111001000001	10		trap
64K	E64K	0110111001000001	10		64K mode

Program Control

CALL	JSR		6		Call subroutine
Mem	Mem	00001MMMDDDDDDDD			uncond, memory
					(PC saved in AC3
RET	POPJ		16		Return from subroutine
		0111010110000001			uncond
RETSW	RET		47		Return from subr 5 wrds
		0110010110000001			move FP to SP, then
					pop PC,FP,AC3-AC0
JMP	JMP		6		Jump relative if
Mem	Mem	00000MMMDDDDDDDD			uncond, memory
INCSZ	ISZ		20		Increment, skip if 0
Mem	Mem	00010MMMNNNNNNNN			memory
DECSZ	DSZ		22		Decrement, skip if 0
Mem	Mem	00011MMMNNNNNNNN			memory
SKIP	SKNV		14		Skip next inst if
NV		0110111011000001			no overflow
IE	SKPBN CPU	011..11100111111	16		interrupts enabled
ID	SKPBZ CPU	011..11101111111	16		interrupts disabled
DN	SKPDN CPU	011..11110111111	16		reserved special use
DZ	SKPDZ CPU	011..11111111111	16		reserved special use
TRAP	TRAP				Trap
		1..........1000			move CA to loc 26
					(27) to PC
HALT	HALT	011..11000111111	4		Leave run mode enter
					console mode
WAIT	WAIT	0110111000000001	4		Wait for interrupt

I/O Operations

NIO [BDC]	NIO [BDC]		12		No data transferred
d	d	011..000CCdddddd			see bdc codes below
SKIP [BDT]	SKP [BDT]		14		Skip on busy/done flags
d	d	011..111CCdddddd			see bdt codes below
INB	READS		12		Input bit
ACn,CSR	ACn	011AA00100111111			accum,console sw reg
INWA [BDC]	DIA [BDC]		12		Input word data, reg A
ACn,d	ACn,d	011AA001CCdddddd			see bdc codes below

```
INWB [BDC]  ! DIB [BDC]  !                 !12! ! Input word data, reg B
   ACn,d     !    ACn,d   ! 011AA011CCdddddd !  ! !   see bdc codes below
INWC [BDC]  ! DIC [BDC]  !                 !12! ! Input word data, reg C
   ACn,d     !    ACn,d   ! 011AA101CCdddddd !  ! !   see bdc codes below
OUTWA [BDC] ! DOA [BDC]  !                 !12! ! Output word data, reg A
   ACn,d     !    ACn,d   ! 011AA010CCdddddd !  ! !   see bdc codes below
OUTWB [BDC] ! DOB [BDC]  !                 !12! ! Output word data, reg B
   ACn,d     !    ACn,d   ! 011AA100CCdddddd !  ! !   see bdc codes below
OUTWC [BDC] ! DOC [BDC]  !                 !12! ! Output word data, reg C
   ACn,d     !    ACn,d   ! 011AA110CCdddddd !  ! !   see bdc codes below
EI          ! INTEN      ! 0110000001111111 ! 6! ! Interrupt enable
DI          ! INTDS      ! 0110000010111111 ! 6! ! Interrupt disable
INTA        ! INTA       !                 ! 6! ! Interrupt acknowledge
   ACn       !    ACn     ! 011AA01100111111 !  ! !   bits 10-15 of accum
            !            !                 !  ! !   = device code
MASKIO  ACn ! MSKO  ACn  ! 011AA10000111111 ! 6! ! Mask out I/O devices
IORST       ! IORST      ! 011..10110111111 ! 6! ! Reset all I/O devices
```

Registers

```
         0            15
       -----------------
ACØ    !               !
       -----------------
AC1    !               !
       -----------------
AC2    !               !
       -----------------
AC3    !               !
       -----------------
SP     ! Stack Pointer !
       -----------------
FP     ! Frame Pointer !
       -----------------
PC     !Program Counter!
       -----------------
PSW    !CKE..........V!
       -----------------


       1 Ø
       ----
       !I ! Interrupt on flag
       ----
```

Flags

```
    C = carry flag
    K = 32Kwrd mode or 64Kwrd mode
    E = trap enable
    V = overflow
    I = interrupt enable
```

Addressing Modes
---------- -----

```
   Univ    Manuf
   ----    -----
   ACx     ACx     - accumulator register
   XX      XX      - register or flag
   PZ a    aa,Ø    - page zero address
```

360

```
RA r         aa,1    - relative address value
(XX)         (XX)    - register indirect
(PZ a)       @aa,0   - page zero indirect
(RA a)       @aa,1   - relative adr indirect
(AC2+n)      aa,2    - indexed
(AC3+n)      aa,3    - indexed
((AC2+n))    @aa,2   - indexed indirect
((AC3+n))    @aa,3   - indexed indirect
```

64K bytes (32Kwrd)	128K bytes (64Kwrd)
Byte Inst - bit 15 used to specify high or low byte.	carry flag used as MSB of the address.
Indirect - bit bit 0 used to indicate indirect address	only one level permitted

Instruction Expansion

	Mem					Accumulator	
Univ	Man	Mode	MMM	DDDDDDDD		Symbol	AA
----	---	----	---	--------		------	--
PZ aa	aa,0	page zero	000	aaaaaaaa		AC0	00
RA r	aa,1	relative	001	rrrrrrrr		AC1	01
(AC2+)n	aa,2	indexed	010	nnnnnnnn		AC2	10
(AC3+)n	aa,3	indexed	011	nnnnnnnn		AC3	11
(PZ aa)	@aa,0	ind_page_zero	100	aaaaaaaa			
(RA r)	@aa,1	ind_relative	101	rrrrrrrr			
((AC2+)n)	@aa,2	ind_indexed	110	nnnnnnnn			
((AC3+)n)	@aa,3	ind_indexed	111	nnnnnnnn			

Inst1

appended to mnemonic: [Carry][Shift][Load]

Carry			Shift			Load		
Ltr	CC	Def	Ltr	SS	Def	Ltr	L	Def
---	--	---	---	--	---	---	-	---
-	00	current	-	00	no shift	-	0	ACd=result
Z	01	C = 0	L	01	rotate left	#	1	no save
O	10	C = 1	R	10	rotate right			
C	11	complement	S	11	swap bytes			

Par1

format: ACs,ACd,[Skip]

Skip		
Ltr	PPP	Def
---	---	---
---	000	no skip
SKP	001	always skip
SZC	010	skip if C=0
SNC	011	skip if C=1
SZR	100	skip if zero
SNR	101	skip if not zero
SEZ	110	skip if zero or C=0
SBN	111	skip if not zero and C=1

	Busy/Done Control				Busy/Done Test
Ltr	CC	Def	Ltr	CC	Def
---	--	---	---	--	---
-	00	no effect	BN	00	Busy is not zero
S	01	Busy = 1, Done = 0	BZ	01	Busy is zero
C	10	0 0	DN	10	Done is not zero
P	11	Pulse the device	DZ	11	Done is zero

Special Memory Locations

```
loc 0000 - Interrupt/Stack fault save address
    0001 - Interrupt vector
    0003 - Stack fault vector
    0010-0017 - auto increment locations
    0018-001F - auto decrement locations
    0026 - ABORT/TRAP address save
    0027 - ABORT/TRAP vector
    00FF - top of page zero
    7FFF - APL start 32K mode
    FFFF - APL start 64K mode
```

Notes

Z8

Z8601, Z8603, Z8611, Z8612, Z8613, Z8681, Z8682, Z8090, Z8094, Z8590, Z8594, Z8800

Data Move

MOV	LD				Move byte
Rs,WRd	WRd,Rs	DDDD1000	6		reg, wrk reg
WRs,WRd	WRd,WRs	DDDD1000	6		wrk reg, wrk reg
WRs,Rd	Rd,WRs	SSSS1001	6		wrk reg, reg
(WRs+v),WRd	WRd,X,WRs	C7	10		insuficient info
		DDDDSSSS			
		VVVVVVVV			
WRs,(WRD+v)	WRd,X,WRs	D7	10		insuficient info
		SSSSDDDD			
		VVVVVVVV			
(WRs),WRd	WRd,aWRs	E3	6		ind wrk reg, wrk reg
		DDDDSSSS			
WRs,(WRd)	aWRd,WRs	F3	6		wrk reg, ind wrk reg
		DDDDSSSS	6		
Rs,Rd	Rd,Rs	E4,SS,DD	6		reg,reg
(Rs),WRd	WRd,aRs	E5,SS,DD	10		reg, ind wrk reg
(Rs),Rd	Rd,aRs	E5,SS,DD	10		reg, ind reg
(WRs),Rd	Rd,aWRs	E5,SS,DD	10		wrk reg, ind reg
Rs,(Rd)	aRd,Rs	F5,SS,DD	10		reg, ind reg
Rs,(WRd)	aWRd,Rs	F5,SS,DD	10		reg, ind reg
WRs,(Rd)	aRd,WRs	F5,SS,DD	10		reg, ind reg
#n,WRr	WRr,n	RRRR1100	6		immed, wrk reg
#n,Rr	Rr,n	E6,DD,SS	10		immed, reg
#n,(Rr)	aRr,n	E7,DD,SS	10		immed, ind reg
#n,(WRr)	aWRr,n	E7,DD,SS	10		immed, ind wrk reg
#n,RP	SRP n	31	6		immed, reg RP
MOVC	LDC				Move byte prog memory

```
        WRs,(WRd) !    @WRd,WRs! D2,SD   !12!       ! wrk reg, ind wrk reg
        (WRs),WRd !    WRd,@WRs! C2,DS   !12!       ! ind wrk reg, wrk reg
                  ! LDCI       !         !  !       !
      +(WRs),(WRd)!    @WRd,@WRs! C3,DS  !12!       ! auto inc mem, ind wrk reg
      (WRs),+(WRd)!    @WRd,@WRs! D3,SD  !12!       ! ind wrk reg, auto inc mem
      MOVX        ! LDE        !         !  !       ! MOVE external data memory
        (WRs),WRd !    WRd,@WRs! 82,DS   !12!       ! data memory, wrk reg
        WRs.(WRd) !    @WRd,WRs! 92,SD   !12!       ! wrk reg, data memory
                  ! LDEI       !         !  !       !
      +(WRs),(WRd)!    @WRd,@WRs! 83,DS  !  !       ! code memory, data mem
      (WRs),+(WRd)!    @WRd,@WRs! 93,SD  !  !       ! code memory, data mem
      POP         ! POP        !         !  !       ! Pop word
        Mem       !    Mem     ! 0101000M !10!      ! reg/ ind reg
      PUSH        ! PUSH       !         !  !       ! Push word
        Mem       !    Mem     ! 0111000M !10!      ! reg/ ind reg
      CLR         ! CLR        !         !  !       ! Clear
        Mem       !    Mem     ! 1011000M ! 6!      ! reg/ind reg
      SWAP        ! SWAP       !         !  !  CZSV! Swap byte halves
        Mem       !    Mem     ! 1111000M ! 8!      ! reg/ ind reg
```

Math Operations

```
      ADD         ! ADD        !         !  ! all ! Add
        Tbl       !    Tbl     ! 0000MMMM !  !     ! srce,dest
      ADC         ! ADC        !         !  ! all ! Add w/carry
        Tbl       !    Tbl     ! 0001MMMM !  !     ! srce,dest
      INC         ! INC        !         !  ! ZSV ! Increment
        WRr       !    WRr     ! RRRR1110 ! 6!     ! working reg
        Rr        !    Rr      ! 20       ! 6!     ! reg
        (Rr)      !    @Rr     ! 21       ! 6!     ! ind reg
        (WRr)     !    @WRr    ! 21       ! 6!     ! ind wrk reg
      INCW        ! INCW       !         !  ! ZSV ! Increment word
        Mem       !    Mem     ! 1010000M !10!     ! reg pair/ind reg
      SUB         ! SUB        !         !  ! CZSV! Subtract
        Tbl       !    Tbl     ! 0010MMMM ! 6!     ! srce, dest
      SBB         ! SBC        !         !  ! D   ! Subtract w/borrow
        Tbl       !    Tbl     ! 0011MMMM ! 6!     ! srce, dest
      DEC         ! DEC        !         !  ! SZV ! Decrement
        Mem       !    Mem     ! 0000000M ! 6!     ! reg/ind reg
      DECW        ! DECW       !         !  ! SZV ! Decrement word
        Mem       !    Mem     ! 1000000M !10!     ! reg pair/ind reg
      CMP         ! CP         !         !  ! CSZV! Compare
        Tbl (rev) !    Tbl     ! 1010MMMM !  !     ! srce,dest
      DA          ! DA         !         !  ! CZSV! Decimal adjust
        Mem       !    Mem     ! 0100000M ! 8!     ! reg/ ind reg
```

Logical Operations

```
      AND         ! AND        !         !  ! ZSV ! Logical AND
        Tbl       !    Tbl     ! 0101MMMM ! 6!     ! srce,dest
      TSTCPL      ! TCM        !         !  ! ZSV ! Test complement
        Tbl       !    Tbl     ! 0110MMMM ! 6!     ! srce, dest
      TEST        ! TM         !         !  ! ZSV ! Test logical AND
        Tbl       !    Tbl     ! 0111MMMM ! 6!     ! srce, dest
      OR          ! OR         !         !  ! ZSV ! Logical OR
        Tbl       !    Tbl     ! 0100MMMM !10!     ! reg/ ind reg
      XOR         ! XOR        !         !  ! ZSV ! Logical Exclusive OR
        Tbl       !    Tbl     ! 1011MMMM ! 6!     ! srce, dest
      CPL         ! COM        !         !  ! ZSV ! Complement
        Mem       !    Mem     ! 0110000M ! 6!     ! reg/ind reg
      RLTC        ! RL         !         !  ! CZSV! Rotate left to carry
        Mem       !    Mem     ! 1001000M ! 6!     ! reg/ ind reg
```

RLWC		RLC				CZSV	Rotate left with carry
	Mem		Mem	0001000M	6		reg/ ind reg
RRTC		RR				CZSV	Rotate right to carry
	Mem		Mem	1110000M	6		reg/ ind reg
RRWC		RRC				CZSV	Rotate right with carry
	Mem		Mem	1100000M	6		reg/ ind reg
SRA		SRA				CZSV	Shift arith right
	Mem		Mem	1101000M	6		reg/ ind reg

Bit Operations

RESF							Reset flag
	C	RCF		CF	6	C	carry
SETF							Set flag
	C	SCF		DF	6	C	carry
CPLF							Complement flag
	C	CCF		EF	6	C	carry

Program Control

CALL		CALL					Call subroutine
	(WRr)		@WRr	D4	20		ind working reg
	(Rr)		@Rr	D4	20		ind reg
	aa		aa	D6	20		abs
RET		RET		AF	14		Return from subroutine
RETI		IRET		BF	16		Return from interrupt
JMP		JP					Jump if
	CC,aa		CC,aa	CCCC1101	12		cond, abs
	UN,(Rr)		@Rr	30	12		uncond, ind reg
	UN,(WRr)		@WRr	30	12		uncond, ind wrk reg
JMPR		JPR					Jump relative if
	CC,r		CC,r	CCCC1011	12		cond, rel adr
DECJNZR		DJNZ					Decrement and jump if not 0
	WRd,r		WRd,r	DDDD1010	12		working reg, rel adr
NOP		NOP		FF	6		No operation

I/O Operations

| DI | | DI | | 8F | 6 | | Disable interrupts |
| EI | | EI | | 9F | 6 | | Enable interrupts |

Registers

144 byte register file

```
loc  0       P0      port 0
     1       P1      port 1
     2       P2      port 2
     3       P3      port 3
   4 - 127   R4 - R127  general purpose
 128 - 239             not used
   240       SIO     serial I/O
   241       TMR     timer mode
   242       T1      timer/counter 1
   243       PRE1    timer 1 prescaler
   244       T0      timer/counter 0
   245       PRE0    timer 0 prescaler
   246       P2M     port 2 mode
   247       P3M     port 3 mode
   248       P01M    ports 0-1 mode
   249       IPR     interrupt priority
   250       IRQ     interrupt request
```

```
251    IMR      interrupt mask
252    FLAGS    program control
253    RP       register pointer
254    SPH      stack pointer high
255    SPL      stack pointer low
```

Most significan 4-bits of the register pointer (RP) specifies one of
eighy sets of working registers within the register file (WR0 - WR15)

```
        0 = loc 0 - 15      4 = loc 64 - 79
        1 =     16 - 31     5 =     80 - 95
        2 =     32 - 47     6 =     96 - 111
        3 =     48 - 63     7 =    112 - 127
```

internal stack R4 - R127 pointed to by SPL
external stack in data memory pointed to by SPL and SPH

Flags

```
C = carry flag     Bit 7
Z = zero               6
S = sign               5
V = overflow           4
D = decimal adjust     3
H = half carry         2
2 = user flag 2        1
1 = user flag 1        0
```

Addressing Modes

```
Univ      Manuf
----      -----

#n        n       - immediate data, 8-bits
Rx        Rx      - register, R0 - R127 and R240 - R255
WRx       WRx     - working reg, WR0 - WR15
aa        aa      - absolute address
(Rx)      @Rx     - register indirect
(WRx)     @WRx    - working register indirect
(X+Rx)    X,Rx    - indexed, register
(X+WRx)   X,WRx   - indexed, working register
r         r       - relative address
```

Notes

16 Bit addresses are stored; MSB even reg, LSB next odd reg.

Instruction Expansion

Tbl

dest	srce	MMMM	Append	Cyc
WRd	WRs	0010	DDDDSSSS	6
WRd	(WRs)	0011	DDDDSSSS	6
Rd	Rs	0100	SSSSSSSS,DDDDDDDD	10
WRd	Rs	0100	SSSSSSSS,1110DDDD	10
Rd	WRs	0100	1110SSSS,DDDDDDDD	10
Rd	(Rs)	0101	SSSSSSSS,DDDDDDDD	10

```
WRd    (Rs)    0101   SSSSSSSS,1110DDDD    10
Rd     (WRs)   0101   1110SSSS,DDDDDDDD    10
Rd     #n      0110   DDDDDDDD,nnnnnnnn    10
WRd    #n      0110   1110DDDD,nnnnnnnn    10
(Rd)   #n      0111   DDDDDDDD,nnnnnnnn    10
(WRd)  #n      0111   1110DDDD,nnnnnnnn    10
```

Manufacturer - destination,source
Universal - source,destination

```
                   Mem
                   ---

Univ   Manu   Desc         M   Append
----   ----   ----         -   ------

Rr     Rr     reg          0   RRRRRRRR
WRr    WRr    wrk reg      0   1110RRRR
(Rr)   @Rr    ind reg      1   RRRRRRRR
(WRr)  @WRr   ind wrk reg  1   1110RRRR
```

aa - address, 16-bits appended, MSB first
WRd - working register, 4-bits appended as 1110DDDD or part of inst
Rd - register, 8-bits appended
r   - relative adr, 8-bits appended
n   - immediate data, 8-bits appended

source reg appended before destination reg
destination reg appended before immediate data

```
              Condition codes
              ---------------

Sym    Disc           CCCC
---    ----           ----

T      always true    1000
F      always false   0000
C      carry          0111   C = 1
NC     no carry       1111   C = 0
Z      zero           0110   Z = 1
NZ     not 0          1110   Z = 0
P      plus           1101   S = 0
M      minus          0101   S = 1
V      overflow       0100   V = 1
NV     no overflow    1100   V = 0
EQ     =              0110   Z = 1
NE     NOT =          1110   Z = 0
SGE    signed > OR =  1001   S xor V = 0
SLT    signed <       0001   S xor V = 1
SGT    signed >       1010   Z or (S xor V) = 0
SLE    signed < OR =  0010   Z or (S xor V) = 1
GE     > OR =         1111   C = 0
LT     <              0111   C = 1
GT     >              1011   C = 0 and Z = 0
LE     < OR =         0011   C or Z = 1
```

Special Memory Locations

 2K on chip ROM
 128 bytes on chip RAM
 62K external prog RAM

366

62K external data RAM

Prog Memory

```
Loc    0 - 11     interrupt vectors
      12 - 2047   on chip ROM
    2048 - 65535  external memory
```

Data Memory

```
loc 0 - 2047  not used
    2048 - 65K  external memory
```

Z80

uPD780, Z80L, MK3880A/B, MPU800, TMPZ84C00P/-3,Z80C00   (1) HD64180

Data Move

MOV	LD				Move byte
Reg,Reg	Reg,Reg	01TTTFFF	4		srce, dest
Mem,Reg	Reg,Mem	01RRR110	7		memory, reg
#n,Reg	Reg,n	00RRR110	7		immed, reg
Reg,Mem	Mem,Reg	01110RRR	7		reg, memory
#n,Mem	Mem,n	36	10		immed, memory
A,(BC)	(BC),A	02	7		reg A, ind BC
A,(DE)	(DE),A	12	7		reg A, ind DE
A,aa	(aa),A	32	13		reg A, abs
aa,A	A,(aa)	3A	13		abs, reg A
(BC),A	A,(BC)	0A	7		ind BC, reg A
(DE),A	A,(DE)	1A	7		ind DE, reg A
I,A	A,I	ED,57	9	-C	reg I, reg A
R,A	A,R	ED,5F	9	-C	reg R, reg A
A,I	I,A	ED,47	9		reg A, reg I
A,R	R,A	ED,4F	9		reg A, reg R
MOVW					Move word
BC,aa	(aa),BC	ED,43	20		reg BC, abs
DE,aa	(aa),DE	ED,53	20		reg DE, abs
HL,aa	(aa),HL	22	16		reg HL, abs
IX,aa	(aa),IX	DD,22	20		reg IX, abs
IY,aa	(aa),IY	FD,22	20		reg IY, abs
SP,aa	(aa),SP	ED,73	20		reg SP, abs
aa,BC	BC,(aa)	ED,4B	20		abs, reg BC
aa,DE	DE,(aa)	ED,5B	20		abs, reg DE
aa,HL	HL,(aa)	2A	16		abs, reg HL
aa,IX	IX,(aa)	DD,2A	20		abs, reg IX
aa,IY	IY,(aa)	FD,2A	20		abs, reg IY
aa,SP	SP,(aa)	ED,7B	20		abs, reg SP
#nn,IX	IX,nn	DD,21	14		immed, reg IX
#nn,IY	IY,nn	FD,21	14		immed, reg IY
#nn,Reg	Reg,nn	00RR0001	10		immed, reg
HL,SP	SP,HL	F9	6		reg HL, reg SP
IX,SP	SP,IX	DD,F9	10		reg IX, reg SP
IY,SP	SP,IY	FD,F9	10		reg IY, reg SP
PUSH	PUSH				Push word onto the stack
BC	BC	C5	11		reg BC
DE	DE	D5	11		reg DE
HL	HL	E5	11		reg HL
AF	AF	F5	11		reg AF
IX	IX	DD,E5	15		reg IX
IY	IY	FD,E5	15		reg IY
POP	POP				Pop word from the stack
BC	BC	C1	10		reg BC
DE	DE	D1	10		reg DE

```
    HL         !   HL        ! E1         !10!  !    reg HL
    AF         !   AF        ! F1         !10!  !    reg AF
    IX         !   IX        ! DD,E1      !14!  !    reg IX
    IY         !   IY        ! FD,E1      !14!  !    reg IY
 XCHGW         ! EX          !            !  !  ! Exchange words
    DE,HL      !   DE,HL     ! EB         ! 4!  !    reg DE & reg HL
    (SP),HL    !   (SP),HL   ! E3         !10!  !    ind SP & reg HL
    (SP),IX    !   (SP),IX   ! DD,E3      !23!  !    ind SP & reg IX
    (SP),IY    !   (SP),IY   ! FD,E3      !23!  !    ind SP & reg IY
    AF,AF'     !   AF,AF'    ! 08         ! 4!  !    reg AF & reg AF'
 XCHGMW        ! EXX         !            !  !  ! Echange trible words
    BDH,BDH'   !             ! D9         ! 4!  !    reg BCDEHL & BCDEHL'
```

Math Operations

```
ADD            ! ADD         !            !  !all! Add byte
    Reg,A      !   A,Reg     ! 10000RRR   ! 4!  !    Reg, reg A
    Mem,A      !   A,Mem     ! 86         ! 7!  !    memory, reg A
    #n,A       !   A,n       ! C6         ! 7!  !    immed, reg A
ADDW           !             !            !  !CNH! Add word
    Reg,HL     !   Reg       ! 00RR1001   !11!  !    reg, reg HL
    BC,IX      !   IX,BC     ! DD,09      !15!  !    reg BC, reg IX
    DE,IX      !   IX,DE     ! DD,19      !15!  !    reg DE, reg IX
    IX,IX      !   IX,IX     ! DD,29      !15!  !    reg IX, reg IX
    SP,IX      !   IX,SP     ! DD,39      !15!  !    reg SP, reg IY
    BC,IY      !   IY,BC     ! FD,09      !15!  !    reg BC, reg IY
    DE,IY      !   IY,DE     ! FD,19      !15!  !    reg DE, reg IY
    IY,IY      !   IY,IY     ! FD,29      !15!  !    reg IY, reg IY
    SP,IY      !   IY,SP     ! FD,39      !15!  !    reg SP, reg IY
ADC            ! ADC         !            !  !all! Add byte w/c
    Reg,A      !   A,Reg     ! 10001RRR   ! 4!  !    Reg, reg A
    Mem,A      !   A,Mem     ! 8E         ! 7!  !    memory, reg A
    #n,A       !   A,n       ! CE         ! 7!  !    immed, reg A
ADCW           !             !            !  !all! Add word w/c
    Reg,HL     !   HL,Reg    ! ED,01RR1010!15!  !    reg, reg HL
INC            ! INC         !            !  !-C ! Increment byte
    Reg        !   Reg       ! 00RRR100   ! 4!  !    Reg
    Mem        !   Mem       ! 34         !11!  !    memory
INCW           !             !            !  !  ! Increment word
    Reg        !   Reg       ! 00RR0011   ! 6!  !    Reg
    IX         !   IX        ! DD,23      !10!  !    reg IX
    IY         !   IY        ! FD,23      !10!  !    reg IY
SUB            ! SUB         !            !  !all! Subtract byte
    Reg,A      !   Reg       ! 10010RRR   ! 4!  !    Reg, reg A
    Mem,A      !   Mem       ! 96         ! 7!  !    memory, reg A
    #n,A       !   n         ! D6         ! 7!  !    immed, reg A
SBB            ! SBC         !            !  !all! Subtract byte w/c
    Reg,A      !   A,Reg     ! 10011RRR   ! 4!  !    Reg, reg A
    Mem,A      !   A,Mem     ! 9E         ! 7!  !    memory, reg A
    #n,A       !   A,n       ! DE         ! 7!  !    immed, reg A
SBBW           !             !            !  !all! Subtract word w/c
    Reg,HL     !   HL,Reg    ! ED,01RR0010!15!  !    reg, reg HL
DA             ! DAA         !            !  !-N ! Decimal adjust Accum
    A          !             ! 27         ! 4!  !
DEC            ! DEC         !            !  !-C ! Decrement byte
    Reg        !   Reg       ! 00RRR101   ! 4!  !    Reg
    Mem        !   Mem       ! 35         !11!  !    memory
DECW           !             !            !  !  ! Decrement word
    Reg        !   Reg       ! 00RR1011   ! 6!  !    Reg
    IX         !   IX        ! DD,2B      !10!  !    reg IX
    IY         !   IY        ! FD,2B      !10!  !    reg IY
NEG            ! NEG         !            !  !all! Change sign
```

```
      A          !               ! ED,44      ! 8!      !    reg A
CMP              ! CP            !           !    !all! Compare byte
    A,Reg        !      Reg      ! 10111RRR   ! 4!      !    Reg, reg A
    A,Mem        !      Mem      ! BE         ! 7!      !    memory, reg A
    A,#n         !      n        ! FE         ! 7!      !    immed, reg A
* MUL            ! MLT           !           !    !    ! Multiply    (1)
*     Reg        !      Reg      ! ED,01RR1100!17!      !    lsb reg x msb reg = reg
```

String Operations

```
MOVS            ! LDD           !           !    !-C ! Mov string, from to count
  -(HL),-(DE),-BC!              ! ED,A8      !16!      !    ind_dec HL, DE, dec BC
                ! LDI           !           !    !-C !
  +(HL),+(DE),-BC!              ! ED,A0      !16!      !    ind_inc HL, DE, dec BC
MOVSR           ! LDDR          !           !    !-C ! Move string repeat
  -(HL),-(DE),-BC!              ! ED,B8      !21!      !    ind_dec HL, DE, dec BC
                ! LDIR          !           !    !-C !
  +(HL),+(DE),-BC!              ! ED,B0      !21!      !    ind_inc HL, DE, dec BC
CMPS            ! CPD           !           !    !-C ! Compare string, to val cnt
  -(HL),A,-BC   !               ! ED,A9      !16!      !    ind_dec HL,reg A,dec BC
                ! CPI           !           !    !-C !
  +(HL),A,-BC   !               ! ED,A1      !16!      !    ind_inc HL,reg A,dec BC
CMPSR           ! CPDR          !           !    !-C ! Compare string repeat
  -(HL),A,-BC   !               ! ED,B9      !21!      !    ind_dec HL,reg A,dec BC
                ! CPIR          !           !    !-C !
  +(HL),A,-BC   !               ! ED,B1      !21!      !    ind_inc HL,reg A,dec BC
```

Logical Operations

```
AND             ! AND           !           !    !all! Logical AND byte
    Reg,A        !      Reg      ! 10100RRR   ! 4!      !    Reg, reg A
    Mem,A        !      Mem      ! A6         ! 7!      !    memory, reg A
    #n,A         !      n        ! E6         ! 7!      !    immed, reg A
OR              ! OR            !           !    !all! Logical OR byte
    Reg,A        !      Reg      ! 10110RRR   ! 4!      !    Reg, reg A
    Mem,A        !      Mem      ! B6         ! 7!      !    memory, reg A
    #n,A         !      n        ! F6         ! 7!      !    immed, reg A
XOR             ! XOR           !           !    !all! Logical Exclusive OR byte
    Reg,A        !      Reg      ! 10101RRR   ! 4!      !    Reg, reg A
    Mem,A        !      Mem      ! AE         ! 7!      !    memory, reg A
    #n,A         !      n        ! EE         ! 7!      !    immed, reg A
CPL             ! CPL           !           !    !NH ! Complement byte
    A            !               ! 2F         ! 4!      !    reg A
* TEST           ! TST           !           !    !all! Test, log AND, byte (1)
*     Reg,A      !      Reg      ! ED,00RRR100! 7!      !    reg, reg A
*     (HL),A     !      (HL)     ! ED,34      !10!      !    ind HL, reg A
*     #n,A       !      n        ! ED,64      ! 9!      !    immed, reg A
RLWC            ! RL            !           !    !all! Rotate byte w/c left
    Reg          !      Reg      ! CB,00010RRR! 8!      !    Reg
    Mem          !      Mem      ! CB,16      !15!      !    memory
    A            !      RLA      ! 17         ! 4!CNH!    reg A
RRWC            ! RR            !           !    !all! Rotate byte w/c right
    Reg          !      Reg      ! CB,00011RRR! 8!      !    Reg
    Mem          !      Mem      ! CB,1E      !15!      !    memory
    A            !      RRA      ! 1F         ! 4!CNH!    reg A
RLTC            ! RLC           !           !    !all! Rotate byte left to/c
    Reg          !      Reg      ! CB,00000RRR! 8!      !    Reg
    Mem          !      Mem      ! CB,06      !15!      !    memory
    A            !      RLCA     ! 07         ! 4!CNH!    reg A
RRTC            ! RRC           !           !    !all! Rotate byte right to/c
    Reg          !      Reg      ! CB,00001RRR! 8!      !    Reg
    Mem          !      Mem      ! CB,0E      !15!      !    memory
```

A	RRCA	0F	4	CNH	reg A
RLWR	RLD			-C	Rotate left w/reg n bits
HL,A,4		ED,6F	18		reg A, reg HL, 4 bits
RRWR	RRD			-C	Rotate right w/reg n bits
HL,A,4		ED,67	18		reg A, reg HL, 4 bits
SLA	SLA			all	Shift left arithmetic
Reg	Reg	CB,00100RRR	8		Reg
Mem	Mem	CB,26	15		memory
SRA	SRA			all	Shift right arithmetic
Reg	Reg	CB,00101RRR	8		Reg
Mem	Mem	CB,2E	15		memory
SRL	SRL			all	Shift right logical
Reg	Reg	CB,00111RRR	8		Reg
Mem	Mem	CB,3E	15		memory

Bit Operations

TESTB	BIT			-C	Test bit
Reg,Bit	Bit,Reg	CB,01BBBRRR	8		Reg, bit
Mem,Bit	Bit,Mem	CB,01BBB110	12		memory, bit
SETB	SET				Set bit
Reg,Bit	Bit,Reg	CB,11BBBRRR	8		Reg, bit
Mem,Bit	Bit,Mem	CB,11BBB110	15		memory, bit
RESB	RES				Reset bit
Reg,Bit	Bit,Reg	CB,10BBBRRR	8		Reg, bit
Mem,Bit	Bit,Mem	CB,10BBB110	15		memory, bit
CPLF	CCF				Complement flag
C		3F		C	carry
SETF	SCF				Set flag
C		37		C	carry

Program Control

CALL	CALL		10		Call subroutine
UN,aa	aa	CD	17		uncond
Z,aa	CZ aa	CC	17		zero
NZ,aa	CNZ aa	C4	17		not zero
P,aa	CP aa	F4	17		positive
M,aa	CM aa	FC	17		minus
C,aa	CC aa	DC	17		carry
NC,aa	CNC aa	D4	17		no carry
PE,aa	CPE aa	EC	17		parity even
PO,aa	CPO aa	E4	17		parity odd
RET	RET		5		Return from subroutine
UN		C9	10		uncond
Z	RZ	C8	11		zero
NZ	RNZ	C0	11		not zero
P	RP	F0	11		plus
M	RM	F8	11		minus
C	RC	D8	11		carry
NC	RNC	D0	11		no carry
PE	RPE	E8	11		parity even
PO	RPO	E0	11		parity odd
RETI	RETI	ED,4D	14		Return from interrupt
RETNMI	RETN	ED,45			Return from NMI
JMP	JP		7		Jump to location
UN,aa	aa	C3	10		uncond
Z,aa	Z,aa	CA	10		zero
NZ,aa	NZ,aa	C2	10		not zero
P,aa	P,aa	F2	10		positive
M,aa	M,aa	FA	10		minus
C,aa	C,aa	DA	10		carry
NC,aa	NC,aa	D2	10		no carry

```
     PE,aa        !  PE,aa     ! EA       !10!   ! parity even
     PO,aa        !  PO,aa     ! E2       !10!   ! parity odd
     UN,(HL)      !  (HL)      ! E9       ! 4!   ! uncond, ind HL
     UN,(IX)      !  (IX)      ! DD,E9    ! 8!   ! uncond, ind IX
     UN,(IY)      !  (IY)      ! FD,E9    ! 8!   ! uncond, ind IY
JMPR            ! JR         !          ! 7!   ! Jump relative
     UN,r         !  r         ! 18       !12!   !   uncond
     C,r          !  C,r       ! 38       !12!   !   carry
     NC,r         !  NC,r      ! 30       !12!   !   no carry
     NZ,r         !  NZ,r      ! 20       !12!   !   not zero
     Z,r          !  Z,r       ! 28       !12!   !   zero
DECJNZR         ! DJNZ       !          !  !   ! Decrement jump rel if not 0
     B,r          !  r         ! 10       !13!   !   dec B, rel
RST             ! RST        !          !  !   ! Restart subroutine via
     t            !  t         ! 11NNN111 !11!   !   t = 0 (00H) to 7 (38H)
HALT            ! HALT       ! 76       ! 7!   ! Stop till interrupt
NOP             ! NOP        ! 00       ! 4!   ! No operation
* SLEEP         ! SLP        ! ED,76    ! 8!   ! Sleep mode
```

I/O   Operations

```
IN              ! IN         !          !  !    ! Input byte
     p,A          !  (p)       ! DB       !11!    !   port p, reg A
     (C),Reg      !  Reg,(C)   ! ED,01RRR000 !12!-C !   ind C, reg
*    p,Reg        !  Reg,(p)   ! ED,00RRR000 !12!-C !   port p, reg  (1)
INS             ! IN         !          !  !    ! Input string
     (C),-(HL),-B ! IND       ! ED,AA    !16!all!   ind C,ind_dec HL,dec B
     (C),+(HL),-B ! INI       ! ED,A2    !16!all!   ind C,ind_inc HL,dec B
INSR            !            !          !  !    ! Input string repeat
     (C),-(HL),-B ! INDR      ! ED,BA    !21!all!   ind C,ind_dec HL,dec B
     (C),+(HL),-B ! INIR      ! ED,B2    !21!all!   ind C,ind_inc HL,dec B
OUT             ! OUT        !          !  !    ! Output byte
     A,p          !  (p),A     ! D3       !11!    !   reg A, port p
     Reg,(C)      !  (C),Reg   ! ED,01RRR001 !12!   !   reg, ind C
*    Reg,p        !  (p),Reg   ! ED,00RRR001 !13!   !   reg, port p  (1)
OUTS            !            !          !  !    ! Output string
     -(HL),(C),-B ! OUTD      ! ED,AB    !16!all!   ind_dec HL,ind C,dec B
     +(HL),(C),-B ! OUTI      ! ED,A3    !16!all!   ind_inc HL,ind C,dec B
*    +(HL),+(C),-B! OTIM      ! ED,83    !14!all!   ind_inc HL, C, dec B (1)
*    -(HL),-(C),-B! OTDM      ! ED,8B    !14!all!   ind_dec HL, C, dec B (1)
OUTSR           !            !          !  !    ! Output string repeat
     -(HL),(C),-B ! OTDR      ! ED,BB    !21!all!   ind_dec HL,ind C,dec B
     +(HL),(C),-B ! OTIR      ! ED,B3    !21!all!   ind_inc HL,ind C,dec B
*    +(HL),+(C),-B! OTIMR     ! ED,93    !21!all!   ind_inc HL, C, dec B (1)
*    -(HL),-(C),-B! OTDMR     ! ED,9B    !21!all!   ind_dec HL, C, dec B (1)
DI              ! DI         ! F3       ! 4!    ! Disable interrupts
EI              ! EI         ! FB       ! 4!    ! Enable interrupts
SETIM           ! IM         !          !  !    ! Set interrup mask
     0            !  0         ! ED,46    ! 8!    !   zero
     1            !  1         ! ED,56    ! 8!    !   one
     2            !  2         ! ED,5E    ! 8!    !   two
* TSTIO          ! TSTIO      !          !  !    ! Test I/O data   (1)
*    #n,(C)       !  n         ! ED,74    !12!all!   immed, ind C
```

Registers

```
        16     8!7      0        16      8!7      0
      -----------------        -----------------
   AF !  A  ! Flags !     AF' !  A'  !  F'  !
      -----------------        -----------------
```

```
BC  !  B  !  C  !    BC' !  B' !  C' !
    -----------------        -----------------
DE  !  D  !  E  !    DE' !  D' !  E' !
    -----------------        -----------------
HL  !  H  !  L  !    HL' !  H' !  L' !
    -----------------        -----------------

SP  ! Stack Pointer !
    -----------------
IX  !   Index Reg   !
    -----------------
IY  !   Index Reg   !
    -----------------
PC  !Program Counter!
    -----------------
      !  I  !  R  !    interrupt vector
    -----------------   memory refresh
```

Flags

    S = sign of result
    Z = zero result
    A = auxilary carry from bit 3
    P = parity
        overflow for math operations
    C = carry
    N = operation type, 1=sub 0=add

Addressing Modes

Univ	Manuf		
#n	n	- immediate data
XX	XX	- register
aa	(aa)	- absolute address
(XX)	(XX)	- register indirect
(XX+d)	(XX+d)	- indexed, reg IX or IY + 8-bit value
-(XX)		- indirect auto decrement
+(XX)		- indirect auto increment
-XX		- register auto decrement
P	P	- port address

Instruction Expansion

Register				Memory			
Byte	RRR	Word	RR	Par	Mode	Inst	Cyc
A	111	BC	00	For single byte basic instructions (xx)			
B	000	DE	01	(HL)	ind HL	xx	0
C	001	HL	10	(IX+d)	indexed IX	DD,xx,dd	12
D	010	SP	11	(IY+d)	indexed IY	FD,xx,dd	12
E	011			For double byte basic instructions (xx,xx)			
H	100			(HL)	ind HL	xx,xx	0
L	101			(IX+d)	indexed IX	DD,xx,dd,xx	8
				(IY+d)	indexed IY	FD,xx,dd,xx	8

    n = immediate data, 8- or 16-bits appended to inst
    aa = address, 16-bits appended to inst
    r = relative adr, 8-bits appended to inst

```
d   = index value, 8-bits appended to inst
bit = bit number, 3-bits part of inst
p   = port adr, 8-bits appended to inst
```

Special Memory Locations

Notes

Z8000

Z80001, Z8002 (AMD)

Data Move

```
MOV         ! LDB/LDRB  !           ! !  ! Move byte
   Reg,(Rx) !   (Rx),Reg! 2E,DDDDSSSS ! 8!  !   reg, ind Rx
   Reg,Mem  !   Mem,Reg ! 6E,MMMMSSSS !11+ !   reg, memory
   Reg,Mem2 !   Mem2,Reg! 32,MMMMSSSS !14!  !   reg, memory
   Reg,Reg  !   Reg,Reg ! A0,SSSSDDDD ! 3!  !   Reg,Reg
   #n,Reg   !   Reg,n   ! 20,0000DDDD ! 7!  !   immed, reg
   (Rx),Reg !   Reg,(Rx)! 20,SSSSDDDD ! 7!  !   ind Rx, reg
   Mem,Reg  !   Reg,Mem ! 60,MMMMDDDD ! 9+ !   memory, reg
   Mem2,Reg !   Reg,Mem2! 60,MMMMDDDD !14!  !   memory2, reg
   #n,(Rx)  !   (Rx),n  ! 0C,DDDD0101 !11!  !   immed, ind Rx
   #n,Mem   !   Mem,n   ! 4C,MMMM0101 !14+ !   immed, memory
            ! LDCTLB    !           ! !  !
   FCW,Reg  !   Reg     ! 8C,RRRR0001 ! 7!  !   FCW flags, reg
   Reg,FCW  !   Reg     ! 8C,RRRR1001 ! 7!  !   reg, FCW flags
MOVW        ! LD/LDR    !           ! !  ! Move word
   Reg,(Rx) !   (Rx),Reg! 2F,DDDDSSSS ! 8!  !   reg, ind Rx
   Reg,Mem  !   Mem,Reg ! 6F,MMMMSSSS !11+ !   reg, memory
   Reg,Mem2 !   Mem2,Reg! 33,MMMMSSSS !14!  !   reg, memory
   Reg,Reg  !   Reg,Reg ! A1,SSSSDDDD ! 3!  !   Reg,Reg
   #nn,Reg  !   Reg,nn  ! 21,0000DDDD ! 7!  !   immed, reg
   (Rx),Reg !   Reg,(Rx)! 41,SSSSDDDD ! 7!  !   ind Rx, reg
   Mem,Reg  !   Reg,Mem ! 61,MMMMDDDD ! 9+ !   memory, reg
   Mem2,Reg !   Reg,Mem2! 31,MMMMDDDD !14!  !   memory2, reg
   #nn,(Rx) !   (Rx),nn ! 0D,DDDD0101 !11!  !   immed, ind Rx
   #nn,Mem  !   Mem,nn  ! 4D,MMMM0101 !14+ !   immed, memory
            ! LDCTL     !           ! 7!  !
   FCW,Reg  !   Reg,FCW ! 7D,RRRR0010 ! !  !   FCW, Reg, FCW
   Refresh,Reg!  Reg,Ref ! 7D,RRRR0011 ! !  !   Reg, refresh reg
   NPSAP,Reg!   Reg,NPSAP! 7D,RRRR0100 ! !  !   NPSAP segment, reg
   NPSAP+1,Reg! Reg,+1  ! 7D,RRRR0101 ! !  !   NPSAP upper offset, reg
   R14,Reg  !   Reg,R14 ! 7D,RRRR0110 ! !  !   R14, reg
   R15,Reg  !   Reg,R15 ! 7D,RRRR0111 ! !  !   R15, reg
   Reg,FCW  !   FCW,Reg ! 7D,RRRR1010 ! !  !   Reg, FCW
   Reg,Refresh! Ref,Reg ! 7D,RRRR1011 ! !  !   reg, refresh reg
   Reg,NPSAP!   NPSAP,Reg! 7D,RRRR1100 ! !  !   reg, NPSAP segment
   Reg,NPSAP+1! +1,Reg  ! 7D,RRRR1101 ! !  !   reg, NPSAP upper offset
   Reg,R14  !   R14,Reg ! 7D,RRRR1110 ! !  !   reg, R14
   Reg,R15  !   R15,Reg ! 7D,RRRR1111 ! !  !   reg, R15
MOVDW       ! LDL/LDRL  !           ! !  ! Move double word
   Reg,(Rx) !   (Rx),Reg! 1D,DDDDSSSS !11!  !   reg, ind Rx
   Reg,Mem  !   Mem,Reg ! 5D,MMMMSSSS !14+ !   reg, memory
   Reg,Mem2 !   Mem2,Reg! 37,MMMMSSSS !17!  !   reg, memory
   Reg,Reg  !   Reg,Reg ! 94,SSSSDDDD ! 5!  !   Reg,Reg
```

#nnnn,Reg		Reg,nnnn	14,0000DDDD	11	immed, reg
(Rx),Reg		Reg,(Rx)	14,SSSSDDDD	11	ind Rx, reg
Mem,Reg		Reg,Mem	54,MMMMDDDD	12+	memory, reg
Mem2,Reg		Reg,Mem2	35,MMMMDDDD	17	memory2, reg
#nnnn,(Rx)		(Rx),nnnn	0D,DDDD0111	17	immed, ind Rx
#nnnn,Mem		Mem,nn	4D,MMMM0111	20+	immed, memory
MOVMWR	LDM				Move multible registers
Reg,(Rx),n		(Rx),Reg, n	1C,DDDD1001 0000SSSS, 0000NNNN	11+	start reg, # reg,to NNNN= # reg-1
Reg,Mem,n		Mem,Reg,n	5C,MMMM1001 0000SSSS, 0000NNNN	14+	
(Rx),Reg,n		Reg,(Rx), n	1C,SSSS0001 0000DDDD 0000NNNN	11+	from, # reg,start reg NNNN= # reg-1
Mem,Reg,n		Mem,Reg,n	5C,MMMM0001 0000DDDD 0000NNNN	14+	
MOV	LDPS			all	Move program status
(Rx),PSW		(Rx)	39,SSSS0000	12+	from ind Rx
Mem,PSW		Mem	79,MMMM0000	16+	from memory
CLR [W]	CLR [B]	[+1]			Move zero to byte [word]
Reg		Reg	8C,RRRR1000	7	Reg
(Rx)		(Rx)	0C,RRRR1000	8	ind Rx
Mem		Mem	4C,MMMM1000	11+	memory
CLRDW	CLRL				Move implied zero to d-word
Reg		Reg	9C,RRRR0000	5	Reg
(Rx)		(Rx)	1C,RRRR0000	11	ind Rx
Mem		Mem	5C,MMMM0000	14+	memory
MOVW	PUSH				Push word onto the stack
Reg,(-Rx)		Rd,Rs	93,DDDDSSSS	9	reg, ind_dec Rx
#nn,(-Rx)		Rd,nn	0D,DDDD1001	12	immed, ind_dec Rx
(Rx),(-Rx)		Rd,Rs	13,DDDDSSSS	13	ind Rx, ind_dec Rx
Mem,(-Rx)		Rd,Mem	53,DDDDMMMM	13+	memory, ind_dec Rx
MOVDW	PUSHL				Push d-word onto the stack
Reg,(-Rx)		Rd,Rs	91,DDDDSSSS	12	reg, ind_dec Rx
#nn,(-Rx)		Rd,nn	0B,DDDD1001	19	immed, ind_dec Rx
(Rx),(-Rx)		Rd,Rs	11,DDDDSSSS	20	ind Rx, ind_dec Rx
Mem,(-Rx)		Rd,Mem	51,DDDDMMMM	20+	memory, ind_dec Rx
MOVW	POP				Pop word from the stack
(+Rx),Reg		Rd,Rs	97,SSSSDDDD	8	ind_inc Rx, reg
(+Rx),(Rx)		Rd,Rs	17,SSSSDDDD	12	ind_inc Rx, ind Rx
(+Rx),Mem		Mem,Rs	57,RRRRMMMM	15+	ind_inc Rx, memory
MOVDW	POPL				Pop d-word from the stack
(+Rx),Reg		Rd,Rs	95,SSSSDDDD	12	ind_inc Rx, reg
(+Rx),(Rx)		Rd,Rs	15,SSSSDDDD	19	ind_inc Rx, ind Rx
(+Rx),Mem		Mem,Rs	55,RRRRMMMM	22+	ind_inc Rx, memory
XCHG [W]	EX [B]	[+1]			Exchange bytes [word]
Reg,Reg		Reg,Reg	AC,SSSSDDDD	6	Reg & Reg
Reg,(Rx)		Reg,(Rx)	2C,SSSSDDDD	12	Reg & ind Rx
Reg,Mem		Reg.Mem	6C,MMMMDDDD	15+	Reg & memory
MOVN	LDK				Load word reg with
#n,Reg		Reg,n	BD,RRRRVVVV	5	4-bit value, reg
MOVBW	LDB				Load word reg with
#n,Reg		Reg,n	1100RRRR, VVVVVVVV	5	8-bit value, reg
LEA	LDA/LDAR				Load efective address
Mem2,Reg		Reg,Mem2	34,MMMMDDDD	15	memory2, reg
Mem,Reg		Reg,Mem	76,MMMMDDDD	12+	memory, reg
					reg=wrd non-seg
					d-wrd segmented

```
TSTSET [W]  | TSET [B]  |[+1]          | !S | Test sign set byte = FFFFH
   Reg      |    Reg    | 8C,RRRR0110  | 7|   |     Reg      [word]
   (Rx)     |    (Rx)   | 0C,RRRR0110  |11|   |     ind Rx
   Mem      |    Mem    | 4C,MMMM0110  |14+  |     memory
```

Math Operations

```
ADD         | ADDB      |              | |all| Add byte
   Reg,Reg  |    Reg,Reg| 60,SSSSDDDD  | 4|   |    Reg, Reg
   #n,Reg   |    Reg,n  | 00,0000RRRR  | 7|   |    immed, reg
   (Rx),Reg |    Reg,(Rx)| 00,SSSSDDDD | 7|   |    ind Rx, reg
   Mem,Reg  |    Reg,Mem| 40,MMMMRRRR  | 9+  |    memory, reg
ADDW        | ADD       |              | |-DH| Add word
   Reg,Reg  |    Reg,Reg| 81,SSSSDDDD  | 4|   |    Reg, Reg
   #nn,Reg  |    Reg,nn | 01,0000RRRR  | 7|   |    immed, reg
   (Rx),Reg |    Reg,(Rx)| 01,SSSSDDDD | 7|   |    ind Rx, reg
   Mem,Reg  |    Reg,Mem| 41,MMMMRRRR  | 9+  |    memory, reg
ADDDW       | ADDL      |              | |-DH| Add double word
   Reg,Reg  |    Reg,Reg| 96,SSSSDDDD  | 8|   |    Reg, Reg
   #nn,Reg  |    Reg,nn | 16,0000RRRR  |14|   |    immed, reg
   (Rx),Reg |    Reg,(Rx)| 16,SSSSDDDD |14|   |    ind Rx, reg
   Mem,Reg  |    Reg,Mem| 56,MMMMRRRR  |15+  |    memory, reg
ADC         | ADCB      |              | |all| Add byte w/c
   Reg,Reg  |    Reg,Reg| B4,SSSSDDDD  | 5|   |    Reg, Reg
ADCW        | ADC       |              | |-DH| Add word w/c
   Reg,Reg  |    Reg,Reg| B5,SSSSDDDD  | 5|   |    Reg, Reg
ADDN [W]    | INC [B]   |[+1]          | |-C| Increment byte [word]
   #n,Reg   |    Reg,n  | A8,RRRRNNNN  | 4|   |    value, reg
   #n,(Rx)  |    (Rx),n | 28,RRRRNNNN  |11|   |    value, ind Rx
   #n,Mem   |    Mem,n  | 68,MMMMNNNN  |13+  |    value, memory
SUB [W]     | SUB [B]   |[+1]          | |all| Subtract byte
   Reg,Reg  |    Reg,Reg| 82,SSSSDDDD  | 4|   |    Reg, Reg
   #nn,Reg  |    Reg,nn | 02,0000RRRR  | 7|   |    immed, reg
   (Rx),Reg |    Reg,(Rx)| 02,SSSSDDDD | 7|   |    ind Rx, reg
   Mem,Reg  |    Reg,Mem| 42,MMMMRRRR  | 9+  |    memory, reg
SUBDW       | SUBL      |              | |-DH| Subtract d-word
   Reg,Reg  |    Reg,Reg| 92,SSSSDDDD  | 8|   |    Reg,Reg
   #nnnn,Reg|    Reg,nnnn| 12,0000RRRR |14|   |    immed, reg
   (Rx),Reg |    Reg,(Rx)| 12,SSSSDDDD |14|   |    ind Rx, reg
   Mem,Reg  |    Reg,Mem| 52,MMMMRRRR  |15+  |    memory, reg
SBB         | SBCB      |              | |all| Subtract byte w/c
   Reg,Reg  |    Reg,Reg| B6,SSSSDDDD  | 5|   |    Reg, Reg
SBBW        | SBC       |              | |-DH| Subtract word w/c
   Reg,Reg  |    Reg,Reg| B7,SSSSDDDD  | 5|   |    Reg, Reg
DA          | DAB       |              | |-N| Decimal adjust byte
   Reg      |    Reg    | B0,RRRR0000  | 5|CZS|   Reg
SUBN [W]    | DEC [B]   |[+1]          | |ZSP| Decrement byte [word]
   #n,Reg   |    Reg,n  | AA,RRRRNNNN  | 4|   |    value, Reg
   #n,(Rx)  |    (Rx),n | 2A,RRRRNNNN  |11|   |    value, ind Rx
   #n,Mem   |    Mem,n  | 6A,MMMMNNNN  |13+  |    value, memory
            |           |              |     |    NNNN=4-bit value -1
NEG [W]     | NEG [B]   |[+1]          | |-DH| Change sign byte [word]
   Reg      |    Reg    | 8C,RRRR0010  | 7|   |    Reg
   (Rx)     |    (Rx)   | 0C,RRRR0010  |12|   |    ind Rx
   Mem      |    Mem    | 4C,MMMM0010  |15+  |    memory
CNVBW       | EXTSB     |              | |   | Convert byte to word
   Reg      |    Reg    | B1,RRRR0000  |11|   |    reg Rx
CNVWDW      | EXTS      |              | |   | Convert word to d-word
   Reg      |    Reg    | B1,RRRR1010  |11|   |    reg RRx
CNVDWQW     | EXTSL     |              | |   | Convert d-word to q-wor
   Reg      |    Reg    | B1,RRRR0111  |11|   |    reg RQx
```

```
CMP [W]      ¦ CP [B]    ¦[+1]        ¦    ¦-DH¦ Compare byte [word]
   Reg,Reg   ¦    Reg,Reg¦ 8A,SSSSDDDD ¦ 4 ¦   ¦    Reg, Reg
   Reg,#n    ¦    Reg,n  ¦ 0A,0000RRRR ¦ 7 ¦   ¦    reg, immed
   Reg,(Rx)  ¦    Reg,(Rx)¦ 0A,SSSSDDDD ¦ 7 ¦   ¦    reg, ind Rx
   Reg,Mem   ¦    Reg,Mem ¦ 4A,MMMMRRRR ¦ 9+¦   ¦    reg, memory
   (Rx),#nn  ¦    (Rx),nn ¦ 0C,RRRR0001 ¦11 ¦   ¦    ind Rx, immed
   Mem,#nn   ¦    Mem,nn  ¦ 4C,MMMM0001 ¦14+¦   ¦    memory, immed
CMPDW        ¦ CPL       ¦            ¦    ¦-DH¦ Compare d-word
   Reg,Reg   ¦    Reg,Reg¦ 90,SSSSDDDD ¦ 8 ¦   ¦    Reg, Reg
   Reg,#nn   ¦    Reg,nn ¦ 10,0000RRRR ¦14 ¦   ¦    reg, immed
   Reg,(Rx)  ¦    Reg,(Rx)¦ 10,SSSSDDDD ¦14 ¦   ¦    reg, ind Rx
   Reg,Mem   ¦    Reg,Mem¦ 50,MMMMRRRR ¦14+¦   ¦    reg, memory
MULDWW       ¦ MULT      ¦            ¦    ¦-DH¦ Multiply word by word
   Reg,RRx   ¦    RRx,Reg¦ 99,SSSSDDDD ¦70 ¦   ¦    reg Rx, reg RRx
   #nn,RRx   ¦    RRx,nn ¦ 19,0000DDDD ¦70 ¦   ¦    immed, reg RRx
   (Rx),RRx  ¦    RRx,(Rx)¦ 19,SSSSDDDD ¦70 ¦   ¦    ind Rx, reg RRx
   Mem,RRx   ¦    RRx,Mem¦ 59,MMMMDDDD ¦71+¦   ¦    memory, reg RRx
MULQWDW      ¦ MULTL     ¦            ¦    ¦-DH¦ Multiply q-word by d-word
   RRx,RQx   ¦    RQx,RRx¦ 98,SSSSDDDD ¦282¦   ¦    reg RRx, reg RQx
   #nnnn,RQx ¦    RQx,nnnn¦ 18,0000DDDD ¦282¦   ¦    immed, reg RQx
   (Rx),RQx  ¦    RQx,(Rx)¦ 18,SSSSDDDD ¦282¦   ¦    ind Rx, reg RQx
   Mem,RQx   ¦    RQx,Mem¦ 58,MMMMDDDD ¦283¦   ¦    memory, reg RQx
DIVDWW       ¦ DIV       ¦            ¦    ¦-DH¦ Devide d-word by word
   Reg,RRx   ¦    RRx,Reg¦ 9B,SSSSDDDD ¦95 ¦   ¦    reg Rx, reg RRx
   #nn,RRx   ¦    RRx,nn ¦ 1B,0000DDDD ¦95 ¦   ¦    immed, reg RRx
   (Rx),RRx  ¦    RRx,(Rx)¦ 1B,SSSSDDDD ¦95 ¦   ¦    ind Rx, reg RRx
   Mem,RRx   ¦    RRx,Mem¦ 5B,MMMMDDDD ¦96+¦   ¦    memory, reg RRx
DIVQWDW      ¦ DIVL      ¦            ¦    ¦-DH¦ Devide q-word by d-word
   RRx,RQx   ¦    RQx,RRx¦ 9A,SSSSDDDD ¦723¦   ¦    reg RRx, reg RQx
   #nnnn,RQx ¦    RQx,nnnn¦ 1A,0000DDDD ¦723¦   ¦    immed, reg RQx
   (Rx),RQx  ¦    RQx,(Rx)¦ 1A,SSSSDDDD ¦723¦   ¦    ind Rx, reg RQx
   Mem,RQx   ¦    RQx,Mem¦ 5A,MMMMDDDD ¦724+¦  ¦    memory, reg RQx
```

Logical Operations

```
AND [W]      ¦ AND [B]   ¦[+1]        ¦    ¦ZSP¦ Logical AND byte/word
   Reg,Reg   ¦    Reg,Reg¦ 86,SSSSDDDD ¦ 4 ¦   ¦    Reg, Reg
   #nn,Reg   ¦    Reg,nn ¦ 06,0000RRRR ¦ 7 ¦   ¦    immed, reg
   (Rx),Reg  ¦    Reg,(Rx)¦ 06,SSSSDDDD ¦ 7 ¦   ¦    ind Rx, reg
   Mem,Reg   ¦    Reg,Mem¦ 46,MMMMRRRR ¦ 9+¦   ¦    memory, reg
OR [W]       ¦ OR [B]    ¦[+1]        ¦    ¦ZSP¦ Logical OR byte/word
   Reg,Reg   ¦    Reg,Reg¦ 84,SSSSDDDD ¦ 4 ¦   ¦    Reg, Reg
   #nn,Reg   ¦    Reg,n  ¦ 04,0000RRRR ¦ 7 ¦   ¦    immed, reg
   (Rx),Reg  ¦    Reg,(Rx)¦ 04,SSSSDDDD ¦ 7 ¦   ¦    ind Rx, reg
   Mem,Reg   ¦    Reg,Mem¦ 44,MMMMRRRR ¦ 9+¦   ¦    memory, reg
TEST [W,DW]  ¦ TEST [B,L]¦            ¦    ¦ZS ¦ Test logical OR w/0
   Reg       ¦    Reg    ¦ 100L110W    ¦ 7 ¦   ¦    Reg
             ¦           ¦ RRRR0100    ¦   ¦   ¦
   (Rx)      ¦    (Rx)   ¦ 000L110W    ¦ 8 ¦   ¦    ind Rx
             ¦           ¦ RRRR0100    ¦   ¦   ¦
   Mem       ¦    Mem    ¦ 010L110W    ¦11+¦   ¦    memory
             ¦           ¦ MMMM0100    ¦   ¦   ¦
XOR [W]      ¦ XOR [B]   ¦[+1]        ¦    ¦ZSP¦ Exclusive OR byte/wrd
   Reg,Reg   ¦    Reg,Reg¦ 89,SSSSDDDD ¦ 4 ¦   ¦    Reg, reg
   #nn,Reg   ¦    Reg,nn ¦ 09,0000RRRR ¦ 7 ¦   ¦    immed, reg
   (Rx),Reg  ¦    Reg,(Rx)¦ 09,SSSSDDDD ¦ 7 ¦   ¦    ind Rx, reg
   Mem,Reg   ¦    Reg,Mem¦ 49,MMMMRRRR ¦10+¦   ¦    memory, reg
CPL [W]      ¦ COM [B]   ¦[+1]        ¦    ¦ZSP¦ Complement byte/word
   Reg       ¦    Reg    ¦ 8C,RRRR0000 ¦ 5 ¦   ¦    Reg
   (Rx)      ¦    (Rx)   ¦ 0C,RRRR0000 ¦12+¦   ¦    ind Rx
   Mem       ¦    Mem    ¦ 4C,MMMM0000 ¦15+¦   ¦    memory
RLWC [W]     ¦ RLC [B]   ¦[+1]        ¦    ¦-DH¦ Rotate left w/c byte/word
```

```
      Reg,1      !     Reg,1   ! B2,RRRR0000 ! 6!    !  Reg, 1 bit
      Reg,2      !     Reg,2   ! B2,RRRR0010 ! 7!    !  Reg, 2 bits
 RRWC [W]        ! RR  [B]     !C+1]         !  !-DH! Rotate right w/c byte/word
      Reg,1      !     Reg,1   ! B2,RRRR0100 ! 6!    !  Reg, 1 bit
      Reg,2      !     Reg,2   ! B2,RRRR0110 ! 7!    !  Reg, 2 bits
 RLTC [W]        ! RL  [B]     !C+1]         !  !-DH! Rotate left to/c byte/word
      Reg,1      !     Reg,1   ! B2,RRRR1000 ! 6!    !  Reg, 1 bit
      Reg,2      !     Reg,2   ! B2,RRRR1010 ! 7!    !  Reg, 2 bits
 RRTC [W]        ! RR  [B]     !C+1]         !  !-DH! Rotate right to/c byte/word
      Reg,1      !     Reg,1   ! B2,RRRR1100 ! 6!    !  Reg, 1 bit
      Reg,2      !     Reg,2   ! B2,RRRR1110 ! 7!    !  Reg, 2 bits
 SLA   Reg,#nn   ! SLAB Reg,nn! B2,RRRR1001 !13!-DH! Shift arith left, n bits
 SLAW  Reg,#nn   ! SLA  Reg,nn! B3,RRRR1001 !13!-DH! Shift arith wrd left, n bits
 SLADW Reg,#nn   ! SLAL Reg,nn! B3,RRRR1101 !13!-DH! Shift arith d-wrd left n bit
 SRA   Reg,#nn   ! SRAB Reg,nn! B2,RRRR1001 !12!-DH! Shift arith right
 SRAW  Reg,#nn   ! SRA  Reg,nn! B3,RRRR1001 !13!-DH! Shift arith right word
 SRADW Reg,#nn   ! SRAL Reg,nn! B3,RRRR1101 !12!-DH! Shift arith right d-word
 SLL   Reg,#nn   ! SLLB Reg,nn! B2,RRRR0001 !13!CZS! Shift logical left n bits
 SLLW  Reg,#nn   ! SLL  Reg,nn! B3,RRRR0001 !13!CSZ! Shift logical left wrd n bit
 SLLDW Reg,#nn   ! SLLL Reg,nn! B3,RRRR0101 !13!CZS! Shift logical left d-wrd
 SRL   Reg,#nn   ! SRLB Reg,nn! B2,RRRR0001 !13!CZS! Shift logical left
 SRLW  Reg,#nn   ! SRL  Reg,nn! B3,RRRR0001 !13!CZS! Shift logical left word
 SRLDW Reg,#nn   ! SRLL Reg,nn! B3,RRRR0101 !13!CZS! Shift logical left d-word
 SHIFTA [W]      ! SDA  [B]    !C+1]         !  !-DH! Shift byte [wrd] arithmetic
      Reg,Reg    !     Rd,Rs   ! B2,DDDD1011 !15+!   !    Reg, dir & # bits
                 !             ! 0000SSSS,00 !  !    !
 SHIFTADW        ! SDAL        !             !  !-DH! Shift d-word arithmetic
      Reg,Reg    !     Rd,Rs   ! B3,DDDD1111 !15+!   !    Reg, dir & # bits
                 !             ! 0000SSSS,00 !  !    !
 SHIFTL [W]      ! SDL  [B]    !C+1]         !  !-DH! Shift byte [wrd] logical
      Reg,Reg    !     Rd,Rs   ! B2,DDDD0011 !15+!   !    Reg, dir & # bits
                 !             ! 0000SSSS,00 !  !    !
 SHIFTLDW        ! SDLL        !             !  !-DH! Shift d-word logical
      Reg,Reg    !     Rd,Rs   ! B3,DDDD0111 !15+!   !    Reg, dir & # bits
                 !             ! 0000SSSS,00 !  !    !
 RLBCD           ! RLDB        !             !  !ZS ! Rotate digit left
      Reg,Reg    !     Rs,Rd   ! BE,SSSSDDDD ! 9!    !    see manual
 RRBCD           ! RRDB        !             !  !ZS ! Rotate digit right
      Reg,Reg    !     Rs,Rd   ! BC,SSSSDDDD ! 9!    !    see manual
```

String Data Operations

```
 MOVS [R]        !             !             !  !P  ! Mov byte string [repeat]
   -(Rx),-(Rx),-Rx! LDDB       ! BA,DDDD1001 !20+!   !   ind_dec Rx, Rx, dec Rx
                 !     [LDDRB]! 0000CCCC,   !  !    !   [X= 0 repeat
                 !             ! SSSSX000    !  !    !     = 1 single]
   +(Rx),+(Rx),-Rx! LDIB       ! BA,DDDD0001 !20+!   !   ind_inc Rx, Rx, dec Rx
                 !     [LDRIB]! 0000CCCC,   !  !    !
                 !             ! SSSSX000    !  !    !
 MOVWS [R]       !             !             !  !P  ! Mov word string [repeat]
   -(Rx),-(Rx),-Rx! LDD [R]    ! BB,DDDD1001 !20+!   !   ind_dec Rx, Rx, dec Rx
                 !             ! 0000CCCC,   !  !    !   [X=0 repeat, =1 single]
                 !             ! SSSSX000    !  !    !
   +(Rx),+(Rx),-Rx! LDI [R]    ! BB,DDDD0001 !20+!   !   ind_inc Rx, Rx, dec Rx
                 !             ! 0000CCCC,   !  !    !
                 !             ! SSSSX000    !  !    !
 CMPS [W,R]      ! CPD [R,B]   !C+1]         !  !ZP ! Compare byte[wrd]string[rep]
   -(Rx),-Rx,Reg !             ! BA,SSSS1X00 !20!    !   string,count,to,condition
      Cond       !             ! 0000NNNN,   !  !    !   [X=1 repeat, =0 single]
                 !             ! DDDDCCCC    !  !    !
                 ! CPI [R,B]   !             !  !    !
   +(Rx),-Rx,Reg !             ! BA,SSSS0X00 !20!    !   string,count,to,condition
```

```
                  Cond          !              ! 0000NNNN, !   !   !
                  !             ! DDDDCCCC  !   !   !
CMPSS [W,R]  ! CPSD [R,B] !(+1)          !   !ZP ! Compare byte[wrd]strings[rep
  -(Rx),-(Rx),-Rx!          ! BA,SSSS1X10 !25!   !   string,string,count,
  Cond          !              ! 0000NNNN, !   !   !   condition
                  !             ! DDDDCCCC  !   !   !   [X=0 single, =1 repeat]
                  ! CPSI [R,B]!              !   !   !
  +(Rx),+(Rx),Reg!          ! BA,SSSS0010 !25!   !   string,string,count,
  Cond          !              ! 0000NNNN, !   !   !   condition
                  !             ! DDDDCCCC  !   !   !
CNVS [R]     !              !              !   ! P ! Translate byte string
  -(Rx),(Rx),-Reg! TRDB    ! B8,DDDD1X00 !25+!   !   string,table,string lth
               ! [TRDRB]! 0000NNNN !   !   !   [X=1 repeat, =0 single]
                  !             ! SSSS0000  !   !   !
  +(Rx),(Rx),-Reg! TRIB    ! B8,DDDD0X00 !25+!   !   
               ! [TRIRB]! 0000NNNN !   !   !
                  !             ! SSSS0000  !   !   !
CNVST [R]    !              !              !   !PZ ! Trans & test byte string
  -(Rx),(Rx),-Reg! TRTDB   ! B8,DDDD1X10 !25+!   !   string,table,string lth
               ! [TRTDRB]! 0000NNNN !   !   !   [X=1 repeat, =0 single]
                  !             ! SSSSXXX0  !   !   !
  +(Rx),(Rx),-Reg! TRTIB   ! B8,DDDD0X10 !25+!   !
               ! [TRTIRB]! 0000NNNN !   !   !
                  !             ! SSSSXXX0  !   !   !
```

Bit Operations

```
TESTB [W]    ! BIT [B]    !(+1)          !   ! Z ! Test bit in byte [word]
  Reg,Rx      !   Reg,Rx    ! 26,0000BBBB !10!   !   reg; Bit in Rx
               !             ! 0000RRRR,00 !   !   !
  Reg,b       !   Reg,b     ! A6,RRRRBBBB ! 4!   !   Reg, bit
  (Rx),b      !   (Rx),b    ! 26,RRRRBBBB ! 8!   !   ind Rx, bit
  Mem,b       !   Mem,b     ! 36,MMMMBBBB !10+!   !   memory, bit
SETB [W]     ! SET [B]    !(+1)          !   !   ! Set bit in byte [word]
  Reg,Rx      !   Reg,Rx    ! 24,0000SSSS !10!   !   reg; Bit(in Rx)
               !             ! 0000RRRR,00 !   !   !
  Reg,b       !   Reg,b     ! A4,RRRRBBBB ! 4!   !   Reg, bit
  (Rx),b      !   (Rx),b    ! 24,RRRRBBBB !11!   !   ind Rx, bit
  Mem,b       !   Mem,b     ! 64,MMMMBBBB !12!   !   memory, bit
SETBIF       ! TCCB       !              !   !   ! Set LSB if
  Reg,Cond    !   Reg,Cond ! AE,RRRRCCCC ! 5!   !   Reg, condition
SETBWIF      ! TCC        !              !   !   ! Set LSB in word if
  Reg,Cond    !   Reg,Cond ! AF,RRRRCCCC ! 5!   !   Reg, condition
RESB [W]     ! RES [B]    !(+1)          !   !   ! Reset bit in byte [word]
  Reg,Rx      !   Reg,Rx    ! A2,0000SSSS !10!   !   reg; Bit(in Rx)
               !             ! 0000RRRR,00 !   !   !
  Reg,b       !   Reg,b     ! A2,RRRRBBBB ! 4!   !   Reg, bit
  (Rx),b      !   (Rx),b    ! 22,RRRRBBBB !11!   !   ind Rx, bit
  Mem,b       !   Mem,b     ! 62,MMMMBBBB !13+!   !   memory, bit
CPLF         ! COMFLG     !              !   !   ! Complement flags
  [C,Z,S,P]   !    flags   ! 8D,CZSP0101 ! 7!   !   flags indicated
RESF         ! RESFLG     !              !   !   ! Reset flags
  [C,Z,S,P]   !    flags   ! 8D,CZSP0011 ! 7!   !   flags indicated
SETF         ! SETFLG     !              !   !   ! Set flags
  [C,Z,S,P]   !    flags   ! 8D,CZSP0001 ! 7!   !   flags indicated
```

Program Control

```
CALL         ! CALL       !              !   !   ! Call subroutine
  (Rx)        !   (Rx)     ! 1F,RRRR0000 !10!   !   uncond, ind Rx
  Mem         !   Mem      ! 5F,MMMM0000 !12+!   !   uncond, memory
CALLR        ! CALR       !              !   !   ! Call subr relative
```

378

```
    dd          |    dd       | 1101DDDD,    |10 |    | uncond, disp x2
                |             | DDDDDDDD     |   |    |
RET             | RET         |              |   |    | Return from subroutine
   CC           | cond        | 9E,0000CCCC  |10 |    | condition
RETI            | IRET        |              |   |all | Return from interrupt
                |             | 7B,00        |16 |    | uncond
JMP             | JP          |              |   |    | Jump to location
   CC,(Rx)      | CC,(Rx)     | 1E,RRRRCCCC  |15 |    | condition, ind Rx
   CC,Mem       | CC,Mem      | 5E,MMMMCCCC  | 7+|    | condition,memory
JMPR            | JR          |              |   |    | Jump relative 2xD
   CC,r         | CC,r        | 1110CCCC     | 6 |    | condition
                |             | DDDDDDDD     |   |    |
DECJRNZ         | DBJNZ       |              |   |    | Decrement jump -2xD if
   Reg,r        | Reg,r       | 1111RRRR,    |11 |    | Reg,not zero
                |             | 0DDDDDDD     |   |    |
DECWJRNZ        | DJNZ        |              |   |    | Decrement jump -2xD if
   Reg,r        | Reg,r       | 1111RRRR,    |11 |    | Reg,not zero
                |             | 1DDDDDDD     |   |    |
TRAP            | SC          |              |   |    | Software interrupt
   #n           | n           | 7F           |39 |    | see manual
HALT            | HALT        | 7A,00        | 8+|    | Stop till interrupt
NOP             | NOP         | 8D,07        | 7 |    | No operation
```

I/O Operations

```
IN [M]          | INB [SINB]  |              |   |    | Input byte
   (Rx),Reg     | Reg,(Rx)    | 3C,SSSSDDDD  |10 |    | ind Rx, reg
   pp,Reg       | Reg,pp      | 3A,DDDD010M  |12 |    | port [MSB], reg
INW             | IN          |              |   |    | Input word
   (Rx),Reg     | Reg,(Rx)    | 3D,SSSSDDDD  |10 |    | ind Rx, reg
   pp,Reg       | Reg,pp      | 3B,DDDD0100  |12 |    | port, reg
INS [M]         | INDB [SINDB]|              |   | P  | Input byte string [MSB]
   (Rx),-(Rx),Rx|             | 3A,SSSS100M  |21 |    | ind Rx,ind_dec Rx,dec Rx
                |             | 0000CCCC,    |   |    |
                |             | DDDD1000     |   |    |
   (Rx),+(Rx),Rx| INIB        | 3A,SSSS000M  |21 |    | ind Rx,ind_inc Rx,dec Rx
                | [SINIB]     | 0000CCCC,    |   |    |
                |             | DDDD1000     |   |    |
INSR [M]        | INDRB       |              |   | P  | Input byte string repeat
   (Rx),-(Rx),Rx| [SINDRB]    | 3A,SSSS100M  |11+|    | ind Rx,ind_dec Rx,dec Rx
                |             | 0000CCCC,    |   |    | [MSB]
                |             | DDDD0000     |   |    |
   (Rx),+(Rx),Rx| INIRB       | 3A,SSSS000M  |11+|    | ind Rx,ind_inc Rx,dec Rx
                | [SINIRB]    | 0000CCCC,    |   |    | [MSB]
                |             | DDDD0000     |   |    |
INWS [R]        | IND [R]     |              |   | P  | Input word string [repeat]
   (Rx),-(Rx),Rx|             | 3B,SSSS1000  |21+|    | ind Rx,ind_dec Rx,dec Rx
                |             | 0000CCCC,    |   |    | [X=0 repeat, =1 single
                |             | DDDDX000     |   |    |
   (Rx),+(Rx),Rx| INI [R]     | 3B,SSSS0000  |21+|    | ind Rx,ind_inc Rx,dec Rx
                |             | 0000CCCC,    |   |    |
                |             | DDDDX000     |   |    |
OUT [M]         | OUTB [SOUTB]|              |   |    | Output byte
   Reg,(Rx)     | (Rx),Reg    | 3E,DDDDSSSS  |10 |    | reg, port ind Rx
   Reg,pp       | pp,Reg      | 3A,RRRR011M  |12 |    | reg, port immed [MSB]
OUTW            | OUT         |              |   |    | Output word
   Reg,(Rx)     | (Rx),Reg    | 3F,DDDDSSSS  |10 |    | reg, port ind Rx
   Reg,pp       | pp,Reg      | 3B,RRRR0110  |12 |    | reg, port immed
OUTS [M]        |             |              |   | P  | Output byte string [MSB]
   -(Rx),(Rx),Rx| OUTDB       | 3A,SSSS101M  |21 |    | ind_dec Rx, ind Rx,dec Rx
                | [SOUTDB]    | 0000CCCC     |   |    |
                |             | DDDD1000     |   |    |
```

```
 +(Rx),(Rx),Rx! OUTIB     ! 3A,SSSS001M !21!   !       ind_inc Rx, ind Rx,dec Rx
               !   [SOUTIB]! 0000CCCC    !  !   !
               !          ! DDDD1000     !  !   !
OUTSR [M]      !          !              !  !:P ! Output byte string repeat
   -(Rx),(Rx),Rx! OTDRB   ! 3A,SSSS101M !11+!   !       ind_dec Rx, ind Rx,dec Rx
               !   [SOTDRB]! 0000CCCC    !  !   !       [MSB]
               !          ! DDDD0000     !  !   !
   +(Rx),(Rx),Rx! OTIRB   ! 3A,SSSS001M !11+!   !       ind_inc Rx, ind Rx,dec Rx
               !   [SOTIRB]! 0000CCCC    !  !   !       [MSB]
               !          ! DDDD0000     !  !   !
OUTWS [R]      !          !              !  !:P ! Output word string [repeat]
   -(Rx),(Rx),Rx! OUTD    ! 3B,SSSS1010 !21+!   !       ind_dec Rx, ind Rx,dec Rx
               !   [OTDR] ! 0000CCCC    !  !   !       [X=1 single, =0 repeat]
               !          ! DDDDX000     !  !   !
   +(Rx),(Rx),Rx! OUTI    ! 3B,SSSS0010 !21+!   !       ind_inc Rx, ind Rx,dec Rx
               !   [OTIR] ! 0000CCCC    !  !   !
               !          ! DDDDX000     !  !   !
DI             ! DI       !              !  !   ! Disable interrupts
   [V,N]       !   [V,N]  ! 7C,000000VN ! 6!   !       V=vectored, N=nonvector
EI             ! EI       !              !  !   ! Enable interrupts
   [V,N]       !   [V,N]  ! 7C,000001VN ! 6!   !       V=vectored, N=nonvector
MBIT           ! MBIT     ! 7B,0A       ! 7!S ! Test multi-micro input line
MREQ  Reg      ! MREQ  Reg! 7B,RRRR1101 !12!ZS! See the manual
MRES           ! MRES     ! 7B,09       ! 7!   ! Reset multi-micro output
MSET           ! MSET     ! 7B,08       ! 7!   ! Set multi-micro output
```

Registers

```
        16   8!7    0                16              0
      ---    ---------------- ---    ---   ----------------- ---
 R0  ! RH0 ! RL0 !            R12  !                 !
RR1   ----------------              RR12   -----------------
 R1  ! RH1 ! RL1 !            R13  !                 !
 ---   ---------------- RQ0    ---   -----------------
 R2  ! RH2 ! RL2 !            R14' ! Sys Stack Ptr !
RR2   ----------------              -----------------   RQ12
 R3  ! RH3 ! RL3 !            R14  !Normal Stack Ptr!
 ---   ---------------- ---    RR14  -----------------
 R4  ! RH4 ! RL4 !            R15' ! Sys Stack Ptr !
RR4   ----------------              -----------------
 R5  ! RH5 ! RL5 !            R15  !Normal Stack Ptr!
 ---   ---------------- RQ4    ---   ----------------- ---
 R6  ! RH6 ! RL6 !
RR6   ----------------              For the Z8002
 R7  ! RH7 ! RL7 !                  -----------------
 ---   ---------------- ---    R14  !                 !
 R8  !               !              -----------------
RR8   ----------------         R15' ! Sys Stack Ptr !
 R9  !               !              -----------------
 ---   ---------------- RQ8    R15  !Normal Stack Ptr!
 R10 !               !              -----------------
RR10  ----------------
 R11 !               !         R14' & R15' Are System mode reg
 ---   ---------------- ---    R14  & R15  Are Normal mode reg

       -----------------       RH & RL are  8 bit reg
(Z8001) !  PC Seg       !      R            16 bit reg
       -----------------       RR           32 bit reg
       !  PC Offset     !      RQ           64 bit reg
       -----------------
```

For Z8001 PC & Stack ptr use SL format below

Z8002 " " " use NS " "

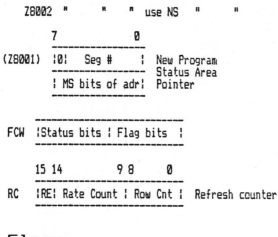

```
             7           0
            ----------------
(Z8001)    |0|  Seg #    |   New Program
            ----------------    Status Area
           | MS bits of adr|   Pointer
            ----------------


            ------------------------------
FCW        |Status bits | Flag bits  |
            ------------------------------


            15 14      9 8     0
            ------------------------------
RC         |RE| Rate Count | Row Cnt |   Refresh counter
            ------------------------------
```

Flags

```
    S = sign of result
    Z = zero result
    H = half carry from bit 3
   DA = decimal adjust
    P = parity
        overflow for math operations
    C = carry
 NVIE = non-vectored inter enable
  VIE = vectored interrupt enable
   SE = stop enable
  S/N = system/normal mode
  SEG = segmetation enable (Z8001 only)
```

Addressing Modes

```
Univ          Manuf
----          -----
Rx            Rx          - register, RHx or RLx = 8-bit, Rx=16-bit,
                              RRx=32-bit, RQx=64-bit
#nn           nn          - immediate data, 4 or 8 or 16 or 32-bits
(Rx)          (Rx)        - reg indirect
aa            aa          - absolute address
dd            dd          - displacement address value
r             r           - relative address value
SS s|aa       s aa        - segmented short address
SL s|aa       s aa        - segmented long address
PP            PP          - port address
(Rx+Rx)       (Rx+Rx)     - indexed register
(Rx++aa)      (Rx++aa)    - indexed absolute, reg Rx + 16-bit adr
(Rx+SS s|aa)  (Rx+ s aa)  - indexed seg short
(Rx+SL s|aa)  (Rx+ s aa)  - indexed seg long
-(Rx)         Rx          - indirect auto decrement
+(Rx)         Rx          - indirect auto increment
```

Notes

All instructions and word data must start at an even adr.(wrd boundry).

Instruction Expansion

Register

Byte	Word	RRR	Byte	Word	RRR	D-Wrd	RRR	Q-Wrd	RRR
RH0	R0	0000	RL0	R8	1000	RR0	0000	RQ0	0000
RH1	R1	0001	RL1	R9	1001	RR2	0010	RQ4	0100
RH2	R2	0010	RL2	R10	1010	RR4	0100	RQ8	1000
RH3	R3	0011	RL3	R11	1011	RR6	0110	RQ12	1100
RH4	R4	0100	RL4	R12	1100	RR8	1000		
RH5	R5	0101	RL5	R13	1101	RR10	1010		
RH6	R6	0110	RL6	R14	1110	RR12	1100·		
RH7	R7	0111	RL7	R15	1111	RR14	1110		

Mem

Parameter	Mode	MMMM	Append
aa	absolute	0000	word adr
SS s aa	seg short	0000	word SS format
SL s aa	seg long	0000	d-word SO format
(Rx+aa)	index abs	R1-R15	word adr
(Rx+SS s aa)	index seg sht	R1-R15	word SS format
(Rx+SL s aa)	index seg lng	R1-R15	d-word SL format

Mem2

dd	rel adr	0000	word displacement
(Rx+dd)	index disp	R1-R15	word displacement
(Rx+Rx)	index reg	R1-R15	index reg Rx & add 40H to 1st byte

```
n    = immediate data, 8-bits appended to inst followed by a zero byte,
                 or 4-bits part of inst
nn   = immediate data, 16-bits appended to the inst
nnnn = immediate data, 32-bits appended to the inst
b    = bit number, 4-bits part of the inst.
pp   = port address, 16-bits appended to the inst
PSW  = program status words, PC and FCW.
aa or s aa - address  (in Z8001 - see NS, SS & SL below
                       in Z8002 - NS only)
```

(Rx)	reg_ind NS	R1-R15
(RRx)	reg_ind SL	RR2-RR14

Condition Codes

NZ	not zero	Z=0	1110	NV	no overflow	P=0	1100
Z	zero	Z=1	0110	V	overflow	P=1	0100
NC	no carry	C=0	1111	SGE	> or =	S xor P = 0	1001
C	carry	C=1	0111	SLT	<	S xor P = 1	0001
PO	parity odd	P=0	1100	SGT	>	Z or (S xor P)=0	1010
PE	parity even	P=1	0100	SLE	< or =	Z or (S xor P)=1	0010
P	plus	S=0	1101	GEZ	logical > or =	C=0	1111
M	minus	S=1	0101	LT	logical <	C=1	0111
NE	not equal	Z=0	1110	GT	logical >	C=0 and Z=0	1011
EQ	equal	A=1	0110	LE	logical < or =	C or Z = 1	0011
UN	unconditional		1000				

Address mode variables appended after any immediate data.

Formats

NS - not segmented   SS - segmented short

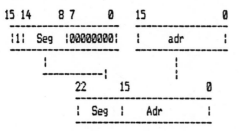

```
15              0            15 14    8 7      0
-----------------            ----------------------
!  16 bit adr  !             !0! Seg  !LSB adr !
-----------------            ----------------------
                                      !         !
                               !-----------!    !
                            22      15      7    0
                            -----------------------
                            ! Seg  !00000000! LSB adr!
                            -----------------------
```

SL - segmented long

```
15 14    8 7      0   15              0
---------------------  -----------------
!1! Seg  !00000000!    !     adr      !
---------------------  -----------------
       !                       !
  !-----------!                !
        22      15             0
        -----------------------
        ! Seg  !   Adr        !
        -----------------------
```

Special Memory Locations

```
       Z8001 Z8002
NPSAP  +8    +4     - unimplemented op code
       +16   +8     - priviledged inst
       +24   +12    - system call inst
       +32   +16    - segment trap
       +40   +20    - non-masked int
       +48   +24    - non-vectored int
       +56   +28    - FCW all vectored int
       +70   +30    - vectored int jump table
       +74   +32    -    "     "  "    "
```

Appendix H

Microprocessor Tables

Manuf	Micro	# Bit	Memory max- ram/rom/eep	C /T	I/O d/s/a	C L K	D M A	M M U	Clk Frq	Inst Set Tbls	Notes
RCA	1802/C	8	64K			Y	Y		6.4	1802	
Sig	2650/A/B	8	32K				Y		1.2	2650	
Inter	6100	12	4K			Y	Y		4	6100	1
Intel	80186	16	1M	3		Y	Y		8	8086	
Intel	80188	16	1M	3		Y	Y		5	8086	
Intel	8020H	8	64/1K	1	13	Y			3.5	8020 *	
Intel	8021	8	64/1K	1	21	Y				8020 *	
Intel	8022/H	8	64/2K	1	28/1	Y				8020 *	
Intel	80286	16	16M	3			Y	Y	10	8086	
Intel	8031/AH	8	128K-128	2	32/1	Y			12	8051	
Intel	8032/AH	8	65K-256	3	/1				12	8051	
Intel	8035	8	64/	1	21	Y				8048	
Intel	8039/AHL/H	8	128/	1	27	Y				8048	
Intel	8040H/AHL	8	256/	1	27	Y			11	8048	
Intel	8042	8	128//2K	1	18	Y	Y		12	8048	2
Intel	8044/AH	8	64K-192/4K	1	32	Y			12	8051	
Intel	8048/H/L	8	64/1K	1	27	Y			8	8048	
Intel	8049/H	8	128/2K	1	27	Y			11	8048	
Intel	8050H	8	256/4K	1	27	Y			11	8048	
Intel	8051/AH	8	128K-128/4K	2	32/1	Y			12	8051	
Intel	8052/AH	8	64K-256/8K	3	32	Y			12	8051	
Intel	8080/A	8	64K				Y		2.6	8080	
Intel	8085	8	64K			Y	Y		3	8080	
Intel	8086	16	1M				Y		5	8088	
Intel	8088	16	1M				Y		8	8088	
Intel	8094	16	64K-232	4	40	Y			12	8096	
Intel	8095	16	64K	4	40/1	Y			12	8096	
Intel	8096	16	64K	4	40	Y			12	8096	
Intel	8097	16	64K	4	40/1	Y			12	8096	
Intel	80C31/BH	8	64K-128	2	32/1	Y			12	8051	
Intel	80C35	8	64/	1	21	Y			11	8048	
Intel	80C39	8	128/2K	1	27	Y			11	8048	
Intel	80C48	8	64/1K	1	27	Y			11	8048	
Intel	80C49	8	128/2K	1	27	Y			11	8048	
Intel	80C51/BH	8	64K-128/4K	2	32/1	Y			12	8051	
Har	80C86	16	1M						5	8086	
Har	80C88	16	1M						5	8086	
Intel	8344AH	8	64K-192/4K	2	32/1	Y			12	8051	
Intel	8394	16	64K-232/8K	4	40	Y			12	8096	
Intel	8395	16	64K-232	4	40/1	Y			12	8096	
Intel	8396	16	64K-232	4	40	Y			12	8096	
Intel	8397	16	64K-232	4	40/1	Y			12	8096	
Intel	8641/A	8	64//1K	1	18	Y	Y		12	8048	2
Intel	8648	8	64//1K	1	27	Y				8048	
Intel	8741	8	64//1K	1	18	Y				8048	2
Intel	8744H	8	64K-192/4K	2	32/1	Y			12	8051	
Intel	8748/AH/H	8	64//1K	1	27	Y				8048	
Intel	8749H	8	128//2K	1	21	Y			11	8048	
Intel	8751/H	8	128K-128//4K	2	32/1	Y			12	8051	
AMD	Am9761H	8	64K-128//8K	2	32/1	Y			8	8051	
RCA	CDP1802/C	8	64K		8	Y	Y		6.4	1802	
RCA	CDP1804/C	8	64/2K	1	/1	Y	Y		5	1802	
RCA	CDP6805E2	8	8K-112	1	16	Y				6805	
RCA	CDP6805E3	8	64K-112	1	13	Y			5	6805	
RCA	CDP6805G2	8	112/2K	1	32	Y				6805	
Fair	F3870	8	64/2K	1	32	Y				F8	

Manuf	Micro	# Bit	Memory max-ram/rom/eep	C/T	I/O d/s/a	CLK	DMA	MMU	Clk Frq	Inst Set Tbls	Notes
Fair	F3872	8	64/4K	1	32	Y				F8	
Fair	F3874	8	64/4K	1	32	Y				F8	
Fair	F38E70	8	64//2K	1	32	Y				F8	
Fair	F9445	16	128K						4	F9445	
GTE	G65SC02	8	65K			Y	Y		4	6502	
GTE	G65SC03	8	4K				Y		4	6502	
GTE	G65SC04	8	8K				Y		4	6502	
GTE	G65SC05	8	4K				Y		4	6502	
GTE	G65SC06	8	4K				Y		4	6502	
GTE	G65SC07	8	8K				Y		4	6502	
GTE	G65SC102	8	65K			Y	Y		4	6502	
GTE	G65SC103	8	4K				Y		4	6502	
GTE	G65SC104	8	8K				Y		4	6502	
GTE	G65SC105	8	4K				Y		4	6502	
GTE	G65SC106	8	4K				Y		4	6502	
GTE	G65SC107	8	8K				Y		4	6502	
GTE	G65SC112	8	65K			Y	Y		4	6502	
GTE	G65SC115	8	4K				Y		4	6502	
GTE	G65SC12	8	65K				Y		4	6502	
GTE	G65SC13	8	4K				Y		4	6502	
GTE	G65SC14	8	8K				Y		4	6502	
GTE	G65SC15	8	4K				Y		4	6502	
GTE	G65SC150	8	64K-64/2K	1	27//2	Y			2	6500	3
GTE	G65SC151	8	64K-64/2K	1	27//2	Y			2	6500	3
Har	HD6100	12	4K						4	6100	1
Har	HD6120	12	32K			Y	Y		5	6100	1
Hit	HD6301V1	8	65K-128/4K	1	29/1				1	6800	
Hit	HD6301X0	8	65K-192/4K	2	53/1				1	6800	
Hit	HD6303R	8	65K-128	1	13/1				1	6800	
Hit	HD6303X	8	65K-192	2	24/1				1	6800	
Hit	HD6303Y	8	65K-256	2	24/1				1	6800	
Hit	HD6305U0	8	128/2K	2	31/1				1	6805	
Hit	HD6305V0	8	192/4K	2	31/1				1	6805	
Hit	HD6305X0	8	128/4K	2	55/1	Y			1	6805	
Hit	HD6305X1	8	12K-128/4K	2	31/1				1	6805	
Hit	HD6305X2	8	16K-128	2	31/1				1	6805	
Hit	HD6305Y0	8	256/8K	2	55/1				1	6805	
Hit	HD6305Y1	8	8K-256/8K	2	31/1				1	6805	
Hit	HD6305Y2	8	16K-256	2	31/1				1	6805	
Hit	HD6309/E	8	64K			Y	Y		8	6809	
Hit	HD63701X0/P	8	65K-192//4K	2	53/1				1	6800	
Hit	HD637A01X0	8	65K-192//4K	2	53/1				1.5	6800	
Hit	HD637B01X0	8	65K-192//4K	2	53/1				2	6800	
Hit	HD63A01V1	8	65K-128/4K	1	29/1				1.5	6800	
Hit	HD63A01X0	8	65K-192/4K	2	53/1				1.5	6800	
Hit	HD63A03R	8	65K-128	1	13/1				1.5	6800	
Hit	HD63A03X	8	65K-192	2	24/1				1.5	6800	
Hit	HD63A03Y	8	65K-256	2	24/1				1.5	6800	
Hit	HD63A05U0	8	128/2K	2	31/1				1.5	6805	
Hit	HD63A05V0	8	192/4K	2	31/1				1.5	6805	
Hit	HD63A05X0	8	128/4K	2	55/1	Y			1.5	6805	
Hit	HD63A05X1	8	12K-128/4K	2	31/1				1.5	6805	
Hit	HD63A05X2	8	16K-128	2	31/1				1.5	6805	
Hit	HD63A05Y0	8	256/8K	2	55/1				1.5	6805	
Hit	HD63A05Y1	8	8K-256/8K	2	31/1				1.5	6805	
Hit	HD63A05Y2	8	16K-256	2	31/1				1.5	6805	

Manuf	Micro	# Bit	Memory max-ram/rom/eep	C/T	I/O d/s/a	CLK	DMA	MMU	Clk Frq	Inst Set Tbls	Notes
Hit	HD63B01V1	8	65K-128/4K	1	29/1				2	6800	
Hit	HD63B01X0	8	65K-192/4K	2	53/1				2	6800	
Hit	HD63B03R	8	65K-128	1	13/1				2	6800	
Hit	HD63B03X	8	65K-192	2	24/1				2	6800	
Hit	HD63B03Y	8	65K-256	2	24/1				2	6800	
Hit	HD63B05U0	8	128/2K	2	31/1				2	6805	
Hit	HD63B05V0	8	192/4K	2	31/1				2	6805	
Hit	HD63B05X0	8	128/4K	2	55/1	Y			2	6805	
Hit	HD63B05X1	8	12K-128/4K	2	31/1				2	6805	
Hit	HD63B05X2	8	16K-128	2	31/1				2	6805	
Hit	HD63B05Y0	8	256/8K	2	55/1				2	6805	
Hit	HD63B05Y1	8	8K-256/8K	2	31/1				2	6805	
Hit	HD63B05Y2	8	16K-256	2	31/1				2	6805	
Hit	HD63L05E0	8	96//4K	1	20/ /1				1	6805	
Hit	HD63L05F1	8	96/4K	1	20/ /1				1	6805	4
Hit	HD63P01M1	8	65K-128//8K	1	29/1				1.5	6800	
Hit	HD63P05Y0	8	128//8K	2	55/1				1	6805	
Hit	HD63PA01M1	8	65K-128//8K	1	29/1				1.5	6800	
Hit	HD63PA05Y0	8	128//8K	2	55/1				1.5	6805	
Hit	HD63PB01M1	8	65K-128//8K	1	29/1				2	6800	
Hit	HD63PB05Y0	8	128//8K	2	55/1				2	6805	
Hit	HD64180	8	512K	2	/2	Y	Y	Y	6	Z80	
Hit	HD6800	8	64K				Y		2	6800	
Hit	HD68000/YZ	32	16M						8	68000	
Hit	HD6801S0	8	65K-128/2K	3	29/1				1	6800	
Hit	HD6801S5	8	65K-128/2K	3	29/1				1.5	6800	
Hit	HD6801V0	8	65K-128/4K	3	29/1	Y			1	6800	
Hit	HD6801V5	8	65K-128/4K	3	29/1	Y			1.5	6800	
Hit	HD6802	8	65K-128			Y				6800	
Hit	HD6802W	8	65K-256			Y				6800	
Hit	HD6803	8	64K-128	1	13/1	Y			3.8	6800	
Hit	HD6805S1	8	64/1100	1	20	Y			1	6805	
Hit	HD6805S6	8	64/1800	1	20	Y			1	6805	
Hit	HD6805T2	8	64/2508	1	19	Y			2	6805	5
Hit	HD6805U1	8	96/2K	1	32	Y			1	6805	
Hit	HD6805V1	8	96/4K	1	32	Y			1	6805	
Hit	HD6805W1	8	96/4K	1	30/ /4	Y			1	6805	
Hit	HD6809/E	8	64K			Y	Y		2	6809	
Hit	HD68A00	8	64K				Y		1.5	6800	
Hit	HD68A09/E	8	64K			Y	Y		1.5	6809	
Hit	HD68B00	8	64K				Y		2	6800	
Hit	HD68B09/E	8	64K			Y	Y		2	6809	
Hit	HD68P01M0	8	65K-128//8K	3	29/1	Y			1	6800	
Hit	HD68P01V07	8	65K-128//4K	3	29/1	Y			1	6800	
Hit	HD68P05V07	8	96//2K	1	32	Y			1	6805	
Hit	HD68P05W0	8	96//4K	1	30/ /4	Y			1	6805	
Har	HM-6100	12	4K			Y	Y		8	6100	
Har	HS-80C85RH	8	64K			Y	Y		5	8080	6
Inter	IM6100	12	4K			Y	Y		5.7	6100	
NS	INS8048	8	64//1K	1	27	Y			6	8048	
NS	INS8049	8	128//2K	1	27	Y			6	8048	
NS	INS8050	8	256//4K	1	27	Y			6	8048	
NS	INS8080A	8	64K				Y		2.6	8080	
Mot	MC146805/E2	8	64K-112	1	16	Y	Y		1	6805	
Mot	MC146805E3	8	64K-112	1	16	Y	Y		1	6805	
Mot	MC146805F2	8	64/1089	1	20	Y			1	6805	

Manuf	Micro	# Bit	Memory max- ram/rom/eep	C/T	I/O d/s/a	CLK	DMA	MMU	Clk Frq	Inst Set Tbls	Notes
Mot	MC146805G2	8	112/2K	1	32	Y			4	6805	
Mot	MC146805H2	8	112/2K	1	24	Y			4	6805	7
Mot	MC1468705G2	8	112//2K	1	32	Y			1	6805	
Mot	MC3870	8	64/2K	1	32	Y			4	F8	
Mot	MC6800	8	64K				Y		2	6800	
Mot	MC68000	16	16M						8	68000	
Mot	MC68008	16	16M						8	68000	
Mot	MC6801	8	65K-128/2K	3	29/1	Y				6800	
Mot	MC6801U4	8	65K-128/4K	3	29/1	Y				6800	
Mot	MC6802/N2	8	65K-128			Y				6800	
Mot	MC6803	8	64K-128	1	13/1	Y			3.8	6800	
Mot	MC6803E	8	64K-128	1	13/1				3.8	6800	
Mot	MC6803U4	8	64K-192	1	13/1	Y			3.8	6800	
Mot	MC6804J2	8	32/1K	1	12	Y				6804	
Mot	MC6804P2	8	32/1K	1	20	Y				6804	
Mot	MC6805K2	8	96/2K/128	2	24/1	Y				6805	
Mot	MC6805K3	8	96/3.6K/128	2	24/1	Y				6805	
Mot	MC6805P2	8	66/1.1K/128	1	20	Y			2	6805	
Mot	MC6805P4	8	112/1.1K/128	1	20	Y			2	6805	
Mot	MC6805P6	8	64/1769	1	20	Y			2	6805	
Mot	MC6805R2	8	64/2K	1	32/ /1	Y			2	6805	
Mot	MC6805R3	8	112/3776	1	32/ /1	Y			2	6805	
Mot	MC6805S2	8	64/1480	2	20/1/4	Y			2	6805	
Mot	MC6805T2	8	64/2508	1	19	Y			2	6805	5
Mot	MC6805U2	8	64/2K	1	32	Y			2	6805	
Mot	MC6805U3	8	112/3776	1	32	Y			2	6805	
Mot	MC6808	8	64K			Y			3.8	6800	
Mot	MC6809	8	64K			Y	Y		1	6809	
Mot	MC6809E	8	64K				Y		1	6809	
Mot	MC68120	8	64K-128/2K	1	21/1					6800	2
Mot	MC68701	8	65K-128/2K	1	29/1	Y			8	6800	
Mot	MC68701U4	8	64K-192//4K	1	29/1	Y			8	6800	
Mot	MC68705P3	8	112//1804	1	20	Y			2	6805	
Mot	MC68705P5	8	112//1804	1	20	Y			2	6805	
Mot	MC68705R3	8	112//3776	1	32/ /1	Y			2	6805	
Mot	MC68705R5	8	112//3776	1	32/ /1	Y			2	6805	
Mot	MC68705U3	8	112//3776	1	32	Y			2	6805	
Mot	MC68705U5	8	112//3776	1	32	Y			2	6805	
Mot	MC68A00	8	64K				Y		1.5	6800	
Mot	MC68A09/E	8	64K			Y	Y		1.5	6809	
Mot	MC68A701	8	65K-128/2K	1	29/1	Y			1.5	6800	
Mot	MC68B00	8	64K				Y		2	6800	
Mot	MC68B09/E	8	64K			Y	Y		2	6809	
Mot	MC68B701	8	65K-128/2K	1	29/1	Y			2	6800	
Mot	MC68HC000	32	16M						12	68000	
Mot	MC68HC01	8	64K-128/4K	1	29/1	Y				6800	
Mot	MC68HC04P2	8	32/1K	1	20	Y				6804	
Mot	MC68HC04P3	8	128/2K	1	20	Y				6804	
Mot	MC68HC04P4	8	128/2K	1	20	Y				6805	
Mot	MC68HC05C4	8	176/4160	1	24/1	Y			2	6805	
Mot	MC68HC09E	8	64K							6809	
Mot	MC68HC11A4	8	256/4K/512	1	24/1/8	Y				6811	
Mot	MC68HC11A8	8	256/8K/512	1	16/2/8	Y			2	6811	
Mostk	MK3880/A/B	8	64K				Y		4	Z80	
STD	MPU800/-1/4	8	64K			Y			4	Z80	
OKI	MSM80C59	8	256/16K	3	32/1	Y			16	8051	

Manuf	Micro	# Bit	Memory max- ram/rom/eep	C/T	I/O d/s/a	CLK	DMA	MMU	Clk Frq	Inst Set Tbls	Notes
NS	NS8040U	8	256/	1	27/1	Y			11	8048	
NS	NS8050U	8	256//4K	1	27/1	Y			11	8048	
NS	NS80CX35	8	64/	1	27	Y			6	8048	
NS	NS80CX48	8	64/1K	1	27	Y			6	8048	
NS	NS87P50	8	//4K	1	27	Y			6	8048	
GI	PIC1650A/XT	8	/512	1	32	Y			1	1650	
GI	PIC1654	8	/512	1	12	Y			4	1650	
GI	PIC1655A/XT	8	/512	1	20	Y			1	1650	
GI	PIC1656	8	/512	1	20	Y			4	1650	
GI	PIC1664	8	512	1	32	Y			1	1650	9
GI	PIC1665	8	1K	2	32	Y			5	1670	9
GI	PIC1670	8	/1K	2	32	Y			5	1670	
GI	PIC16C55	8	/512	1	20	Y			1	1650	
GI	PIC16C63	8	512	1	32	Y			1	1650	9
Rock	R6500/1	8	64/2K	1	32	Y			2	6502	
Rock	R6501/xx	8	65K-192	2	32/1	Y			2	6502	
MOS	R6502	8	65K			Y	Y		3	6502	
MOS	R6503	8	4K			Y	Y		3	6502	
MOS	R6504	8	8K			Y	Y		3	6502	
MOS	R6505	8	4K			Y	Y		3	6502	
MOS	R6506	8	4K			Y	Y		3	6502	
MOS	R6507	8	8K			Y	Y		3	6502	
Rock	R6511/xx	8	65K-192	2	32/1	Y			2	6502	
Rock	R6511Q	8	65K-192	2	32/1	Y	Y		2	6502	
MOS	R6512	8	65K				Y		3	6502	
MOS	R6513	8	4K				Y		3	6502	
MOS	R6514	8	8K				Y		3	6502	
MOS	R6515	8	4K				Y		3	6502	
MOS	R6541/xx	8	4K-64	2	24				2	6502	
Rock	R6541Q	8	4K-64	1	23				2	6502	2
Rock	R6542	8	4K-64/1.5K	1	47				2	6502	
Rock	R6543	8	4K-64/256	1	23				2	6502	
Rock	R65C02	8	65K			Y			4	6502	
Rock	R65C102	8	65K			Y	Y		4	6502	
Rock	R65C112	8	65K				Y		4	6502	
Rock	R65C21	8	64K-128	2	52	Y			4	6502	
Rock	R65C29	8	64K-128	2	52	Y			4	6502	8
Rock	R65F11		16K-192	2	16/1	Y			2	6502	10
Rock	R65F12		16K-192	2	40/1	Y			2	6502	10
Rock	R68000	16	16M						12	68000	
SAB	SAB8031/A	8	128K-128	2	32/1	Y			12	8051	
SAB	SAB8051/A	8	128K-128/4K	2	32/1	Y			12	8051	
SAB	SAB8086-x	16	1M				Y		10	8088	
SAB	SAB8088	16	1M				Y		5	8088	
SAB	SAB80286	16	16M	3			Y	Y	8	8086	
Tosh	TMP8048xx	8	64/1K/4K	1	27	Y			11	8048	
Tosh	TMP8049xx	8	128/2K/4K	1	27	Y			11	8048	
Tosh	TMP8085AP	8	64K						10	8080	
Tosh	TMP80C48xx	8	64/1K/4K	1	27	Y			11	8048	
Tosh	TMP80C49xx	8	128/2K/4K	1	27	Y			11	8048	
Tosh	TMP80C50xx	8	256/2K/4K	1	27	Y			11	8048	
Tosh	TMPZ84C00P	8	64K				Y		4	Z80	
TI	TMS32010	16	8K-288			Y			5	32000	11
TI	TMS320M10	16	8K-288//3K			Y			5	32000	11
TI	TMS7001	8	64K-128	3	32/1				2.5	7000	
TI	TMS7002	8	256/4K	3	12/1	Y			8	7000	

Manuf	Micro	# Bit	Memory max- ram/rom/eep	C/T	I/O d/s/a	CLK	DMA	MMU	Clk Frq	Inst Set Tbls	Notes
TI	TMS70120	8	64K-128/12K	1	32				2.5	7000	
TI	TMS7020	8	64K-128/2K	1	32				2.5	7000	
TI	TMS7040	8	64K-128/4K	1	32				2.5	7000	
TI	TMS7041	8	64K-128/4K	3	32/1				2.5	7000	
TI	TMS7042	8	256/4K	3	32/1	Y			8	7000	
TI	TMS70C00	8	64K-128	1	32				1.75	7000	
TI	TMS70C20	8	64K-128/2K	1	32				1.75	7000	
TI	TMS70C40	8	64K-128/4K	1	32				1.75	7000	
TI	TMS70P161	8	64K-128//16K	3	32/1				2.5	7000	
TI	TMS7742	8	256//4K	3	32/1	Y			8	7000	
TI	TMS9900	16	64K				Y		4	9900 *	12
TI	TMS9940A	16	2K-128/2K			Y	Y		2.5	9900 *	12
TI	TMS9980A	16	16K				Y		2.5	9900 *	12
TI	TMS9981	16	16K			Y	Y		2.5	9900 *	12
TI	TMS9995	16	64K-256	1	/1	Y	Y		4	9900 *	12
WDC	W65C02	8	65K			Y	Y		4	6502	
WDC	W65C802	16	64K				Y		10	65816	13
WDC	W65C816	16	16M				Y		10	65816	13
WDC	W65SC02	8	65K			Y	Y		4	6502	
WDC	W65SC03	8	4K				Y		4	6502	
WDC	W65SC04	8	8K				Y		4	6502	
WDC	W65SC05	8	4K				Y			6502	
WDC	W65SC06	8	4K				Y		4	6502	
WDC	W65SC07	8	8K				Y		4	6502	
WDC	W65SC102	8	65K			Y	Y		4	6502	
WDC	W65SC103	8	4K				Y		4	6502	
WDC	W65SC104	8	8K				Y		4	6502	
WDC	W65SC105	8	4K				Y		4	6502	
WDC	W65SC106	8	4K				Y		4	6502	
WDC	W65SC107	8	8K				Y		4	6502	
WDC	W65SC112	8	65K			Y	Y		4	6502	
WDC	W65SC115	8	4K				Y		4	6502	
WDC	W65SC12	8	65K				Y		4	6502	
WDC	W65SC13	8	4K				Y		4	6502	
WDC	W65SC14	8	8K				Y		4	6502	
WDC	W65SC15	8	4K				Y		4	6502	
WDC	W65SC802	16	65K				Y		10	65816	13
WDC	W65SC816	16	16M				Y		10	65816	13
WDC	W65SC902	16	16M				Y		10	65816	
Zilog	Z8									Z8 *	
Zilog	Z80/L/C	8	64K				Y		4	Z80	
Zilog	Z8001	16	8M				Y	Y	10	Z8000	
Zilog	Z8002	16	64K				Y	Y	10	Z8000	
Zilog	Z8090	8	256/2K	2	24				4	Z8 *	14
Zilog	Z8094	8	256//2K	2	24				4	Z8 *	14
SGS	Z80C00	8	64K						4	Z80	
Zilog	Z84C00/-4	8	64K				Y		4	Z80	
Zilog	Z8590	8	256/2K	2	24				4	Z8 *	15
Zilog	Z8601	8	62K-128/2K	2	32/1	Y			8	Z8 *	
Zilog	Z8603	8	62K-128//2K	2	32/1	Y			8	Z8 *	
Zilog	Z8611	8	60K-128/4K	2	32/1	Y			8	Z8 *	
Zilog	Z8612	8	60K-128	2	32/1	Y			8	Z8 *	9
Zilog	Z8613	8	60K-128//4K	2	32/1	Y			8	Z8 *	9
Zilog	Z8681	8	128K-144	2	24/1	Y			8	Z8 *	
Zilog	Z8682	8	124K-144	2	12/1	Y			8	Z8 *	
Zilog	Z8800	8	128/325	2	32/1	Y	Y		12	Z8 *	
AMD	iAPX-186	16	1M	3		Y	Y	Y	8	8086	

Manuf	Micro	# Bit	Memory max-ram/rom/eep	C/T	I/O d/s/a	CLK	DMA	MMU	Clk Frq	Inst Set Tbls	Notes
AMD	iAPX-286	16	16M	3		Y	Y	Y	10	8086	
NEC	uPD70108	16	1M						5	8086	16
NEC	uPD70116	16	1M						5	8086	16
NEC	uPD780	8	64K						6	Z80	
NEC	uPD7800	8	64K-128	1	32/1		Y		4	7800	
NEC	uPD7801	8	60K-128/4K	1	48/1		Y		4	7800	
NEC	uPD7802	8	48K-128/6K	1	48/1		Y		4	7800	
NEC	uPD7807	8	64K-256	3	40/1	Y	Y			7800	
NEC	uPD7809	8	64K-256/8K	3	40/1	Y	Y			7800	
NEC	uPD7810	8	60K-256	3	42/1/8	Y			12	7800	
NEC	uPD7811	8	60K-256/4K	3	42/1/8	Y			12	7800	
NEC	uPD78C05	8	64K-128	1	24/1	Y				7800	
NEC	uPD78P09	8	64K-256//8K	3	40/1	Y	Y			7800	
NEC	uPD8021	8	64/1K	1	21	Y				8020	*
NEC	uPD8039HL	8	2K-128	1	16	Y			11	8048	
NEC	uPD8041A	8	64/1K	1	18	Y	Y			8048	2
NEC	uPD8048H	8	64/1K	1	16	Y				8048	
NEC	uPD8049H	8	128/2K	1	16				11	8048	
NEC	uPD8085A	8	64K			Y	Y		3	8080	
NEC	uPD80C35	8	64/	1	16	Y			6	8048	
NEC	uPD80C39	8	2K-128		16	Y			8	8048	
NEC	uPD80C48	8	64/1K	1	16	Y			6	8048	
NEC	uPD80C49	8	128/2K		16	Y			8	8048	
NEC	uPD8741A	8	64//1K	1	18	Y	Y			8048	2
NEC	uPD8748	8	64//2K	1	16	Y				8048	
NEC	uPD8749H	8	128//2K	1	16	Y			11	8048	

Manufacturers

```
AMD   = Advanced Micro Devices
DG    = Data General
Dig   = Digital
Fair  = Fairchild
Fer   = Ferranti Electric
GI    = General Instrument
GTE   = GTE Microcircuits
Har   = Harris Semiconductor
Hit   = Hitachi America, Ltd.
Intel = Intel Corp.
Inter = Intersil
MIT   = Mitsubishi Electronics
MOS   = MOS Technology
Mostk = Monolithic Systems Corp.
Mot   = Motorola
NEC   = NEC Electronics
NS    = National Semiconductor
OKI   = OKI Semiconductor
Pan   = Panasonic
R     = Rockwell
RCA   = RCA Solid Stat Division
SAB   = Siemens
SGS   = SGS Tech & Service
Sig   = Signetics
SM    = Solid State Micro Tech.
```

Memory

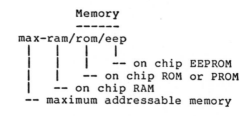

```
max-ram/rom/eep
 |   |   |   |
 |   |   |   -- on chip EEPROM
 |   |   -- on chip ROM or PROM
 |   -- on chip RAM
 -- maximum addressable memory
```

I/O

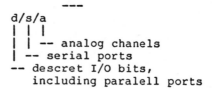

```
d/s/a
| | |
| | -- analog chanels
| -- serial ports
-- descret I/O bits,
   including paralell ports
```

```
STD    = Standard Microsystems Corp. |
TI     = Texas Instruments.          |
Tosh   = Toshiba, America            |
WDC    = Western Design Center Inc.  |
WD     = Western Digital             |
White  = White Technology Inc.       |
WS     = Wafer Scale Integration     |
Zilog  = Zilog                       |
```

Notes

-----

1 - PDP-8 compatible	2 - Controller
3 - Networks	4 - LCD Driver
5 - PLL Logic	6 - Radiation resistant
7 - Tone generator	8 - Dual CPU
9 - Developement chip	10 - Fourth based
11 - Signal processor	12 - Emulates 990
13 - Cache memory	14 - Z Buss
15 - Non multiplexed	16 - 8080 Mode

UNIVERSAL ASSEMBLER

The Universal Assembler, MOPI, described in this book was developed, and is distributed, by VOCS. Detailed information about and ordering instructions for the assembler can be obtained by writing to the address below.

The Proposed Assembly Language Standard on which this book is based was also developed by VOCS. All comments relating to the proposed standard should also be directed to the following address.

Voice Operated Computer Systems
Book 2730
TAB BOOKS Inc.
P.O. Box 40
Blue Ridge Summit, PA 17214

Index

Index

Other Bestsellers From TAB

☐ **THE ILLUSTRATED DICTIONARY OF MICROCOMPUTERS—2nd Edition**

Meticulously researched and thoroughly updated to include all of the most recent terminology and usage related to the microcomputer industry, this is an essential sourcebook for technically and nontechnically oriented alike—businessmen, hobbyists, students, and professionals. Provides clear, concise definitions and explanations for more than 8,000 key terms. 360 pp., 357 illus. 7" × 10".

Paper $14.95   **Hard $24.95**
Book No. 2688

☐ **SUPERCOMPUTERS OF TODAY AND TOMORROW: THE PARALLEL PROCESSING REVOLUTION—Jenkins**

A view of future technology from the birth of modern computer science to the development of today's most advanced fifth generation computers. You'll discover what technological breakthroughs are being made in parallel processing and artificial intelligence research and the expected impact of these developments. 208 pp., 26 illus., 4 Full-Color Pages.

Paper $14.95   **Hard $21.95**
Book No. 2622

☐ **DATA COMMUNICATIONS AND AREA NETWORKING HANDBOOK**

With data communications and LANs being the area of greatest growth in computers, this sourcebook will help you understand what this emerging field is all about. Singled out for its depth and comprehensiveness, this clearly-written handbook will provide you with everything from data communications standards and protocols to the various ways to link together.

Hard $25.00   **Book No. 2603**

☐ **COMPUTER TECHNICIAN'S HANDBOOK—2nd Edition—Margolis**

Cash in on the multi-million dollar computer repair business! Written by a successful microcomputer repairman, the *Computer Technician's Handbook* starts with the basics and takes you one step at a time through the process of breaking down and repairing a personal computer. Here's all the electronics background you'll need, and detailed diagrams and schematics. 490 pp., 284 illus.

Paper $16.95   **Book No. 1939**

☐ **THE MICRO TO MAINFRAME CONNECTION—Brumm**

Highlighting the data handling capabilities offered when microcomputer versatility is combined with mainframe performance power. Brumm supplies planning checklists, details on computer linking techniques and software packages LANs (local area networks), and public network systems. It's a complete guide to state-of-the-art options available for taming your ever-increasing flow of paperwork. 224 pp., 54 illus.

Paper $15.95   **Hard $22.95**
Book No. 2637

☐ **THE COMPUTER SECURITY HANDBOOK—Baker**

Electronic breaking and entering into computer systems used by business, industry and personal computerists has reached epidemic proportions. This up-to-date sourcebook provides a realistic examination of today's computer security problems, shows you how to analyze your home and business security needs, and gives you guidance in planning your own computer security system. 288 pp., 61 illus. 7" × 10".

Hard $25.00   **Book No. 2608**

☐ **ONLINE RESEARCH AND RETRIEVAL WITH MICROCOMPUTERS—Goldmann**

This time-saving guide shows you how to turn a micro into an invaluable research "tool" for digging up information from databases across the country. Using Nahum Goldmann's "Subject Expert Searching Technique," businessmen, engineers, physicians, lawyers, professors, and students can quickly and easily retrieve information in the comfort of their work station. 208 pp., 119 illus. 7" × 10".

Hard $25.00   **Book No. 1947**

☐ **COMPUTER USER'S GUIDE TO ELECTRONICS—Margolis**

Assembly language will be easier to learn . . . you'll be able to do your own interfacing with peripherals . . . and most importantly, you can perform simple repair procedures yourself when you rely on this exceptional sourcebook which includes more than 250 diagrams and illustrations. In fact, the savings realized by changing one bad chip yourself will more than pay for this handbook! 320 pp., 250 illus. 7" × 10".

Paper $15.95   **Hard $24.95**
Book No. 1899

Other Bestsellers From TAB